Public school finance

Public school finance

Its background, structure, and operation

Paul R. Mort, Ph.D., Litt.D., LL.D.

PROFESSOR EMERITUS OF EDUCATION
TEACHERS COLLEGE, COLUMBIA UNIVERSITY

Walter C. Reusser, Ph.D., Litt.D.

PROFESSOR OF EDUCATIONAL ADMINISTRATION
UNIVERSITY OF WYOMING

John W. Polley, Ed.D.

PROFESSOR OF EDUCATION
TEACHERS COLLEGE, COLUMBIA UNIVERSITY

Third Edition

McGRAW-HILL BOOK COMPANY, INC.

New York   Toronto   London   1960

PUBLIC SCHOOL FINANCE

Preface

I n the preface of the first edition of this book, written at the end of the Great Depression, this statement appears: "Since educational finance is in large part a reflection of educational objectives, financial organization and operation must be conceived as dynamic. A static concept of educational finance would tend to set patterns of organization and operation that would retard needed development and change and tend to freeze outworn objectives." The second edition, published in 1951, covered a decade's evolution in development spurred by war and its aftermath. This second rewriting reflects the strains of the 1950s in their accelerated demand for dollars arising from growing school population, rising costs, improved standards of living and their effect on the market for school personnel, and the urge for more effective education. Also, it reflects considerable development in background theory during this period.

The first three sections of the book (Parts One, Two, and Three) present the major components of the legal-fiscal community structure and their roles in school finance. In a sense they represent the theoretical background for legal structure and fiscal operation. The other two sections (Parts Four and Five) discuss the actual legal-fiscal operations against this theoretical background.

The four chapters comprising Section 1, The Fiscal Setting, give a unified picture of public education from the angle of the control of policy. These four chapters cover and supplement the policy control aspects treated in the first three chapters and Chapters 19 and 20 of the second edition. The approach is simplified by the omission of financial statistics of the character that appeared in Chapter 1 of the second edition.

Chapters 5, 6, and 7, comprising Section 2, Evaluation, bring together and supplement the considerations dealing with fiscal evaluation, treated in the second edition in Chapters 4 to 7, and in Chapter 13. Chapter 7 in this edition presents a great deal of evaluation material of a "quality control" character not available a decade ago.

The three chapters of the taxation section, Section 3, Chapters 8, 9, and 10, present a treatment of taxation—local, state, and federal—greatly expanded from that given in Chapters 11 and 28 of the second edition. They seek to emphasize the tax issues of special pertinence to educators within a setting of common interest to workers in all fields of government.

The eight chapters of Section 4 (Chapters 11 to 17) deal with the long-time and current trends in the participation of central government (state and federal) in public school support. They are presented as a more readable and more teachable treatment of these problems than was provided by the second edition in Chapters 19 to 29. The approach is markedly different, buttressed to a much larger degree by analysis of current practice and the roots of present practice in the past. Considerable attention is given to a reappraisal of the work of Cubberley, Updegraff, and Morrison, the omission of which from the second edition proved to be a disappointment to users of the first edition.

The eight chapters that comprise Section 5, Operational Finance, present a reorganization of the materials treated in Book 2 of the second edition. The exception to this coverage is that the tax chapter now is covered in Section 3, and the cost analysis chapter is now included in the section on evaluation. The task assayed in these eight chapters is that of detailing the system of management of financial matters on the local level, where the theory and the fiscal structure are put to ultimate tests in the hands of school boards and administrators.

On the whole, it is believed that this edition reflects to a considerable degree the maturation of public school finance that proceeded at a rapid rate in the turbulent fifties.

In acknowledgment the authors want to thank those authors and publishers who have generously given permission to quote from books and articles and to various users of the earlier editions whose suggestions have proved extremely helpful. It is a pleasure to acknowledge the special helpfulness of analyses made, at the request of the publishers, by the following: Prof. Eugene S. Lawler, Prof. William R. Odell, Dr. A. W. Schmidt, Prof. Maurice J. Thomas, Dr. Raymond H. Harrison, and Prof. H. B. Woodward, Jr.

Paul R. Mort
Walter C. Reusser
John W. Polley

Contents

List of tables

PART ONE

The fiscal setting of public school finance in the United States

CHAPTERS 1 to 4 describe the setting of governmental responsibility, principles of our culture, and the legal structure in which fiscal arrangements operate. Chapter 5 deals with the issues of cost related to the quality of education as evaluated in terms of the character of the offering. Chapter 6 assesses the impact of school support on the culture and the economy. Both of these chapters have a bearing on the evaluation of public education as a public investment; they deal with issues that are the basis for a strong public posture toward education. Chapter 7 points out the uses of financial data in assessing the wholesomeness of provisions made for education in a given community or a state.

1. Levels of government and public education

THIS CHAPTER sketches the national posture in regard to public education in terms of the division of financial and curriculum responsibility among local, state, and federal agencies of government.

Financial support of the schools operating in a given community is derived from several sources. A large proportion of districts receive some funds from the federal government; all, with few exceptions, receive funds from the state government; and most receive support from local governments. The local support may be from an independent school district—a government purely for school purposes—or it may come from municipal government. There may be support from some larger unit of local government such as the county. The proportions from the various sources vary greatly among school districts within most states and among states. In many school districts in Delaware, for example, there is no local support; in Nebraska school districts, there is generally only a modicum of state support.

The responsibility for what the educational program will be in a community is likewise shared but in a different way. The federal government keeps clear of responsibility; it moves in where it is interested through persuasive special aids but takes no responsibility for the over-all program. The state government takes responsibility for setting the metes and bounds of the program in terms of compulsory education and years of schooling; it usually sets the qualifications of teachers, designates fields to be taught and areas to be avoided; it may set minimum salary schedules, establish tenure for employees, and require provision for retirement pay; it may regulate operation by statutory rules ranging from specifications for school buses to course content. Although, unlike the federal government, the state government is theoretically unlimited in its power, state governments often use the device of special aids to

3

affect practice just as the federal government does. While a few states, when it comes to paying the cost of education, take much the same attitude as the federal government, most states assume considerable financial responsibility. In 40 per cent of the states, half or more of the cost is met from state funds.

With few if any exceptions, however, the bulk of the responsibility for what the program will be falls to the local school district. Here is decided what will be built as an educational program. Federal influence can be accepted or rejected with little financial gain or loss; the same can be said of the special-incentive aids provided by the state. State requirements, being essentially minimum, leave the top open. The degree to which local school districts take advantage of their power, however, varies enormously in each state. This talent of local power is dealt with much as in the story of the talents in the Bible. Some communities invest it; some keep it.

The above summarizes how we as a people now view the nature of the support of and responsibility for American public education. It shows the position we have reached in a long evolution of our national attitude, expectancy, or posture with respect to the control and support of public education. As faith in education burgeons into an understanding of its potential for us as persons and as a nation, and as our sovereign states struggle individually to shape governmental forms for achieving their expectations, our national posture will change. We may look for more agreement on expectations; the correction, by some means, of situations where these expectations cannot generally be realized; and perhaps, though not necessarily, a narrower range of practice among states in terms of the spread of responsibility and the allocation of support within their borders.

THE LEGAL FOUNDATIONS

This section and the sections that follow give more detail on the points made above. They deal with the constitutional framework in which the schools operate.

Our national Constitution gives no recognition whatever to education as a problem of the federal government. So far as the national Constitution is concerned, it is left to the states to decide whether education is to be at public or private expense. The lack of provision for education in the federal Constitution at the time of its adoption cannot, of course, be taken as indicating a lack of appreciation for the importance of education of the young at that time. Rather, it should be taken as a decision to leave this matter to the states or to the people as the individual states should decide.

Uncertainty as to whether responsibility should be allocated to the government or to families singly or in concert is reflected in the all but complete absence of provisions for education in the state constitutions. The constitutions of most states simply affirm that the legislature shall be responsible for the establishment of a system of education. Even these directives came relatively late in the evolution of the state constitutions.

House Bars U.S. Control In Schools

Amendment To Federal Aid Bill

By The United Press

WASHINGTON, July 24.— The House voted today to forbid any form of Federal interference in public-school education under the proposed $1,500,000,-000 Federal school-aid program.

The amendment, approved by voice vote, would forbid the government to exercise any control over local school personnel, school books, school curriculum or school administrative policies.

THE STATE AND EDUCATION

Dr. James E. Allen Jr., New York State Commissioner of Education, sent to Governor Harriman and members of the Legislature a week ago a program of recommendations by the Board of Regents for increased aid to education. The Regents "firmly believe," said the Commissioner, "that the program is essential as a minimum and that the people, weighing both need and cost, are ready and willing to supply the needed financial support."

The program unanimously adopted by the Regents "for maintaining and improving the quality of elementary and secondary education" included this statement from the Regents: "The Regents appreciate that inherent in their proposals are added responsibilities for the taxpayers of this state. They are fully aware that increased taxes may be necessary. * * * The Regents believe that the time has come when the American people must devote an increased proportion of their income to educational purposes."

Fig. 1-1   Exhibits on our national posture in regard to education. *Left: New York Herald Tribune,* July 25, 1957. *Right: The New York Times,* editorial, February 6, 1958.

But this uncertainty on the part of those who shaped the early constitutions has not been necessarily a deterrent to action. Legislatures and the Congress have extremely broad powers. Exercising these broad powers, the various state legislatures, and to a degree the Congress, have been in the process of shaping our national posture in respect to education through legislation of a constitutional character which they have passed over a century and a half. They have created agencies of government, granted them powers, set limits within which they may exercise the powers, and stated principles to guide them. Such legislation is of a constitutional character, whether it is found in the constitution itself or in statutes.

What has resulted is a highly complex structure for education in which federal agencies, state agencies, and local agencies exercise control and make financial arrangements. It is the multiplicity of the agencies, the variations in the character of their financial powers, and the necessity for keeping the sum total of financial effects in proper alignment with the revenue system (local, state, and federal) that accounts for the colorful character of American school finance. The complexity and liveliness of American school finance may be contrasted with the simple structure of finance in a centralized system (such as that of France, for example) where all educational fiscal responsibilities are concentrated in the national government, in the same package as the plenary powers over fiscal matters in general.

THE LIMITED RESPONSIBILITY ASSUMED
BY THE FEDERAL GOVERNMENT

In spite of efforts, sporadic over a century and continuous since World War I, to achieve congressional recognition of national financial responsibility for at least a minimum of wholesome educational conditions in all the states, no such recognition has been achieved. These efforts have been bent toward congressional action since the lack of specific constitutional provisions for education would appear not to be a legal barrier to action. Parallel action has been taken in other fields not specified in the Constitution, under the constitutional authority stemming from the general-welfare clause, as the general-welfare clause has been interpreted.

Education in general is still a problem "for the states or for the people." As a people represented in our national government, we maintain that whatever is done by the people of a state in the light of their own concerns and ability and willingness to pay is not a national concern; whether the schooling is good or poor is not our national responsibility.

But we are not without national interest in education. We note shortcomings dramatized by this or that event, and from time to time we take action designed to sway the states in what they do by aiding certain programs. Thus the concern of the national government has taken a financial turn in attempts to correct what are considered to be dangerous specific shortcomings in our national life. In this category would fall the federal aids for agriculture and the mechanic arts and aid for the improvement of the teaching of science and mathematics. The purpose of such financial help is to persuade.

Apart from such specialized educational concerns, federal participation in the financing of education has been incidental to other aims such as the disposal of surplus food, caring for war veterans, and providing relief to federally impacted communities where, owing to the exemption of federal property from taxation, local taxing power is insufficient to serve the expanded population.

In quite a different category, the federal government has entered into the educational field in a very high degree in the provision of training for its own employees, both civilian and military.[1]

To recapitulate, we as a nation have not assumed financial responsibility for education through our federal government. So far as carrying the burden of a system of universal public education is concerned, the expenditures of the federal government are all but negligible. They amount to about one-third of one per cent of total expenditures for public education.

It follows that, with respect to the day-to-day operations of the school system, problems in federal public school finance are limited to those associated with special grants—their amounts, how they are obtained, how they are distributed, how they are accounted for. Beyond these matters, considerations are hypothetical.

Consideration of potential federal action may take three directions:

Special Aids

Accepting the present federal policy, further exploration would be limited to the examination of additional spots deserving of special federal attention and the use of federal aids in the attempt to influence the states.

Federal Responsibility

If a more vigorous federal policy were desired, exploration in the direction of a more inclusive assumption of federal responsibility would be indicated, as in plans for general aid that would provide some minimum of financial support for education.

Tax Collection

A third line of development would assume the desirability of the federal government's providing assistance in collecting taxes without assumption of educational responsibility. It would be an inquiry into the possibilities of using federal tax-collecting machinery to collect money for the states, to be returned to them in some manner that would

[1] See James E. Russell, *Federal Activities in Higher Education after the Second World War*, King's Crown Press, New York, 1951, for a portrayal of the amazing reach of the educational undertakings of the federal government.

not commit the government to broad policy responsibilities so far as public education is concerned. Clearly this last would be aid of an administrative character; it would presumably require no assumption of federal responsibility for education. It could be purely fiscal.

THE ALLOCATION OF RESPONSIBILITY WITHIN THE STATES

Our stand as a people in relation to public education has been and continues to be actively shaped in the state arenas. Perhaps the most interesting aspect within the states is the development of a special state agency of local jurisdiction, the school district. To this agency, almost universally by legislative rather than constitutional act, broad governmental powers are allotted. The agents holding the powers are typically the voters themselves and their boards of education. In kind, the powers of these local agencies are similar throughout the states. They are powers to set standards, to determine offerings, to levy and collect taxes, and to spend public monies. The constituting legislation surrounds these grants of powers with various kinds of limits. In the field of offerings, there are usually state laws or regulations which require the teaching of certain subjects and may deny the right to teach certain other subjects. The taxing power may or may not be held within rigorous limits. The spending power may be exercised with complete freedom or under rather rigorous checks by state-level agencies.

It is in the character and scope of these various kinds of limits to school district action and in the character and scope of the taxing power allotted to school districts that we find one important aspect of our posture in relation to public education being developed—our attitude toward "home rule" for education. In its immediate applications, public school finance must be concerned with the workings of the system as it is and with the seeking of principles which will guide further development of this instrumentality. For those who believe that this almost uniquely American device of "home rule" for education should be weakened, there may be concern for developing methods of diluting or eliminating it.

Each state has one or more central agencies working in conjunction with the state agencies of local jurisdiction. The chief central agency is the state department of education, which serves a variety of functions:

Police power. It is responsible for policing state mandates.

Legislative power. It has power to establish rules and regulations that have the force of law. In some instances, as in Maryland, legislatures have delegated to this agent the curriculum-determining powers still exercised directly by many legislatures.

Service. It administers the state-aid laws, sometimes with considerable discretionary power: it certifies teachers; it collects information; it issues reports.

Supervision. It develops courses of study, provides supervisory assistance to communities, and in some instances constructs and administers student examinations.

Judicial. In all instances it gives advisory interpretation of laws and in some instances serves as a court of appeals. In New York State the Commissioner of Education is legally the court of last resort for matters for the adjudication of which appeal is to the Commissioner.

Leadership. It provides leadership to the legislature and to the public in revision of the school laws.

Other functions. To these more customary duties most states add one or more other responsibilities, such as responsibility for a state library, for teachers' colleges, for film censorship, and for basic educational research.

In some states, the legislature has assigned more or less limited responsibilities to other central agents. Among these are the highway department, the Civil Service Commission, the audit department, a budget commission, and the state tax commission.

State departments of education vary considerably in the extent of their powers and services. Some are established by the constitution, others by statute. Some have an over-all policy board; others are headed by one official. In some states the chief educational officer is elected, in others appointed by the state board of education or by the governor. Some departments (in Maryland, for example) have immunity from executive review for their financial recommendations based on law; others have their budgets merged in a single executive budget. Some are well staffed; others are scantily staffed. Some are expected to make independent policy recommendations on school matters; others are expected to make their recommendations in accordance with state executive policy.

Within each of the states, conflicting views of the state's educational responsibility are held by various groups and individuals within groups. The dominant concept in a given state may vary markedly from that in another. Some states look on education as largely a community affair. What the state does is largely in response to the influence of various pressure groups. State aid in such instances is not purely fiscal; it is an instrument of influence, of persuasion. At the other extreme, the state takes over. Local administrations hesitate to ask for local support for program improvements; they tend to wait for a cue from the state in special aid, or permissive legislation, or regulation. In between is an arrangement more like a partnership, where the communities are expected to lead but the state stands ready to keep fiscal conditions wholesome.

DEVELOPMENTS AFTER 1900

As is pointed out in Chapter 11, which gives a more detailed story of the evolution of the financing of public schools, the present posture was fairly well established by the turn of the present century.

The period since the turn of the century has seen the formulation of what may be the major lines of the posture of American education. During the nineteenth century some tremendous hurdles had been cleared. The idea of tax support for public education had been established. The idea of compulsory attendance, stimulated and extended through the urge to take up the slack of technological unemployment perhaps as much as by the desire for schooling, had been established. Professionalization of teaching had been established in principle. There had evolved a sense of the state's responsibility for providing real fiscal aid to poorer school districts rather than just granting funds to encourage this or that subject or service.

Given these accomplishments, a great increase in school enrollment and in cost of education; a broadening of the school offering, making it possible to care for children through the high school years even though they are not of college-preparatory caliber; and even the slow response to dramatic discoveries in the psychology of learning that has now consumed half a dozen decades were all foregone conclusions.

These developments of the present century were implicit in the decisions made by 1900. We might add that the American people are now beginning to insist on the kind of education that has been made possible through the experimentation that has proceeded regardless of wars, depressions, inflations, sputniks, and other national crises. As one leader has put it, "Our frontier in education for the next 20 years is quality. Basically, in the last century, the battle of quantity has been won. There are many skirmishes and rear-guard actions still to come, but the principle of extensive and universal education is firmly established. As quantity was the primary goal for the past century, so will quality be our chief aim for the next. We have been concerned that every child get into school. Now we must ask how much each child gets out of school." [2]

It is in this setting that this book seeks to assess the problems of today and the problems of public school finance in the United States.

QUESTIONS FOR STUDY AND DISCUSSION

1. The route the nation traveled to arrive at this present educational posture was a slow and tortuous one. There were no dramatic moves like that made

[2] William G. Carr, Executive Secretary, National Education Association.

by the federal government during the 1930s in changing the whole structure
of the welfare aspects of our government—a change so drastic and so far-
reaching that many people never realized that the old universal system of
locally supported poorhouses was being replaced by a system strongly supported by the federal and state governments. The fact that this welfare aspect
of government had been closely held locally since colonial times and yet responded to such dramatic change should be an indication that equally dramatic
changes might occur in our national posture toward education if sufficiently
dramatic conditions should materialize.

Apart from some such unforeseeable eventuality, we may expect the evolution of the national posture toward education to continue its slow pace toward
a resolution of the inevitable conflict between a three-level taxing system
(local, state, and federal) and an integral economic system.

An acquaintance with the landmarks along the road the nation has already
traveled is rewarding in its own right and occasionally helpful in achieving
an understanding of present problems. Here are a few of them: the early developments in the Massachusetts Bay Colony, Connecticut, and New Amster-
dam; the Charity Schools in the Middle and Southern colonies; the Ordinance
of 1787; rate bills; the struggle between two cultures in achieving tax-supported
education in Indiana; the part of labor in achieving tax-supported education,
particularly in Ohio; the preview of our present-day posture provided by
Horace Mann of Massachusetts and Henry Barnard of Rhode Island and Connecticut in the 1840s; the sweep of state school systems through the South in the
last third of the nineteenth century; the Kalamazoo case. Most of these have
been cited in the chapter on the evolution of state aid (Chapter 11). With some
of them most readers are familiar. Those who wish to pursue others will find
helpful materials in the selected references.

2. Attempting to describe our national posture in regard to education is not
unlike trying to describe the European or the Latin-American posture. The
result is likely to fit no particular state exactly. Our states are sovereign states.
There is no legal reason why two American states should be any more alike
than Holland and Spain, or England and Denmark. Why is this so? It is suggested that you outline your own state's posture in regard to education, including the role of the federal government, of course. In what respects does it
vary from what has been said in this chapter? Compare notes with representatives of other states.

3. In recent years, particularly, historians of education have concentrated
on matters of curriculum and issues arising between citizens and public authorities. Since Cubberley, the history of control and support has been given but
sketchy consideration. The readings should be helpful to those wishing to
delve more deeply into these matters. For example, the story of the rate bill
is a very exciting one. Laid to sleep nearly a century ago, along with toll
roads, it also has experienced a new birth in financing community colleges
in some states. It has been growing by accretion in state universities for three
or four decades. Why has what seemed so bad become so good? Perhaps it is
an example of Finnagle's dictum: "Nothing in finance ever dies; it just awaits
new occasions."

4. One thing seems certain: we are always in midpassage. Slowly government forms yield to what is in men's minds—through changed laws or changed interpretations of their meaning. Where is your mind leading with respect to our national posture?

5. Is uniformity among the states necessarily good? Do you detect ambivalence in the attitude of the writers in the last sentence of the first section of this chapter?

SELECTED REFERENCES

Benton, William: *This Is the Challenge,* College Presses, New York, 1958.

Bereday, George Z. F., and Luigi Volpicelli: *Public Education in America,* Harpers & Brothers, New York, 1958.

Cubberley, Ellwood P.: *Public Education in the United States,* rev. ed., Houghton Mifflin Company, Boston, 1934.

Lippmann, Walter: *Education for Leadership,* National Citizens Commission for the Public Schools, New York, 1954.

Mort, Paul R., and William S. Vincent: *Introduction to American Education,* McGraw-Hill Book Company, Inc., New York, 1954, chap. 4.

National Education Association, Educational Policies Commission: *The Contemporary Challenge to American Education,* Washington, 1958.

Rockefeller Brothers Fund, Inc.: *The Pursuit of Excellence: Education and the Future of America,* Doubleday & Company, Inc., New York, 1958.

Russell, James E. (ed.): *National Policies for Education, Health and Social Services,* Doubleday & Company, Inc., New York, 1955, pp. 2–45.

Strayer, George D.: *The Structure and Administration of Education in American Democracy,* National Education Association, Educational Policies Commission, Washington, 1938.

2. Characteristics of government and the financing of schools

ARRANGEMENTS for financing public schools are a vital facet of the system of public control. Their form is shaped for the governmental framework in which they are suspended. Their form is shaped also in response to strong public expectations, some of them educational, some applying to all government, all more or less related to the prime function of the financial arrangements.

This chapter discusses three clusters of "demands" on the design and operation of financing arrangements. In the first cluster are characteristics of American government that have been developed specifically for the government of the school system; in the second are characteristics of government that to a greater or less degree are pertinent to financial arrangements for both schools and municipal government; in the third are characteristics of the culture that continually influence the structure of government, particularly educational government, and its operation.

SPECIALIZED CHARACTERISTICS OF GOVERNMENT
FOR THE SCHOOLS

Education has a place quite as unique in the governmental system of the United States as the courts. Constitutional provisions and statutory laws reflect the tendency in all states to make differential arrangements for the government of public education. While most of us are more familiar with this in the local arrangements for education, separated from municipal government as educational government is in most states by statutory law, such a trend may be noted also in the arrangements which are made on the state level. Just as our federal and state constitutions establish a system of courts and the separation of executive from

13

legislative powers, most state constitutions have defined a state-level agency specifically designed to deal with educational matters, leaving to the legislature plenary powers to define its powers and responsibilities.

Limited Recognition of the Unique Place of Education

One of our very serious difficulties today is that the unique aspects of educational government are not generally enough recognized. The unique place of the courts is recognized. It is customary for people in all groups of our society to come to their protection. We teach in our schools that government is divided into the legislative, the administrative, and the judicial. We accept the unique place of the courts as a matter that is now commonplace. We look with a jaundiced eye on the development of trends in the field of the judicial system which threaten the independent place that has been established by tradition for that system.

Certainly those who are concerned with the operation of the judicial system today are not responsible for the unique place of the courts any more than those who are responsible for the operation of the educational system are responsible for the evolution of the unique place of public education. Yet any infringements upon our traditional concepts of the judicial system are attacked by citizens in general—not just by those who operate the judicial system. This is not true to anywhere near the same extent for the educational system. Today the defenders of the specialized place of the educational system in our governmental organization are most likely to be the educators and the educators alone—those who are concerned with the operation of the educational system. Those who have taken as their field of competency the general field of government show a strong tendency to overlook the unique historical development of public education and to seek to force public education into the system of general government in such a way as to destroy the fruits of the century and a half of experience in our governmental evolution.

Political Theory and Education. During the half century just past a great deal of effort has been spent on codifying our government experience in the various states. Those concerned with the codification of the educational experience have, naturally enough, limited themselves to the rich experience in the field of public education. The structure of education gives them a separateness. The titles they carried—superintendent of schools, commissioner of education, professor of education—tended to keep them within the limited areas.

But those concerned with the other phases of government bore no such limiting titles. They were professors of government, of political science, and later, of public administration. They dealt with many relatively small services that required amalgamation. In the codifications of experience they sought for generalizations that would fit the police service, health service, highway construction and maintenance, fire protection, water systems, sewer systems, care of the poor, care of the insane, prisons, and a multitude of other specialized services. They tended to ignore differentiating tendencies, among them the persistent differentiating tendencies for education that had been gradually built up over the years.

Thus we have on one hand the educators accepting education as unique [1] and ignoring other governmental development and on the other the political scientists ignoring the history of educational development and seeking for generalizations that they apply to education along with other governmental functions. Sooner or later the canons of these two groups were bound to come in conflict as they have done increasingly in recent years as the influence of the public administration specialists on those concerned with the noneducational phases of government has grown. We can see the effects in state legislation, flowering, for example, in the multiplication of central departments that have been given control or leadership functions over the public schools. It is revealed in the tardiness of improving the structure of controls and finances in the city systems in line with the teachings of the century of varied experience with education under city charters.

There are conflicts also between the officials of the greatly expanded central function and the local operational agents arising from the assumption that the central agents have or ought to have a line relationship between local agents and the legislature.

Resolution of the Differences. There are promising signs of attempts of each to understand the other. Students of school administration have been giving increasing attention to the work of the public administrators, and public administrators have given occasional recognition to the phenomena peculiar to education which their taxonomies provide no place for. The following quotation from Caldwell is to the latter point: [2]

> The extensive character of state concern for education, the numbers of people employed in the schools, the large proportion of state and local money spent for educational purposes, and the relative independence of education from other functions and services of government explain occasional reference to the state educational system as "the fourth branch of the state government."

But we are still too far from understanding each other. As a result, we see such flagrant violations of educational canons as the action in one state giving county supervisors the right to establish discretionary

[1] See Charles A. Beard, *The Unique Function of Education in American Democracy*, National Education Association, Educational Policies Commission, Washington, 1937.
[2] Lynton K. Caldwell, *The Government and Administration of New York*, American Commonwealths Series, Thomas Y. Crowell Company, New York, 1954, p. 317.

taxes for the support of schools, thus tending to give the county supervisors control over educational policy. This is a conflict between the canons of public administration and the canons of school administration. As another example we see the growth of the power of auditors over educational policy in violation of the principles governing *ultra vires* acts of boards of education as established down through the generations by the courts.

These conflicts more and more color all financial legislation particularly, and there is a great need for a clarification. It is believed that most of the differences can be resolved by a fuller sharing of the empirical evidence on which the canons of each group are based.

The Integral Character of the Educational Enterprise

School government as it has grown up in our national history has been constructed differently from other government. To view it as divisible into state aspects and local aspects is to ignore the facts as to its character. At one and the same time it has vastly important local manifestations and strategically important central aspects. It must be viewed as an integral whole, with its roots deep in the family, the individual life, its trunk in the community, its branches reaching into state service agencies, and its highest boughs reaching into the constitution. Yet it is a single enterprise. No major part can be dispensed with— roots, trunk, or branches. It is indivisible. By the same token it must be treated as what it really is, a form of government parallel with, but not intertwined with, other government. Decisions made on the assumption that it is like other departments of government, state and local, are likely to be destructive.

Scope of Application. The principle has an important bearing on the development of services on a state level and on the establishment of relationships with municipal government on the local level.

The increasing complexities of fiscal arrangements, among other things, have resulted in a situation where many agencies participate in the operation of the schools. As a result, conflicts have arisen in the conceptions of the place of education, of the responsibility of the state legislature, of the relationships of educational and local government, and of the functions of central service agencies. These conflicts, in no small degree, may be traced to the fact that during our national history the states have bit by bit built up two systems of operating governmental functions—one for education and one for other government.

Difference in Function. In reviewing the steps taken through the years, it is easy to see why students of governmental arrangements for education have come to the conclusion that there is something inherent in the educational function which has resulted in different governmental treatment. State controls of a rather rigorous character came early into the educational picture. At the same time, a large measure of local control has been retained. The result is that the educational system reaches down to the people in every community, not just as a service—as the post office—but as a function of closely controlled popular government. At the same time the educational system reaches up through a highly specialized state agency of control, service, and leadership—up to special protective provisions in the state constitution itself.

Education neither "State" nor "Local." The "different" character of education is well summarized by Beard in the following statement: [3]

Thus, disturbing events bring forcibly to the foreground the necessity for assuring to educational authorities throughout the entire school system a wide range of freedom in the determination of policies and the conduct of the schools. They are not entitled to, and do not seek, a position of impregnable irresponsibility against society or its matured judgments. They do not deny the validity of the claim that community budgets must be balanced, by curtailment if necessary, in times of stress. They accept the broad principle of democratic control.

It is against the ravages of transitory politicians engaged in mere inquisitorial expeditions that they demand protection. They object to having teaching positions, in schools and universities, turned into the spoils of office, with continuous unsettlements and turnovers from election to election. They protest against allowing any legislative or administrative authority, chosen for other purposes and mainly engrossed in other business, to intervene at will in educational administration, to threaten college presidents, superintendents, and teachers with reprisals, to upset carefully arranged curricula for petty reasons, to dictate the purchase of books and materials, to locate school buildings with respect to real estate projects, and otherwise to subject the school to passing tempers and the demands of private interests.

In stating their position, school authorities merely say that those responsible for educational policies and administration should be in fact responsible, should have powers commensurate with their duties, and should be immune against sporadic raids by men who are not responsible. In so contending they simply assert a fundamental principle of democracy and sound administration. As a unique form of public service, having obligations different from and transcending other services, education must insist upon measures of law designed to assure it that form of autonomy in which it can best discharge its particular functions.

The education system resists that classification as "state" or "local" which students of other phases of government have found to be a simplifying concept. Such classification is destructive to education. The educational system resists absorption into the political system we have found reasonably satisfactory for other phases of government. It resists amalga-

[3] Beard, *op. cit.,* pp. 125–126.

mation with strictly central or state agencies on the one hand and with municipal agencies on the other. To flourish, it must suffer the onus of standing alone and apart. This seems to be the verdict of the people, and the weight of evidence is that to deviate from it is to court ineffectiveness in serving the purposes peculiar to education.

Principle and Practice. What this section deals with is a principle of governmental organization comparable to the integrity of the courts: the separation of legislative, judicial, and executive powers. It is a principle still being shaped, as all such principles are, for that matter.

It is well to remember that in the political arena no such principles are completely realized. Common as is the acceptance of the idea of integral courts, we see the great growth in recent years of "administrative justice" at both state and federal levels. And the courts themselves are not immune from encroachments; the maintenance of what has been achieved toward the ideal is a task for every generation.

What we are trying to say is perhaps better said in the words of Howard Lee McBain, quoted on pages 25 and 26.

Education a State Function

The various constitutional provisions making it incumbent on the legislature to provide for a system of public education is the basis for the oft-repeated principle or fact that education is a state function.[4] This has been used to justify all sorts of legislative acts, most of which would have been within the plenary powers of the legislature anyway. Its chief importance, therefore, has been in charging the legislature with responsibility to act and interest in acting and in guiding the courts in disentangling school boards and local governmental officials from controversial situations in local support and control. In the latter case, however, it may be said that the different ways of looking at municipal government and school districts were usually the cause of the complication that the principle was called upon to resolve. One chief interest in it is as a structural fact to be taken account of in local financial organization and operation. It carries with it (1) the supremacy in school matters of state regulation over city home-rule charter; (2) the status of all school officers, no matter how appointed; (3) the responsibility of local school officers to all the people of the state, rather than just to the people in the locality; and (4) the prudential responsibility of school

---

[4] Legal theory, itself an indispensable tool for interpretation of law, also makes education a state function. The constitutional provision endorses and strengthens legal theory. In legal theory state functions may include education, eminent domain, public utilities and their regulation, and election. Of course, individuals differ as to the application of legal theory. The above is a list given by the eminent jurist Louis Marshall in the 1915 New York State Constitutional Convention.

agencies of state-wide jurisdiction in protecting the interests of all the people in the individual school districts.

Education in Sovereign States. The recognition of the principle that the final authority in matters of education rests with the state and not alone with the local school units has resulted in the development of fifty school states, differing in many respects as to details of organization and administration but much alike in broad outline. That the people have delegated large powers to the local units in matters of organization, construction of school buildings, employment of teachers, provision of materials, supplies, teaching methods, and supervision and in many other ways means only that the districts are recognized subordinate parts of the state for the purpose of administering the schools in conformity with local demands and local needs. The supremacy of the state resides in the recognition of the importance of education to all the people rather than to certain local groups and the necessity of making educational requirements that are to be met by all districts. It is the expression of the electorate of the state, through the legislature and the state department of education, of the importance of the schools and of entrusting the control of them to all the people rather than to certain minority groups.

Limited Power of School District. The fact that the school districts are legalized gives them only the powers to carry on certain functions that have been entrusted to them; they have no inherent rights of their own. In most states the state legislature may at any time alter their boundaries, grant more or less authority to them, or eliminate them entirely. In actual practice a large measure of authority has been given to the districts. This makes it incumbent upon the people of the state to see that the authority granted is wisely used in the administration of the local schools. For this purpose, states have established certain minimum requirements—such as compulsory attendance, certification of teachers, minimum salaries, minimum length of school term, uniform records and reports, and certain standards relating to buildings and equipment—which all local units must meet. Beyond the enforcement of these minimum requirements, the function of the state is largely one of providing for stimulation, guidance, and leadership for the encouragement of local communities to improve their schools beyond the minimum requirements and to undertake programs that will more adequately meet local needs. No small part of the state's responsibility is to institute means for adequate support, both local and state-wide, not only to insure the minimum requirements, but also to provide for the financing of programs that are in advance of minimum requirements.

Limited Powers of Central Agents. A closer examination of the principle of state responsibility is desirable at this point. Sometimes it is interpreted as the sovereign right of the legislatures to do as they will or of the state boards of education or state department of education officials. But this is not what it means. The legislatures have no sovereign rights. State boards of education and state department of education officials are no more state agents than are the school boards in the smallest communities. They differ only in their jurisdiction. Invoking state responsibility for education is not invoking the legislature or the state board of education or the state department of education, but it is invoking something of which they are the agents and of which, likewise, local boards of education are the agents. In the sense in which the term "Education is a state responsibility" is used, the local boards of education are as truly state legislatures as is the one that meets in the state capitol. The range of powers that they exercise is more limited, the area over which they have jurisdiction is different, but they have the same roots.

State-wide Concern the Key Concept. What is this state responsibility, if it is not something that can be associated with legislatures, state boards, or chief state school officers? By "Education is a state function" is meant that by the very nature of educational service that which is done in any community is the concern not of the people of that community alone, but of all the people of the state. Education is a state-wide interest, a state-wide concern. If the people of a state, working through the various mechanisms that have been set up to express their will, permit unsatisfactory education to be offered in any part of the state, they are failing to perform their duty. It is their concern if their mechanisms, state legislatures, state boards of education, state departments of education, and local boards of education are failing.

Other aspects of local government fall within a different class. People are delegated powers to do, through government, what they might choose to do through private enterprise. As an extreme example of this, one may cite the case of a municipal lighting system. Particular localities may be permitted to operate electric lighting plants or bus lines as a governmental service. It is of no concern to all the people of the state whether they do this or do not do it. It is only of remote concern to the people of the state whether they have electric lights or gas lights or no lights at all. So governmental services operating in this realm are of a different kind. Governmental machinery may be established to permit such activity. But the failure of the successful operation of any such activity is of far less concern to all the people of the state than the failure of a unit of the educational system.

This is something of the justification for the favored status of education, but fundamentally the difference goes back to constitutional provisions. Some municipal activities may be of wide importance to the entire state but may not have been legally recognized as such. Education is legally recognized as such.

Not Applicable to Devices. The principle of state responsibility for education, then, means that all the arguments about district organization and financing and control are not arguments on fundamental rights. They deal only with the question of what are the most adequate devices for getting the job done. If it is considered wise to establish local school authorities with broad powers, it must be in the belief that through such a device the interests of all the people will be best served. The people might choose to operate the schools entirely from one central office located in the state capitol, just as the great "state" of the city of New York is operated from one central office or as the schools of the Cape Province in the Union of South Africa, which is as large as Texas, are operated from one office in Cape Town. If it could be shown that, all things considered, this device would best serve the interests of all the people, this is the device that should be used. Or it would be possible to set up a system by which the entire responsibility for support and control would fall on small units of the state. If a system of complete local responsibility could be shown to be the one that would best serve the interests of all the people of the state, that device should be favored.

Use in Court Decisions. There are important connotations of the principle that education is a state function. Some flow from court interpretations. Courts in the various states have interpreted cases which indicate that on a question of responsibility for acts, even in those communities where boards of education are fiscally dependent on municipal authorities, the board of education is the responsible agent, not the municipal government. Other cases have ruled that in the absence of state regulation, the rules of the board of education as a state agent have the force of law in the school district and supersede any contrary rules passed by municipal agencies. The court rulings accordingly emphasize the separateness of the educational function from the municipal function, frequently tracing their reasoning to the constitutional injunctions on the legislature with respect to education. This is one of the most significant meanings of the principle that education is a state function—that education is separate, that it does not participate in and of municipal local government.

Another implication flows from the long history of mandatory legislation and state regulation. It is that the state has the responsibility, by whatever means are necessary, to assure to all children a satisfactory foundation education. Since the middle of the last century it has become increasingly clear that this imposes responsibility either for complete state support of a foundation program or for major state equalization aid, simply for the very practical reason that there is no other way to assure support in less able districts.

The Posture of Legislators. Not the least of the difficulties faced by those concerned with the improvement of the structure of public education is the attitude often evidenced by members of the legislature that they are particularly representative of central agencies of government. Those who have this viewpoint feel antagonism toward those concerned with public education.

The effective operation of the governmental system by which the state (the people) gets its work done requires a legislature that can maintain an even-handed relationship with central agencies and those that operate locally.

There appears to be a strong tendency on the part of some of the groups concerned in the development of state policy to look upon the legislature as peculiarly closely related to the functions operated on the state level. It is true that the legislature is the basic policy board for the state-operated governmental functions. It is also true, however, that the legislature has the responsibility, in large degree, for establishing the structural pattern and over-all operational rules according to which all locally operated governmental functions are managed. In the latter sense, then, the legislature is no more closely affiliated with state central agencies than with local government. It would, accordingly, be unfortunate if, in the differences that inevitably arise between the central government agents and local government agents, the legislature were to find itself consistently taking sides with one of these groups.

This is particularly true under the system in those states where, except through the constitutional conventions, the people have no direct hand in initiating the law-making process and carrying it through without participation by the legislature.

Those nineteen states which utilize the devices of the initiative and the referendum have a protection against a legislature with biased assumptions.[5]

Overuse of the Principle. Apart from these significant meanings, what we have to learn from a review of the evidence would seem to be that

[5] In twelve states action thus initiated may be directed at constitutional amendment, but in all nineteen action may be directed to legislation having a status comparable to that of action by the legislature. Popular initiative for constitutional amendment or the enactment of statutes is provided in Arizona, Arkansas, California, Colorado, Massachusetts, Michigan, Missouri, Nebraska, North Dakota, Ohio, Oklahoma, and Oregon. Popular initiative for statutory action only is provided in Idaho, Kansas, Maine, Montana, South Dakota, Utah, and Washington. See Owen Love, *Constitutional Provisions for Education in the Forty-eight States*, New York State Educational Conference Board, Albany, N.Y., 1958.

those concerned with education, those deeply interested in the place of education as a social instrument (and these persons are by no means limited to those professionally engaged in education), must realize that education became a concern of all the people of the state early in our history and is likely to be worthy of remaining a concern of all the people of the state. What those in the noneducational field may learn from this is that the fact that educators may have tended to rest their case too fully on expressions of intent of our forefathers is really no justification for any failure of themselves as citizens or as members of the legislature or as representatives of other agencies to give the functions of education continued attention. In short, all of us should look to the function to be performed, to the need to be served in our day. Between that need and the other needs that we as people have by virtue of the fact that we live together in a state, there is no necessary and essential conflict.

"Home Rule"

When we have established that education is a state function, we have established that there is no inherent right of local self-government in education. This tradition dies so hard, however, that it may be well to state that legal experts recognize no inherent right of home rule even in municipal matters, although municipal government is thought of as more local in its responsibility. American municipal governments operating with wide freedom from legislative regulation do so under powers expressly granted through constitutional provisions or legislative action. Where the origin of the power is the constitution, it is a granting of power by the state, not a recognition of inherent powers by a sort of bill of rights.

This may be contrasted to the sovereign rights of states to operate in areas which the people have not specifically assigned to the federal government or with the earlier status of German municipalities, which, after 1812, had power comparable to our states as members of the federal system. The distinction that recognition as a state function gives to education as compared with municipal government is that education thereby partakes of certain rights and immunities of the sovereign not shared by a municipality as a licensed public corporation.

De Facto Home Rule. This is the legal interpretation. In the light of experience and court decisions, it is not particularly helpful. As a matter of fact, there seems to be a sort of home rule in the American school system for which the legal theorist as yet has no name.

In setting metes and bounds to the initiative of central and local agents, a bias operates in favor of maintaining local power or strengthening it. This emphasis toward keeping the control close to the people has been maintained for a century and a half during which legislatures have maintained an all but constant interest in the educational enterprise. Its roots are deep. This is what is meant by home rule as the term is applied to education.

The degree that this has permeated thinking in the past is reflected in the unique arrangements for the people in small communities in a number of states to meet together to decide on the character and extent of the budget to be supported and to order the levying of the necessary local taxes.

This principle has a bearing on the making of a decision to achieve quick reform by allocation of powers to central agents without regard to the effect of transferring the power, either on long-time efficiency or on the people as individuals and citizens.

In this principle are the roots of the insistence of educators and parents and citizens in general who make educational matters their concern upon maintaining within the localities the right to make decisions on the character of education. This structural organization for education accounts for the use of the term home rule in education—a term which comes close to describing a situation approaching as nearly an inherent right to home rule as anything we have in government. The use of the term home rule by educators, in spite of the fact that it has come to have the technical meaning associated with a form of government of cities stemming from constitutional or statutory provision, is a source of confusion. It may be worth while to point out that, when educators use the term home rule, they are seeking for a term to express a fact of governmental organization for schools, not to draw comparisons with home rule for municipal government. There seems to be no other satisfactory term. Local initiative, close popular control, local right to determine the destiny of the schools within the bounds set by the state might be more accurate terms.

Trend of Court Decisions. It is of interest that this concern over close popular control of education is found pretty generally throughout the United States. As a matter of fact, in a long series of court decisions stemming from the Kalamazoo case in 1872, courts have declared that the local authorities have the right to determine the character of the educational program—the curriculum, as they put it—so long as they do not fail to carry out the injunction of the law or of regulations by central authorities made in accordance with law, and do not contravene such provisions detailing offerings which they may not give. A perusal of these cases shows that the courts have had a hard time to square these judgments with legal theory. In legal theory no local operating authority has the right to perform any act not specifically designated in the law unless it is necessary for the carrying out of an act designated in the law. In legal theory we have no such thing in American states as inherent home rule, so the arguments usually turn on the tie-in of the act of the local authorities with some legally designated right. But there can be little doubt that what has influenced the court is this "something" which we see recognized in educational government that has never been fully taken into account by our legal theory, deriving, as that legal theory did, from our pre-Revolutionary government in charters and our parallel government in constitutions that followed the Revolution.

The fact remains that the people in many states, boards of education, and professional educators have a high regard for the maintenance of local leeway for action in providing educational programs and with the support of the courts have been able to maintain it to date in a high degree.

Roots of the Conflict in Theory. When such a far-reaching phenomenon as that under discussion does not gibe with an accepted theory, it would seem to be time to question the theory, on the one hand, and to seek out the fundamental causes for the phenomenon, on the other. A guess may be hazarded that the cause for the phenomenon lies pretty deep in our aspirations for self-government. Whatever the forms for governing ourselves we have been able to develop in our brief history as a nation, it is probable that they are not altogether in keeping with our aspirations. We have a way periodically of getting very much excited over the results to be achieved and tending to disregard the methods of their achievement. Yet our whole governmental experiment seems to have been postulated on experimentation in method. At the heart of it was the desire for men to have a say in determining their own destiny, the closer the better.

The following statement by McBain shows the relationship of such an urge to the legal system: [6]

It would be folly to deny that in a general way the principle of local self-government is one of those principles that lie at the foundation of American political institutions. Of like character are the principles of democracy, of representative government, of civil liberty,. and of the tripartite separation of governmental powers. These are principles, or doctrines, of our political theory which, to the extent that they have been incorporated into our fundamental laws, have found more or less concrete expression in our institutional life and development. But not one of these principles has been completely realized in the practical operation of our institutions, partly for the reason that our constitutions have never attempted their complete establishment and partly for the reason that our government, like all governments, is one of men as well as of laws. It is therefore a legal doctrine of no trivial significance which asserts

[6] From Howard Lee McBain, "The Doctrine of an Inherent Right of Local Self-Government," reprinted from *The Columbia Law Review,* March and April, 1916.

that an abstract political theory—no matter how important a place it may occupy in the philosophy of our politics—may by the courts be translated into a positive legal right, wholly in the absence of any constitutional provision giving substantial expression to the theory.

Traditionally we have opposed doing things by government that we could do as individuals; we have opposed doing things by state government that we could do by local government; we have opposed doing things by the federal government that we could do fairly well by state government. *We are biased toward keeping the control close to the people.* It is of interest that this bias has shown up so clearly in that most intimate of governmental forms—the school system. Apart from highways there is no aspect of government that so nearly reaches all the people. In addition, it deals with matters which are of intimate personal concern to the public—the education of children. Here, whatever may have been our sampling of remote government accepted purely for efficiency's sake, we have sought to maintain control close to the people.

If we may judge from the writings on local self-government in this and other lands, the importance of the method of government to the people participating may not be overlooked in assessing its values. We must not only ask what results it gets in the function under consideration, they tell us, but we must also ask what effect does the method of government have upon the people themselves. Close popular government, many claim, provides a school for citizens. It safeguards the people against the capture of government by despotically inclined persons, and in every operation it provides a means of personal realization comparable perhaps to building a cathedral or raising a fine herd of cattle or painting a picture.[7] However anyone may personally assess these claims, it cannot be overlooked that for these or for some other deep-lying reasons we have maintained our traditional bias for local control in this field of education, itself undeniably a matter of great state-wide concern.

We may conclude that in allocating responsibility for carrying out the enterprise or for the spending of money in carrying out the enterprise, we must look further than the immediate advantage of quick action by a central agent selected to do a specific thing at a specific time. We must look beyond this to the long-time probabilities that, in the common sense of the people operating in close oversight over the schools, the solutions that may develop tomorrow may be better than those which the central agent would provide for today. And we must look further than this beyond the results in the activity itself to the effect of the enterprise on the

[7] A review of the arguments for and against local government appears in Paul Studenski and Paul R. Mort, *Centralized versus Decentralized Government in Relation to Democracy,* Bureau of Publications, Teachers College, Columbia University, New York, 1941. See also Paul R. Mort and Donald H. Ross, *Principles of School Administration,* 2d ed., McGraw-Hill Book Company, Inc., New York, 1957, pp. 42–66.

people who carry it out—on their training for citizenship, on our long-time protection from dictatorship, on the creative opportunity afforded to participants in the arts of government.

Resolution of the Conflict. We may conclude from this that, when it is charged that educational officers cannot make up their minds because one moment they are invoking the fact that education is a state function and the next moment they are invoking the right to local control, the charge has its roots to a degree at least in misunderstanding. Clearly, we must look at education with a broad enough conception to embrace these two phenomena. It is proposed that such a broad conception is that education, whether we look upon it in its local aspects or in its state aspects, is a continuous, integrated whole. It is a state function left to a tremendous extent to the responsibility of people locally and subject always to the checks and safeguards of legislative action and the action of those agents whose duty it is to work in the enterprise from a central vantage point.

The establishment in our educational structure of two correlative agencies—the state department of education and the school district—is a continuous source of conflict. Much of this has been resolved by the practice of legislatures in making the assignment of responsibilities to agencies of state-wide jurisdiction specific, and the responsibilities of local authorities general and open-ended. The practice of making specific allotments of powers to the agencies of state-wide jurisdiction is all but universal. The practice of providing general powers to the local agencies is much less uniform. It varies from almost complete home rule to a high degree of restriction through budgetary preview and wide-ranging audits by state agencies.

The restrictive tendency is probably due to the strong prudential strain in our culture. It has resulted in some states in a situation where nobody really has much power to act outside of the habituated methods of operation, a situation which results in a very low degree of adaptability in the system. The rationale for the limitation of powers of the local agents is found in the legal "principle" that an agency of local jurisdiction has only those powers that are specified in the law, or, as the courts frequently say, those that are specified in the law or are necessary for the carrying out of what is specified in the law.

Courts versus Administrators. Actually this ancient principle, stemming from juridical theory, has given far less trouble when interpreted by courts than when used as a guide by administrators. The courts over and over again have interpreted the principle as permitting amazing latitude. We may say that the great degree of freedom exercised by local authorities in our states flows more from these court interpretations of a restrictive legal principle than from attempts to correct the situation in law.

As a matter of fact, if the principle is clear, it is simple enough to handle in law. The law could state, for example, that boards of education shall have the power to expend funds for educational purposes approved according to the established processes, unless such expenditures are specifically denied by law. With such a provision in the law, the occasion for applying the legal principle will not arise. It is a principle to be used where there is lack of clarity of intention in the law. It is not a principle to guide in the construction of the basic law. So far as is known, no law granting broad powers to agencies of local jurisdiction has ever been challenged by a court in terms of the legal principle.

It is helpful to remember that this legal principle is not constitutional law—rather, it is part of a system of juridical thinking for resolving difficulties when the law is not sufficiently clear. The principle is not that in the nature of things the powers of local authority *should* be specific rather than general. Rather, the principle is that in case of doubt as to the intent of the legislature, this rule is a good one to start with in resolving the dilemma. Courts always seem to find ways of coming out with what may appear to the layman as a contrary ruling, if in their judgment the occasion demands it. The Kalamazoo case is an excellent illustration of this.

A Rule for Developing Legal Structure. As a rule to guide the development of the legal structure it is proposed that the following is in line with the evolution of our school system: *Powers of the agency of local jurisdiction should be broadly defined in law; powers of agencies of state-wide jurisdiction should be specifically defined.* This principle is drawn from the all but universal character of state legislation making the powers of state agencies specific and the somewhat less general policy of state legislation in making the powers of local agencies broad. But the effect of defining the powers of local agencies specifically rather than broadly is offset by a multitude of individual court decisions which appear on the surface to go contrary to the widely accepted legal principle that agencies of local jurisdiction have only those powers that are specifically delegated to them.

It is believed that following this rule in the clarification of legislation and as a guide for interpreting ambiguous legislation, at least as a foil to the ancient legal rule, will have a salutary effect in strengthening both central and local educational agencies in their proper spheres.

INTEGRAL SCHOOL GOVERNMENT; BURGEONING ECONOMY; AND THE THREE-LEVEL TAX SYSTEM

The financing of an integral (not state, not local) government poses problems that can in major degree be avoided by governmental functions that can more readily be broken down into local functions and state functions. This has brought to the fore the first of the two vital issues dealt with in this section. Of a quite different character is the issue raised by the impact of a rapidly changing economy on the school system which only in recent years has begun to reap the fruits of a strengthened state-local partnership in financing schools. This is the second issue treated in this section.

Both issues are clear-cut in education. However, it would seem that they are bound to be of increasing importance in other phases of government as increasing responsibilities of two or more levels of government come more and more to overlap indivisible functions. Public health, welfare, and police protection, for example, seem to be becoming more like school government as described in the preceding section and less like government as traditionally viewed.

Independence of Finance and Control

The changes in the degree of participation demanded of the state and federal governments as the result of economic changes bring one face to face with disturbing implications of the long-accepted canon that control not only does but should follow the dollar, even within different state agencies. If this were followed, there would arise the sheer necessity of disrupting the traditional system of major control by educational agencies of local jurisdiction. In recent years this position has been challenged as representing an unrealistic interpretation of our educational structure.

The position challenged is one that has been commonly held by legislators, governmental administrators, laymen, and educators: that control must necessarily emanate from the agencies which provide the support. Writing in 1897, Webster observed that state aid "naturally and necessarily" led to state control.[8] Fairlie noted the close relationship between state control and support but pointed out that state control was more for the purpose of supervision and that grants were not made for the purpose of control.[9]

In 1905, Cubberley found that states were distributing aid on the basis of educational need as measured by the number of children of school age and on the basis of reward for effort made by communities in carrying on special features of their educational programs.[10] It is quite likely that the latter method of distributing state subsidies has tended to fix in the minds of many the necessity of some regulation and control of the funds

---

[8] William C. Webster, "Recent Centralizing Tendencies in State Educational Administration, doctoral dissertation, Columbia University, Faculty of Political Science, New York, 1897, p. 13.

[9] John A. Fairlie, *The Centralization of Administration in New York State*, Bureau of Publications, Teachers College, Columbia University, New York, 1898, p. 57.

[10] Ellwood P. Cubberley, *State School Funds and Their Apportionment*, Bureau of Publications, Teachers College, Columbia University, New York, 1905, p. 202.

thus distributed and has tended to perpetuate the control-support idea. Although in more recent times we may find those who believe that some degree of state control must inevitably follow increased state support, there has been a clarification of the principles of control and support that shows the two to be not necessarily interdependent. The controls over education or any part of it may be allocated to the local communities or to central agencies quite independently of the source of support.

It is not intended to suggest that accidental shifts in control are the only ones worthy of observation. On the contrary, it is highly desirable that certain differences in conception as to the criteria or principles which should determine a change in control should be ironed out. There are two such conceptions that are particularly troublesome.

The Piper and the Tune. The conception that the amount of control exercised over the expenditure of money should be determined by the percentage of the money supplied by a given level of government has been an oversimplification drawn from private enterprise. It conceives of the state government as having so many votes on the governing body of the corporation and the local government having so many votes, depending upon the number of shares they own. This dichotomy does not fit the facts with respect to education. As a matter of fact, whether the money is collected by a central agency or collected by a local agency, it is paid by the people. The central government and the local government are simply two agencies of the people. The people may use one agency for collecting money and the other agency for control if, and this is the important point, this way of dividing these responsibilities promises to get the best results.

It is true that this canon flows from experience with efficient operation in a limited sense of economy or prudence or even in the broader sense which would include results achieved for money spent, but it is experience from private life. The canon is not borne out by the facts of governmental operation, at least as far as operation of schools is concerned. It is conceivable that there may be more justification for this canon in dealing with phases of government which classify more easily as local or central. In the case of education, which is an integral enterprise rising through both so-called levels of government and an enterprise operated closely under the eyes of the people themselves, the canon does not fit the case.

In lieu of this canon, the rule should be followed that the control should be placed where it is most likely to get results in the long run, all things being considered—both economy in the narrow sense and economy in the broad sense of measuring results over against the investment. Parenthetically, it may be said that consideration should be given also to the effects upon those exercising the control in terms of the entire enterprise as well as the effects on the particular aspect under consideration.

The Tax Collector and Operation. Closely related to the foregoing is the misconception that the only way to shift the support from local agencies to central agencies is by the process of shifting the function itself to the central agent. Operating on this canon, extensive attempts were made early in this century, extending well up toward the present time, to adjust to the narrow local tax base by shifting functions from local to state operation. We saw this procedure with highways, with certain police functions, with welfare, with training of teachers. Not in every instance were these shifts of functions made solely to adjust to the financial stringency on the local level. But the studies of government, particularly in the 1920s, show many indications of a search for functions that could be transferred in order to relieve the local tax base. There is still much talk of this method of adjusting the tax structure. It is not unusual to hear suggestions made by citizens of high standing that the way to handle education is to transfer its operation to the state. Students of taxation and of public administration in general seem to have abandoned this as any solution for present conditions, but one gets the impression that the abandonment is because of the fact that sufficient transfer cannot be achieved to meet the financial stringency rather than for reasons of its bearing on long-term effectiveness of governmental operation.

The ease with which the public accepts these transfers is another disconcerting evidence that, however extensive the belief in this canon may be, there is all too little concern over the effects of allocation of government as between local agents and remote agents. There is need to be on the watch for reasoning on the shift of governmental functions that tends to accept this canon as a good and sufficient reason by and of itself.

These Misconceptions Not Universal. These misconceptions are not the possessions of any particular group. They will be found among the professional educators as well as among those concerned with other phases of government. As a matter of fact, a number of leaders in the field of public administration have repudiated these canons and have advanced the fundamental reasoning that the long-run wholesomeness of the situation should be the criterion for the allocation of control of a function or for responsibility of operation. The following quotations, one from a New York Legislative Commission Report and one from a textbook on public administration, are illustrative:

The function of developing and operating a tax system (hereafter briefly referred to as "administering taxes") is just as much a governmental activity as providing education or building and maintaining roads. This is obvious, but its implications are not always obvious. One implication is that it is possible that the function of administering certain kinds of taxes is most effectively performed by one unit of government (*e.g.*, the state), while some other function that depends upon these taxes for sustenance is most effectively performed by another unit (*e.g.*, the county or the city). When the two functions do not fit the same administrative pattern, budget disequilibrium results: the tax-administering unit has a surplus, the other unit has a deficit. State aid (in all senses except complete state assumption of functions) forms a means whereby the budget surplus of the one political unit is drained off to make good the budget deficit of the other. Without state aid, there would be a strong temptation to do damage to the tax-administering function by forcing it into a pattern that, although conforming to the pattern of the other functions, might be wasteful and inequitable from a taxation standpoint. The alternative would be state assumption of some of the functions, such as education and the building and maintaining of roads. This might indeed occur, and, as was implied in the preceding section, the other forms of state aid are to be thanked for allowing avoidance of transferring these functions merely to fit the proper pattern of the revenue-raising function. State aid, in all its aspects except complete state assumption of functions, works both ways, when the pattern of the tax-administering function does not coincide with the aggregate pattern of the other governmental functions—it makes it unnecessary to distort either pattern so that it will coincide with the other.[11]

Unfortunately, the most advantageous distribution of governmental service functions according to the canon of functional fitness does not coincide with the optimum distribution of tax administration. Local governments are best fitted to perform the larger proportion of the service functions. State governments are better fitted to levy, administer, and collect most of the taxes. Unless an equalizing factor is introduced, local governments are compelled either to restrict their functions below a socially desirable point or else to press to an unbearable extent upon the property tax and other revenues available to them. And so we come to the third canon of state-local fiscal interrelationship: The states must to an ever increasing extent devise means to put revenues they collect at the disposal of their local units.[12]

Center of Gravity of Control. The enterprise of education, in a manner peculiar to that function, cuts across both state and local levels of government as usually conceived. We can think of it at any given time as having a control center of gravity. Considering the powers—administrative, legislative, and judicial—given state agents, one might think that the center of gravity of control was close to the central level. A closer examination would doubtless lead to the contrary conclusion. For example, the recent upsurge of local tax rates in many states to maintain schools in spite of price rises did not flow from a central agent. It flowed from control close to the people.

The control structure as it exists is a result of legislative acts through the years. The control relationship between boards of education and city government in many states has been molded by the interactions of in-

---

[11] "Report of the New York State Commission on State Aid to Municipal Subdivisions," *Legislative Document,* no. 58, Albany, 1936, pp. 48–49.

[12] William J. Schultz, *American Public Finance,* Prentice-Hall, Inc., Englewood Cliffs, N.J., 1942, p. 721.

dividual cities and the legislature. The powers that are exercised by all central agents are the powers that were given them by the legislature or the constitution. The size of school boards, their manner of election, the manner of determining the amount to be spent in localities were all determined by state legislation.

One cannot but wonder as to whether or not the center of gravity of control that now exists is as close to the people as it could be to the benefit of the enterprise and of the people themselves. One cannot but wonder as one sees the crop of new laws coming year by year whether or not these changes in control have resulted from some carefully considered judgment on the part of the legislature as to their effects upon the welfare of the enterprise as a whole.

The writing of financial legislation is a particularly dangerous enterprise when it comes to the question of unintended shifting of the center of gravity of control. For example, the long series of special-aid laws passed in the first decades of this century—well intentioned as devices for promoting local support for specific enterprises—tended to carry along the conception that nobody but some central agent really knew what was satisfactory practice in the specific fields.

In summary, the agency (or government level) responsible for raising the revenue does not necessarily need to be the agency (or government level) that has ultimate discretion in spending. To hold otherwise is to have the first three principles outlined above destroyed by the impossibility of adjusting the taxing power of the local and state agency (and also federal agency) in accordance with the effective distribution of the control of services on the local, state, and federal levels.

Responsiveness to Change at the State Level

The analysis of state and local responses to increasing need for school support appearing in Chapter 12 shows that, over the years, this response on both levels has been little short of miraculous. The fact that state adjustments tended to be correctives for intolerable conditions faced by communities does not lessen the significance of the fact that legislatures have been responsive to the needs of the schools. Also, when the proportion of state support was less, the disturbing effect of delay in keeping up the state's share was not so great.

Current Strains on Capacity to Adapt. Today, with the states increasingly taking the responsibility of collecting revenues from non-property taxes and channeling them back to the schools, delay in legislative action has more serious effects.

In addition, since the Second World War we have been experiencing unprecedented needs for increase in school money. Today there seems to be a continuous need for revising financial arrangements. The problem cannot be met, on the part of the state, with the sporadic attention that characterized the past. State-level school finance is almost as urgently an annual problem as local-level school finance.

This increased need for attention to education finds legislatures busier than ever before. In the past few decades state government has burgeoned. Every expansion of state services and every move to centralize formerly local government functions has been accompanied by increased legislative responsibility.

Reducing Burden on the Legislature. Accompanying this increase of legislative burden we see a gradual reshaping of the powers of central agencies. The federal government is not alone in experimenting with new patterns of handling legislative responsibility such as that exemplified by the Special Services. That education has been affected is shown by the rapid spread of the adoption of the state school board with its own executive to take over the functions formerly exercised by an elected state superintendent of schools.

Further Steps Needed. The problem we are dealing with here suggests that a further step be taken to relieve legislatures of at least part of the now continuous fiscal responsibility for education.

As a minimum the state board of education should be required to make annual reports to the legislature and to the public on the fiscal needs of the schools. A few states—Rhode Island, for example—have such a legal provision. In addition, it would appear to be appropriate to ask whether the state board of education might not be given the leeway to keep in a wholesome balance the support afforded education from state-collected revenues and the support coming from the locally collected revenues. Or, since this particular problem involves municipalities as well as school districts, whether the state board of education in conjunction with some agency representing the municipalities in a similar fashion might not be required to carry this responsibility to the extent, at least, of providing annual review and recommendations to the legislature and to the voters.

Whatever the arrangements, the principle is clear. Powers to maintain the proper alignment of the revenue system and the demands of locally operated and state-operated governments should be so disposed on the state level that the locally operated governmental units will not be handicapped by failure of prompt response to rapid changes in dollar valuation, population increase, governmental costs, or general betterment of educational services.

IMPACT OF THE CULTURE

Back of constitutions, statutes, and governmental structure are the public expectations they were designed to serve, the public sanctions that test them, the common sense of the culture.

Like the power of a legislature, these expectations are not exhausted by exercise. Constitutions, laws, and governmental forms are changed to bring them into better alignment. Those responsible for operating the government—whether it be schools, highways, police, or welfare—move in an atmosphere of these expectations.

In drafting school legislation or in the local administration of financial affairs, these expectations must be taken into account. Here two of them —equality of opportunity and adaptability—are discussed in their relation to school finance. These two are of critical importance to the structure of state-aid systems. For local financial arrangements and operation, as well as for their bearing on state-aid laws and state-level services, we might well have added a dozen others: stability, flexibility, and two series that could be classed as humanitarian and prudential.[13] It may be added that the discussion of "home rule" above would have fitted in this section. The underlying principle discussed there is what Mort and Ross speak of as structural democracy. Viewed as a principle it belongs with the two discussed here.

Equality of Opportunity

The period from the beginning of the twentieth century to the present is one in which the acceptance of the principle of equalization of educational opportunity stands out as a dominant characteristic. Not that this ideal has now in any sense been achieved on a nationwide scale or that it was unrecognized before, but this recent period has been one in which increasing clarification of the principle and increasing emphasis upon it have carried it to the point of actual practice in a large number of states. Equalization of educational opportunity was an ideal expressed by the founders of our country. It was in part achieved when the battles for free, tax-supported schools was won. Again it was partially achieved in legislative acts in some of the New England states in the latter part of the nineteenth century when state aid was distributed to the more needy districts. Cubberley found that in 1905 six states distributed state aid in greater amounts to poor than to wealthy districts.[14] McGuire shows that by 1920 as many as twenty states had recognized the principle in one way or another.[15]

Most of the earlier efforts of the states to aid poor school districts may be classed as weak district laws; they did not in any real sense contemplate adequate equalization of a minimum educational opportunity for all children in the state. New concepts of the principle of equalization of edu-

[13] For a treatment of fourteen such sanctions in relation to finance as well as other aspects of school administration, see Mort and Ross, *op. cit.*

[14] Cubberley, *loc. cit.*

[15] S. H. McGuire, *Trends in Principles and Practices of Equalization of Educational Opportunity*, George Peabody College for Teachers, Nashville, Tenn., 1934, p. 31.

cational opportunity were first clearly stated by the Educational Finance Inquiry Commission in 1923.[16] Following this formulation of the equalization principle, a long series of individual studies developed the techniques by means of which finance programs within the states could be set up to equalize a minimum educational opportunity for all the children. The National Survey of School Finance [17] carried on further research along this line, and the Joint Commission on the Emergency in Education did much to show the need of equalization.[18]

Equality of educational opportunity is a principle that is fundamental in American education—a principle based upon the assumption that our democracy is best served by extending to all the children an equal minimum opportunity to attend schools adequate for the achievement of self-realization, economic efficiency, civil efficiency, and efficiency in human relationships. To deny this principle is to thwart the basic purposes of American education as they were conceived by its founders and as they have been developed to meet the needs of a modern civilization.

Equality of educational opportunity means, not an identical education for all children, but the provision by state or local means of at least certain minimum essentials of financial support. The acceptance of education as a function of the state and the insistence that, in the main, certain minimum educational standards are the concern of all the people in the state rather than that of certain minorities make it incumbent upon the state to provide the machinery through which the principle may be effectively realized. The classical statement of the implications of the principle of equality of educational opportunity, as given by the Educational Finance Inquiry Commission in 1923, recognized the obligation of the state to require at least minimum schooling for all the children, to place the support of this minimum schooling squarely upon the resources of the state, and to make supervision an important element in the state's program.[19]

The implications of this conception appear to do for the idea of equalizing opportunity what the national legislation of the 1930s did for welfare. It has taken education out of the posture of helping the poorer communities provide a more adequate pittance. In its place it has centered the responsibility squarely on the state government to provide a minimum

---

[16] George D. Strayer and Robert M. Haig, *The Financing of Education in the State of New York,* report of the Educational Finance Inquiry Commission, The Macmillan Company, New York, 1924, vol. I, p. 174.

[17] American Council on Education, "State Support for Public Education," *Report of the National Survey of School Finance.* Washington, 1933.

[18] National Education Association, Joint Commission on the Emergency in Education, *Report of National Conference on the Financing of Education,* Washington, 1933, p. 23.

[19] Strayer and Haig, *op. cit.*

of educational support adequate in terms of our needs as a people. To make it possible for the "poor" community more easily to provide education up to its own standards is not enough; all communities must support education on a level at least as high as the state standard of adequacy. This minimum of support constitutes the foundation program, dealt with at some length in Chapter 3.

Underlying the equality principle is the concept of assuring a minimum without placing a ceiling on opportunities—the idea of helping those handicapped by their economic and social environment. Equality of opportunity demands leveling up, not leveling down. It demands helping the weak, not hobbling the strong.

Adaptability

The success of the school, like the success of any other institution, depends upon the extent to which it serves present needs and can accommodate itself to present-day social, economic, and political contingencies. In a rapidly changing social and political structure, no institution can be in the vanguard or even keep reasonably up to date unless it has the capacity to make changes in its structure, in its methods, and in its purposes—unless it is adaptable.

Any new developments in the organization of public education, any changes in the allocation of control, any new methods of financial support must be evaluated, at least in part, with respect to their contribution to adaptability. They must favor the adaptive mechanism within their own structure and must make the schools more pliable, more sensitive to new needs, and more ready to produce necessary changes in methods or administrative practices. This concept of adaptability has been defined as follows: "Adaptability is the capacity for adaptation. It may be thought of as being conditioned by the environmental setting in which a school system must operate, by the structural nature of the school system, and by the use of the adaptation processes of public and private agencies within or without the school systems." [20]

It is a well-known fact that there is much in our existing educational system that had its origin in another century and was intended to serve past generations. Witness, for example, the subjects taught in the present-day college-preparatory curriculums—Latin, French, algebra, geometry, physics, chemistry, and the like—all of which as now taught are largely a perpetuation of the academic tradition and ill adapted to the large proportion of children who will not continue their education beyond the twelfth grade. When the secondary schools were highly selective and attracted only a small proportion of the young people of high school age,

[20] Paul R. Mort and Francis G. Cornell, *American Schools in Transition,* Bureau of Publications, Teachers College, Columbia University, New York, 1941.

these pupils were usually of the group that had both the ability and the purpose to pursue academic subjects. For the great masses of our high school pupils today such subjects are inappropriate. To emphasize them is obviously very wasteful of time, money, and the learning opportunities of the pupils.

The continuance in the schools of practices that belong to the past and are ill adapted to the present is frequently tolerated to the point where the situation becomes absurd. Often there is a sudden break with tradition, resulting in hurriedly formulated policies and ill-considered practices that, while they introduce change, do not accomplish the most desirable improvement of the system. If such breaks in our educational systems are to be avoided, the schools must constantly keep in touch with the changing social, economic, and political scene, and they must be willing to adapt their methods so as gradually to absorb the new and slough off the outworn in an ever-continuing process of adaptation. This process must go on within the school so as to keep the institution ever alert to the problems and needs of the day, ever moving forward at a pace with changing conditions of the community and the state.

It is recognized that many educational services have been forced upon the schools by outside community pressure and that not a few—such as playgrounds, libraries, and health clinics—are often conducted as community enterprises quite apart from the schools. During the depression of the 1930s certain educational services were carried on by the federal government entirely outside the public schools. It may be that these are signs of the failure of the schools to adapt their programs to changing conditions and new needs. Can it be that the more progressive citizens in a community must look outside the schools for newer educational developments? Whether this is the situation or not, there is urgent need to build into our public school system those elements of adaptability that will enable it to accommodate itself to needs as they arise in a community and to meet those needs. The design of the system for financing schools abounds with opportunities for enhancing adaptability.

SUMMARY

The form that fiscal arrangements take in American states is profoundly influenced by what have come to be widely accepted as specialized characteristics of government for the schools, by the problems of adjusting a school government that is an integral combination of state and local functions with a burgeoning economy and the three-level tax system, and by expectations the American people have of all government—expectations that are exemplified by our governmental arrangements but have not been exhausted by those governmental arrangements.

Specialized characteristics for the government of the schools are as follows: (1) School government as it has grown up in our national history has been constructed differently from other government. To view it as divisible into state and local aspects is to ignore the facts as to its character. At one and the same time it has vastly important local manifestations and strategically important central aspects. It must be viewed as an integral whole. (2) It is a legal fact that education is a state function. The implications of this are not as far-ranging as is often supposed. The key concept involved is state-wide concern. The fact is not particularly useful in resolving issues as to administrative devices. It has been widely invoked in court decisions in the establishment of the separateness of the local phases of school government from local government. (3) When we have established that education is a state function, we have established that there is no inherent right of local self-government in education. However, there seems to be a sort of home rule in the American school system for which the legal theorist has as yet no name. For example, in the long series of court decisions stemming from the Kalamazoo case in 1872, courts have declared in effect that the local authorities have the right to determine the character of the educational program, so long as they do not fail to carry out the injunctions of the law or of regulations by central authorities made in accordance with law and do not contravene such provisions detailing offerings which they may not give.

Two rules are helpful in resolving the conflicts that arise from using the three-level system of local, state, and federal taxation to finance an integral (state and local) system: (1) Powers of the agency of local jurisdiction should be broadly defined in law; powers of agencies of state-wide jurisdiction should be specifically defined. (2) The agency (or government level) made responsible for raising the revenue does not necessarily need to be the agency (or government level) that has ultimate discretion in spending.

Today, with the states more and more taking the responsibility for collecting revenues from non-property taxes and channeling them back to the schools, delay in legislative action has serious consequences. Some steps have been taken to relieve legislators through the allocation of powers to administrative agencies, but this has not occurred to any large degree in education. It is suggested that steps be taken to relieve legislatures of at least part of the now continuous fiscal responsibility for education. The requirement in some states that the state board make periodic reports on the fiscal needs of the schools is helpful. Consideration might well be given to allocating to the state board of education the power to keep in wholesome balance the support of education coming from state-collected revenues and the support coming from locally collected revenues.

Back of constitutions, statutes, and governmental structure are the public expectations they were designed to serve. Two that are particularly critical in the structure of state-aid systems are equality of opportunity and adaptability.

QUESTIONS FOR STUDY AND DISCUSSION

1. What is the status of school government in your state with respect to the issues discussed in the first section of this chapter?

2. What is the position taken in your state (by teachers' organizations, superintendents of schools, board members, state department of education, legislators, public figures in general) on the issues discussed in the first section of this chapter?

3. Does the legal responsibility for initiating changes in your state laws governing state aid or local financial arrangements rest with the legislature itself or has it to any degree been delegated to the state department of education or to some fiscal agent or body other than the state department of education?

4. Have there been any important changes in the laws governing your state department of education in recent decades? Did the changes touch on the place of the state department of education in shaping state fiscal policy?

5. In the introductory paragraphs to the second major section of this chapter, reference is made to a dozen additional cultural sanctions that have greater or less impact on school finance. You may be interested in selecting some financial topic and running down references to it in the index of Mort and Ross, *Principles of School Administration*. The index carries twenty-four references to the budget, four to the audit, seven to accounting, sixteen to taxation, twenty-four to control, and fifty-two to school districts.

SELECTED REFERENCES

Anderson, William A.: *American Government*, Henry Holt and Company, Inc., New York, 1938.

Beach, Frederick F., and Andrew Gibbs: *The Structure of State Departments of Education*, U.S. Office of Education, Miscellaneous Bulletin 10, Washington, 1949.

Chase, Francis S., and Edgar L. Morphet: *The Forty-eight State School Systems*, Council of State Governments, Chicago, 1949, chap. I, pp. 4–9.

Cocking, Walter D.: "The Role of the States in Education Since 1900," *State Government*, vol. 23, no. 6, pp. 119–123. June, 1950.

Cubberley, Ellwood P.: *Public Education in the United States*, rev. ed., Houghton Mifflin Company, Boston, 1934.

Finer, Herman: *English Local Government*, Columbia University Press, New York, 1934.

Garber, Lee O., and William B. Castetter: "Functions of Government in Educational Control," *Annals of the American Academy of Political and Social Science*, vol. 265, pp. 25–34, Philadelphia, 1949.

Gittell, Raymond G.: *Political Science*, Ginn & Company, New York, 1933.

Hamilton, Robert R., and Paul R. Mort: *The Law and Public Education*, The Foundation Press, Chicago 1959.

Holcombe, Arthur N.: *State Government in the United States*, 3d ed., The Macmillan Company, New York, 1931.

Mott, Rodney L.: "Strengthening Home Rule," *National Municipal Review*, vol. 29, no. 4, pp. 172–177, April, 1950.

National Council of Chief School Officers: *Our System of Education*, Washington, 1950.

National Education Association, Educational Policies Commission: *The Purposes of Education in American Democracy*, Washington, 1938.

————: *The Structure and Administration of Education in American Democracy*, Washington, 1938.

————: *The Unique Function of Education in American Democracy*, Washington, 1937.

Ross, Donald H. (ed.): *Administration for Adaptability*, Metropolitan School Study Council, New York, 1958.

Schultz, William J., and C. Lowell Harris: *American Public Finance*, 6th ed., Prentice-Hall, Inc., Englewood Cliffs, N.J., 1954.

Taylor, James E.: "Texas Moves Forward in Education," *State Government*, vol. 23, no. 1, pp. 13–16, January, 1950.

U.S. Commission on Organization of the Executive Branch of the Government: *The Hoover Commission Report*, McGraw-Hill Book Company, Inc., New York, 1949, part XIX, pp. 443–460.

Weltzin, J. Frederick: *The Legal Authority of the American Public School*, The Mid-west Book Concern, Grand Forks, N.D., 1931.

3. State and local responsibility: the foundation-program concept

T HE CONCEPT of the foundation program has a strategic place in clarifying the fiscal relationships of state governments and school districts and bids fair eventually to bring clarity into the maze of relationships between the federal government and the states involved in federal aid to education. This concept calls for the spelling out of a program of education in terms of over-all cost in each school district, which program shall be a joint responsibility of state-level government and the school districts. What the community spends on its own initiative, beyond the foundation level of support, is its own responsibility.

In addition to the purpose it serves in state-aid programs, this concept goes a long way in guiding the clarification of responsibility and the delimitation of authority of the state-level agencies and the school districts which, as was noted in Chapter 2, must operate simultaneously, as partners, on the same enterprise.

FISCAL ADVANTAGES AND DISADVANTAGES OF LOCAL AUTONOMY

The practice of local support of education in American states led to variations in expenditure levels from community to community for two reasons: (1) the communities vary in ability, and (2) the communities vary in vigor of local support. The reasons for the variation in ability are apparent. The variation in vigor of local support is a dynamic concomitant of the American emphasis on local support and control. Individual communities pioneer both with ideas and with the concept of how much a community is willing to tax itself for education. Communities having the same ability to support schools vary greatly in vigor of support unless low tax ceilings are set by law.

42

The differences in vigor among communities make it possible for those of average ability or better to create laboratories for improving education. They provide the pilot plants, the lighthouses. They are released from dependence on the uniformity of ability and vigor that characterizes a centralized system.

We have interesting examples of economically able and potentially vigorous communities thwarted from providing leadership in all large cities and in many of our larger county systems. These are exceptions in American practice but are the rule in most countries, since most countries have completely centralized support. Unhappily, with the growth of population and the accompanying widespread adoption of the large school district, the number is increasing rather alarmingly. Restricting tax limitations have worked in the same direction in many of our states.

While the average and better communities are freed by the system of local support, the poorer communities are handicapped. An extremely poor community cannot provide even a defensible minimum of support regardless of its vigor. In a centralized system with uniform support comparable to what the average community might have if decentralized, the very poor communities fare better than in a decentralized system. Witness the relatively favorable conditions found in the poorer sections of our city and county school districts when they are viewed alongside independent communities of similar wealth.

It is with the handicap of poorer districts under a decentralized system that equalization deals. In centralized systems the problem we attack through equalization does not exist. The problem in the decentralized system is how to deal with the disadvantages without losing the advantages and without involving inequitable treatment of communities with like ability but with different vigor. It boils down to this: What do districts lose in support by the system of local autonomy when compared with the support that would be available if the program were a centralized state program?

We can answer this question if we can get an estimate of what the state-wide program would be if there were no local-support districts. Having got the answer, we can then arrange for the granting of central funds sufficient to make up the lacks, assuming vigor of support comparable to what would characterize the state if it were to provide uniform support throughout, as now happens in city and county systems and the centralized systems of many countries.

EMERGENCE OF THE FOUNDATION-PROGRAM CONCEPT

To arrive at the estimates of lacks we must be able to compute the cost of the program which the state would be justified in supplying all schools if there were no local support. To estimate its cost we must first visualize the program. It is this visualized "state-wide program" which constitutes the foundation program. Net shortages from it in any district that through state and local taxes exercises vigor of support equal to that which the state as a whole would exercise to support such a program represent the losses it suffers, which, unless they are made up some way, must be either loaded as overburden on local taxpayers or foregone.

The discovery of a satisfactory solution to the equalization problem through the maze of other issues to be taken into account thus awaited the foundation-program concept evolved in the work of Strayer and Haig in 1923. Early attempts to meet the problem were not only generally inadequate but also fraught with undesirable effects on adaptability and the center of gravity of control.

Accordingly, it is safe to say that the foundation-program concept has been the most valuable single tool for clarifying the fiscal relationships of state and localities. It provides a basis for dividing the expenditures by local districts into those for which the state has a responsibility and those which are a solely local responsibility. When this division is made, the local variations in expenditure due to local variations in vigor are ruled out of the state-local fiscal picture.

In its 1949 report the National Education Association Committee on Tax Education and School Finance appraised the foundation-program concept in these terms:

The concept of the "foundation" program is that of establishing an equitable fiscal partnership between the state as a whole and the individual school systems charged with the responsibility and privilege of operating the public schools. Its purpose is to assure the financing of an acceptable educational offering in all school systems regardless of their taxpaying abilities.[1]

In its 1958 report the committee has the following to say:

At first the movement to implement the concept of state foundation programs was slow and halting. But during recent years the state foundation program concept has steadily spread, and with this spreading have come refinements of the concept and improvements in its application. As states have initiated and revised their foundation programs, they have usually incorporated the best features of programs existing in other states with adaptations from their own experience. Through this process of borrowing, adapting, and revising, better state-aid programs and concepts have evolved.[2]

[1] National Education Association, Committee on Tax Education and School Finance, *Guides to the Development of State School Finance Programs,* Washington, 1949, p. 5.
[2] National Education Association, Committee on Tax Education and School Finance, *Guides to the Improvement of State School Finance Programs,* Washington, April, 1958, p. 28.

Strayer and Haig introduced the foundation-program concept as it is now understood. Their original statement of it is as follows: [3]

To carry into effect the principle of "equalization of educational opportunity" and "equalization of school support" as commonly understood it would be necessary (1) to establish schools or make other arrangements sufficient to furnish the children in every locality within the state with equal educational opportunity up to some prescribed minimum; (2) to raise the funds necessary for this purpose by local or state taxation adjusted in such manner as to bear upon the people in all localities at the same rate in relation to their tax-paying ability; and (3) to provide adequately either for the supervision and control of all the schools, or for their direct administration, by a state department of education.

The basic concept having to do with the equalization of educational opportunity, in contradistinction to equalization of school support, is:

... to establish schools or make other arrangements sufficient to furnish the children in every locality within the state with equal educational opportunities up to some prescribed minimum.

The remainder has to do with equalization of burden and with the question of local vigor of school support.

Cost and Quality

The combination of these complex principles as given here resulted in a very considerable amount of confusion in the years immediately following the publication of the Report of the Educational Finance Inquiry. The idea of a minimum program gave a concept for a bench mark. Strayer and Haig gave no guidance as to what the height of this bench mark should be. They advised that we find out the cost implications for the ideas we have regarding the minimum educational program and then do the obvious thing with it of equalizing the burden so that it would become possible in the poorer communities as well as in the average and abler communities.

The idea that education has a price mark was more or less revolutionary. Most people agreed that some money is necessary for schools, but after they got the schools open, the amount of money to be spent on the schools seemed to them to be little related to the quality of the educational program. They could see that adding health service or shopwork would cost more money, but they could not see the relationship

[3] George D. Strayer and Robert M. Haig, *The Financing of Education in the State of New York*, report of the Educational Finance Inquiry Commission, New York, 1924, by permission of The Macmillan Company, pp. 173–175. This section of the report is quoted at greater length in Chapter 12.

of money to such aspects of the educational program as character development.

Today we have the advantage of a considerable number of studies of the relationship of the quality of education to expenditure level. They are discussed in Chapter 5. The detailed studies of this relationship were first introduced in the early 1930s. Even as late as 1933 the idea that money was related to quality in education was still a matter of conjecture.

Today we can speak with considerable confidence on the relationship between expenditure level and quality. We now have evidence covering a range of expenditure levels from near the lowest in the country to near the highest. We can say that we may expect such and such things to occur in a school on a given expenditure level. Accordingly we have a basis for prescribing a minimum in educational opportunity and for determining the expenditure level that it implies. As we see the quality unfold, it becomes apparent that, whatever interim steps we may take to equalize foundation programs somewhere near average practice or somewhere above the actual minimum practice in a state, we can hardly be content with expenditure levels short of a figure far beyond the national average. These higher expenditure figures become the goal toward which we should work, whatever the state.

Once we realize that the task is to assure the defensible foundation program to the children in even the least able communities, we see that the task of equalizing educational opportunity is, in fact, the task of making such an opportunity available, not the task of equalizing the burden of an adequate educational opportunity. The task of equalizing the burden is really in another category. It is a way of implementing the desired program. Any group that examines the facts as to the relationship between quality and expenditure level cannot but be forced to the realization that some financial provisions must be made for the poorer communities in all states, for without such financial aid the program that can be defended as the one we should have if we had no local taxing power for education cannot possibly be available to the children in certain communities in any state. The same holds for the poorer states in the Union.

Every program must be assessed in terms of how far it gets us along the road to the adequate equalization of a defensible educational opportunity, whatever other tests are pertinent. The essential problem of equalization becomes then the problem of making arrangements to provide the kind of education men of good will can honestly support as the minimum necessary for the achievement of our national ends—our welfare as a people and our fullest life as persons. It requires a more realistic assessment of what schools are doing in the individual states and in the nation as a whole. It requires a comparison of the poorest with the best. It requires judgment on the part of individuals and groups interested in the problem and their endorsement of what they consider to be a defensible stand to be taken by the agencies to which the responsibility for determination of policy has been delegated.

Quantity Measures Related to Cost

Consideration of the foundation program is simplified by the use of measures of quantity that can be related to cost. With such measures of quantity to account for the different amounts of education required in communities different in size and other pertinent characteristics available, it is possible to determine cost simply by multiplying the quantity units by an amount representing the unit cost desired. For example, if we could assume that a given quality of education would cost so much a pupil regardless of the size or other characteristics of the community, we could readily divide the expenditure of a district, whether large or small, by the number of pupils and get a figure which would represent the price tag on the education provided—its educational level. We could thus compare expenditures of communities. Or if we decided that the foundation program should be the kind of education that we could expect to buy for $400 per pupil, all we should need to do to find the cost of the foundation program in a community would be to multiply the number of pupils by $400.

Such a measure of quantity of education is known as a measure of educational need. Clearly the number of pupils to be educated is a rough measure of educational need. Likewise the number of teachers employed is also a rough measure, superior to the number of pupils in that it reflects differences in sparsity conditions affecting cost but inferior in that it reflects differences in support policy among communities. Likewise, the number of inhabitants of a district or the number of miles of highway would also be rough measures.

The weighted elementary pupil unit has proved to be the most satisfactory measure of educational need thus far developed. The concept of the weighted elementary pupil unit is a simple one. Under like conditions expenditures in education vary rather closely with the number of pupils. Accordingly, it is reasonable to assume that larger expenditures per pupil will give better returns if there is a relationship between expenditure level and the quality of education. The only problem is to refine this pupil measure to the point that differing conditions outside community control will be taken into account. For example, although costs of a like service vary with the number of pupils, they do not vary exactly with the number of pupils. If the pupils are in high school, the cost is in practice greater than if the pupils are in elementary school.

Similarly education is more expensive per pupil in rural schools that must transport the children than in schools where the children can walk to school. Or it is more expensive in rural schools that do not transport the children, because of the impossibility of getting as many children in a class as is found satisfactory in more thickly populated areas. Again the same quality of education costs more per pupil in communities where cost of living is higher than in communities where it is not so high. The problem of determining a defensible measure of educational need is simply the problem of taking into account those factors which cause the cost per pupil of a given educational program to vary from community to community.

When all the corrections are made, a single figure can be obtained which will represent so many equal "cost units," each of them equivalent to the cost of one pupil for a given program in a village or city elementary school having more than 300 pupils.

Sometimes the weighted elementary classroom unit is used. This is obtained by dividing the number of weighted elementary pupil units by a constant. Accordingly the number of weighted pupil units is simply a multiple of the weighted elementary classroom units. The pupil unit is the simpler and in most cases the measure to be preferred, but mathematically the choice is like choosing yards or inches as units of measurement. Either one will serve the purpose.

In the discussions that follow, the weighted elementary pupil unit is used exclusively as the measure of educational need. The detailed methods of developing a measuring rule calibrated in weighted elementary pupil units appear in Chapter 7.

THE LEVEL OF THE FOUNDATION PROGRAM

While the foundation-program concept has implications for state-control legislation and for the character of the work of state departments of education, fiscally we are concerned with its over-all unit cost. We are concerned fiscally primarily with the question: What *minimum unit expenditure* must be made possible in communities handicapped by the system of local support so that their children shall not be denied a program at least as good as might be expected from a satisfactory system of complete central support if that hypothetical system of central support were responsive to the needs?

In the decades since the foundation-program concept was brought to the fore by Strayer and Haig, the following approaches to an answer to this question have emerged:

1. The establishment of the fiscal implications of state mandatory legislation and state department regulations

2. The determination of level of expenditure in satisfactorily organized school districts of average wealth

3. The determination of the level of expenditure at which a reasonable level of adaptability is noted

4. The determination of the level of expenditure that reasonably assures an educational program acceptable in our times in terms of our social and personal needs as persons and as a people

The first two obviously have reference to a particular state. The other two are independent of state advantages and limitations. In the remainder of this section the strengths and weaknesses of each of these approaches are discussed. In general, the first two make less rigorous demands than the third, with the exception of three states—New York, New Jersey, and California—and in all states the first three make less rigorous demands than the fourth. All are helpful in reaching a judgment on the foundation program to be defended in any state at a given time.

Fiscal Implications of State Mandates

It is always enlightening to appraise the requirements for educational offerings as they have been established by state law or by central agency regulations having the force of law. In such an attempt it quickly comes to light that most such requirements can be met through a very low performance. For example, a requirement that United States history be taught is met if the school district makes the meagerest provisions for teaching United States history. Or a requirement that so many minutes a day be given to physical exercise may be met as well, as a mandate, by the school that has meager facilities as by the school well equipped with physical facilities and with specially trained teachers. The school system with high standards and the resources to meet them may find the special requirements very costly. The school system that lacks resources or lacks interest finds it possible to meet the letter of the requirement without adding to the costs. Such mandates are, of course, meaningless as far as assuring an adequate foundation program is concerned, and they give us no clue to the cost of such a program unless we introduce the idea of what such requirements ought to involve in cost.

These limitations do not apply in the same degree to out-and-out financial requirements such as minimum-salary laws. But even a minimum-salary schedule set by the state can be met by communities with limited resources or interest through provisions that must be far short of what was envisioned by those who drafted the law. The actual demands of the requirements may be watered down by the employment of teachers with a minimum of experience and training and, in all but the very smallest school districts, by employing fewer teachers than would be required if the needs were reasonably assessed.

Districts of Average Wealth

An analysis of expenditures in the well-organized districts of average wealth provides a test of consumer demand. Districts that do not vary markedly from the state average in taxable valuation (equalized) per weighted elementary pupil unit are selected. From these are removed any districts considered too small or too large to exercise local autonomy effectively—certainly one-teacher districts and city districts with more than 100,000 population. The median of their unit expenditures is then used as the unit cost of the foundation program. In states which have not made any great headway with equalization, the expenditure so determined is typically from two to four times that of the school spending the least. This criterion, therefore, sets a high standard, at least in terms of the task to be done in individual states.

The Adaptability Test

Both the mandate and average-wealth approach give strong emphasis to vigor of local support as it reflects the concern of people in many communities with education as they have understood it and their concern with tax rates as a sort of detached and independent criterion. The relatively recent studies of the rate of adaptation of schools to reflect improved methods and newly realized needs reveal conclusively that any such standards of "ability and willingness to support" cannot but reflect what is still a general unawareness of the relations between support level and quality and of two or three decades of adjustment to unparalleled changes in insight into social and economic implications of education as a social instrument. In contrast, the adaptability test reflects these new developments as does the social and economic test that is fourth in our list.

The first broad-scope study of adaptability, a study of Pennsylvania, revealed that communities differ in ability to slough off less efficient practices and to take on more efficient ones and that they differ in their ability to change their programs in line with improved insight into educational needs. In the report of the study referred to, this point is expressed in these words: "... some school districts are pioneers, some are early followers, some are late followers, and some never move without compulsion from central authority." [4] This study shows that, of the scores of factors which might help account for this difference in adaptability, expenditure level is one of the most important. This finding has been supported by later studies in Rhode Island, New York, West Virginia, Mississippi, and the metropolitan area about New York City, in-

---

[4] Paul R. Mort and Francis G. Cornell, *American Schools in Transition,* Teachers College, Columbia University, New York, 1941, p. 83.

volving communities representative of nearly every expenditure level in the entire range of school expenditure.

Vital as this approach would appear to be, it has not been widely used. The difficulty with this approach is that degrees of adaptability of a school system have not as yet been made translatable into meaningful categories. There is always a justification for a higher expenditure since no place in practice has been reached where increased expenditure is not associated with enhanced adaptability. The problem is: What degree of adaptability is essential for our times?

In attempting to isolate meaningful degrees of adaptability, recourse has always been taken to static descriptions of the schools. Few if any attempts have been made to describe a given level of adaptability in terms of how vital the school system is, how dynamic, responsive, flexible, elastic, imaginative, creative, inventive. Efforts at interpretation have been through static descriptions. The question asked has not been: What characterizes a given level of vitality (creativity, inventiveness, elasticity, etc.)? Rather, it has been: What do schools look like today which are characterized at a given level of adaptability? Such static descriptions of a dynamic characteristic have validity for a given time and have had some use in getting an understanding of the level of expenditure that should be assured. In a sense they answer the question: What level of support makes it probable that schools will be achieving today in such and such areas? The implication is that those that are achieving at such and such levels today have achieved this level by adapting. By implication they will continue to be achieving at about the described degree beyond the general run of school systems.[5]

The invocation of the criterion of adaptability would certainly put all but two or three states in a position of seeking a level of support considerably above the present average. A plan involving the adoption of such a minimum level of support would hardly be espoused unless there were a very real concern in the state for upgrading the whole system. There have been instances of action of a comparable strategic character in the history of most states although rarely in finance. Such a move in the realm of finance occurred in Rhode Island in 1955 when the state established a foundation program which utilized a higher minimum expenditure than was found at that time in any community in the state.[6] It involved increase in support both from the school districts and from the state. This step was taken in the face of the showing that

[5] For further discussion of the adaptability approach, see Paul R. Mort, *The Foundation Program in State Educational Policy*, The University of the State of New York, The State Department of Education, Albany, N.Y., 1957, pp. 47–58.

[6] Rhode Island State Board of Education, *State and Local Financing of School Operation*, Staff Study No. 3, Providence, R.I. 1955.

the schools were already as well supported as the schools in states with comparable ability.

Adequacy for Our Times

Perhaps the increased public concern with the schools, coupled with the widespread belief that schools are not adequate for our times, will result in more states, or even the national government, moving away from the bit-by-bit tactical approach to school finance that has characterized much of the fiscal activity during this century. A new look is reflected in the 1955 report to the New York State Educational Conference Board in a seven-page discussion of the demands of our times on education, leading to this recommendation "that . . . the people of this state take further steps to find the kind of foundation program of education required for the future in terms of citizenship, scientific and technological foundations, economic well-being, personal happiness, and other important objectives of education. . . ."

There would seem to be no basis for doubting that this is the approach we need. Before it can be used effectively, considerable broad-range creative thinking needs to be done. There are indications here and there that educators and others are beginning to realize that we are prepared—now, after more than a half-century of research, experimentation, and minor invention—to design a school system adequate to our times.

This stronger posture is showing up in a good many communities in support levels for schools three or four times the national average. It is having a marked effect on a few entire states. Perhaps the best approach for any state would be to seek to understand what the high-expenditure-level schools are doing. Interestingly enough, this was the approach followed in the Rhode Island study that eventuated in the adoption of a foundation level higher than the expenditure level of any community— in spite of the fact, as was noted earlier, that Rhode Island, when compared with its peer states, made an acceptable showing.[7] More detailed suggestions based on this approach appear in Chapter 7.

COST RELATED TO ABILITY

The foregoing considerations deal with what kind of education is desired—with what is in the market place and the price tag on it. In deciding

[7] Current information on expenditure levels in communities with strong support can be obtained from the financial studies of study councils serving areas around New York, Philadelphia, Pittsburgh, Detroit, Buffalo, Rochester, Syracuse, and Albany. Some of them issue current-year budget data at the middle of the school year. Data from wider ranges of school systems are published by the National Education Association Research Service, the Associated Public School Systems, the New England School Development Council, and the New York State Central School Study.

on the level of support, the feeling of prosperity, one assessment of ability to pay, can hardly be divorced from the assessment of good to be derived. In every such decision, a judgment on willingness to sacrifice is made whether consciously or unconsciously. There are indications that people of communities and of an entire state vary considerably in their feeling of prosperity. This variation is probably one of the strong factors, other things being equal, that show up in variation in what has been called "vigor of support." Accordingly, studies of relative effort or vigor and facts on relative economic ability have an important contribution to make to the process of deciding on the level of the foundation program to be set as a goal in a state.

A very important item is the amount of actual increase in expenditure that would be required (whether state or local) in the achievement of any given program. The fact can be determined by the simple process of computing the total amount that would be required to supplement present expenditures of districts below the proposed foundation program up to the foundation program. If the state average were accepted as a foundation program, the actual increase in expenditure would be amazingly small.

Studies made by Norton and others are helpful in orienting the people of a state with respect to their relative effort and serve to keep those designing fiscal policy from getting unknowingly out of line with practice. These studies should not, however, be taken as other than the norms established by a generation that has been greatly concerned with hot and cold wars, inflation, population increase, teacher shortages of all kinds, missiles, and space travel—a generation that perhaps has tended to take public education too much for granted, to consider it adequate as it was inherited from the nineteenth century and needing only a little attention to school houses, teacher recruitment, reading, and science. There is little sign that education has yet gained any extensive consideration as a potentially powerful social and economic instrument in the lives of communities, states, or the nation. Accordingly, in the use of comparative data on ability, the idea that the most vigorous effort on the part of any state is other than a favorable variation in a rather unmarked modern phenomenon should be avoided. The considerations reviewed in Chapter 6, coupled with personal knowledge of states and communities, lead the present authors to the opinion that the people of any state could with profit embark on a vigorous educational program which would represent effort far beyond what any state has yet made.

Scope of the Foundation Program

The foundation program should embrace (1) all the activities the state wishes to assure the communities of least ability to support schools and (2) the whole range of expenditure involved.

It should exclude aspects of the program that may be thought of as the pioneering of the abler districts, at least until the state is ready to meet the financial implications fully in the poorest districts. If aid is to be granted for the developments to stimulate their growth, it should be done outside the foundation program.

Also it should include the capital costs as well as the current costs, for to do otherwise is either to deny the less able communities and rapidly growing communities adequate buildings or to load upon them a burden of debt service that will encroach upon the ongoing program.

Attention is called to the fact that throughout this chapter discussion has been in terms of current costs. The reason for this is that current costs must be used to make valid comparisons among communities because of the fact that building cost or debt service in *any one year* bears no constant relationship to the education program. Increasing current cost figures by 14 per cent will give a figure that covers current costs and the cost of capital outlay evened out over the years; for example, what has been referred to as a $400 program connotes a program costing $400 annually for current purposes and an average of $56 a year, in perpetuity, for capital outlay (see Chapter 16).

Educational versus Financial Implications

While most discussions of the foundation program will be found associated with state aid or federal aid, the concept has other implications that warrant independent consideration. If, as is maintained in this chapter and in most treatments of it, it is a definition of the state-wide responsibility for education, it should provide a guide for the reexamination of mandates and regulations that have evolved over the years in the state. In most cases examples of mandates will be found that are absurdly high and others that are absurdly low, their implications, if not their absolute requirements, in present-day education considered. The questions to be asked are: Is it reasonable to expect what is patently implied by the mandate, assuming that the funds are available for the kind of a foundation program which is, in fact, possible in the state, current fiscal policy considered? If fiscal policy were brought into line with the demands of a defensible foundation program, could what is patently implied by the mandate be expected?

The first of these two questions can readily be answered by comparing what is done in the poorest school districts to meet the mandates. Surely opening the windows and putting children through a calisthenics drill in the classroom are not in line with a state mandate for so many minutes of physical education per day.

In brief, the foundation-program concept should help bring order and realism into the growth of mandates and regulations that have accumulated on the statute and state regulation books over the years.[8] It should help give them unity and balance. Perhaps it should substitute for them or add to them a minimum financial requirement to be met by the district as a prerequisite to continued existence as a governmental unit charged with the state's business of providing public education.[9]

Minimum Requirements versus State Aid

The treatment of the foundation program as proposed above facilitates differentiation between the foundation program as a mandatory requirement and the foundation program as a basis for computing state aid. So considered, the state may require the district to provide adequate funds so that its discretionary acts do not encroach on the foundation program. This sometimes occurs in the transportation of pupils. Some communities choose to transport children who live but a few rods from the school. Others may elect to reduce transportation to the minimum required by the state. Quite clearly, in the former case, a total expenditure just equal to that required by the computed cost of the foundation program would be short somewhere, since part of it would go to this optional transportation. Another problem is that some districts may be operating unnecessary one-teacher schools. "Luxury" expenditures on such schools should not be credited to the foundation-program expenditure required.

By-products

To develop the foundation-program concept it was necessary to refine the concept of expenditure level and to supplement available measures of school-system quality that would reflect what has been happening to education itself in the past few years. Entirely apart from their use in the development of state-aid programs, both concepts are central to the continuous evaluation of local school systems.

Interestingly enough, very little of the technical work that has been done in the refinement of measures of expenditure level has been done outside the state-aid studies. The uses of these measures in evaluation are dealt with in Chapter 7.

[8] See A. W. Schmidt, *The Development of a State's Minimum Educational Program,* 1932, and J. K. Flanders, *Legislative Control of the Elementary Curriculum,* 1925, Bureau of Publications, Teachers College, Columbia University, New York.

[9] See Paul R. Mort and Donald H. Ross, *Principles of School Administration,* 2d ed., McGraw-Hill Book Company, Inc., New York, 1957, p. 348, for this type of mandate in the school code for the state of New Osceola.

CRITICAL DECISION ON THE FOUNDATION PROGRAM

Central to the principle of equalization of educational opportunity is the assurance, by some manner, of the kind of program the people of the state want to assure as a minimum in every community—the program below which no community shall be allowed to go. Nothing that is done simply to make a given foundation program fair to all communities will offset the error of selecting a foundation that, when achieved, does not assure to the least favored community the kind of educational program that the people of the state would want if they knew all the facts and implications. By all odds, the step of choosing a foundation level as a goal is the most important in the series of steps required to achieve effective fiscal policy.

Because of lack of fiscal power in some communities, state aid is required. But state aid is not all that is required. The foundation-program concept demands a review of mandates and sanctions, district organization, and services of central agencies.

SUMMARY

The concept of the foundation program has proved highly useful as a device for differentiating the responsibility of the state as a whole from the additional responsibilities assumed by local communities on their own initiative. This poses a complex problem faced only by those states or nations which have built local support of education into their educational structures.

The utilization of local support in American states has led to variations in expenditure levels from community to community, (1) because of differences in ability among the communities and (2) because of community differences in vigor of local support. It has made it possible for communities of better than average ability or better than average vigor to create laboratories for shaping better education. At the same time it has resulted in handicapping poorer communities unless proper steps have been taken by the state to supplement local taxing power by means of state funds.

The amount that the poorer districts suffer from the decentralized system in operation in American states can be gauged by comparing what they can achieve through local support with the kind of support they would have under a centralized program.

The foundation program is the program which we would have a right to expect the state to provide all districts if there were no local support.

In the study of fiscal policy we are interested in the cost of the foundation program. This cost may be expressed as so much per some unit of measurement that can be related to cost—by definition, a unit of educational need. The expenditure per unit of educational need, such as so many dollars per weighted elementary pupil, is the unit cost of the foundation program, or the "level of the foundation program."

In establishing a satisfactory cost level for the foundation program, four approaches have been used:

1. The establishment of the fiscal implications of state mandatory legislation and state department regulations.

2. The determination of level of expenditure in satisfactorily organized school districts of average wealth.

3. The determination of the level of expenditure at which a reasonable level of adaptability is noted.

4. The determination of the level of expenditure that reasonably assures an educational program acceptable today in terms of our social and personal needs as a people and as persons.

The foundation program should embrace all the services the state wishes to assure all communities at minimum acceptable levels. It should exclude aspects of the program for which the state is not as yet ready to meet fully the financial implications in the poorest districts.

The educational implications of the foundation-program concept are of such importance that it is wise to treat the definition of the foundation program in state statutes independently of the state-aid program.

QUESTIONS FOR STUDY AND DISCUSSION

1. What is the foundation-level "goal" which educational bodies in your state have accepted as an ultimate objective?

2. Write a description of the kind of school you would have a right to expect if your state were to establish its present average as a foundation program. What would be the strong contributions of such a program to the great mass of individuals who would experience the program and to our nation as a nation? What would be its outstanding lacks in both these respects that could reasonably be achieved on a level of support you could defend in terms of personal needs and the needs of our way of life? Use the descriptions of schools referred to in this chapter as a basis for your description.

3. What would you state as the possible results of a step that would yield a national foundation level of support of $400 per weighted pupil?

4. Dewey stated the following: "What the best and wisest parent wants for his child that must the community want for all its children. Any other ideal is narrow and unlovely. Acted upon it destroys our democracy." What would the fiscal implications of this statement mean for your state? The social implications? The economic implications?

SELECTED REFERENCES

Burke, Arvid J.: *Financing Public Schools in the United States*, rev. ed., Harper & Brothers, New York, 1957 (see index).

The Cooperative Study Policy Committee: *Education for Our Times, A State Action Program*, Maryland State Department of Education, Baltimore, Md., May, 1959.

Cornell, Francis G., and William P. McLure: in R. L. Johns and E. L. Morphet (eds.), *Educational Problems and Issues in Public School Finance*, Bureau of Publications, Teachers College, Columbia University, New York.

Mort, Paul R.: *The Foundation Program in State Educational Policy*, The University of the State of New York, The State Department of Education, Albany, N.Y., 1957.

National Education Association: *Guides to the Improvement of State School Finance Programs*, Washington, 1958.

National Education Association Research Bulletin, vol. 36, no. 1, February, 1958.

New York State Educational Conference Board: *Toward More Quality Education*, Albany, N.Y., August, 1958.

————: *Your School Budget, Its Setting, and the Challenge of the Times*, Albany, N.Y., September, 1959.

Ross, Donald H. (ed.): *Administration for Adaptability*, Metropolitan School Study Council, New York, 1958.

4. Local fiscal machinery

O NE OF the prime functions of the school district as an agency of government is to make financial decisions within the metes and bounds established in the legislation that created and maintains it. This chapter discusses the variety of forms which arrangements for financial decision making have taken, goes into some detail on one much discussed facet, the relation with municipal government, and finally seeks to sketch the issues of control of decision making in a somewhat broader framework than it has become the custom to utilize.

MACHINERY FOR MAKING TAXING AND EXPENDITURE DECISIONS

Nationwide, the plan for making local decisions respecting taxes to be levied locally for the schools and the pattern of expenditure to be followed centers responsibility in a board of education, answerable both to the state and the local electorate. The law stipulates the tax base to be used. All but universally, however, there are certain matters reserved to the electorate. An example is bond issues.

Variations in Arrangements—Boards of Education

When an attempt is made to be more specific than this, variations are met with on every hand. The board is usually elected, but it may be appointed by the mayor of the city, appointed by the courts, or, as in most Maryland communities, appointed by the governor. The final decision as to the amount of money to be spent for school purposes in any year is typically in the board itself, but it may be in a town meeting, in a special school town meeting, in a ballot vote by the electorate, in a city board of estimate, in a county reviewing body, or in a state-wide reviewing body. The tax base is usually the property tax, but the property tax may be supplemented by a poll tax (with the rate set by law or allowed to vary within limits), by payroll taxes, by income taxes, by sales taxes, or by one or more of a variety of minor taxes. The property tax may be available without legal limits or may be subject to legal limits of greater or less restrictiveness.

The taxes may be collected by the board of education or by some other government agency—municipal government or county. Boards vary in size, in length of term, and in their representativeness—whether elected by subareas or at large. If elected, the election may be at a separate, nonpartisan, school election or at a regular election. If at a regular election, candidates may be listed on party ballots or all may be listed on all party ballots. Most but not all boards serve without pay.

All these variations are provided by law. Most states have at least two patterns, in some instances varying with size of the districts—in others, with specific provisions in city charters. In some instances, as in New Jersey, communities are given a choice as to type of budgetary control; in several states they have a choice as to the size of the board.

Variations as between Boards and the Electorate

There are certain functions that are almost universally referred back to the electors of a district before any action is taken. The most important example of this type is the determination of the question of the erection and equipment of buildings through the issuing of school bonds. Conditions surrounding the issuing of school bonds are usually quite rigidly prescribed by the laws of the states and almost universally require a favorable vote of the electors. While it is impossible to give a summary of the various types of provisions, both legal and regulatory, surrounding the levying of taxes for school purposes, the following summary gives a few of the more outstanding provisions common in the several states.

1. State laws usually prescribe the maximum indebtedness that a school district may incur, in terms of some set percentage of taxable property. There are also legal provisions that regulate the maximum term of the bond issues, the rates of interest, and the plans for the payment of the principal of the issue.

2. Usually some legal provision is made for boards of education to incur short-term indebtedness for current operations, but only in very rare cases can boards of education incur indebtedness for the purpose of erecting and equipping school buildings. This usually requires a favorable vote of the people.

3. A third provision is that of requiring the vote of the people for exceeding a given specific tax levy. Frequently there are maximum levies which the board may not exceed without the consent of the people.

Until recently there was a strong tendency on the part of students of school administration to assume that the best ultimate answer to the control of the budget was to leave it in the hands of the board of education. There was a tendency to deplore such arrangements as are found in New England towns, where the town meeting decides on the budget for the schools either in detail or in toto at the same meeting at which it decides on the budget for municipal purposes. Similarly the situation that obtains rather generally in the states of New York and New Jersey, except in large communities, where in the former case people in a district meeting have the power to determine the character of the budget and in the latter case the total amount of the budget, has been looked upon as unduly complex. By the same token, provisions found in states such as West Virginia, Ohio, Michigan, Oklahoma, and California, where boards of education have the power to set the tax rate limited by a maximum tax rate, the exceeding of which requires a vote by the people, have been considered as unduly limiting on the power of the board of education.

Certain observations made during the period of stress caused by loss of purchasing power of the dollar following the Second World War seem to give some grounds for a review of this attitude. A check made by the senior author in the spring of 1948 from a sampling of school systems throughout the United States showed that, in communities where the budget is decided on by the electorate rather than by the board of education, the average expenditure per pupil both in 1940 and 1947 was considerably higher than the average expenditure per pupil in communities where the decision was made by the board of education or by the board of education with review by some municipal authority. The advantage of the "electorate-determined budget" over the budget determined by a representative body held for communities when classified by size groups up to but not including the largest group of districts having electorate control (35,000 to 50,000 population).

The lack of comparative data on ability to support schools in poorer school districts from state to state made it impossible to discover whether or not the above findings might be due to differences in ability. There was some ground for doubts on this score because of the fact that two high-ability states, New York and New Jersey, have the electorate-determined budget as the predominant type—number of districts considered.

However, a recheck of the data, limiting the comparison to boards in the same expenditure category and the same region of the United States, at least partially offset this shortcoming and still gave results that indicated a tendency toward a better showing in the districts that operate with a voter-controlled budget.[1] From this there would seem to be a basis for a renewed interest in this type of budget control. The point is enlarged on later in this chapter in connection with the discussion of the issue of fiscal independence of school boards.

It is of interest that the voter-controlled budgets persist in greater or less degree in fifteen states. In New England the town-meeting system operates over schools and municipal government in most communities, the sizable cities being the exceptions for the most part. In New York and New Jersey voter control is as predominant as in New England— in New York through a sort of special town meeting operating for schools only and in New Jersey, except in districts that elect to follow the alternative plan provided by law (mostly cities), through submission of the budget to the voters for acceptance or rejection by ballot. In Kansas, Minnesota, Oregon, and Wyoming, the town-meeting plan operates in small school districts; in Kansas, in common school districts and rural high school districts; in Minnesota and Wyoming, in common school districts; in Oregon, in districts with fewer than 200 pupils and in all districts in case the budget rises over a specified percentage. In California, Michigan, and West Virginia, voters must approve tax levies beyond certain statutory limits.[2]

Variations Interrelated

The variations are not entirely independent of each other. Four examples are given: (1) Where the state law calls for an over-all tax limit on property, either arrangements must be made for a set division of the available base between schools and other government or the decision on the amount for schools must be left with some authority other than the school board. (2) Where the people do not vote on the appropriations annually, there will more likely be found a check on the representative authority (board or municipal government) in the form of legal tax limits. (3) An appointed board is rarely given the ultimate authority over the amount to be spent, but there are notable exceptions. (4) Large school districts are the more likely to have appointed boards.

Local School Government Still Experimental

Quite clearly we are still in a formative stage on this matter of the shape of local school government. In time many of these variations may be expected to fall by the wayside of their own weight—such variations

[1] Reported in an article by Paul R. Mort entitled "Voter Control vs. Board Control of the Budget," *School Executive,* vol. 70, pp. 34–37, July 1, 1951.

[2] For the above information the authors are indebted to the Chief School Officers for supplying the information in response to a special request sent them in the fall of 1949.

as overlarge boards (over nine, for example) or oversmall boards (under five, for example).

Up to now, the only variation that has been subjected to intensive study for more than one-third of a century is that having to do with the relationship of school government to municipal authorities—the issue of fiscal independence. It may be noted that it is the issue that runs through the four interrelationships listed above. Where there is a tax limit, fiscal dependence is likely to follow (1). Where the people don't vote on the annual appropriation, there are usually tax limits (2) and therefore fiscal dependence (1). Large districts are less likely to retain fiscal decision in the voters (4) and thus are more likely to have tax limits and, in turn, fiscal dependence. Large districts are more inclined to have appointed boards (4) and therefore to have fiscal dependence (3). Here the core issue that emerges is fiscal independence.

Turning the argument the other way around, where school districts are not overlarge, there is more likelihood that there will be voter control. Where there is annual voter decision on the amount to be spent, there is little likelihood that there will be tax limits. From this the core issue appears to be closeness of popular control.

THE CRITICAL ISSUES

Quite clearly these two issues are interrelated. The fiscal-independence issue would appear to respond more readily to resolution if the popular-control issue were grappled with. The footings of fiscal independence are in the integral character of school government, and it would appear to need no other justification. The footings of the popular-control issue are in the principle of adaptability. To justify fiscal independence we need only to show that it is not intolerably wasteful (which it certainly is not, as shown by the long series of studies). To justify close popular control to the degree that some school districts have it, we must show its fruits in better schools, for the alternative rules out completely any concomitant advantages of close popular control claimed under the "home rule" principle—the principle of structural democracy.

FISCAL INDEPENDENCE AND THE ROOT PROBLEMS INVOLVED

Most evaluations of the problem of control have dealt solely with the fiscal-independence issue. These studies are reviewed here.

While there are a good many smaller school systems that are fiscally dependent on some body outside the school framework, it is particularly a problem of large districts—cities and county systems.

The control situation in large districts is in a state of uncertainty and transition. The finding of a good solution out of the great variety of practices that has grown up as cities became outsize and the county-unit system developed is one of the challenging current problems.

Fiscal Control in Cities

McLaughlin posed seven questions for determining the fiscal status of a board of education in relation to municipal government: [3]

1. Does the board of education have the power to estimate and finally determine the amount of the current expense budget?
2. Does the board of education have the power to levy or cause to be levied taxes sufficient to raise the revenue necessary for the established budget?
3. Is the board of education free to establish accounting procedures, purchasing methods, budgeting practices, the handling and payment of funds, the hiring and control of all personnel and like matters, independent of outside control?
4. Is the taxable wealth available to the board of education sufficient to provide ample funds for a good school program?
5. Is the tax base possessed by the school board so circumscribed as to be of limited use in providing funds for the school system?
6. Does the board of education have a reserve of taxable wealth beyond that being utilized currently for the support of schools and other governmental functions, sufficient to enable it freely to adapt school practices to the expanding needs of the community?
7. Does the board of education clearly demonstrate a responsiveness to the voice of the people in regard to educational matters?

The first two items are the central ones, even though, as McLaughlin points out, it is possible to answer these two questions in the affirmative and still have hampering conditions that nullify the critical budget power. The seventh could be considered as questioning the policy of transferring from the electorate's hands as much power as is customarily sought.

The concern over fiscal independence of boards of education expressed in an extensive series of studies beginning in the early 1920s reflects the fact that American cities are still seeking for a good answer to a difficult question. The long search for a satisfactory substitute for the public meeting in the control of education has been going on during the last century throughout the whole range of American cities. At the present time about one-half of the boards of education in American cities are fiscally independent. The recent trend has been toward a slight increase

[3] From Frederick C. McLaughlin, "Fiscal and Administrative Control of City School Systems," *Fiscal Policy for Public Education in the State of New York*, Staff Study 4, New York State Educational Conference Board, Albany, N.Y., January, 1949.

in fiscal dependence. Reasons for this trend were the increase of property-tax limitations on the one hand and the activity of groups interested in achieving what they considered simplicity of governmental organization on the other.

Effective tax limitation results in fiscal dependence either of the municipal government on boards of education or of the board of education on municipal government unless a division is made in the tax limit so that part of it is allocated to the schools and part of it to municipal government. Only one case has come to notice where the board of education was given the upper hand. This is in the city of Auburn, N.Y., where the city charter provided for the school board's supplying its own needs first, thus setting the limits to what is available for municipal government. This proviso has recently been superseded by a general law providing fiscal independence to all school boards in New York cities with less than 125,000 population.

The other factor that probably has had something to do with the slowing down of the trend toward fiscal independence of boards of education is the conflict in conceptions of what constitutes simplicity in government—the position that all locally operated government can be put in one governmental package as opposed to the argument that school government, state and local, is the proper packaging. This point has been discussed in Chapter 2. The evidence shows that the argument for dependence has to be based on this inapplicable concept of simplicity. Every extensive test of economy and efficiency that has been made has either favored the separation or shown no difference. In brief, fiscally independent boards of education do not spend more but they spend more effectively. They do not spend more effectively all the time or on every phase of the program, but on the whole, and generally, they spend more effectively.

Under the circumstances it is strange that we have been so long in bringing the control of education in our cities into line with the weight of experience. The reason for our tardiness with cities doubtless lies in the complexity of problems of government in these cities. For many years there was no attempt to associate school districts with the cities. When the move toward amalgamation into more satisfactory units went forward, however, there was a tendency to make these larger school districts coterminous with cities and to seek to find the answer for their government in the city pattern. This was the only experience that people in these communities had had in working as a larger community. The larger amount of dissatisfaction with the arrangements indicated by the changes in city charters would seem to suggest that those who followed the separation principle had fewer difficulties.[4] They are those who did

4 *Ibid.,* p. 18.

not despair of maintaining close relationship between education and the people in spite of the complexity of the city.

Salient Points of Comparison Studies

Frasier compared groups of school systems so organized with respect to an efficiency index which he developed. He found that the medians of the index numbers computed for the various groups of cities varied from plus .75 for the first group to minus 2.70 for the ninth group. When the first five groups were combined and classed as independent and the last four groups combined as dependent school boards, a correlation of minus .27 was attained between dependence and school efficiency, as measured by the index numbers; that is, according to Frasier's index, the more dependent, the less efficient.[5]

Two points of view have developed with respect to the desirability of fiscally independent boards of education. The one, advocated largely by school administrators, is that, since education is a function of the state, it does not properly belong under the jurisdiction of the city government. The other, usually advocated by authorities in municipal government, holds that education is but one activity carried on by the city and that greater economy and efficiency can be achieved by coordinating all activities carried on by the city authorities.

Frasier summarizes the case for fiscal independence under six points as follows:

1. Fiscal independence is right in principle.
2. Fiscal independence is not a violation of the principle of taxation.
3. Fiscal independence works better in practice.
4. Fiscal independence makes for a continuity of educational policy.
5. Fiscal independence provides adequate financial safeguards for the community.
6. Fiscal independence tends to keep politics out of the schools.

McGaughy conducted an investigation in which he included 377 cities divided into fiscally independent and fiscally dependent ones.[6] In this study, he found certain financial and education factors to be significantly larger on the average in independent than in dependent cities. These are

School tax rate per $100 real valuation.
Percentage that school tax rate is of total municipal tax rate.
Percentage that school bonded debt is of total municipal bonded debt.
General control expense per pupil in A.D.A.

[5] G. W. Frasier, *The Control of City School Finances*, The Bruce Publishing Company, Milwaukee, 1922, chap. VI.

[6] From J. R. McGaughy, *The Fiscal Administration of City School Systems*, The Education Finance Inquiry Commission, New York, vol. V, pp. 2–3. By permission of The Macmillan Company, 1924.

Maintenance of plant per pupil.

Fixed charges per pupil.

Capital outlay per pupil.

Debt service per pupil.

Percentage of increased cost of living from 1913–1914 to 1919–1920 that was met by increased salaries for women elementary teachers.

Percentage of sixteen- and seventeen-year-old children in school.

Percentage of pupils having 60 sq. ft. or more of playground each.

Percentage of children enrolled who attend school all day and in adequate buildings owned by the city.

Frasier's Index of School Efficiency.

Financial and educational factors that were found to have a significantly higher average for dependent cities than for independent ones are the following: [7]

Percentage of real valuation at which taxable property is assessed.

Municipal bonded indebtedness outstanding per capita.

Percentage that total municipal bonded debt is of total real valuation of taxable property.

Instructional services, per pupil.

Teachers' salaries, per pupil.

Percentage of women elementary teachers having six or more years of training above eighth grade.

More recently, Henry and Kerwin have reported a nonstatistical study of the problem in cities having 50,000 or more population. They point out that the state legislature has the power to assign the operation of its schools to an agency of its own choosing and that, therefore, legally there can be no question of the soundness of fiscal dependence. They then proceed, as indeed did McGaughy and Frasier, to apply the pragmatic test. They considered in this the advantage of both the schools and municipal government.

They compared the two types of organization on such matters as amount of cooperation on common problems and considered such matters as common service bureaus. They found no marked difference in cooperation on community problems and discovered political interference present under both control conditions in some instances and absent in others. Since they seemed to have accepted the point of view that simplicity required one system locally (in contradistinction to simplicity through the integration of the school system, state and local, as presented in Chapter 2), they read their results as favoring, or at least as not opposing, fiscal dependence.

Woodward in the late 1940s made a study covering much the same ground as the McGaughy study of a quarter-century earlier. His study

[7] *Ibid.*, pp. 55–56.

embraced 338 cities over 25,000 population. With the exception of the state of Pennsylvania, fiscally dependent cities were concentrated chiefly in the Eastern section of the United States, fiscally independent cities were found largely in the Western section, cities falling in the special category were centered largely in the Great Lakes region, and in the Southern states a general mixture of independent, dependent, and special cities was found, with the dependent cities predominating.

Woodward made an analysis of expenditure in 85 cities between 100,000 and 1,000,000 population over the period 1929–1930 to 1943–1944. During this period the mean per pupil expenditure was highest in the fiscally dependent cities. They spent about 4 per cent more than the independent districts in 1929–1930 and nearly 12 per cent more in 1943–1944. The differences appear to be mainly in the instruction and operation of plant items. He calls attention to the need for a more searching analysis than his data made possible and outlines a series of such studies.

Woodward states that there was no significant change in status in this group of cities in the quarter of a century since McGaughy's study.[8]

Fuller gives a cogent summarization of the problem: [9]

Local programs of education are now governed almost everywhere by local boards of laymen selected and serving on a nonpartisan basis. More than 85 per cent of local school boards are fiscally independent from municipal governments. In the older parts of the country, where most of the 15 per cent of school districts with some remaining fiscal dependence on municipal governments are located, establishment of debt and tax limits for education apart from debt and tax limits for municipal government promises to eliminate the political veto of the school budget. The large cities will be the last to reform, but even there less resistance is found lately—since many municipal politicians have discovered that school budgets are too large to be political assets, and especially since the people commonly insist that school funds are more out of bounds for political fence building than are other tax funds. Public education is legally a state function, and local school board members are legally state officials locally selected. They are not municipal officials. Local boards of education have expert professional administrators seldom matched in the municipality by professional city or town managers. The superintendent of schools and his board must be protected from aspects of municipal politics detrimental to schools. It would often be almost impossible to operate effective schools if school government were to be merely a part of municipal government.

[8] Henry B. Woodward, "The Effect of Fiscal Control on Current School Expenditures," doctoral dissertation, Teachers College, Columbia University, New York, 1948, p. 14. In 1920, 42.8 per cent of cities above 30,000 were fully independent; in 1947, 43.1 per cent.

[9] From a paper on *Education in the Reorganization of the Federal Government* by Edgar Fuller, Executive Secretary, National Council of Chief State School Officers, Jan. 27, 1950.

Fiscal Control in County Systems

The development of large local units not spurred on by urbanization bids fair to throw us into the same sort of a control problem as that which has accompanied the growth of cities. Only in Utah and Alabama and the new large districts in Idaho has the power been placed in the board of education.

DIRECT POPULAR CONTROL VERSUS DELEGATED CONTROL

Fiscal dependence of boards of education on some external authority may be viewed as a system of checks and balances placed upon a representative body when direct control of the electorate was given up. As a matter of fact the question of fiscal independence or dependence does not arise except in those cases where the power has been given up by the electorate. The question may well be raised whether or not this issue of electorate control should not be brought into the picture in seeking solution to the problems of fiscal independence and fiscal dependence. Perhaps it should not be fiscal independence as opposed to fiscal dependence but rather more direct control by the electorate as opposed to control either by the board of education or by the board of education subject to some external checks and balances.

An interesting example of how the search for checks and balances may proceed when close popular control is sacrificed is given by the experience of West Virginia in the 1930s. When West Virginia moved from the district system to the county system, the power over the budget within certain limits was placed in the county board of education. It was not long until someone developed the idea that the county board of education should be subject to some system of checks and balances. Noting the general lack of vigor of local support of public education, the survey staff, to its own satisfaction at least, traced the cause to the remoteness of control introduced by the county system.[10]

The historical development of delegated control of education would be worthy of a more complete historical treatment than it has been given. The general conception seems to be that, when school districts became too populous and the town-meeting type of control thus became too unrepresentative, the answer was to delegate control to a board of education or to the municipal authorities. Even a modicum of looking about has revealed that this has not always held. There are a goodly number

[10] George D. Strayer, Director, *A Report of a Survey of Public Education in the State of West Virginia*, State of West Virginia, Legislative Interim Committee, Charleston, W.Va., 1945, pp. 114–117. Somewhat more extensive discussion of this appears on pp. 548–551 of this same report.

of New England towns of sizable population that have been experimenting with a plan which appears to be much closer to the town-meeting control than to board control. Greenwich, Conn., affords a striking example.

The town of Greenwich (population 50,000) operates under a plan which provides for the election of a representative assembly. Each member of this representative town meeting represents approximately 100 qualified voters. The assembly performs the functions of the town meeting in smaller communities and of the popular balloting on the budget in many larger communities. This is an experiment in self-government worthy of consideration for wider use. In the case of Greenwich, the representative town meeting controls municipal affairs as well as school affairs. There would seem to be no good reason, however, why it could not be adapted for school affairs alone as an adaptation of the school-meeting plan that has been operating in New York State villages and smaller districts since 1812.

Intermediate Districts

The use of an agency intermediate between the state central agency and the local operating agency is not new. The county superintendent of the Midwest and West, the district superintendent of New York State, the regional "state supervisor" in Connecticut and Maine, all performed vital functions in communication and in selection of teachers and supervisors in the early days, and all played a strategic role in the school-district reorganization movement. The county superintendents of New Jersey and Pennsylvania came rather early to play an important financial role in the smaller districts.

In recent years there has been a strong movement to utilize these intermediate offices or to create new intermediate offices to administer and, in some instances, to finance services that can be shared by a number of districts. This step appears to give the consolidated, village, and small city districts the critical advantage of bigness without the disadvantages of the loss of close popular control that comes with the utilization of large populations or large areas as the prime local operating agency.

Among the challenging current developments of the intermediate agency are the county services in California, liberally financed by the state, the county services in Pennsylvania, and the cooperative-boards arrangement in New York State. The New York State development is interesting in that it involves a lay board as well as professional administration.

A NEW LOOK AT THE LOCAL FISCAL ARRANGEMENTS

With this background the studies of fiscal independence versus fiscal dependence might readily be viewed as a search to discover which of two poor ways of controlling policy is the better.

The New York State Educational Conference Board grappled with this problem of determining broader fiscal-control machinery for districts of various sizes in a report published in 1956. At the time of the study, school districts in New York State were organized as follows:

1. Six city school districts varying in population from 125,000 to 8,000,-000, all fiscally dependent because of a constitutional over-all tax limitation.

2. Sixty fiscally independent, smaller city school districts, operating by school board control within a tax limit for schools only.

3. Six hundred village and consolidated school districts operating without tax limit and with control of amounts to be spent resting in the voters, either by ballot or by "district meeting."

4. Several hundred one-teacher districts remaining from the 8,000 operating a third of a century ago and for the most part consolidated into "central school districts" or merged with neighboring larger districts.

The Conference Board grappled mainly with the fiscal organization "within" these districts. The steps identified in the report follow: [11]

1. The elimination of oversmall school districts wherever this is not hindered by geographic conditions and population distribution, and the recognition, through state aid and state leadership, of the special problems to be overcome in those which cannot be brought up to the minimum size.

2. The development of stronger public responsibility in communities within school districts of greater than the minimum size. Two promising approaches are pointed out: (a) the use of representative district school meetings in communities up to 50,000 or 60,000 population; (b) the establishment of legal community responsibility with a limited and carefully selected grant of powers to subareas within communities of over 60,000 population.

3. The continued elimination, wherever desirable, of remnants of school districts that lie in the periphery of small cities.

4. The guidance of district reorganization in the suburbs of large cities so as to avoid the shortcomings of large city school districts.

[11] New York State Educational Conference Board, *School Quality and Local School Government*, Albany, N.Y. 1956.

QUESTIONS FOR STUDY AND DISCUSSION

1. Without fiscal powers a school district would be a tame affair. Their development and protection should be a matter of central and continuous concern. In your state, what are the arrangements for levying taxes and making decisions on what is to be spent for what?

2. Try your hand at restating the provisions covering public education in your state constitution so as to make them more meaningful in terms of this and the preceding chapters.

3. Examine the preamble and Chapter 1 of *The School Code for the State of New Osceola* [12] to discover how it treats the issues discussed in this chapter. Then examine the parallel treatment in your own state school code. What changes would you suggest in either?

4. Analyze in a similar way *The Administrative Code of Green Willows* [13] and the administrative code of your own board of education (rules and regulations).

5. Chart all various governmental bodies that, taken together, have the control of education in your state. What are the major functions of each? Who determines the budget under which each operates?

6. In many states schools operate in city school districts according to special arrangements in individual city charters which operate to supplement general provisions of the school code. In addition, in some states some school districts operate under special legislation. Studies of fiscal control based on the state school codes often overlook these special arrangements. Are there any such in your state? How do these districts operate? Considering them as special experiments rather than as undesirable deviations, what insight do they give you on the vexing problem of budgetary control?

SELECTED REFERENCES

Frasier, G. W.: *The Control of City School Finances,* The Bruce Publishing Company, Milwaukee, 1922.

McGaughy, J. R.: *The Fiscal Administration of City School Systems,* The Education Finance Inquiry Commission, New York, vol. V. By permission of The Macmillan Company, 1924.

McLaughlin, Frederick C.: "Fiscal and Administrative Control of City School Systems," *Fiscal Policy for Public Education in the State of New York,* Staff Study 4, New York State Educational Conference Board, Albany, N.Y., 1949.

Mort, Paul R.: "Voter Control vs. Board Control of the Budget," *School Executive,* vol. 70, pp. 34–37.

———— and Donald H. Ross: *Principles of School Administration,* 2d ed., McGraw-Hill Book Company, Inc., New York, 1957.

[12] Paul R. Mort and Donald H. Ross, *Principles of School Administration,* 2d ed., McGraw-Hill Book Company, Inc., New York, 1957, Appendix C.

[13] *Ibid.*

New York State Educational Conference Board: *School Quality and Local School Government,* Albany, N.Y., 1956.

Polley, John W., Joseph O. Loretan, and Clara F. Blitzer: *Community Action for Education,* Bureau of Publications, Teachers College, Columbia University, New York, 1953.

Strayer, George D., Director: *A Report of a Survey of Public Education in the State of West Virginia,* State of West Virginia, Legislative Interim Committee, Charleston, W. Va., 1945.

Woodward, Henry B.: "The Effect of Fiscal Control on Current School Expenditures," doctoral dissertation, Teachers College, Columbia University, New York, 1948.

PART TWO

Evaluation

CHAPTER 5 deals with the issues of cost related to the quality of education as evaluated in terms of the character of the offering. Chapter 6 assesses the impact of school support on the culture and the economy. Both of these chapters have a bearing on the evaluation of public education as a public investment; they deal with issues that are the basis for a strong public posture toward education. In contrast, Chapter 7 points out the uses of financial data in assessing the wholesomeness of provisions made for education in a given community or state.

5. Cost and character of education

TODAY IT can be said, with considerable assurance, that communities spending more for education get more of what promises results desired by people in general. Expenditure level is one of the highly important factors in achieving good education. This has always been an important question in communities that have provided more in the way of educational support than their neighbors. Such communities had their own specifications, which to them were undoubtedly sufficient. They might point to the larger percentage of children entering college, to the greater amount of individual attention their children received because of more adequate staffing, to longer school terms, to more adequate provision of supplies at public expense, to well-kept school buildings, to better holding power in high school, to less in the way of retardation of children, or to a combination of these results or services. In the last analysis it would seem to boil down to the quality of the teachers and the quality of the provisions for helping teachers do their work. An Ohio layman once told the senior author that he came from a rural community in that state where, down through the years, it had been a tradition to employ the best trained teachers they could find. He then recounted the number of persons of distinction who had come from that small community as a justification for this tradition. He ended his discourse with the statement that a good teacher is a "pillar of fire."

When our major task was that of providing any schools at all or providing school terms more than a few months in length or providing supplies or custodial services, the question of returns for money spent was a rather simple one. It was obvious to anyone that longer school terms, though they might not cost proportionately more, still cost more than shorter school terms; that the purchase of supplies by the board of education required more public money than when supplies were purchased by individual families; that the provision of custodial service out of pub-

lic funds increased the cost of education. The results were tangible,
observable, and desired by the communities that made the expenditures.
In recent years, the problem has shifted. We have a vast number of school
systems that have a fairly satisfactory length of term, a fairly satisfactory
provision of teachers as far as numbers and training are concerned, and a
fairly satisfactory provision of custodial service, supplies, and materials of
instruction. To show that the length of term, provision of supplies, provision of health inspection, provision of nurses, etc., were related was to
prove the obvious. Such studies were interesting but unnecessary. Accordingly studies made in the first two or three decades of this century
were more concerned with discovering the degree to which states had
actually provided minimum terms, well-trained teachers, supplies at public expense, custodial service, etc. This doubtless explains the fact that
Ayres only parenthetically introduces the question of the relationship
between expenditure and results in education in connection with his
Index Number for State School Systems. In his *Index,* Ayres used 10
items, 5 of which had to do with financial arrangement and 5 of which
had to do with tangible characteristics of the program, such as length of
school term. He found that the two sets of factors had an intercorrela-
tion of .78.[1] It certainly was not surprising to discover that states which
spent more money had longer school terms and were reaching more children. In commenting on these results, Ayres had the following to say: [2]

We can, however, secure from the data presented in this volume convincing
evidence that there is a real relationship between expenditure and results in
education. We cannot prove that the higher paid teacher is individually more
skilled than the lower paid one, but it can be shown that as salaries increase,
attendance improves, and more pupils are found in the high schools. It can
further be shown that as salaries increase, expenditures for purposes other than
salaries also increase and this results in better buildings and equipment. It is
further evident that, in general, the purely educational items of the index tend
to increase as the financial items grow larger even where there is no functional
connection between the two sets of data.

In more recent years interest has tended to shift to the results that are
achieved among schools with the same length of term, the same general
range of services, but with differences in expenditure levels. The question
might well be phrased: Does a higher expenditure level under these conditions in any degree assure commensurate returns? If so, what is their
nature? Does more expenditure assure more teachers who are "pillars of
fire"? The question is of interest to those concerned with setting a minimum of financial support for the state or nation. It is of concern, likewise,
to those who would like to know whether or not there are returns to be

[1] Leonard P. Ayres, *An Index Number for State School Systems,* Russell Sage
Foundation, New York, 1920.
[2] *Ibid.,* p. 55.

expected from greater vigor of support than that which would be required to meet minimum standards.

As Arvid J. Burke has recently remarked, we have every right to expect a high relationship between expenditure level and quality of schools. Money is not put into the schools for purposes other than for the production of education. Either the money spent was well spent and thus produced the quality hoped for, or it was poorly spent. Deviations from a one-to-one relationship between expenditure and quality would thus be laid to other conditions, such as errors in measurement and differences in efficiency of administration.

MEASUREMENT PROBLEMS INVOLVED

The study of the relationship of cost and quality has required the selection of two types of measures: (1) a measure of expenditure level and (2) a measure of quality.

Expenditure Level

There are classes of expenditure that are not expected to enhance educational quality. Their purpose is to offset environmental conditions that would otherwise get in the way of education. Accordingly care is necessary to take these into account in comparisons of communities. Among these are: expenditures for transportation; expenditure for small classes quite out of relation to the task to be performed, as is found in small schools; expenditure for children sent to other districts and not showing up in the quality measurement of the local school.

Unless communities are of the same type with respect to such matters, rough comparisons on a per capita or per pupil basis will be clouded. To use expenditure per pupil to compare quality in a small one-teacher school with expenditures in a large school is only less absurd than using the gross expenditure in a large city with that of a small town. These distortions must be removed from the expenditure figure if meaningful comparisons are to be made.

What is needed is a measure of the intensity or level of support that will rule out the necessary but qualitatively extraneous factors. Added expenditure on transportation, for example, does not increase the intensity of support of education; it should not be counted in determining the *expenditure level* of the community.

The technical problems involved are discussed in Chapter 7. For the immediate purpose it should be sufficient to state that in the discussion that follows cost is considered in terms of *expenditure level*. The relationship discussed is that between expenditure level and quality—not between quality and over-all cost, current cost per capita, or total cost per pupil.

Measurement of Quality

The twenty-four studies of cost and quality listed in the References at the end of this chapter have made use of a variety of ways of assessing quality. Sixty-four per cent rated school systems on what were considered good indications of what makes for good education. The items used ranged from short lists of external factors such as length of term and holding power to long lists of items descriptive of what is taught and how it is taught. Twenty per cent used tests of achievement and the remaining sixteen per cent used social and economic characteristics of the population with expenditure levels of some year or years in the past.

Most of the studies that used descriptions of school practice were associated with finance surveys. Their purpose was to identify the educational programs that were associated with different expenditure levels. The study of the cost-quality relationship was incidental. But these studies do have the advantage of a range of evaluation that cannot be approached by testing the product. And it may be pointed out that while what is being evaluated is more remote from the real test—effective living throughout life—it is only one step more remote than tests of children and young people during or shortly following the educational experience. From such measures we estimate the quality of the product from the quality of the process.[3] From tests we estimate the quality of the product by the perfection of its more measurable parts as they are completed.

What we need, of course, is a life test. The manufacturer can speed up life testing of the product so that ten years' wear can be compressed into a period of from two weeks to two months. No one has yet designed any comparable scheme for giving a "life test" to the products of our schools.

Four of the studies listed in the Selected References at the end of the chapter attempted life testing of a sort: Bagley (1925), Thorndike (1939), Clark (1945), and Bowyer (1948). The cost-quality aspect of these studies was incidental to an interest in the economic and social outcomes associated with education. Chapter 6 deals with them in that frame of reference.

THE COST-QUALITY RELATIONSHIP

The presumption from the results obtained from the twenty-six studies reviewed is that the relationship is strong. Here are three pertinent statements that will serve to summarize the findings:

[3] For a lucid discussion of facets of quality evaluation, see James E. Allen, Jr., "Evaluating Our Schools," *Harvard Graduate School of Education Alumni Bulletin,* June, 1957.

1. Regardless of the method of measuring quality, a relatively strong relationship holds through all levels of expenditure as yet experienced in public education, from the lowest as exemplified by Mississippi, through the middle group as exemplified by West Virginia, Maine, Rhode Island, Illinois, and Pennsylvania, to the highest as exemplified by New York and New Jersey.[4]

2. Even the highest expenditure public schools do not begin to approach the point, if there is one, where the relationship drops off, and no school is so poorly supported as to be lacking in important values.

3. The relationship appears to be an accelerating one. Those who spend more tend to add to the range of education, on the one hand, and on the other, to do a better job of focusing on the needs of children and young people throughout the range of ability.

Woollatt's Study

Most of the studies were completed before 1950 and were reviewed in detail in the second edition of this book and by the senior author in *Problems and Issues of Public School Finance*.[5] Perhaps the most illuminating of these studies was one done by Woollatt using data from a group of relatively high expenditure schools in the New York metropolitan area—the membership of the Metropolitan School Study Council.[6]

The quality measure was obtained by an application of the observation instrument, *The Growing Edge*.[7] This is an instrument designed to show the relative responsiveness of communities to the challenge of what are considered better methods of teaching and of operating schools. In other words, it measures quality with emphasis on the adaptability of the systems. The range of the instrument was such as to give a good measure of quality as judged by what Allen calls "institutional behavior."[8] But the fact remains that adaptability was emphasized throughout. Since much of our policy, both state and local, is concerned with change and responsiveness to change, this would seem to be an advantage rather than a shortcoming from the standpoint of the use of the results made in this report. The instrument is limited to four facets that seem to be observed in the high-expenditure schools: (1) the teaching of skills in a

---

[4] The titles of these studies are listed in the References at the end of the chapter.

[5] R. L. Johns and E. L. Morphet (eds.), *Problems and Issues in Public School Finance*, published by the National Conference of Professors of Educational Administration, distributed by the Bureau of Publications, Teachers College, Columbia University, New York, 1952, chap. 2.

[6] Lorne H. Woollatt, *The Cost-Quality Relationship on the Growing Edge*, Bureau of Publications, Teachers College, Columbia University, New York, 1949.

[7] Paul R. Mort, William S. Vincent, and Clarence A. Newell, *The Growing Edge*, Metropolitan School Study Council, New York, 1946.

[8] Allen, *op. cit.*

real or realistic fashion and the teaching of a wider range of skills, (2) the teaching of areas of knowledge realistically, (3) the discovery and development of special aptitudes of individuals through test and try-out, and (4) the development of gross behavior patterns, like citizenship, character, and thinking, which are assumed to be developmental characteristics.

Woollatt's study showed that, within this group of high-expenditure schools, there is a direct relationship between these factors taken together and expenditure and between each one individually and expenditure (see Figure 5-1). The correlation between the over-all score and the expenditure level was .59.

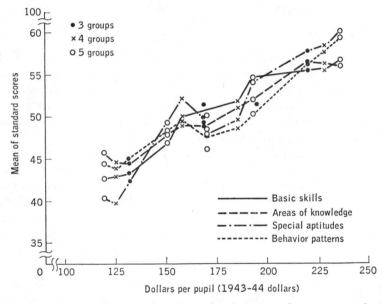

Fig. 5-1 Phases of educational quality related to expenditure per pupil. (From Lorne H. Woollatt, *The Cost-Quality Relationship on the Growing Edge,* Bureau of Publications, Teachers College, Columbia University, New York, 1949, p. 56.)

Studies since 1950

Since 1950 five additional studies have been made. Four of them confirm the findings of the earlier studies. One, a study of Connecticut, found significantly less relationship between quality as measured (achievement tests) and expenditure level as measured (a two-year average expenditure per pupil, presumably without the use of sparsity corrections).

A study of New York State school systems made under the auspices of the Educational Conference Board was published in 1954. This report deals with an evaluation of 126 public elementary schools throughout the State of New York. "Types of school programs are described in terms of what the schools are doing to attain ten important objectives." Among the instruments used were standardized tests in reading vocabulary, reading comprehension, and arithmetic. The results are summarized as follows: [9]

The significant findings are: First, the schools differ widely in mastery of basic skills. Second, the schools that rank highest in mastery of the Three R's usually have the most comprehensive programs for attaining other important elementary school objectives. (It appears that the schools that challenge pupils' interests and make learning most meaningful contribute most to mastery of basic skills.) Third, the schools which achieve the highest mastery of essential skills and do the most to promote all objectives cost the most.

Smith studied the relationship between expenditure level and central school quality as measured by an instrument relatively rough compared with those used in other recent studies. Smith's findings may be summarized as follows: "We may conclude, therefore, that the central school cost-quality correlation of .35 is approximately what previous studies would lead one to expect, when the narrow range of expenditure per pupil and the many common community factors of these schools are considered." [10]

The fourth study was made by Furno, using a wealth of data from the Metropolitan School Study Council and exploring particularly the period of lag between a change in expenditure policy and its maximum effect on school quality. From Furno's findings it would appear that expenditure policy today may be expected to have ineradicable effects, good or bad, over a period of at least twenty-five years into the future. This is discussed in some detail in the next section.[11]

In 1955 Bloom studied results of the Armed Forces Test of General Educational Development as applied to products of the schools in all forty-eight states. The results supported the findings of the previous studies.[12]

[9] *What Do Good Schools Do for Children?* New York State Educational Conference Board, Albany, N.Y., 1954, p. 2.

[10] Stanley V. Smith, "Quality of Education Related to Certain Social and Administrative Characteristics of Well-financed Rural School Districts," unpublished dissertation, Teachers College, Columbia University, New York, 1954.

[11] Orlando F. Furno, "The Projection of School Quality from Expenditure Level," unpublished dissertation, Teachers College, Columbia University, New York, 1956.

[12] Benjamin S. Bloom, "The 1955 Normative Study of the Tests of General Educational Development," reprinted from *The School Review*, March, 1956. University of Chicago Press, Chicago.

STRENGTH OF THE RELATIONSHIP

In the wholesomeness setting we are bound to raise the question of how strong the relationship is as compared with the relationships with quality of other possible aspects of the school setting. Isolation of expenditure level for a unique place in fiscal policy would seem to assume that it is among the strong building blocks of state strategic policy with respect to education. The same holds for the use of expenditure level as an evaluation measure.

Certain of the above studies throw light on this matter. The series of studies of adaptability that began with the Pennsylvania study, reported in *American Schools in Transition* [13] in the early 1940s, explored the relationship between school quality and some hundreds of measurable items of community and educational provisions. Of the sixty-seven items studied by Mort and Cornell in Pennsylvania, there were only two anywhere near as closely related to school quality as current expense per weighted elementary classroom unit. These two were the percentage of business and professional workers (.59) and the percentage of a sampling of the public with a high cultural level as measured on the McCall Educational Background questionnaire (.56). In the next group of strength fell such items as percentage of the teaching staff with a high level of understanding of education as determined from the poll *What Should Our Schools Do* (.52), a similar measure of a sampling of the public (.50), percentage of eighth grade graduates and college graduates in the community (.54 and .51), and percentage of unskilled labor (−.51). In this group also was the average of the sampling of the public on the McCall measure (.51). Quite clearly few, if any, of these could be readily controlled as a matter of state policy.

Pierce's study with the Metropolitan School Study Council data confirms these results. Of the twenty-four measures of community which he studied, only two showed a relationship with quality as measured by the elementary *Growing Edge* instrument [14] anywhere near the relationship between expenditure level and quality, as determined for the same communities by Woollatt. These two measures were again the percentage of business and professional workers (.56) and a wealth measure (.61). Woollatt found the relationship between expenditure level and school quality of these same communities to be .59.

Other items studied by various members of the staff of the Institute of Administrative Research for these same communities in the same years

[13] Paul R. Mort and Francis G. Cornell, *American Schools in Transition,* Bureau of Publications, Teachers College, Columbia University, New York, 1941.

[14] *The Growing Edge,* an instrument for measuring the adaptability of school systems, by Paul R. Mort, William S. Vincent and Charles A. Newell, *op. cit.*

showed a comparably high relationship for the percentage of elementary staff with five or more years' training beyond high school (.58), percentage of staff that had had travel experience (.57, .59), and average salary of staff (.51). There were no comparably high relationships found for the secondary school staff as related to the measure of secondary school quality.[15]

A restudy of the Council communities in the middle 1950s establishes again the relationship of approximately .60 between expenditure level and school quality as measured by *The Growing Edge* (in this case a combination of elementary and secondary school scores). Other relationships of comparable strength covering the same range of items referred to above are:

Wealth (a combination of assessed
valuation, tax rate, and tax leeway) .... .59
Population characteristics presumably
related to wealth .... .43
Expenditure level for instruction .... .63
Expenditure per pupil for current purposes
other than professional salaries .... .40

In the analysis of scores of factors presumably related to the production of quality, no others were found of strength comparable to that of expenditure level. Note that in these measures there is little reflection of such matters as district organization, mechanism of budgetary control, or administrative organization.[16] From the standpoint of our consideration here, this is a serious omission. The omission in this series of studies is not due to an underestimation of their possible importance; rather, it is due to the necessity for centering upon the characteristics of community, financial policy, and staff, all of which are of long-time origin and which, if ignored, confuse the analysis of administrative organization, operational plans, budgetary control, and district organization. Those concerned with these studies believe that the time is now approaching when these disturbing factors can be held under control. When this time comes it is believed that sharp studies will be possible

[15] Donald H. Ross (ed.), *Administration for Adaptability*, Metropolitan School Study Council, New York, 1958.

[16] It is of interest, notwithstanding, that such simple critical aspects of district organization as size of the school population and area did not hold up well enough in the earlier studies of Pennsylvania and the Metropolitan School Study Council communities to warrant their placement in the 32 measures selected as efficient predictors of quality. These studies did not embrace the very small districts and districts with more than 100,000 population. They involved very few districts of more than 50,000 total population.

defining the effects of such other forces, large or small. In the meantime, it would seem to be a wise course to consider district organization, budgetary control, and administrative structure as elements comparable to expenditure level in their effects on quality.

In the studies of the Council data for the mid-1950s, a correlation between expenditure level and quality taken for the same year dropped rapidly from the .59 established in the Pennsylvania study and in the Council data of the mid-1940s. An analysis of this situation by Furno led to a realization that the inflationary period we had gone through in the preceding decade had a tremendous impact on the schools, even the relatively favored schools of the Metropolitan School Study Council. Realizing that communities do not make their adjustments uniformly, Furno investigated the idea of taking the average of three years of expenditure level. This uniformly increased the relationship. Following this idea still further, he investigated the effects of the known fact that a change in expenditure cannot be expected to influence the character of the education instantaneously. These studies indicate that the effect of an expenditure-level quality change is measurable even after twenty-five years, and that the maximum impact occurs in about seven years. He developed a formula measuring expenditure levels which, applied to the twenty-five years prior to 1955, increased the correlation from the low .40s to .63. The same applied to the less turbulent (surprisingly perhaps) twenty-five years prior to 1945 resulted in an increase in the correlation from .59 to .62. From this he concludes that the relationship between expenditure level, as refined, and quality may be safely thought of as that relationship shown by a correlation of .60.[17] Bloom found a correlation of .75, perhaps because of the wide range of expenditure and quality he was dealing with.[18] The writers are of the opinion that .60 is the most useful value for the relationship.

UTILITY OF THE FINDINGS

It seems difficult now to believe that there could ever have been any serious doubt as to the relationship between expenditure level and quality. But there was much wishful thinking that after sufficient money had been spent to get a school established, the effect of the expenditure level would taper off. The doubt, whatever its origin, had a great deal to do with the prosecution of the cost-quality studies. That there has as yet appeared no indication of a point on the scale beyond which an expenditure level does not yield commensurate returns is therefore significant. It seems hardly likely that this issue can be pertinent within any

[17] Furno, *op. cit.*
[18] Bloom, *op. cit.*

range of probable improvement in expenditure level in public schools, at least so long as education retains anything like its present priority among the things which the American people desire to buy.[19]

The central purpose back of the various studies of cost and quality has varied. Most of them were made by persons who were not concerned with the question per se. Their interest was in finding a sort of actuarial basis for determining the cost level of a foundation program. Strayer and Haig in their clarification of the foundation-program concept had taken for granted that there is a strong relationship between cost and quality. The question became: What quality is associated with what cost?

It is all the more interesting to discover that the factor of expenditure level selected by Strayer and Haig appears to be the most closely related to school quality of all those members of the family of factors related to quality which lend themselves to simple objective measurement. The wide use of this approach in state-aid laws is discussed in Chapter 11.

But there is another use of the fact that expenditure level is at one and the same time one of the most powerful predictors of quality and one of the simplest measures to obtain. Expenditure level is a key element in the kind of evaluation of school quality and the conditions producing it that both state and local school systems are initiating. This use is discussed in Chapter 7.

QUESTIONS FOR STUDY AND DISCUSSION

1. Discuss the implications of the term "expenditure level."

2. There are places where there is no substitute for expenditure. There are other places where high-expenditure levels seem to provide favorable conditions in which all sorts of good things develop, good things which represent only differences in behavior of staff and cannot be traced directly to a cost factor. For example, half of the characteristics noted in the report *What Education Our Money Buys* do not seem to be directly related to cost, and yet they will be found far more frequently in higher expenditure schools than in middle-expenditure schools and hardly at all in low-expenditure schools. List some of the characteristics that differentiate higher expenditure schools from lower expenditure schools which can be directly related to cost. Make a second list of such characteristics that are not so closely related to cost. How do you explain the second list?

3. From the relationship between expenditure level and adaptability of school systems, what implications do you see for the amount of aid which

[19] This paragraph and much of the preceding section appeared in approximately the same form in Paul R. Mort, *The Foundation Program in State Educational Policy*, The University of the State of New York, The State Department of Education, Albany, New York, 1957,

should come from the state to the community or from the federal government
to states?

SELECTED REFERENCES

Reports Referred to in This Chapter

Ayres, Leonard P.: *An Index Number for State School Systems,* Russell Sage
Foundation, New York, 1920.

Bagley, William C.: *Determinism in Education,* Warwick and York Incorporated, Baltimore, 1925.

Bloom, Benjamin S.: "The Normative Study of the Tests of General Educational
Development," *The School Review,* March, 1956.

—— and Charles R. Statler: "Changes in the States on the Tests of General
Educational Development from 1943 to 1955." *The School Review,* vol.
LXV, no. 2, Summer, 1957.

Bowyer, Vernon: "Measuring the Economic Value of Education to the States,"
Improving Educational Research, Official Report, American Educational
Research Association, Washington, 1948.

Clark, Harold F.: *Education Steps Up Living Standards,* Chamber of Commerce of the United States, Washington, 1945.

Connecticut Citizens for the Public Schools: *A Study of Factors Related to
Academic Achievement in the Public Schools,* Hartford, Conn., June, 1957.

Ferrell, D. T.: *Relation between Current Expenditure and Certain Measures
of Educational Efficiency in Kentucky County and Graded School Systems,*
George Peabody College for Teachers, Nashville, Tenn., 1936.

Furno, Orlando F.: "The Projection of School Quality from Expenditure Level,"
unpublished dissertation, Teachers College, Columbia University, New
York, 1956.

Governor's School Survey Commission: "Reconstruction of the System of Public
School Support in the State of New Jersey," *Report of the Commission,*
vol. II, supplement I-B, pp. 76–112, Trenton, N.J., 1933.

Grace, A. G., and G. A. Moe: *State Aid and School Costs,* McGraw-Hill Book
Company, Inc., New York, 1938, pp. 324–329.

Grimm, Lester R.: *Our Children's Opportunities in Relation to School Costs,*
Department of Research, Illinois Education Association, Springfield, Ill.,
1938.

Maine School Finance Commission: *The Financing of the Public Schools of
Maine,* Augusta, Maine, 1934, chap. III, pp. 64–97.

McLure, William P.: *Let Us Pay for the Kind of Education We Need,* Report
of a Study of State and Local Support of Mississippi's Schools, Bureau
of Educational Research, University of Mississippi, University, Miss., 1948,
chap. II, pp. 3–29.

Mort, Paul R., and Francis G. Cornell: *American Schools in Transition,* Bureau
of Publications, Teachers College, Columbia University, New York, 1941,
chaps. VII–VIII, pp. 139–195.

Pierce, Truman L.: *What Do Good Schools Do for Children?* New York State Educational Conference Board, Albany, N.Y., 1954.

Powell, Orrin E.: *Educational Returns at Varying Expenditure Levels,* Bureau of Publications, Teachers College, Columbia University, New York, 1933.

Rhode Island Commission on the Legal Structure of Rhode Island Public Education: *Schools for Our Children,* Providence, 1941, vol. I.

Smith, Stanley V.: "Quality of Education Related to Certain Social and Administrative Characteristics of Well-financed Rural School Districts," unpublished dissertation, Teachers College, Columbia University, New York, 1954.

Strayer, George D., Director: *A Report of a Survey of Public Education in the State of West Virginia,* State of West Virginia, Legislative Interim Committee, Charleston, W.Va., 1945, pp. 582–597.

Thorndike, Edward L.: *Education as Cause and as Symptom,* The Macmillan Company, New York, 1939.

Vincent, William S.: *Emerging Patterns of Public School Practice,* Bureau of Publications, Teachers College, Columbia University, New York, 1945.

———: *What Education Our Money Buys,* New York State Educational Conference Board, Albany, N.Y., 1943.

Woollatt, Lorne H.: *The Cost-Quality Relationship on the Growing Edge,* Bureau of Publications, Teachers College, Columbia University, New York, 1949.

Other Readings

Johns, R. L., and E. L. Morphet (eds.): *Problems and Issues in Public School Finance,* National Conference of Professors of Educational Administration, Teachers College, Columbia University, New York, 1952, chap. II.

Mort, Paul R.: *The Foundation Program in State Educational Policy,* The University of the State of New York, The State Department of Education, Albany, N.Y., 1957.

Russell, James E. (ed.): *National Policies for Education, Health and Social Services,* Doubleday & Company, Inc., Garden City, N.Y., 1955, pp. 46–72.

Vincent, William S., John W. Polley, and Orlando F. Furno: *Does Money Make a Difference?* Associated Public School Systems, New York, 1958.

6. Education, the culture and the economy

IN CHAPTER 5, five studies of the economic and social impact of education are referred to in terms of their bearing on the cost-quality issue. But their authors, including such names as Bagley and Thorndike, and their sponsors, including the United States Chamber of Commerce, are the clue to the concern of these studies with an arena markedly different from that required for the exercise of the cost-quality concept as customarily viewed. These studies attempted to see the effects of education on goodness of life (Thorndike), cultural patterns (Bagley), and economic patterns (Clark). These attempts to see educational effects on adult life and society would appear to be an approach to the life test of the effectiveness of education.

Chapter 5 deals with the relation of expenditure level of education to the kinds of things people judge to be good education, for whatever reason. This chapter deals with the longer view—the effects of education on adult life.

DISTINGUISHING EFFECTS FROM GOALS

No nation can rise above its people. The quality, character, and intelligence of a people determine the character of a nation. Natural resources may be present in abundance, but they must be developed by people who are resourceful and energetic and who have the knowledge and skills to turn them into goods for general consumption. There are examples of countries that possess vast natural resources but do not have the human resources to develop them, whereas other examples show how human intelligence has built high levels of civilization in countries relatively poor in natural resources,

90

But the effects are not limited to the economic. Norton sets the wider scene in these words:

Education is both affected by and is a part of the social scene. On the one hand, the schools are inevitably and properly conditioned as to purpose and procedure by the culture. On the other hand, educational institutions are part of the culture and wield significant influence in shaping its evolution. This is especially true in a society such as that of the United States where there is clear recognition that a general diffusion of knowledge is essential to the perpetuation and progress of the society we wish to maintain, and where it is public policy to make education available to all.

Education in the United States has important effects on many facets of the culture. It contributes to the general enlightenment which is essential for a society of free men. It teaches much of the background of ideals and knowledge upon which such a society rests. It is one of the essential ingredients of technology. The highly productive economy of the United States would be impossible without the contributions of education.[1]

Clearly, important as they are, the economic effects of education are but a facet of its total effect. Public schools had spread throughout the nation before any great concern was expressed over their economic effects except on the earning power of the individual. The very fact that the hands of the federal government have been kept off the schools is one indication that as a nation we have believed that if the objectives accepted by parents and communities were followed, the people would be so equipped that the needs of the economy would be adequately met.

This does not deny that schools do have tremendous economic effects. They raise consumer demand—a function on which our economic system spends directly almost as much as is spent on public education. They provide basic skills which our complex production and distribution systems rely on—reading, for example, and simple arithmetic. They provide a keeping place for young people until they have reached the age at which our customs and laws permit them to enter the labor market.

A school system designed from the top will be strongly influenced by economic and political objectives while one that has grown up from the people will be found emphasizing the rearing of strong, self-reliant persons. Both influences are needed. The American system is an as yet unresolved mixture. It cannot be subsumed fully either under a theory limited to the "public" purpose or to the "personal" purpose. This is the root difficulty with so many of the educational "simples" that come

[1] John K. Norton, "The Contemporary Scene," chap. II in Roald F. Campbell and Russell T. Gregg (eds.), *Administrative Behavior in Education*, Harper & Brothers, New York, 1957, p. 41.

to the fore in times of stress. Their authors usually envision education all one way or all the other.

The point is made here as a sort of warning that the effects of education are not to be confused with goals. The confusion of concomitant effects with goals to be sought can lead to serious warping of education away from its prime goal—the promotion of life, liberty and happiness of persons, objectives which appear in the long run to be as acceptable to the human spirit as economic security.

Vastly important as are the economic concomitants of education—and the better the education the stronger the effects—the writers cannot accept the dictum that "the educational system must, in the long run, earn its way by contributing to the national economy." Of course effective education will affect the economy. Its products will operate and shape the economy, just as they will shape the nation's behavior in all respects. It probably pays its way many times over. But to put critical emphasis on the inescapable concomitants of education, economic or other, is to lose sight of the central task of the schools to lend a hand in the rearing up of a strong people.

It may be added that as educators we are too prone to accept at face value every claim of the value of education to the operation of our economy. We see the vast growth of the use of school methods in industry without asking whether those responsible, for example, for the multiplication of printed instructional materials have not accepted it as a fact that all people can be taught to read at the expected levels—a fact that has by no means been demonstrated. Having allowed this position to go unchallenged, we are then faced with the necessity of accepting as a mark of failure of the schools the fact that the schools have not done what may well be impossible. Perhaps the schools can be forgiven for trying to bring all pupils to a high level of reading ability—impossible as it appears to be by any known method; after all, these schools are chiefly reading machines. But is that any excuse for industry to accept achievement as actually attained? Better by far to encourage industry to use simpler communication devices, since it patently has no moral compulsion to try to teach reading. Nor does the lessening of the use of reading as a communication device necessarily indicate that schools should abandon their attempts to develop reading skills to reasonably attainable levels.

CULTURAL EFFECTS

The two classic studies seeking to assess the cultural effects of education were made by Bagley and Thorndike. Both studies compared educational provisions at one time with social phenomena two or three decades later.

Bagley's Study

In the early 1920s Bagley assembled data from many sources for the purpose of comparing the effects of educational provisions at one time to later behavior of people. He first selected the states that had 55 per cent or more of their population native to the state in 1910. He obtained a rating of the extent of provisions for education in these states in 1880, 1890, 1900, 1910, and 1918. He then correlated these ratings with test scores obtained for army recruits in the First World War and with a number of social and economic measures for the states. The results are shown in Table 6-1.

Table 6-1 Correlations between Median School Ratings for Education and Certain Measures of Present-day Intelligence, Leadership, and Economic Efficiency

	Correlation between median school rating for education and median 6 present measures					
Year	*Adult white literacy, 1920*	*A and B scores, Army Alpha, 1918*	*Median white, Alpha, 1918*	*Per capita circulation, (10 mag.), 1922*	*Birth- states, present leaders*	*Per capita income (Knauth), 1919*
1880	.70	.83	.83	.90	.92	.78
1890	.80	.83	.82	.92	.86	.88
1900	.89	.88	.89	.96	.87	.86
1910	.89	.87	.87	.97	.87	.84
1920	.82 *	.82 *	.83 *	.93	.79	.63

* School ratings for 1918.

Table 6-1 is taken from the chapter in *Determinism in Education* entitled "Do Good Schools Pay?" Bagley's interpretation, in part, is as follows:

Of particular significance are not only the uniformly high correlations that we find, but also the fact that, *without exception, the highest correlations fall where they should if our theory of the influence of schooling is correct.* The Army tests show the closest resemblance to school conditions in 1900 and 1910, as they should. The distribution of present-day leaders coincides almost perfectly with the distribution of school facilities in 1880. The *per-capita* circulation of magazines shows very high correlations with school conditions for all of the decades, and especially for 1900 and 1910. Present-day *per-capita* income is closely associated with school efficiency during the decades when the present dominant generation was in school, the resemblances being closest for the years 1890 and 1900. Recent school conditions have not affected the present dominant generations, but school conditions twenty, thirty, and forty years ago did have a profound effect if our figures tell the truth.[2]

Bagley went on to make inferences in terms of intelligence. Stopping short of any such inferences, the data and his interpretations as quoted would appear to be applicable to the subject of this chapter, the social and economic effects of education.

Thorndike's Study

Thorndike built up a checklist of items describing social phenomena selected as indicators of goodness of living (his G Index). Using this index, he scored states and cities, using census data for 1930. He then got (1) a measure of the extent and character of educational provisions for 1900, using five educational items from the Ayres Index and the Bagley Index; (2) a five-item measure indicative of intelligence, morality, and devotion to the home (personal qualities of residents); and (3) current expenditure per pupil in average daily attendance. He ran correlations between his 1930 G scores and the three measures for 1900. His results for states were as follows:

1. School provision in 1900 and 1930 G score—.41
2. Personal qualities of residents in 1900 and 1930 G score—.59
3. Current expenditure per pupil in 1900 and 1930 G score—.41

Thorndike's conclusion as it bears on education (Items 1 and 3, above) and population (Item 2) points out a stronger effect of population characteristics than of education. His results for cities show an even stronger weighting for the population characteristics.

Thorndike notes that the quality of the population in 1900 might well have been influenced by the quality of education in earlier years. The study does not reveal how much the G score may have risen generally between 1900 and 1930 (presumably in part due to education) since it dealt only with variations among states (or cities) in 1930. Nor does it account for effects of pre-1900 education on 1930 G scores or the 1900 effects that would not show up for another decade or so.

We might summarize Thorndike's findings by saying that they confirm what everybody knows, if he thinks about it, that life thirty years from now will be considerably influenced by the kind of people we are today and the way we educate our children. But after all, one of the jobs of the scientist is to clarify the meaning of the obvious. His summation is chastening:

[2] William C. Bagley, *Determinism in Education*, Warwick & York Incorporated, Baltimore, 1925, p. 82.

Mankind has its genes, its tools and apparatus, its customs and institutions. We should make the most and best out of all of these. The way to do so is to learn the truth about them and act accordingly. School education is one of the most important of human institutions, and free schooling for those who can use it for human welfare is one of the finest and most beneficent. But we honor education more by understanding it than by praising it, and we should not ask too much from it. There is a certain attractiveness in thinking that education has limitless possibilities and appealing to it, whatever our difficulty or distress may be. But the attractiveness of such an attitude is like the attractiveness of an infant's appeal to his mother in confidence that she can gratify his every wish. After childhood such appeals seem, and are, weak and stupid. So should the appeals of this, that, and the other public or private interest to education to save this, that, and the other valuable, or at least valued, feature of life. Least of all should educators expect too much of education. Like men of science they should measure and know, and like good engineers they should when advisable allow a factor of safety. What is more contemptible than an ignorant educational reformer (or conservative) selling his wares to a trustful public, taking a profit from spreading guesses and lies! [3]

World War II Data—Illiteracy

Ginzberg and Bray, in their study *The Uneducated*, throw a great deal of light on the relation of at least a minimum of education to acceptance into and success in the military forces in times of war. They found that "the twelve states with the lowest expenditure per pupil in 1929–30" accounted for five out of every seven rejectees.[4] Complementary to this they detail the success of the army in bringing illiterates up to operational efficiency by a comparatively brief period of intensive schooling.[5]

Education and Specialized Talent

The Commission on Human Resources and Advanced Training goes into the relation of education to resources at the other end of the scale. It points to the growing need for specialists and turns to education as the means for finding and developing vast untapped human resources. The concluding paragraph of the report is given as an appropriate ending for this section.[6]

The brains of its citizens constitute a nation's greatest asset. From the minds of men will come future scientific discoveries, future works of art and literature, future advances in statesmanship, technology and social organizations, in short,

[3] Edward L. Thorndike, *Education as Cause and as Symptom*, The Macmillan Company, New York, 1939.

[4] Eli Ginzberg and Douglas W. Bray, *The Uneducated*, Columbia University Press, New York, 1953, p. 54.

[5] *Ibid.*, p. 98.

[6] Commission on Human Resources and Advanced Training, Dael Wolfle, Director, *America's Resources of Specialized Talent*, Harper & Brothers, New York, 1954, p. 283.

all future progress. Since there can be no argument over this proposition, the practical problem becomes one of devising the best means of nurturing the talent which exists in the population. A nation which has had the ingenuity to conquer the air, to eradicate age-old diseases, to send radio messages around the world, to achieve a higher standard of living than has ever been seen elsewhere in the world can surely overcome the barriers of doubt, of unequal opportunity, of financial handicap, and of inadequate motivation and education which interfere with the fullest development of the industrial, educational, intellectual, and moral leadership which our kind of society increasingly requires.

ECONOMIC EFFECTS

The profound interdependence of education and the economy is fairly obvious. It is accepted without question by those who criticize the schools when there is a shortage in any of the vast and increasing number of occupational fields that require a background of science or mathematics (see the manpower studies listed in the "readings"). Its acceptance was demonstrated by the movements to introduce vocational and commercial courses, vocational guidance, and even "driver education" into the schools. It has been accepted by those responsible for the long series of studies showing the relationship between educational level and income. It can be noted by inquiry into the community of origin of the men giving the orders in large industries and businesses.

But sometimes the full implications of the obvious are overlooked. Studies such as Clark's inquiries into education and standard of living of nations and his tracing of the effects of curriculum changes on clothing, housing, and food consumption have served to dramatize the implication for financial support on the one hand and for curriculum development on the other.

Education and Productivity

An analysis of the production capacity of a people reveals several factors which are quite definitely influenced by intelligent skill and initiative. Economists usually group the factors of production comprising land, labor, and capital and show how each of these factors is dependent upon managerial skill to such an extent that management may be thought of as a fourth factor. In one of its publications the Educational Policies Commission shows how these factors of production are influenced by the level of education maintained. The following paragraph identifies the factors: [7]

Economists differ on details in analyzing the basic elements in the productive process. Their discussions, however, generally recognize four basic factors.

[7] National Education Association, Educational Policies Commission, *Education and Economic Well-being in American Democracy*, Washington, 1940, pp. 7–8.

Labor, whether of brain or of brawn, is identified as an essential element. Natural resources, involving the raw materials of land, water, and climate upon which production rests, constitute another basic factor. A third element in production is capital, including such factors as tools and machinery, factories, warehouses, and inventories. The efficient use of all factors of production depends upon organization and management. These have become so important in industrial economy that some class them as a fourth basic element in production.

It can readily be demonstrated that the intelligence and efficiency of the workers vitally affect production. America has been called the "land of opportunity" in which each person can progress in accordance with his capabilities and skills. This stimulus of personal initiative is a strong factor in the improvement of workers on all levels and tends to promote the productive capacity of the nation. Over a period of time industry has employed more and more skilled workers and relatively fewer unskilled workers.

The emphasis on vocational education has prepared young people to assume their place as producers in our national life. This result of education has tended to prepare more and more persons for the growing demands of industry. Not only has education produced more skilled workers, but the programs of health and safety have generally resulted in fewer industrial accidents and less loss of time due to illness and have promoted general health and well-being.

In order to maintain a high proportion of skilled workers, education must continue to train each oncoming generation in the habits, skills, and abilities that are needed to maintain the productive capacity. Education in our national economy is an ongoing process and cannot be slowed down during periods of economic stringency and increased during periods of prosperity but must be continued at a high level of efficiency throughout changing economic conditions.

The conservation of our natural resources, so evidently needed, must be realized and practiced by persons who understand the importance of such results to national well-being. Already much of our topsoil has been lost through wind and water erosion and cannot be restored except over long periods of time. Forests have been reduced to the point where only long-range programs can replace them. Irreplaceable resources such as coal, oil, iron ore, and other minerals must be carefully conserved if they are not ultimately to become depleted.

Through the study and practice of conservation, each generation can be taught to make the fullest and wisest use of its resources without waste or depletion. Already programs of conservation in agriculture, forestry, and mining are protecting resources. Wasteful methods are being checked and agricultural practices improved in order that productivity of the soil may be maintained at a high level.

The wise use of capital, whether it be in cash or in the tools of production, is dependent upon the intelligence and skill with which it is used. Science and technology have shown how new products may be developed and how new uses may be made of existing resources. Our entire program of research has resulted in greatly improved production and has raised our industrial achievement to a higher level.

In all these developments management has been one of the most important factors. The great complexity of business and industry has been developed and must be operated by persons with knowledge and skill acquired through the educative process. The Educational Policies Commission stated the different contributions of management in the following paragraphs; they are as true today as they were the day they were written: [8]

Education has provided an environment in which children and youths of all classes have rubbed elbows and have developed a community of understanding essential to a reasonable degree of social cooperation in the productive enterprise. The influence of the common school is one of the factors which has retarded the development of class lines. Education has also provided a means whereby genius and energy might rise to positions of leadership. Many economists have recognized the economic importance of this educational function.

Schools have long provided literacy and other elementary education which even the "self-made" man has possessed. The tendency recently has been to emphasize the importance of formal training as a qualification for leadership in business enterprises.

Colleges, technical schools, and universities train scientists, engineers, and technologists who provide expert knowledge for the business executive and who in some cases themselves assume managerial ability. Graduate schools of business are training growing numbers of young men, who first enter minor executive positions from which are recruited those who rise to positions of major managerial importance.

Education and Wealth

While it is true that generally more money is spent for education in the relatively prosperous communities than in the poorer ones, the overwhelming evidence that can be marshaled on this point agrees consistently that a high national economy depends upon an efficient school system and that high levels of education among the people are a direct cause of high national prosperity. Clark's study of nations [9] has demonstrated this in the world arena. Bowyer's study, referred to in Chapter 5, gives interesting evidence at home. In a study of the measurement of the

[8] *Ibid.*, pp. 24–26.
[9] Harold F. Clark, *Education Steps Up Living Standards,* Chamber of Commerce of the United States, Washington, 1945.

economic value of education to the states, Bowyer reaches the following conclusions: [10]

1. When the percent of wealth or income expended for public schools is taken as an index of the educational status of the various states, a positive relationship is found between this index and subsequent economic progress for the period 1890 to 1946. The relationship is so generally consistent as to indicate that the work of the schools has had a causal bearing upon economic development.

2. School support, in the terms previously indicated and considered for the period mentioned above, apparently has begun definitely to affect economic progress within ten or twelve years after the date of the school expenditures and has continued this positive influence for several years thereafter. At the end of about twenty years, the influence of school support upon economic progress begins to wane, or at least evidence of it becomes submerged by the influence of a more recent period of school support.

3. The amount of economic return apparently resulting from such school support has become sufficient within ten or twelve years to cover not only the original school expenditures but also a liberal rate of interest for the intervening years.

SUMMARY

Care should be taken to differentiate effects from goals. Not all good effects are consciously sought after. The studies of Clark and others demonstrate that the economic impact of the schools is far reaching. They raise consumer demand, they provide basic skills that facilitate the operation of our complex production and distribution system, they serve as a waiting place for young people pending the opening of employment opportunities.

But important as they are, the economic effects of education are but a facet of its total effect. Public schools had spread throughout the nation before any great concern was expressed over their economic effects except on the earning power of the individual. The very fact that the hands of the federal government have been kept off the schools is one indication that as a nation we have believed that if the objective accepted by parents and communities were followed, the people would be so equipped that the economy could remain "political."

The Bagley and Thorndike studies give strong support to the position that education influences our national behavior as a people; that it plays an important role in building a strong nation.

Ginzberg and Bray, accepting the role of the school as a positive one,

[10] Vernon Bowyer, "Measuring the Economic Value of Education to the States," *Improving Educational Research,* Official Report, American Educational Research Association, Washington, 1948, p. 178.

show the effects of failure to educate on our national defense posture, and the Commission on Human Resources and Advanced Training takes the potential of education for granted as an instrument capable of finding and developing untapped human resources.

QUESTIONS FOR STUDY AND DISCUSSION

1. Give the arguments for and against the following: "The best education for adult life is that education directed to a good life during the years of schooling."

2. Give the strengths and weakness of the position indicated by the following: "You educate them; we will provide the training we need on the job."

3. Give your reaction to this statement: "We have the teaching materials and the teachers to train men to be foremen; the men are ready and willing, but they can't read the materials."

4. What is the economic role of vocational guidance?

5. Discuss: "Our troubles do not come from lack of ability to run machines but with lack of ability to get along with people."

6. Discuss the following: "Young people coming from the schools don't know how to assume responsibility."

7. Consider the cultural and economic implications of the following position: "The function of the schools is to discover and develop leaders; anything else is a waste of time and money." Would this position have been acceptable to Bagley and to Thorndike?

SELECTED REFERENCES

Bagley, William C.: *Determinism in Education,* Warwick and York Incorporated, Baltimore, 1925.

Bowyer, Vernon: "Measuring the Economic Value of Education to the States," *Improving Educational Research,* Official Report, American Educational Research Association, Washington, 1948.

Clark, Harold F.: *Education Steps Up Living Standards,* Chamber of Commerce of the United States, Washington, 1945.

Commission on Human Resources and Advanced Training, Dael Wolfle, Director: *America's Resources of Specialized Talent,* Harper & Brothers, New York, 1954.

Ginzberg, Eli, and Douglas W. Bray: *The Uneducated,* Columbia University Press, New York, 1953.

National Education Association, Educational Policies Commission: *Education and Economic Well-being in American Democracy,* Washington, 1940.

Norton, John K.: "The Contemporary Scene," chap. II in Roald F. Campbell and Russell T. Gregg (eds.), *Administrative Behavior in Education,* Harper & Brothers, New York, 1957.

Thorndike, Edward L.: *Education as Cause and as Symptom,* The Macmillan Company, New York, 1939.

7. Expenditure level and other facts of great yield

CHAPTERS 5 and 6 have demonstrated the extreme complexity of the task of evaluating the products of a school system. Schools, in common with other public services, do not have the handy ultimate test of profit and loss. They can make an assessment of sorts of the state of the product as schooling is completed or in various stages along the way, but they have only the vaguest conception of how the product will stand up in the test of life. They have not as yet found access to the power system, as it were; they must content themselves with measuring the smoothness of the burnishing the schooling has given.

DIMENSIONS OF EVALUATION

But a manufacturer does not rest with a balance sheet and the life-tests of the product. He too must be alert to how the customers like the product before negative reaction to its "feel of solidity" or "class" has resulted in a reduction of sales and eventually in an unfavorable balance sheet. Like educators, he must spend a great deal of time on matters of little functional significance.

Beyond this his evaluation processes go back into the production process. Where is waste showing up through too many rejections of parts? Is the "burden," as he calls administrative costs, getting out of accepted tolerances? Is there excessive labor turnover? Are the "standard time allotments," estimated by the wise old production engineer when the process was set up, realistic? Are the "input" materials up to specifications?

The manufacturer has found a hundred places to look to test the fitness of the conditions that are creating his product.

Apart from the profit and loss sheet, the task of the school administrator is not particularly different. He has the reports of his "salesmen" on consumer reaction; he has the description of the input: intelligence, education of parents, home background, community environment. He can estimate progress in the mastery of skills and knowledge; he can assess the conditions under which skills and knowledge are developed, and the selection of the skills and knowledge so as to achieve a reasonably good estimate of their dynamic potential in life. He can dip into his pupil progress and placement statistics for another perspective that will keep him from losing track of materials that are just going round and round in the mill. He can examine his financial statistics for clues as to the wholesomeness of conditions. How about the support level—could it fairly be expected to produce the kind of product he is advertising? Is the expenditure for betterment relatively too great or too little?

FACTS OF GREAT YIELD

This chapter deals with financial data that have proved to be "facts of great yield" in assessing the wholesomeness of conditions for producing education and in planning the financial program from year to year.

All the items discussed here have long been in use in one form or another, but not always with a full appreciation of their power. They are those items that have proved their worth in studies of the relation of hundreds of factors to the quality of education. Refinements have been suggested in the light of scores of studies carried on since the early 1940s by the Institute of Administrative Research of Teachers College, Columbia University. The items and the refinements are those now in use in the continuous evaluation studies being carried on by the Metropolitan School Study Council, the Associated Public School Systems, and the Central School Study. Figure 7-1 shows how they have been grouped with certain other facts of great worth in one of the periodic evaluation studies of the Associated Public School Systems. The "report card" from which Figure 7-1, page 103, is drawn uses thirteen over-all measures and contains supplements with nine additional measures and thirty-one submeasures (from which major measures are built up) for use in diagnostic analysis.

EXPENDITURE LEVEL

No single item of information about a school system has been identified that yields as much insight into the character of the education it may be expected to produce as the expenditure level. Even rough measures of it, such as expenditure per pupil in attendance or membership, fre-

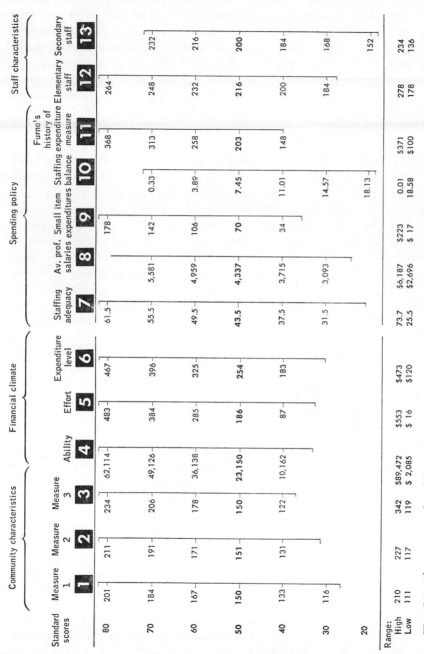

Fig. 7-1 The Associated Public School Systems report card. *Note:* Numbers here are standard scores. Their values change from year to year. The data presented here are for the school year 1955–1956.

103

quently show strong relationships with quality. Note the studies by Bloom and Thorndike, discussed in Chapters 5 and 6. The value of the refined measure in predicting quality has been confirmed so often that it is now reasonable to suspect some error in measurement when contrary results appear. Low expenditure levels will rarely if ever be associated with first-class schools, no matter how well administered; high expenditure levels will rarely fail to be associated with first-class schools, however badly the schools are administered.

In a Setting of Measures

This is not to say that we can rest our case with expenditure level. What is being said is that an educational-expectancy table can be built on expenditure level just as a life-expectancy table can be built on age. But policy cannot be built on expenditure level solely or any other factor standing by itself. One of the most striking findings of the search for order in the maze of forces that come into play in producing education is that *nothing really counts of and by itself.* There would seem to be no phase which can be drawn out from its setting for exclusive attention. Any factor, whether it be expenditure level, district organization, concern with special phases of the program, or what have you, is only effective in partnership with other forces. This point is stated by Smith as follows:

Schools operate in a complex environment. They are continuously subjected to the interplay of forces from within and without. The sum total of these forces, large and small, measured and yet-to-be-measured, gives a school its particular quality of education.[1]

Furno states it as follows, bringing in the dimension of time:

Education is a complex function. Its quality is as much a function of past policies as it is of present ones. Some policies tend to provide nurture for the educational program, and adaptability burgeons forth and blossoms. Other policies react unfavorably upon the ongoing educational program, and adaptability withers. Expenditure level is conditioned by community policy. Both present and past policy condition expenditure level.[2]

Vincent makes a point that retains the emphasis on the key position of the expenditure level:

Level of finance, because of the many benefits which flow from adequate expenditures, may be considered a critical condition of better schools whether those schools be situated in communities of favorable type or not, or whether

[1] Stanley V. Smith, "Quality of Education Related to Certain Social and Administrative Characteristics of Well-financed Rural School Districts," unpublished dissertation, Teachers College, Columbia University, New York, 1954.

[2] Orlando F. Furno, "The Projection of School Quality from Expenditure Level," unpublished dissertation, Teachers College, Columbia University, New York, 1956.

(within the limits of the size studied—under 200,000) they be large school systems or not. That increase in size of school system up to a point and existence of favorable community conditions also react favorably upon character of education cannot be denied, but possibly with the exception of certain unusual situations outside the horizons of this study such factors operate within the limits of adequate financing.[3]

Since money is an inescapable necessity for the operation of schools, it will certainly not be one of those things that is entirely set aside. The importance of these findings is that expenditure level is in all likelihood the central conditioning factor. While each of the factors is dependent on the others, it would seem to be a safe assumption that dependence of all factors on expenditure level is more universally strong. While the studies showing the degree to which one factor can vary from the expectancy of the total group without being destructive are only in their infancy, the studies of Brickell,[4] Teresa,[5] and Campbell[6] provide the basis for a strong hypothesis that the expenditure level as the base line for measuring variance of the wholesomeness of other conditions could well be the most critical base line available.[7]

Three Tests of the Measure

Long-time Effect. Expenditure policy casts a long shadow. The deleterious effects of low expenditure level (and the salutary effects of high expenditure level) are not quickly erased. This year's policy as it affects teacher employment, for example, will leave measurable effects for more than a quarter of a century.

Validity. On reviewing the studies of expenditure level and quality, it cannot but be noted that the strong relationship found appears to be independent of the method used for measuring quality. If quality is measured in the simple ways used in the studies of the 1920s; if it is judged by extensive checklists like those used in the early 1930s; if it is measured by carefully developed instruments such as those used in the

[3] William S. Vincent, *Emerging Patterns of Public School Practice*, Bureau of Publications, Teachers College, Columbia University, New York, 1945.

[4] Henry M. Brickell, "An Analysis of Certain Non-Instructional Staff Expenditures," unpublished Ed. D. project, Teachers College, Columbia University, New York, 1953.

[5] Anthony J. Teresa, "An Analysis of the Effect of Various Specific Items in School Accounting," unpublished Ed. D. project, Teachers College, Columbia University, New York, 1955.

[6] James A. Campbell, "Small Item Expenditure and School Quality; A Cost-Quality Study," unpublished Ed. D. project, Teachers College, Columbia University, New York, 1956.

[7] The material in the foregoing section and that in the section which follows was adapted from Paul R. Mort, *The Foundation Program in State Educational Policy*, The University of the State of New York, The State Department of Education, Albany, N.Y., 1957.

late 1930s and 1940s; if it is measured by standardized tests; if it is measured by projections into adult life; if it is measured in any of these ways, the relationship with expenditure level is strong. Here it would appear that we have at least one valid measure of the complex factors producing school quality which we can use as a key element in assessing the wholesomeness of conditions for producing good education.

Stability. The relationship appears to be relatively free from secular influences. The relationship held in the 1920s, in the 1930s, in the 1940s, and in the 1950s. While the tremendous turbulence of expenditure policy over the previous decade, arising from inflation and rapid expansion of school population, did disturb this relationship as measured in the middle 1950s, the fact remains that these effects themselves appear to be subject to prediction and correction, as Furno has demonstrated.[8]

Another important finding on stability comes from the current work of the Institute of Administrative Research. A recent test of the thirteen most efficient predictors of school quality to discover the degree that each retained the same relationship with the other twelve measures when applied to 1945 data and 1955 data of the Metropolitan School Study Council showed that expenditure level rated highest in terms of maintaining over this decade the same relationships with the other predictors.

How It Works

How this factor of expenditure level works so as to have its effect on quality is fairly obvious. People in the community want to do something. To do something often requires money. The additional money increases the expenditure level, whatever its special purpose. Higher expenditure levels, therefore, are a reflection of efforts made to bring improvement of quality. That the relationship is not stronger can be laid to many things, including the soundness of judgment on the effectiveness of the particular items of expenditure.

But there are observations that can be made that are not so obvious. Vincent discovered that approximately half of the items used in describing schools in the Conference Board study of the early 1940s and which differentiated between better-supported schools and schools of low support did not require an additional outlay of money. Yet they consistently appeared in the better-supported schools and not in the poorer-supported schools. An engaging hypothesis that has come from a study of these relationships is this: When money is added for any particular purpose, the expenditure level is raised and thereby value is added other than that which is sought. Hence, according to this hypothesis, meeting immediate goals builds toward a new expenditure level and tends to enhance the whole educational program. According to this hypothesis, such addi-

[8] Furno, *op. cit.*

tions to expenditure may not be assessed *alone* in terms of their specific goals; in fact, they could miss their immediate goals and still be salutary. Vincent suggests an explanation of this phenomenon:

It cannot but have been an object of some note to the careful reader that many of the practices itemized in this monograph, though presented as related to amounts of expenditure in schools, do not in and of themselves cost more to have in a school program than not to have. In fact, one entirely separate investigation conducted by the writer showed that of 165 noteworthy adaptations (unusual and outstanding practices to meet specific and local needs) observed by fieldworkers in middle and high expenditure schools (as against only 13 noted in low expenditure schools) about half (48%)—because they required no extra equipment, supplies or teachers—did not in and of themselves cost any more to have than not to have.

The ratio between items such as these which require no special outlay of money to the total measure of adaptability of better-supported school systems is, in the opinion of the writer, a rough measure of the "resourcefulness, imagination, and intelligence of the teachers which the salaries paid by these (better-supported) schools have been able to attract . . . (and) of the additional effort which derives not alone from teachers, but from any human beings, surrounded with stimulating conditions—suitable equipment, adequate materials, respected colleagues, sound standard of living." [9]

Computing Expenditure Level

Expenditure level is measured in terms of so many dollars of presumably educationally effective expenditure per some measure of amount of service to be supplied. The rough measure expenditure per pupil fulfills the conditions approximately. We would say that in two communities comparable except for size, the one with 10,000 pupils could be expected to be spending ten times as much as the one with 1,000 pupils, assuming a similar kind of service. If the first community were spending $5,000,000 and the second $500,000, they would be on the same expenditure level. For the first community the expenditure component of the measure would be $5,000,000; the amount of service to be supplied or educational-need component would be 10,000 pupils.

To obtain a better measure of expenditure level it is necessary to refine these two components.

The Expenditure Component. The first step in obtaining a useful expenditure component is to remove all expenditures that are not customarily spread evenly over the years. Capital outlay and debt service are normally the only items in this category. When they are removed what is left is current expenditure. If, however, such normally current items as expenditure for library books are counted as capital expenditures—

[9] William S. Vincent, *What Education Our Money Buys*, New York State Educational Conference Board, Albany, N.Y., 1943.

as they are in some instances—it is appropriate to treat them as current expenditures in computing expenditure level.

The second step is to remove current expenditures for sizable items that presumably do not affect quality. Chief among these is expenditure for transportation. Lunchroom expenditures that are recovered from sale of food should also be excluded if the amount is sufficient to influence the computed expenditure level materially.

The third step is to add expenditures made through some other agency for services provided in the schools that are normally paid for from school funds. Sometimes school librarians and school nurses are paid from city funds. In other instances the maintenance and lighting of school buildings are not charges on the school budget. To obtain a figure comparable with those of other communities, such expenditure should be added.

The test of whether or not to exclude or include items is of course whether they are of any sizable significance. In the vast majority of communities the only items that need to be considered are capital outlay, debt service, and transportation.

The above assumes the use of attendance data on all pupils, whether they are residents or nonresidents. If resident pupils alone are to be considered, the expenditure figures should be reduced by the amount received on account of the nonresident pupils from the sending district and any state aid received directly on account of these nonresidents.

The Expenditure Component for "Sending" Districts. In school systems that send a sizable proportion of their children to other districts, additional adjustments are required. To obtain a useful measure of the level of education in the home schools, payments to the other districts should be subtracted from the expenditure component.

The Expenditure-Pupil-Unit Component—Units of Educational Need. Basically educational costs vary with the number of pupils to be educated. The only major distortion to this in large school systems with one or more high schools enrolling approximately 700 pupils each is the variation in the percentage of pupils who are in the higher, more expensive grades. This can be cared for by counting each pupil in Grades 7 to 12 as 1.3 pupil cost units (weighted pupil units).[10] Thus a school with 1,200 pupils in elementary grades and 1,000 pupils in Grades 7 to 12 would be credited with 1,200 plus 1.3 × 1,000, or 2,500 weighted pupil units.

With the expenditures identified as in the preceding section, and with the corrected pupil figure obtained, division of the former by the latter produces expenditure level.

The Expenditure Pupil Unit for Smaller Schools. Where there are fewer than 700 pupils in the secondary grades (Grades 7 to 12) the

[10] New York State experience (see Table 7-1).

Table 7-1 Small-school Corrections for Use in Computing Expenditure Pupil Units—Weighted Pupils or Weighted Classroom Units

(x equals average daily attendance)

	Norton and Lawler 1940 [*]	New York State 1943–1944 [†]	West Virginia 1944–1945 [‡]	Mississippi 1946–1947 [§]	Illinois 1947–1948 [¶]
Elementary average daily attendance	Under 21 ....27 21–42 ....$1.286x$ 43–135 .. $54+0.87(x-32)$ Over 135 x	1 teacher ....22 2 or more teachers: Under 45 ....$1.56x-25$ 45–109 ....$57+0.82x$ 110–315 ....x Over 315	1 teacher ....30 2 or more teachers: 51 or less ....$1.18x$ 52–196 .. $60+1.034(x-51)$ 197–332 .. $210+0.88(x-196)$ Over 332 x	1 teacher ....30 2 or more teachers: 70 or less .. $17+1.5(x-7)$ 71–304 .. $112+0.82(x-70)$ Over 304 x	Under 81 ....$3+1.4x$ 81–288 .. $115+0.83(x-80)$ 289 and over x
Secondary average daily attendance	Under 45 .. $25+1.35(x-8)$ 45–724 .. $75+0.955(x-45)$ Over 724 x	Under 69 ....$14+1.68x$ 69–391 ....$59+1.02x$ 392–695 ....$153+0.78x$ Over 695 x	Under 70 ....$1.37x$ 71–719 .. $96+0.96(x-70)$ Over 719 x	Under 75 ....$1.81x$ 76–685 .. $136+0.9(x-75)$ Over 685 x	Under 98 ....$34+1.23x$ 98–673 .. $155+0.9(x-98)$ Over 673 x
Sec. elem.:					
Salary ratio	1.23	1.18	1.20	1.27	Not given
Class-size ratio ..	1.08	1.10	1.25	1.36	1.20
Combination ratio	1.33	1.30	1.50	1.73	Not given
Stabilizing ratios: [a]					
Elementary	27	22	30	30	24
Secondary	25	20	24	22	20
Grade range:					
Elementary	K–8	K–6	K–8	K–8	K–8
Secondary	9–12	7–12	9–12	9–12	9–12

[*] John K. Norton and Eugene S. Lawler, *An Inventory of Public School Expenditures in the United States*, American Council on Education, Washington, 1944, pp. 375–401.
[†] Paul R. Mort and A. W. Schmidt, "Technical Aspects of State Aid," *Fiscal Policy for Public Education in the State of New York*, Staff Study 10, New York State Educational Conference Board, Albany, N.Y., 1947, pp. 9–12.
[‡] George D. Strayer, Director, *A Survey of Public Education in West Virginia*, State of West Virginia, Legislative Interim Committee, Charleston, W. Va., 1945, pp. 612–614.
[§] William F. McLure, *Let Us Pay for the Kind of Education We Need*, University of Mississippi, Bureau of Educational Research, University, Miss., 1948, pp. 58–60.
[¶] William P. McLure and Francis G. Cornell, *Financing Education in Efficient School Districts*, University of Illinois, Bureau of Research Service, Urbana, Ill., 1949, pp. 143–144.
[a] For use in transmuting weighted pupil units to weighted classroom units.
Note 1: For treatment of junior colleges, see Questions for Study and Discussion.
Note 2: If some measure other than average daily attendance is used, the limits of the categories should be appropriately adjusted.

task is more complex. In these smaller school systems the average number of pupils that can be cared for by a teacher declines. This can be compensated for by allowing more educational-need units for smaller schools. In state-aid systems these allowances are either set according to average practice in supplying teachers in schools of different sizes or by some rule-of-thumb method. For developing comparable figures it is suggested that one of the systems of correction given in Table 7-1 be used. The New York State figures have four advantages that have been operating over several decades: (1) the schools operate without state class-size controls, (2) all schools are strongly aided, (3) there are large numbers of schools in each category, and (4) the schools are in general well supported. After the proper corrected figures are obtained, the figures for secondary pupils (Grades 7 to 12) are increased by 30 per cent as in the case of the larger schools. The norms change, but they change slowly.

The expenditure-level figures obtained by using such corrections for the pupil figures in small schools may be compared with expenditure levels for large schools.

It should be clear from this that studies using expenditure levels derived from uncorrected expenditure figures or unweighted pupil figures must be used with extreme care. But even with all corrections made, the predictability for school quality is subject to distortion because of cost-of-living differences and their effect on costs, and perhaps, in the case of some large cities, the heavy extra load incident to providing fair opportunities for children of families immigrating from educationally underprivileged areas. While there have been excellent cost-of-living studies, the problem of assessing the differential effects on school costs has not been satisfactorily solved. What they do suggest is that the distortion in the cost of education is much less than many people have assumed.[11] Accordingly, it is left to the individual to assess such differential effects as cost of living, attractiveness of rural life, attractiveness of suburban life, and attractiveness of climate in appreciating or depreciating the purchasing power of his school system. It is to be hoped that in doing so he will proceed with caution, whatever his teacher-recruitment brochures or the home-town-development league may say.

Expenditure-level Norms

We are clearly in midpassage today between an education designed to give the ready and willing his chance and an education designed to

---

[11] David P. Harry, Jr., *The Cost of Living of Teachers in the State of New York,* Bureau of Publications, Teachers College, Columbia University, New York, 1928.

bring education to all, ready and willing or no. Vincent has estimated the nature of this change as follows: [12]

As schools have increased their expenditures during the past ten to twelve years, what have they bought with the additional money in excess of what inflation has absorbed? It would appear from the evidence that, even in the face of inflation, schools of the state with the resources to do so have increased the quality of their educational program in at least five important areas:

1. Attention to individual growth and development of pupils.

2. Improvement of the setting in which desirable intellectual and character attributes of individuals may develop.

3. Greater realism in the manner in which the educational program is organized and presented.

4. Greater variety in the courses and opportunities offered for the development of special skills and talents in pupils.

5. Broader evidences of highly skilled teaching.

Evidence is clearest for the first of these, and the indications are that it is the oldest of the five trends.

The great majority of our schools give lip service to the "school in the making" but are still trying to achieve it by mass methods that were quite satisfactory for the earlier ideal. Obvious failure with the dull, the bright, and the talented has lead many of the "better" schools to set up separate classes for these groups. But what is happening to the remaining 95 per cent does not look good when compared with what is happening to them in schools with excellent teachers in adequate numbers so that there is enough time to reach each youngster as a growing person.

The lowest-expenditure schools are on the first level. The ready and willing emerge and shed glory on the whole school. It is difficult to imagine what would have happened to another ten, or hundred, or thousand under a good education. Bagley, growing up in the Thumb of Michigan, found his chance in spite of the poverty of the school; he went from the eighth grade to the State Agricultural College—possible in those days. How many who were a little less able or inspired than Bagley were passed over? At the same time Thorndike was attending Wesleyan, where he, along with many lesser men, was getting all a fine school could provide. Thus the American system took care of two of the ready and willing. It was a wonderful system—as far as it went.

The school that is emerging is not content to stop so soon. Whatever it may cost, America will pay. What it will cost even in present-day dollars

[12] William S. Vincent, *Educational Betterment in New York State Public Schools since 1920*, New York State Educational Conference Board, Staff Study No. 1, Albany, N.Y., November, 1957.

is anybody's guess. But it will probably not be less than the most vigorous communities in most states are now spending. The average communities in two or three states, for example, are well on their way, and the adjustment has been accelerating rapidly. But their schools are neither the old schools wholly nor the schools they are on the way to becoming.

In this time of changing dollar values, the best that can be done is to make an estimate from the studies of the characteristics of schools on different expenditure levels, as in Figure 7-2. Observe along the left margin the notes characterizing the education associated with the various expenditure levels.

FORTUNES OF EXPENDITURE

Figure 7-2 has another purpose. It gives the Woollatt index correction for cost level. This index reflects both cost of living and, to a degree, the general rise of standard of living as it has impact on the employment of teachers.[13] Expenditure levels charted for a community will show whether expenditure status is being bettered or worsened as adjustments to changing cost levels occur. If the line is horizontal, it indicates no change. If it rises from left to right it indicates increasing purchasing power; if it drops, it indicates diminishing purchasing power.

A blank scale is provided at the right for entering the Woollatt scale for the current year. If current figures are not available, they should be estimated.

The application of this chart to all the school districts in one state in the midst of the turbulent 1950s showed a decline in every school district in spite of what appeared to be rapidly expanding expenditures.

HISTORY OF EXPENDITURE

In a search for ways of allowing for the distorting factors in a period of rapid price rise, Furno discovered that a strong prediction measure could be obtained by a combination of three expenditure-level figures: the average of three recent years, a three-year average nine years earlier, and a three-year average eighteen years earlier. This appears to adjust for secular disturbances. It becomes a splendid measure to reveal the effect of expenditure policy during a period of two decades on present-day school quality. It drives home the fateful character of the expenditure decisions the community is making today.

[13] Lorne H. Woollatt, *The Cost of Education Index,* Baltimore Public Schools, 1956. (Revised periodically).

School year

	1947-1948	1948-1949	1949-1950	1950-1951	1951-1952	1952-1953	1953-1954	1954-1955	1955-1956	1956-1957	1957-1958	1958-1959	Current year
Type A: (pioneering support level)	$400	412	416	436	480	480	500	516	536	568	600	648	—
	$350	361	364	382	420	420	438	452	469	497	525	567	—
Type B: (minimum support level for broad range program)	$300	309	312	327	360	360	375	387	402	426	450	486	—
	$250	258	260	273	300	300	313	323	335	355	375	405	—
Type C: (frugal support level)	$200	206	208	218	240	240	250	258	268	284	300	324	—
	$150	155	156	164	180	180	188	194	201	213	225	243	—
Type D: (scant support level)	$100	103	104	109	120	120	125	129	134	142	150	162	—
	$50	52	52	55	60	60	63	65	67	71	75	81	—
	0	0	0	0	0	0	0	0	0	0	0	0	

Fig. 7-2 The fortunes of school support over the period 1947–1948 to 1958–1959. (Expenditure levels are expressed in dollars.) Expenditure level is adjusted for price levels of education by use of the Woollatt index. The base year is 1947–1948 = 100. Thus, a community would have to provide $150 in 1957–1958 for every $100 it provided for education in 1947–1948 in order to keep up with inflationary costs. The support level is net current expenditure divided by weighted pupil units (EPUs). The expenditure pupil units are average daily attendance corrected for sparsity as it affects class size (pupil-teacher ratio) and for the higher costs of high school education. A close estimate can be found by dividing net current expenditure by ADA (average daily attendance) and reducing the result by 10 per cent. The net current expenditure is total expenditure for schools less the following: (a) expenditures for capital outlay and debt service; (b) expenditures for transportation; and (c) payments for pupils sent to schools other than those of the town or city. The result is that measure of expenditure level that will best predict the quality of the schools operated by the school district. Data for 1957–1958 and 1958–1959 are estimated.

ALLOCATION OF EXPENDITURES

Teachers, supervisors, administrators must be paid; instructional equipment and supplies must be purchased; custodians and what they work with must be supplied; buildings must be paid for and maintained; in most school systems transportation must be made available. How these monies are kept in balance appears to have considerable influence on the quality of education provided and reflects to no small degree the expectations staff and community have for their schools.

Assuming a vigorous recruitment policy, the quality of new teachers in the schools today and of old teachers ten, twenty, thirty, and forty years from now is influenced by salary levels, teaching load, quality of buildings, adequacy of supplies, the level of community expectation for their schools, and the goodness of the community as a place for a teacher to live his life and pursue his profession. So much for the long-time effects of the pattern of expenditure. Furno's studies showed a comparable correlation of .31 between the expenditure level in 1930 and quality in 1955, a depression, two wars, and a recession later. This was what spurred Furno's study of ways of adjusting for fiscal turbulence, resulting in his "history of expenditure" measure (measure 11). This measure shows a correlation of .63 between expenditures before and during the period of turbulence and quality in 1955.[14]

As to immediate effects, all these same factors influence the quality of the day-to-day service of teachers. Perhaps the relative effects are not the same, but all these factors are among those that shape the school today and will influence it as long as those recruited this year are a part of the school system. Put another way, the quality of the schools of today is the product of expenditure policy not only of this year, but also of last year, ten years ago, twenty years ago, forty years ago.

The point is that decisions on the amount of money made available for schools and on how it is allocated are fateful decisions. They are strategic —not tactical.

One of the first fruits of the more or less uniform system of accounting adopted by the states early in this century was the establishment of norms for the distribution or allocation of expenditure (see Chapter 21). Students of school administration in the 1920s were expected to memorize the percentages normally allotted to administration, instruction, maintenance, etc. Such norms served and still serve a useful purpose in evaluation and budget development.

A series of studies pursued by the Institute of Administrative Research of Teachers College, Columbia University, appears to have opened up a new phase in such development of norms. It was initiated by Martin's study inquiring into the possibility that the percentage allocation would vary with expenditure level.[15] Interestingly enough, it does not. This of

[14] Furno, *op. cit.*
[15] Robert R. Martin, "Implications of Patterns of Expenditures for Budgeting and Accounting," unpublished Ed. D. project, Teachers College, Columbia University, New York, 1951.

course may indicate that the norms now in use for three or four decades have become a sort of Procrustean bed.

The current status of this line of inquiry is reflected in the items of Figure 7-1: teachers' salaries, staffing adequacy, small items (current expenses reduced by the subtraction of transportation, teachers' salaries, and maintenance), debt service, and the variation of staffing numerical adequacy from what would be predicted by average salary and "small-item" expenditures. These topics are discussed below.

From these studies it is now clear that (1) accounting classifications need refinement and (2) balance is important as well as gross amounts. The latter idea suggests the possibility of evolving tolerance norms— for example, safety bands of expenditure for salaries in relation to materials, safety bands for numerical staffing adequacy in relation to salary levels and expenditure on materials and services other than instruction.

The facts of great yield isolated in the work to date are discussed below.[16]

Salary Levels

The average salary of teachers is one of the most potent predictors. Furno's studies show that it closely parallels the expenditure level.

Small-item Expenditures

From Martin's study it was obvious that the accounting system at present does not reflect the differences in practice between the lower-level-expenditure school systems he studied and the high-level systems. Probing for vital elements was begun by Brickell.[17] He ran correlations between the quality measure and all the subitems in the administration, operation, and maintenance categories and found some surprising results. Teresa [18] followed with a rerun, using a more acceptable quality measure. Out of this the powerful "small items" factor was evolved.

All of this work was done within the framework of the present accounting system. A highly promising new phase was initiated by Campbell [19] when he examined 25,000 vouchers in five school systems, all in small-items areas. This case study gives strong indication that the vital differentiating element is expenditure for goods and services beyond those required for the operation of the school in the accustomed manner. The expense of the field-worker method used by Campbell in this pioneering

---

[16] For correlations of these items with "Quality" as measured by The Growing Edge, see Donald H. Ross (ed.), Administration for Adaptability, Metropolitan School Study Council, New York, 1958, pp. 607–624.

[17] Brickell, op. cit.

[18] Teresa, op. cit.

[19] Campbell, op. cit.

study delayed collection of data on these items until through the work of Recktenwald [20] and Bothwell a method was developed for collecting the information by the questionnaire method. The first fruits of the application of the method give norms obtained from Associated Public School Systems data.[21]

Staffing Adequacy

Staffing adequacy, the number of professional employees (instructional) per 1,000 staffing pupil units, is roughly the inverse of the long-used pupil-teacher ratio. It is a powerful determinant of expenditure level—comparable to the average salaries paid. Some school systems are supplying staff in the proportion of 25 per 1,000 staffing pupil units; others provide as many as 90 per 1,000.

There are indications that the major educational adjustment taking place across the land today requires an increase in the staffing complement of our schools. In New York State, where the state-aid system is free from controls on this factor and where the expenditure level of districts of average wealth increased from $72 in 1921 to $440 in 1957, staffing adequacy increased in the same period from 36 per 1,000 staffing pupil units to more than 50. This is the trend of individual community decisions in the state that has, by and large, the most adequate school support.

Staffing adequacy is measured by dividing the number of professional staff members by the number of thousands of staffing pupil units. The number of professional staff members is the sum of the classroom teachers, administrators, supervisors, guidance officers, and school nurses. The number of staffing pupil units is determined in the same way as expenditure pupil units except that the number of pupils in Grades 7 to 12 (corrected for small schools) is multiplied by 1.1 instead of by 1.3. Put another way, it is expenditure pupil units less .2 the number of pupils in Grades 7 to 12.

Staffing Balance

Staffing balance, as it appears in Figure 7-1, is the amount of variation (up or down) of the staffing-adequacy measure from the staffing adequacy that would be predicted from the community's position as to average salary and small-items expenditure. It is obtained by taking the variation

[20] Charles F. Recktenwald, "A Report of the Development of an Instrument to Collect Data of Small Item Expenditures," unpublished Ed. D. project, Teachers College, Columbia University, New York, 1958.

[21] Bruce Bothwell, "Creative Expenditures for Quality Education," Associated Public School Systems, New York, 1958.

of the community's position on staffing adequacy (Measure 7, Figure 7-1) from the position that would be predicted from the community's position on Measures 8 and 9.[22] This difference (whether above or below) is then charted as Measure 10.

This measure is of interest quite as much for the promise it gives that tolerance standards are achievable as for its own value.

Building Costs

The fact that in smaller communities it frequently happens that one generation is required to shoulder the costs of building for three becomes a serious threat to the wholesomeness of conditions for producing good education. Sometimes its effects are felt over a period of a quarter of a century. This is the extremely serious situation in which some communities—and not always poor communities—find themselves and that has spurred the development of state aid for school buildings in the 1940s and 1950s.

The over-all problem is discussed in Chapters 16 and 22. Here consideration is limited to clues to the evaluation of unwholesome conditions. The problem is to keep the debt service associated with capital outlay from getting out of bounds and, if it is not possible to keep it within reasonable bounds, to make it a subject of sufficient consideration in the community so that the extra burdens will be accepted as such—as the extra burden of a new sewer system would be accepted—without encroaching on current support of the schools.

As a clue to overburden, Grossnickle[23] estimates that over many decades capital outlay will average about 14 per cent of current costs (other than transportation). When the debt-service ratio gets much beyond this it should be a call to action.

It is difficult to formulate a rule of thumb that will be generally applicable because of the variation among states in the percentage of the current costs met by the state. A rule that comes near to being universal

[22] For example, assume that Community A has an Average Professional Salary of $5,600 (Measure 8), Small-item Expenditures of $142 per weighted pupil (Measure 9), and a Staffing Adequacy of 54 (Measure 7). To calculate Staffing Balance (Measure 10), subtract from Staffing Adequacy the sum of .45 times Average Professional Salary (in $100's), .04 times Small-item Expenditures, and the constant 25.22. The resulting figure taken without regard to sign is the measure called Staffing Balance. Thus for Community A, Staffing Balance (Measure 10) is obtained as follows:

$$\text{Staffing Balance} = |[54 - \{(.45)(56) + (.04)(142) + 25.22\}]|$$
$$= |(54 - 56)| = 2.00$$

[23] Foster E. Grossnickle, *Capital Outlay in Relation to a State's Minimum Educational Program*, Bureau of Publications, Teachers College, Columbia University, New York, 1931.

is as follows: When the local tax rate for debt service, computed in terms of full market value of taxable property, exceeds two dollars per thousand, and when the total tax rate for schools so computed is in excess of 1½ times the state average, there is a strong possibility that debt service is warping the ongoing program.

The rule proposed in the APSS Report Card [24] of which Figure 7-1 is a part suggests that when the tax rate for debt service exceeds 20 per cent of the total tax rate, it should be taken as a signal for careful analysis of the local financing of schools.

Clearly neither of these rules would make sense in Hawaii where the central government meets all the operating costs.

ABILITY AND VIGOR

One of the most strategic tasks of administration is the assessment of the economic ability of a community to meet the challenges and, as a correlative, the intensity of the community's use of its resources—its effort, its vigor of support. In the first place we may assume that all communities feel poor and all feel that they are vigorous in support of schools, considering the fact that they are poor. The most fateful error is for the administrator to accept this as a useful assessment. He must know how poor, how vigorous. This section deals with the measurement of these characteristics.

Taxpaying Ability

The achievement of a measure of the ability of one community is of little assistance unless there are comparable figures for other communities. Since in an absolute sense all communities feel poor, this year anyway, for one reason or another, we must resort to measures of relative ability—of relative wealth (or poorness—certainly not poverty). Communities then can be arranged according to degree of ability and an assessment of the potential of any one community thus can be achieved within the framework of a nation we all accept as wealthy, poor as we hold all its constituent parts to be.

The spur to the development of ways of assessing community ability has been the trend toward equalization-type state aid, particularly since 1920. But the results are applicable to local evaluation as well as to the achievement of just state-aid laws.

The measure of ability is obtained by dividing the tax base of the community by ability pupil units.

[24] *APSS Report Card,* Associated Public School Systems, An Affiliate of the Institute of Administrative Research, Teachers College, Columbia University, New York, 1958.

The Tax Base

For these purposes the measure of ability must be in terms of the ability of the community to pay taxes under the tax system as established by the state. If the property tax is the sole or chief tax base available to the community, the ability measurement must be either a direct or an indirect measure of the ability of that tax base to pay taxes when a uniform rate is applied. Under such circumstances the fairest index for comparing the relative ability of two or more communities is the amount of taxable property, fairly assessed, back of each weighted pupil unit. Similarly, the fairest measure of local vigor of support is the tax rate computed by dividing the amount of money actually raised for education by the amount of taxable property fairly assessed. By the same token the best index of the amount a school district should be expected to pay toward the cost of the foundation program is the amount of taxable property fairly assessed.

When localities are permitted generally to levy taxes on other tax bases than property so that the yield is significant compared with the yield of the property tax, the ability to pay taxes on such bases must be taken into account in obtaining the ability measure. This requires some sort of weighting.

The concept underlying fair ability measures is simple enough, but its achievement in practice is not easy. No function of government has been held so closely in the control of relatively small governmental units in the state as the assessment of property. The result is that what is considered fair assessment in one section of the state is not considered fair assessment in another section of the state. Accordingly data drawn from the assessment rolls are not directly usable for comparing communities with respect to their ability to support schools. The tax rates based on these assessments are not comparable, since a 5-mill tax in one community based on 50 per cent of fair valuation is only half as great a true tax rate as a 5-mill tax in another community based on a 100 per cent valuation. Similarly the assessment figures if used in a state-aid formula tend to favor the communities that assess their property low in relationship to its fair value and to penalize the communities that assess their property nearer its true value.

If all property were assessed at a fair value, actual assessed value of property would be the ideal index of relative ability of school districts, where, as in most instances, the property tax is the only tax of any importance that can be generally utilized in school districts, large and small. A consideration of the problem of measuring relative ability, then, may take the form of considering the means of getting either fair assessments of property or adequate estimates of fair assessments. In most cases this is a very difficult task, inasmuch as common practice is to have property assessed by locally elected persons who, on the one hand, have no great skill at assessments and who, on the other hand, are influenced by various forces tending in the one case to increase assessments and in the other case to decrease them. Communities seeking new population sometimes follow the policy of assessing property at full value or something approaching full value, in order that the tax rates levied may appear low. Other communities, interested in reducing taxes, may seek to inflate the appearance of heavy taxes by the use of low assessments and accompanying high tax rates. The result is chaos as far as the comparability of actual assessments is concerned.

Obtaining a Useful Measure. In a state where the state tax commission performs the service of determining assessment ratios, the problem of comparing data for various communities within the state is reduced to finding out what assessment ratio is assigned to each. The assessed value of property in a given community is then divided by the ratio. For example, if the assessment ratio is 50 per cent, the total assessed value is divided by .50. The result is an equalized valuation twice as large as the assessed valuation.

Just what the revised figure is, other than a basis for comparison with other communities in the state, depends on what the tax commission uses. Sometimes the base is called true value, or market value. But even this does not necessarily mean 100 per cent. All figures may be referred to what were considered true values five years ago. So it is well to ask, "true values as of when?"

Comparison on the basis of true values among communities in different states is extremely difficult. Some attempts are made to achieve this in the studies of the Associated Public School Systems, as will be noted in Figure 7-3. The instructions for those reporting the data for school systems are as follows:

Full valuation is the total as it would be if all properties were assessed at their current market value. Possible sources for this information are: report of State Tax Commission, local assessors, local real estate dealers, building and loan association officers, insurance company officials, Annual Bulletin of the Bureau of Governmental Research, Detroit.

Please give your own best appraisal in the light of any such data that are available. Perhaps you will want to check your figures with the actual experiences of a half-dozen or so of your associates who own real property. Take into account the possibility that homes, businesses, and industrial properties, as groups, may be assessed at different ratios of their current market value.

The chances are that the distribution of ability obtained by using the resulting figures is fairly authentic, since there would be a tendency for errors in one direction to cancel out errors in the other direction except at the ends of the distribution. Since the communities in the scale are

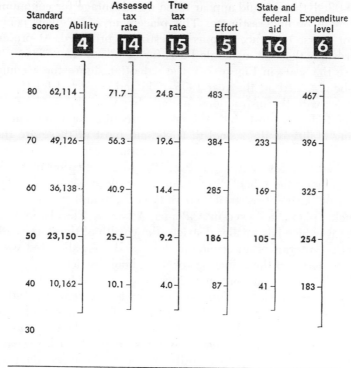

Sources of expenditure

Standard scores	Ability 4	Assessed tax rate 14	True tax rate 15	Effort 5	State and federal aid 16	Expenditure level 6
80	62,114	71.7	24.8	483		467
70	49,126	56.3	19.6	384	233	396
60	36,138	40.9	14.4	285	169	325
50	23,150	25.5	9.2	186	105	254
40	10,162	10.1	4.0	87	41	183
30						

Range:
High $89,472   97.5   34.4 $553 $286 $473
Low $ 2,085   1.0   0.8 $ 16 $ 10 $120

4 Ability--full property valuation per ability pupil unit (in dollars).

14 Tax rate on assessed property valuation (in mills)

15 Tax rate on full property valuation (in mills)

5 Effort--amount raised locally per EPU (in dollars)

16 State and federal aid per EPU (in dollars)

6 Expenditure level--net current expenditure per EPU (in dollars)

Fig. 7-3 What are the ingredients of your expenditure level?

This chart will help you get a good look at them. The ingredients of expenditure level flow from characteristics of the local community as well as those of the state. A part of the community wealth potential becomes available through taxation. This is expressed in terms of the amount raised locally per EPU (Measure 5). The tax rates indicate a community's local effort—especially tax rate on full property valuation. When monies from the state and federal governments are added to this, the result is the community's level of expenditure. These expenditures are used to buy the materials with which the staff is to work and to pay salaries. In conjunction with the kind of community which has produced these conditions, the level of expenditure attracts and retains a certain kind of staff. What this staff does with the students is the school program. Thus, the sources of expenditure of a community and the effort exerted by the community will in time affect the quality of education children are receiving day by day and will receive in future years.

not identified, there would appear to be no advantage for communities to overestimate or underestimate. The placement of a given community would of course be as accurate as the estimate provided. At present, this scale provides the best available basis for comparison.

To use the scale in Figure 7-3, the valuation figure for a community should be obtained for the year 1955–1956 and corrected *for that year* in accordance with the instructions quoted above.

Use of Indexes. Most state-aid systems require some measure of the taxpaying ability of the school districts and most of these are the local assessments corrected by the assessment ratios assigned by the state tax commission. In a few states, however, the total valuation of the state is prorated among the school districts in terms of an economic index. This can be done fairly satisfactorily where the county unit system is in operation. Such a plan is followed in Alabama, Arkansas, Florida, and Georgia.

In Texas, which has smaller districts, the wealth of the state is allocated to counties in terms of an economic index and then allocated within the counties in terms of the valuations of the school districts.

It is to be hoped that someone will succeed in developing an economic index applicable to smaller units than a county. Currently a study in this direction is being pursued by Thomas Shea of the New York State Department of Education. This study, begun by Shea when he was working with the Associated Public School Systems, may take a first step in this direction. Shea is seeking to identify predictive localized data not now available but collectible by a simple polling device. When and if such a measure becomes available it will provide an instrument of prime value to local administrators, whether or not it proves useful in state-aid systems.

The Ability Pupil Unit

The wealth figure is all that is needed in most state-aid systems. For evaluation uses, however, once the figure for wealth is obtained, the problem remains of expressing wealth in terms of some measure of the size of the educational job. Such a measure requires the use of all children attending public schools *who reside in the district,* whether they attend school in the district or in another district. This is to be contrasted to the expenditure pupil unit which usually uses all the children who attend in the district regardless of their places of residence.

When this base figure is obtained, it is first subjected to the same corrections as are outlined for the expenditure pupil unit (see Table 7-1). The simplest procedure for small school systems is first to compute the attendance pupil units and then subtract the actual average daily attendance (or comparable figure) from the total, being sure to count each secondary pupil as 1.3 units.

To the resulting figure is added one derived by dividing the expenditure for transportation by the expenditure level in dollars per expenditure pupil unit. This is a rule-of-thumb method devised to reduce to a minimum the distortion from varying transportation loads.

Use in State-aid Systems. State-aid systems customarily do not require the use of unit figures but call instead for an application of a uniform rate to the tax base. Also, transportation is usually dealt with as a special problem, as discussed in Chapter 16.

Community Vigor

The best measure of community vigor is the true tax rate for school purposes. It is obtained by dividing the total amount raised by local taxes by the full valuation of property. The same result will be obtained by multiplying the actual tax rate by the assessment ratio. For example, if the property on the average is assessed at 25 per cent of its full market value, and the tax rate is $20 per thousand, the true tax rate is 25 per cent of $20, or $5.

The distribution of true tax rates in the APSS schools in 1955–1956, as shown in Figure 5, ranged from 80 cents per $1,000 to $34.40 per $1,000. The mean was $9.20; the middle two-thirds fell between $4.00 and $14.40. While these school systems represent every part of the United States, it is probable that they show up somewhat but not markedly higher than a true sampling would show. As in the case of the ability data, these are the only broad-range data available. They are subject to the same comments as were made with respect to the ability figures.

SUMMARY

Properly processed, expenditure data provide the best single clue to the wholesomeness of quality-producing conditions in a school system. For evaluation purposes it should be associated with demographic data descriptive of the community, ability measures, measures of vigor of support, measures of the distribution of expenditures by amounts and balance, measures of the characteristics of the staff, and an assessment of operational conditions in the schools.

There are two expenditure-level facts of great yield: the expenditure level itself and the "history of expenditure." The expenditure level is measured by a refined figure for expenditure per pupil, both the expenditure component and the pupil component requiring refinement. The history of expenditure is a combination of expenditure levels for three periods over an eighteen-year span.

What has been happening to expenditure level in the net can be determined by use of a chart that corrects for year-to-year changes in cost levels of education.

Among the more detailed measures that have proved to be facts of great yield are salary levels, small-item expenditures (for betterment), staffing adequacy, and staffing balance.

The tax burden incident to building costs is another critical fact.

Associated with the expenditure policy outlined above are the facts on community ability to pay taxes and on true tax burden. Important as these measures are, they are obtained only with extreme difficulty. But they cannot be ignored with impunity.

The refined measures of expenditure level and ability are essential to the achievement of a just and adequate system of state aid.

QUESTIONS FOR STUDY AND DISCUSSION

Table 7-2 Information on Three School Districts (A, B, and C)

	Community A	Community B	Community C
Expenditures			
Total school expenditures	$ 2,587,000	$1,883,000	$1,407,000
Capital outlay	79,000	51,000	22,000
Debt service	181,000	57,000	134,000
Tuition payments to other districts	13,000	7,000	3,000
Transportation expenditures	44,000	37,000	1,000
Full property valuation ($100's)	129,398,000	78,669,000	67,605,000
Assessed property valuation	60,817,000	12,889,000	16,080,000
Amount of money raised on property	2,241,000	553,000	1,064,000
Total current expenditures	2,327,000	1,775,000	1,251,000
Average daily attendance, grades K–6			
All pupils attending	1,190	7,794	1,698
Pupils attending who live outside the district	4	0	15
Pupils residing in district attending school in other districts	5	0	3
Average daily attendance, grades 7–12			
All pupils attending	1,093	3,736	1,360
Pupils attending who live outside the district	8	120	290
Pupils residing in district attending school in other districts	3	70	8

1. Compute the following: expenditure level, ability, true tax rate

2. Make a table comparing the three communities in these three measures. Compare your results with a similar table using current expenditure per pupil in average daily attendance, assessed valuation per pupil in average daily attendance, and tax rates on assessed valuations.

SELECTED REFERENCES

The research on which the computation of expenditure level and the pupil-cost unit associated with it is based is reviewed extensively in the second edition of this book, Chapters 4 and 25 and Supplement C.

The many studies on which the selection of the measures is based are referred to in the text. They all appear in abstract form in the following:

Ross, Donald H. (ed.): *Administration for Adaptability*, rev. ed., Metropolitan School Study Council, New York, 1958.

The three references below provide an excellent coverage of the issues involved in obtaining ability measures and in estimating taxpaying ability:

Johns, Roe L., and E. L. Morphet (eds.): *Problems and Issues in Public School Finance*, Bureau of Publications, Teachers College, Columbia University, New York, 1952, chap. 7.

National Education Association, Committee on Tax Education and School Finance: *The Index of Local Economic Ability in State School Finance Programs*, Washington, 1953.

———: *Equalization of Property Assessments*, Washington, 1958.

PART THREE

Taxation

CHAPTERS 8, 9, and 10 seek to outline the major issues in the general governmental field of taxation. Only in the sense that the issues treated are those that are inescapably involved in financing public education are these chapters educationally oriented.

8. Local taxation for education

THE IMPORTANCE of local taxation cannot be overemphasized. While in amount it runs third [1] to federal and state taxation, it performs a uniquely important function. It gives body and substance to local autonomy. Each time the state either by neglect or by direct action limits still further the extent of local taxation, by just that amount does it limit local autonomy as a workable function.

Local property taxes are levied for county, municipal, and school purposes, sometimes jointly, sometimes separately. Traditionally the source of local taxation has been the property tax but as revenue demands have intensified there have been more frequent attempts to use various forms of sales and business taxes and, less often, the personal income tax. Local revenue for the support of education has come in overwhelming proportion from the property tax.

The decline in relative importance of the property tax has been more dramatic than it has been indicative of weakness. In 1933 the property tax produced more revenue than all other taxes put together. In 1941 it was still the largest single revenue producer, but by 1956 it had declined to approximately 11 per cent of the total. However, the change is in large part due to the awesome increase in federal taxation, to a lesser extent to increases in taxes at the state level, and to a minor extent to the interesting development of new forms of local taxation. Despite the decline the property tax produced $2\frac{1}{2}$ times as much revenue in 1956 as it had any time prior to the depression. In 1953, when the total amount raised by property taxes was $9 billion, the average was $60 per capita across the United States and even in a state considered poor, such as Mississippi, the per capita revenue was $25.

[1] In 1956, federal revenue amounted to approximately $72 billion, state revenue to $14.6 billion, and local revenue to $13 billion. Of the local revenue an estimated $11 billion came from property taxation.

The large amounts of money which the property tax raises make it important to know what property taxation is about. Anyone who is concerned with education should have a thorough understanding of this tax. Often it is the sole local support for the operation of the public schools.

THE NATURE OF THE PROPERTY TAX

The property tax is the very life blood of the independent and responsible local operation of public education. Some $4.5 billion were raised for education in 1954 through this tax.

There is no question but that the property tax furnishes a smaller and smaller proportion of total local taxation. Where once it was almost the sole source, now a great variety of taxes are levied in various places.

Criticisms of the property tax have been legion. Much has been said about the continuing overburden on the property tax. Some have maintained that the property tax is too expensive to collect since it involves assessment, the maintenance of records of valuation, the collection of taxes, and their distribution to government units where they are used. The inequities and inefficiency of the assessment process have been widely proclaimed and acknowledged. The regressivity of the property tax is well known. Despite all these shortcomings the property tax is here to stay and there are abundant reasons for this, some valid and some less than valid.

1. The property tax has been levied for centuries and for that reason alone is expected and accepted.

2. Property, despite the tremendous diversification of wealth, still represents with some justice a rough measure of wealth.

3. What possible substitute is there for it? Any tax which produces more than $11 billion a year cannot easily or quickly be replaced.

4. The property tax alone of all taxes is the one where the amount of money to be spent is determined first and the money raised to meet this demand. All other taxes work in quite a different manner. The amount to be collected does not depend on the budget but may exceed or fall short depending on business conditions and the accuracy of the original estimate.

5. The demand for revenue on the local level is increasing. The increased population, the improved standards of living (both public and private), the needs caused by inflation, and the scarcity of well-qualified school personnel combine to cause great increases in the outlays for local governmental services.

6. While the property tax is slow to respond to rising prices, it is also slow to respond to a downward change. It is stable and dependable in yield, a fact which enables long-range fiscal plans to be made with some confidence.

7. Property valuation, a concomitant of property taxation, is deeply imbedded in the whole state and local fiscal structure. It is used in many ways in various states:

    a. In the apportionment of state aid for schools

    b. In the apportionment of certain municipal aids

    c. In the provision of special tax privileges in the form of exemptions for homesteaders, veterans, clergymen, volunteer firemen

    d. In the determination of the debt limits for local government

    e. In the apportionment of costs of county government

THEORY OF PROPERTY TAXATION

The general property tax is a tax on wealth, both tangible and intangible, levied at a uniform rate in the taxing jurisdiction upon a value known as assessed valuation. It is frequently called an ad valorem tax.

Many governmental services, such as fire protection, police protection, garbage collection, sewage, and others, are direct benefits to the property owners and it is argued that taxation of property for these purposes is justified.

In practice the benefit principle does not work as smoothly as theory would suggest. Government services contribute to the value of property, but such values are diffused among properties and cannot always be attributed to any specific piece of property in relation to its value or the tax that it pays. Perhaps the benefit theory does not have as much validity today as it once did. In a changing economy in which the proportions of local, state, and federal spending have been greatly altered, the protection of property is not as important relatively as it once was.

The ability-to-pay theory of taxation does not apply as much to property taxation as it does to certain other types, such as the income tax. The application of this theory requires the assumption that the value of property is an index of ability and that taxes assessed on property are in a broad sense levied in accordance with the income and ability to pay. This is not strictly true. The income-producing value of a piece of property may be roughly comparable in the long run to its value, but under specific conditions there may be wide variation between the value of a piece of property and its income-producing ability. Furthermore, there are today many forms of wealth which are only incompletely represented in property values. Personal property has increased many fold. Much of the productivity of today's economy does not arise from what the land will produce but arises from the skills and knowledges which men possess. Also, intangible property rights such as stocks, bonds, and mortgages have become increasingly common. It is extremely difficult to tax this kind of property. Attempts to do so lead to problems of evasion, double taxation, and shifting of burden.

HOW THE PROPERTY TAX WORKS

In outline the property tax is certainly not complex. Each parcel of property in a taxing jurisdiction is given a value by assessors. These values are entered on a tax roll, the total of which forms the total assessment value of the jurisdiction. The competent body—whether it be the people, the board of education, the city council, or another group—votes an annual tax levy. Each owner of property in the jurisdiction must then pay his proportionate share of the levy which is expressed in mills, cents, or dollars. Proportional assessment of property taxes is of long standing. Despite many efforts, no satisfactory substitute for it has been evolved.

For example, assume that School District A has an assessed valuation of $1,000,000 and it has voted to raise $10,000 for the support of education. By dividing the $1,000,000 into the $10,000 the assessed tax rate is determined. This would be 10 mills or $.010 per dollar, $1 per hundred, or $10 per thousand.

Similarly in School District B, individual and total assessed valuation have been determined by the assessors. Assume that the latter is $2,000,000 and that $25,000 has been voted for the support of education. The assessed rate is then 12.5 mills or $.0125 per dollar, $1.25 per hundred, or $12.50 per thousand. Here is the point at which many err in discussing taxation. Presumably the tax rate in School District B is higher than that in School District A. Certainly it is higher on assessed value.

However, it is inexact and highly erroneous to draw any conclusions as to the burden of taxation between two local governmental units on the basis of assessed value. Variations in the ratio of assessed to true value as between governmental units are extreme in all states. For example, in New Jersey in 1957 there were thirteen municipalities with assessment ratios below 10 per cent and ten with ratios of more than 50 per cent. None were at 100 per cent.[2] In Maryland in 1952, counties ranged in ratio from 25 to 60 per cent, and in Wisconsin, one of the leading states in terms of efforts to improve property taxation, the ratios by counties in 1954 ranged from 32 to 81 per cent.[3]

To return to the example, assume that School District A is assessed at a ratio of .50 of assessed to true value, while School District B is assessed at a ratio of .25. By multiplying the rate of taxation on assessed valuation by the ratio of assessed to true valuation, the actual full or true tax

[2] New Jersey Commission on State Tax Policy, *The General Property Tax in 1958*, Trenton, 1958, pp. 94–95.

[3] Federation of Tax Administrators, *Equalization Programs and Other State Supervisory Activities in the Property Tax Field*, Preliminary Report, Chicago, 1957, p. 76.

rate is determined. The rate in School District B is actually less than that in A.

The method of determining the ratio of assessed to true value which is called equalization will be discussed under assessment procedures.

The process of equalization would be quite simple if each property were assessed at the same exact standard of value but that is not the case. There are also great variations in assessments among categories or classes of property. Since many states still assess personal as well as real property there are still further discrepancies in this area.

ASSESSMENT

Equitable assessment is an extremely difficult undertaking. The values for different kinds of property depend on quite different factors; a home differs from a business property as does a business property from a factory. In many states both real and personal property are assessed, often at differing rates. The most difficult and complex assessments, e.g., railroad and public utilities, are made in most states by state assessors. But there are exemptions which must be taken into account, billions of dollars of property being wholly or partially tax exempt for a variety of reasons. There are tax limitations setting a ceiling on the levy a community may set. The first problem then is to get fair assessments.

Assessments vary widely in quality within the same taxing jurisdiction. This is not to be wondered at for even expert property appraisers, given ample time and complete opportunity to do a thorough and exact job of assessment, will often vary greatly in their evaluation of the worth of a property. It is not expected or even necessary that assessors do as complete and thorough a job as this. What is needed is at least an approximation of even-handed justice. One of the great difficulties with the assessment process is that it has accumulated all the errors of a century of neglect and administration by persons lacking in training as well as the errors both advertent and inadvertent due to political manipulation. The assessment process has many, many shortcomings. There is no question but that variations in assessment give rise to serious injustices.

There are many different kind of inequities in the property tax. Perhaps the most important of all is the inequality of assessment among individual properties. For example in New York State in 1956, farm properties ranged in the ratio of their assessed to full value from approximately .10 to more than 1.25. Within one taxing district it is common to have variations of ratios of assessed to full value ranging more than 50 per cent.

Another source of inequity is the inequality among various categories or classifications of property. In order to do a more accurate job of assessment, rules and formulas have been developed for assessing different types of property such as farms, residences, business properties, factories, utilities, vacant lots, timber land, and others. But, as is often the case, if one type of property is consistently overassessed or under-assessed in relation to another type of property, each type or classification will necessarily bear a much heavier or lighter portion of the tax load than its fair share. Over and over again personal property has come off lightly because of the difficulty of evaluation and ease of evasion.

Study after study has shown that the property tax tends to be rather highly regressive. In other words, properties of large value tend to be underassessed in comparison with properties of lower value.

Another inequity is intercounty inequality of assessment. This occurs primarily in states where there is no state oversight of full valuation. There is an inequity which arises between various municipalities making up a county. This is important in every state because county functions are largely financed through property taxes. Most counties have some sort of county equalization of property valuation to care for this particular difficulty.

Exemptions

A different type of inequity grows out of the exemption of various types of property. Each exemption increases the taxes of every taxpayer within that taxing jurisdiction. The total amount of exemptions is enormous. For example in New York State in 1957, with taxable property values of some $52 billion, some $11 billion more of property values were tax exempt. Much of this exemption is in the property of units of government, of churches, and of educational, charitable, and scientific institutions. Homestead exemptions came rapidly into being during the depression, especially in the Southern and Midwestern states. Florida, for example, has almost abolished residential property taxes with a $5,000 homestead exemption combined with low assessments. While other states are not quite so generous, this exemption has made serious inroads on the property tax in every state where it has been adopted. Fortunately the spread of this exemption halted with the end of the depression.

There are other new and growing exemptions. For example in New York State and primarily in New York City a billion dollars in tax-exempt housing has been added to the property rolls in the past ten years. In many cases this property replaces taxable property. Without questioning the social and human values represented in this development, the question must be raised as to what this does to other important social and human values which are fostered by institutions supported by property taxation.

The exemptions of the federal government create a growing and very important problem in many communities. If there is a defense plant owned by the federal government which attracts large numbers of workers, school districts and other units of government must bear greatly increased burdens. In some cases the burden is offset by grants of various kinds. But in no case is the property subject to taxation. This is certainly injurious to local government.

Of more than passing interest too are the inequities created by the attrition of the property tax. Each time a new superhighway is built, thousands of acres of land and many buildings are removed from the tax rolls. Some communities will benefit from new building stimulated by this development but the poorest communities are the least likely to have anything to replace the loss. The restaurants and gas stations along some of these highways are tax exempt. Revenue from these does not even go into the state treasury; it goes to some supergovernmental agency. The same criticism applies to airports with their bars, restaurants, shops, and parking facilities. Again there is no question of the value of such developments but thought must also be given to the preservation of other long-established values.

Ratios of Assessed to True Value

Some idea of the vastness of the property tax base may be gained from the Department of Commerce publication, *Assessed Values and Sales Prices of Transferred Real Property:* [4]

Property subject to local general property taxation in the United States is officially valued on the tax rolls, altogether, at approximately $280 billion. This total, as shown in earlier publications of the 1957 Census of Governments, consists of $210 billion of locally assessed real estate, $48 billion of locally assessed personal property, and $22 billion of State assessed property—mainly railroads and other utilities.

In 1922, according to the governmental census for the year, property assessments in the United States totaled $125 billion. The corresponding aggregate in 1890 was about $25 billion. The national total reported for 1860 was $12 billion.

The breakdown of the relationship to aggregate value for each of the main categories of property is contained in the same report:

Non-farm residential property accounts for about one-half of all locally assessed realty in the Nation, both in terms of numbers of properties and in aggregate assessed value. . . .

About one-seventh of the total assessed value of real property carried on the assessment rolls in the Nation is for acreage and farm properties. . . .

[4] U.S. Bureau of the Census, *Assessed Values and Sales Prices of Transferred Real Property, 1957 Census of Governments,* Washington, p. 1.

Vacant lots account for only 2.3% of total valuations of real estate. . . .

Despite their limited numbers, commercial and industrial properties account for more than one-fourth of the total locally assessed valuation.[5]

The above four categories account for approximately 98 per cent of assessed value of locally assessed real properties. The remainder is contained in properties which are not reported in the publication. A rough estimate of the full value of property in all four categories is approximately $750 billion.

State-wide assessment ratios invariably are less than 100 per cent with wide variations among states. On a simple sales-based average, assessment ratios shown for transferred residential property range from 6.1 per cent in South Carolina to 60.7 per cent in Rhode Island. The average for the United States is 27.3 per cent.

On the same basis the ratio for farm acreage and properties is somewhat lower in most cases than for residential properties. The ratios range from 6.9 per cent in Montana to 49.1 per cent in Rhode Island. The average for the United States is 22.9 per cent.

Sales of commercial and especially industrial properties are much fewer in number. Therefore reliable ratios are more difficult to obtain. The range for commercial properties among the thirty-eight states having sufficient sales for a sample in 1956 was from 11.7 per cent in Arkansas to 78.7 per cent in New York. The United States average was 41.4 per cent. In only six states were enough data obtained to compute ratios for industrial property. The range among them was from 17.8 per cent in California to 79 per cent in New York. The United States average was 39.3 per cent.

While more data might be helpful it seems reasonably safe to conclude that farm properties are generally assessed less than other categories of property across the United States and that industrial and commercial properties are the highest-assessed categories.

Assessment at a Uniform Valuation

Very few if any communities and no entire states have property assessments which even approach 100 per cent on full valuation despite laws in almost every state requiring assessment at 100 per cent of value. One hundred per cent value is variously defined: current market value as established in a transaction between a willing buyer and a willing seller, fair market value, or full cash value. All such definitions denote a value determined by sale in the open market. In fact one of the most pressing problems in property taxation at the present time in many states is a decision on what fraction of value shall be adopted as a re-

[5] *Ibid.*, pp. 6, 8, 11, 12.

quirement for uniformity. In practice the 100 per cent valuation which should provide uniformity has been allowed to become something quite different with consequent variations which provide tremendous barriers to 100 per cent assessment. It appears that the chief reason for allowing less than 100 per cent valuation may be an attempt to keep debt limits at low levels.

In New Jersey, a state heavily dependent on the property tax, valuation at 100 per cent or some fraction thereof has been the subject of a considerable portion of legislative debate for several years. The following quotation from a statement by a New Jersey Senator, Wayne Dumont, Jr., sums up the bitter reality of the problem which is far from New Jersey's alone.

The two principal problems referred in 1956 by the New Jersey Legislature to the State Tax Policy Commission and which are the subject of this report are most difficult and complex. Inescapably interwoven with municipal assessment and taxation of real and personal property is the second question of where to find more revenue to meet the steadily rising costs of State and local government directly reflected in the requests of the citizens of New Jersey for more State and local services.

It is an unfortunate paradox that the procedures and percentages applied by municipal assessors and governing bodies throughout New Jersey to assessment of real and personal property differ so much that grave doubts must be raised as to whether any mandatory uniform Statewide ratios can operate effectively and fairly, even though the very motive and reason for uniformity is fair play to everyone. Certainly the present law which has been interpreted to mean that all real property shall be assessed at 100 per cent of true value has over the years been observed principally in the breach and has proven to be neither practicable nor workable. Yet unless this law is soon repealed or a time extension granted, the decision of the New Jersey Supreme Court requiring full value assessing of both real and personal property will take effect on January 1, 1959.

While the 40 per cent recommendation contained herein would seem to be much more realistic than 100 per cent assessing, any percentage when applied uniformly could require substantial tax adjustments in some areas of our State. . . .[6]

As the foregoing statement implies the problem came to the fore in New Jersey when the courts interpreted the New Jersey law which requires equality of treatment according to the same standard of value, the standard of value being true value, to mean just that for both real and personal property.[7] However, the court did grant a period of grace before this standard is to apply.

[6] New Jersey Commission on State Tax Policy, *The General Property Tax in 1958*, Trenton, 1958, p. xiii.

[7] Switz and Middletown Township, 23 N.J., 580 (1956).

As has been indicated, assessment at 100 per cent valuation would affect markedly the pattern of assessment and of tax collection in most states in the United States. It would mean that in a great majority of the states the law now on the statute book would actually be observed.

Assessment at 100 per cent valuation would mean a tremendous change in assessed-value tax rates. The change would be purely psychological, however, unless the property owner had previously had an assessment ratio different from the ratio for his assessing district. The assessed tax rate would decline in an amount commensurate with the increase in the tax base. In New Jersey in 1957 this would have meant that the average state rate for all purposes would decline from $8.30 to $2.05 per $100 of assessed valuation.

The tax base would also change. In New York State in 1956 when the state as a whole moved in terms of full value from a former full value of approximately $34 billion to what at least came closer to a 100 per cent valuation, full value changed to $51 billion.

The greatest difficulty in changing to 100 per cent assessment would arise from the changes in individual tax rates—a shift in the burden. All taxpayers whose individual assessment increased less than the local municipal average increase would have to pay less taxes; those whose assessment increased more would have to pay more taxes. In New York State in 1956 the change in full valuation did not affect the local assessment so that the only change in tax rates was in terms of what the new full valuations accomplished in equalizing values.

There would also be changes in the impact of taxes on the various categories or classes of property. Across the nation industrial property appears to be bearing the heaviest burden of taxation. Assessment at 100 per cent valuation would relieve industrial property in those states where it is now overassessed and require another or several other categories to bear an increased load of taxation.

Like any generalization, this one runs the danger of being misinterpreted. Not in all states is industrial property more heavily assessed than other classes. In New York State in 1956, for example, farm property was most heavily assessed. In 169 townships out of 227, farm property was overassessed in comparison to industrial property according to the State Commission on Equalization and Assessment. In New Jersey under the 100 per cent proposal of the State Commission on Tax Policy in 1957: [8] "All classes of property except farm property would realize a tax decrease (and farm property would experience a $321,000 tax increase ...). Commercial and industrial real estate would realize a tax decrease of $64,736,000 but this would be more than offset by a tax increase on personal property used in business amounting to $93,942,000."

[8] New Jersey Commission on State Tax Policy, *op. cit.* 9th Report, p. 55.

The principal net effect would be to transfer some $30,750,000 from residential real estate and household goods to commercial and industrial personal property.

Still another effect would be to decrease the value of homestead, veterans', and other exemptions in terms of tax dollars because of the lower rate which would apply. In New Jersey, for example, this was estimated to reduce the tax value of veterans' exemptions by some $9,000,000.

One hundred per cent valuation would increase the borrowing power of tax districts in those states where limits on borrowing are based on assessed value and not on full value. Likewise, it would increase tax leeway for the tax districts where there are tax limits based on assessed value.

Assessment at 100 per cent valuation, or to a lesser extent at any uniform proportion of value, would mean tremendous improvement in property taxation. It is heartening to note that New York State moved a considerable distance toward this in increasing full values by almost 50 per cent.

THE PROCESS OF EQUALIZATION

The necessity for equalization of property valuations comes about because assessors in the various assessment districts use different ratios of full value in carrying out their function, despite the fact that the law in most states requires that property be assessed at full value or at some set percentage of full value. Therefore some means must be provided for arriving at the proportion assessed value bears to full value in each district. This affects state aid and it affects local taxes. In many states, a good deal of state money is distributed back to school districts or to municipalities on the basis of valuation. Unless this valuation is fair to all, each district will receive a greater or lesser proportion depending on how clever the officials are in evading the requirement of full valuation or the set proportional assessment.

To return to the example used previously: School District A has an assessed value of $1,000,000. The ratio of assessed value to true value is .50. School District B has an assessed value of $2,000,000 and a ratio of .25. By dividing the assessed value by the ratio of assessed to full, the full valuation is determined. The full valuation then is four times as great in District B as in A. If for county or state purposes each school district were to pay taxes on assessed value, District B would pay twice as much as A. However, if the tax were levied on full value B would pay four times as much as A.

Similarly, if state aid were distributed on the basis of property valuation without provision for equalization, assuming each district had the same number of children, District B would fare much better using assessed value than if full value were used.

Many states distribute state-aid funds to individual school districts on the basis of property valuations, either assessed or equalized. Since the level of assessments varies widely from district to district in any state, the injustice of using assessed values must readily be apparent. This farcical situation would quickly turn the assessment process into a race to see who could come up with the lowest assessment in order to qualify for the highest amount of aid. And, of course, such use of assessment grossly inhibits the use of the property tax on a local basis. The situation in some states has actually fallen not far short of this. Therefore, it becomes essential that some means of establishing full valuation be provided. This may be done by the county board of supervisors acting as a board of equalization or by a state equalization commission doing the same job.

The process is much more complicated than has been indicated thus far. In the first place it requires that each type of property be categorized under such headings as farm, residential, public utility, business, and others. Then sales prices must be arrived at through inspecting sales that have been made and through appraisals by competent individuals. These figures must then be compared with assessed values and an average ratio of assessed to full value be prepared for each class of property. The various classifications must then be brought together and a ratio of full to assessed valuations arrived at. This is a complex job which requires a great deal of detailed work. It can be done, however, as has been done in many instances, by careful and painstaking work by competent people. When the state assessors have compiled full-valuation figures on a sufficient number of properties in a classification, they may take the median ratio of assessed to full as the ratio of that classification of property for the entire municipality and determine full valuation for that classification by the use of the median ratio. The same is done for each classification of property in the municipality.

There is one great difficulty with this process. While it produces at least a rough estimate of equalized values and certainly means greater justice in both local taxes and the distribution of state aid back to individual districts, it places great reliance on the local assessor. For example, if one class of property has been overvalued in relation to another, and this is very often the case, this type of property must bear an undue share of local taxes for local purposes and the district having a greater proportion of this property will be penalized in terms of the state aid that is returned to it.

The great difficulty with this state or county oversight is that it does nothing at all in terms of equalizing inequities and values within the local taxing district in states which allow a variable ratio of assessments. That is the work of the assessor. No matter what kind of inequities may show up in the state equalization process, the local assessor's figure is the one which determines the amount of tax which the local taxpayer must pay.

To cite another example, this might be the case in one municipality. When assessed values are converted to full valuation, the total full valuation for all types of property is $3,000,000. Dividing the assessed valuation by the total full value the ratio assessed value bears to full is .66⅔ as shown in Table 8-1.

Table 8-1   Property Values According to Category

Type of property	Assessed value	Median ratio assessed to true	Full value
Farm	$1,000,000	.80	$1,250,000
Residential	750,000	.60	1,250,000
Industrial	250,000	.50	500,000
Total	$2,000,000		$3,000,000

Ratio of assessed value to full value for the municipality equals .6667

How does this affect the payment of taxes? Continuing the hypothetical situation posed above, assume that in this municipality $45,000 must be raised for school purposes. A tax rate of $22.50 per thousand will have to be levied on assessed value to raise this amount. This converts to $15 on true value, of course, but it is levied on assessed value. Note how this affects various classes of property. If one class or category is over-assessed in comparison to the others, this means that that category of property must bear an unfair portion of the total tax burden for the taxing district. In other words, that category of property will be over-taxed while other categories may escape part of their just tax load. This is shown in Table 8-2.

Table 8-2   Effect of Levying Taxes on Inequitably Determined Assessed Valuations

Type of property	What they paid		Correct share	
	Assessed rate	Total	Full rate	Total
Farm	$1,000,000 × $.0225 =	$22,500	$1,250,000 × $.015 =	$18,750
Residential	750,000 × .0225 =	16,875	1,250,000 × .015 =	18,750
Industrial	250,000 × .0225 =	5,625	500,000 × .015 =	7,500

Actual rate paid on full value for each class of property, in dollars per thousand: farm $18.00; residential $13.50; industrial $11.25.

However, the process of equalization does offer information to the local taxpayer. The records of the equalization commission are open to all and the local taxpayer may ascertain what kinds of property are over-valued or undervalued in relation to other types. He can then take this information to his local assessors and ask that they bring about equal values among all classes of property. This still leaves considerable leeway for inequities in the valuation of property within any class.

Table 8-3   Intent of Equalization Programs for Nineteen States, 1955 *

State	Variable ratio, no direct effect on local tax base	Uniform ratio, direct effect on local tax base
Arkansas	x	
California		x
Illinois		x
Iowa		x
Kentucky		x
Maine	x	
Michigan		x
Minnesota	x	
Missouri		x
Nebraska		x
New Hampshire	x	
New Jersey	x	
New York	x	
Ohio		x
Oregon	x	
Pennsylvania	x	
Washington	x	
West Virginia	x	
Wisconsin	x	

* National Education Association, Commission on Tax Education and School Finance, *Equalization of Property Assessments*, Washington, January, 1958, p. 28.

There is still another remedy for inequities revealed by the state process of equalization. If one type of property is consistently overvalued or undervalued in relation to another throughout a state, in effect there exists a classified property tax. The classified property tax simply means that one type of property is consistently valued at a greater rate than another. It was used by states to some extent several decades ago, particularly to get a better collection of taxes on personal property. It was not widely successful but it is still in use.

However, there does seem to be this possibility: if one type of property is consistently overvalued or undervalued in relation to another, a state may recognize this tendency in its state-aid system. Full valuation could be determined on the basis of classified values which would be set at the relative levels which state-wide practice has shown to exist.

In summary, equalization programs have four different purposes. (1) They may be used to change local assessments for local tax purposes. In states where this is done the local levy would be correspondingly reduced. (2) They may be used for the purposes of a state property tax levy. (3) They may be used in the process of state assessment of locally taxed property. (4) They may be used for the distribution of state aid. Table 8-3 shows the intent of equalization programs in nineteen states which have some form of equalization program.

IMPROVEMENT OF THE PROPERTY TAX

Property taxation consists of three steps: assessment, levy, and collection. Of these the assessment process is by far the most complex and in its workings the most antiquated. Indeed, the assessment process in many tax-collection districts is not much different now from what it was 100 years ago. However, many communities are moving rapidly toward or have already achieved modern systems of assessment.

It is not surprising that there is considerable activity in many states in the improvement of the property tax system. The pressure for revenue at the local level is becoming increasingly strong and since property taxes across the nation have doubled in the past ten years it is going to be much more difficult to meet the new demands. Such demands are many. They are brought about by a rapidly increasing number of children in school, by rapidly growing total population, and by accelerating urbanization, plus the expansion of public services to match the rapidly developing complexity of private life.

Since assessment makes up such a large part of property taxation practice, most of the ideas for improving property taxation center around this important area. The goal is uniform assessment in practical terms. Because of the complexity of the assessment problem no one expects 100 per cent equality. There is simply no way of evaluating that perfectly.

Changes in Assessment Practice

Proposals for improving assessment deal with state oversight, the employment of competent full-time assessors, the use of objective formulae in the assessment process, and the cooperative involvement of the taxpayer in the assessment process.

State Oversight. Almost all states have some assessing body at the state level. Commonly it lacks both authority and funds to make its work effective. The purpose of the office should remain as it is now: to provide information, assistance, and leadership to local assessors. There is no thought of removing assessment from local hands. Normally this office would assess railroads, mineral land, and utilities. Similarly, where equalization is involved, it would be expected that this office would carry on studies of the effects of local assessment which would provide equitable figures for the purpose of equalization. But the primary purpose would be the stimulation of improved local assessment. The issuance of assessment manuals, the conduct of schools and conferences, the development of increased public understanding of the assessment process should be the foremost aim of such an office. Supervision and assistance, however, are no substitute for careful, accurate, original assessments. This criterion is closely related to the following one.

The Establishment of an Assessing District of Adequate Size. Most assessing districts are far too small and have too few resources to operate an adequate tax-assessing office. The establishment of the assessing office on a county and city basis is a necessity if the job is to be consistently well performed. This criterion implies that an office will also be maintained where careful records and files are kept and where there is enough competent clerical assistance. Records should include sales, appraisals, and costs of construction. Chief among the tools to be used is a tax map. The National Association of Assessing Officers has this to say about tax maps: [9]

Assessors working without the aid of tax maps seldom make an accurate inventory of all taxable land within their districts. Inaccuracies usually take the form of omissions of entire parcels or the listing of parcels for smaller areas than they actually contain. Occasionally the error is in the opposite direction and a single parcel is doubly listed or is listed at an excessive area. Consequently, even the smallest district cannot afford to allow the assessor to work without an accurate map. The expense and uncertainty of other methods of checking the assessment roll against the actual land area of the district make their use undesirable, while the failure to make an accurate check places the repute of the whole assessment process in jeopardy.

Without a tax map, the assessor has little more than last year's rolls and the declarations of taxpayers against which to check his enumeration of taxable properties.

Maps are of several kinds. They include land-value, tax-district, public-utility, soil, land-use, and aerial maps. Their purposes are threefold: to discover, to describe, and to appraise the property. Such maps are well known, reasonably simple to construct, and comparatively inexpensive, yet there are still thousands of tax districts without them. In the absence of this desirable practice is a strong argument for reorganizing the office.

The Employment of a Competent Full-time Assessor. Many assessors are appointive, civil service employees but many more are elective, often

---

[9] National Association of Assessing Officers, *Construction and Use of Tax Maps*, Assessment Practice Series No. 1, Chicago, 1937, p. 5.

filling a part-time position at a ridiculous rate of pay. The continuation of such a system is purely political. The only excuse for it, a poor one indeed, is that it means a few more jobs to keep the party machine operating. It is not within reason to expect a good job of assessment from men who are politically chosen and paid a few hundred dollars as most assessors in small districts are.

The salary should be attractive, appointment should continue only during good performance of duties, and civil-service-type examinations should govern appointment to the position.

The Use of Objective Formulae in the Assessment Process. Too often, it is the accepted practice in assessment simply to copy the previous year's tax roll with the obvious additions and changes. Such a practice means that every several years there may be a slight general over-all increase in times of rising prices but only if the need for revenue is great.

There are many sources of carefully defined formulae which are based on the front footage and depth of the property in urban areas as well as its location, or the acreage and types of soil in rural areas plus building dimensions and characteristics and adequate allowances for depreciation.

The complexity of the job is illustrated even by the brief examples given above. How often can an assessor or a team of assessors be expected to do a careful job of assessing all types of properties? Present laws usually call for yearly assessment. Biennial assessment is certainly more realistic and this may be a considerable undertaking. Certainly, a yearly assessment is not necessary to keep the tax rolls in line with changing property values.

The Involvement of the Taxpayer in the Assessment Process. The New Jersey Commission on State Tax Policy speaks of the "armed conflict" theory of assessments. It is an apt phrase for the whole process is carried on with the assessor operating in the dark with respect to information the taxpayer could give him, and the taxpayer paying his tax in almost complete ignorance of how his assessment, which determines the amount of the tax, is arrived at.

The New Jersey Commission has this to say: [10]

One of the principal weaknesses in the administration of the property tax has been the lack of cooperation of the taxpayers in the assessment process. In the case of excise taxes, it has become routine for the taxpayer to expect to provide reasonably comprehensive and accurate data as the basis for the assessment of the tax. In such taxes, in fact, self assessment by the taxpayers is used as often as not. But the property tax still retains the notion that the assessor should work in the dark, the darker the better in ascertaining the facts to make a good assessment.

[10] New Jersey Commission on State Tax Policy, *The General Property Tax in New Jersey: A Century of Inequities,* Sixth Report, Trenton, 1953, p. 160.

The Commission goes on to recommend: [11]

The general tax law should be amended to require upon suitable penalty, that every owner of real property should file with the assessor a confidential, informational return setting forth so far as possible the original cost, date of construction, cost of additions and modifications and dates thereof, annual gross rentals for income producing properties, the consideration for which the property was last conveyed, insurance coverage (exclusive of land and foundation), and if it is currently for sale, the price at which it is offered, together with all encumbrances on the property. In addition, the information return should contain such further information and data with respect to the nature and character of the property and its value as may be required by the State Director of the Division of Taxation.

Such information would infinitely simplify the job of the assessor, but it must be remembered that cooperation is a two-way street. Therefore, information might well be supplied the taxpayer by the assessor. There is no reason why the assessor should not mail to the taxpayer copies of the formulae by which his property has been assessed, together with the percentage of market value at which he is assessing each class of property.

Such information would be a powerful incentive for uniformity in assessment within classes of property and for similar uniformity among the various classes. How long would residential property be assessed at a ratio of .40, business property at .30, and vacant land at .10, or in reverse ratio, if one group of taxpayers knew they were carrying more than their fair share of the burden?

Levy

The second part of property tax administration is the levy. It appears that the total burden of the property tax is not nearly so important as the assessed rate in determining resistance to changes in education which might cost money.

All too often objections of taxpayers to the payment of property taxes, when traced to their source, will be found to lie not in the amount of taxes they pay, but in the feeling that they are paying more than their fair share of the burden assessed against the property taxpayers in the community. The feeling of injustice is visited upon the schools, the best known users of property tax yields.

There are some indications that high tax rates tend to make people less receptive to change in education. When a citizen discovers that his tax is higher than that of a neighbor, he immediately tends to think that he is being unjustly treated. There are some indications that when

[11] *Ibid.*, p. 162.

a community has adopted a high tax rate consciously and knows that it is a higher tax rate than those of its neighbors, this negative effect does not occur.

The interesting fact is that the negative relationship between tax rate and up-to-dateness of schools is associated with assessed tax rates, not with actual relative tax burdens. Pierce's [12] studies showed that there is a negative relationship between school tax rates and certain measures of school quality. This was when the actual assessed tax rates as they spoke of them in the community were used. When Pierce corrected these tax rates to take into account variations in the ratio of assessed to true value so that the tax rates would be comparable as indicators of burden carried, the relationships were considerably lower.

Similar results were obtained when total tax rates for all local purposes were used instead of school tax rates. The negative relationship of total tax rate was considerably higher than that of the school tax rate. The total tax rate showed only one positive relationship out of three, whereas school tax rates showed two positive relationships when an adjusted tax rate was used, but in no case was the relationship of any significance when an adjusted tax rate was used. This gives a strong argument for the use of a basis of assessment that will make tax rates comparable among communities.

Pierce's studies showed further that it is desirable to have property assessed at a high ratio of assessed to true value. The school districts that he studied varied from a relatively low percentage of true value to full value. He discovered that the ratio of assessed to true value was positively correlated with adaptability. This is what we should expect if people are affected by the crude tax rate.

Effects of Tax Competition. The effect of the level of property taxation as a factor in inducing either business or residents to settle in one state or district as against another is open to considerable question. If any individual or a corporation gives very much attention to this, he is overlooking entirely the great leveling effect of the federal income tax. The offsetting effect of the deductibility of state and local taxes from income for federal income tax purposes means that a considerable portion of state and local taxation either of individuals or of corporations will be paid by what is saved on federal taxation.

The 1956 *Report of the Governor's Minnesota Tax Study Committee* gives strong evidence: [13]

[12] Truman L. Pierce, *Controllable Community Characteristics in Relation to the Quality of Education*. Bureau of Publications, Teachers College, Columbia University, New York, 1947, p. 10.
[13] *Report of the Governor's Minnesota Tax Study Committee*, St. Paul, Minn., 1956, pp. 25–26.

The fact that governments in Minnesota rely more heavily upon property taxation than do governments in most other states, coupled with the impact of the system of property classification in this State, suggest that comparable business firms pay higher taxes in Minnesota than they do, typically, in other states. Computation of the tax liability incurred by a hypothetical firm alternatively located in Minnesota, Illinois, Iowa, Missouri, Nebraska, North and South Dakota and Wisconsin supported this suggestion. State and local taxes were found to be about the same in Minnesota and Wisconsin, but less than half as high as in Illinois, Missouri, Nebraska, and South Dakota and one-quarter to one-third lower in North Dakota and Iowa. However, when deductibility of state-local taxes from income for federal income tax purposes and the federal tax liability are taken into account, the percentage differential in total tax liabilities between Minnesota and Nebraska, the lowest tax state, is reduced to less than 6 per cent.

Pyramiding. The pyramiding of tax levies among overlapping districts also poses a problem. When state, county, municipal, and special fire, sewage, and police district taxes are all added together they may become prohibitive. While this is a special problem which occurs in relatively few cases, it is likely to become more common with the increasing urbanization which is now accompanying population growth.

Modernizing Collections

Many states have taken steps to make the property tax less burdensome by providing more convenient ways of payment than a single lump sum or, as is still often the case, two payments, one for schools and one for municipal and county taxes. Usually this takes the form of dividing the tax into quarterly installments. Most states and communities now mail tax bills to the taxpayer and permit payment by mail.

Accompanying provisions to make payment more convenient should be sure methods of collecting from delinquent taxpayers with no possibility allowed of a reduced settlement if taxes are allowed to accumulate. Interest rates on delinquent taxes should be high enough to discourage the accumulation of back taxes. There should be ample notice of the delinquency of the tax and the penalties attached. Tax sales should be inevitable if delinquency continues.

Finally, the tax collector should be appointive on civil service qualifications rather than elective.

Personal Property Taxation. Personal property assessment has never been satisfactory. Its use was stimulated when the forms of wealth became increasingly diverse. So long as property taxation was the chief source of revenue there was probably considerable justification for this tax, but as income taxation has developed there is much less justification. There are many criticisms of the tax. It is difficult to locate, identify, and value the items. There is little uniformity in the methods of various assessors in assessing household items. Indeed, the process often takes on the aspects of negotiation rather than taxation. In the case of business and industrial establishments where the assessment is made on a given day, inventories are often shifted so as to minimize the amount on hand on that date.

There have been various attempts at the solution of this problem. Three states have abandoned the taxation of personal property—Delaware, New York, and Pennsylvania. Only four states still tax a large portion of intangible property through the general property tax—Arkansas, Maine, New Mexico, and Texas. Several states, notably Minnesota, have tried the classification of property and taxation at varying levels in order to make the tax more equitable and more effective. The *Report of the Governor's Minnesota Tax Study Committee* has this to say about Minnesota's system: [14]

Among the outstanding features of property taxation in this state is the rather complex system of classification under which taxable or assessed value ranges from 50 per cent of "full and true" value for iron ore to 5 per cent for rural electric transmission lines and zero for exempt property such as the facilities used in the mining and concentration of taconite and the first $400 of the full and true value of household goods. Some features of this system are readily justified in terms of administrative feasibility or encouragement to resource use and development, but others appear to be the result of political pressures and compromise and have little or nothing to commend them.

Classification has not been widely used nor does it seem to have been significantly helpful in improving the administration of personal property taxation.

Authorities in the field of taxation generally agree that personal property taxation should be abolished.

Tax Limitations. The effect of the size of the assessment base on property taxation is often overlooked. If a state provides for assessment at 50 per cent of value as do some states it is unlikely that as much revenue will be raised as with 100 per cent assessment even though a doubling of the tax rate would theoretically provide the same revenue.

Still another form of limitation is that used in Michigan where a county board is used to divide the maximum total tax rate among counties, townships, municipalities, and school districts. In Washington a maximum of 40 mills is set for all purposes and then by constitutional provision 14 mills is allocated to the schools.

Many states have a maximum millage which can be levied for school purposes. Most Middle Western states allow a change in the millage by local voters.

[14] *Ibid.,* p. 26.

Closely related to limitations on spending are limitations on the amount of indebtedness. Every state has some sort of building-indebtedness limit. The provision usually takes the form of a percentage of either assessed or full value. In states where this has currently proved too restrictive, special state provisions for financing school buildings have been adopted.

The practice of having reviewing boards, either state or local, pass upon school budgets or the amount of revenue that may be raised locally is another form of limitation that was depression born. With the increase in assessed valuations during the postwar period there was some relaxation of this practice, although it has persisted in many states. This form of limitation is likely to place fiscal control of the schools in the hands of groups not directly concerned with education.

Sly and Miller point out that "as a result of some twenty years of experience with a wide variety of property tax rate limitations, competent observers are generally agreed that such limitations may sometimes succeed in restraining the taxation of property, but generally fail to restrict the total tax burden; and even tend to increase it by compelling the adoption of new and additional forms of taxation at the state level. This conclusion is based upon a considerable variety of tax limitations and their operation in the depression period, 1932–41—a time during which a number of property tax limitations were adopted together with state sales or income taxes." [15] It is observed that the notion of limiting the burden of taxation is not achieved through property tax limitations. Conditions that existed in depression times when rate limitations were most commonly imposed no longer exist. In a very real sense legislation to limit tax rates is in effect an expression by legislators that they do not place confidence in the people of the local taxing district. As stated above, there may be some actual limitation in revenue raised in certain cases, but by and large the best judges of how much local tax should be levied and how much the people are willing to tax themselves are matters of local-community ability and desire. Tax rate limitations are generally considered as undesirable and have little or no effect in curtailing the burden of taxation.

LOCAL NON-PROPERTY TAXES

The growth of local non-property taxes since World War II has been tremendous. The burden on the property tax has been such that these alternative forms of revenue have been eagerly sought out and adopted. The proportion of over-all revenue is still small, but the amounts raised

[15] John S. Sly and William Miller: *Tax Policies in Utah,* Utah Legislative Council, Salt Lake City, 1954, p. 68.

are sizable and the proportion is growing. In 1954 these taxes comprised 6 per cent of total local government revenues, but they were almost 15 per cent of the property tax and amounted to $1.4 billion.[16]

The great bulk of local non-property taxes is levied in cities and it is there that their use is growing the fastest. Almost two-thirds of the cities over 10,000 population levy one or more such taxes. According to the Committee on Tax Education and School Finance of the National Education Association, the proportion of such taxes in cities of 100,000 or more population increased from 8 per cent of total tax revenues in 1930 to 23 per cent in 1948. Each year sees substantial increases in the number of cities levying local non-property taxes and in the number of taxes levied.

The effect of local non-property taxes on school finance is profound. Here is a new tax development which is substantially changing the local tax base. Property taxation is becoming progressively less important. School personnel must recognize what this does to the revenue potential for education. It can directly broaden the total school tax base if schools are allowed to share in this type of taxation as they are in property taxation. Or by relieving the property tax (as is the case when non-property taxes are reserved to municipal government) it may simply increase the tax leeway of the local school district.

Every city of over 1,000,000 population has a sales or an income tax. Twelve of the nineteen cities with more than 500,000 have income or sales taxes. This will have a profound effect on public school finance, especially in those cities which levy separate taxes for schools. Since the broadest possible tax base is possibly even more important to education than to other units of local government, educational authorities must be alert to share in the changing tax base. For example, in 1917 in New York City, the board of education was given 24 per cent of the current property tax base. If the board had retained the same 24 per cent of today's tax base, this together with the current state aid for education would make the board of education in this great city essentially financially independent.

While local non-property taxation definitely contributes to tax base broadening for whatever local unit to which such taxes are assigned, it contributes nothing to the equalization concept. The community which can get little from the property tax will get little from non-property taxes; the community which can raise a large amount by property taxation will find non-property taxes equally lucrative.

[16] Municipal Finance Officers Association, *Municipal Non-property Taxes*, 1956, Supplement to "Where Cities Get Their Money," Chicago, pp. 2–3.

AUTHORIZED NON-PROPERTY TAXES

There are literally myriads of different local non-property taxes if each local variation is taken into consideration. However, there are really only three productive types of taxes: the property tax, the sales tax, and the income tax. Actually most of the local non-property taxes will fall under the sales tax heading.

New York State and Pennsylvania led the way in non-property taxation with permissive legislation in 1947. Other states have followed. Especially wide use is made of the sales tax in California and Illinois and of admissions and income taxes in Ohio.

New York State

The New York State legislature made a broad list of taxes available to counties and cities in 1947. In the counties the funds were to be used for the support of education. This limitation was removed several years later. The only non-property taxing power specifically given to school districts, and this only to city districts, is the power to tax consumers' utility bills not to exceed 3 per cent. It has not been widely used (five cities) although it is estimated to produce equivalent to $.50 per thousand in most districts. However, in cities under 125,000 the city authorities are authorized to levy for school purposes on the request of the school board any of the taxes available to the city. Table 8-4 shows authorized non-property taxes in New York State in 1955.

Table 8-4   Authorized Local Non-property Taxes, 1955, New York State

Unit of government	Taxes authorized on	Maximum rate
Cities (including New York City) and villages over 5,000 population	Gross income utilities	1%
Counties	Pari-mutuel pools except at harness meetings (rate reduced by 1% annually beginning January, 1952; not available after 1955)	5%
Counties and cities (except New York City) *	Retail sales and compensating use of tangible personal property	2% (3% for New York City)
	Restaurant charges of $1.00 or more	3%
	Consumers' utility bills †	3%
	Privilege of selling liquor, wine, or beer at retail for on- or off-premise consumption	25% of state license fees

Table 8-4   (Continued)

Unit of government	Taxes authorized on	Maximum rate
	Admission, certain membership fees, and cabaret charges	5%
	Coin-operated amusement devices	$25 per year
	Motor vehicle use	$5 and $10 depending on weight
	Occupancy of hotel rooms costing $2.00 or more	5%
	Admissions to flat racing	15%
	Admissions to harness racing (only cities over 100,000 and counties with no city over 100,000)	15–30%
New York City	All above-listed taxes except parimutuel pools and in addition:	
	Gross income of conduit companies	3%
	Privilege of doing business (business gross receipts tax)	a) ¼ of 1%, general businesses b) 1%, financial businesses
	Cigarettes	1 cent per pack
	Payroll tax (paid equally by employer and employee) ‡	½ of 1%
School districts located wholly or partly in cities of under 125,000 population	Consumers' utility bills	3%

In addition, on request of school authorities, cities of under 125,000 population are authorized to impose for school purposes any of the taxes which the city may impose for city purposes and provided that the rate of tax if levied for both city and school purposes does not exceed the statutory maximum for either.

* A business privilege tax similar to New York City's was authorized for other cities and counties, but in 1952 a moratorium was declared on this type of tax (except in New York City). Only Monroe County had enacted such a tax.

† Gas, electricity, water, and telephone and telegraph.

‡ Authorized in 1953, this tax is tied to the establishment of a transit authority and has not yet been imposed.

SOURCE: Adapted from State of New York, Temporary Commission on the Fiscal Affairs of State Government, *A Program for Continued Progress in Fiscal Management,* Vol. 1, February, 1955, pp. 287–289; and other sources.

New York City makes the widest use of non-property taxes of any municipality in the state. It uses almost every tax permitted. None of the receipts are specifically earmarked for schools although the broadening of the tax base is certainly of great benefit. The wide use of non-property taxes by the city is undoubtedly the result of the need for revenues and is reinforced by the fact that the city is tight up against property tax limitations. The returns are tremendous, reaching approximately 20 per cent of a $2 billion budget. This is equivalent to about half of the amount raised by the property tax.

The experience of Erie County in New York State (the city of Buffalo is within the county) illustrates clearly the impact of non-property taxes on school support. As permitted by law, Erie County has levied a 1 per cent sales tax for schools. The revenue has been eye-opening. The $8.7 million raised in 1954 amounted to almost $80 per pupil and it has continued at this level for many years. Over the years the returns from the 1 per cent sales tax have averaged almost 50 per cent of the property tax or one-third of the local school support.

Monroe County and the cities of Niagara Falls, Syracuse, and several others also levy a sales tax which yields substantial income. Most of the other taxes authorized are levied somewhere in the state but not widely.

There seems little doubt that many of the non-property taxes would have been widely used if they had been available to school districts as is the case in Pennsylvania. The fact that they must be levied through the county, which has no connection with school districts, is extremely cumbersome and takes control of school revenue out of the hands of the responsible school authorities. In addition, the per capita method of sharing the revenue is questionable. It treats the rich and the poor, the large and the small, the elementary and the high school pupil exactly alike.

Pennsylvania

Pennsylvania's Public Act 481 permitted any unit of local government to levy any tax which the state government was authorized to levy but was not actually using. This is by far the broadest authorization of non-property taxation made by any state. It has been widely used by all local units—cities, boroughs, towns, townships, and school districts—large and small. Certain limitations on these taxes were adopted in 1949. Chief among them is a prohibition of taxation on coal and other natural resources and on manufactured and farm products, a $10 limit on poll taxes, 1 per cent on earned income, 2 per cent on retail sales, 10 per cent on admissions, 1 per cent on transfer of real estate, and 1 per cent on wholesale transactions. Double taxation is prohibited; if two units covering the same area levy the same tax, the combined rate may not exceed the maximum and one-half the return is supposed to go to each.

The aggregate amount of taxes annually is limited to an amount equal to a 10-mill property tax in municipalities and a 15-mill property tax in school districts.

The taxes have been widely used. By 1955, almost 60 per cent of the local units eligible were levying one or more taxes. This included approximately 71 per cent of the 2,500 school districts. Total taxes collected in 1953 amounted to approximately $42 million of which almost half went to school districts. The big revenue producers were the income tax and the per capita tax followed by the mercantile (gross receipts), amusement, and deed-transfer taxes. All these produced substantial revenues.

A recent development in Pennsylvania has been the joining together of a number of tax-collection districts (both municipal and school) in the collection of whatever tax is imposed. This colonizing makes the levy of the tax less open to criticism, reduces cost of collection, and enables more efficient methods of collection to be used.

TAXES LEVIED

The taxes most commonly levied on a local basis are income, sales, admissions, cigarette and liquor, motorist, licenses, and utilities.

Income Taxes

Washington and Philadelphia were the first cities to levy an income tax (1939). Ohio cities use this tax widely. As has already been noted, it is used even more widely in Pennsylvania. About 420 income taxes were levied in Pennsylvania by 1955, including those levied by 262 school districts. A tax ranging from ½ of 1 per cent to 1 per cent was levied in seventeen cities there in 1956. All income taxes in cities are levied by municipal authorities—none by school boards. Kentucky and Missouri cities also levy such a tax. Revenue is substantial even at the most common rate of a flat 1 per cent. Table 8-5 shows that it is equivalent to 65 per cent of the property tax in the forty-eight cities where it is levied. One argument used for it is that it obligates nonresidents who work in the city to help pay the cost of central city government. However, if reciprocity is extended, as in Pennsylvania, it means that there will be a ring of communities around the central city taxing income and this special advantage is lost.

Local Sales Tax

New York City levied the first city sales tax in 1934. The tax is most widely used locally in California and in Illinois, where 189 and 617 municipalities, respectively, used the tax in 1955. There are many varieties of sales tax. The retail sales tax, as the title indicates, is a tax on goods sold at retail. A general sales tax is broader, being imposed on wholesale as well as retail sales. A selective sales tax applies only to specific goods such as cigarettes or gasoline. A gross receipts tax includes taxation on professional fees as well as sales. A "use" tax complements the sales tax and is levied outside the city. It is designed to discourage purchases outside the city with the specific purpose of avoiding the sales tax.

Sales taxes are especially advantageous to resort communities since they are also paid by the "resorters." The tax has been found easy and inexpensive to administer. Merchants themselves normally do the collecting. Rates normally run around 1 per cent. It also is an extremely lucrative tax. As shown in Table 8-5, in 171 cities of over 10,000 population it returned collections amounting to 32.66 per cent of the property tax. In gross amount it is the largest of the local taxes, amounting to over $400,000,000 in 1955 when receipts from all units of local government are totaled. When this figure is totaled with gross receipts of cigarette and gasoline taxes, the yield is over $600,000,000.

One of the most interesting developments in the use of this tax is that in several states such as Florida, Illinois, California, Mississippi, and New Mexico, some or all local communities may impose the tax and have it state collected and returned to the local unit. This may well decrease the cost and increase the effectiveness of local collection.

Table 8-5 Municipal Non-property Taxes, Cities Over 10,000, 1955

Tax	Average rate	Yield, in thousands	Population affected, in thousands	Number of cities	Per cent of property tax
Admissions and amusement	5.86%	$21,607	25,012	197	1.96
Cigarette	2.6¢	37,198	19,640	84	3.52
Gasoline and motor fuel	1.2¢	19,527	3,737	39	22.52
Gross receipts: business license	2.3%	145,264	25,290	189	11.58
Income	.7%	108,631	6,687	48	65.3
Liquor and alcoholic beverage	. . .	11,652	5,248	37	6.75
Motor vehicle	. . .	42,503	19,491	135	4.22
Public utility gross receipts	2.69%	98,476	42,548	341	5.69
Sales	.76%	391,823	24,112	171	32.66

SOURCE: Municipal Finance Officers Association, *Municipal Non-property Taxes*, 1956, Supplement to *Where Cities Get Their Money*, Chicago, 1956, Appendix A, pp. 33–35.

Other Taxes

As Table 8-5 shows there are a number of other local taxes which yield substantial revenue. The admissions tax is easy to administer and not excessive in rate. This tax has been widely used in Pennsylvania, Illinois, New York, Ohio, and Washington. However, it has been dropped by many smaller communities in recent years. Cigarette taxes, like other sales taxes, are relatively easy to collect. Since states use such taxes widely, this tax has not been imposed extensively on a local basis. Taxes on motorists are extensive at the local level. Gasoline is taxed locally in five Southern and Western states. License taxes are imposed locally in Illinois, Missouri, and North Carolina. Receipts from parking meters are extensive. A survey of sixty-two cities of over 10,000 indicates that each meter will average about $75 annually. Licenses have always been an important part of local revenue and continue to be widely used. Liquor taxes are not widely imposed because communities often tax this source through license fees. The poll tax appears to continue to decline in use. The objection which once applied to it, however, would seem to be no longer applicable. Public utility gross receipt taxes are extremely numerous. They apply in most states and to a variety of utilities which may be taxed in many ways. An extremely large amount of revenue is raised by the public-utility complex of taxes. As shown in Table 8-5 in the 341 cities of over 10,000 population where these taxes were imposed they raised almost $100,000,000.

Non-property Tax Problems

Many of the problems of collection have already been mentioned. Foremost among these is the difficulty of obtaining efficient operation of tax collection in small units. Few local non-property taxes can be collected inexpensively and without evasion in small areas and those that can raise the lesser amounts of revenue. Solutions to this problem are appearing. In Pennsylvania many local units are combining to levy the income tax. State collection and return of the sales tax is established in several states such as California and Illinois.

Most local non-property taxes are regressive. No doubt this difficulty has been overemphasized. In an economy where the average per capita income is close to $2,000 and where there is a steeply progressive income and inheritance tax this argument would seem to have less and less validity.

There are, of course, the complexities presented by overlapping tax jurisdictions. As taxes become more numerous, these will increase, adding to the harassment of the already harried taxpayer. Such problems, however, are largely administrative.

The cost of collection is a definite concern. Generally the income tax has been the most expensive to collect at the local level. Costs range up to 10 per cent but are reduced as larger units are used. The sales tax is somewhat more reasonable, running around 5 per cent for effective operation. Business and social conditions change and change the effectiveness of a tax. When the federal government dropped its amusement tax from 20 per cent to 10 per cent in 1954 it was expected that states and localities would benefit. The fact that they did not and that this tax was dropped locally in many communities was undoubtedly due to the effect of television.

Table 8-6   Number of States in Which Selected Municipal Non-property Taxes are Levied, 1956

Tax	Number of states levying
Admissions	17
Business gross receipts	26
Cigarette and tobacco	3
Deed transfer	3
Gasoline	5
Income	8
Liquor and alcoholic beverage	10
Motor vehicle	10
Hotel occupancy	5
Poll	13
Public utility gross receipts	35
Sales	10

SOURCE: Municipal Finance Officers Association, *Municipal Non-property Taxes,* 1956, Supplement to *Where Cities Get Their Money,* Chicago, 1956, p. 16.

THROUGH A GLASS DARKLY

The tax picture for the future is presumably as it always has been: not especially bright either for education or for municipal government. Population, combined with the delaying effects of depression and war, has far outstripped the tax structure. There are only two choices. The first is to revise the tax structure; the second, to limit drastically the standards of public service. The first is difficult but not impossible. The second is extremely unlikely. So long as we can achieve high standards of living in our private lives, we will continue to demand at least somewhat comparable standards of public service. Furthermore, it is impossible to see how we can survive as a nation unless high standards in education, health, and welfare are not only maintained but improved.

Three definite trends point to better services at the local level: (1)

the increase of local financial aid through federal- and state-collected, locally distributed taxes; (2) the long history of absorption by state and nation of functions which are local in character but which cannot readily be financed locally; (3) the broadening of the local tax base by every available means. The first trend is well established in most states and is exemplified in state aid for education or welfare. The second is exemplified by state care for the mentally ill. The third trend requires that the state make unused taxing power available to local units of government and that the state return to local units those taxes which can best be utilized locally. The trend is exemplified by the increased local use of non-property taxes and by proposals to return to the states such federal taxes as amusement and gasoline. The state in turn might then make such taxes available locally. There may well be still another step necessary, however, if a strong local autonomy is to be preserved, and this may be state collection and return to the source of such taxes as cannot be administered locally. This is best exemplified by the proposals made over the past many years, none taken seriously, that the community levy and the state collect and return a portion of the income tax for local use.

None of these remedies is exclusive. It is likely that all three will play some part in the future financing of education and other local governmental functions.

SUMMARY

The taxation of property is an old and well-established method of raising revenue, although it is criticized more than any other form of tax. While it is desirable to supplement the local property tax by other means of raising revenue in the local community as well as in the state and nation, it is certain that the local property tax will continue to be an important source of revenue for public schools. Since this is the case, it is desirable that the property tax be improved and strengthened through the development of better methods of assessment and more uniform and adequate methods of levying and collection, by consideration of the exemptions to be allowed, and in other ways. The importance of the general property tax in school support may be gained from an understanding that in 1953–1954 more than 54 per cent of school support was provided by this tax.

Other means of raising local revenue have gained considerable acceptance, especially in large cities. Non-property taxes are changing the local tax base. School authorities must be alert to the possibilities of obtaining school revenues from such sources and must encourage tryout and experimentation with new ones. While many of the non-property taxes are productive of considerable revenue, others would seem to be administered better on a state-wide basis.

QUESTIONS FOR STUDY AND DISCUSSION

1. Outline the method of property taxation for public schools in your state. Show the method of assessment, the rate at which the tax is levied, limitations, and exemptions.

2. How are local taxes collected in your state? From recent reports, give an estimate of property tax delinquencies.

3. Outline a plan for the assessment of real and personal property which you consider to be ideal. Select material from a number of state laws.

4. What local non-property taxes are authorized in your state? To what extent do such taxes broaden the local tax base?

5. Show the trend of assessed valuations in your district or state for the past ten years. Plot the curve of increase or decrease.

6. What proportion of educational costs is met by taxation on the district, county, and state levels in your state?

SELECTED REFERENCES

Burke, Arvid J.: *Financing Public Schools in the United States,* Harper & Brothers, New York, 1957.

————: "New Look at Property Taxes," *School Executive,* vol. 74, pp. 19–21, May, 1955.

Goodman, Archie B.: "Essentials of State Assessment Supervision," *Taxes, The Tax Magazine,* vol. 24, pp. 1049–1053, November, 1946.

Hutchins, Clayton D., and Albert R. Munse: *Public School Finance Programs in the United States,* U.S. Office of Education, 1954.

———— and ————: *Trends in Significant Facts on School Finance, 1929–30 to 1953–54,* U.S. Office of Education, Circular No. 498, Washington, 1957.

Kendrick, M. Slade, and Wallace C. Strevell: "The Potentialities of the Property Tax as a Fiscal Instrument in New York State," *Fiscal Policy for Public Education in the State of New York,* Staff Study No. 7, New York State Educational Conference Board, Albany, N.Y., 1947.

Murray, William G.: "State Action for Better Assessments," *State Government,* vol. 28, pp. 90–94, April, 1955.

National Association of Assessing Officers: *Construction and Use of Tax Maps,* Chicago, 1948.

National Citizens Commission for the Public Schools: *How Do We Pay for Our Schools?* New York, 1954.

National Education Association, Committee on Tax Education and School Finance, *Equalization of Property Assessments,* Washington, 1958.

————: *The Index of Local Economic Ability in State School Finance Programs,* Washington, 1953.

————: *Tax Losses from Property Tax Exemptions* (Michigan Pilot Study), Washington, 1954.

National Education Association, Research Division: *Improving the General Property Tax as a Source of School Revenue,* Washington, 1950.

————: *Tax Limitation Laws,* Washington, 1956.

New Jersey Commission on State Tax Policy: *The General Property Tax in New Jersey: A Century of Inequities,* Sixth Report, Trenton, 1953.

————: *The General Property Tax in 1958: Toward a Balanced Tax Structure,* Trenton, 1958.

North Central Land Tenure Committee, Subcommittee on Tax Assessments: *Improving Property Assessments in the Midwest,* Ames, Iowa, 1954.

Norton, John K., and Arvid J. Burke: "The Potentialities of the State Tax System in the Financing of Public Schools in New York State," *Fiscal Policy for Public Education in the State of New York,* Staff Study No. 2, New York State Educational Conference Board, Albany, N.Y., 1947.

Polley, John W.: *The Non-property Tax Potential of New York State,* Staff Study No. 3, New York State Educational Conference Board, Albany, N.Y., 1957.

Rosenstengel, William Everett, and Jefferson N. Eastmond: *School Finance: Its Theory and Practice,* The Ronald Press Company, New York, 1957, chap. 7, pp. 113–136.

Shultz, William J., and C. Lowell Harris: *American Public Finance,* 6th ed., Prentice-Hall, Inc., Englewood Cliffs, N.J., 1954.

The Tax Foundation: *Facts & Figures on Government Finance, 1956–57,* New York, 1957.

U.S. Bureau of the Census: *Assessed Values and Sales Prices of Transferred Real Property,* G-CGA 7, Washington, 1958.

9. State sources of school revenue

S TATE REVENUES for public education are not new in concept but in both amounts and proportion they have recently undergone startling change. State aid, however modest in amount, dates from the early days of the republic. The amounts involved were never great until the state patterns of revenue were revised and expanded.

All state school systems today are supported by the joint contributions made by the federal government, the states, and the local communities, however widely the proportion of support from the various agencies may differ. It was pointed out in a previous chapter in this volume that in some states local support constitutes more than 90 per cent of school income and again, in other states, nearly 90 per cent of the support of schools is derived from state sources.

There were sixteen states in the union in 1953–1954 that provided more than 50 per cent of school revenue from state sources, whereas thirty-two states provided less than 50 per cent of current operational costs of public elementary and secondary schools.[1]

The principle of state taxation for public schools is now well established. It is generally conceded that the states have tax resources not available to local communities and that certain taxes are better administered on a state-wide basis than on a local basis. Raising revenue on a state-wide basis with the subsequent distribution of some of the proceeds to school districts through acceptable measures of capacity and need is a fundamental concept in programs of financing education.

THE DEVELOPMENT OF THE STATE TAX STRUCTURE

At the turn of the century property taxes and licenses, those taxes least responsive to economic change, produced the bulk of state revenues. But

[1] Clayton D. Hutchins and Albert R. Munse, *Public School Finance Programs in the United States,* U.S. Office of Education, 1954, p. 14.

as shown in Table 9-1 the decline of the property tax as a source of state revenue was comparatively rapid. Where in 1902 it had produced 52.6 per cent of state revenues, by 1922 it had declined to 36.7 per cent and by 1942 it had almost reached today's level of 3.5 per cent. What the inflation and prosperity of World War I did not accomplish the depression of the 1930s did. The need for greater local revenue plus the development of lucrative new taxes led state after state to abandon the property tax to local use. Today only seven states derive any substantial revenue from property taxation at the state level.

New taxes have developed rapidly during this period. The state income tax, introduced in Wisconsin in 1911, spread rapidly. By 1929 twenty states had adopted either a personal or a corporate income tax or both. Today thirty-three states levy this tax. It is interesting to note from Table 9-1, however, that the proportion of state taxation from this source has not changed as rapidly as many others. Nor has it been as lucrative at the state level as either various sales taxes or the various taxes on motorists.

Taxes on motorists paralleled the development of state income taxation and increased rapidly both in proportion and amount of revenue raised. Such taxes are used in every state in the union. The latest comers, however, the various sales taxes, have become the largest producers of income on the state level, both in total amount and in proportion. The sales tax in its present form did not appear until the 1930s but it has spread widely. Selective sales taxes are used in every state and the general sales tax is now used in thirty-four states.

Although taxes on income, motorists, and sales provide the bulk of state revenue, there are many other lucrative taxes. Some of these vary tremendously in yield from state to state, others do not. Licenses continue to produce goodly amounts of state funds; severance, stock-transfer and pari-mutuel taxes yield considerable revenue depending on the state which levies them. Inheritance and admissions taxes are widely used.

As the states moved to more broad-based taxes the receipts mounted rapidly. From $156 million in 1902 they increased to $14,531 million in 1957. On a per capita base, state tax collections grew from $2.02 in 1902 to $87.31 in 1957. The collections on a per capita base vary tremendously. The low in 1957 was $50.92 in New Jersey and the high $137.76 in Nevada.[2]

In comparing state taxation with federal and local, as in Table 9-2, it can be seen that combined state and local taxes were greater than federal taxes until well into the depression. State taxes, however, reached the level of federal taxes at only one time and then dropped back to about the

[2] U.S. Department of Commerce, *Compendium of State Government Finances in 1957*, Washington, 1958, p. 52.

Table 9-1 State Tax Collections by Specific Source
(in millions of dollars and per cents)

Year	General and selective sales, use, gross receipts *		Income tax		Motor vehicle and operators' licenses and fuel		Property		Other		Total	
	Amount	Per cent	Amount	Per cent	Amount	Per cent	Amount	Per cent	Amount	Per cent	Amount	Per cent
1902	..	..	..	..	..	..	82	52.6	74	47.4	156	100
1913	2	.7	..	..	5	1.7	140	46.5	154	51.2	301	100
1922	..	..	101	10.7	165	17.5	348	36.7	333	35.2	947	100
1932	27	1.5	153	8.1	862	45.6	328	17.4	520	27.4	1,890	100
1942	1,075	27.3	518	13.3	1,373	35.1	271	6.9	674	17.3	3,903	100
1952	3,197	32.5	1,736	17.6	2,794	28.4	370	3.8	1,744	17.7	57	100
1956	4,160	31.2	2,258	16.9	3,974	29.8	468	3.5	2,476	18.6	13,335	100

* Includes alcohol and tobacco sales and licenses.

SOURCE: The Tax Foundation, *Facts and Figures on Government Finance*, 1956–1957, pp. 136–137. (Excludes unemployment compensation taxes.)

same relationship they had had previously. But comparing state and local, a different picture emerges. It was not until the 1950s that state taxes achieved the same level as local taxes. During the 1950s the relationship had not changed greatly.

The use of new sources of revenue changed state and local relations far more at the municipal level than at the educational level. Mort, in the Cooperative Study of the Maryland Public Schools, describes the change: [3]

Table 9-2   Tax Receipts of Federal, State, and Local Governments
(in millions)

Year	Federal	State	Local	Total
1902	$ 517	$ 156	$ 704	$ 1,377
1913	673	301	1,308	2,282
1922	3,656	947	3,069	7,672
1932	1,807	1,890	4,274	7,971
1942	13,382	3,903	4,625	21,910
1952	63,909	9,857	9,466	83,232
1956 *	72,159	13,335	13,000	98,494

* Preliminary.

SOURCE: The Tax Foundation, *Facts and Figures on Government Finance, 1956–1957*, New York, 1957, p. 104.

This tapping of newer sources gave the federal government and the states fiscal power out of proportion to the requirements of governmental services operated on those levels. Accordingly, some services formerly supported on a local level were shifted bodily to the state, or to the state and the federal government, as in the case of welfare. When the need for more extensive highways developed, the states stepped in to relieve the localities of what had been traditionally a local governmental function. This step was repeated for a whole series of services either formerly operated on a local level or of such a character that they would traditionally have been assigned to the local levels.

Not so with education. Our people were willing to give up highways, police protection to a degree, relief and welfare, to state government, but resisted any comparable transfer of educational functions. Such shifting was largely limited to the training of teachers. There is hardly any new educational function of any fiscal consequence, no matter what its character, that has not been added to the local budget of educational responsibility.[4]

[3] Paul R. Mort, *State Action toward More Quality Education*, Cooperative Study of Maryland Public Schools, State Department of Education, Baltimore, Md., 1959, p. 25.

[4] It should be stated that in comparing the increase in cost of education with increase in cost of other public services, it is a mistake to compare education and municipal (local) government. In 1900, for example, government consisted of locally financed education, locally financed municipal government, and a relatively thin slice

Changes in the revenue structures of the states for the support of elementary and secondary schools are constantly taking place. Certain general trends are emerging. Perhaps the most important single trend is the decline in allocating specific sources for the use of schools and the increase in the tendency for the states to make legislative appropriations to schools from their general funds. This shift in sources in state school revenue has been in progress for many years, and although there was a temporary increase in the number of states that allocated specific taxes for schools following the period of the depression, the great increase in school revenue required since World War II has caused many states to depend more and more upon legislative appropriations.

Legislative Appropriations

Of the various sources from which state school funds are derived, 80.4 per cent were made by legislative appropriations in 1953-1954; 18.2 per cent were derived from earmarked state taxes; and 1.4 per cent were derived from permanent endowments. Perhaps the chief advantage in the legislative appropriation of money for schools lies in the flexibility that this plan provides for the state school system. In a time of rising costs and expanding school programs, it is difficult to provide adequately for school needs during any school year by means of allocated sources of revenue. Appropriations make it possible to increase or decrease state aid in such a way as to meet the needs of the schools. The method of appropriating from the state's general fund is to be recommended. The recent increases in teachers' salaries and foundation programs in general have required larger and larger amounts of state support which could not have been foreseen in prewar years.

Although there has been an increase in the number of states that provide for direct appropriation of money for aid to schools, it is unlikely that specifically allocated taxes and revenue sources will be eliminated. In 1953-1954, thirteen states appropriated 100 per cent of state aid for public elementary and secondary schools. Nineteen other states provided from 80 to 99 per cent of all state school revenue through legislative appropriations. At the other extreme there were three states—Minnesota,

---

of expenditure across the top for state services. Interestingly enough, in those days the federal government budget too was amazingly small. Over the years what was formerly municipal government has become state or federal government. What would normally have become municipal government except for the tax problem became state government. Education, on the contrary, kept pretty much within the same scope. Additional demands for the education of more children for longer periods, additional demands for services, all piled up as the cost of locally operated education. A comparison then would be more illuminating if we were to compare education with municipal plus state government rather than education with municipal government alone.

New Mexico, and North Dakota—that did not provide any state school money through legislative appropriations. Three other states provided less than 10 per cent of state funds through appropriations. These were Alabama, 1.5 per cent; Kansas, 2 per cent; and Wyoming, 6.3 per cent.

The states that provided 100 per cent of their state school revenue through legislative appropriations from general funds were: Arkansas, California, Connecticut, Georgia, Illinois, Kentucky, Maryland, New Mexico, North Carolina, Pennsylvania, South Carolina, Tennessee, and Vermont.

Revenue from Permanent Endowment

Under permanent endowments are included primarily those funds that have been built up by the federal land and money grants, those accumulated by the states, and the value of the remaining unsold school lands. Land grants were made to all Western states except Texas and Oklahoma. Texas retained title to its lands on admission. Oklahoma received a money grant. A number of money grants were made to all states. The original states had all established permanent endowments, many of them prior to the Revolution. The land grants were extensive. Beginning with the Northwest Ordinance the land grants were later liberalized. Approximately 319,500 square miles of land were included.

Although educational endowments have not always been well administered in the past, there are yet considerable portions of these funds remaining in a number of states. The income from such funds, either through interest on invested money or receipts from leases of unsold school land, constitutes a substantial amount in some states. For the United States as a whole the school receipts from this source are relatively small, amounting to only $41,883,350 or 1.4 per cent of state receipts in 1953–1954. In that year only four states reported no income from this source. These were: Georgia, Maryland, North Carolina, and South Carolina.[5]

Forty-four states reported some receipts from permanent school endowments, although only thirty-nine states actually had reserve funds invested and earning interest for the schools. Some of the states with the largest portion of state income from permanent school funds were: [6] Nebraska, 76.2 per cent; South Dakota, 37 per cent; Montana, 39.1 per cent; Wyoming, 25.7 per cent; New Mexico, 23.7 per cent; North Dakota, 17 per cent; Colorado, 16.6 per cent; Idaho, 14.5 per cent. All other states derived less than 10 per cent of their state school revenue from this source. Many of them had very small amounts. It should be observed that the percentages given are of state funds for schools and not per-

[5] Hutchins and Munse, *op. cit.*, p. 23.
[6] *Ibid.*, p. 20.

centage of total school revenue. Some of the states with high percentages of state revenue from this source have in reality a small proportion of school revenue derived from the state.

The status of permanent school endowments shows that such funds remaining as reserve funds or invested funds amount to almost $1 billion and that the principal of these permanent endowments is increasing at an annual rate of $50 million. There are approximately 43 million acres of unsold school land that have an estimated value of $238 million.

All states but nine—Alabama, Georgia, Illinois, Kentucky, Maryland, Michigan, Mississippi, South Carolina, and Tennessee—have permanent endowments existing as reserve or invested funds. The total amount of these funds is $992,299,170. In addition, seven states have what may be termed perpetual state-indebtedness funds. These are Alabama, Illinois, Kentucky, Michigan, Mississippi, Ohio, and Tennessee. The total amount of these perpetual state-indebtedness funds in 1953–1954 was $23,649,659.

TYPES OF STATE TAXES

A great variety of taxes is levied at the state level. One expert places the number at 142. The principal ones together with the total revenues they raise and their rates are listed in Table 9-3.

State Property Tax

The rate of state taxation on property is usually relatively low so that a small proportion of state school revenues is derived from this source. Wyoming derived the largest proportion of state school revenue from the state property tax with a 6-mill general property tax earmarked for schools. This source furnished 27.4 per cent of state school revenue.

The decline in state property taxes as a source of revenue for schools may be shown by the fact that in 1948 there were twenty-seven states that levied state property taxes as a revenue source for schools. Only seven of them raised any substantial amount of revenue from this source.

Income Taxes

During the first half of the present century there has been a marked increase in the establishment of income taxation. Although this form of tax was not entirely new, it was not considered successful until about 1915. Such taxes have been developed to a relatively high degree in foreign countries where they have been in operation for a much longer period. An early attempt at income taxation in the United States was the tax levied in 1840 in the state of Pennsylvania at the rate of 1 per cent on all salaries. During the Civil War several of the Confederate states and some of the Border states levied state income taxes. By 1903

Table 9-3 Totals of Principal State Taxes Collected, 1957 *

Tax	Amount of revenue, in millions	Rate †
General sales	$3,373	.5–3 per cent
Motor fuel	2,828	3–7¢ per gallon
Motor vehicle and operators' licenses	1,367	
Individual income	1,569	Commonly 1–2 per cent in lowest bracket
Corporate income	984	1–8 per cent normally flat rate
Corporate license	408	
Alcoholic beverage	569	$.75–$3.60 per gallon on distilled spirits
Operation state liquor stores	210	
Tobacco sales	556	2–8 cents per pack
Property tax	579	
Insurance company gross premiums	428	
Stock transfer	80	
Severance tax	388	
Public utilities gross receipts	343	
Death and gift	338	
Pari-mutuel	225	3–11 per cent

* Department of Commerce, *Compendium of State Government Finance in 1957,* p. 6.

† The Tax Foundation, *Facts and Figures on Government Finance,* New York, 1957, pp. 144–171.

sixteen states had adopted income taxes but few remained in operation and they were generally regarded as a failure. Poor local administration leading to evasion was the cause of the poor showing. The present federal income tax dates from the year 1913 and the first successful state income tax from 1911. In 1958, thirty-three states levied either individual or corporate income taxes or both. Two of these levied the individual income tax only. There is not much question but that the level of federal taxation has retarded the state use of this tax. No state had added the income tax to revenue sources since 1937 until Delaware and New Jersey added the corporation income tax in 1957 and 1958. Seven states earmarked all or a portion of state income taxes for the use of schools. These states were Alabama, Massachusetts, Minnesota, Montana, New Mexico, Utah, and Wisconsin.[7]

Although the net proceeds of state income taxes were considerably increased after World War II, the percentage that such proceeds were of

[7] *Ibid.,* p. 22.

total state revenue showed only a slight increase. Theoretically a state income tax at a relatively low and graduated rate and with reasonable exemptions appears to be one of the soundest methods of raising revenue. Although the relatively high federal income tax has tended to reduce the widespread acceptance of state income taxes, there is little question but that the latter presents a fair means of raising state revenue from a large number of taxpayers. Perhaps the most objectionable feature of income taxes is the fact that both states and federal government use this form of raising revenue.

Personal exemptions are relatively high in most state income taxes. In 1956 only eight states had exemptions as low as the federal government's are. Eight states allow exemptions of $1,500 for a single individual. Fifteen of the states make federal income taxes deductible.

Without increasing rates most states could considerably increase their tax income from this source simply by lowering exemptions. For example in New York State, which had a $1,000 exemption for a single person and $2,500 for a married couple, returns were received in 1955 from 4 million taxpayers while the federal government received returns from more than 6½ million New York State taxpayers.[8] Tax experts have generally favored the application, however slight, of the income tax to all persons possessing income.

The income tax has much to recommend it. It is a direct tax. It cannot be shifted. The costs of administering it are reasonable. It is perhaps less regressive than many other taxes although the rates at the state level are not particularly progressive. Indeed flat rates are levied by four states. Like all other taxes except the property tax, returns are not stable; fluctuations with economic conditions are to be expected. It has been stated that the income tax has the highest income elasticity. A rise in income will produce a more than proportionate rise in collections and the converse is also true.

Corporate Income Tax

A wide variety of taxes is levied to reach the resources represented by business enterprise. In New York State, for example, taxes which come under this heading are corporate income, franchise, transportation, insurance, banks, and unincorporated business. Such a pattern reflects the development of taxation but does not have much more than tradition to recommend it. Tax experts generally agree that a more uniform system of business taxation would be preferable.

Minimum rates of taxation in the states levying a corporate income tax vary from 1 per cent to 8 per cent. Rates in the highest bracket also

[8] J. W. Polley, *The Non-property Tax Potential of New York State*, New York State Educational Conference Board, Albany, N.Y., pp. 10–11.

reach only to 8 per cent. Twenty-five states levy a flat rate. Newcomer has this to say about the flat rate: [9]

There would seem to be no reason for levying progressive rates on business income in proportion to the size of the income, as is done in many state corporation taxes. The justification of the progressive rate for personal income tax rests with the theory of diminishing utility, and the income of a single business unit may be shared by an indefinite number of individuals, so that a very large business income may bring only a small sum to each of the participants.

The corporate tax liability is determined, however, not so much by the rate as by the exemptions. Fifteen states allow the deduction of federal income tax and there are a variety of other types of exemption. The biggest difficulty with the administration of corporate income tax is the allocation of income in the case of businesses engaging in interstate business.

Sales Taxes

The sales tax in its various forms has gained rapidly in favor until it is at the present time the most important single source of state revenue. In one form or another it is levied by all states. The various types of sales taxes have been defined in the previous chapter. In 1956 thirty-three states levied a general sales tax at rates varying from 2 to 3.5 per cent. The median percentage of state revenues received from sales and gross receipts taxes in 1956 was 61.6 per cent. The range was from a low of 24.9 per cent in Oregon to a high of 84.7 per cent in West Virginia.

The general sales tax was first levied in West Virginia in 1921. Many states adopted the tax during the 1930s when they were forced to look for more revenue. There have been a number of adoptions of the sales tax since World War II. In all these cases, however, food has been exempted. When food is taxed it forms the principal source of sales tax revenue.

In a number of states the proceeds of general sales taxes have been earmarked in whole or in part for schools. Among these states are Kansas, Michigan, New Mexico, South Dakota, Tennessee, and Utah.

Objection to the general sales tax is frequently made on the grounds that it is regressive, that is, it taxes lower incomes in greater proportion than higher incomes. The income tax cannot reach low incomes without increasing collection costs. The sales tax on the other hand requires relatively less bookkeeping. For that reason a combination of the two has won favor in many quarters. It is assumed by some that the one fills in where the other falls short, but this is not always borne out in practice.

The selective sales taxes such as those on liquor, cigarettes, and gasoline are big revenue producers in view of the fact that they are levied

[9] Reported in Paul R. Mort, *Federal Support of Public Education*, Bureau of Publications, Teachers College, Columbia University, New York, 1936, p. 154.

on one commodity each. They are very widely used, all states levying taxes on liquor and gasoline and forty-one levying a tax on cigarettes.

The rate on gasoline ranges from 3 to 7 cents a gallon. Each year the revenue from this tax increases. In fact it tripled in the ten-year period from 1946 to 1956, which would indicate that few if any states have achieved the maximum in returns as yet.

The alcoholic beverage tax is also levied by the gallon but is much more complex because of the varieties of rates involved. On distilled spirits, for example, it has ranged from $.75 to $3.60 per gallon. The revenues from alcoholic beverages have not increased as much as those from gasoline, but there has been a 36 per cent increase in the same ten-year period.

The tax on cigarettes makes up the bulk of the state tobacco taxes, the rates ranging from 2 to 8 cents per package. The revenue from this tax has also leaped ahead, increasing 159 per cent in the ten-year period.

Taxes on Motorists

The most lucrative tax on motorists has already been treated under the selective sales tax. Every state also levies taxes on motorists in the form of motor vehicle and operators' licenses. These are also productive taxes. These taxes have increased 194 per cent in the ten-year period and give indication of continued expansion.

There is a comparatively new tax in this field which may be expected to expand rapidly. This is a weight-mile tax levied on trucking. In New York State, while it is still a minor revenue producer, it has been expanding at the rate of almost $2 million per year.

The taxes derived from motorists have largely been considered benefit taxes and have often been earmarked for highways, although occasionally a state will earmark a portion of them for education.

Other Taxes

There are several other widely used taxes such as the inheritance tax which is levied in all states except Nevada. It is not a large revenue producer and the yield is very unstable because of the extreme influence of an especially large estate or the lack of such. Exemptions are normally high. This tax has also shown a large increase, more than 100 per cent in the ten-year period.

State severance taxes are based on the principle that those who profit by the extraction of minerals or forest products from the soil impoverish the state and, therefore, should be taxed for this privilege. The term "severance tax" applies to the extraction of all minerals, raw materials, forests, and other products from the soil, except agricultural products. In practice, however, the tax is frequently limited to certain types of natural resources depending upon those found within the state levying the tax.

Twenty-eight states levy some form of severance tax, but only in a few of them are the proceeds in whole or in part set aside for the use of public schools. Louisiana and Texas are examples of states which earmark this tax for schools. The revenue derived from the tax in Louisiana in 1957 was $83 million. In Texas it produced $198 million, slightly more than half the United States total of $388 million.

A number of states have taxes on mineral products such as oil, gas, and coal, but they cannot truly be considered as severance taxes. They are rather in the nature of production taxes since the mineral products are usually taxed as property at the mines.

Two other taxes which have only limited application are the stock-transfer and the pari-mutuel taxes. As with the severance tax, only a few states can benefit from the stock-transfer tax because there must be an active stock exchange to make it worthwhile. The pari-mutuel tax is more widely used; it has been levied in twenty-four states but it produces substantial revenues in only about half of these.

TAXPAYING CAPACITY AND EFFORT

It is impossible to gain an adequate concept of a state's taxing system merely by listing the various types of taxes that are levied and their yield over a period of years. In addition, it is necessary that one take into consideration the total wealth and income of a state and the extent to which the tax structure is designed to tap that wealth and income. Since taxes must be paid from income, the various types of wealth within a state must be viewed in the light of their income-producing capacity.

In a study of the taxpaying capacity and tax effort in the state of West Virginia, Newcomer said: [10]

It is important to distinguish between taxpaying capacity and tax effort. The first is a measure of a state's ability to pay taxes. The second is a measure of the extent to which a state has utilized its taxpaying capacity. There is no absolute standard of either taxpaying capacity or tax effort, but there are a number of useful measures of relative taxpaying capacity and effort. And it is reasonable to assume that any state falling much below the national average for any acceptable measure of tax effort can be expected to contribute further to the support of government functions if such support seems desirable.

Perhaps the most useful single test of taxpaying capacity is the income per capita within the state. This test applied to any state will show the state's rank. Even in those states that rank relatively low there are certain

[10] George D. Strayer, Director, *A Report of a Survey of Public Education in the State of West Virginia,* State of West Virginia, Legislative Interim Committee, Charleston, W.Va., 1945.

taxpaying resources that may not be adequately taxed by the common types of taxes. Other measures of taxpaying capacity are the estimated yield per capita of a specified uniform tax system and per capita wealth. When taxpaying capacity is measured in terms of income, an income tax properly designed and administered on the state level would appear to be one of the most adequate taxes.

In the discussion of local tax effort, the study by Samuelson and Mushkin may be cited.[11] In this study three tests of tax effort are discussed: (1) tax performance, (2) relative use of tax capacity, and (3) tax severity. The first of these tax tests is a comparison of the yield of different taxes from one state to another. It shows how much tax is collected without any consideration of the potential yield of the tax. The second one, relative use of tax capacity, relates to the yield of different taxes in terms of the tax base; the third, tax severity, takes into account the matter of shifting and incidence of the different types of taxes. A relatively large dependence on state sales taxes indicates a rather regressive tax system, although when combined with other types of taxes, this may not be the case.

The adaptation of the taxes levied in any state to that state's resources and the nature of its location and population constitute a very important test of the total tax structure.

THEORIES AND PRINCIPLES OF TAXATION

The distribution of the tax burden among all the taxpayers of the state has always been a topic of prime importance. There is always a choice to be made among the taxes to be levied and there is always a choice of the rates at which various taxes are levied. Stability, collection costs, and equity must be considered. There is need for a general understanding of the fundamentals of tax questions.

There are many theories on which taxation is based. Two of the most commonly discussed are the benefit theory and the ability theory. As revenue needs have mounted these theories have received less attention. Primary concern has been focused on the productivity of the tax. Similarly, whether or not a tax is regressive has been an important standard of judgment.

The benefit theory is simply what the name implies. Does the person or business that pays the tax derive benefit from it? The difficulty is that benefit is hard if not impossible to measure and thus the theory becomes a rather befuddled argument for almost any type of taxation. Often the

[11] J. Wilmer Samuelson and S. J. Mushkin, *The Measurement of State and Local Tax Effort*, U.S. Social Security Board, Bureau of Research and Statistics, Bureau Memorandum 58, Washington, June, 1944.

benefit theory has been exploited as an argument for earmarking certain
taxes, such as the gasoline tax for highways. Carried to its nonlogical
extreme each tax would go for some specific function related to the
source from which it is derived, leaving no funds for those functions of
general welfare which require the greatest amounts such as health, welfare, and education.

The ability theory is based on the postulate that all persons benefit
directly or indirectly from most governmental services and should therefore pay for them according to their economic capacity. The federal income tax with its progressive rates is the best example of a tax based on
this theory. From this theory has arisen the criterion of regressiveness.
The chief problem in the application of this theory is the definition of
ability. It is certain, however, that a taxing structure which imposes only
a slight levy on intangible property and ignores income but taxes real
property misses completely all the tenets of a good system of taxation.
Such a structure clashes violently with the principle of ability.

There is every reason to believe that stocks, bonds, and the like make
up the greatest portion of wealth. In 1939 a study of probated estates in
the state of Washington showed them to be made up of realty 40 per
cent, tangible property 3 per cent, and intangible personalty 57 per
cent.[12] This was at the end of the depression. The proportion of intangible wealth would be much greater today. State tax systems cannot
ignore this source without ignoring ability and greatly overburdening
other sources.

The question of tax incidence, meaning who bears the burden of payment of a particular tax, is one of the most complicated of economic
problems. Undoubtedly the incidence of a tax such as the sales tax
depends on a variety of circumstances such as rate and business conditions.

Taxable capacity means different things to different people. Those in
favor of a particular project assume capacity is without limit; those who
favor limiting taxes generally feel capacity has already been reached
and passed. Taxable capacity may be defined as the capacity to raise
revenue without extreme interference with productive capacity and the
operation of the economy. There are no precise mathematical limits. The
larger the portion left of national income after providing for essential
private consumption, the greater the capacity.

To be considered in assessing taxable capacity are (1) the incentive
to establish new businesses, (2) the incentive for existing business to
expand, (3) the incentive to invest, (4) the incentive to work.

The form and scope of the tax system are also important. The larger

[12] Reported in Maurice W. Lee, *Tax Structure of the State of Washington*, The
State College of Washington, Pullman, Wash., 1950, p. 56.

the number of revenue sources available, the greater the capacity. A variety of taxes, rather than a few, means that rates will not be unbearably high and that the imperfections of any one tax will not bear too heavily on any group of taxpayers.

All writers on taxation list a number of tests of the soundness of a tax system. Since most systems of taxation are not systems at all but the result of the needs for revenue which have developed over centuries, it is perhaps surprising that state tax systems apply as many of the principles as they do.

Usually the first principle to be stated is productivity. Will the taxes levied produce adequate revenues? The broad range of taxes levied in each state, with but few exceptions, has been more than adequate up to this point.

The elasticity of revenue yield is closely related to productivity. Can the system be expanded quickly if need arises or is every tax already levied at its maximum rate?

Stability has already been mentioned in this chapter. Commodity and property taxes are the most stable, income the least. It is necessary in a sound tax system to use taxes which will hold up in hard times as well as in times of prosperity.

Diversity of source has also been mentioned. A skillful balancing of sources is required to reach all groups.

Adaptability is as important in taxation as in all other phases of life. Times and conditions change and what may have been entirely satisfactory taxation at one time no longer meets the need. A good example of this is the shift away from the property tax at the state level.

Simplicity is another universal principle of good administration. The more simple and clear the better. However, modern accounting makes possible the successful levy of the income tax, which is something less than simple.

Certainty is closely related to simplicity. The amount, dates due, and method of computation should be known to all concerned with the tax. This is one of the strong points of the income tax and one of the weaknesses of the property tax in its present method of application.

Convenience is a necessity if a tax is to produce large revenues. The withholding feature of the federal income tax is a good example of an added convenience of relatively recent origin.

Economy refers to the costs of the administration of the tax. Some taxes cause more bookkeeping than others and are more difficult to enforce. When this is the case, costs rise and the principle of economy is lost. Some taxes must be levied and enforced in order to strengthen the tax system. As in the case of the use tax, which is extremely difficult to enforce, it may be desirable to spend extra funds to enforce it in order to strengthen the application of the sales tax.

Taxation should be just. It should bear equitably on various groups and classes of income in accordance with both benefit and ability. Needless to say, this is not always the case. Standards are not possible which make taxation that exact.

While individual taxes often fail on several of the above principles, state systems more and more tend to meet them well. There are no perfect systems for all states; indeed, there is no state which could not improve. But even in our complex economy and with all the divergent effects of both local and federal taxation, better than rough approximations of applying the principles have been made.

SUMMARY

The increase in state support for schools that has taken place during the past two decades has come largely from various new sources of revenue such as the income tax, sales tax, severance tax, inheritance tax, and a number of others. Although these new sources have been utilized extensively, the older state property tax continues to yield some revenue in a few states.

There has been a trend in the direction of state appropriations for schools rather than fixed earmarked funds. Perhaps the chief advantage of this method lies in its flexibility to adapt revenue to public school needs. Income from permanent school funds constitutes a minor source of school income in a number of states, perhaps of more historical interest than present significance.

In seven states a state-wide tax on general property is levied for public elementary and secondary schools. In general the states have placed less emphasis on state-wide property taxes in recent years than formerly. A few states still depend to a considerable extent on this source.

Until 1957 during the past two decades there had been no increase in the number of state income taxes, probably because the emphasis that the federal government has placed on this source of revenue has made it less attractive as a state source. State sales taxes have increased greatly in significance from the standpoint of revenue yield in recent years and now form the most important single source of state revenue.

Consideration should be given to the types of taxes levied in any state and to the types of wealth and the total wealth and income of the state to determine the taxpaying capacity and the tax effort.

QUESTIONS FOR STUDY AND DISCUSSION

1. Enumerate the types of state taxation for public schools in your state and show the approximate proportion of school revenue derived from each. If school revenues are derived from the general fund, prorate the amounts.

2. Outline the provisions, if any, for state-wide property tax for schools in a particular state with which you are familiar. Indicate the minimum tax rate, proportion allocated to schools, funds to which the proceeds are assigned, and the purpose for which money from this source may be expended.

3. Describe the provision for income taxation for public schools in one or more states. Indicate the rates of the tax, the exemptions, the proportion of proceeds devoted to schools, and the purpose for which money from this source may be expended.

4. What are the provisions for a severance tax in one or more states that levy such a tax? On what products or raw materials is the tax levied? What proportion of the proceeds is allocated to schools?

5. Show the details of sales taxation in one or more states that levy this tax. Give the rates of the tax, the exemptions, the method of collection, the allocation of the proceeds to various governmental purposes.

6. To what extent are the proceeds of the inheritance tax in certain selected states devoted to schools?

7. Describe any other form of state-wide taxation that is used in whole or in part for the support of public schools.

8. Compare a number of states relative to their income per capita and show the relative tax effort that is made.

SELECTED REFERENCES

Buehler, Alfred G.: *Public Finance,* McGraw-Hill Book Company, Inc., New York, 1948.

Burke, Arvid J.: *Financing Public Schools in the United States,* Harper & Brothers, New York, 1957.

Hutchins, Clayton D., and Albert R. Munse: *Public School Finance Programs in the United States,* U.S. Office of Education, 1954.

Kendrick, M. Slade: *Public Finance,* Houghton Mifflin Company, Boston, 1951.

Lee, Maurice W.: *Tax Structure of the State of Washington,* The State College of Washington, Pullman, Wash., 1950.

Mort, Paul R., Director: *State Action toward More Quality Education,* State Department of Education, Baltimore, Md., 1959.

National Education Association, Committee on Tax Education and School Finance: *Guides to the Improvement of State School Finance Programs,* Washington, 1958.

Polley, John W.: "The Non-property Tax Potential of New York State," Staff Study No. 3, *1957 Review of the Fiscal Policy for Public Education in New York State,* New York State Educational Conference Board, Albany, N.Y., 1957.

Samuelson, H. Wilmer, and S. J. Mushkin: *The Measurement of State and Local Tax Effort,* U.S. Social Security Board, Bureau of Research and Statistics, Bureau Memorandum 58, Washington, June, 1944.

Strayer, George D., Director: *A Report of a Survey of Public Education in the State of West Virginia,* Legislative Interim Committee, Charleston, W.Va., 1945.

The Tax Foundation: *Facts and Figures on Government Finance, 1956–57,* New York, 1957.

United States Department of Commerce: *Compendium of State Government Finances in 1957,* Washington, 1958.

10. Federal sources of revenue

THE FEDERAL GOVERNMENT stands in a unique place in the three-level taxing system. It has moved in a relatively short period of time into a position where it collects the overwhelmingly largest portion of the tax dollar. There are only three legal limits on its power to tax. It cannot tax exports to foreign countries, state government functions, or the ownership of property according to its value.

The federal government has far greater financial powers than state or local governments. It has access to the entire economic resources of the nation. It is not restricted by the tax competition which limits the action of state and local governments. It has tremendous borrowing power and, as the record of the past twenty-five years amply indicates, it is not restricted as are many states to an annually balanced budget. The development of an increasingly complex economy makes certain types of taxation by the largest governmental unit far more practical than state or local taxation.

The federal government has enormously increased its revenues over the past twenty-five years. The expansion has followed the demand for increased outlays for military purposes and also for increased services. As the expansion has continued little recognition has been given the over-all needs of education. Rather the emphasis has been on promoting those aspects of the program in which some current problem has brought recognition of need. Federal interest in education has a long history beginning with the formation of the republic itself, but despite the enormous extension of federal aid to the states in the welfare and highway programs only minor concern has been shown for education.

The amount of federal taxation which goes to the support of education is extremely small. But such is the dominant place of the federal government in the taxation field that whatever the federal government does profoundly influences revenues available to the schools. Furthermore,

180

there are many who advocate substantial federal support of education in all the states of the union. An understanding of federal revenues is essential to a knowledge of the problems of federal support for education.

The federal government has limits other than legal to its revenue resources. First of all, it is committed to a huge program of expenditure which by its very nature must recur annually. This means that new programs require new taxes. Adding to the already huge debt is a serious step. There is the added requirement to watch carefully each new revenue for its effect on the total economy.

Although consideration in this volume has focused on three levels of revenue, there is only one economy from which all levels of government derive their revenues. The problem of fostering fiscal balance among the three arises out of the nature of the economy.

THE DEVELOPMENT OF FEDERAL REVENUES

The increase in federal revenue is shown in Table 10-1. By 1956 it had increased to $75,848,424,000 from a mere $528,493,000 in 1900. Where in 1900 only 37.5 per cent of taxation was levied by the federal government, in 1956 this had increased to 72.3 per cent. Such an increase has had tremendous effects on the revenue patterns of the states. It has retarded the use of the income tax and fostered the use of sales taxes. Because of the progressive effect of federal taxation the regressive nature of state and local taxes has lost much of its importance.

The first revenue measures adopted by Congress in 1789 were a tariff followed shortly by an excise tax on liquor. Other excises quickly appeared. The internal taxes were difficult to collect and were soon largely repealed, leaving only the customs duties. From time to time the excise taxes were reimposed as the need for revenue became great. This was the pattern of federal taxation until the Civil War.

With the Civil War came a drastic change. The modern version of taxation began. As Kendrick describes it: [1]

Articles that had been taxed during the War of 1812 again appeared on the list of revenue sources. Others not used or available in the earlier period were added. Thus auction sales, beer, ale, porter and other malt liquors, distilled spirits and carriages were again subjects of taxation.

Taxes on yachts, billiard tables, and plate were added. Special licenses were required of persons and corporations doing business. Railroads were taxed on gross receipts. Banks, trust companies, and insurance companies were made to pay on dividends declared. A 3 per cent levy was imposed on receipts from advertising. Legacies were taxed. The personal income tax was retained (it had

[1] M. S. Kendrick, *Public Finance*, Houghton Mifflin Company, Boston, 1951, pp. 141–142.

been imposed earlier in the war), but the rates were made slightly progressive and the exemptions were reduced to $600. Revenue stamps had to be affixed to every instrument of exchange.

The big revenue producer during the war and directly following was the income tax. From 1863 to 1872 when it was repealed it yielded $347 million. From then on, the income tax was not levied until authorized by the adoption of the Sixteenth Amendment in 1913.

Great increases in taxation were made during World War I. However, in contrast to the Civil War only the most productive sources of revenue were taxed. The big producers were the income and corporation taxes which yielded approximately 70 per cent of the revenues in 1918.

Table 10-1   Federal Tax Collections, 1789–1956
(in thousands)

Year	Total taxes	Income	Customs	Others
1789–91	$4,399	$ . . .	$4,399	$
1830	21,935	. . .	21,922	12
1870	379,438	37,776	194,538	147,124
1900	528,493	. . .	233,165	295,328
1910	623,617	20,952	333,683	268,982
1920	5,727,934	3,944,949	322,903	1,460,082
1930	3,626,296	2,410,987	587,001	628,308
1940	5,700,891	2,125,325	348,591	3,226,976
1950	39,890,112	28,262,671	422,650	11,204,791
1956	75,848,424 *	56,633,738	704,898	18,509,741

* Includes funds from various retirement and unemployment insurance funds.
SOURCE: The Tax Foundation, *Facts and Figures on Government Finance*, New York, 1957, p. 111.

The decade of the 1920s was marked by tax reduction but the 1930s brought a return to high income taxes and many excises plus the tightening of tax laws to make escape from taxation difficult. In the search for revenue in the 1930s, the federal government and the states which formerly had used different sources now turned to the same ones. Personal and corporate income, inheritance and estates, tobacco, gasoline, and alcoholic beverages became basic parts of both tax structures. During this period when state and local government expenditures increased, much of the expansion came from federal grants. Expenditures for state and local governments had increased by $2 billion a year by 1939 over the 1929 level. Almost half of the increase came from the federal government.

With the coming of World War II there was little change in the pattern of taxation. Rates were drastically revised upwards but no new major taxes were adopted.

Since the close of World War II revenue from taxation at the federal level has continued to increase. While there was a slight downward trend in the late 1940s international tension caused an increase in taxation until in 1956 the federal government revenue was well over $70 billion. In the period from 1950 to 1956, as shown in Table 10-1, revenue from the income tax doubled and revenue from the various excise taxes and similar sources increased more than 60 per cent. The various forms of income tax constitute by far the most important part of the tax structure. Excise taxes are, however, far from negligible. The third major source is the employment taxes.

The Personal Income Tax

In 1956, the personal income tax yielded $35.3 billion out of a total tax yield of $75.8 billion. This amounts approximately to $275 per capita, an amount considerably in excess of the per capita state and local tax collections. Prior to World War II corporate income had exceeded personal income in revenue but since the early 1940s personal income has been the chief revenue source of the federal government. The tax has provided substantial revenue since World War I. It yielded 31 per cent of federal revenue in 1929. Although it dropped to 19 per cent in 1933, it increased throughout the early 1940s and in 1956 it provided 47 per cent of the federal revenue.

The federal income tax is the best example of a tax based on the ability-to-pay principle. In 1955, a single person with no dependents and a net income of $2,000 would have paid at the rate of 14 per cent, while a person with a net income of $100,000 would have paid at the rate of 66.8 per cent.

The development of withholding in World War II makes the collection of the tax on smaller incomes much more practical. While there may be loopholes in this tax such as provision for gifts, capital gains, or the exemption of the income of municipal securities, the revenue yielded by the tax has been remarkable in amount. The yield of the tax depends on the exemptions allowed but the increasing level of income has brought more and more people into income-tax-paying status. The number of individual income tax returns has increased from 4 million in 1925 to 56 million in 1952, the increase being almost 6.5 million from 1945 to 1952.

The Corporate Income Tax

The corporate income tax has yielded large revenues except during the 1930s. In 1929 it provided 35 per cent of federal revenues and although it dropped to 20 per cent in 1933 it had increased to 23 per cent in 1939 and to 28 per cent in 1956. As shown in Table 10-2, it amounted to $213 billion in that year. It is especially easy to administer because of the relatively small number of corporations paying and the size of the payments which they make. In contrast to the personal income tax, the number of returns in 1952 was only 242,000 greater than in 1925. In 1952, there were 672,071 returns. The tax has often been criticized on the grounds that it constitutes double taxation since the same funds are first taxed as corporate profit and then taxed again as income in the hands of the corporation owners.

Income taxes and corporate-earning taxes are closely associated in the minds of many people. Hence arises the concept of double taxation. However, other taxes are not considered double taxation and quite obviously all taxes must be paid out of income and income is taxed in numerous ways.

Table 10-2   Source of Federal Tax Collections, 1956

Tax	Amount, in millions
Individual income	$35,337
Corporate income and profits	21,297
Manufacturers excise taxes	3,456
Alcoholic beverages	2,921
Tobacco	1,631
Other	2,096
Estate and gift taxes	1,171
Employment taxes	7,330
Customs	705

SOURCE: The Tax Foundation, *Facts and Figures on Government Finance, 1956–1957,* New York, 1957, p. 110.

The very high wartime rates contained in the excess profits feature have been eliminated. In a complex tax such as this many other problems are involved. However, it is an important revenue producer and with federal expenditures at record levels it is likely that the main reason for the levy, that of producing adequate revenue, will be sufficient reason for it to continue.

The sensitiveness of the personal and corporate income taxes to business conditions is well illustrated by federal government revenues in 1958. As a result of the business recession which occurred during that year, the largest peacetime deficit in the history of the national government is anticipated.

Employment Taxes

The employment taxes on wages are primarily those contained in the social security act. They are designed to finance old age annuities, survivors' benefits and unemployment insurance payments. The chief difficulty has been to keep the program self-supporting and yet in the early years not to build up such a reserve as to upset the whole fiscal structure of the nation. In 1956, receipts were outrunning expenditures, as they have consistently since its inception in 1939.

Consumption Levies

The federal government levies taxes on many articles of consumption which the states also tax as shown in Table 10-2. In addition it taxes jewelry, furs, luggage, toilet preparations, oil pipelines, transportation, telephones, telegrams, sugar, coal, and electricity. Rates have been consistently reduced in this area since the war and more liberal exemptions have been allowed.

The matter of tax overlapping is one to be watched with some care. Certainly overlapping will grow. It has several disadvantages, including not only inconvenience and annoyance to the taxpayer but increases in the cost of tax administration. On the positive side a more balanced and stable tax structure is possible if many taxes are levied than if each level of government were limited to a few.

Borrowing

Borrowing has formed a consistent part of the federal revenue picture since the 1930s. Up to 1956 the federal government had had a surplus of receipts over expenditures in only three years. The debt reached a level in excess of $275 billion in 1958. While this amount sounds staggering, it must be remembered that the federal government debt is quite unlike private debt and that the amount is not extremely large in terms of the national income. Furthermore, the burden of the debt charges in comparison to national income is less than it was in the World War I period, less even than in the 1930s.

The management of the federal debt is an extremely complex problem and one which has great effects on the national economy.

Impact of Present Revenue Sources

At present the federal revenue system, largely dependent on progressive income taxes, tends to vary directly with the level of business. Revenues rise when business is good—fall when business slows down. This variation has been accentuated by the use of withholding taxes and the payment of corporate income taxes within six months. State and local taxes are much more stable, depending to a great degree on property taxation plus the sales taxes on necessities or the seminecessities of daily living. Tax collections have become a large portion of total economic activity. With the exception of the war years about one dollar out of four has gone for the support of government for the past twenty years.

The net result is that if tax rates remain unchanged during the entire business cycle the existing revenue system will have considerable effect in stabilizing prices, consumption, and employment and in maintaining the present distribution of the national income.

The Keynesian theory of economics which has received wide attention in recent years provides for a stable kind of federal revenue. This theory in simplified form holds that government expenditures should be financed during periods of depression primarily by borrowing, since tax rates would be reduced to stimulate purchasing power, and conversely that during periods of prosperity tax rates should be increased in order to pay back the loans, to decrease purchasing power, and to retard inflation.

Proposals for Federal Revenue

There are many proposals in regard to federal taxation. Some have as their goal the curbing of inflation or deflation, others are aimed at eliminating loopholes in the present tax law, while still others have the primary aim of more revenue from a greater variety of sources. Some, perhaps all, of the taxes discussed will never be enacted into law. They do, however, give some clues as to what further tax developments might be apart from rate changes.

It has been suggested that the level of taxation should be changeable as necessary month by month. Thus the rate of tax would increase or decrease if money income increased or decreased by a certain amount during the month. A spendings tax was recommended during World War II and again during the Korean War. The tax would be levied on money spent, savings would be exempt. The object is to control consumption. It has been urged also as possibly a much more progressive substitute for excise taxes. A purchase tax, as now used in Great Britain, would apply at the wholesale level on selected commodities. It is a combination of a luxury tax and a tax on scarce raw materials.

The distribution of the tax load has strong bearing on possible new taxes and also on the distribution of federally collected taxes back to the states. In dealing with this problem the following information is important: [2]

Unfortunately, the distribution of the tax load is not known because Federal tax collections by State, as reported by the Internal Revenue Service, do not reflect the source of tax payments. For example, more than three-fourths of the manufacturers' excise taxes on automobile parts are collected in Michigan, and over half of all tobacco taxes are collected in North Carolina, but these taxes are ultimately paid by car owners and smokers throughout the Nation.

[2] Committee on Government Operations, *Federal–State–Local Relations: Federal Grants-in-aid,* Government Printing Office, Washington, 1958, p. 42.

Although it is theoretically possible to trace the origin of federal taxes on a State basis, such an allocation involves assumptions as to the incidence and effects of taxation about which there is presently no general agreement.

Income taxes like excise taxes may be reported in a different state from that in which a person resides. For example, the individual income tax returns which General Motors withholds from its employees are filed in the district in which the principal place of business is located. The tax for a General Motors' subsidiary which is located in Chicago is paid from the central office in Detroit. Only a balance of tax due over withholding is paid at the residence.

SOME CONSIDERATIONS IN A SYSTEM OF TAXATION

The size of the federal budget, the great federal debt, and memories of the long depression of the 1930s point to the need for careful management of federal finances. In fact taxation, expenditure, borrowing, and debt payment have a much greater relationship to the level of the national income than in times when they were of lesser magnitude.

Traditional economics has always assigned a limited role to government in fostering the financial welfare of the nation. In the tradition of Adam Smith business was best left alone and government was assigned the job of policeman.

As Lindholm describes the part government policy plays, it becomes a considerably more active participant: [3]

Gradually, as the modern economies of today have evolved economists have become aware that the role of government must be considerably greater than that of "a night watchman" and that it is incorrect to assume that the best government is the cheapest government. This change of attitude has arisen from an abundance of experience which has shown that more government does not necessarily destroy the foundations on which a private capitalist economy is built. Instead, experience has shown that more government can strengthen the foundations.

Because of the availability of federal revenues—that is, the federal government can both increase taxes and borrow money more easily than state and local governments—the federal government is under constant pressure to use its greater revenue resources to provide services at the state and local levels. Not only does the federal government have greater revenue resources but also it may be more responsive to certain pressing local problems. For example, there are constantly growing and con-

[3] Richard W. Lindholm, *Introduction to Fiscal Policy*, Pitman Publishing Corporation, New York, 1955, p. 2.

stantly increasing numbers of metropolitan areas in this country. As defined by the Census Bureau, a metropolitan area is one that includes a central city of 50,000 or more population and an urban fringe. There are 170 of them. Because they often cross state lines and because state legislatures are frequently rurally dominated, such areas often look to the federal government for aid in economic and social problems. Such problems naturally enough include education.

The variety of demands on government plus the extent and number of services it already provides has led to consideration of what are the limits, if any, on taxation. How great a portion of the national income may be taken in taxes before the economy begins to suffer? Those who favor rapid expansion of tax-supported public functions assume that taxation may be increased almost without limit. Those who regard any increase in taxation with horror often take the position that limits of taxable capacity have been reached and passed long ago and that salvation is possible only through a tax cut.

Such a debate appears to be largely academic. Increases in taxation come about in periods of rising prices when the growth of the economy will provide increased revenue and hence the possibility of increased service, or in periods of emergency such as war or depression when whatever steps are presumed necessary meet with little or no opposition because the immediate goal of survival is the chief concern.

A sidelight on increases in taxation is provided by Galbraith.[4] He points out that liberals are obliged to argue that services should be paid for by progressive taxation which will reduce inequality. They must oppose sales and excise taxes. Conservatives oppose the use of income tax although not necessarily the service. Since the debate over the means of providing the service cannot be resolved, the service becomes a casualty of the debate. In this provocative treatment of public and private spending, Galbraith takes the position that public spending for desirable services contributes more to the economy than much private spending and that it is a necessity at our high levels of income in order to keep production and consumption in balance.

The Brookings Institution examined the taxation picture in 1950:[5]

In a nation faced with heavy governmental requirements, it is essential that the adverse effects of taxation on economic incentives be held to a minimum. The crux of the fiscal problem is to raise the required revenues without unduly affecting the volume of production and the level of the national income. In this

[4] John K. Galbraith, *The Affluent Society*, Houghton Mifflin Company, Boston, 1958, p. 262.

[5] Lewis H. Kimmel, *Taxes and Economic Incentives*, The Brookings Institution, Washington, 1950, p. 195.

study we have been concerned mainly with the effects of taxation on four incentives that are fundamental to an enterprise economy: (1) the incentive to establish new business, (2) the incentive for existing business to expand, (3) the incentive to invest, and (4) the incentive to work. The analysis has been focused on the four principal classes of taxes now used in the United States—income, sales and excise, property, and payroll; these taxes account for almost 95 per cent of the combined revenues of federal, state and local governments.

The conclusion reached is that the encroachment of taxes on incentives is primarily an income tax problem and especially that of the level of corporate taxation. Since the time of the report, corporate taxes have been reduced.

SUMMARY

The federal government has moved to a dominant place in our three-level taxation system in the past twenty-five years. The present-day patterns of taxation had their origins in many cases in taxes which were first widely used during the Civil War. Despite the fact that comparatively small amounts of revenue for the direct support of education are drawn from federal sources, a knowledge of federal taxation amplifies a knowledge of state and local taxation. It is also essential to an understanding of the problems of federal support for education.

Federal revenues have been drawn largely from income taxes and a few excises. So large do the economic activities of the federal government loom in the total economic activity of the nation that any change in the pattern may well have important connotations for state and local revenues.

QUESTIONS FOR STUDY AND DISCUSSION

1. List the sources of federal revenues and the funds obtained from each source for the current year.

2. List the taxes levied by both federal and state governments.

3. How many more persons filed income tax returns this year than last? Use data for the latest year available. In what income brackets did this increase occur?

4. Determine the federal aid going to the largest city in your state. Compare this on a per capita basis with federal aid going to a rural county. What conclusion do you draw?

5. Define a regressive tax, a progressive tax, a proportional tax. Give examples of each.

6. What is meant by the terms "incidence," "impact," "shifting"?

SELECTED REFERENCES

Buehler, Alfred G.: *Public Finance,* McGraw-Hill Book Co., Inc., New York, 1948.

Burke, Arvid J.: *Financing Public Schools in the United States,* Harper & Brothers, New York, 1957.

Commission on Intergovernmental Relations: *A Report to the President for Transmittal to the Congress,* Government Printing Office, Washington, 1955.

Committee on Government Operations: *Federal–State–Local Relations,* Government Printing Office, Washington, 1958.

Galbraith, John K.: *The Affluent Society,* Houghton Mifflin Company, Boston, 1958.

Johns, R. L., and E. L. Morphet (eds.): *Problems and Issues in Public School Finance,* Bureau of Publications, Teachers College, Columbia University, New York, 1952.

Kendrick, M. Slade: *Public Finance,* Houghton Mifflin Company, Boston, 1951.

Kimmel, Lewis H.: *Taxes and Economic Incentives,* The Brookings Institution, Washington, 1950.

Lindholm, Richard W.: *Introduction to Fiscal Policy,* Pitman Publishing Corporation, New York, 1955.

Part four

State and federal participation in school support

CHAPTERS 11 to 16 deal with the issues and techniques involved in participation by a central government (the state) in the support of local school systems. Chapter 17 considers the unique problems faced in federal sharing in school support in the light of the rationale of central support as developed in Chapters 11 to 16.

11. The evolution of state-aid systems

T HE FIRST section of this chapter reviews the beginnings of state participation in the support of public schools and traces the evolution of patterns of support up to the turn of the present century. The second section outlines the evolution of the patterns of support from 1890 to the present. With the first two sections as a backdrop, the third section traces the evolution of theory to the pattern of support to which it is suggested we are now tending. This third section includes a brief discussion of current developments in tax theory that are diverging somewhat from what the authors believe to be the logical outcomes of developments in education, and treats two recent developments in practice that may possibly affect future patterns. The final section discusses the inadequacy of present state-aid systems in reflecting the purposes they are presumably meant to serve.

EIGHTEENTH AND NINETEENTH CENTURY BEGINNINGS

Four lines of influence on the evolution of programs for state aid to education have been identified. Strands from each of them can be found in our practices and controlling traditions today. One strand came from the states that were experimenting with public education in the eighteenth century; one from the states that initiated their programs early in the nineteenth century; the third from the states carved out of the Northwest Territory; and the fourth from the states of the Southeast which delayed the establishment of public education until after the War between the States. Perhaps a fifth group should have been included— the states newly formed about and after the turn of the present century.

The Eighteenth Century

At the time the Constitutional Convention decided to leave education "to the states or to the people," tax-supported education was limited
to the older New England states. To the large majority of the original
states, public education was an unknown quantity. Of the twelve states
which adopted constitutions in this period, only seven mentioned education; only three of these offered definitions (Massachusetts, New Hampshire, and Vermont). Forty years were to pass before New Jersey,
Pennsylvania, and Rhode Island entered the list of states having tax-
supported schools; eighty years were to elapse before most of the remainder were to make their beginnings. The wilderness west of the
Alleghenies was more committed to public education than the majority
of the older states because of the land-grant policy adopted by the
Continental Congress in 1787. This included the earmarking of land for
school purposes in every township of the Northwest Territory. The
policy was extended eventually to all the new states and brought to them
a total land area equal to 150 Rhode Islands.

The early Massachusetts law (1647) had depended on mandate. Since
it worked with reasonable effectiveness through local support, the issue
of state aid did not rise in the early years. It was Massachusetts, however, that had pioneered the idea of school land grants in the wilderness
to encourage settlement of what later became Maine.

Connecticut, which had followed the Massachusetts Bay Colony's early
lead in 1650, likewise depended on local support until 1795, when provision was made for the distribution of the money it received from the
sale of its western lands. While this money was presumed to be used to
supplement money available from local taxation, the requirement was not
firm and local support fell off. What was designed as a supplementary flat-
grant aid (to use our present-day terminology) became in fact state
support.

At the end of the eighteenth century neither Connecticut nor Massachusetts was a particularly bright and shining example of this new
development, public education. Both dependence on the localities and
the fear of large state support that is in the tradition of many states
today have their roots, no doubt, in some degree in these early experiences.

New York was a newcomer to this eighteenth century group. In 1795
funds were granted to municipalities to be used for schools and to be
supplemented locally by half the amount. This law was enacted to operate
for five years but in spite of apparent success was not renewed. A commission appointed in 1811 cut to the roots of the problem. On its recommendation a law passed in 1812 created a system of local school govern-

ment, gave the new government agencies taxing power, and required them to match the state grants. The New York law of 1812 was destined to have wide influence both on methods of finance and methods of local fiscal control.

The Early Nineteenth Century

The first third of the nineteenth century was a period of gestation. Apart from the brilliant example of New York in 1812, education in the East was in the doldrums. Massachusetts and Connecticut were declining, prior to the awakening led by Horace Mann and Henry Barnard. The larger cities were experimenting with church schools, charity schools, Lancastrian schools, and public school societies. Jefferson's friend, the first DuPont, was designing a national system of education. There were many "viewings with alarm" and appeals to justice. There were also bright spots, however.

Ohio, the first state shaped from the Northwest Territory (1803), provided in its constitution for right of entry of pupils to any school profiting from the federal land grants, but made no provision for state or local support. Indiana in its constitution (1816) went the further step of calling on the legislature to set up a complete system of public schools "as soon as circumstances will permit." The schools were to be tuition free. "Circumstances did not permit" until thirty years had elapsed. Also, in 1811, South Carolina established free schools at state expense—one for each member of the House of Representatives. Provision was made for a first call on the schools for "poor orphans and the children of indigent and necessitous parents."

By 1830 the shape of public education began to appear—a system of public control, a method of financing. Within the brief space of a half-dozen years significant steps were taken by Rhode Island, New Jersey, and Pennsylvania, calling for public tax support and, in the case of Rhode Island and Pennsylvania, for small amounts of incentive aid. In the decades immediately following the new states espoused tax-supported education and, in these instances, had already at hand money from the federal land grants to use as a stimulus to local action.

Among the states that had taken action before 1850, there are today only two that provide as much as 50 per cent of the cost of education from state taxation. These are Michigan and South Carolina. None of the original four New England states today exceeds 25 per cent in the support provided by the state.

Late Nineteenth Century

By the middle of the century the issues covering public education had been clarified. Horace Mann in Massachusetts, Henry Barnard in Rhode

Island and Connecticut, Caleb Mills and John Pierce in those extensions of New England—New York, Indiana, and Michigan—had made the decade of the 1840s a decade of crystallization. Late-blooming older states and the new states had a program of education to talk about—not just an appeal to justice and ideals. Accordingly, as a group they were ready to forge ahead. When legislatures acted to provide education, they provided money also—and enough to go a long way in the support of the schools, not just incentive money.

Table 11-1   Per Cent of Support from State and Federal Funds, 1890

Less than 15%	15–19%	30–49%	More than 50%
Colorado (+1)	Connecticut °	Arkansas (+1)	Alabama °
Illinois (+1)	Delaware (+2)	Indiana °	Georgia °
Iowa °	Florida (+2)	Louisiana (+)	California °
Kansas (+1)	Minnesota °	Maine (−1)	Kentucky (−1)
Massachusetts (+)	Missouri °	Maryland °	New Jersey (−2)
Michigan (+3)	Nebraska (−1)	Mississippi (+1)	North Carolina °
New Hampshire °	New York (+1)	Nevada °	South Carolina °
Pennsylvania (+2)	North Dakota °	Utah °	Tennessee °
Rhode Island (+1)	Ohio (+1)		Texas °
South Dakota °	Oregon °		Virginia (−1)
Vermont (+1)	West Virginia (+2)		
	Wisconsin °		
Totals 11	12	8	10

An asterisk indicates that the state fell in the same category 65 years later.

The number in parentheses indicates change in this period, e.g., Kentucky has moved 1 column to the left (−1); Louisiana 1 column to the right (+1); Michigan 3 columns to the right (+3). Only 5 states have moved to a lower-percentage category: Kentucky, New Jersey, Virginia, Maine, and Nebraska; 20 have retained their category; 16 have moved to a higher-percentage category. Only 6 of the 21 states that have changed have bridged one or more categories; 5 of them have moved to higher categories.

Thus we find that in 1890 (by which time tax-supported public education was an accomplished policy in all the states) one-fourth of the states were providing more than half of the costs of public education from state taxation. Dominant in this group were the late bloomers, the states of the South: Alabama, Georgia, North Carolina, South Carolina, Tennessee, Texas, and Virginia. The two others in the group were California, a late comer, and New Jersey, a very temporary exception to the rule. In the 30 to 49 per cent group were to be found at that time Arkansas, Mississippi, Louisiana, and Maryland, together with the late comers, Nevada and Utah. Indiana was also in this group.

These four streams of influence can be seen in the financing practices of the states in 1890 (see Table 11-1). By that time the die was cast. The pattern of 1890 still survives in broad outline at least, as is shown by the comparable statistics for 1956 as they appear in Table 11-2.

Of the eighteen in the two higher-percentage groups in 1890, only two are now found in the lower-percentage group. Of the twenty-nine in the two lower-percentage groups, only seven are now found in the higher-percentage group. Clearly the posture of the several states in regard to state support had already become fairly well fixed by 1890.

Table 11-2 Per Cent of Support from State and Federal Funds, 1956

Less than 15%	15–29%	30–49%	50% or more
Iowa	Connecticut	Arizona	California
Nebraska	Colorado	New York	Washington
New Hampshire	Idaho	Montana	Nevada
South Dakota	Illinois	Wyoming	Michigan
	Kansas	Ohio	Texas
	Maine	Indiana	New Mexico
	Massachusetts	Maryland	Louisiana
	Missouri	Pennsylvania	Delaware
	North Dakota	Utah	Florida
	Vermont	Kentucky	North Carolina
	Wisconsin	Virginia	Oklahoma
	New Jersey	Oregon	West Virginia
	Rhode Island	Minnesota	Tennessee
			Georgia
			South Carolina
			Alabama
			Arkansas
			Mississippi
Totals 4	13	13	18

TRIAL BY EXPANSION, INFLATION, DEPRESSION, AND BETTERMENT

Since 1890 there have been four periods which have subjected the system of school financing to great stress. Three of these were periods when a large increase in the school population combined with economic inflation to make necessary great expansion of school support. Following a fairly mild period of thirty years when the chief call for money had been from increased attendance (1870 to 1900), the first fifteen years of the present century showed a doubling of per pupil costs. This, together with betterment and inflation, resulted in a trebling of the total costs. The periods following World War I and World War II were similar in character and even more rigorous in their demands. The other period of severe stress was the depression of the 1930s. The response of the states to the stresses of these four periods is reviewed here.

Expansion: 1900 to 1915

The comparison of Table 11-1 with Table 11-2 shows that this new system that had only just taken form in the last decades of the nineteenth century had the capacity to hold to the lines laid out.

After this over-all fact, perhaps of greatest significance is the showing of responsiveness on the local level. Down through the years this had been a central concern—to arouse vigorous local interest. The first test period revealed that the task had been well done. From 1900 to 1915 state aid was increased 1½ times, but local support was increased nearly 2 times. The average percentage from state funds dropped from 20.3 to 18.4. This showed responsiveness on both local and state levels. On neither side was there a turning back.

Of course the states varied in their response. Major surgings ahead in state support were made by Delaware, Iowa, Maine, Michigan, New Hampshire, and Tennessee. Faltering was shown by Nebraska, Kansas, North Carolina, Pennsylvania, and South Carolina. But only North Carolina and South Carolina showed an actual decrease in the amount of state aid.

Expansion: 1915 to 1930

For the period 1915 to 1930 the story is much the same. State aid was increased 2½ times, but local support outran it, bringing the average percentage of state aid down from 18.4 in 1915 to 17.3 in 1930. This was in spite of an increase in one state alone equal to the total for all states twenty years before. While there was thus a general decrease, the percentage of state aid was doubled in this period in four states—Florida, Massachusetts, New York, and South Carolina. Two states decreased the gross amount of state aid—Colorado and Montana.

Expansion: Since 1948

For the expansion period following World War II the story is repeated. From 1948 to 1956 state aid increased in gross amount in every state but one. In sixteen states it more than doubled. In spite of this, local support outran state support in twenty-seven states. In every instance where the percentage showed an increase, there had been a major upward movement in state aid.

The Stress of Depression

The same tests applied to the periods of the depression and of World War I seem to indicate that local vigor tends to fall off more than state vigor in times of depression and war. The surging of local action ahead of state action in the two expansion periods between 1900 and 1930 had resulted in the disappearance from the 50 per cent or over group of all the states listed in the 50 per cent or over column in Table 11-2. There was only one state in that column in 1930—Delaware, a newcomer to the list. By 1940, however, this group had built up to nine and by 1948 to sixteen—all those listed in Table 11-1 except Texas, plus one other, Oklahoma. At the other extreme, in 1930 there were twenty states in the less than 15 per cent group, while by 1940 this group had dropped to fourteen and by 1948 to five. While total expenditure increased about 10 per cent from 1930 to 1940, local support was less in 1940 than in 1930.

Response to Stress

It would appear that our systems of support gain over-all stability from the differential responsiveness of state and locality. In good times the localities lead; in bad times the state is a tempering force. Perhaps out of more experience policies will evolve that will keep the two types of agencies of the people in a firmer partnership—alert together to the needs for expansion, alert together to maintain strength in bad times. Whatever the economic picture, the twin facts of our immersion in world affairs and the emergence of new and stronger designs for education out of a half-century of research and experimentation spell for American schools a new period of fiscal challenge. This new period of challenge, as significant as that which sparked the great period of creativity following Horace Mann and Henry Barnard, bids fair to prove an even greater test of the stability and adaptability of our school system than the periods of stress reviewed here. To the writers, at least, this underlines the need for a more stable partnership between state and localities.

PURPOSES AND DESIGN

This section reviews the attempts that have been made to find order and principle in the practices of the forty-eight laboratories in which the people of this country have grappled with the problems of financing education.

Cubberley's Analysis

The first extensive analysis of state-aid practice was made by Cubberley.[1] At the time of his study, practice in the states was almost identical with that summarized in Table 11-1. The time was the beginning of the first three expansion periods discussed in the preceding section.

In reviewing these conditions he came forward with what he considered to be the major activating principles that had emerged—equaliza-

[1] Ellwood P. Cubberley, *School Funds and Their Apportionment*, Bureau of Publications, Teachers College, Columbia University, New York, 1905.

tion and reward for effort. Finding these simple principles in the maze of school practices, he made them available to the educational world and the American people. As a result, many states made more progress in the next two decades than those that had painfully carried through the experiments had been able to make in three-quarters of a century. He proposed as a formula for action that it is wise for the people to use state funds to help economically backward districts. Coming as it did at the beginning of a great period of expansion in the educational program, at a period of rapid concentration of favorable economic factors in some communities and rapid decadence in others, he served these two decades as a cloud by day and a pillar of fire by night.

However, the very rapidity of changes in the educational world and in economic conditions that made Cubberley's 1905 proposals the key to action in that period resulted in their becoming outmoded within fifteen years. Whatever the disabilities of poor districts may have been in 1905, by 1920 they had been greatly multiplied by economic shifts, on the one hand, and by the expanding educational program, on the other. It was no longer possible to build a sound economic base under poor communities by the use of a few hundred dollars of aid. The concentration of wealth had left many sections of our states on a subsistence level. Technological unemployment was increasing the number of children in the elementary school and pressing them blindly on into the high schools. The development of educational science necessitated professional leadership. The old pattern of district organization, typical in America, cracked under the burden.

The people were forced to consider whether or not their district system could safely be entrusted with the state's educational responsibilities. But the decision to change to larger districts involved vast financial questions. There was a tremendous loss involved in recapitalizing one-room rural school houses as corncribs. There was an increase in cost involved in the transportation of children to centers in which attendance was adequate. There was a great increase in cost in obtaining adequate educational personnel. What educators in 1905 thought of as an equalization job involving hundreds of thousands of dollars of state aid emerged as a job involving millions.

As better information services were set up in state offices, and as the survey movement got under way, there was awakened an increasing realization that the process of modernization of education was exasperatingly slow. Updegraff, noting that the granting of special aids for individual functions ignored the economic weakness of vast sections of states, held that reward for effort conceived in terms of individual projects was too narrow in scope. He proposed this formula to give all districts the equivalent of the average of the state in financial ability: the granting of such aid that, whatever the community's tax rate, the total of local taxes and state aid combined would equal the amount which that tax rate would yield in the average community. He did not question Cubberley's reward-for-effort principle, but he dared to look at its implications in a far more realistic fashion than anyone before his time had done. The authors remember it was said of a certain manufacturer that when other men were satisfied to paint signs on fence boards, this man was covering entire barns. Updegraff's proposals bear a similar relationship to the proposals generally made during the second decade of this century.

Practice Outrunning Theory

Four states in that period also went far beyond the implications typically recognized by the educational leaders of the time. The most outstanding example is that of Delaware. The General Education Board made a survey of the state of Delaware in 1918. In it the board stressed the need for special aid to help poor districts in the state, following closely the Cubberley 1905 pattern. In establishing the political feasibility of such a plan, it stressed the fact that education is a state function. A group of interested citizens in Delaware, after considering the problem, recommended the support of a relatively high cost program entirely from state funds. This plan was enacted into law in 1921 while educational leaders were still giving great stress to the question: What percentage of the total cost should be supplied from state funds? Action of a similar nature but not so far-reaching was taken in Maryland in 1922. Here again a survey made by the General Education Board was a stimulating factor that was outrun in its realization. After reviewing the inequalities that resulted from the distribution of the state's funds that was then in effect, the chief recommendation of the survey was that more local effort be made than that required as a condition for participation. As a result, the equalization law was enacted. In it the question of effort originally tied up with the notion of special aids was sublimated to mean general local support. All communities were required to levy a comparatively low minimum tax, which was then supplemented by state-aid funds up to an amount determined by computing the cost of teacher's salaries according to a set schedule and adding to it a certain percentage for other current expenditures.

The same year, under the leadership of State Superintendent Finegan, ably supported by Senator Edmonds, the state of Pennsylvania made provision for the financing of a minimum program by means of a combination of state and local support. The minimum program was computed in terms of teachers' salaries. Instead of supplementing the local tax as in the case of the Maryland law, however, the districts of the state were divided into wealth categories, the amount given each wealth group being inversely related to the wealth per teacher.

This eventful year also saw the extension of the unique California plan of large state grants on a per pupil basis, supplemented by a mandatory county contribution, which raised the funds available to local districts from state and county sources to a total exceeding all funds available then in the average American school district. All four of these laws went far beyond any of the equalization laws that had previously been passed. Where the state support was liberal, the local support required was either nothing, as in the case of Delaware, or relatively low.

In contrast with this we may cite the more typical equalization law that had previously developed, taking Indiana as an example. In this state the equalization law passed in 1905 provided for state aid to supplement the yield of the maximum tax sufficiently to pay for the minimum school term. Here, as in the case of the Delaware, Maryland, and Pennsylvania laws, was a recognition of the minimum-program concept. The chief difference in theory was the relatively high rate of local taxation required for participation in equalization aid. In Pennsylvania, Delaware, and Maryland, aided communities could supplement the state equalization aid without difficulty if they so desired. In the case of Indiana this was legally impossible. In Pennsylvania and Maryland the extent of the minimum program was determined by a more or less objective index of cost per unit of educational service (educational need). In Indiana the definition of what should constitute an eight-months' program was left to the discretion of the state department of education.

During this same period other states were active in reorganizing their financial programs. Michigan and Minnesota introduced primitive equalization plans in 1921. Some of the pioneer states made worthwhile improvements over their first attempts, notably New Hampshire in 1921, Indiana in 1922, and North Carolina in 1922 and 1923.

Strayer and Haig—The Equalization Principle

There was obviously a need once more for taking stock of the developments. This need was met by the Educational Finance Inquiry (1921 to 1924) in a survey of nationwide scope. It must be remembered that at that time the steps taken in Pennsylvania, Maryland, and Delaware were not thought of as having particularly great significance. They were commonly appraised in terms of the 1905 Cubberley pattern. Updegraff's work, alone in making an attempt to establish a new frame of reference, had just reached its highest point in the report of the New York Rural Survey in 1922.

The Educational Finance Inquiry was interested in a broad study of the facts of school finance. It attacked this problem by making intensive, descriptive studies of conditions in New York, Iowa, California, and Illinois. These were supplemented by a nationwide study of fiscally independent and dependent cities and of unit costs in higher education.

As one examines the aspects of these studies that bear on the role of the state in financing education, he notes the study by McGaughy on the fiscal independence of cities [2] and the guidance given to appraisal efforts by state officers through studies of unit costs and other methods of portraying financial data. But he finds only sketchy materials looking toward a more adequate frame of reference for considering what should be done through state agencies in the financing of local school programs.

The analysis of the California, Illinois, and Iowa data did not result in the forming of a conceptual pattern superior to that which had emerged from the Cubberley 1905 analysis. But almost hidden in the New York study (Strayer and Haig), in the chapter on "The Size of the Unit for School Support and the Problem of State Aid," was a new frame of reference which gave significant meaning to the Delaware, Maryland, and Pennsylvania acts and a conceptual basis for much of the intense activity in reorganizing state financial relationships during the next fifteen years. At the end of the chapter there appear two pages under the subtitle, "Equalization of Educational Opportunity," in which we find the conceptual pattern that has had and today is continuing to have such far-reaching significance. Considering the part that these two pages had to play in the succeeding years, one is surprised to find them given so little emphasis. We repeat them here in full,[3] because they represent one of the milestones in the conceptual evolution of the relationship of state and local agencies in exercising the responsibility of all the people with respect to public education.

There exists today and has existed for many years a movement which has come to be known as the "equalization of educational opportunity" or the "equalization of school support." These phrases are interpreted in various ways. In its most extreme form the interpretation is somewhat as follows: The state should insure equal educational facilities to every child within its borders at a uniform effort throughout the state in terms of the burden of taxation; the tax burden of education should throughout the state be uniform in relation to tax-paying ability, and the provision for schools should be uniform in relation to the educable population desiring education. Most of the supporters of this proposi-

[2] J. R. McGaughy, The Fiscal Administration of City School Systems, Report of the Educational Finance Inquiry, vol. V, The Macmillan Company, New York, 1924.

[3] George D. Strayer and Robert M. Haig, The Financing of Education in the State of New York, The Educational Finance Inquiry Commission, New York, 1924, by permission of The Macmillan Company, pp. 173–175.

tion, however, would not preclude any particular community from offering at its own expense a particularly rich and costly educational program. They would insist that there be an adequate minimum offered everywhere, the expense of which should be considered a prior claim on the state's economic resources.

This proposal assumes, of course, that the interest of the state in providing an equal educational opportunity for each child outweighs the possible economic objection that the operation of such a plan involves a subsidy to economically backward communities, with its attendant possibilities of misdirected economic effort. It is proposed in this section to examine some of the fiscal implications of this principle.

To carry into effect the principle of "equalization of educational opportunity" and "equalization of school support" as commonly understood it would be necessary (1) to establish schools or make other arrangements sufficient to furnish the children in every locality within the state with equal educational opportunities up to some prescribed minimum; (2) to raise the funds necessary for this purpose by local or state taxation adjusted in such manner as to bear upon the people in all localities at the same rate in relation to their tax-paying ability; and (3) to provide adequately either for the supervision and control of all the schools, or for their direct administration, by a state department of education.

The simplest method of financing the school system to achieve the aims of the principle would be through uniform state-wide taxes on ability-to-pay. Such a proposal, however, encounters serious obstacles such as the difficulties of centralizing the administration of school funds, in large states particularly, without deadening local interest and initiative, and the difficulties of developing a suitable revenue system with the necessary central control of assessments and rates. The strength of position in favor of local control of schools and of school finances makes it desirable to inquire what measure of responsibility for financial support may be left to the localities, if the aims of the principle are to be gained. The essentials are that there should be uniformity in the rates of school taxation levied to provide the satisfactory minimum offering and that there be such a degree of state control over the expenditure of the proceeds of school taxes as may be necessary to insure that the satisfactory minimum offering shall be made at a reasonable cost. Since costs vary from place to place in the state, and bear diverse relationships to the tax-paying abilities of the various districts, the achievement of uniformity would involve the following:

1. The local school tax in support of the satisfactory minimum offering would be levied in each district at a rate which would provide the necessary funds for that purpose in the richest district.

2. This richest district then might raise all of its school money by means of the local tax, assuming that a satisfactory tax, capable of being locally administered, could be devised.

3. Every other district could be permitted to levy a local tax at the same rate and apply the proceeds toward the costs of schools, but—

4. Since the rate is uniform, this tax would be sufficient to meet the costs only in the richest districts and the deficiencies would be made up by state subventions.

The Adaptability Principle: Local Initiative and Tax Reform

The first application of the Strayer-Haig definition of equalization, in the actual development of a program in New York State, followed closely upon the work of the Educational Finance Inquiry. This plan, developed by Mort under the sponsorship of Strayer and Haig, proposed a program to cost $70 per weighted pupil, or approximately $1,900 per elementary classroom unit. It was proposed to provide such state aid to supplement a tax of 36.4 cents on $100, the required funds to be obtained from additional revenue. The rate for the local communities, 36.4 cents, was set at the point that would bring about an equalization of the program not already supported by state funds. The program actually adopted by the New York Legislature brought about the type of equalization recommended. The bill provided also for an increase in flat grants, the net effect of which was to give more aid than equalization would require. As a result of the work of the Friedsam Commission,[4] this law was changed a year later to provide for an increase in the minimum level and for a reduction of the local rate of contribution. The net effect of this change was to bring large increases in aid, particularly to the able districts.

This law, it will be noted, provided for much more aid than was demanded by the equalization principle as defined by Strayer and Haig. As a matter of fact, if equalization had been the sole purpose of the state-aid law, there would have been justification for withdrawing all aid to the ablest communities instead of increasing it. The increase to able districts was justified as a tax measure rather than for any known educational implications. People of the state said, in effect, "We wish to raise a considerable amount of money by state taxes and send that money back to the communities for their use for local functions of government or for relief of their local property taxes."

During the next half-dozen years this same problem was met over and over again in other states. Commissions in state after state facing the need for getting more aid for the poor districts could not accept it as reasonable to take money away from able districts and thus actually increase the burden on their property tax. The question was not entirely one of taxation. Faced with the actual problem of taking aid away from the able communities, it was difficult to see how this could be done without harming the educational program. Naturally the question was raised as to whether it was necessary, in order to improve conditions in one part of the state, actually to make conditions worse in other parts

[4] "Financing Education in Cities," *Report of Special Commission Appointed to Study the Subject*, Michael Friedsam, Chairman, Legislative Document 92, J. B. Lyon Company, Printers, Albany, N.Y., March 22, 1926.

of the state. While the Educational Finance Inquiry had awakened grave doubts as to the desirability of reward for effort, there were few who wanted to take the responsibility of saying that the people, through their state agencies, should actually penalize effort. Gradually there developed the realization that taking money away from able districts and thereby throwing extra burdens on the property tax was, in effect, handicapping local initiative.

Cubberley had said that it was desirable to encourage communities to do more than they otherwise would do to improve their education. He had supported, for this purpose, the payment of special grants-in-aid for particular functions. The Educational Finance Inquiry showed that such grants-in-aid tended to go to the able districts rather than to the poor districts. Hence, use of money for special aids at all comparable with money used for equalization tended to offset the equalizing effects.

But whatever was done about special grants-in-aid as a device, it became clear that there was a basic underlying principle that could not be ignored. A search was started to find a more acceptable interpretation of the phenomena of state stimulation through special aid. A careful study of the various surveys shows a gradual mounting of the realization that the state has an interest in the schools of the abler communities which transcends its interest in the better education of those children who are immediately benefited. At the same time, those who had accepted for nearly two decades the idea of payment for effort as a fundamental principle did not accept without a struggle the Strayer and Haig conclusion that payment for effort should be ruled out. Mort proposed that the principle underlying the payment-for-effort idea was sound, but that payment for effort was only one device for serving this underlying principle. Following this lead, Neulen's investigation [5] showed that many states had made progress in the introduction and diffusion of new ideas without the use of special aid. It was an easy step from there to the proposal that the state should be concerned with all ways and means of promoting progress. This notion was proposed as the "promotion principle" in the Kansas Survey,[6] as the "efficiency principle" in the Missouri Survey,[7] and as the "progress principle" in the Colorado Survey.[8]

[5] Lester N. Neulen, *State Aid for Educational Projects in the Public Schools*, Bureau of Publications, Teachers College, Columbia University, New York, 1928.

[6] Kansas School Code Commission, *Some Problems Confronting the School Code Commission, with Supporting Data*, vol. I, Topeka, Kan., June, 1928.

[7] Missouri Survey Commission, *Financing Education in Missouri*, State Department of Education, Jefferson City, Mo., 1929.

[8] Colorado Education Association, "Report of the Reconstruction of the System of Financing Public Schools in the State of Colorado," *Bulletin*, vol. 4, no. 2, Denver, 1931.

In the light of these analyses it became clearer that our whole emphasis on local control and operation of schools had as a very important purpose a potential contribution to adaptability. This was what people meant when they said that local control and support encouraged experimentation. These measures embolden communities to try new ways of meeting old problems and to contrive ways of meeting newly emerging problems. What had been dismissed by a few vague phrases as experimentation began to take on broader meanings. Questions were raised concerning the best ways of financing local initiative as well as the best ways of financing a minimum program.

The National Survey of School Finance followed its chapter on equalization of burden with a chapter on financial provisions for local initiative. This chapter pointed out the hampering effects on local initiative of tax-limitation laws and of central budgetary reviewing boards.[9] It pointed to the necessity of realizing that education is a function of all the people and may be controlled by their agencies as they see fit, but that there is no necessary identity between the agency of the people that collects the taxes and the agency of the people that determines the nature of the educational program. Finally, it made far-reaching proposals with respect to responsibility of the people for seeing that an adequate minimum program of education is supplied without exhausting the local taxpaying power necessary to support local initiative over and beyond this minimum program.

One of the most far-reaching implications claimed for the adaptability principle has to do with local initiative. Throughout this period of reconstruction of state finance, the question of allocation of controls to local and state governments has been to the fore. Most of the proposals for change in control would, in the net, narrow the scope of local initiative. It appeared in the earlier studies that local initiative was one of the chief devices by which the adaptability principle was served. Assuming this to be true, the financial structure of public education should be such as to stimulate, not hamper, local initiative. The minimum program should be high enough to favor rapid diffusion of proved adaptations, and there should be a considerable number of districts with expenditure level sufficiently high to provide conditions favorable for experimentation (well-trained teachers and supervisors, excellent working materials, free funds, varied special services, and small classes).

It is not sufficient to equalize burden; in addition, it is necessary to see that the property tax, which supports local initiative, is not unduly burdened as compared with other taxes. It is not sufficient to have an adequate tax base; the locality must have tax leeway, hence tax-limitation

[9] American Council on Education, "State Support for Public Education," *Report of the National Survey of School Finance*, Washington, 1933.

laws should be opposed. Nor is it sufficient to have tax leeway and an adequate tax base, but it is necessary also that the local authorities have final judgment with respect to a wide range of expenditures. Hence, it is essential to oppose central budgetary reviewing and the type of school auditing that would give auditors power to disallow items in the school budget.

In brief, the adaptability principle serves as a check on the other principles, particularly the equalization and prudential principles. It demands that we consider the financial health of the abler districts as well as that of the poorer districts of the state and thus frustrate the tendency to equalize down as well as up. It defines the bounds within which the prudential principle may operate, frustrating the attempts to place prudential management uppermost in the relation of the central agencies with the localities.

Updegraff and Morrison—Other Approaches

Two outstanding variations from the main stream of thinking in the field may not be omitted from any adequate consideration of this problem: the work of Updegraff and the work of Henry Morrison.

In the period following Cubberley's study in 1905, and preceding the report of the Educational Finance Inquiry, the most stimulating thinker in this field was Harlan Updegraff. His work, centered around the years 1919 and 1922, was associated with studies made in Pennsylvania and New York.[10] In his attempts to implement the interpretation of Cubberley's payment-for-effort and equalization principles, he departed from the customary interpretation and drew new and more daring inferences. He tied these inferences closely with a plan for equalization more thoroughgoing than any proposed by the theoretical workers in the field, surpassed though they were by the plans put into operation in Maryland and Delaware contemporaneously with his studies.

Cubberley called the payment of part of the cost of a new activity "payment for effort." This was a poetical interpretation of these phenomena, meaning no more to most interpreters than the phenomena on which it was based. Updegraff, however, taking the expression of payment for effort apart from the phenomena which it reflected, accepted it as a fundamental principle and built a logical structure upon a more literal interpretation of the word "effort." He showed that effort was

[10] Harlan Updegraff, *Application of State Funds to the Aid of Local Schools,* University of Pennsylvania, Bulletin 1, 1919, University of Pennsylvania Press, Philadelphia, 1919; also (with L. A. King) *Survey of the Fiscal Policies of the State of Pennsylvania in the Field of Education,* Part II, Citizens' Committee on Finances of Pennsylvania, 1922, and *Rural School Survey of New York State: Financial Support,* Joint Commitee on Rural Schools, Ithaca, N.Y., 1922.

more truly measured in terms of tax rate than by the offering of a new activity, thus foreshadowing the findings of the Educational Finance Inquiry. He proposed a plan for New York which called upon the state to provide financial conditions such that any effort on the part of a community of less than average wealth would yield tax returns equal to those of the same effort exercised by the communities of average wealth. Here was the merging of the equalization principle and the payment-for-effort principle, which in effect was much farther reaching than the equalization principle as defined by Strayer and Haig. Looking back on it in the light of our present interpretation of the payment-for-effort phenomena in terms of adaptability, it has many challenging implications which will doubtless cause it to come up again and again for consideration as this field develops. Interpreted in terms of the minimum implications of Strayer and Haig's definition of equalization, it means penalizing communities that go below the minimum in proportion to their effort, and rewarding those that go beyond in proportion to their effort.

The proposals of Morrison given in his *School Revenue* [11] were foreshadowed by his Illinois study [12] made as a part of the Educational Finance Inquiry. In this he was much concerned with terminal costs—the idea that when the laggards were brought up to standard, all schools would spend alike. It is but a short step from such a consideration to a picture of a state system of public education completely financed up to such a satisfactory level that the question of permitting variation above this level becomes an academic one. It was such a proposal that he made in his *School Revenue*, building it upon the concept of a citizenship school. Here was an independent consideration of educational objectives, building not on tradition but on the concept of formulating a structure of educational finance that would truly meet the educational needs of our society.

One cannot consider this proposal without the hint that perhaps he is foreshadowing a condition that will exist some time in the future and without the feeling that our emphasis upon local taxation may be a function of the transitional period in which we are tremendously concerned with bringing 90 per cent of American schools up to a really satisfactory level. While one may doubt whether we shall ever come to a time when local initiative will not have a part to play in bringing about continued adaptation of schools to changing needs, it is not difficult to conceive of the possibility that the concern for local taxing

[11] Henry C. Morrison, *School Revenue,* University of Chicago Press, Chicago, 1930.
[12] Henry C. Morrison, *The Financing of Public Schools in the State of Illinois,* Report of the Educational Finance Inquiry Commission, vol. IX, The Macmillan Company, New York, 1924.

power will be of much less consequence once America has met fully its problems of financing public education.

It is not inconceivable, then, that the immediate acceptability of the conservative interpretation of equalization and payment for effort given us by Cubberley was in a sense a first step ahead of an intolerable condition being made constantly more intolerable by the acceleration of differentials in ability among various communities in the state; that the Strayer and Haig demands, much more drastic than those of Cubberley, were no more ahead of their day than Cubberley's were ahead of his. How long will the Strayer and Haig interpretation be in the forefront? Is the time approaching when the drastic recommendations of Updegraff may prove acceptable toward promoting a more rapid mopping-up process with respect to the financing of school systems laggard in attitude or forced always to be lagging by the sharp increase of costs due to inflation, population increase, and betterment? When such a mopping-up process nears completion, will the pattern proposed by Morrison become applicable? While it is unlikely that either of these proposals in their present form will prove to be the ultimate pattern, the present writers suggest that it is equally unlikely that they will prove to be as futile as the results in this brief period of their history would now make them appear.

Tax Reform

Running through the foregoing discussions are issues of equalization, taxation, and local initiative. In recent years the special problems of taxation have come more into the open. The tax issues appear to be more insistent in their demands at present than either of the others. When the result of tax reform is an increase in the percentage of state aid it would appear to have no necessary effects on the equalization and local initiative issues.

The percentage of state aid does not seem to be significant in its effects on local vigor. As noted earlier, the position of the states was fairly well established by the methods used in the early years of their operation of school systems. Tests made on expenditure level, ability considered, and effort in terms of the percentage of personal income spent on public education do not favor any percentage group particularly. Apart from early tradition, the factor most affecting the allocation of support among local communities appears to be the evolution of the taxing system in the states. To a lesser degree in its effect on the percentage of state aid, it is the concern with wholesomeness of taxing conditions in communities of less than average wealth—equalization. Taken alone, equalization in this sense would rarely if ever require a percentage greater than 30 per cent of the total cost of education in a state with vigorous local support. Any marked change in percentage in any state is bound to be more a tax problem than an educational problem.

This century has seen the development of state aid in large amounts for municipal government as well as for schools. Here there was no appeal to the principle so widely used in education—that a state function was involved. As we review the history of this movement we see it following a long period of adjusting revenue to needs by transferring functions such as highways and welfare to the state and federal levels of government.

This might well have occurred in education, as it did to a degree in such matters as teacher education, had there not been strong resistance to the idea of centralizing education. As the transfer of functions began to lag behind the need, states resorted to shared taxes and per capita grants to municipalities. A difference was that the "anxious mother" attitude associated with special aids to education was not in the background of municipal government. While the making of educational grants was hailed as an opportunity to bring about this or that reform by compliance requirements, the aids to municipal government tended to be free of restrictions.

Eventually economists made their voices heard as to the cause of the clamor—the need either to shift governmental functions to state-level (or national-level) government, where a major part of practical power to tax our economy lies, or the evolution of some plan for central taxation with the returns made available to the local governments in the communities from which the tax money comes. This is exactly what had been happening over a century, with particular emphasis on the centralization of functions of municipal government.

At the present time many students of the problem are holding that we have approached the limit of practical centralization of municipal government. Within the states we must either centralize education or find some major way to supplement the property tax in reaching the resources of the communities. Within the nation, they hold, we must either centralize government away from the states or find some way for the federal government to collect taxes for the states.

In this development it is clear that to many protagonists of tax reform education is but a pawn in a game of developing a better tax system. Accordingly the result is proposals for federal taxes shared with the states for all purposes, or state taxes shared with municipalities or school districts without regard to equalization. This would be fairly satisfactory if it were not for the problem of central responsibility for a foundation program—within the states, certainly, and almost as compulsively among our states as a national group.

Centrally collected taxes could be returned to the jurisdiction of origin on some index of taxpaying ability. But this would not care for that part of the clamor that rises from poor districts in states and from poor states. Seeking to get around this without close analysis of the need, such proposals as that made by Ruml call for a distribution on a per capita basis.[13] On closer analysis it would appear to be wiser to return the money to the states (or communities) of origin and then make a straightforward complementary attack on the equalization problem. To deal with the equalization problem by a flat grant would require money in vastly greater amounts, perhaps in greater amounts than could be justified in the interest of tax reform.

This seems to be where the tax reform movement gets us. It has great fiscal strength; it is independent of the yearning to shape destinies in detail; it is not considerate of equalization. The first two of these characteristics are of fateful importance. They are characteristics that are lacking in many of the educational aid laws.

New Challenges to Scope and Purpose

Two relatively recent developments should be noted here. The first is a challenge to the scope of public support, just as the Civilian Conservation Corps was in the 1930s. The second raises interesting questions as to potentialities for regional cooperative action.

Aid to Students. A development worth attention was initiated by the acts of Congress providing aid to veterans attending school. So far as the support of public institutions is concerned, this was of little positive fiscal importance. By adding to attendance it increased the costs at the expense of the states and communities. Perhaps it is not stretching the point too far to classify state and federal scholarships for able students on the college level in the same category. It is at least within the realm of conjecture that a variation of this scholarship idea may develop to indemnify young people now held in the schools against their readiness or willingness, as a device for keeping them off the labor market. Theirs is a problem that remains unsolved. Will payments that will make it possible for them to hold up their heads as young adults be one of the answers?

The central question here may well be whether this is the beginning of a significant move to extend the scope of public support for education to include living costs. The point has often been made that schools cannot be effectively free until the time that the state requires youngsters to give up from productive work, for whatever reason, and to spend in school—presumably to the benefit of all and sundry—is compensated for directly to the student. The point brings to mind the demands made

[13] Beardsley Ruml, "Long Term Problems of Public School Finance," address given before the American Association of School Administrators, April, 1955.

by parents in a remote Western community many years ago that the school board provide spending money to children living at home comparable to that made available to children who were housed in dormitories at public expense, in lieu of transportation.

Interstate Cooperation. In addition to these two a movement fiscal in character carried on among states of the Southeast is worthy of note. By agreement entered into under the auspices of The Southern Regional Education Board, several states undertake specialized developments in their universities in such a way that all may be served by a specialized offering in one of them. A similar cooperative development among school districts within counties or ad hoc intermediate units suggests, if we may indulge in a little brainstorming, the possibility that some of the specialized offerings found in the public schools of our largest cities might, by interstate cooperation, be made available in less populous states, perhaps utilizing some of the governmental forms that have been evolving in connection with such interstate agencies as the Port of New York Authority.

Recapitulation of Purposes

In way of summary it may be stated that whether we view state-aid practice today in the various states or the historical development of state aid in any one of the older states, we shall find it designed to serve some or all of the following purposes:

1. The assuring of a defensible level of support for communities that cannot provide such a level of support with their own tax resources.

2. The equalizing of the burden among communities for a generally accepted program, adopted either through local initiative or through mandates or influence of central agencies.

3. The stimulating of curriculum or service developments in neglected areas of the program that is already established.

4. The organizing of schools or services for the maintenance of which many present districts are not well adapted.

5. The stimulating of local vigor in support of education.

6. The modernizing of the local tax base by (*a*) broadening, through state aid or local non-property taxes, to take account of economic developments, and (*b*) improving the tax machinery to assure more justice in such tax bases as the property tax.

7. The stimulation of "lighthouse communities" and special experimentation.

8. The providing of an instrument for enforcing compliance with state law.

All the issues in our list of eight are important today, but there are four overarching issues: assuring a defensible level of support for communities that cannot provide adequate support from their local resources (1), modernizing the tax base (6), the stimulation of local vigor (5), and the provision of lighthouses (7). Of these, the assurance of a defensible level of support makes inescapable demands upon state aid and federal aid. Modernizing the tax base may take advantage of state aid as a choice and may even come into the federal-aid picture. These two considerations set the framework of state aid. Carrying out the first purpose (1) involves equalization of burden (2). Variations in control provisions or special earmarking may be made to serve certain of the other purposes, particularly the stimulation of curriculum or service developments (3 and 4), and the very existence of state aid provides an instrument that may be used to enforce mandatory laws (8).

To these, of course, we must add a ninth: making education "effectively free" by maintenance grants to pupils. Whether this last is a passing incident or a speck of cloud that is destined to spread across the sky is a matter of conjecture.

These purposes are being shaped into a theory that gives them functional balance. This theory for our times accepts the clear-cut division of state responsibility from local responsibility by the defined foundation level. It calls for a foundation level that will assure wholesome financial conditions for the support of education adequate for our day and time. It calls for the support of the foundation program in such a way that the burden is equalized among communities and among tax bases so that adequate leeway is left for local initiative beyond the foundation program —a matter of special emphasis in the Strayer and Haig report. In the consideration of the balance on tax bases it calls for state policy that will bring about balance, not within the public school system alone, but within all public services which utilize the same tax bases as education, thus assuring even more firmly a place for local responsibility in educational matters. It sets the metes and bounds of special aids. It closes off the blind alley of oversimplified solutions such as that which has consumed the thinking of so many—the idea that there is a set optimum percentage of the cost of education to be paid by the state, applicable to all states.

In this theory we see the recognition of the strength of the long-time efforts along two streams: (1) the improvement of the wholesomeness of conditions for the production of education locally and (2) the state concern with the improvement of education in detail, whether through special aids, provision of state supervisors, or other means. It calls for the removal of barriers to the free exercise of local responsibility. In doing this it does not call for neglect of prudential considerations but, rather, for the keeping of such prudential features as state auditing, specific laws, state rules, and the operation of state agencies within the bounds where they do not become barriers to the achievement of the central purposes of the educational system.

In contrast with this, the Cubberley theory of small amounts of money for special aids and aid to the needy, the Updegraff emphasis on rewarding vigor, the Morrison concern with spelling out the implications of terminal costs and/or complete state support, the tax specialists' concern with tax adjustment without regard to function—all loom up as inadequate approaches to the fiscal aspects of state educational policy.

DISTRIBUTION METHODS AND PATTERNS

Practical state-aid systems more or less successfully seek a balance in achievement of their purposes by a combination of distribution methods. Unhappily or not, no distribution method bears any close relationship with any recognized purpose. That there is still a great deal of unprofitable discussion of state aid in terms of these methods as such is probably due in part to the dramatic writings of Cubberley in the early years of this century.

The simplest method, the flat grant, bristles with implications for equalization; but it has even greater implication for adjusting the tax base. By the selection of the unit on which it is based—as, for example, using attendance instead of enrollment—it may have elements of incentive in it. So-called equalization methods are often tax measures rather than equalization measures, and they may be shot through with incentives and punishments.

Accordingly it is wise to avoid associating a particular purpose with a form of distribution. Rather, it is wise to assess each proposal for distribution, whether a simple or combination method, in terms of all the purposes. Above all, it is wise to disassociate the concept of values from distribution methods. Values should be associated with the purposes served. Their evaluation requires more than a superficial inspection in terms of method per se.

Methods of Distribution

The three dominant distribution methods are discussed briefly below. They are treated in detail in Chapters 12, 13, 14, and 15.

Flat Grants and Shared Taxes. Aid distributed on some population basis (e.g., pupils in attendance, pupils enrolled, weighted pupil cost units, school census, total population) or wealth. More strictly, "flat grants" refer to distributions in terms of some population base; shared taxes refer to distribution in direct proportion to wealth.

Special Aids (Grants-in-aid, Subventions, Incentive Aids). Payments in all or in part for some specific phase of education, e.g., salaries of supervisors, payments for classes for mentally retarded or bright children, partial payment of superintendent's salary, payments for adult education classes.

Equalization Aid. Aid paid roughly in inverse proportion to wealth, usually the excess of some predetermined cost figure (e.g., x dollars per pupil) over the yield of a given local tax.

Patterns of State-Aid Systems

In practice the various methods of distributing state aid are now pretty well merged into systems. These systems can be classified under the five patterns listed here. The differentiating characteristic is "apparent" (not necessarily actual) emphasis on equalization. In this list no separate category is given for incentive aids. In one way or another incentive aids are injected into all five patterns. No state system could be classed as a system of incentives. If the list were to embrace the federal aids to education, there would be justification for an added category, incentive aids. Also, tax sharing is not listed separately. As a distinct method it does not appear in any of the systems of aid to education; however, as is explained in Chapter 12, it, like the incentive idea, is embraced in greater or less degree in all the five patterns given here. All states give some aid that can be considered tax sharing money.

If categories for shared taxes and incentives were provided they would lead the list, with shared taxes coming first, incentives second, flat grants third.

As is brought out in the chapters which follow, such a classification of state-aid systems, while it approximates the frame of reference that has been dominant since Cubberley made his classic analysis, is of little utility in studying functions.

Here are the five patterns:

1. *Flat grants—only educational need considered, differences in ability disregarded.* Distribution of state money on some basis that more or less accurately reflects the size of the job to be done. Distribution of so much per pupil (attendance, enrollment, or census) or so much per teacher employed are examples. Distribution in terms of expenditure pupil units (Chapter 7) would be an attempt to enhance the justice of the distribution. Payment of the full cost of a foundation program, with the cost determined by approved budgets (as in Alaska, Delaware, Hawaii, North Carolina, and South Carolina), could be classed as a form of flat grant. Burke separates this "full-cost" group which he designates "completely state-supported equalization programs." [14]

---

[14] Arvid J. Burke, *Financing Public Schools in the United States*, Harper & Brothers, New York, 1957, pp. 434ff.

The larger the flat grant, the more consequential the injustices of distribution bases that fall short of being good measures as developed in Chapter 7, and the more consequential the injustices arising from warpings of the measure to reward certain types of behavior.

2. *Flat grants plus "equalization"—both need and ability considered.* Equalization-type formula but with the flat grants and incentive grants not charged against the communities in computing equalization aid. Under such a plan the true foundation-program level is the sum of the flat grants and the foundation program as computed for equalization. Deviation of the distribution base for flat grants from a true measure of educational need is added to the errors that arise from similar deviations in the method of computing the cost of the foundation program.

3. *Flat grants with "equalization"—both need and ability considered but flat grants nullified.* Equalization-type formula apparently supplemented by flat grants, or by incentive aids that through time have taken on the character of flat grants, but actually not so supplemented since the flat grants are charged against the foundation program along with the specified local support when equalization aid is being computed. Under this plan errors in the measurement of educational need that is used as a distribution base for flat grants affect only those receiving aid solely on the flat-grant basis.

4. *"Equalization"—both need and ability considered, plus minimum guarantee.* Equalization-type formula supplemented by a minimum guarantee for the able districts and usually supplemented by minor incentive aids. The effects are the same as in the case of Plan 3.

5. *"Equalization" only—both need and ability considered.* Equalization-type formula, usually supplemented by minor incentive aids.

Table 11-3 lists the states according to the formula type they were following when this book went to press. The states are grouped according to the percentage of support supplied from state and federal funds in 1956. Thirty-nine states make some use of the need and ability formula (Columns 2, 3, 4, and 5). Only six of these states use it as an outright supplement to flat grants (Column 2). One-third have dispensed with flat grants (Columns 4 and 5), and one-half have nullified the influence of flat grants on districts receiving equalization aid (Column 3). Seventeen of the fifty states still maintain flat grants as the sole distribution method (Column 1) or in a compartment by themselves (Column 2). The other thirty-three have either eliminated them entirely (Columns 4 and 5) or in some degree nullified their differential effects (Column 3).

Purposes Served not Discernible from These Patterns

What all this leads up to is that there is no rule-of-thumb method for judging what state-aid systems do, either by the character of the

Table 11-3 State-aid Patterns in Practice in the Various States in 1958

| State and federal support 1956, per cent | Flat grants only—ability disregarded (1) | Flat grants plus equalization | | Flat grants nullified in equalization distribution | | Equalization plus minimum guarantee (4) | Equalization—no minimum guarantee, except incentive aids in most cases (5) |
		Flat grant greater (2a)	Equalization greater (2b)	Flat grant greater (3a)	Equalization greater (3b)		
Above 75	Delaware Hawaii South Carolina				Alabama		Georgia (4.0) † New Mexico *
50–74	Alaska North Carolina	Nevada	Mississippi	California Louisiana Texas Washington	Arkansas Michigan Oklahoma	Tennessee	Florida (0) West Virginia (1.4)
30–49	Arizona	Kentucky		Maryland Minnesota Ohio Virginia Wyoming Oregon	Montana	New York	Indiana (1.5) Pennsylvania (1.5) Utah (2.8)
15–29	Colorado Connecticut Vermont Nebraska		Wisconsin	Rhode Island North Dakota	Kansas Illinois *	Idaho Missouri New Jersey	Maine (9.3) Massachusetts (6.0)
Below 15	Iowa South Dakota New Hampshire						

Need and ability patterns

* Classification doubtful (Type). † Per cent aids classed here as incentive aids, outside equalization.

distribution methods used or the percentage of the cost of education paid by the state.

All five of these patterns involve equalization; all five as they are now operating serve the function of helping communities get access to their own resources; all five in greater or less degree are used to shape the educational program by earmarking the expenditures, by the choice of methods of computing the cost of the foundation program, or by compliance provisions.

As to the percentage paid by the state, each group, except the group of four states that supply 15 per cent or less of the cost from state revenues, range across the board as to pattern of distribution. Large state support could rationally be associated with the flat-grant distribution method, small state support with equalization emphasis. Yet it is of interest that three of the six states in which more than 75 per cent of the cost is paid by the state do not rely on flat grants, and only two of the four states with less than 15 per cent make even minor use of the need and ability formula.

The three chapters that follow seek to come to grips with the basic issues involved.

SUMMARY

Four lines of influence upon the evolution of programs for state aid to education have been identified. Strands from each of them can be found in our practices and controlling traditions today. One strand came from the states that were experimenting with public education in the eighteenth century; one from the states that initiated their programs early in the nineteenth century; the third from the states carved out of the Northwest Territory; and the fourth from the states of the Southeast which delayed the establishment of public education until after the War between the States.

The states that introduced tax-supported education in the eighteenth century depended largely on local support; those that introduced tax-supported education during the first half of the nineteenth century gave somewhat more impetus to support through state aid; those that initiated their public school systems in the latter half of the nineteenth century went still farther in state support.

The pattern of state and local support was fairly well fixed by 1890. Of the eighteen in the two higher-percentage groups in 1890, only two are now found in the lower-percentage group. Of the twenty-nine in the two lower-percentage groups, only seven are now found in the higher-percentage group. Clearly the posture of the several states in regard to state support had already become established by 1890.

The responsiveness of the finance system to stresses of expansion and depression since 1890 indicates that the systems gain stability from the differential responsiveness of state and locality. In good times the localities lead; in bad times the state is a tempering force.

At the turn of the century Cubberley sought to find order and principle in the practice of the various states. He settled for two basic purposes, equalization and reward for effort. During the next two decades practice in some states gave far more emphasis to equalization than Cubberley had envisioned. In the early twenties Strayer and Haig came forward with a clear-cut definition of the equalization concept, expressed as the equalization of the support of a minimum program for all communities through state aid. The Strayer and Haig concept, more or less supplemented by considerations of the adaptability issue, gained a wide following.

Two nonconforming proposals came to the fore in this period. Updegraff (1922) proposed reward in proportion to tax effort; Morrison (1930) proposed a system of complete state support.

The present authors propose an approach to analysis of state-aid systems that takes into account net provision for equalization, special problems of taxation, and local initiative. They propose that this analysis be applied to municipal aids as well as educational aids.

New challenges are being faced by the developments in aid to students and in interstate cooperation.

While state-aid systems may be classified according to their superficial characteristics, such classification gives but little help in identifying their actual effects in solving the problems that are at the root of the need for state aid.

QUESTIONS FOR STUDY AND DISCUSSION

1. What has been the history of the development of state aid in your state? Can you identify the effects of the various stages through which thinking in this field has evolved?

2. Is your state properly classified in Table 11-1? If there has been a recent change, what is its nature and purpose?

SELECTED REFERENCES

Burke, Arvid J.: *Financing Public Schools in the United States,* Harper & Brothers, New York, 1957.

Mort, Paul R.: *The Foundation Program in State Educational Policy,* The University of the State of New York, State Department of Education, Albany, N.Y., 1957.

————: *Fiscal Readiness for the Stress of Change,* University of Pittsburgh Press, Pittsburgh, Pa., 1957.

Rosenstengel, William E., and Jefferson N. Eastmond: *School Finance: Its Theory and Practice,* The Ronald Press Company, New York, 1957.

Thurston, Lee M., and William Roe: *State School Administration,* Harper & Brothers, New York, 1957.

See also: Periodic reports on school finance systems published by the Research Division of the National Education Association and the U.S. Office of Education, Washington, D.C.

12. Tax sharing: access to community resources

T HE UNDERLYING purpose of tax sharing—a device for giving communities, rich and poor, access to their own resources, be they great or little—is present in some degree in all state-aid plans for schools. But it is never identified as such. This fact is at the root of the difficulty we face in seeking functional categories for classifying state-aid systems (See Chapter 11). Preparatory to an analysis of state-aid systems, this section seeks to clarify the tax sharing objective of state aid and the characteristics of state-aid systems that serve it.

TAX SHARING THROUGH STATE AID

We have been particularly remiss in education in failing to differentiate distinctly educational concerns from the central purpose that today underlies the major part of state aid, municipal and educational, in most states. Our distinctly educational concerns are (1) stimulating educational improvement in chosen particulars, and (2) assuring help to districts that are patently lacking in local taxpaying ability. The purpose we have failed to keep in focus is that of getting revenue for local school and municipal governments through the agency of state (or federal) taxation. This tax-collection purpose centrally accounts for the greater part of the large increases in state aid to education during the past half-century and for an even larger proportion of the proportionately still greater increases in aid to municipal government.

The tax-collection purpose has been confused by the names applied to it and the nature of the appeals for public support. Those promoting municipal government aid may have dramatized the increase in terms of the need for highways and hospitals, or may have appeared only to

222

provide for sharing new taxes with local government as a means of getting support for the new taxes. Similarly those promoting the large aids for schools may have dramatized the need for higher salaries for teachers and may have made discernible gestures toward considering the greater needs of poorer districts.

Basic to the movement in both fields, however, has been the insistent problem of adjusting the tax system to a changing economy. That the adjustment has frequently been made in proportion to the squawk instead of as a result of careful analysis does not remove the fact that the squawks had an economic origin. With exceptions such as those states that, using the squawk-measuring device instead of analysis, have practically put the property tax out of operation,[1] the sum total of adjustments bears some relation to the basic need.[2] Since all methods of distribution except distribution in direct proportion to wealth and certain types of special aids have an equalization effect, and since, as shown in Chapter 13, most so-called equalization formulas bear heavier on the tax-collection purpose than on the equalization purpose, it would appear to be important to identify the effects of any distribution plan on each function. Hardly otherwise will a wholesome financing system result. The method variously known as "putting the grease on the squeaks" or "weighing the goose by the squawks" leaves too many bearings dry, too many goslings underfed.

Cubberley and Shared Taxes

In his classic analysis of state aid, published in 1905, Cubberley[3] began with shared taxes (distribution with respect to taxes and wealth), moved through a maze of flat grants and incentive aids, and ended up in an equalization dilemma.

Cubberley saw no merit in the "shared tax" plans. He was centrally concerned with spending small amounts of state money on the principle: "Collect the money where the money is and send it where the children

---

[1] Witness the fact that the assessed value of personal property exceeds the assessed value of real property in South Carolina, almost equals it in West Virginia, and equals two-thirds of it in Montana. Perhaps even more dramatic would be the effect of exemptions, bad enough in any state, but particularly severe in the form of wide-sweeping "homestead" exemptions as in Oklahoma and Florida. See U.S. Bureau of the Census, *Property Tax Assessment in the United States*, 1957 Census of Government, Advanced Releases, 1957, p. 12.

[2] To assess the adjustment a state has made would require first a consideration of the extent of the need for adjustment and the use made of ways of making the adjustment other than through increasing state aid. Two alternative ways are centralization of local government—as has been done to a large degree with highways and welfare—and the development of local non-property taxes.

[3] Ellwood P. Cubberley, *State School Funds and Their Apportionment*, Bureau of Publications, Teachers College, Columbia University, New York, 1905.

are." The idea of adequacy played little part in his analysis. The phenomenon noted in Chapter 11, that at the time of his study one-fourth of the states were providing more than 50 per cent of the cost of the schools, evidently escaped him. In his earlier chapters he discussed state taxation for schools in terms of what it showed about public concern. He did not refer to the tax problem that, temporarily perhaps, has become the major determiner of state aid—helping communities get access to their own resources.

Solution by Centralization

This is not said in criticism. The process of adjusting the tax system to the changing economy was already under way, but it was moving according to the squawk method. It was taking the form of centralization of governmental functions. Even the economists, who at that time took a dim view of the possibility of devising broader-based taxes for local use, did not invoke state aid as a solution until considerably later. Their solution was centralization.

By the turn of the century the problem was already nearing the point where opposition was setting limits to the centralization solution. New York had embarked on aid to municipalities in 1898—a century after its first state aid to schools. By 1920 aid to municipalities had caught up with and outrun state aid to schools. For four decades, without fanfare, state aid for municipal government has kept up with the vastly expanded state aid for schools in New York State, the latter wrought at the cost of gargantuan appeals to the favored constitutional position of schools and the great needs of children and teachers. By 1942 such aids to municipal government throughout the nation, almost entirely lacking in 1900, had accumulated to the point that the total exceeded the total of aid to education. This held in the year 1947 for twenty-five states but by 1956 the number had dropped to fourteen.[4] In eleven other states in 1956, aid to municipal government was nearly as large as aid to education. Also in 1947, thirty-eight states had already gone beyond the specific aids to highways, welfare, health, and hospitals to general aid to municipal government. In that year general aid for municipal government[5] (not including highways, welfare, etc.,) exceeded school aid in Arizona, Connecticut, Iowa, Massachusetts, Rhode Island, and Wisconsin.

[4] The fourteen states were Arizona, Colorado, Illinois, Iowa, Kansas, Maryland, Massachusetts, Nebraska, New Hampshire, New York, North Carolina, Ohio, Rhode Island, and Wisconsin. From 1947 to 1956 total aid for municipal government and schools increased from $2.5 to $6.5 billion. Of the $4 billion increase, $2.4 billion was for schools, $1.6 billion for municipal government. U.S. Department of Commerce, 1957, Compendium of State Government Finance in 1956.

[5] U.S. Department of Commerce, State Aid to Local Government, State and Local Government Studies #28, 1948.

The Schools and the Tax Reformers

To a considerable degree state aid for schools increased because the schools provided a wider channel to the communities than other forms of government. In the early 1930s Governor Roosevelt was instrumental in having the state-aid penalty for one-teacher schools removed in New York State. It had been put in the law on the educational theory that it is not wise to aid unsatisfactory district organization. Removal of the penalty was a good way to get state money to the farmers. It ran contrary to the prudential arrangement then favored by educators, but the penalty was removed and the farmers got their aid.

In 1931 the New York State Commission for the Revision of the Tax Laws gave the senior author the task of determining the capacity of the school-aid system for channeling money back to the communities. This was nearly three decades after Cubberley had missed the point, yet it appealed to the senior author as a strange task indeed.[6]

It is certain also that in the development of a state-aid system for schools, this sweeping development cannot be ignored. In the future this will be even truer since in many states there are no costly universal services which are locally financed other than education to be aided or centralized. Recently a case came to attention where educators protested against a proposal to use the school "aid" system for channeling a considerable sum to the localities of a state. The educators proposed that the aid be given to municipal government instead. Their argument was that the increased aid would be interpreted as additional money for schools. The response was that the only local government service universally found in that state was county government and the whole cost of county government was less than the amount under consideration.

How the Purpose of Tax Sharing Changed

The plans that Cubberley discussed for distributing money on the basis of local taxes paid or on the basis of wealth probably had their early roots in a desire to stimulate local vigor in the support of schools and municipal government and to stimulate realistic assessment of property. Where such plans exist today in combination, as in the aid for municipal government in Rhode Island, the rationalization has changed. Now it is claimed that the plan is used as a substitute for satisfactorily comparable assessment figures.

With the increasing availability of equalized assessment data, on the one hand, and of usable economic indexes, on the other, there is no longer

[6] New York State Commission for the Revision of the Tax Laws, *State Support for Public Schools in New York as Related to Tax Relief and Educational Expansion,* Albany, 1932.

need for such makeshifts (Chapter 7). For a tax that can be traced to its source, such as the state income tax, the whole or any part of the yield of the tax can be sent back to the jurisdiction of origin. This is done in Maryland. The state income tax thus becomes in part a local tax, collected by the state.

More commonly, however, the shared tax distribution is hidden in a "flat grant" or "equalization grant." In the former case, the part that the community gets that came from the community in the first instance is shared taxes; the remainder, if any, is usually equalization. In individual cases a wealthy community may receive money in excess of what it provided, because of inequities in the distribution system used or incentive aids.

How to Disentangle Tax Sharing Aid

The money returned to the ablest districts is from that part of the total that is being sent back to the communities where it originated, and the total of the aid that is really being sent back to the communities of origin can be estimated by multiplying the amount the ablest community gets by the ratio of the total wealth of the state to the wealth of the richest district or, practically, the richest large district.

Here is an example. In a state using the flat grant method of distributing a sizable amount of aid in 1958, the ablest large district received $450,-000 in aid. Clearly this aid was not for equalization, for equalization is aid to the poorer districts. It was money collected in the community by the state and returned for local use. This community had within it $\frac{1}{34}$ of the wealth of the state. Accordingly, it presumably received $\frac{1}{34}$ of the money distributed back to the source. The total money returned to source then must have been 34 times the aid received by the district, or $15.3 million. Since the total aid for all purposes distributed by the flat grant method was $27 million, the flat grant method distributed $15.3 million in shared taxes (57 per cent) and the remainder, $11.7 million, for equalization (43 per cent).

Another example is drawn from the municipal field. Polley analyzed the nearly one-half billion dollars a year of state aid to municipalities in New York State (excluding school aid). This money is distributed in a variety of ways but chiefly by flat grants, part in terms of population and part in terms of actual money expended. He concluded that of $483 million, $302 million (62 per cent) was aid returned to county of origin and $181 million, equalization aid.[7]

---

[7] John W. Polley, *The Non-property Tax Potential of New York State,* Staff Study No. 3, New York State Educational Conference Board, Albany, N.Y., 1957.

Shared Taxes in Equalization Plans and Flat Grants Compared

"Equalization" formulas usually differ from flat grant plans in that they have features designed to assure more help to the poorer communities than flat grants provide. The actual number of dollars involved in these corrections tends to be relatively small. It is not surprising then that an analysis similar to the above for a state considered a strong equalization state shows 44 per cent of the money being returned to where it came from. Only 56 per cent was for equalization.

Equalization Not Affected

The test for adequacy of equalization is not the percentage of state aid that goes to equalization. As we shall see in Chapter 13, the tests are of a quite different character. Also in itself a system is neither good nor bad because it serves as a channel for returning taxes collected by the state to the communities of origin. What needs to be tested here is the balance of the state and local tax system as a whole. Conceivably the tax system could be kept in balance without utilizing a system of aid to schools. And conceivably, large aid to schools could be associated either with a tax system still throwing too great a burden on the revenue bases on which schools draw locally or with a tax system thrown out of balance in the other direction by the toleration of artificial barriers to the use of the property tax or of grossly inefficient administration of assessment and collection of property taxes. (See Chapter 8.)

This is a field that has been neglected both by educators and by specialists in public administration to the great detriment of education, and presumably also not without harm to municipal government. The two groups should join to assure that the combined steps taken in education and municipal government provide wholesome conditions for both. Readjustments made without due regard to the need may do more harm than good.

Tax Sharing May Not Be Ignored

The point of all this discussion is that state aid to schools may not be considered in an educational vacuum. It is essential to know how it fits in with the administration of the total tax system, state and local, and it is essential to be able to look below the labels appended to the formulas of distribution to see how the essentially educational functions of state aid are faring.

It is important to realize that the lion's share of the increase in municipal aid in this century and only a lesser share of the increased school aid has been simply money collected by the state through taxes not available locally and returned to the local government—whether municipal or school. The lion's share hasn't been aid at all. It has gone back to its source. The rich got much because they paid much, the poor little because they paid little.

This is not necessarily bad. It was usually justified, no doubt by the need to keep the tax system attuned to the nature of the economy. In those circumstances, whether the money went to school or municipality, the local taxes were in a better position to support local initiative except in those instances where offsetting restrictions were imposed on local taxation.

Equalization Shouldn't Get Lost

Of the total money involved in the transaction, only a fraction went to adjust for discrepancies in ability among school districts, and this is not necessarily bad. Large amounts of tax sharing may be associated with poor equalizing arrangements or with good ones. Each objective must be clearly identified and justified in terms of the problems it is associated with. But above all, the fact should not be lost sight of that equalization is an inescapable function of state aid and may not be neglected with impunity. While there are alternative ways to achieve an adjustment on the tax base (e.g., local non-property taxes instead of state collection and return), there is no alternative method for achieving equalization.

The dangers to equalization are all the greater when an equalization-type formula is used as a tax-sharing formula. This is so because the tax-sharing potential is all but fully independent of the adequacy of the foundation program or of the justice of the methods used in computing the cost of the foundation program. The school districts that will get most of the aid have but little selfish concern with these matters so critical to the poorer districts; to them they may appear inconsequential. The result can be that an "equalization formula" may turn out to achieve far less equalization than would appear on the surface. Of twenty-four states with equalization-type formulas and with state-aid percentages meeting the minimum estimate as to percentage of state aid required for equalization,[8] six of the plans appear to have no net equalization effect whatever and four others fall below the 15 per cent test; none of these ten states pay less than 25 per cent of their school costs from state funds, three more than 40 per cent.

Tax Sharing and Control

The same factors that make the equalization money in an "equalization formula" small and thus easily subject to neglect, make it easier for the individuals and groups always present with a miracle-working incentive or compliance requirement to make themselves heard. The com-

[8] See Chapter 13.

munities receiving most of the aid will already have what the incentive is meant to stimulate or what the compliance requires. Their natural reaction appears to be that the poorer communities lack these things because of innate laggardness while their own advanced status is due to greater native insight. At this point equalization stands to lose another battle, since the effect of compliances is to deny full aid to those who may desire to spend their resources on something other than the particular miracle workers under consideration.

TAX SHARING IN PRESENT PROGRAMS

Table 12-1 shows the results of an attempt to identify approximately the percentage of state aid that is in effect tax sharing. It is based on the school year 1956–1957 and on forty-seven states. The method used was explained earlier in this chapter. State departments of education were asked to provide comparable figures on the wealth of the state and of the ablest large district (the key district). In addition they were asked for the total state aid and the aid supplied to the key district. While the results would probably be considerably at variance in some states from what would be obtained from a more exhaustive study, they should provide a fairly good estimate of the general situation.

Table 12-1   Percentage of State Aid Returned to Communities
of Origin—Tax Sharing—Compared with Percentage
of State Aid, 1956–1957

Per cent of cost of education from state aid	Percentage of aid for tax sharing				
	0–29	30–49	50–69	70 or more	Total
Over 60	1	2	2	4	9
40–59	5	6	1	3	15
20–39	4	2	2	8	16
Under 20	1	1	1	4	7
Total	11	11	6	19	47

Note that there is very little relationship between the percentage that state aid is of total cost and the percentage of state aid that comprises shared taxes. However, states with less than 40 per cent of their costs coming from state aid tend to emphasize tax sharing more than those with larger percentages of state aid. The states that emphasize tax sharing the least, as a group, are those falling in the 40 to 59 per cent bracket of state aid. They have a median of 32 per cent going to tax sharing; all others have a median of 70 per cent going to tax sharing. It is of interest that there are instances in nearly every percentage level where the tax shar-

ing is 100 per cent (not shown). As is pointed out later, this is probably
not intentional tax sharing but rather a warping of flat grant and equalization aids by incentives and compliance features so that the net effect is
to return the money roughly to the communities of origin.

That the percentage of aid going to tax sharing cannot be predicted
from the type of distribution system is shown by Table 12-2 (forty-six
states). While more of the flat grant states (five out of nine) have a
higher percentage of their aid in the highest tax sharing bracket and
the reverse is true for those with some equalization (fourteen out of
thirty-seven), the difference isn't marked. The five states with the
minimum-guarantee plan of assuring all communities aid showed a strong
tendency to emphasize tax sharing; the "equalization only" states tended
to fall below 50 per cent in the proportion of such aid going to tax
sharing.

Table 12-2 Percentage of State Aid Returned to Communities
of Origin—Tax Sharing—Compared with State-aid Pattern,
1956–1957

	Percentage of aid for tax sharing				
Pattern of state aid	0–29	30–49	50–69	70 or more	Total
Flat grant	2	2	—	5	9
Equalization plus flat grant	4	8	1	8	21
Equalization alone and equalization plus minimum guarantee	3	2	3	4	12
Total	9	12	4	17	42

One point this emphasizes is that the present ignoring of tax sharing
in classifying state-aid programs is unrealistic. Half of the state-aid systems today are more tax sharing plans than equalization plans. A classification based on this differentiation would rearrange the five categories
presented in Chapter 12 as shown in Table 12-3.

A CONSTRUCTIVE APPROACH TO TAX SHARING

The achievement of arrangements whereby communities of whatever
ability can tax the resources within them without throwing undue burdens on one class of taxpayers is of no less importance to education by
virtue of the fact that such achievement in the last analysis must be
brought about through cooperation of state, municipal, and educational
agencies. Without the achievement of such arrangements the century
and more of successful struggle to arouse a sense of local responsibility
for education goes for naught. Accordingly, educators must be interested

in the steps taken in the financing of municipal government through state assumption and state aid and through local non-property taxes. These steps cannot be taken without helpful or harmful effects on schools, harmful particularly if they become associated with tax relief instead of tax-base strengthening and bring down an avalanche of restrictions on the property tax. And they should be taken as a part of a concerted plan of tax development for state and local government, both educational and municipal.

Table 12-3 Comparison of Equalization—Tax Sharing Classification with Traditional Classification

	Predominantly tax sharing	Predominantly equalization
Flat grants only—ability disregarded	South Dakota Nebraska Vermont Delaware South Carolina	North Carolina Arizona Connecticut *
Flat grants plus equalization	Nevada Kentucky Iowa	Mississippi Wisconsin
Flat grants nullified in equalization distribution	Kansas Montana Oregon Wyoming Ohio Rhode Island Minnesota	Alabama North Dakota Oklahoma Maryland Virginia California Michigan Washington Arkansas Texas Louisiana
Equalization plus minimum guarantee	Tennessee New York Missouri New Jersey Idaho	
Equalization—no minimum guarantee, except some incentive aids	Florida Indiana West Virginia	Georgia New Hampshire New Mexico Utah Pennsylvania Massachusetts Maine
Unclassified		Colorado Illinois

* Connecticut on borderline.

What is involved here is essentially the adaptability of the system. At any time, and particularly in times like these, it is essential that conditions be made wholesome for the vigorous use of local initiative—wholesome in adequacy of district organization, wholesome in respect to the system of control the people and the profession are given over fiscal decisions, wholesome with respect to an available—not relatively overburdened—local tax base.

Some idea of how local initiative is working could be gained from studying the rise in a state's median expenditure under the challenges of population increase, rises in price levels, and the general betterment of education. This would not be a conclusive test because the action of the state in increasing state aid would have to be ruled out some way.

There is a simpler test—the ratio of the highest-expenditure levels in the state to the median. In applying this test it should be held in mind that the highest-expenditure levels do not all fall in the wealthiest communities. The compensatory effect of tax vigor comes into play. A district with average wealth and double the average effort will usually fall in the highest expenditure brackets. Within the range of vigor among communities, it is not at all unlikely that some of the highest-expenditure-level communities will be found to have less than average wealth.

A situation where communities—rich, poor, and average—wait for a nod from the state, through permissive legislation, state aid, mandates, or legal interpretation, is one to be concerned about. A situation where state officials are promoting leadership by such means only and are not concerned with the signs of local fiscal liveliness (or lack of them) is one to be concerned about.

METHODS OF USING THE AID SYSTEM
AS A TAX SHARING CHANNEL

To proceed now from evaluation to action, the following discussion is presented as suggestive of the types of action possible.

Taxes Shared through the Equalization-type Formula

The only form of state aid that is strictly tax broadening in character is the shared tax. Perhaps the reason that shared taxes are not more widely used is that usually, when fiscal adjustments are being made by legislation, the legislature is faced with the problems of all kinds of communities and must accordingly consider demands rising from needs for equalization as well as the demands for tax broadening. This underlies the important shifting of the system of aid to municipal government in New York State brought about in 1946, when all shared taxes were done away with and in their place were substituted the forms of aid which were in effect flat grants based on an index of municipal government need.

But even when the desire is to adhere to the tax-broadening idea through a system of shared taxes, difficulties arise in achieving a situation where the community receives from the taxes collected by the state the exact amount of money it paid. When the money is paid to local tax collectors, as in the case of the mortgage tax, for example, this is quite simple; when the collecting district is not the same as the tax district in which the taxpayer resides, as is the case with the sales tax, serious difficulties arise.

One way around the complexities that has been somewhat used is the distribution of the yield of the state taxes in terms of the wealth of individual communities as measured by the valuation of property for tax purposes. Such measures are usually referred to as tax-relief measures, but they need not be so considered. Actually there is a rather high relationship between the amount of property in communities, by and large, and the yield of non-property taxes. In the early 1930s Cornell showed that the ability of communities to pay taxes in areas as large as counties could be predicted rather well from economic indexes. In the 1947 study of fiscal policy by the New York State Educational Conference Board a comparison was made between the equalized value of property in counties and the computed yield of five authorized non-property taxes. These two independent measures of counties correlated rather highly (.76).[9] Accordingly there is a rather rough justification for the use of value of property as a basis for sharing state-levied non-property taxes.

The idea certainly has the merit of simplicity. For example, if a state has a valuation of $10 billion and desires to distribute $50 million for the purpose of sharing a state tax with the localities, the $50 million could be allotted to the communities either in proportion to the amount of taxable property they hold or in amounts equal to what a 5-mill tax would raise on the taxable property valuation in the communities. The two results would clearly be identical. In other words, $50 million distributed to the communities in proportion to their property valuation would give each community what 5 mills would yield on its property valuation.

This provides a clue for the interpretation of equalization-type formulas that use rates of local contribution lower than those which could be justified for equalization purposes alone. If a 9.4-mill local rate of contribution is what would be obtained by computing the cost of the foundation program in the key district, the use of a 5-mill local rate would have the effect of giving each community the yield of 4.4 mills on its valuation in addition to what it is justified in receiving as equalization aid. Where the rate used is lower than the highest rate justified for equalization, the difference between the rate actually used and the justifiable rate is an index

[9] New York State Educational Conference Board, *Fiscal Policy for Public Educa-tion in the State of New York*, Albany, N.Y., 1947, p. 103.

of the amount of aid being distributed by the formula for tax-broadening purposes. This rate applied to the total valuation in the state gives a close approximation of the amount of aid used for tax-broadening purposes.

Two Plans for One

The danger to equalization arising from the use of an equalization-type formula to distribute tax sharing money has been stressed earlier in this chapter. The danger could be avoided by attacking each problem directly. The equalization formula could be limited to equalization and the tax-sharing money distributed under an entirely separate section of the law.

For most districts (all districts in county-unit states) the same result would be obtained if the equalization aid were distributed by use of a strict equalization formula and the remainder of the aid distributed in proportion to the tax on property in the school districts. In the example given above, 9.4 mills would be used as the local rate of contribution in the equalization formula, and a separate provision of the law would call for the distribution of additional aid to each district equal to the computed yield of a 4.4-mill tax.

Flat Grant Plus Equalization

One approximation of this sort of provision has the merit of driving home the fact that an "equalization formula" is not necessarily all equalization. One formula is retained, but before equalization is computed an amount per pupil (or per classroom unit) equal to that which the ablest district would receive is spread over all districts (either as a flat grant or as a minimum guarantee). This reduces the amount apparently needed for equalization, but has the advantage of overcompensating. Flat grant money, as we have seen, is neither fish nor fowl. It contains within it a considerable measure of equalization.

However, if the flat grant were made in terms of the yield in each district of the tax rate necessary in the ablest district (or key district) to raise the amount of money granted the key district, it would be perfectly clear that the amount of money involved is for broadening the tax base, and that the "equalization money" is truly equalization money.

SUMMARY

The underlying purpose of tax sharing—a device for giving communities, rich and poor, access to their own resources, be they great or little— is present in some degree in all state-aid plans for schools. But it is never identified as such.

We have been particularly remiss in education in failing to differentiate distinctly educational concerns from the central purpose that today underlies the major part of state aid, municipal and educational, in most states. Our distinctly educational concerns are (1) stimulating educational improvement in chosen particulars, and (2) assuring help to districts that are patently lacking in local taxpaying ability. The purpose we have failed to keep in focus is that of getting revenue for local school and municipal governments through the agency of state (or federal) taxation. This tax-collection purpose centrally accounts for the greater part of the large increases in state aid to education during the past half-century and for an even larger proportion of the proportionately still greater increases in aid to municipal government.

Basic to the movement in both education and municipal government, however, has been the insistent problem of adjusting the tax system to a changing economy. That the adjustment has frequently been made in proportion to the squawk instead of as a result of careful analysis does not remove the fact that the squawks had an economic origin.

Cubberley did not identify tax sharing as a purpose of state aid. At the time of his study, however, much had already been done through the medium of centralizing functions of government formerly financed locally. During the past half-century there has been a large growth of aid to municipalities as a supplement to the tax adjustment that had been achieved through centralization. Much of the large increase in aid to education has had the same basis.

Most of the aid that has tax sharing at its roots is hidden in flat grant or equalization distribution formulas.

The money returned to the ablest districts is from that part of the total that is being sent back to the communities where it originated, and the total of the aid that is really being sent back to the communities of origin can be estimated by multiplying the amount the ablest community gets by the ratio of the total wealth of the state to the wealth of the richest district or, practically, the richest large district.

In itself a system is neither good nor bad because it serves as a channel for returning taxes collected by the state to the communities of origin. What needs to be tested here is the balance of the state and local tax system as a whole. Conceivably the tax system could be kept in balance without utilizing a system of aid to schools. And conceivably, large aid to schools could be associated either with a tax system still throwing too great a burden on the revenue bases on which schools draw locally or with a tax system thrown out of balance in the other direction by the toleration of artificial barriers to the use of the property tax or of grossly inefficient administration of assessment and collection of property taxes.

The dangers to equalization are all the greater when an equalization-type formula is used as a tax sharing formula. This is so because the tax sharing potential is all but fully independent of the adequacy of the foundation program or of the justice of the methods used in computing the cost of the foundation program.

There is very little relationship between the percentage that state aid is of total cost and the percentage of state aid that comprises shared taxes.

The achievement of arrangements whereby communities of whatever ability can tax the resources within them without throwing undue burdens on one class of taxpayers is of no less importance to education by virtue of the fact that such achievement in the last analysis must be brought about through cooperation of state, municipal, and educational agencies.

QUESTIONS FOR STUDY AND DISCUSSION

1. Over the past three-quarters of a century what steps have been taken in your state to meet the tax problem of communities by centralizing functions of government formerly financed locally?

2. Chart the growth of aid to municipal government in your state.

3. How much of the state aid for education in your state goes back to the communities from whose taxpayers it came?

SELECTED REFERENCES

Allen, Edward D., and O. H. Brownlee: *Economics of Public Finance*, Prentice-Hall, Inc., Englewood Cliffs, N.J., 1947.

American Municipal Association: *State-collected, Municipally-shared Taxes*, Report 165, Chicago, Ill., 1948.

Bowen, Howard R.: "English Grants-in-aid: A Study in the Finance of Local Government," *University of Iowa Studies in Social Science*, vol. XI, no. 1, Iowa City, 1939.

Burke, Arvid J.: "A Century and a Half of Financing Locally Operated Functions of Government in New York State," *Fiscal Policy for Public Education in the State of New York*, Staff Study 1, New York State Educational Conference Board, Albany, N.Y., 1948, chap. III, pp. 36–45.

Cornell, Francis G.: "Grants-in-aid Apportionment Formulas," *Journal of the American Statistical Association*, vol. 42, no. 237, pp. 92–104, March, 1947.

De Marco, Antonio De Viti: *First Principles of Public Finance*, Harcourt, Brace and Company, Inc., New York, 1936.

Department of Commerce, Bureau of the Census: *Governmental Finances in the United States, 1902–1957*, Washington, March, 1959.

Dewhurst, J. Frederick, and Associates: *America's Needs and Resources*, The Twentieth Century Fund, Inc., New York, 1955.

Grodzins, Morton: "State-Municipal Fiscal Relations: A Critical Commentary," *National Tax Journal,* vol. III, no. 1, pp. 1–17, March, 1950.

Groves, Harold M.: *Financing Government,* rev. ed., Henry Holt and Company, Inc., New York, 1945, part II, pp. 25–407.

————: *Trouble Spots in Taxation,* Princeton University Press, Princeton, N.J., 1948, chaps. IV-V, pp. 70–105.

Jensen, Jens P.: "The General Property Tax, the Mainstay of Local Fiscal Autonomy," *Annals of the American Academy of Political and Social Science,* Philadelphia, 1936, vol. 183, pp. 124–129.

Kendrick, Myron S.: *Public Finance,* Houghton Mifflin Company, Boston, 1951.

Lamitie, Robert: *Leeway in the Property Tax—An Index of Relative Use by States,* Associated Public School Systems, New York, 1959.

Lawler, Eugene S., and Procter Thomsen: "Taxation and Educational Finance," in R. L. Johns and E. L. Morphet (eds.), *Problems and Issues in Public School Finance,* Bureau of Publications, Teachers College, Columbia University, New York, 1952.

Ross, Donald H. (ed.): *Administration for Adaptability,* rev. ed., Metropolitan School Study Council, New York, 1958.

Schultz, William J., and C. Lowell Harris: *American Public Finance,* Prentice-Hall, Inc., Englewood Cliffs, N.J., 1949.

Stout, Randall S.: *Recent Trends in State Grants-in-Aid and Shared Taxes,* Bureau of Business Research, Bulletin 36, State College, Pa., 1948.

U.S. Bureau of the Census: *State Aid to Local Government,* State and Local Government Studies, Washington, 1954.

13. The equalization objective

THE DISTRIBUTION of state-collected monies back to the communities of origin (tax sharing), discussed in Chapter 12, is not aid in the sense of a grant from some outside source. Rather, it is use of the state-aid system as an administrative convenience. Theoretically the same result could be obtained by broadening local taxing powers. In contrast, aid for equalization brings money, in the net, from communities of above average wealth to communities of below average wealth. There is no way of doing this except through state aid. Accordingly, whatever is done through the system of state aid, it is essential to know just what part of it is really equalization aid.

In this chapter the equalization effects of state-aid systems are assessed in so far as available data make it possible, the foundation-program test of equalization is discussed, and the impact on state-aid systems of the problems involved in raising expenditure levels is dealt with.

The purpose of the chapter is to disentangle equalization—the one inescapable function of state aid—from the complex of functions to which any formula or combination of formulas for distributing state aid to education seems inevitably to get harnessed—particularly tax sharing and state control through rewards and punishments.

EVALUATING THE EQUALIZATION EFFECTS
OF A STATE-AID SYSTEM

In the final analysis the adequacy of the equalization aid is determined by comparing the amount of such aid with the amount required to equalize the burden of an acceptable foundation program. To apply this test to the states requires a case study of each state. Data are not available for any such application, but certain indirect approaches can be made which yield a fairly good over-all picture. This section applies these indirect methods to all the states and territories for 1949–1950 and to forty-three states for 1957. The results are likely to be fairly typical for a considerable length of time, for in achieving equalization along with

238

all the other purposes and traditions that weigh down a state-aid system, progress is slow.

For the reader not interested in the detail, this section can be summed up with the statement: In one-half of the states less than 40 per cent of the aid has an equalizing effect; no state professes to equalize an acceptable foundation program and yet no state passes the test of assuring to all even the foundation program it professes to equalize.

The Amount of Aid for Equalization

The idea of extending aid with regard to both need and ability has made great strides since Cubberley in 1905 rather apologetically proposed that states should have a reserve fund for communities still found to be needy after other aids had been distributed. At that time seven states had such plans, most of them involving infinitesimally small amounts of money. Today the idea is applied far more forcefully in thirty-nine states. Instead of being a supplementary provision, the need and ability formula has become the dominant method of distributing state aid in many states. It embraces what was formerly done by the flat grants. It has proved extremely useful as a means for channeling state-collected taxes back to communities of origin. It has all the potentialities of incentive aids and a few extras for achieving the purpose of influencing the character of local programs. The aura of equalization has been spread over all the functions of state aid.

In this process the equalization dilemma that confronted Cubberley has been in part resolved, but not nearly as satisfactorily as the amount of money paid under so-called equalization formulas or under what Burke calls "completely state-supported equalization programs" [1] would suggest. Equalization as used in the laws has been appropriated as the name for all these functions but, as this chapter shows, in most states equalization itself still sits humbly below the salt.

A Method of Identifying Equalization Aid. It is possible to approximate the amount of aid going to equalization from the total of state aids paid to education by the simple process of separating the amount of aid that is in effect tax sharing. The way of doing it is explained in Chapter 12. The method may be expressed in equation form as follows:

$$\text{Equalization aid} = \text{Total aids} - \text{Aid to key district} \times \frac{\text{Wealth of state}}{\text{Wealth of key district}}$$

in which the key district is the ablest large district.

[1] Arvid J. Burke, *Financing Public Schools in the United States*, Harper & Brothers, New York, 1957.

This method was applied for 1956–1957 data for forty-three states. The data were supplied by the state departments of education. The results for any one state may be at considerable variance from what would have been obtained if it had been possible to assemble the evidence on all districts or a good enough sample to be certain that there were not conditions that would make the particular district chosen unrepresentative of the higher ability districts. But it is believed that the general pattern as used here is fairly representative of the over-all picture in 1956–1957.[2]

Percentage of Aid that Equalizes. Table 13-1 gives the distribution of the results obtained by applying the formula to the data for forty-three states. The states are grouped by the patterns of aid they use and again by the percentage of school support that comes from all aids combined. For example, there is one state in the flat grant group in which the state aid meets more than 40 per cent of the cost but in which less than 5 per cent of the aid is for equalization. More than 38 per cent of the 40 per cent goes back to communities (in general) where it comes from.

Of the forty-three states represented, thirty-four have "equalization" laws. But the median percentage of the aid going for equalization falls short of 50 per cent. The showing for the nine flat grant states is almost the same. In four of the nine flat grant states and in eight of the thirty-four "equalization" states, the equalization effect has been pretty well squeezed out by the measurement methods used or by the use of incentives.

Table 13-1   Percentage of Aid Going to Equalization—by Patterns
of State Aid and Percentage of Support
from the State, 1956–1957

Patterns of state aid	Per cent of support from state	Percentage of aid going to equalization					
		0–4	5–29	30–49	50–69	70–94	95–100
Flat grant	40 or more	1	1		1		
	Under 40	3			1	2	
Equalization plus flat grant	40 or more	3			7	2	1
	Under 40	4	2	1	1	1	
Equalization and equalization plus minimum grants	40 or more		1	2		1	2
	Under 40	1	2	1	2		
Totals	40 or more	4	2	2	8	3	3
	Under 40	8	4	2	4	3	

[2] This method actually exaggerates the equalization aid. Strayer and Haig selected the wealthiest district as the key district for reasons of administrative practicality. Theoretically the average district is the key district so far as *net* equalization is concerned.

Percentage of Costs from Equalization Money. As was indicated in Chapter 12, the percentage going for equalization does not provide a test of the system. But the fact that one-fourth of the states are in the 0 to 4 per cent equalization column is a good indication that things are not what they seem. Also, when in one-half of the states tax sharing money comprises more than one-half the aid, it would appear to be shortsighted to continue to speak of the aid systems as if they were all attributable to the equalization objective.

A different view of the situation is provided by Table 13-2. The table shows the percentage of the total cost of education, state and local, that is met by equalization aid (whatever the method of distribution). Here we see that seventeen states represented in the table give less than 10 per cent of the support of education through money that is not directly proportional to the ability of communities. In the 10 to 19 per cent group is to be found the State of New York, which has worked diligently on equalization since the middle 1920s. Maryland and Pennsylvania, which began a strong program of equalization in the early 1920s, are to be found in the 20 to 29 per cent group and the 30 to 39 per cent group, respectively. California is in the 30 to 39 per cent group and Rhode Island and Wisconsin are in the 10 to 19 per cent group, along with New York.

Table 13-2 Percentage of Support, State and Local, Coming from State Equalization Aid

Per cent of state support	Percentages								
	0–9	10–19	20–29	30–39	40–49	50–59	60–69	70–79	80+
60 or over	2	1	1	1	1				1
40–59	3		3	5	3	1			
20–39	8	6	2						
Under 20	4	2							
Total	17	9	6	6	4	1			1

This would suggest that a fairly wholesome proportion for equalization might comprise as little as 20 per cent, in some states perhaps as little as 15 per cent, of the total cost of education.

Of course the figures in Table 13-2 are not highly satisfactory tests since the percentage would be reduced either by vigorous local initiative or by failure of the poorer communities to spend up to the assumed foundation level.[3] But it indicates that a job as good as New York is doing could be achieved, under some conditions, with less than 20 per cent of the total cost being attributable to equalization aid extended by the state, and it raises the question as to wholesomeness of conditions in general,

[3] Because of overzealous compliance features, unjust warpings of the need measures, lag between state aid and expenditure, etc.

state and local, if the part of the cost represented by equalization money rises much above 35 or 40 per cent.

The State-aid Pattern and Equalization Effects. The conceptions of the equalization job to be done through state aid seem to fall in two groups: (1) the Cubberley approach: flat grants plus special help to the poor and (2) the over-all equalization formula approach. Table 11-3 in Chapter 11 identifies these two approaches roughly. States in Column 1 either ignore the equalization problem, as in Nebraska and South Dakota, or seek to alleviate it by comparatively large flat grants, taking the form of complete state support of a foundation program in some instances—notably Delaware, South Carolina, North Carolina, Alaska, and Hawaii. Those in Columns 2a and 3a introduce an equalization provision as such and those in 2b and 3b distribute more money as equalization than as flat grants. Only those in Columns 4 and 5 have taken the over-all equalization approach.

Table 13-3   The State-aid Pattern and Equalization Effects

Number of states	Column *	Number meeting test	Per cent meeting test
9	1	2 †	22
3	2a	0	0
2	2b	1	50
11	3a	7	64
8	3b	5	62
5	4	2	40
10	5	6	60
9	1	2	22
14	2a and 3a	7	50
10	2b and 3b	6	60
15	4 and 5	8	53

* Columns referred to are in Table 11-3.

† One of the "complete state support" states fails the test.

But the equalization effects are not assured by the pattern of support. If we set as a minimum that at least 15 per cent of the cost of education must come from equalization money (as opposed to tax sharing money) we find the results shown in the upper part of Table 13-3. Counting them in terms of superficial emphasis on equalization, we have the results given in the lower part of the table. The showing in total is not a good one (48 per cent).

The Foundation Program Approach to Evaluation

But small as its demands are, equalization is the one objective that has first priority on state aid. Accordingly there is need for a critical test of the adequacy of provisions which a state-aid law makes for equalization. The foundation-program concept, discussed in Chapter 3, provides the key. Regardless of how large or how small the percentage of state aid, the real test of equalization is how nearly the level of support in the poorest district approaches the state median or average; or, more sharply, how much will the state aid plus a reasonable local tax make available in such a district.

Unhappily current data are not at hand to make this sort of an assessment possible. However, the studies of expenditure made at the U.S. Office of Education [4] make it possible to see the situation in each state at the end of each decade. At this writing the latest study gives data for 1949–1950. It shows that in nine states the second percentile of expenditure was less than 43 per cent of the state median. The most extreme case was Mississippi with approximately 17 per cent.

At the other end of the scale were eight states in which the second percentile was above 74 per cent of the median—the best showing being made by Utah with a percentage of 91. Interestingly enough, Delaware, with the highest percentage of state aid in relation to total expenditure, is not one of these eight. The eight with the poorest showing included two with state-aid percentages above 50; the other group, three. One in the poorer group had a state-aid percentage of 18; one in the other, 16. In the middle half, those with the poorer showing ranged from 29 to 40 per cent; those with better showing, 36 to 52 per cent. This indicates some relationship between the percentage of total aid and the variation in level of support among localities. But it demonstrates again that a large percentage of state aid gives no assurance of good equalization, and a relatively low percentage no assurance of lack of it.

Of course there are factors that make such comparison faulty. States with large local units tend to vary less. They rarely have extremely poor districts. Such a comparison favors these states. However, county-unit states constituted half of each group. Also, the higher the expenditure level the more strain is placed on poor communities to meet the demands on local taxes. They are penalized in the kind of comparisons made here. Interestingly enough, however, half of the group with a better showing were on higher-expenditure levels than any of the states making a poorer showing, and half making the poorer showing were lower than any of those in the group making the better showing.

In spite of the move to recognize equalization, it is quite clear that

---

[4] These were planned for ten-year intervals before the turbulence of the 1940s and 1950s. The speed with which they get out of date would seem to counsel a shortening of the interval. The time between the year of the data used in the mid-century report and this writing has already seen an approximate doubling of expenditure. According to the present schedule the next report will not be available until another five years have elapsed.

equalization still is an ideal to strive for—by no means an accomplished fact. In a large number of states it is treated in much the same way as Cubberley envisioned it in 1905—as a sort of minute but troubling problem, one that distracted attention in Cubberley's day from getting longer school terms and more textbooks; in our day from getting driver training, guidance specialists, classes for the bright, or care for the underprivileged. Few states are practicing the philosophy that the prime responsibility is to provide wholesome conditions for local thinking and acting.

FAULTS IN THE STATE-AID SYSTEM

The explanation for the fact that even large amounts of state aid may fail to achieve a high degree of equalization may lie in any one of a number of places. It may lie in the elements of the over-all structure of the plan, in the provisions for keeping the state's share in balance with the local share, or in earmarking or compliance features. There are instances where provisions in one of these three areas have been sufficiently inept to destroy the equalizing effects of an otherwise superior program.

The most likely area, however, is the first—the structure itself.

The Structure

The Level of the Foundation Program. The anchor part to every equalization-type program is the assumption as to what foundation program is to be achieved. This is the most fateful decision so far as equalization is concerned.

It is now more than one-third of a century since the Strayer-Haig proposal was made and surprisingly little attention has been given to what would seem to be this most critical aspect of the proposal "that there be an adequate program offered everywhere, the expense of which should be considered a prior claim on the State's economic resources." The Strayer-Haig proposals came at a time when those concerned in writing state-aid laws were, on the one hand, still under the domination of the bit-by-bit concept of school improvement so well expressed in Cubberley's state-aid theory, and on the other, faced with the demand for distributing state aid in amounts vastly greater than Cubberley's theory had envisioned. So the Strayer-Haig formula came widely into use without much appreciation of its qualities other than its amazing potentiality for distributing large amounts of money that could be rationalized without too much difficulty by the Cubberley theory. The fact that the local rate of contribution could be manipulated in association with any foundation program, however inadequate, so as to absorb vast amounts of state aid apparently without violating the equalization of burden aspect of the

Strayer-Haig theory probably was in considerable part to blame for the comparative neglect of what now appears to be the most crucial aspect of the Strayer-Haig proposal—the adequacy of the foundation-program level.

The nub of the matter seems to be that the mechanism of the equalization formula, adaptable as it is to the distribution of aid for general assistance to all districts, has got far too much credit for achieving the central purpose for which it was originally designed—the assurance of an adequate foundation program.

Viewed from the standpoint that state actions should provide wholesome conditions, the level of the foundation program would seem to be crucial—more so, certainly, than exact distribution of the burden of its cost.

Effect on Poor Districts. The reason that the level of the foundation program is a crucial matter lies in the fact that the poorest districts will have very little more money to spend on education than that provided by the foundation program. This is true regardless of the rate of local contribution. Here is an example drawn from New York State under the law in 1958. A New York school district with a valuation of $3,000 per pupil, for example, pays less than $21 per pupil toward the cost of the present foundation program. It receives $309 from the state. If the local rate of contribution were raised to 10 mills, it would raise locally only $30 and it would still receive $300 from the state. If the rate were raised to 20 mills for current operation, it would raise only $60 locally and would receive $270 from the state.

Or look at it another way: A community with a valuation of $3,000 can now have a $330 program after levying 6.8 mills. If this community were to levy an additional 7 mills (total tax of 13.8 mills) for operational purposes, it would increase its expenditure level only from $330 to $351. Take a less extreme case—a community with a valuation of $6,000 per unit. This community under the present law contributes $41 (actually $40.80) to the cost of the program and receives $289 aid. Even if the local rate of contribution were raised to 20 mills, this community would still be receiving $210 from the state; or, if this community were to supplement the foundation program with a tax of 7 mills for operational purposes, it would raise the expenditure level only from $330 to $372.

Contrast with the above a plan that would set up a $200 foundation program with the *total cost coming from the state*. The community with the $3,000 valuation, if it were to raise 14 mills locally, would have only a $242 expenditure level as compared with the $351 above. The community with $6,000 under like circumstances would have a $284 level as compared with $372 above.

Offhand, the $200 program completely supported would seem more liberal than the $330 program supported with a local rate of 6.8 mills. Quite clearly this conclusion would be grossly erroneous.

The point here is that the level of the foundation program is a fundamental consideration for the poorer communities. The basic reason for this is that the amount of state aid largely determines the expenditure level of such communities, regardless of their local vigor in support of schools.

Effects on Able Districts. If this sort of analysis were carried through for the average community or the able community, it would readily be seen that so far as these communities are concerned the level of the foundation program used in computing aid is of relatively little importance. The community with a valuation of $25,000 under the present law would raise $170 locally and receive $160 from the state. If the foundation level were $200 and completely supported, this community would receive $200 from the state. With an additional tax for current operation of 7 mills under present circumstances, the community with a $25,000 valuation could have an expenditure level of $505. With a $200 foundation program completely supported by the state, a 14-mill tax would raise $350 locally. Added to the $200 from the state, this would give a $550 expenditure level.

The fact that the level of the foundation program is of less significance than the local rate of contribution to communities of average wealth and above probably accounts for the neglect of a rigorous examination of the implications of adequacy for a foundation program. It has permitted a rationalization of inadequate state-aid programs in terms of the whole idea of "helping" the poor rather than in terms of the Strayer-Haig concept of an acceptable minimum for all.

State Practice

In the majority of state-aid systems the foundation program is explicitly stated in terms of dollars, as so many dollars per some kind of pupil cost unit or teacher cost unit. In others it is difficult even to identify it.

Here are examples, chosen from the highest-expenditure states, the middle-expenditure states, and the low-expenditure states (as of 1958).

California. $212 per elementary unit of average daily attendance ($232 for poor districts). Small districts approximately $5,300 per teacher employed. High school, $280 ($350 for poor districts). Adult same as high school. Junior college $380 per unit of average daily attendance. Transportation aid added on equalization basis.

Connecticut. Average daily membership weighted according to size, amounting to $52.50 at average daily membership of 1,000. Small schools more. Schools of 125, $100 per average daily membership. Transportation cost ignored.

Florida. Instruction units determined on average daily attendance basis; varies with school size. Then cost computed by allowing from $2,900 to $3,950 according to the degrees held by staff. Less for those without degrees. One-fifth added for those employed for twelve months. For each instruction unit $300 added for operation and $400 for capital outlay.

Hawaii. Full budget for instructional costs.

Illinois. $200 per unit of average daily attendance. Transportation aid added.

Indiana. Teacher units: one for thirty-two elementary; one for twenty-eight high schools (9 to 12). Supervisory units added. Units multiplied by "average minimum salary." Transportation aid added (equalization basis).

Kentucky. Classroom units based on twenty-seven pupils (average daily attendance). Salary allotments in terms of schedule varying with training. $600 per classroom unit added for other operating expenses; $400 for capital outlay. Transportation aid added. (Plan not fully implemented because when state appropriations are short, it is prorated. Currently at about 70 per cent). To above is added about $1,100 per unit on flat grant distribution (census basis) not incorporated in computing equalization aid.

Maine. Average expenditures for current purposes two years preceding biennium in which aid is paid.

Maryland. Amount of state minimum salary schedule, teachers and principals, increased by 25 per cent. Supervisory allowances and transportation added. Teachers allowed based on membership in October, weighted for school size.

Massachusetts. $130 per census child aged seven to sixteen (increased at rate of $1 for each $100,000,000 of assessed value). In places with population under 5,000, however, $2,875 per professional employee. Transportation aid added—all over $5 per pupil per year.

Michigan. $150 per unit of elementary average daily membership; $170 high school; $2,225 for a one-teacher school. Transportation allowance added.

New Jersey. $200 per unit of average daily attendance. Transportation aid added at 75 per cent of cost.

New York State. $330 per equated elementary pupil in average daily attendance; $412.50 per equated high school pupil (about three-fourths of state median)—less for districts with fewer than eight teachers. Transportation aid added at 100 per cent of formula.

Ohio. Average daily membership. Elementary $137.50; high school (9 to 12) $160. Plus portion of transportation cost.

Oregon. The lesser of two: (1) $1.15 per aggregate days membership or (2) amount expended for current purposes, transportation excluded. No case less than $3,000 per teaching unit allowed.

Rhode Island. $300 per pupil in average daily attendance, weighted for small schools. Transportation cost included.

South Carolina. Salary schedule with pupil-teacher ratio limit on number counted (enrollment and attendance), plus $5 per pupil enrolled, plus actual expenditures for transportation.

Virginia. $145 per average daily attendance unit. Transportation aid added.

Washington. 57¢ per unit of aggregate daily attendance (e.g., 200 days, $114) plus $1,190 per certified employee (estimated at $40 per unit of average daily attendance). Attendance given more weighting for junior high schools, high schools, Grades 13 and 14, plus 60 per cent of transportation approved cost. Minimum guarantee in terms of a state board "minimum financial program" that increases the above amount as a measure of the foundation program.

Wisconsin. $315 per resident pupil in average daily attendance (in better organized districts, $352.50). (It is of interest that aid is paid in proportion to tax levied from minimum of 3 mills up to maximum of 15 mills.) Transportation allowance added.

Adequacy of the Foundation-Program Level in the States

The adequacy of these levels may be judged by comparing them with the estimated expenditure levels in Table 13-4. In the table these are estimated by increasing the median for 1949–1950 [5] by 50 per cent and with a higher constant level, $400, which is somewhere near what the national median would be if all the states were exercising an effort comparable to that of states which were taxing themselves most vigorously for education in 1949–1950.

The foundation-level figures for each state are translated into terms roughly comparable with the New York and California figures—weighted average daily attendance. This reduces costs to equivalents of expenditures per pupil in grades below the seventh.

The four columns at the right show what taxes would be required, supplementary to any required for supporting the foundation program, in two districts of comparatively low but not extremely low wealth, if they were to reach the state median (Columns 5 and 7) or the $400 level (Columns 6 and 8). In most cases the rate, expressed on 100 per cent property valuations as they are, would be fantastic. This of course assumes that they have already achieved the foundation level, an assumption that is not sound due to limiting provisions of one sort or another controlling the distribution of aid.

[5] Clayton D. Hutchins and Albert R. Munse, *Public School Finance Programs in the United States,* U.S. Office of Education, Washington, 1954.

This table disregards watering down for small schools, any inaccuracies in the application of the measure to schools of different sizes or conditions, the varying ways of dealing with transportation and capital outlay, and the method of sharing the cost as between the state and the localities. Forgetting all about such additional disturbing matters, it should be quite apparent that the critical decision as to foundation level may predetermine a surprisingly low rating on the equalization function.

Table 13-4 Foundation Levels Provided in Various States
Compared with State Median Expenditure Levels—
Estimated as Applicable to 1958 *

State	Foundation level provided	Estimated 1958 state median	Per cent foundation program is of		Supplementary tax, dollars per hundred on full valuation required to supplement state aid to reach levels indicated			
					A $4,000 district †		A $6,000 district	
			State median	$400	State median	$400	State median	$400
N.Y.	$330	$420	79%	83%	$2.25	$1.75	$1.50	$1.16
N.J.	180	350	51	45	4.25	5.50	2.83	3.67
Ill.	180	345	52	45	4.12	5.50	2.75	3.67
Ore.	120	330	36	30	5.50	7.00	3.50	4.67
Calif.	212	320	66	53	2.70	4.70	1.80	3.13
Conn.	50	310	16	13	6.50	8.75	4.33	5.83
Wash.	154	305	50	39	3.78	6.15	2.52	4.10
Mass.	100	300	33	25	5.00	7.50	3.33	5.00
R.I.	270	295	92	68	.63	3.25	.42	2.17
Mich.	167	274	61	42	2.67	5.82	1.78	3.88
Ohio	153	259	59	38	2.65	6.17	1.76	4.12
Md.	180	255	71	45	1.87	5.50	1.25	3.66
Wis.	284	247	115	71	. . .	2.90	. . .	1.93
Va.	131	190	69	34	1.47	6.72	.98	4.48

* All expressed in weighted elementary pupil units.
† $4,000 full value back of each pupil cost unit.

Deviations from Equal Treatment of All Districts

What look like little compromises in the measurement of need and ability—in introducing special-aid or earmarked aspects of the program as essential to improvement, in invoking compliances to canalize improvement, and in defining the scope of the foundation program—warp the equalizing effect of some "equalization" programs and presumably of some flat grant programs. In some instances it would appear that poorer districts would receive as much or more aid on an out-and-out return to them of the money paid by their residents. Note, for example, that in

Table 13-1, four of the nine presumably flat grant states have distributed the flat grants in such a way that less than 5 per cent of the money has an equalizing effect. It is not conceivable that a true flat grant would have less than a 3 per cent equalization effect; even among the states in the United States approximately 25 per cent of a true flat grant would go for equalization.[6] The two flat grant states that are credited with from 50 to 69 per cent of total aid as equalization aid probably have distributive systems relatively free from warping.

Measurements of Need and Ability. Whether the plan followed is complete state support of a foundation program (flat grant type) or a need and ability (equalization type) formula, variations from a just measure of the cost of like programs should be made only with full knowledge of the effects. The same holds for ability measurements in the case of the need and ability formulas, but the more usual variations here, troublesome as they are prudentially, are of far less educational consequence. Shortchanging on the need measure shortchanges educational opportunity; errors or purposeful deviations in the ability measure tend to be limited to their effects on the taxpayer.

Deviations in the measurement of need appear in neglect or watering down of the correction for small schools, transportation, and debt service. They appear also, but with milder disturbances, in the use of aggregate days of attendance or membership instead of average daily attendance or membership, or in the choice of average daily attendance over average membership, or the choice of school census over either.

Deviations in the measurement of ability appear in the neglect of proper measures to obtain equalized valuation of property and in variation in the rate of local contribution to the foundation program for different classes of districts.

The methods of achieving acceptable measures of need (expenditure pupil units or their equivalent, expenditure classroom units) and acceptable measures of ability are discussed in Chapter 7.[7] The reasons underlying the deviations, other than sheer oversight, are discussed in Chapter 14.

Earmarking, Special Aids and Compliances

Whenever a state-aid law is being written, everybody, it seems, has some special miracle worker that will induce or press the schools into making progress. The denial of full participation to "poorly organized schools," the granting of so many dollars "if you spend it for these particu-

---

[6] The percentage of a flat grant made in terms of expenditure pupil units that goes to equalization is the same as the percentage of state aid required to equalize a given foundation program expressed in terms of expenditure pupil units.

[7] See also discussion of Cubberley's analysis, Chap. 12.

lar purposes" (or the adding of special aids for the same purpose), the computation of the cost of the foundation program so that schools must expand expenditures by hiring better-trained teachers (if they can) and not by hiring more teachers, the determination of the cost of the program by budgets that must pass state-office inspection, the payment of aid as reimbursement instead of in terms of commitments for the current year—these are the little things that squeeze the equalization out of state-aid programs. In this list of "short cuts to progress" will be found in considerable measure the causes for the poor showing of the brave equalization or "complete support" programs revealed in the preceding section.

The writers believe that the "short cuts" represent disturbing and totally inadequate solutions to a very real problem—that of expanding the support of education in the communities handicapped by lack of wealth or lack of vision, or both. State departments must be staffed with more people who can see the whole range of the problems involved in a major increase in expenditure level; they may not continue to be satisfied with supervision limited to specialists. What is needed is more able, broad-range persons who know education from kindergarten to community college and from curriculum to finance, and who have faith that the communities will respond if they can be helped with (1) recruiting adequate staffs and (2) supplying them with a favorable setting for their work—materials and special services, of course; public faith in them as persons and professionals, most certainly.

Further attention is given to this in Chapter 14 as one of the major problems to be weighed in achieving a balanced policy.

SUMMARY

Aid for equalization brings money, in the net, from communities of above average wealth to communities of below average wealth. There is no way of doing this except through state aid. Accordingly, whatever is done through the system of state aid, it is essential to know just what part of it is really equalization aid.

In the final analysis the adequacy of the equalization aid is determined by comparing the amount of such aid with the amount required to equalize the burden of an acceptable foundation program.

The idea of extending aid with regard to both need and ability has made great strides since Cubberley in 1905 rather apologetically proposed that states should have a reserve fund for communities still found to be needy after other aids had been distributed. At that time seven states had such plans, most of them involving infinitesimally small amounts of money. Today the idea is applied far more forcefully in thirty-nine states. Instead of being a supplementary provision, the need and ability formula has become the dominant method of distributing state aid in many states.

It is possible to approximate the amount of aid going to equalization from the total of state aid extended to education by the simple process of separating the amount of aid that is in effect tax sharing.

Of the forty-three states represented in Table 13-1, thirty-four have "equalization" laws. But the median percentage of the aid going for equalization falls short of 50 per cent. The showing for the nine flat grant states is almost the same.

This would suggest that a fairly wholesome proportion for equalization might comprise as little as 20 per cent, in some states perhaps as little as 15 per cent, of the total cost of education.

The conceptions of the equalization job to be done through state aid seem to fall in two groups: (1) the Cubberley approach: flat grants plus special help to the poor and (2) the over-all equalization formula approach.

There is need for a critical test of the adequacy of provisions a state-aid law makes for equalization. Regardless of how large or how small the percentage of state aid, the real test of equalization is how nearly the level of support in the poorest district approaches the state median or average; or, more sharply, how much will the state aid plus a reasonable local tax make available in such a district.

In spite of the move to recognize equalization, it is quite clear that equalization still is an ideal to strive for—by no means an accomplished fact. In a large number of states it is treated in much the same way as Cubberley envisioned it in 1905—as a sort of minute but troubling problem.

The explanation for the fact that even large amounts of state aid may fail to achieve a high degree of equalization may lie in any one of a number of places. It may lie in the elements of the over-all structure of the plan; in the provisions for keeping the state's share in balance with the local share; or in earmarking or compliance features.

The mechanism of the equalization formula, adaptable as it is to the distribution of aid for general assistance to all districts, has got far too much credit for achieving the central purpose for which it was originally designed—the assurance of an adequate foundation program.

The reason that the level of the foundation program is a crucial matter lies in the fact that the poorest districts will have very little more money to spend on education than that provided by the foundation program. This is true regardless of the rate of local contribution.

So far as average and able communities are concerned, the level of the foundation program used in computing aid is of relatively little importance.

What look like little compromises in the measurement of need and ability—in introducing special-aid or earmarked aspects of the program as essential to improvement, in invoking compliances to canalize improvement, and in defining the scope of the foundation program—warp the equalizing effect of some "equalization" programs and presumably of some flat grant programs.

Whether the plan followed is complete state support of a foundation program (flat grant type) or a need and ability (equalization type) formula, variations from a just measure of the cost of like programs should be made only with full knowledge of the effects. The same holds for ability measurements in the case of the need and ability formulas, but the more usual variations here, troublesome as they are prudentially, are of far less educational consequence.

The denial of full participation to "poorly organized schools," the granting of so many dollars "if you spend it for these particular purposes" (or the adding of special aids for the same purpose), the computation of the cost of the foundation program so that schools must expand expenditures by hiring better-trained teachers (if they can) and not by hiring more teachers, the determination of the cost of the program by budgets that must pass state-office inspection, the payment of aid as reimbursement instead of in terms of commitments for the current year —these are the little things that squeeze equalization out of state-aid programs.

QUESTIONS FOR STUDY AND DISCUSSION

1. How much of the state aid extended in your state actually acts as equalization aid?

2. What is the lowest expenditure level of the least well supported schools in your state? How does it compare with the state average?

3. Are there any provisions in your state-aid law that militate against its equalizing effects in the districts identified in Question 2?

SELECTED REFERENCES

Burke, Arvid J.: "A Century and a Half of Financing Locally Operated Functions of Government in New York State," *Fiscal Policy for Public Education in the State of New York*, Staff Study 1, New York State Educational Conference Board, Albany, N.Y., 1948, chap. III, pp. 36–45.

Cornell, Francis G., and William P. McLure: "The Foundation Program and the Measurement of Educational Need," in R. L. Johns and E. L. Morphet (eds.), *Problems and Issues in Public School Finance,* Bureau of Publications, Teachers College, Columbia University, New York, 1952.

Morphet, Edgar L.: "Characteristics of State Support Programs," in R. L. Johns and E. L. Morphet (eds.), *Problems and Issues in Public School Finance,* Bureau of Publications, Teachers College, Columbia University, New York, 1952.

Mort, Paul R.: *The Foundation Program in State Educational Policy,* The University of the State of New York, The State Department of Education, Albany, N.Y., 1957.

U.S. Office of Education, *Public School Finance Programs in the United States,* Washington, 1955.

14. Design for state-aid systems

THE HALF-CENTURY-LONG ideological battle for equalization appears to have been nearly won. Most states have the elements of good financial structure in law. The problem now is to shape them more precisely to the intended purposes—to achieve balance.

This is the first of three chapters dealing with the design of a balanced system of state aid. This chapter deals with the critical structural and operational elements involved. The first major part reviews the elements. The second major part develops design, first in terms of the recognition of the two fiscal purposes and then in terms of provision for adjustment to changing conditions. The impact of neglect and of control arrangements that often warp a state-aid system out of proper relationship to its fiscal functions is dealt with in Chapter 15; the special problems associated with transportation and capital outlay are dealt with in Chapter 16.

ELEMENTS OF DESIGN

All state-aid systems are written in terms of (1) flat grants, (2) flat grants and special aids, or (3) equalization (need and ability considered), with or without flat grants or their equivalents in minimum guarantees. As we have seen in Chapters 12 and 13, plans written in such terms do not reveal their relative emphasis on equalization and tax sharing, the two basic fiscal purposes. Neither do they reveal the degree of warping of these two fiscal purposes by the injection of control through compromises in measurement of need and through compliances.

Four Schools of Thought

There are four schools of thought on state-aid systems. The "incentives school" makes incentives central; the "equalization school" makes help to poorer districts central; the "tax-reform school" makes tax sharing

255

central; the "wholesomeness school" focuses on the achievement of whole-some balance of all three underlying purposes.

The tax sharing school of thought predominates with respect to munici-pal aid in some states. Each of the other three schools of thought is dominant with respect to aid to schools in one or more states today.

The writers believe that the movement in all states, in both school and municipal aid systems, should be toward recognition of the fact that the special purposes represented by the first three schools are present in some degree by conscious or unconscious decisions in all state-aid systems and need consciously to be kept in wholesome balance. In other words, they align themselves with the fourth school.

Cubberley's Analysis

It may be helpful to review Cubberley's analysis of the problems in-volved as a backdrop to the approach made in this chapter.

Cubberley's analysis moved from shared taxes to flat grants and finally to equalization. He finally endorsed flat grants subject to incentive modification and supplemented by an emergency equalization fund. Cubberley was trying to move his readers away from a complete reliance on state collection of local taxes to a plan that would at one and the same time care for overburdened school districts and stimulate progress in detail. Essentially, the plan he favored was a flat grant system.

While he rejected the tax collection function, he did not go so far as to say: "Use the money in the poor districts and let the able look after themselves." [1] Perhaps this would have denied him a hearing. More likely he was influenced by his high regard for using state aid as a means of influencing the educational programs of school districts. He was the key protagonist of the first school. This was a purpose that was perhaps sufficient considering that, apparently, he thought of state aid as in-volving relatively small amounts of money.

Cubberley's Analysis of Distribution Bases. Having accepted the flat grant as superior to aid distributed in terms of wealth, Cubberley pro-ceeded to analyze various bases. First he considered total population. He rejected this because it is not a good index of school cost. He pointed out that the number of children of school age varied considerably from community to community. He showed that in 1900, Springfield, Mass., employed 5.1 teachers for each 1,000 inhabitants while Lowell's ratio was 3.2.

He then took up the school census. (This is still embedded in the constitutions of sixteen states as a basis for the distribution of income from the federal land grants, but in at least ten states it is nullified in

[1] Ellwood P. Cubberley, *State School Funds and Their Apportionment,* Bureau of Publications, Teachers College, Columbia University, New York, 1905.

its differential effects by being counted toward equalization.) While he considered this better than the total number of inhabitants, he found that this basis also failed to approximate costs, because of the small-school problem, and that it left unusually poor communities in a bad way. When in Indiana the grants were figured in terms of number of teachers actually employed, however, Brown County, the delight of the budding sociologists of that day, was receiving 50 per cent more than Benton, which was listed as having several times the per capita wealth of Brown.

Cubberley next considered membership and attendance. He found that the number of children in school reflected the problem better than the total number of children in and out of school, and he liked the connotations of the former for encouraging attendance. Deploring, however, that schools with longer terms got no more money than those with short terms, he recommended that those who had the vigor and the means to run longer terms be aided in proportion, by the device of using aggregate days of attendance. This measure is still used in Colorado, Iowa, Oregon, and Washington. In all but Colorado its effects have been largely nullified by being counted toward equalization.

After building up the attendance basis to take care of the ready, able, and willing, Cubberley discovered that he had so distorted the distribution that poor districts were less well served than rich districts and that the census basis was better than the attendance basis if only one method could be used. Here we have illustrated the ambivalence arising from the need to equalize and the urge to shape destinies that plagues us to this day; it has resulted in "equalization" laws with the effect of the equalizing features utterly destroyed by "betterment" provisions.

At this point Cubberley discovered that the number of teachers employed gave a clearer indication of the actual cost than any pupil or population basis. Here he approached the simplifying foundation-program idea, associated with the measurement of what the educational need really is, regardless of wealth and regardless of ability, willingness, vigor, or predilections as to how the money ought to be spent. But this idea had to await the passage of another two decades. Five pages later Cubberley had fallen into the incentives trap again. There he states, "Its best feature is that it places a premium on the employment of a sufficient number of teachers to teach the children properly." [2]

Next Cubberley shows that the best thing to do is to combine the two measures—number of teachers employed and aggregate attendance—with all the evils and advantages of each. [3]

[2] *Ibid.*

[3] For the present-day solution of this dilemma, see the discussion of expenditure pupil cost units in chap. 7.

But Cubberley's conscience would not allow this recommendation to stand alone. There was still Brown County without enough money to run schools. Reviewing the feeble efforts in seven states to recognize the problem, and viewing again the effects of his prescription of aggregate attendance and number of teachers, he adds, "even after a distribution had been made on such a combination . . . there still probably would be heavy burdens to be borne by some poorer communities, in which case a certain 'reserve fund' should be set aside, to be distributed by some responsible educational body, for the relief of those communities which have made the maximum effort allowed by law and yet are unable to meet the minimum demands of the state and those whose peculiar circumstances make some additional assistance particularly desirable." [4]

Few studies in education have been so carefully done, so far-searching as this work of Cubberley's. It gives the most detailed picture of state aid in the United States that has ever been written. This and his analysis of trends were its great contributions—a marvelous job indeed, considering that it was done half-way back to Horace Mann.

But he was limited by his assumption that there was a magic index for a flat grant of small amounts of money. He didn't find one; there isn't any. He came very close time after time to the frame of reference that would have resolved the conflicts and shown the way out of the wilderness.

This work has been reviewed, not for what it contributed to a solution, but because it illustrates so well the traps that educators and public administration people are still falling into today. Every generation discovers them anew.

It should be obvious that flat grants are neither fish nor fowl. They are vestigial remnants of past approximations based on faulty assumptions. They are a snare and a delusion; a delusion because they sound so sensible, a snare because, unless they go most of the way in support, they still leave us with Brown County. The best flat grants extant today are those that have been neutralized by being absorbed into local support in computing equalization aid. As Table 11-3 shows, this has been done in nineteen states. In time these states will follow the lead of the thirteen states that have eliminated them entirely, protecting the few communities that would lose by the elimination by substituting a minimum guarantee as in Idaho, Missouri, New Jersey, Wyoming, and Tennessee, or finding no need even for a minimum guarantee as in Florida, Georgia, Indiana, Maine, Massachusetts, Pennsylvania, Utah, and West Virginia.

At least a quarter of the states are operating today in essentially the Cubberley pattern.

[4] Cubberley, op. cit., p. 252.

A BALANCED PROGRAM OF STATE AID

In the period since 1905 the equalization dilemma that confronted Cubberley in his use of flat grants has been resolved theoretically by Strayer and Haig, and the tax problems underlying tax sharing have come into the picture.

States have not been particularly aware of the tax problem. They have, however, developed greater concern for poor districts and they have never lost faith in the possibility of achieving progress through the age-old device of giving incentive money, and the equally venerable device of denying money to those who do not conform. Since emphases vary, the result is the equalization school of thought and the incentive school of thought.

These two concerns both breed a sort of paternalism in state-local relations that has provided a rationale for denying the poor districts what justice would require. They have made it more difficult to develop the sense of equal partnership of central and local agencies that seems to be demanded by the magnitude of the problems we now face in the financing of education. The achievement of such a partnership would seem to require a system built in terms of the basic economic problems involved —both structural and dynamic. The incentives purpose should not be allowed to intrude until the just treatment of the communities, in terms of the basic economic problems, has been determined.

The Structural Elements

The framework of the state-aid system should be determined in terms of the needs for equalization and tax sharing. The needs for equalization stem from the considerations involved in the foundation program (Chapter 3). The needs for tax sharing are discussed in Chapter 13. This section shows how the two needs, once defined, can be joined in an equalization formula.

The Equalization Requirements. If there were some way to get the localities fully to support the foundation program, equalization (in the sense of assuring such a program, as a minimum, to all children) would be achieved. But the element of justice to taxpayers, and, for that matter sheer inability of some communities, requires state sharing of the burden.

It was lack of ability that Cubberley invoked in his 1905 analysis. It was to justice that Strayer and Haig appealed two decades later.

The demands of justice are met effectively when all communities pay toward the cost of the foundation program at the rate that the wealthiest large district (referred to previously as the key district) would require to support the cost of the foundation program without aid. Placing any larger share on the communities results in injustice—the higher the share, the more injustice to the communities receiving aid.

The important point here is that equalization does not require a lower rate than that required for complete support in the key district. If a lesser local rate is used, it does not result in an improvement of equalization. The increased state aid, required by lessening the local support, actually goes to the communities in exactly the same way as it would go if it were distributed in terms of the wealth base used in the law.

Here is an example. If the rate required in the key district were 10 mills, this would be the lowest local rate of contribution that equalization demands. If the rate used in the law were 8 instead of 10 every community would pay 2 mills less on the value of its property and the loss would be made up in state aid. The increased aid is obviously what 2 mills would raise in each community. In a community with a valuation of $3,000 per pupil, using 8 mills instead of the allowed 10 would increase its aid by the amount of its local saving, $6 per pupil; in a community with a valuation of $20,000 per pupil, using 8 mills would likewise increase its aid by the amount of its local saving, $40.

Relation to Tax Sharing. But this is exactly what has been the objective in the moves to have the state collect taxes for communities, returning the yield to the community of origin. Accordingly, aid in excess of that required for equalization is "tax sharing" aid.

Consequently any decision to use a rate of local contribution higher than the maximum tolerable for equalization results in inequality of burden; any decision to use a lower rate does not enhance the equalizing effect but rather it introduces a tax sharing function.

There may be every justification for a tax sharing function. But it rapidly expands state aid without enhancing the foundation program. The quality of equalization of educational opportunity is enhanced by raising the level of the foundation program—not by increasing the state's share of the cost of a given foundation program.

Flat Grant and Equalization—Dangers. Actually many combined flat grant and equalization plans are really equalization plans with an intolerably low foundation program and an intolerably high local rate. What this does is to overemphasize tax sharing (which is practically meaningless to the community limited in resources) at the expense of equalization. It keeps everybody happy who is not concerned with equalization. Since those who are affected seriously by the need for equalization usually lack the local leadership or the means to be represented at meetings of the leaders, decisions too frequently are made with no voice raised for authentic equalization. Decisions are made to increase "equalization" aid to all. State "equalization aid" is increased, but true equalization is not materially enhanced; it may even be diluted by "compliances" and "incentive" features written by men of little under-standing of the problem of school improvement in poorer areas.

It should be quite clear that when an unusually high percentage of the cost of education is coming from the state and a defensibly high foundation level is conspicuous by its absence, equalization is being sacrificed to tax sharing. In such a case someone is being fooled. To equalization, state aid is indispensable; to readjustment of the tax base, state aid is only one of several available tools.

Flat Grants, Tax Sharing, and Equalization

It may be helpful to realize that the combination of flat grants and equalization is a marriage of convenience. It makes no sense whatever until it is broken down into the equalization and tax sharing components.

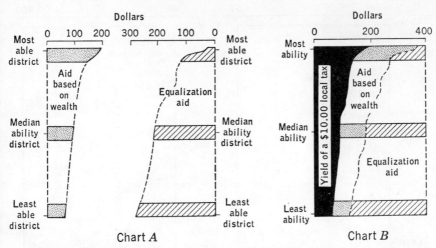

Fig. 14-1 How distribution on basis of wealth and distribution of equalization aid may be combined in an equalization-type formula.

Figures 14-1 and 14-2 show how an equalization-type formula can be translated into an equivalent formula made up of a flat grant and an equalization part. In this case, the key district is the wealthiest district, and the use of the flat grant idea makes no change whatever in the grants to individual districts. Chart A, Figure 14-1, shows aid based on wealth or tax-broadening aids. This is given at the left. Equalization aid is given at the right. Chart B binds the two parts in Chart A in the two sectors of the chart at the right, leaving the black section at the left as the part of the foundation program which must be cared for by local taxation.

Expressed as an equalization formula, state aid is the difference between the cost of a $400 foundation program and a $10 rate of contribution. What the wealthiest community gets is entirely based on wealth, a tax-broadening aid. The communities of median ability get considerably less aid based on wealth and a sizable amount based on equalization. The communities of least ability get little aid based on wealth and a great deal based on equalization.

It will be noted from Chart B that the same effect could be achieved if every community were granted first $200 per weighted pupil and then the difference between the other $200 per weighted pupil and the $10 local rate of contribution. In other words, there would be a $200 flat grant and then an equalization formula for equalizing the remainder of the $400 not taken care of by the $200 flat grant.

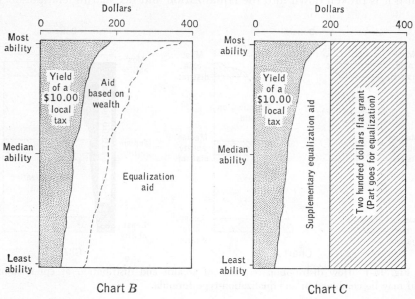

Fig. 14-2 Comparison of the effects of two methods of writing a state-aid law. (Adapted from New York State Educational Conference Board, *Fiscal Policy for Public Education in the State of New York,* Albany, N.Y., September, 1947, p. 69.)

This can be seen more readily in the two charts that make up Figure 14-2. Chart B in Figure 14-2 is the same as Chart B in Figure 14-1, except that the three types of communities are not crosshatched. Chart C in Figure 14-2 shows the $200 flat grant and the supplementary equalization aid.

In comparing Charts B and C it should be quite clear that a great deal of the flat grant money is equalization money. Enough of the flat grant money is equalization money to supplement the equalization aid sufficiently to make the area in Chart C for equalization aid equal to the area in Chart B for equalization aid. This would leave, of the flat grant for aid based on wealth, a part equivalent to the section in Chart B designated as aid based on wealth.

It should be clear that the only difference between these two plans, except as Chart C might make a minimum guarantee to very wealthy districts above the key equalization districts, is in its psychological effect. Chart C says, in effect, that the state is paying for half of the foundation program outright and "equalizing" the other half. It is paying for half of the foundation program outright because of the fact that, when equalization and tax broadening are both taken into account, the result is that the key district is entitled to half of its foundation program from the state. Superficially, however, it also denotes a state-wide concern that would be obvious to those who might not take the trouble to see through the component parts of the aid as it is fundamentally presented in Chart B. In other words, it is a matter of choice which pattern of the formula is to be used.

Of course, the same results as those shown in Chart C could be achieved by saying that the state would pay the difference between a $400 program and a $10 rate of local contribution, but not less than $200 per unit of need. This, however, has the effect of isolating the relatively small number of able districts that get the minimum guarantee and putting them at some disadvantage. Where such districts are inadequately organized, their aid should be reduced in some way or their local mandated tax increased or both. Where they are well organized, such districts should be looked to as potential lighthouses in the system. The amount of aid that goes to them which could not be justified on the pure equalization basis is of little consequence. This flat grant as a minimum guarantee protects them against the kind of criticism that periodically arises against favored communities from persons who do not fully appreciate the potential contributions of such communities to the general welfare of the system.

The Dynamic Elements of a State-Aid System

In recent years it has become more and more apparent that the character of a state-aid system must in no small degree be measured in terms of its dynamic qualities. However good it may be in its structure, its effectiveness depends upon its responsiveness to change: change in population, change in the value of money, and change in public expectancy.

It was noted that since 1890 we have experienced three major periods characterized by increased school population, rising price levels, and educational improvements. During each of these periods the state part of the state-local partnership has responded, but the local partner has responded more. The local responsiveness is a rather continuous process from year to year or by surges every two or three years. The state expansion has tended to come more sporadically. There have gradually developed various devices by which the responses of the state partner can be made smoother.

Commitment to a Program Instead of to a Fixed Sum. In the early days of state aid it was quite customary for a state to set up a specific amount of money or take the yield of certain invested funds or of a given tax and distribute it according to some base, such as number of children living in the community or the number of children in school. As population increased, the allotments became thinner and thinner. This was what happened in Connecticut where the returns from the sale of its western reserve were at first sufficient to operate the schools completely and over the decades became less and less adequate without a compensating response on the part of the localities. If Connecticut had been committed to complete support for education, the history of American school finance might be quite different.

Gradually, as they have taken on greater responsibility, states have shifted from the distribution-fund approach to the program approach, but there are still a number of states in which the state-aid laws carry a provision for prorating the state aid when it is not sufficient to carry out the program. While there may be no legal way absolutely to assure that the legislature will provide the funds necessary for a given program, state-aid laws should certainly not make neglect easy by providing partial payment formulas. Maryland went a long way in the right direction in the constitutional revision of 1910. It provided that the estimates of the state department of education as to the cost of schools under the statutory program should not be subject to modification by budgetary officers.[5]

Quite clearly, unless the state government takes its commitments seriously, any talk of a firm partnership between the state and locality is inapplicable. Of course this is a protection for times of retraction as well as for times of expansion. The temptation for the legislature to fail to provide the full demands of statutes may be even greater during depression periods than during periods of expansion.

Adjustment to Population Change. All state-aid plans of any fiscal consequence utilize some distributive measure which reflects increase in school population. They use the number of pupils, the number of teachers, or actual expenditure. All of these measures respond to population increase. The only problem is to have the state committed to maintain the levels of support for larger populations and to provide means of

---

[5] The Wilmington *Journal Every Evening* of June 24, 1959, reports a ruling by the Delaware State Attorney General that "contracts of the State Board of Education with school employees are binding regardless of funds cut or appropriated by the General Assembly."

easing the financial problems of the localities which are suffering a loss of population.

State systems vary considerably, however, with respect to their responsiveness to change. Most state-aid systems are built on a reimbursement principle. During a given year the state pays in terms of the program of the previous year, a second previous year, or a combination of previous years. More and more emergency funds have been associated with such plans to help rapidly growing districts.

Some states have discovered, however, that this lag in responsiveness of the state partner is not necessary. State aid is usually paid in two or more installments. It is entirely feasible for the early installment to be made on estimates of the current year's distribution data (pupils, teachers, expenditures, or whatever) and corrections to be made for errors of estimate in the latest distribution or in the distribution of the succeeding year. Of course the states that use the budget plan as a basis for state aid—Alaska, Delaware, Hawaii, and North Carolina—are not faced with this lag problem.

Adjusting the Level of the Foundation Program. The increase in cost due to population increase is a sort of horizontal increase. If there is neither change in the purchasing value of the dollar nor general enhancement of the education program, no difficulty arises from a fixed foundation level such as those used in most of the states.

The trouble is that neither of these factors resists change for any length of time, and the indications are very strong that at least the factor of betterment will be a highly disturbing one in the decades ahead as the American school system squares away for the task of providing more adequate education. State after state is faced with the dilemma that a fixed program written in the law one year on the basis of data for the preceding year is already outdated when it goes into effect the succeeding year. Whatever happens to price levels, this will continue to be true as the schools in America readjust themselves to insights that have arisen out of the experimentation and research that were keyed off by the psychological discoveries at the turn of the present century. There are many signs that we are definitely in this adjustment period, a period in which we will come more and more to adjust the schools through having well-trained teachers in sufficient numbers to do the job we all want done. The Educational Policies Commission's report, *The Contemporary Challenge to American Education*,[6] was one of the first indications of the recognition of this grass-roots fact on a high policy level.

What this will require of financing programs is some kind of an escalator to keep the objective plans of the foundation program, in terms of cost units of some sort, abreast of the unfolding program as it is influenced

[6] National Education Association, Educational Policies Commission, *The Contemporary Challenge to American Education*, Washington, 1958.

both by policy changes and by the long trend towards betterment. Today states that use the budget plan of determining the foundation program—Alaska, Hawaii, Delaware, and North Carolina—presumably provide for automatic adjustment to some degree, at least. The states that make their allowances in terms of a percentage of the actual cost, as a number of states do for transportation, and as Alaska does for the general program, presumably provide fully for automatic adjustment.

The only state with an objective method of determining the cost of the foundation program that has an automatic adjustment feature is the State of Indiana, where the number of units determined objectively is multiplied by the average salary of teachers. If a single element were to be selected to get a measure of the response of the local school systems to the burgeoning forces which affect their operation, this would be the best one. There is, of course, the possibility of going the whole way, as was suggested by the New York State Educational Conference Board in its *1957 Review of Fiscal Policy:* "It is recommended that, upon the attainment of a proper adjustment in the level of the foundation program and other controlling factors of the state aid formula, the factors be adjusted each year thereafter by the use of an index, for example, one based upon the change . . . in the median expenditure of districts within 10 per cent of the average valuation per true weighted pupil cost unit in the state." [7]

The Conference Board recommendation calls attention to the fact that an automatic correction to the foundation program alone will tend to disturb the balance existing in the system as between the equalization money and the tax sharing money. Put another way, it tends to throw out of balance the relative proportions carried by the state and the localities. The Conference Board proposal recognizes this by asking that the index be applied to all controlling factors. These would be the foundation program, the local rate of contribution, and any arrangements providing minimum guarantees (flat grants nullified except for communities not receiving equalization aid, or outright minimum guarantees).

This is not a problem in the instance where the foundation program is completely state supported, as in Alaska, Delaware, Hawaii, and North Carolina. It would be a factor in the sort of correction that the Indiana law provides since under the present arrangements the increase in the foundation program would be carried completely by the state. This is not necessarily bad. It might be used as a planned arrangement for a gradual increase in the state's share.

[7] New York State Educational Conference Board, *1957 Review of Fiscal Policy for Public Education in New York State,* Albany, N.Y., August 1957, p. 8.

Low Expenditure Problems. There is always the problem of the districts that fall below the foundation level.[8] A recent review of what happened in two of the strong pioneer equalization states, Maryland [9] and New York,[10] showed that in spite of the great emphasis equalization has been given in these two states since the middle 1920s, the pattern of expenditure has not flattened out on the lower end. It has improved, however, and the gap between the foundation program and where the low communities are now operating is one that could conceivably be crossed through increased local vigor. One shudders to think of the situation these schools would be in if the localities alone had been faced with the necessity of bridging the tremendous gap between their ability and present expenditure standards. A study of what happened in these two states over a third of a century is chastening but exceedingly revealing. While it is by no means discouraging, it does suggest some changes in emphasis.

Reasons for lag. Without inflation, rising living standards, wars, and educational betterment, possibly the Strayer-Haig conception of the foundation level, to be achieved without local initiative, would have come to pass. Actually, however, there are few, if any, states that have come anywhere near to a situation where no schools are operating financially below the presumed foundation level.

There are many difficulties in reaching this ideal. In the first place, many states have despaired of attaining their true foundation level in the small school districts that have not given way to reorganization. In these cases there has been a general willingness to accept far less than what could be achieved in these areas even under the outmoded organization. The theory has been that if schools were made as good as they could be, the people would not want to reorganize.

Another cause for delay is lack of willingness on the part of some districts to levy the minimum taxes required for the foundation level. Most states have some way of recognizing this by reducing the aid to districts that do not fully meet the taxing standard that the law establishes as a minimum.

The standard of preparation of teachers to which communities may be

[8] State accounting procedures may show all districts up to the level as measured in terms of compromises injected into the law. Such compromises appear in the exclusion of certain classes of districts; in the use of watered-down expenditure pupil units, in budgets approved, and in counting debt service or transportation expenditure as though it contributed to the expenditure level (chap. 7).

[9] William S. Sartorius, *The Fortunes of Equalization Since 1920*, Maryland State Department of Education, Baltimore, Md., 1959.

[10] Bernard H. McKenna, *The Achievement of Equality of Educational Opportunity in the State of New York*, Staff Study No. 5, New York State Educational Conference Board, Albany, N.Y., November, 1957.

committed is another source of difficulty. Many communities have an appreciable proportion of teachers below the standards adopted by the state. Where they are a minority, they do not disturb people too much in their thinking about raising expenditure levels. Where their numbers are dominant, it is difficult for people to see that raising expenditure levels is a way to salvage those that can be salvaged and discourage those that cannot be.

A less tangible reason for the slowness of response of communities is the phenomenon of expenditure-level habit. Furno's study of expenditure level of the Metropolitan School Study Council schools over thirty-five years suggests that expenditure level in a community tends to stay in much the same relationship with its neighbors, decade after decade.[11] The shifting of a community expenditure level to a markedly higher one is evidently something of a traumatic experience, whether the community be rich, average, or poor. The realization of this phenomenon tends to make us a little more sympathetic with the people and administrators in communities that are asked by the state to change their way of life. Also, a realization of this point should make us a little less fearful that communities of high ability, which exist in every state, would deteriorate if placed under a plan such as the Wisconsin plan but without restrictions.

The Wisconsin approach. One of the most challenging attacks on this problem has been made by Wisconsin. Instead of requiring all communities to tax at the level established for the foundation program in order to get any or all of the equalization aid desired, Wisconsin has provided that, for whatever level the community is operating on, the state's proportionate share and the local proportionate share shall be the same as they would be at the prescribed foundation level. For example, if the state aid to which a community would be entitled if it were operating the full foundation program were a third of the total, then in case the community is operating at only half the foundation level, it will still get a third of the cost from the state and provide two-thirds locally. There is a limit set on this which presumably defines the foundation level toward which the state is directing its efforts and the local contribution associated with it. While the law does not state these amounts or identify them, they are apparently $315 and 15 mills.

The more common method is to set the foundation level and local rate in the law and then to withhold state aid equal to that which the community saves by using a lower rate. The Wisconsin method, in effect, withholds only that percentage of state aid which the amount saved locally is of the specified local rate.

[11] Orlando F. Furno, "The Projection of School Quality from Expenditure Level," Ph.D. dissertation, Teachers College, Columbia University, New York, 1956. (Typewritten.)

Raising the Level in All Districts. When the problem is to raise the level not just of the minority of districts but of all the districts in the state, the merits of such a plan as the Wisconsin plan appear to be even greater. This need is more general than would at first appear. Six decades of ferment in the schools following the discoveries at the turn of the century concerning the nature of learning combined with the increasing reliance on education as a social and economic tool (Chapter 6) would appear to have demonstrated to anyone who will look at the facts squarely the need for financing education at higher levels than any state has yet achieved. Even in the fiscal turmoil of the 1950s arising from expanding school population and inflation, there has been a surging forward in many communities and in entire states.[12]

Accordingly any set foundation level that is automatically responsive only to population increase and changes in dollar values would appear to be always out of date during this period of betterment. It may well be a period spanning from three to five decades. This underlies the discussion earlier in the chapter on adjusting the level of the foundation program. The issue is raised here again because the Wisconsin approach with modifications seems to provide an attractive alternative to the set foundation level.

A modified "Wisconsin plan." By and large, many states that have had a consciousness of need for catching up, as it were, have attacked this problem through the device of allowing the foundation program to reflect the level of training of teachers. This purpose must have been in the background of the establishment of the plan for imputing a budget from teachers' salaries that are based on a state salary schedule in which training and sometimes both training and experience are taken into account. These states include Alabama, Delaware, Georgia, Idaho, Kansas, Maryland, South Carolina, Tennessee, Texas, and Virginia.

In the light of our discussion here, it would appear that there may be more hope in the Wisconsin plan, which permits local adjustments of the program as it evolves, than in the plan that seeks to guide improvement through rewarding districts that employ highly trained teachers. In the Wisconsin plan if more is paid for teachers, it is recognized in state aid. It is presumably the district leaders' responsibility to see that all things which make for better teaching, including certification and experience, will be taken into account. There is certainly no assurance that rewarding the training of teachers and, as most states do, penalizing, as it were, the employment of more teachers is the only way to salvation.

If the Wisconsin alternative were followed in situations where there is general assumption that no districts are doing well enough, then it

---

[12] William S. Vincent, *Educational Betterment in New York State Public Schools Since 1920*, New York State Educational Conference Board, Staff Study No. 1, Albany, N.Y., November, 1957.

would appear to be wise to remove the limitations which Wisconsin has placed on the sharing arrangement, or to relax the limitations materially. To do this, all that would seem to be necessary would be to establish the ratio of reimbursement for each community somewhat in the Wisconsin or Pennsylvania pattern, and then to apply this to the expenditure level, whatever it might be. When the more vigorous communities reach levels which could be considered high enough to be realistic in terms of present-day needs, a limitation such as the Wisconsin limitation could be imposed. This is not likely to happen in less than several years.

The Updegraff plan. In reviewing the evolution of a conceptual basis for state aid, the first edition of this book, published in 1941, discussed the proposal of Updegraff for tying up aid with the local tax effort and of Henry Morrison for complete state support. They were treated as "nonconforming proposals." [13] The second edition (1951) did not refer to these two proposals. What the preceding section says is that perhaps the time has come when the Updegraff approach can be a useful tool in the transition in school finance that is now upon us. It has been proposed for such use in Maryland. [14]

The Cubberley Approach as an Alternative to the Equalization Formula

In this chapter, up to this point, the analysis has been in terms of fitting an equalization-type formula to the two objectives of equalization and tax sharing. From an examination of Table 11-3 in Chapter 11, it can be concluded that states are now moving strongly in this direction. But the analysis of equalizing effects given in Chapter 12 lends itself to another interpretation. This other interpretation is that the great majority of states (perhaps all but the eleven in Column 1 of Table 11-3 and the nine in Column 5), more or less unconscious of the tax sharing objectives, are following the Cubberley pattern of flat grant plus equalization supplements.

This suggests the policy of proceeding on the flat-grant basis (analyzed we hope in terms of its tax sharing and equalization effects) and dealing with equalization as a special problem much as we have suggested in Chapter 16. With respect to transportation and capital outlay we suggest the reduction of the inequalities to tolerable limits rather than complete justice in a theoretical sense. While the reasons in these instances are technical, there would appear to be no reason why the same approach should not be used to the equalization problem remaining after flat

[13] See pp. 200–201.

[14] Cooperative Study Policy Committee, *Education for Our Times—A State Action Program*, Maryland State Department of Education, Baltimore, Md., May, 1959.

grants have been applied, even though in this case the reason for doing it is theoretical rather than technical.

If we assume that in a given state the over-all need for equalization can be met by pure equalization money equal to 20 per cent of the cost of education, a flat grant amounting to one-half the cost of the foundation program will reduce the required equalization money to 10 per cent. Accordingly it is not outside the bounds of reason to make flat grants computed on some basis such as the expenditure pupil unit, supplemented by aids for (1) residual equalization, (2) transportation, and (3) capital outlay.

If the people of a state see the problem as essentially taxing the wealth where it is and sending the money where the children are, and are not willing to embrace the logical outcome—complete state support of the foundation program—this method of dealing with the equalization problem that is not cared for by flat grants short of 100 per cent support may be the logical one. Designed with the same regard for the basic objectives, a plan involving flat grants and residual equalization could have effects identical with those of an equalization-type over-all plan.

SUMMARY

All state-aid systems are written in terms of (1) flat grants, (2) flat grants and special aids, or (3) equalization (need and ability considered), with or without flat grants or their equivalents in minimum guarantees. Plans written in such terms do not reveal their relative emphasis on equalization and tax sharing, the two basic fiscal purposes. Neither do they reveal the degree of warping of these two fiscal purposes by the injection of control through compromises in measurement of need and through compliances.

There are four schools of thought on state-aid systems. The "incentives school" makes incentives central; the "equalization school" makes help to poorer districts central; the "tax-reform school" makes tax sharing central; the "wholesomeness school" emphasizes the achievement of wholesome balance of the three underlying purposes.

Cubberley's analysis moved from shared taxes to flat grants and finally to equalization. Finally he favored flat grants subject to incentive modification and supplemented by an emergency equalization fund. Cubberley was trying to move his readers away from a complete reliance on state collection of local taxes to a plan that would at one and the same time care for overburdened school districts and stimulate progress in detail. Centrally, the plan he presented was a flat grant system.

At least a quarter of the states are operating today in essentially the Cubberley pattern.

In the period since 1905 the equalization dilemma that confronted Cubberley in his use of flat grants has been resolved theoretically by Strayer and Haig, and the tax problems underlying tax sharing have come into the picture.

The framework of the state-aid system should be determined in terms of the needs for equalization and tax sharing. The needs for equalization stem from the considerations involved in the foundation program (Chapter 3).

If there were some way to get the localities fully to support the foundation program, equalization (in the sense of assuring such a program, as a minimum, to all children) would be achieved. But the element of justice to taxpayers and, for that matter sheer inability of some communities, requires state sharing of the burden.

The demands of justice are met effectively when all communities pay toward the cost of the foundation program at the rate that the wealthiest large district (referred to previously as the key district) would require to support the cost of the foundation program without aid. Placing any larger share on the communities results in injustice—the higher the share, the more injustice to the communities receiving aid.

Any decision to use a rate of local contribution higher than the maximum tolerable for equalization results in inequality of burden; any decision to use a lower rate does not enhance the equalizing effect but rather it introduces a tax sharing function.

It should be quite clear that when an unusually high percentage of the cost of education is coming from the state and a defensibly high foundation level is conspicuous by its absence, equalization is being sacrificed to tax sharing. In such a case someone is being fooled. To equalization, state aid is indispensable; to readjustment of the tax base, state aid is only one of several available tools.

The combination of flat grants and equalization is a marriage of convenience. It makes no sense whatever until it is broken down into the equalization and tax sharing components.

In recent years it has become more and more apparent that the character of a state-aid system must in no small degree be measured in terms of its dynamic qualities. However good it may be in its structure, its effectiveness depends upon its responsiveness to change: change in population, change in the value of money, and change in public expectancy.

There is always the problem of the districts that fall below the foundation level. There are few, if any, states that have achieved anywhere near a situation where no schools are operating financially below the presumed foundation level.

One of the most challenging attacks on this problem has been made by Wisconsin. Instead of requiring all communities to tax at the level established for the foundation program in order to get any or all of the equalization aid desired, Wisconsin has provided that, for whatever level the community is operating on, the state's proportionate share and the local proportionate share shall be the same as they would be at the prescribed foundation level.

When the problem is to raise the level not just of the minority of districts but of all the districts in the state, the merits of such a plan as the Wisconsin plan appear to be even greater.

Designed with the same regard for the basic objectives, a plan involving flat grants and residual equalization could have effects identical with those of an equalization-type over-all plan.

QUESTIONS FOR STUDY AND DISCUSSION

1. In the light of this chapter analyze the design of the state school-aid system in your state, considering all aids to education as constituting a "system."

2. Make a similar analysis of the design of the state aid to municipal government in your state.

3. How do the two systems of aid complement each other in achieving equalization of the burden of school and local government and balance in the tax system?

SELECTED REFERENCES

Burke, Arvid J.: *Financing Public Schools in the United States,* rev. ed., Harper & Brothers, New York, 1957.

Cooperative Study Policy Committee: *Education for Our Times—A State Action Program,* Maryland State Department of Education, Baltimore, Md., May, 1959.

Cornell, Francis G.: "Grants-in-aid Apportionment Formulas," *Journal of the American Statistical Association,* vol. 42, no. 237, March, 1947, pp. 92–104.

Johnson, Byron L.: *The Principle of Equalization Applied to the Allocation of Grants-in-Aid,* Federal Security Agency, Bureau of Research and Statistics, Memorandum 66, Government Printing Office, Washington, 1947.

National Education Association, Educational Policies Commission, *The Contemporary Challenge to American Education,* Washington, 1958.

New York State Department of Education: *Summary Report of 1957–58 Studies in State Aid to School Districts,* The University of the State of New York, Albany, N.Y., 1958.

New York State Educational Conference Board, *Fiscal Policy for Public Education in the State of New York,* Albany, N.Y., 1947.

Rockefeller Brothers Fund, Inc.: *The Pursuit of Excellence,* Education and the Future of America, Doubleday and Company, Inc., New York, 1958.

Ruml, Beardsley: *Financing Public Education in the Decade Ahead,* National Citizens Commission for the Public Schools, New York, 1954.

15. State aid as an instrument of control

THE LONG history of using state aid for schools as a means to stimulate and canalize practice has left its imprint on all school aid systems and is likely to continue to counsel mandates, compliances, and other departures from the uniform treatment of districts which is assumed in the discussion of tax sharing and equalization. The first major section of this chapter discusses the variations from uniform treatment that are practiced. The second major section seeks to resolve the conflict between the theory underlying such practices and the general "wholesomeness of conditions" approach that motivates tax sharing and equalization.

VARIATION FROM LIKE TREATMENT

Three types of variation from uniform treatment are dealt with here: incentive aids, prudential controls, and oversimplification.

Incentive Aids

Special aids as such are rapidly disappearing from the scene. The older ones are being absorbed into the equalization program. Some still surviving are really general aids and no longer serve the stimulation function. They might well be repealed or absorbed into the equalization program. What remain are fiscally inconsequential.

Attention should be called, however, to the fact that although special aids may not show up on the statute books, they may still be in the picture. A great many state-aid systems, whether of the flat grant type or the equalization type, carry provisions for additional money to be granted communities operating classes of one sort or another. Such

274

payments certainly are not needed to adjust a measure of the cost of the foundation program. They are in the law for stimulative effect only and might just as well be included frankly as the special aids they are. Their appeal comes from the fact that more money goes to those who perform the educational task in a way that those who pass on the task approve. Others who may have just as satisfactory a way of doing the job, along with those who do nothing about it, are of course not given the additional help.

Such steps have been defended as a means of expanding the scope of the foundation program. If their proponents can demonstrate that the particular activities specified generally represent the best possible use of that amount of money—that there are no acceptable alternatives—this method of expansion could conceivably be justified. The alternative is to raise the level of support and then bring state leadership into play. If the new money should in fact go to special classes, or adult education, or to summer schools, or to community colleges, communities should be found responsive to leadership. Giving the community an either/or choice would appear to be a rather low level of state leadership.

It should be clear that earmarking of extra money for various purposes is not essential for a just operation of a state-aid program. What is needed is an index of educational need which will have high "actuarial" relationship with school quality. The expenditure pupil unit discussed in Chapter 7 meets the test. Any additions to meet peculiar conditions should reflect causes (such as sparsity of population and the uneven burden of capital outlay), not variations in programs.

This holds for such mutations of the basic pupil index as expenditure classroom units, or expenditure teacher units. Computations based on these can be identical in their effect. The trouble with them is that they invite comparison of the number of units of need with the number of teachers employed in individual districts (two quite different things) and hence the imposing of controls that require a given number of teachers to be employed for a given number of pupils.

Most of the plans using the teacher salary as a base do not recognize local cost distributions that allocate more for teachers with less training (or less training and experience) or more for nonsalary expenses than that used in determining the total budget from salaries. An example of this is the Maryland law which computes nonsalary current cost (other than transportation) at 25 per cent of the computed salary cost, even though every county in the state exceeds this figure.

Under such plans the community must make the transition to higher expenditure levels by following the state pattern. Any other plan is penalized.

Invariably associated with this approach is the confusion of teacher cost units (often computed quite justly from attendance or enrollment corrected for population sparsity) with the number of teachers, with the result that penalty is visited on a community choosing to employ fewer teachers, and to put the money in higher salaries or in other aspects of expenditure. This is incentive aid with a vengeance.

This is not an argument against the use of special aids but rather an appeal to keep their use in perspective. Whether they are frankly provisions of the general finance program or show up as earmarking in the foundation program itself, their justification is in their efficiency as a device to achieve real improvement as compared with either less restrictive approach. As Burke has pointed out, so long as they are available to all communities—a condition that requires complete support of the activity by the state—they do not have disequalizing effect. They can go to the poor as well as to the rich. Under those circumstances they must be judged purely as promotional devices. Even when this condition is not met, the disturbance of the general fiscal program caused by the relatively small amounts going to special aids in one way or another is infinitesimal as compared with the disturbances that will be discussed in a later section of this chapter. They are inconsequential. But the warpings arising from projecting the cost of the foundation program from a state salary schedule are far from inconsequential.

Prudential Controls

Attention has already been called to the provisions in state-aid laws that deny full participation to some districts and make drastic cuts in aid to communities that fall below the standards set. To these might well be added the denials visited upon the poorer communities that find it difficult either through inept administration or through lack of funds to recruit good teachers. In the frame of reference in which these laws were written, this no doubt seems entirely justified. Judging it from the standpoint of broader financial policy, however, one wonders how such communities can overcome the kind of handicaps they have. Every state-aid system should be examined to discover the covert or unintended penalizations made in accordance with an oversimplified notion of how progress can be achieved in the poorer districts. Such penalties are one of the causes for failure of these poorer communities to bridge the chasm between their own expenditure level and that presumably made possible by the state. One questions, for example, how long we shall deny education to children in what are considered poorly organized districts as a means of forcing their elders to accept governmental forms more palatable to educators. Wouldn't it be wiser to let these communities have a taste of the best education that can be provided? The children at least will not suffer. Their elders may then be more interested in changing governmental organization if it indeed does promise to improve the quality of education.

By and large, the present writers believe that we have been caught too long in a rather narrow notion of what good district organization is. There seems to be a strong probability that the ideals we give lip service to were established in terms of a transitional conception of a good school —a school with mass instruction for most of the children and special classes for the unusual. We have come to see that this school is not adequate. There should be enough doubt, at least, of the miracle-working powers of trading teachers for bus drivers to carry us to the point of eliminating these penalties.

Not that a consideration of adequate district organization is unimportant. The trouble is that it appears more and more probable that district organization hampers education quite as much when school districts are oversized as when they are undersized and that the key characteristic to look for is not size but the character of the popular control of budget and policy.[1]

The psychologists tell us that punishment is not the opposite of reward—that punishment is poison and should be administered as medicine only by experts and only after the most careful analysis of the needs of the patient and his physical capacity to take the punishment. Some of this point of view might well influence our thinking about the use of compliances in state-aid laws. The writers would settle for one compliance—that the state aid for operation should be spent, and spent for operation. Even this is more than our municipal government brethren seem to find necessary in connection with a considerable share of the aid to municipal government. Perhaps they go too far the other way. Educators reared in a culture that believed that the task of the state was to stimulate local vigor and that miracles could be performed by fiscally unimportant aid measures—the Cubberley notion—certainly must be alert to the possibility that they may go too far in this matter of compliances.

Oversimplification

One of the most prolific producers of injustice in state-aid systems is the tendency to oversimplify provisions for determining the cost of the foundation program. The methods reviewed earlier—developed since Cubberley made his brilliant analysis—should be applied. When such measures have been developed, avoiding compromise, deviations from standard practice can be based upon the results with full knowledge of their effects on individual communities. To assume without actually

[1] New York State Educational Conference Board, *School Quality and Local School Government,* Albany, N.Y., 1956.

knowing that this or that approximation will be adequate is to court injustice, discontent, and often ill-considered revisions of the law. Too many state-aid laws today use measures that cause the system to depart amazingly from justice in its operation. The variations are a result of a combination of incentives, prudential requirements, and oversimplification—all representing guesses that what is done is of minor effect on the system.

TOWARD A BALANCE OF FISCAL AND CONTROL PURPOSES

This section seeks to differentiate between two theories of state policy: (1) the production of wholesome conditions for local action in which the foundation program is the keystone of a structure of interrelated items, and (2) the bit-by-bit, vectorial approach, according to which the foundation program is just one more narrowly defined and relatively independent aspect.

In the Strayer and Haig proposal it was assumed as axiomatic that the assurance of a minimum level of support for education and the achievement of a just distribution of the burden for its support would be good for schools. They saw a conflict with these objectives in the policy of building the state-aid program bit by bit, awarding separate grants for the promotion of specific aspects of the educational program. Their analysis of the twenty-two special aids which at that time comprised the state-aid system of New York indicated that such aids went to the abler communities in undue proportion and thus tended to magnify the injustices of the system of support rather than to correct them. They considered this conflict serious, presumably because they had not fully conceived of the demands of their principle upon state aid. Actually the carrying out of the Strayer and Haig principle requires scores of millions of dollars of state aid whereas the special-aid approach can be satisfied with millions. Inequalities introduced by special aids associated with an adequate program for equalization of the burden of a minimum program of even modest dimensions would disturb the total justice in the distribution of burden but little. Evidently they were combating the notion, that was then generally held as a result of Cubberley's 1905 analysis, that an adequate state program would be made up of about equal parts of promotional aids and help to the poor communities (equalization aid).

The proposal by Strayer and Haig for equalizing the burden for a minimum program, associated with their opposition to special aids, provides a corollary to the assertion noted above. This corollary is that any system of aid that runs counter to the objective of assuring a minimum program with a just distribution of burdens is to be avoided, regardless of its value in the promotion of specific aspects of the program.

The Bit-by-Bit Approach

When the studies by Neulen [2] and Wrightstone [3] demonstrated that special aids were by no means infallible devices for promoting the spread of a specific practice, even this justification of special aids was brought into question. But they are still greatly favored as a means of promoting special concerns of groups interested in particular phases of the educational program. Because of this faith, the Burke principle is of high practical importance. Some two decades after the analysis of special aids by Strayer and Haig, Burke pointed out that special aids sufficient in amount to pay the total cost of the special phase of education to be favored make the new phase available as readily to the poor communities as to the able and thus circumvent the Strayer and Haig objection. The Burke principle has been followed fairly consistently in connection with special aids that have been brought into the New York State finance program in recent years. A notable instance is adult education. Whether or not such special aids augmented according to the Burke principle are efficient as devices for promoting the spread of new practices remains to be tested. But those favoring such devices can have the satisfaction of knowing that they are not violating the Strayer and Haig corollary if they adhere to the Burke principle.

The conflict between the Strayer and Haig equalization proposal and special aids runs deeper than this. It can now be seen as a conflict between two theories as to how state agencies can be mobilized for the betterment of education.

When we realize that since the Strayer and Haig proposal was made, the base of state aid in New York State granted in accordance with it has mounted from $23 million to more than $600 million, we cannot but conclude that great faith has been manifest in the soundness of the principle, "... that the assurance of a minimum level of support for education and the achievement of a just distribution of the burden for its support would be good for schools."

But it is highly unlikely that Strayer and Haig put their fingers on the only elements in the situation that control the wholesomeness of conditions and that are potentially subject to state influence. The great interest evidenced in New York State over this same period in the reorganization of school districts may be seen as a parallel move. Accordingly it is but

[2] Lester N. Neulen, *State Aid for Educational Projects in the Public Schools*, Bureau of Publications, Teachers College, Columbia University, New York, 1928.

[3] J. Wayne Wrightstone, *Stimulation of Educational Undertakings: A Study of School Support in New York Cities and Villages Under Earmarked and Non-earmarked State Subsidy Plans*, Bureau of Publications, Teachers College, Columbia University, New York, 1932.

a slight step to the generalization of the Strayer and Haig assumption in the following terms: The development in all communities of wholesome conditions for the production of education is a major concern of the state and is a challenge to state leadership.

It is in this challenge that a basic conflict can be seen between the Strayer and Haig approach and the special-aids approach. The special-aids approach was a manifestation of the conception of state leadership which saw the task of the state department of education as that of selecting critical elements in the educational program for special attention and giving them sanction through rules and regulations or law. Finally, in the words of Finegan, "the injustice and inequalities developed by this method of legal sanction becomes apparent to all." It is a bit-by-bit philosophy, which explains the wide prevalence, first of inspectors and later of supervisory officers, special reports on new practices, special aids, and, in the final stages, penalties. This bit-by-bit philosophy that largely dominated conceptions of state leadership a third of a century ago left little place for the purpose which Finegan ascribed to the law of 1812 when, in speaking of the first superintendent of common schools in New York State, he said "this officer was given sufficient directory and supervisory authority to initiate proceedings to set the machinery into operation and the power to bind the schools together into one strong, aggressive force to accomplish the purposes for which the State created it."[4]

Doubtless the strong emphasis on the bit-by-bit philosophy was in some degree grounded in misconceptions as to the nature of adaptation processes and the tempo of change. Not until the middle 1930s was there any awareness that it is not unusual for a half-century or more to elapse between the realization of a need and the discovery of an acceptable way of meeting it. Once the acceptable way of meeting the need has appeared, an additional fifteen years may elapse before 3 per cent of the communities have embraced it or the adaptation has even come to the attention, through the educational literature, of the leadership in the state departments of education and elsewhere. No one realized that legal sanctions and the appointment of state supervisory officers is typically delayed until after this fifteen year introduction, or until sixty-five years after the emergence of the insight, and that diffusion is then relatively rapid regardless of whether or not the state takes a hand with supervisory or financial help. Take, for example, Finegan's statement of the problem of change appearing in *Free Schools* in 1921:

All social and educational progress passes through three stages. First, the need becomes a conscious conviction in the minds of a few leaders who en-

[4] Thomas E. Finegan, *Free Schools*, The University of the State of New York, Albany, N.Y., 1921, p. 52.

deavor, through constant agitation, to enlighten the general public. Second, the demand for legal sanction arises from a few communities that begin to see the advantages their people might gain by adopting such principles. Then third, the injustice and inequalities developed by this method of legal sanction becomes apparent to all and the demand for legal compulsion results.[5]

There is no indication that Finegan or anyone else during this period realized that the first stage is typically sixty-five years and that an additional period of twenty years typically elapses before it is feasible to control it by mandate. This misconception of tempo of change then extant could well explain the great emphasis on the bit-by-bit approach.

The Wholesomeness Approach

Since the ability of our school systems to keep fiscally in adjustment with our needs has become increasingly important as the implicit demands of our society on education have multiplied, there is need for a thorough evaluation of the scope, emphasis, and adequacy of our current conceptions of the place of the state in the educational program. Fundamentally the question is not how adequate is the bit-by-bit approach as far as it goes (and this certainly warrants some critical inquiry), but what should be done that has not been done to promote the wholesomeness of conditions for producing good education.

It is hardly conceivable that the two factors identified by Strayer and Haig—the foundation program and the equalization of burden—even when supplemented by improvement of district organization, can exhaust the lines of development of wholesomeness. Furthermore, it is essential that haphazard state policies in areas that might not at first glance seem to be related to education—such, for example, as the nature and quantity of municipal aid—should be assessed to discover their possible contribution to wholesomeness of conditions for producing good education and whether there are conflicts that could be removed or changes made which would enhance wholesomeness.

Research on the tempo of change and the factors that explain the differences in community productiveness with respect to education throws light here and there on this problem. As the Strayer and Haig formula has evolved, the idea of equalizing the burden of the foundation program as among school districts has been supplemented by the objective of achieving a situation where the tax base used for local support will not be overburdened, relative to other tax bases. Whatever else might be said about this, its justification in terms of fairness to taxpayers is apparent. However, there are educational concomitants. This is on the theory that a just distribution of the burden on taxpayers is one of the determiners of wholesome conditions for the production of good education not

[5] *Ibid.*

only from the standpoint of willingness to pay taxes but even of willingness to think about educational problems.

Three studies have subjected this to test: Mort and Cornell [6] found some indications of positive relationship between the leeway for local taxation and a measure of the up-to-dateness of thirty-six public school systems in Pennsylvania. Knott [7] found similar results in a study of New York State communities. The third was the series of studies of *facts of great yield* for predicting school quality. This is one of the thirty-one measures that survived out of the several scores examined over a period of years.[8]

What this line of thinking seems to demand is that attention be given not only to equalization of burden among communities but to the maintenance of a situation where the burden on the property tax or other taxes used for local support of schools is just, compared with the burden on other taxpayers, and that the assessment of the taxes is fair, as among individuals within the community.

In the conflict between the Strayer and Haig proposal and special aids, then, we have the conflict between two lines of strategy—the one, the bit-by-bit approach, and the other, the achievement and maintenance of wholesomeness approach.

Resolution of Purposes

A central weakness in the bit-by-bit theory of state policy is not so much in its own limitations in terms of its avowed purposes as in the tendency it has had of commanding the center of the stage to the exclusion of the less specific but vastly more penetrating wholesomeness approach. What is needed is a state policy sufficiently broad to encompass both. So long as it is realized that the maintenance of conditions for wholesome production of education locally is by the very nature of its demands a prime state responsibility, there would seem to be no necessary conflict between its objective and the more specialized, perhaps more opportunistic, objectives of the vectorial theory.

The first requisite of a workable correlation of these two theories is that what is done under the vectorial theory shall not dilute the wholesomeness of the general situation. This possibility is well expressed by Suzzalo in the following remarks about special aids, in this case federal aids:

[6] Paul R. Mort and Francis G. Cornell, *American Schools in Transition*, Bureau of Publications, Teachers College, Columbia University, New York, 1941, p. 165.

[7] W. D. Knott, *The Influence of Tax Leeway on Educational Adaptability*, Bureau of Publications, Teachers College, Columbia University, New York, 1939.

[8] Donald H. Ross, (ed.), *Administration for Adaptability*, Metropolitan School Study Council, New York, 1958.

Federal standards of procedure when first inaugurated generally represent the best selections from the then existent, widely divergent, and spontaneous experiments of many local communities. Such experimentation tends to be discouraged and restricted after a decade or more of standardization under central governmental influences, and progress halts with the retardation of free inquiry and experiment.[9]

Once there is assurance that a step taken in line with the vectorial theory does nothing to dilute the wholesomeness of the whole general situation, the proposed step can then be tested in terms of its efficacy in achieving its immediate and presumably well-defined objective. To take an example from the earlier discussion, Strayer and Haig opposed special aids because they thought that they would essentially offset the efforts for equalizing the burden of a foundation program. This was because of the tendency for special aids as normally dealt with to go in greater proportion to abler communities than to less able communities. When in the application of the Burke principle this particular effect is eliminated (through the payment of the total cost of the activity aided), the Strayer and Haig objection does not apply. When this is established, and not until then, the special aid can be defended in terms of its effects in speeding up the introduction and spread of some specialized aspect of the educational program.

This is not to deny the possibility that the instruments of the vectorial theory might serve to increase the general wholesomeness of conditions. An example of this might be special aids to provide more funds for research and development. From the vectorial standpoint the gaining of more attention to research and development might be considered as an immediate objective that is worthy in its own right. But if such a step were in fact to promote more research and development, the indications from the Brickell, Teresa, Campbell, and Bothwell studies reviewed in Chapter 7 are that the communities would become more adaptable and that education would improve.

SUMMARY

The long history of using state aid for schools as a means to stimulate and canalize practices has left its imprint on all school-aid systems and is likely to continue to counsel mandates, compliances, and other departures from the uniform treatment of districts which is assumed in the discussion of tax sharing and equalization.

Special aids as such are rapidly disappearing from the scene. However, although special aids may not show up on the statute books, they

[9] National Advisory Committee on Education, *Federal Relations to Education,* Part I, Washington, 1931.

may still be in the picture. A great many state-aid systems, whether of the flat grant type or the equalization type, carry provisions for additional money to be granted communities operating classes of one sort or another. Such payments certainly are not needed to adjust a measure of the cost of the foundation program. They are in the law for stimulative effect only and might just as well be included frankly as the special aids they are.

It should be clear that earmarking of extra money for various purposes is not essential for a just operation of a state-aid program. What is needed is an index of educational need which will have high "actuarial" relationship with school quality.

Most of the plans using the teacher salary as a base do not recognize local cost distributions that allocate more for teachers with less training (or less training and experience) or more for nonsalary expenses than that used in determining the total budget from salaries. Under such plans the community must make the transition to higher expenditure levels by following the state pattern. Any other plan is penalized.

Special aids can be kept in perspective by applying the Burke principle. So long as they are available to all communities—a condition that requires complete support of the activity by the state—they do not have disequalizing effects.

Every state-aid system should be examined to discover the covert or unintended penalizations made in accordance with an oversimplified notion of how progress can be achieved in the poorer districts.

One of the most prolific producers of injustice in state-aid systems is the tendency to oversimplify provisions for determining the cost of the foundation program.

The special-aids approach was a manifestation of the conception of state leadership which saw the task of the state department of education as that of selecting critical elements in the educational program for special attention and giving them sanction through rules and regulations or law. Finally, in the words of Finegan, "the injustice and inequalities developed by this method of legal sanction becomes apparent to all." It is a bit-by-bit philosophy which explains the wide prevalence, first of inspectors and later of supervisory officers, special aids, and, in the final stages, penalties.

Doubtless the strong emphasis on the bit-by-bit philosophy was in some degree grounded in misconceptions as to the nature of adaptation processes and the tempo of change.

Since the ability of our school systems to keep fiscally in adjustment with our needs has become increasingly important as the implicit demands of our society on education have multiplied, there is need for a thorough evaluation of the scope, emphasis, and adequacy of our current conceptions of the place of the state in the educational program. Fundamentally the question is not how adequate is the bit-by-bit approach as far as it goes (and this certainly warrants some critical inquiry), but what should be done that has not been done to promote the wholesomeness of conditions for producing good education.

A central weakness in the bit-by-bit theory of state policy is not so much in its own limitations in terms of its avowed purposes as in the tendency it has had of commanding the center of the stage to the exclusion of the less specific but vastly more penetrating wholesomeness approach. What is needed is a state policy sufficiently broad to encompass both.

SELECTED REFERENCES

Chisholm, L. L., and M. L. Cushman: "The Relationship of Programs of School Finance to the Reorganization of Local School Administrative Units and Local School Centers," chap. III in R. L. Johns and E. L. Morphet (eds.), *Problems and Issues in Public School Finance*, Bureau of Publications, Teachers College, Columbia University, New York, 1952.

Cooperative Study Policy Committee: *Education for Our Times—A State Action Program*, Maryland State Department of Education, Baltimore, Md., May, 1959.

Mort, Paul R.: *The Foundation Program in State Educational Policy*, The University of the State of New York, The State Department of Education, Albany, N.Y., 1957.

New York State Educational Conference Board: *School Quality and Local School Government*, Albany, N.Y., 1956.

16. State aid for transportation and capital outlay

IN THREE-FOURTHS of the states, state-aid laws recognize the disturbing effects of the cost of transportation on the ability of school districts to support schools. An increasing number are providing aid for capital outlay.

TRANSPORTATION

In some school systems, more than 20 per cent as much is spent on the transportation of children to and from school as on the work of the school itself. In the 500 New York State centralized districts, transportation costs average about 8 per cent of the total current expenditure.[1]

Whatever benefits there may be from the transportation function, no claim has come to the fore that expenditures for that purpose are what we might call educationally effective. They are not a part of the expenditures that should be considered in determining expenditure level (Chapter 7) and should not be included in comparisons among communities except for the purpose of measuring ability or effort. When used in comparisons that consciously or unconsciously are assumed to predict the quality level of education they can lead to grossly misleading interpretations. It is one thing to compare communities in terms of what they spend for all purposes for education, per capita of population or per

[1] There are some indications that as schools are better financed the related burden for transportation will fall into more reasonable limits. For example, in the New York State rural districts the percentage of current expenditures going to transportation dropped from 11 per cent in 1944 to 8.4 per cent in 1954—a drop of almost one-fourth. In ten districts selected for the high proportion of transportation expenditure in 1947, the decade following showed transportation costs rising only two-thirds as much as other current expenditures.

school child. In some circumstances such comparisons have value. They reflect burden. But it is quite another thing to compare communities in terms of the *level* on which they support education. In the latter comparison it is essential to omit transportation costs and other costs that are associated with educationally noneffective practices, however necessary they may be.

Aid for Transportation in the Equalization Formula

Financing a foundation program involves a special case of expenditure comparison. It is essential to obtain a measure of what it is necessary to spend to achieve a given level of education. It is education we are seeking to equalize. Expenditure level is a device by which we translate a given level of education into dollars. Not that a given expenditure level has a one-to-one relationship with quality. It is only the best objective actuarial measure for translating a given level into dollar values, a step essential to the development of a good state-aid system.

In computing the cost of a given foundation level, then, it is necessary directly or indirectly to add the total cost of transportation to the cost figure obtained for the actual school operation—whether that cost figure is obtained by the unit cost method used in most states, the "approved budget" method, or the budget imputed from teachers' salaries. If the cost of transportation is added, the aid is increased over what it would otherwise be by the total amount allowed for transportation. Theoretically this should be 100 per cent of all necessary cost.[2]

More than half of the states aiding transportation consider the costs of transportation as a part of the foundation program cost.

Separate Aid for Transportation

Several states do not actually add transportation cost to the foundation program, but deal with it as a separate item. If the state-aid plan for other purposes pays equalization aid to all communities, this separate plan for transportation will carry the same number of dollars to the same communities as the plan of counting it as a part of the foundation program—providing it pays 100 cents on the dollar allowed. When some communities do not obtain "equalization" aid, the separate payment plan will pay money to most of the communities excluded from equalization in excess of what they would get under the combined plans. It may have a more or less significant disequalizing effect. This is particularly likely in states with large flat grants or large minimum guarantees, or extremely high requirements for local contributions.

[2] In Delaware and North Carolina transportation is operated and paid for by the state.

Determining Necessary Transportation Costs by Formula

Whichever plan is followed, the central task is to decide what are necessary transportation expenses. Taking the community's desires on this is usually not considered prudent. Attempts to get an answer to this question have led to the development of elaborate schemes, usually involving mileage traveled and bus size, and sometimes involving complicated allowance for bus driver salaries, for depreciation of buses, etc. Many states are using or have recently used such elaborate plans. Examples are New York and Ohio.

Determining Transportation Cost by Expenditure

Another approach is that pioneered by New Jersey many years ago: the payment of a percentage of whatever is spent—in the case of New Jersey, 75 per cent. This has the effect of reducing the inequalities due to transportation to 25 per cent of what they would otherwise be. For the great mass of districts this amount of inequality is not significant. The disturbing inequalities the additional 25 per cent represents could be reduced to a negligible factor by allowing districts the same proportion of this extra cost as they get for their basic foundation program— the reimbursement fraction idea used in the Pennsylvania law. Or the state could pay a large fraction of the excess left over beyond some mileage figure as has been proposed for debt service in Rhode Island and Maryland. Bus purchase costs could be dealt with along with building capital outlay, as proposed later in this chapter.

Some such method of reducing inequalities has much to commend it over the methods of more exact measurement now being used. The elimination of harmful inequalities is what we are concerned with—not a meticulous sharing of state largess.

Another variation of this is to apply the reimbursement fraction idea to the entire operating expenses for transportation, as Pennsylvania does. Using this method reduces the amount of aid markedly. Under this plan the remaining cost of transportation in the general run of communities would not be disturbing. But it would be an added cost over and beyond what districts without transportation would have to pay. Where this plan is under consideration a check should be made of its effects on communities with a high burden for transportation and relatively low ability.

Over-all Sparsity Corrections

Perhaps it is hoping against hope, but the authors still look with interest on the possibility of developing an over-all sparsity correction that will get to the source of the need of both transportation and small-school corrections.

In the middle 1930s Mort and Lawler developed a sparsity index for entire states which would predict the combined small-school correction and transportation correction.[3] It was a decade later that the opportunity was afforded to apply this approach to the determination of a sparsity correction for the educational need measure in units as small as counties. This opportunity was offered in the West Virginia Survey. Using West Virginia data, McLure developed a sparsity formula which ranged in correlations for various parts of the curve from .85 to .92. The criterion was the sum of the small-school correction and transportation cost for each county. For all the complicated rules on small-school corrections for elementary and secondary schools and for the budgetary item measure for transportation it was possible to substitute the following: [4]

A sparsity correction shall be computed to care for transportation needs and the need for operating small schools in rural areas. It shall be that percentage of the average daily attendance of rural pupils obtained by adding (a) and (b) below.

a. A basic correction of 11 per cent shall be allowed all counties having .56 or less square miles of area per mile of highway as reported by the State Road Commission; all counties having .64 or more square miles of area per mile of highway shall receive a basic correction of 15 per cent. Those falling between .56 and .64 shall receive proportionate basic corrections; for example, in a county having .57 of a square mile of area per mile of highway, the basic correction shall be 11.5 per cent; in a county having .58 of a square mile per mile of highway, the correction shall be 12 per cent.

b. To the basic correction in (a) shall be added a percentage equal to 1.6 times the miles of highway in the county per rural pupil in average daily attendance.

The modification of this, enacted into law in West Virginia in 1947, reads as follows: [5]

"Sparsity Factor" shall be a number derived as follows:
The number five divided by the sum of (1) the weighted net enrollment divided by the total miles of designated roads in the county, and (2) the weighted net enrollment divided by the number of square miles of area in the county.

"Miles of Designated Roads" shall mean miles of primary and secondary

[3] Paul R. Mort, *Federal Support for Public Education*, Bureau of Publications, Teachers College, Columbia University, New York, 1936, pp. 81–96.

[4] George D. Strayer, Director, *A Report of a Survey of Public Education in the State of West Virginia*, State of West Virginia, Legislative Interim Committee, Charleston, W.Va., 1945, p. 559.

[5] Enrolled Committee Substitute for House Bill 344 (originating in the Committee on Finance), pp. 4–5, West Virginia, Passed Mar. 6, 1947; in effect July 1, 1947.

roads and highways in any county designated as such by the state road commission.

"Square Miles of Area" means the area of a county to be taken from the latest figures furnished by the West Virginia Geological Survey.

McLure later extended the study and in his monograph gives a wide variety of useful alternatives and approaches. Later McLure had the opportunity of applying this approach to the state of New York for areas approximately as large as counties. He used a similar procedure. He worked out the small-school corrections for all the schools and the transportation corrections and used them as a criterion for developing an empirical formula. This formula developed from New York State data gave results correlating with the criterion to the extent of .97. The New York State formula is as follows: [6]

The sparsity formula may be stated as a method for obtaining the sparsity correction in weighted elementary pupils from a correction factor which is multiplied by the average daily attendance in kindergarten through grade 12 living in the open country or in population centers (places defined in the federal census as incorporated or unincorporated) of less than 4,000, referred to hereafter as the base group. The correction factor shall be .16 plus 1.239 times the average distance in miles between pupils in the base group. This average distance shall be the distance across the average plot of land in the district for each pupil in the base group, diminished by the number of population centers of 4,000 or more in the district for each lot of 63 pupils in the base group, the amount of diminution not to exceed 10 per cent of the sum stated in the preceding sentence.

This may be expressed mathematically as follows:

$$\text{Correction factor} = 1.239 \sqrt{\frac{\text{Land area of the Dist. in sq. mi.}}{\text{A.D.A. (Base Group)}}} \; plus\; .16\; minus\; \frac{63\,(\text{Number of pop. centers over 4,000})}{\text{A.D.A. (Base Group)}}$$

Following this, McLure applied the same technique to the states of Mississippi and Illinois. His formula for Illinois, simplified so as to be predictable from a density measure of pupils per square mile and broken into segments, is as follows: [7]

1. For counties with an average of 6 or fewer rural pupils per square mile: $X_1 = 0.7700 - 0.0567X_2$.

2. For counties with an average of more than 6 rural pupils per square mile, but not more than 11: $X_1 = 0.5860 - 0.0260X_2$.

---

[6] "The Intermediate District in New York State, Special Studies," University of the State of New York, *Bulletin* 1356, Albany, N.Y.: The State Department of Education, Albany, N.Y., Nov. 15, 1948, p. 108.

[7] *Financing Education in Efficient School Districts*, pp. 152–153, a study of school finance in Illinois by the Bureau of Research and Service, College of Education, University of Illinois, Urbana, Ill., 1949.

3. For counties with an average of more than 11 rural pupils per square mile, but not more than 22: $X_1 = 0.4100 - 0.0100X_2$.

4. For counties with an average of more than 22 rural pupils per square mile: $X_1 = 0.3000 - 0.0050X_2$.

The reported correlation of the results with the criterion was .973. Figure 16-1 shows the lines represented by the four equations in the above formula and how they are related to the estimates of sparsity corrections obtained by combining a transportation correction and a small-school correction.

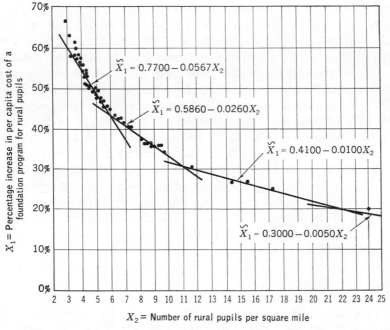

Fig. 16-1 Distribution of Illinois counties according to density of rural pupils and percentage increase in cost of a foundation program. (From Francis G. Cornell and William P. McLure, *Financing Education in Efficient School Districts*, University of Illinois, Urbana, 1949, p. 152.)

Such an over-all sparsity correction has a great many advantages: It eliminates certain special difficulties arising from the use of the small-school correction, particularly that arising from the situation in which a community might have avoided small schools through a different type of organization. In the case of transportation corrections, all methods that have been developed rely upon expenditure practice in the communities. If the community spends more than the amount computed by formula, it receives only the amount computed by formula. If by some combination of circumstances it saves and spends less than the amount computed by the formula, the state gets the advantage of the saving rather than the community. This takes away some of the spur to economy that would arise if the community could have the funds justified and then could utilize the savings for other purposes. When the grants are made to the community for the sparsity correction to be used either for small-school correction or transportation or both, this spur to economy in the local operation is present inasmuch as the community by saving, more efficient organization of schools, or more efficient operation of transportation can utilize the savings on its own program.

The difficulty with the over-all sparsity correction is that it is not directly applicable to districts smaller than such counties as are found in New York or West Virginia. Where, as in West Virginia, the local school district is the county, this poses no difficulty. Where, however, as in many states, the unit is smaller than such counties, this device is not directly usable. The difficulties may be more apparent than real, however. The committee working on the development of an intermediate unit in the state of New York demonstrated the applicability of the over-all index to such intermediate units and proposed a plan for allocating aid to the intermediate board and the constituent districts. One plan considered allowed aid on the straight per pupil basis, corrected for the difference between high school and elementary cost, to go directly to the constituent districts, whereas the sparsity correction aid would go directly to the intermediate unit board. The intermediate unit board would make allotments to the individual districts for small school corrections and would provide the necessary transportation for all the districts within the intermediate unit. Any savings would be available for educational purposes other than sparsity correction.

The simplification introduced by such a plan in computing state aid on the one hand and in eliminating the necessity for discretionary decisions on such matters as transportation routes and special controls for grants to small schools counsels the invention of ways and means by which the index could be used in states with township or district units. The grant of the sparsity correction could be made to the county school authorities. If there were no board of education, a board could be set up which would have the responsibility for allocation of grants for small schools and for the payment of transportation. If such a board had no power to provide educational facilities to supplement those of the small districts, the resulting savings from such a program could be allocated to the individual districts for their use. Discretion would be involved in making the allotments for small-school corrections, but the discretion would be in the hands of a body relatively close to the people rather than in the hands of a remote state department of education. Local policy under these circumstances could not affect the amount of state aid that would go to a county. Injustices in allotments within a county would affect only the communities within the county and would therefore be likely to result in movements for a correction of injustices within the county itself.

AID FOR SCHOOL BUILDINGS

Until the 1940s aid for school building was limited to incentive aids to encourage reorganization of school districts. Philosophically the general belief was that the provision of school housing should be a local affair. While this opinion was not held universally by any means, practically it hardly seemed wise to complicate equalization laws by constructing them so as to embrace what, taken over the years, is but a minor fraction of the total cost—approximately one dollar in eight, according to Grossnickle's study made in the 1920s.[8]

A 12 per cent error was a minor one indeed compared with the fateful compromises in the level of the foundation program characteristic of state-aid laws.

The trouble is that however small the capital outlays may be when spread over the life of a building—and Lo Cicero's findings [9] covering the twenty-five year period prior to 1955 show the Grossnickle findings to be fairly realistic—the fact is that there are no methods available to the small community or to the rapidly growing small or middle-sized community to spread them out over the building life. A reasonably wealthy community may find itself carrying a debt service load 40 per cent as high as its current operations load over a quarter of a century.[10] This is a threat to the operation of schools in any community—rich or poor. In a community that has one-half of its operating cost carried by state aid, a debt load of 40 per cent is 80 per cent of the locally raised share of the current expenditures. In a community that has three-fourths of its operating load carried by the state, such a percentage represents a debt load more than 50 per cent greater than its operations load.

An analysis of Rhode Island communities in 1953–1954 showed that more than one-third were carrying taxes for debt service 50 per cent or more above the "normal." Of these, only one had a current expenditure level above the state average. To quote the report, "This is disturbingly

[8] Foster E. Grossnickle, *Capital Outlay in Relation to a State's Minimum Educational Program*, Teachers College, Columbia University, New York, 1931.

[9] Benedict Lo Cicero, "Debt Service Expenditures in the Metropolitan School Study Council Schools from 1920–1955," Ed.D. report, Teachers College, Columbia University, New York, 1957. (Typewritten.)

[10] *Ibid.*

strong confirmation of the theory that obviously high debt service rates tend to militate against adequate current support." [11]

In a period of relatively stable population only the poorer communities and the comparatively small number of rapidly growing communities were faced by this problem. There was a tendency to overlook the poorer communities except in those cases where capital outlay aid was used as a reorganization incentive; the others were few in number. But as rapid population growth in urban and suburban areas became the rule, this problem came strongly to the fore. In 1949 Chase and Morphet reported that a score of states had already entered the field of state aid for capital outlay.[12] By the middle 1950s the number had markedly increased.

Some of the plans in use in 1949 and some in use today had quite different roots. They are plans designed to circumvent constitutional debt limits based on assessed values made unrealistic by the failure of assessed values of property to keep pace with true values. In this category is the state building commission idea, used in Pennsylvania. They provide no relief for the economic problem outlined in this book. They have the same effect as a modification of the tax-limit laws or constitutional provisions, leaving the problems arising from poverty and rapid growth unsolved. Such plans, together with state loan funds, are discussed in Chapter 22.

The Fixed Annual Payment

The simplest of the plans is that followed by Florida, Georgia, and South Carolina. It calls for an allowance for building outlay of a fixed amount per classroom unit or per pupil unit in computing the cost of the foundation program.[13] This is paid to each district each year, regardless of building costs. When, as in Florida, all districts are of sizable population, there is little likelihood that the district will be paying at any one time for buildings for much more than one-third of the school population. Where such conditions obtain the cost of school buildings tends not to get out of line with operational costs.

This plan of payment of the annual allowances is less practical where some school districts are small. Such districts frequently build for several generations, and the generations that pay must carry a heavy

[11] Rhode Island State Board of Education, *The Financing of School Buildings*, Staff Study No. 4, Providence, 1955.

[12] Francis S. Chase, Research Director, and Edgar L. Morphet, Associate Director, *The Forty-eight State School Systems*, Council of State Governments, Chicago, 1949.

[13] Strevell's study shows that the classroom unit or pupil unit corrected for sparsity is to be preferred over number of pupils as an index of capital outlay need. Wallace Strevell, *State Aid for Central School Building*, Bureau of Publications, Teachers College, Columbia University, New York, 1949.

extra burden. It is also less practical where there are rapidly growing districts, regardless of their size, as in the case of suburban counties.

Conceivably this plan could be made to work in other states for the county or some comparable intermediate unit dealt with as Texas deals with the county index of valuation. The allotment could be made to a building board for the area, with authority to dispose of it according to immediate need in its area.

Of comparable simplicity is the Alabama plan for including debt service as a foundation program cost.

Fixed Annual Allotment—Payment on Need

Theoretically there would appear to be no difficulty in working out an arrangement to credit each district for capital outlay each year with an amount equal to a given percentage (say 14 per cent) of the aid granted for current purposes. This would then become a drawing account to be called on by local districts at any time their debt-service load exceeded an established danger level. Provision could be made for advanced drawing also. Such a proposal was made in Rhode Island in 1955.[14] It would result in the reduction of debt service to approximately 30 cents per hundred dollars full valuation in the most extreme cases. If such a plan is carried to its logical conclusion, close state oversight over building costs would appear to be essential for prudential reasons.

The "Reductio ad Absurdum" Basis

As in the case of transportation costs, attempts to achieve absolute justice in capital outlay can lead to complicated proposals and, inevitably, to close controls. As in transportation, it may be a matter of wisdom to utilize a plan that will keep all communities reasonably harmless from the impacts of capital outlay by a direct attack on the patently harmful spots. The percentage-payment plan appears to afford a means for reasonable achievement of practical justice.

In the Willis proposal for Maryland outright grants are proposed for 75 per cent of the debt-service costs beyond the yield of a tax of 20 cents per $100 full valuation.[15] The theory is that this will keep the debt service in most districts from rising above 20 or 25 per cent of the current costs. Provision for further aid is made for poorer districts by applying to the local 25 per cent the same proportion of state aid as is paid on

---

[14] See Rhode Island State Board of Education, *op. cit.*

[15] Debt service computed on the basis of 25-year bonds, in case of shorter term bonds or direct outlay. Charles W. Willis, *A Program of Financing School Construction Designed to Safeguard the Current Operating Program in Maryland,* State Department of Education, Baltimore, 1958.

the operating expenses. This last provision would result in the poorest county in Maryland receiving 80 per cent of the cost over 20 cents per $100 full valuation.

The 75 per cent figure is selected as that which requires enough local support to encourage economy. What this should be is a matter of judgment. Studies some years ago indicated that the 75 per cent figure operated satisfactorily in New Jersey from the economy angle. Experiences in some states with larger percentage allowances in welfare aids were not as happy, perhaps because of the larger allowances, perhaps because of the difference in the functions. Whether or not the provision for further aid to poorer communities would require closer state oversight in those communities receiving "imprudently large" percentages in total is a matter of judgment. In any case the provision for state oversight of expenditures could be much more limited than in the case of the plan outlined in the preceding section.

The Pennsylvania plan of applying the reimbursement ratio to certain building costs could be classified in this category, as could the Georgia plan of paying $200 per classroom unit plus 50 per cent of certain additional costs.

The real test of any such plan for a state, whether in this or in an earlier category, would be the effect it has in reducing debt service in all districts to a tolerable level.

THE BETTERMENT CHALLENGE

If, as the authors believe, we are in a sort of educational harvest period that will see a rather rapid spread of the more powerful educational practices that have emerged from the past half-century of research and experimentation, it seems highly likely that we will find ourselves short of adequate school housing. More attention in planning for capital outlay may therefore well be given to increasing the estimates of cost above those projected from population increase and prevailing prices for the kind of housing that is found satisfactory for the transition period. The probable improvement of the ratio of professional staff per 1,000 staffing units (Chapter 7) provides one way of making allowances for the probable future trends. An example of such consideration appears in a Rhode Island State Department study published in 1955:

Column I shows the needs of June 30, 1954; Column 2 the additional needs that will mature by 1960. These are conservative estimates. They are based upon the costs of housing for school programs as they were in 1954, school programs that were apparently seriously underfinanced. The foundation program envisioned by the 1955 school finance act would increase this estimate by a considerable fraction. The program proposed in Staff Study No. 3 would increase the cost further. For, over the long run, housing adequate for a school program costs in proportion to the cost of operation of the program.[16]

SUMMARY

Most state-aid laws recognize the disturbing effects of the cost of transportation on the ability of school districts to support schools. An increasing number are providing aid for capital outlay.

Transportation expenditures should not be considered in determining the expenditure level of a school district; to consider them would be to assume that they of themselves enhance the quality of education. Rather, they should be considered as educational expenses required in some districts before educationally effective expenditures begin. Theoretically, necessary transportation expenses should be carried entirely from state funds.

Adding the cost of transportation to the computed cost of the foundation program results in a 100 per cent payment by the state in those districts in which equalization aid exceeds the cost of transportation.

Dealing with transportation under a separate provision of the law results in payments to any districts not eligible for "equalization" aid; where all districts receive equalization aid, 100 per cent payment of transportation aid under a separate legal provision has essentially the same effect as adding the cost of transportation to the computed cost of the foundation program.

One hundred per cent payment on either plan poses a difficult task of determining what are necessary transportation expenses. Some states use highly complex formulas for this purpose.

Intricate systems of determining necessary expenditures can be avoided by compromising a bit with absolute justice and following the principle that what is sought is the reduction of the burden for transportation to the point that it is not a threat to effective expenditures. This has been attempted in New Jersey by the simple means of paying 75 per cent of all expenditures; in Pennsylvania by applying a reimbursement fraction, i.e., by paying the same percentage of transportation as the state pays for the foundation program.

It still may prove possible to develop a formula for predicting the combined effect of population sparsity on need for transportation and need for the small-school correction discussed in Chapter 7. The McLure approach is promising.

Until the 1940s aid for school building was largely limited to incentive provisions designed to spur school consolidation. The neglect of depression and war years augmented by the rapid expansion of population,

[16] State Board of Education, *op. cit.*, p. 11.

however, has magnified into a major burden what is only a relatively small item of expenditure when spread over the life of a building. As a result many states now have some plan of aiding school districts in school building construction.

Florida and South Carolina make regular payments of so much a pupil or so much a classroom unit. This plan is satisfactory unless a district is small or subject to such growth that housing for considerably more than a third of its pupils is being paid for at any one time. The Rhode Island State Department of Education has proposed a plan to help districts faced by unusual building demands by making advanced payments sufficient to reduce the load for debt service to approximately 30 cents on a hundred dollars of full valuation. Willis has proposed a plan for Maryland that would supplement other aids in such a way as to have approximately this effect.

The real test of any plan would be the effect it has in reducing debt service in all districts to a tolerable level.

In planning programs of school building finance it would be well to consider the probable effect on housing needs of betterment of the educational program in the years ahead.

QUESTIONS FOR STUDY AND DISCUSSION

1. How effectively does your state's legislation reduce the local costs of transportation and school buildings to the point that they do not jeopardize the ongoing educational program?

2. What objective seems to have motivated the aid for transportation and buildings in your state? (a) incentive, (b) complete equity, (c) save harmless, (d) other.

SELECTED REFERENCES

Burke, Arvid J.: *Financing Public Schools in the United States,* rev. ed., Harper & Brothers, New York, 1957.

Committee on Tax Education and School Finance, *Proceedings of the National Conference on School Finance Problems,* National Education Association, Washington, 1958.

Rhode Island State Board of Education, *The Financing of School Buildings,* Staff Study no. 4, Providence, R.I., 1955.

Willis, Charles W.: *A Program of Financing School Construction Designed to Safeguard the Current Operating Program in Maryland,* State Department of Education, Baltimore, Md., 1958.

17. Federal financing of education

A GENERALLY accepted conceptual basis for federal aid to public education has been slow in emerging. It appears now to be following strongly the line of development followed in the states in the 1920s and 1930s—at least in terms of the emphasis given bills introduced into Congress. In recent years these bills have given an out-and-out recognition of the foundation-level principle. This recognition followed by two decades its development in the pioneering states. In addition there has emerged a considerable body of literature supporting the concept of equalization of a foundation program as applicable to federal aid for other forms of government and some discussion of the idea of encompassing federal aid for education in more inclusive plans of federal assistance to states.

FEDERAL GOVERNMENT INTEREST IN EDUCATION

The early federal interest was in an educated citizenry—in a qualified electorate. Beginning with the Morrill Act of 1862, federal interest became specialized: the technological preparation of the people in the colleges of agriculture and mechanic arts, the diffusion of the fruits of the research of the colleges of agriculture in the various extension measures (county agent, experiment stations), the extension of agricultural and technological training through the Smith-Hughes provisions affecting high schools.

In the second quarter of this century other interests of the increasingly socially conscious federal government came into the picture. The Public Health Service, with concern for mental hygiene; the Department of the Interior, with concern for conservation and the protection of miners; the Department of Justice, with a helping hand for all law enforcement officials; the Department of Labor, seeking to promote apprentice train-

299

ing; the U.S. Maritime Commission, seeking to make up for the lack of the glamour of the sea that went with the sailing ships; the Department of Commerce, seeking to help small business, all these took upon themselves what they considered the appropriate action through one sort of "extension" service or other—only the work with small business being channeled through existing institutions, public or other, in the states.

Other departments turned to the schools. Trade and industry courses were added to the high school courses on agriculture and mechanic arts at United States government expense; the Department of Commerce spent vast sums to develop air-mindedness and to provide all sorts of aids to teachers to this end; the Federal Security Agency lent a federal hand to schools for the blind and to the rehabilitation of persons disabled in industry; the Department of Justice provided a citizenship education service to encourage public schools and colleges to take a hand in preparing immigrants for citizenship; the U.S. Maritime Commission lent a hand to state institutions training mariners; the Army continued the policy of using high schools and colleges for military training (introduced in colleges with the establishment of the colleges of agriculture and mechanic arts in 1862); the Department of Agriculture distributed largess to schools in the form of surplus foods; the U.S. Treasury got into the act by spending a quarter of a million annually in an attempt to infiltrate thrift into various school courses; and most recently the Atomic Energy Commission undertook to step up technological preparedness by helping students and institutions that were willing to turn their attention to the new challenges of the physical, medical, and biological sciences.

Passing over the most dramatic of all, the educational aid to veterans that must stand along with the munificent land grants to the new states as a symbol of national faith in education and people, attention may be called to the discovery of the universities and colleges as research and service agencies to the government enterprise itself. No less than ten government departments and agencies now contract with universities for research. Allen lists the following in this category: the Department of Agriculture, the Atomic Energy Commission, the Department of Commerce, the Federal Security Agency, the Department of Interior, the National Advisory Committee for Aeronautics, all three branches of the military establishment, and the Tennessee Valley Authority.[1] He lists nine agencies as utilizing available colleges and universities in the inservice training of their personnel: the U.S. Civil Service, the Department of Commerce, the Public Health Service, the Housing and Home Finance Agency, the Department of the Army, the Department of the

[1] Hollis P. Allen, *The Federal Government and Education*, McGraw-Hill Book Company, Inc., New York, 1950, pp. 23-56.

Navy, the Department of State, the Department of the Treasury, and the Veterans' Administration.

Most of the concern of the federal government is with the details that happened to be recognized in governmental agencies: conservation, mine accidents, shortages in the merchant marine, mental diseases, surplus of farm production, the mysteries of the atomic world, the need to sell government bonds, military security. The task of raising children healthful in mind and body, schooled in the languages of communication, business transactions, and technology, alert to the glories of life and its values, these matters are clearly of little concern to those who draw their pay from the federal government. So we hand out a few millions here and a few millions there to seek by some magic wand to correct the mounting deficiencies in these fundamental realms and do not give much consideration to the fact that, if some of our states are to provide more than a horse-and-buggy education, billions in federally collected taxes will be needed, to be spent without the necessary intrusion of the special-mindedness that tends to capture all government workers who are far from the oversight of the people except as it is revealed by censuses and polls.

THE SEARCH FOR A CONCEPTUAL PATTERN
FOR FEDERAL AID

Until the report of the National Advisory Committee on Education, the controlling conceptual basis of federal aid was that federal aid should be used to stimulate the correction of weaknesses in state school systems, particularly in those areas in which national interest had evolved. This, of course, was not true in the early land grants. The policy, which had its origin in the granting of land in what is now Maine by the state of Massachusetts following the French and Indian War, was for the purpose of encouraging settlement. Its adoption as national policy in the provisions of the Ordinance of 1785 was for purposes general in character. According to this provision, endorsed by acts of Congress when the various states were accepted into the Union, a designated area of federal land was set aside for the purpose of schools in each township. With the passage of the first Morrill Act in 1862, the conceptual basis for federal aid was set in the "stimulation of special activity" pattern, and this was carried on through the Hatch Act in 1887, the second Morrill Act in 1890, the Smith-Lever Act in 1914, and the Smith-Hughes Act in 1917.

The proposals made by the Emergency Committee in 1918 followed this same pattern in that they earmarked funds for improving health service, eliminating intolerable conditions in the rural schools, improving the training of teachers, and correcting the illiteracy situation. For these purposes the commission recommended $50 million a year. In addition, it recommended $50 million to help equalize opportunities or, in other words, to help equalize the burden of support of public education in general. This provision for equalization represents the emergence of the broader notion of general aid that was expressed later in the Strayer-Haig definition of equalization of educational opportunity.

This new emphasis gained headway in the next decade to the point that the National Advisory Committee on Education, appointed by President Hoover in 1929, recommended the dropping of the emphasis on special aids and the expanding of the emphasis on the general-aid idea. In the period following 1931 the depression difficulties of the schools greatly increased interest in the problems of federal aid. A joint commission of the National Education Association and the Department of Superintendence, under the chairmanship of Professor John K. Norton, was active over a four-year period in bringing light to bear upon the actual situation with respect to our schools. A special conference called by this commission in the summer of 1933 reached the following conclusions: [2]

1. Federal support for education is in accord with the development of national policy with respect to education.

2. The need for national aid to the states, apparent from the beginning, has been increased by the development of the machine and power age.

3. The federal government should enable the states to support a foundation program of education for all children within the nation.

In the fall a conference of representatives of many national organizations was called by the U.S. Commissioner of Education, G. F. Zook. Out of this conference grew a specific program for the emergency and much discussion of the long-time implications of the facts that were being collected. The activities implemented by this conference, however, have since been pointed largely to the problem of emergency aid. The program agreed upon included aid to the poorer states to keep schools open, aid on a more general basis to assist the property tax in carrying the burden of schools during the depression, school construction aid with particular attention to the rehousing of rural schools, the use of federal credit for refunding certain district indebtedness, and aid to college students.

In this period there was wide activity on the part of various lay and

---

[2] From *Report of National Conference on the Financing of Education*, held under the auspices of the Joint Commission on the Emergency in Education of the National Education Association and the Department of Superintendence, Columbia University, July 31 to Aug. 11, 1933, National Education Association, Washington, pp. 77ff.

educational groups. In 1934 the American Association of University Women issued a syllabus for study groups covering the problems of state and federal support. School board associations, parent-teacher associations, teachers' associations, and other organizations, in innumerable instances, passed resolutions favoring federal support. States all up and down the line of ability were represented by these resolutions. In the year 1934–1935 the question of federal aid was made a subject for high school debates throughout the country. While much of the activity had to do with the emergency situation, there was apparent, throughout, an undercurrent of conviction that the educational phase of the problem existed before the depression and would continue to exist after recovery. This conviction, that there was something structurally wrong with leaving the financing of education entirely to states and localities, was doubtless due in no small degree to the increasing array of evidence collected by various commissions and individual researchers.

Norton's study, *The Ability of the States to Support Education,* indicated that there was a range of six to one in the ability of states.[3]

The National Survey of School Finance gave detailed evidence on expenditure in communities and in states. Many persons took this type of evidence to indicate the necessity for federal aid to education. Others, however, contended that the ability data were faulty. They held that, if the states were to modernize their tax systems, no such differences as then existed would continue to obtain. They held, in effect, that the economic indexes of ability developed by Norton were not in fact reliable indications of taxpaying power. Studies made by Chism[4] and Newcomer[5] bore out the essential soundness of the conclusions drawn from Norton's data. Chism and Newcomer both sought to develop an index of the taxpaying ability of states under a defensible tax system.

When Ashby compared the ability of states with the cost of the average program in the United States, the answer as to the necessity for financing in larger units than the state was conclusive, assuming a national interest in the operation of a program approximately as good as the average in the country. Ashby's study[6] indicated what would happen if states were

---

[3] John K. Norton, *The Ability of the States to Support Education,* National Education Association, Washington, 1926. It is of interest that in 1949 the divergence had lessened to four to one, as judged from the income per classroom unit.

[4] Leslie L. Chism, *The Economic Ability of the States to Finance Public Schools,* Bureau of Publications, Teachers College, Columbia University, New York, 1936.

[5] Mabel Newcomer, *An Index of the Taxpaying Ability of State and Local Governments,* Bureau of Publications, Teachers College, Columbia University, New York, 1935.

[6] Lyle W. Ashby, *The Efforts of the States to Support Education as Related to the Adequacy of Financial Support Provided and the Ability of the States to Support Education,* National Education Association, Washington, 1936.

to make a like effort as well as correct their basic financial structures. His investigations show that the average state carries one and one-half times as heavy a burden, as far as effort is concerned, as the state which makes the least effort. The two studies showed further that to expect the poorest states to provide an adequate minimum of educational opportunity would require that they carry nearly four times as heavy a burden as the average state.

Concurrent with the studies by Chism, Newcomer, and Ashby, investigations were going forward seeking to develop a formula for federal aid that would utilize objective measures of need and ability. It will be remembered that the National Advisory Committee on Education, appointed in 1929 and reporting in 1931, had favored the shifting of emphasis in federal aid from the special-aid idea to the idea of general aid. The recommendations, however, were not definitive. In this sense they were comparable to Cubberley's 1905 recommendations in state support. There was no basis by which it was possible to determine how much federal aid there should be. It is possible to interpret their findings in two ways. The first interpretation is that they were interested in a general pushing up of the educational program, with emphasis on the states of lower ability. This was the Cubberley 1905 concept. The other possible interpretation is that this implied the Strayer and Haig concept of the minimum, or foundation, program.

Taking the latter interpretation, Mort, Cornell, and Lawler sought to establish a defensible level for a national foundation program of education and then to develop measures of educational need and of relative ability of states which would implement this interpretation.

Parallel work being carried on at the same time by committees of the National Education Association was reflected in the various educational aid bills introduced into Congress. In addition to seeking more refined measures of need and ability, Mort, Cornell, and Lawler drew the adaptability concept into the picture and came forward with a specific formula based upon the application of the equalization and adaptability principles. They summarized their arguments in support of the foundation-program concept, as follows: [7]

The arguments advanced in favor of federal responsibility for an adequate minimum of education are based mainly on the hypothesis that the benefits of public education, or the penalties arising from lack of it, cannot be localized either within a community or within a state. It is held, on the contrary, that these benefits from adequate education, or penalties from lack of it—civic, social, or economic—are widely diffused throughout the nation. Some of the arguments are accordingly pointed to the need of improving education in

[7] Paul R. Mort, *Federal Support for Public Education*, Bureau of Publications, Teachers College, Columbia University, New York, 1936, pp. 10–13.

order to insure general welfare. Others look upon the same problem as the task of removing festering sores in our civic, social, and economic system. Either line of argument leads to the conclusion that states must have the ability to support a defensible foundation program. Viewpoints of the extent of this program vary from those which would insure the nation against the worst penalties of lack of education to those which would insure a major contribution to the national welfare.

Supporting the negative phase of this hypothesis, we can point to the fact that the more inadequately educated persons cannot be barred from migrating from place to place. An example of the infusion of the educationally under-privileged Negroes of the South into the Northern communities is perhaps the most dramatic. The civil, social, and economic unfitness of this vast num-ber of migrants is well known. But there are other phases of the problem which, while not so dramatic, are perhaps equally important. It is a well-known fact that the quality of education provided by a community or state bears a close relationship to its economic ability. Those who live in the com-munities least privileged, from the standpoint of economic ability, are the most poorly educated. Upon this group living in the marginal economic areas of our country there is a particularly strong pressure to migrate to other com-munities. Some of these persons by sheer cleverness rise to a high place in these communities. Others will be found gracing the relief rolls. All are handi-capped personally and in their contributions to the general welfare by the early denial of adequate educational opportunities.

These shifts in population are influenced in no small degree by a differential in birth rate in urban and rural areas. Recent studies by Dr. O. E. Baker, Senior Agricultural Economist connected with the United States Department of Agriculture at Washington, D.C., show that a shortage in urban birth rate is offset by an excess in rural birth rate, when the criterion is the number of births necessary for the maintenance of a given population. This social situa-tion provides a great suction pump that will continue to draw in the excess population of the rural areas to make up the deficiency in urban population. In order to hold their own, the cities must recruit from rural areas a sufficient number to make up from one-tenth to one-third of the future urban popula-tion. This, coupled with the well-known fact that the rural schools of America are at least a generation behind the urban, represents a problem of no small moment. Evidence collected by the National Survey of School Finance shows that the average level of rural schools in America, in at least 90 per cent of the counties, is below a defensible minimum. In these underprivileged schools no small proportion of the urban population of tomorrow is now being educated.

Nor is the limit of the general welfare defined by the degree of migration of population. Limited educational opportunities are associated with limited standards of living. Limited standards of living mean subnormal consumption of goods. Subnormal consumption of goods affects the economic welfare of our abler communities. Similarly, limited education is associated with limited pro-ductive capacity. This at one and the same time limits the purchasing power of the individuals concerned and their potential contribution to the economic welfare of others throughout the nation. Finally, the existence in great areas in our country of people with limited education not only influences the economic and social pattern of the nation at large, but also provides a rich area of support for selfish pressure groups that help to set the civic as well as the social and economic pattern of the nation.

While national equalization of a defensible foundation program seemed imperative, there did not appear to be so strong an impulsion for federal aid to broaden the tax base in all the states as is found in the relationship of state government and school districts, a position that is now vigorously questioned. The same possibilities for utilizing an equalization-type formula are, of course, available. The discussion referred to above continues with this treatment of tax-broadening aid.[8]

In addition to the argument based on the diffusion-of-benefit hypothesis, much has been written in the last decade and a half favoring federal taxation for the support of fundamental phases of government, such as education, because of the advantage which some states obtain fortuitously from the working of our economic system. The point is made, for example, that because of the complex nature of our economic system, a state like New York can collect taxes on incomes actually created in large part in our most remote states. It is argued from this that the federal government should collect the taxes and send back to each state at least as much as it produces.

A further argument leading in the same direction arises from the difficulties which states encounter in collecting many of the newer types of taxes. Recent writers in taxation have claimed that it would be a distinct advantage if the federal government were to act as a tax-collecting agency, thereby eliminating the difficulties which arise because of interstate commerce, the economic accidents mentioned above, and such difficulties as bootlegging taxable materials or removing tax situs across the state lines.

These arguments from the field of taxation, it will be noted, are not arguments for federal aids to education specifically. Federal aid to education comes in as a possible method of distribution of taxes collected by the Federal government. Tax coordination is a matter involving both tax collection and tax distribution. The distributive aspect is the problem of supporting the various phases of state and local government. To the extent that a plan for financing public education would serve as a channel for the flow back to the states of funds collected by the federal government, thereby relieving state or local taxes, or both, it will serve the purpose desired. It is of interest that a system supporting public education can be made to serve as a channel for the flow of central funds to the states in perfect relationship to the relative ability of the states to support education, either with or without the use of ability measures. This holds, even though an ability measure lacking in complete validity is incorporated in the distribution plan.

[8] *Ibid.*, pp. 13–14.

It is of interest that in the introduction of the above report the acceptableness of the equalization principle was mentioned first among sixteen problems proposed as problems that must be determined as matters of public policy rather than by research. It is also of interest that thirteen years after the formulation of the Strayer and Haig definition of equalization there appeared still to be uncertainty as to the acceptance of the equalization principle as applied to federal aid. As a matter of fact, the out-and-out recognition of the foundation-program idea was not made in any proposed federal-aid legislation until the middle 1940s. The concept had been basic to the computations made for these plans, but the formulas had always been written in an indirect fashion.

This in general was the situation which obtained when the problem was approached by the Advisory Committee on Education appointed by President Roosevelt in 1937. The studies of this committee multiplied the information on inequality and brought clear light to bear upon the actual federal-aid practices. We seek in vain in the general report, however, for any clear-cut answer to the question, "Does the equalization principle as defined by Strayer and Haig apply to the national situation?" Like the findings of the National Advisory Committee on Education, the report takes a stand against special aid. It points out, however, certain weaknesses that the commission thought were so important as to require the earmarking of funds granted by the federal government.

As we have noticed in the case of the states, those who see a conflict between general and special aid may be in error. There may be no essential conflict. It is entirely possible that a restrained and careful use of reward-for-effort aids may continue to be an important function of the national government even after steps have been taken adequately to assure a defensible minimum program in all states. As a matter of fact, a general-aid program should make it possible more easily to dispose of the special aids after they have served their purpose. Furthermore, with a more adequate foundation, smaller aids may prove as stimulative as the larger aids used in the past. This would avoid at least part of the evil effects pointed out by students of the problem—the drawing of funds from other functions so as to make possible the support of the aided function. This has not been a serious difficulty except in the states that are providing inadequate general programs at the cost of a great effort.

The apparent conflict between federal aid to education and the legal fact that education is a function of the states has been a subject of much discussion ever since the first proposals for federal aid of a general nature. This is the issue on which most of the arguments have turned. The various positions taken may be summarized as follows:

1. We are in favor of federal aid because of the financial need, and

we believe that it can be arranged in such a way as to avoid the growth of federal control.

2. We believe in federal aid because it would give the federal government a chance to eliminate intolerable conditions.

3. While we see the desirability of federal aid from a financial standpoint, it would give the federal government control over the schools.

Those taking the second position favor either earmarked aids or the granting of wide discretionary powers to the national administrative agency concerned. Those taking the first position seek to develop a plan of distribution objective in nature and with the very minimum of discretionary power on the part of the administrative agency. Those taking the third position apparently doubt the efficacy of measures proposed to safeguard the states' control. The problem is not simplified by the tendency of many persons to shift between the objective of position 2 and the fear of consequences represented in position 3.

One major issue involves the first and third positions. It is essentially the question of the separability of finance and control as discussed in Chapter 2. Application of this hypothesis to the national situation requires that we look upon certain of the interests of education as transcending state lines—as interests of all the people of the nation. It assumes that the people may choose to use their federal tax-collecting powers to raise funds partially to aliment state-aid funds of the states and to allot to their state agencies the full power of disposal of such funds.

Some evidence on the practicality of this point comes from experience with general national aids in the Union of South Africa. The elementary and secondary schools are operated by the four provincial school systems, but the national government makes an allotment to each province sufficient to support an educational program roughly equal to the average educational expenditure in the United States. While the grant is a flat grant per elementary and secondary pupil in attendance, it is not restricted in any way—not strictly restricted even to education. This system has been in operation for more than a third of a century without encroachments on the control of the provinces.[9]

A second issue involves positions 1 and 2. It has to do with the desirability of shifting considerable control to federal agencies. Viewing the undesirable conditions in many parts of the country, one can easily get enthusiastic over the idea of trying to use federal agencies directly, to affect the operation of schools as well as to improve the probabilities of improvement by helping to correct defects in the financial structure. Proponents of position 2 at least imply that there is no adequate reason

[9] *Official Yearbook of the Union of South Africa*, No. 16, 1933–1934, Chaps. IV and XXII, Pretoria: Printed in the Union of South Africa by the Government Printer.

why we should not face the issue of reallocation of controls over education as between the federal government and the states. This appears to be the position taken by the Advisory Committee on Education.

The reasonableness of this point makes it appear likely that the issue between positions 1 and 2 will come to be one of emphasis. Those holding position 2 may concede the necessity of safeguarding against unintended shifts in control, and those holding position 1 may concede the desirability of transferring certain specifically defined powers to national administrative agencies.

The sections that follow illustrate the developments of positions 1 and 2, in both instances certain concessions being made to the other position. Position 3 counsels no action and therefore needs no legislation.

APPLICATION TO FEDERAL AID WITH EMPHASIS ON POSITION 1

Two extensive studies have sought to apply the emerging conceptual pattern for federal aid represented by position 1, discussed in the preceding section. The first of these, directed by Mort, was published in 1936.[10] It represents an attempt to develop the measures necessary to a general-aid plan of the type recommended by the National Advisory Committee in 1931. The National Survey of School Finance had collected the data necessary for the development of norms for an index of educational need. These data made it possible to make adaptations in the index, refining it for interstate comparisons and simplifying it. Simplification was possible because of the fact that units as large as states do not present all the problems faced in dealing with school districts.

The practice of communities of average wealth in the United States was taken as a basis for determining the unit cost of the foundation program. Independent measures were developed for the relative ability of states to pay taxes under a model tax plan based on the ability-to-pay criterion. Consideration was given to the amount of aid over and beyond that required for equalization that might be used to assist in tax reform in the states. The result was the recommendation of a method of approach to an eventual program that would fall in between equalization and the complete support of the foundation program. Half of the cost of the national minimum program in every state would be paid outright to every state, and the remainder would be equalized.

The other study, directed by Mort and Lawler, was made for the Advisory Committee on Education.[11] This study tested the measures that

[10] Mort, *op. cit.*
[11] Paul R. Mort and Eugene S. Lawler, *Principles and Methods of Distributing*

had been developed in the earlier study in terms of 1930 data by applying them to 1935 data. It utilized the same unit cost for the foundation
program but shifted the unit of educational need from the average daily
attendance to the school census basis. From Heer's study [12] it was apparent that, assuming the desire to utilize federal tax collections to ex-
pedite tax reform, it would be feasible to support the entire foundation
program from federal taxes—essentially the flat grant idea widely
espoused later by Ruml and others. The study also considered the possibility of a formula that would fall short of equalization and still be defensible and proposed such a program as one of three possibilities.

The three alternatives proposed by Mort and Lawler are as follows: [13]

Plan I—Realizing the Defensible Foundation Program

Granting Federal aid to the States on the basis of the differences between
present State and local expenditures and the cost of the defensible foundation
program would require a reduction of expenditures in many communities in
all but a few States if the defensible foundation program were to be maintained
in all communities without increasing the State and local tax burden.... A
plan of basing Federal aid upon 87 per cent of average effort would give aid
to all States of less than average ability and to that group of States which falls
between average and 15 per cent above average ability. [About a fourth of the
states would get no aid.] Moving the 87 per cent up to 100 per cent would
eliminate the group of States just above average ability. It is assumed that this
group of States, by making approximately 15 per cent greater effort than they
now make, could raise their actual minimum levels up to the level of the
defensible foundation program without Federal aid. These States, however,
would have the additional burden of contributing through Federal taxes to a
Federal aid fund. There is grave danger that under these circumstances either
equalization up to the national defensible program would not take place, or
that, if it did take place, it would be at the expense of the abler communities
in these States. In a sense, then, this group may be considered the critical
States. They would be harmed by a plan that did not give them sufficient
Federal aid to raise their present minimum programs to the defensible foundation program.

*Plan II—Realizing the Defensible Foundation Program and Equalizing the
Financial Burden*

Plan II is designed to achieve the defensible foundation program and to
equalize the financial burden. It gives aid to all but the 3 ablest States. It uses

---

Federal Aid for Education, Report of the Advisory Committee on Education, Staff
Study No. 5, Government Printing Office, Washington, 1939.

[12] Clarence Heer, "Federal Aid and the Tax Problem," *Report of the Advisory
Committee on Education*, Staff Study No. 4, Government Printing Office, Washington,
1939.

[13] Mort and Lawler, *op. cit.*, pp. 23–27.

the largest State of high ability, New York, as the criterion State. The plan involves a very slight deviation from strict equalization, but States receiving aid would bear a burden only slightly less than 1 per cent above the average.

Plan III—Realizing the Defensible Foundation Program, Equalizing the Financial Burden, and Assisting in Tax Reform

It has already been pointed out that Plan I would realize the defensible foundation program without placing additional handicaps on local initiative, and that Plan II would equalize the financial burden and incidentally include some measure of assistance to local initiative. Plan III is specially designed to rehabilitate local initiative.

It has been stated that local units cannot effectively exercise control over educational programs and adapt them to their own local conditions or to changing economic and social needs without an opportunity for experimentation. This requires some financial leeway. If funds for the defensible foundation program come principally from the property tax, the only major tax which can be used effectively by local units, freedom to exercise initiative is in fact denied to local units. The necessary relief to the property tax can be brought about only by the reorganization of existing tax systems. Ultimately this might be accomplished through the slow process of State action, but the difficulty of tax reform through individual State action leads to the conclusion that the Federal Government may well hasten the process by serving as a tax-collecting agency. If the Federal Government distributed aid in proportion to the total educational need, the aid in excess of that allocated by Plan II would be returned to the States in proportion to their financial ability.

Plan I carries a slight measure of tax relief to those participating States now making efforts greater than approximately 115 per cent of the average; Plan II carries a still larger measure of tax relief to those States now making greater than average effort. In addition, relief for the property tax is afforded in both of these plans largely to the extent that the funds collected from individual States through Federal taxes are returned to them as aid. Plan III would afford relief for the property tax in all States.

Guides for Appraisal of Federal-aid Plans

These are the ultimate patterns to be used as guides for immediate steps. Those interested in the immediate steps proposed will find them in the studies cited. But they also provide guides for appraisal of a given proposal. Their use as guides is treated in Chapter IV of the Mort-Lawler report, as follows: [14]

In using these plans to appraise various proposals for Federal aid, the following objectives with which they are associated should be kept in mind:

*Objective 1—To provide the defensible foundation program without placing additional handicaps on local initiative.—*Any plan which gives aid in proportion to financial need to all but the 10 or 12 ablest States serves this objective.

[14] *Ibid.,* pp. 29–31.

Objective 2—To equalize the burden of the defensible foundation program among the States.—Any plan which distributes aid in proportion to financial need to all but 2 or 3 of the ablest States serves this objective in addition to Objective 1.

Objective 3—To assist States in improving the financial base of local initiative.—Any plan which grants aid to all States serves this objective in addition to Objectives 1 and 2.

Proposals frequently made to grant aid in proportion to financial need to only the poorer States are evidently directed solely toward the attainment of Objective 1.

. . . . . .

A plan which distributes aid to all States in proportion to financial need serves Objective 3 to the extent that the total amount of aid granted exceeds the amount which would be granted by a plan that excludes the two or three ablest States.

The adequacy of any given plan must also be appraised in terms of the validity of the measures of educational need and financial ability used and in terms of the total amount of money made available. . . .

The association of the Federal aid plans described above with definite objectives makes it possible to appraise any Federal aid proposal in terms of the objectives served, without further technical analysis.

Measures of Need and Ability

The chief differences between the measure of educational need for states and that for school districts discussed in Chapter 7 are: 1. A measure usable in a Federal law can utilize a sparsity measure to take care both of the small class and of transportation corrections. 2. There is considerable justification for use of census data rather than attendance data. The measure of ability must, however, be radically different. Within the states the local tax system is set by the state. The federal government has no such control over state tax systems. Therefore, while presumably there is uniformity of tax systems among school districts in a state, there is no such uniformity among states. To obtain a fair measure of the relative ability of states to support education, it is necessary to use some uniform tax plan as a basis of estimate.

As an approach to this, Newcomer worked out estimates of the yields of "ability" taxes. Such taxes as the motor fuels tax, not customarily used for education, were eliminated. Cornell then sought through government-collected data for economic data from which the closest approximation to Newcomer's estimate could be obtained. The best combination of these measures was taken as the index of relative ability of states to pay taxes.[15]

[15] A complete account of Lawler's work on refining the index of educational need and the work of Newcomer and Cornell in developing the ability measure is given in Mort, *Federal Support for Public Education, op. cit.* A report of later tests of these measures appears in Mort and Lawler, *op. cit.*, Chap. V.

Various other attempts have been made to get at a defensible measure of the fiscal ability of the states.[16] Most of them have missed the potentialities of an empirical formula such as the one developed by Cornell utilizing Newcomer's estimates of taxpaying ability of states. Instead they have attempted to develop a logical basis for measuring fiscal ability. Accordingly they deal with various ways of handling the income of individuals. They fail to inquire into the possible profits of the development of formulas by empirical methods which have proved so useful in the development of measures of relative ability for units within states.

The federal-aid bills proposed in recent years utilized measures of fiscal capacity of states in terms of income. Applying the test of predictability of taxpaying ability of the states, such measures fall considerably short of what can be obtained through the empirical approach. While the error in using such measures of fiscal ability of states is relatively small as long as the proposals for federal aid remain in the modest stage, it is rather regrettable that, when they do become established and the basis for support extended, the errors involved will be multiplied. They will then become difficult to correct because correction will mean the loss of special advantages.

Control Features

Those holding that federal aid should be for the purpose of strengthening the financial structure and should avoid intended or unintended shifts of control to the federal government would provide the very minimum of compliance features. They would have a federal act for general aid indicate the purpose for which Congress accepts the establishment of the proposed plan, but they would not make the attainment of these purposes the condition for the receiving of aid. They would require, however, a full reporting of the use of funds to be made to the federal government after the fact, these reports to be used as a means of general public information and as a basis upon which Congress can shape future policies with respect to the extension of the proposed program.

With respect to the advantage of financial audits referred to above, the following statement from the Report of the National Advisory Committee on Education is to the point: [17]

Complete financial audit gives the publicity that protects the Federal Government and is an adequate safeguard against state expenditure of federal funds for anything outside the broad educational purposes contemplated.

[16] Byron L. Johnson, "Principle of Equalization Applied to the Allocation of Grants in Aid," Federal Security Agency, Social Security Administration, *Memorandum 66*, September, 1947, pp. 114ff.

[17] "Federal Relations to Education," *Report of the National Advisory Committee on Education*, Washington, The Committee, 1931, part I, p. 32.

Wisdom in state allocation and expenditure of funds given by the Federal Government is best guaranteed by full and detailed reports to the Federal Government. The printing and wide distribution of the same by the Federal Government will inform public opinion, the only competent check upon which popular government may rely in the long run.

APPLICATIONS TO FEDERAL AID WITH EMPHASIS ON POSITION 2 [18]

While the 1938 report of the Educational Policies Commission leaned to the position basic to the preceding section, the Advisory Committee on Education, reporting in the same year, leaned to the position that the federal government should become actively engaged in improving the educational services at clearly defined points. This is indicated both in the special aids and in the compliance features proposed.

Special aids recommended were as follows: improved preparation of teachers and other educational personnel, construction of school buildings to facilitate district reorganization, administration of state departments of education, educational services for adults, library services for rural areas, cooperative educational research demonstrations and planning. Their proposal for general aid gave general aid almost twice as much emphasis as all these special aids combined.

The committee favored the allocation of the general aid on an objective basis but recommended that the formula be defined in principle and left to administrative agencies to work out from year to year. On this point the report carries the following: [19]

The allocation of funds among the States in accordance with their financial needs involves the use of technical procedures of measurement. Technical studies have been made of the cost of various levels of educational service in rural, small urban, and large urban areas, of the ability of the States to support social services through taxation, and of the share of their tax-raising ability that should be devoted to the support of education. On the basis of these studies, a large amount of effort has been devoted in recent years to the development of formulas to measure the relative financial needs of the States with respect to education.

The Committee has given consideration to these formulas, has carried on additional studies, has developed experimentally a number of new formulas, and has had the advice of the most expert counsel available. It believes that the existing studies indicate the factors to be considered and in general the procedures to be followed. The Committee has been reluctantly forced to the conclusion, however, that the statute providing for the proposed grants should

[18] See p. 308.
[19] Advisory Committee on Education, *Report of the Committee*, Government Printing Office, Washington, 1938, pp. 70–73.

avoid the specification in exact detail of any formula for the allocation of the funds to States, but should specify instead the general procedure to be followed and the policies to be considered controlling.

This recommendation could conceivably give the same results as the methods of approach offered in the preceding section.[20] Here there is an evident interest in eliminating unforeseen controls. But the special aids and the compliance features show a very strong interest in allocating certain large specified controls.

Special aids were proposed for improving teacher preparation, school buildings, and state departments of education.

FEDERAL AID FOR BALANCING THE TAX BURDEN

To the student of school finance, the most important aspects of federal taxation are those which have a bearing on the desirability of using federal funds in large amounts over and beyond that amount necessary to assure a minimum acceptable national standard of education with a defensible, equitable distribution of burden upon the people in all states. If Plan I, discussed above, is accepted as reasonably equitable in its distribution of burden and a defensible minimum of educational opportunity is set at some multiple of $50 per weighted census pupil, the area of federal taxation in which we are interested is that which would be utilized in providing eventually something more than $600 million annually from federal funds for each $50 of the foundation program. If equalization of burden to the extent of Plan II were demanded to meet the criterion of reasonable equity, the area of taxation to be considered here is that which would be drawn upon to yield federal aid in excess of $1 billion annually for each $50. Of course the issue comes in much earlier, inasmuch as the pattern of federal aid, long before it has reached the above amounts, will be built in terms of either an ultimate plan demanding reasonable equalization only or an ultimate plan envisaging more federal aid than that which reasonable equalization requires.

We have seen that aid over that demanded for the equitable support of a national foundation program must be justified, if at all, as a means of facilitating the tax reform necessary for relieving the property tax to the extent necessary to make it a solid foundation for local initiative. Theoretically, since the states, with certain exceptions, are sovereign with respect to taxation, the power to bring about an equitable burden as between property and other taxes lies within the states themselves.

In the relation between the state government and the local districts, the situation is quite the reverse. Here the power over taxation lies only with

[20] See pp. 312–313.

the central government. Local agents must operate in the framework established by the central government. As a matter of fact, however, the compelling reason why the desired objective of proper distribution of burden on various taxes cannot be attained by local governments lies in the fact that the range of taxes that can be administered locally is at present very narrow, limited in most districts largely to the property tax.

When we compare state governments with the federal government, we are faced with the same condition but in lesser degree. In spite of the theoretically broad scope of taxes available to state governments, there are distinct limitations to this scope, arising from federal constitutional limitations on the one hand and from the lack of taxable resources on the other.

LIMITATIONS OF TAXING POWER

The most serious limitation on federal taxing power is the federal constitutional restriction on direct taxes. This leaves the direct property taxation to the states and localities. Inasmuch as the phase of tax reform in which we are interested is the shifting of the burden from the direct property tax to other taxes, this limitation on the federal government is not in effect a limitation in scope as far as our problem is concerned. On the other hand, the states are limited from imposing direct burdens on interstate and foreign commerce. In addition to these constitutional limitations, there are practical limitations imposed by interstate competition. In his detailed treatment of the problem under consideration in this chapter, Heer has the following to say on this point: [21]

Interstate competition. The unequal distribution of taxable resources among the States is not the only factor that weakens the revenue-raising power of State and local tax systems. In comparison with the Federal Government, the States suffer from certain disadvantages which prevent them from effectively utilizing the resources which they have. Many of the subjects of State and local taxation, other than real estate, are more or less mobile. In their efforts to tap these mobile sources, the States are handicapped by the limited areas over which their taxing powers extend, by the diversity of State taxing systems and rates of levy, and by the ever-present threat of interstate tax competition. Any State that departs too widely from the general pattern of taxation set by its neighbors invites wholesale tax avoidance and evasion and runs the risk of seeing valuable taxable assets drained away.

The extent to which the taxing powers of the States are weakened by interstate competition is clearly apparent in the case of the personal income tax.[22]

[21] Clarence Heer, "Federal Aid and the Tax Problem," *Report of the Advisory Committee on Education,* Staff Study No. 4, Government Printing Office, Washington, 1939, pp. 47–49. See chap. 9 for more extensive treatment.

[22] The Tax Research Foundation, *Tax Systems of the World,* 7th ed., Commerce Clearing House, Inc., Chicago, 1938, pp. 137–143,

The reason for this moderation on the part of the States is plain. High income tax rates can be applied only against very large incomes. The recipients of such incomes reside for the most part in a few industrial States. Individuals of means, especially the beneficiaries of large income from investments, however, constitute a fairly foot-loose group, and some of them might be induced to change their State of residence if it became sufficiently worth their while. This possibility tends to deter the industrial States from adopting scales of income tax progression that are much above those prevailing in the rest of the country, although it might otherwise be profitable for them to do so. The agricultural States, on the other hand, have little to gain from steeply graduated rates since they have few large incomes to tax. Their legislators may, in fact, believe that they have more to gain by keeping their rates in their upper income brackets low, or by having no income tax at all, with a view to attracting residents from other States.

The personal income tax is not the only revenue source which the States are unable to exploit as effectively as the Federal Government. Interstate competition threatened the productivity of State inheritance taxes until congress adopted an amendment to the Federal estate tax which permitted payments on account of State death taxes to be used as a credit against amounts due under the Federal tax up to a specified limit. This so-called crediting device tends to equalize the combined burdens of Federal and State death taxes throughout the country, but it protects the States from interstate competition only to the extent that they keep their death rates within the limit of the Federal credit.

In the field of business taxation the States are likewise hampered by potential competition.[23]

In the case of State taxes that enter directly into business costs and are added to prices, it is necessary, of course, to keep an eye on the practices of other States. No State can afford to place its producers for a national market at competitive disadvantage. Thus, although the Federal Government derives considerable amounts of revenue from the manufacturers' excise taxes, the States make very little use of this type of taxation. Even in their use of the retail sales tax, the States must keep their rates low enough to discourage an undue amount of out-of-State buying.[24]

From the standpoint both of scope and of meeting the administrative difficulties in bringing about tax reform, there seems to be a distinct advantage in utilizing the federal tax machinery for bringing about the desired results.

Lack of Taxable Resources

Considering the vast range in abilities of states to obtain revenue from various taxes, we may well ask whether tax reform in an individual state

[23] *Ibid.*, pp. 144–145. Oregon has a flat rate of 8 per cent. In South Dakota, the 8 per cent rate applies to net income in excess of $318,000. Pennsylvania taxed 1936 income at 10 per cent, but the rate for 1937 and 1938 net income is 7 per cent.

[24] See chap. 10 for a more complete discussion.

that brings about a fair burden of taxes would bring about a condition favorable to local initiative in the poorer states. In states that are largely agricultural, it is not possible to shift the burden from the property tax to anywhere near the degree that is possible in the industrial states. We might readily conclude from this, then, that even with tax reform carried on by the states, some of the states would find themselves in a position where the adaptability principle, as far as it is served by property-tax relief, could not be adequately cared for. It is possible, as we understand the full implications of this principle, that this may become a very strong argument for the use of federal tax machinery. At the present stage of understanding of the problem, however, it can hardly be brought forward as a compelling argument. When we reach a situation where there is a fair distribution of burden among the various taxes in a state and the effects of this on the educational program are appraised, we may see the necessity as compelling for equalizing local initiative, as it were, as we now see equalizing the burden of the foundation program. At the present time the weight of the argument for federal aid over and beyond that for equalization would seem to lie in the relative scope of the taxing powers of the federal and state governments and the relative ease with which a unified program of tax reform could be brought about by federal legislation as compared with state legislation.

AID FOR EDUCATION AND OTHER GOVERNMENTAL PURPOSES

Table 17-1 gives the federal aid to states for education and other purposes. Note that education plays a relatively minor role—$204 million out of $6,468 million. The school lunch program absorbs three-fourths the amount of the aid for educational purposes.

During the 1940s there developed a great deal of interest in simplifying federal aid for all state and local purposes. A series of studies has been developed by various federal agencies, including the U.S. Treasury and the Federal Security Agency, by the Council of State Governments, the Hoover Commission on Organization of the Executive Branch of the Government and by the Department of Health, Education, and Welfare. These studies show a strong tendency to pass over the history of experience in the field of education and draw upon the shorter but admittedly far more dramatic experience with aid in the health, welfare, security, and highway fields.[25]

[25] This tendency to ignore education as having any special stake was reflected in the act to establish a National Commission on Intergovernmental Fiscal Relations to be made up of persons appointed by the President, Senate, and House of Representatives, supplemented by persons to be nominated by the Council of State Governments and the United States Conference of Mayors. Senate Bill 810, 1950.

Table 17-1 Federal Aid Payments to State and Local Units of Government and to Individuals Within States

	1950 (actual)	1957 (actual)
Part A. Payments to States and Local Governments		
1. Department of Agriculture—total	$207,365,227	$306,606,406
a. Experiment stations—regular grants	12,243,522	28,329,098
b. Extension work—regular grants	31,025,919	48,692,857
c. School lunch and school milk	81,213,235	155,625,339
d. Projects in marketing research	1,339,582	2,754,949
e. Value of commodities purchased and donated, then distributed	64,023,959	236,146,641
f. Shared revenues	8,042,343	29,157,633
g. Other	9,476,667	42,046,530
2. Department of Commerce—total	462,188,553	987,293,137
a. Bureau of Public Roads	428,780,277	954,732,612
b. C.A.A.—airports program	32,782,999	20,629,109
c. State marine schools	157,761	292,523
d. Shared revenues	467,516	1,472,476
e. Other	. . .	10,166,417
3. Department of Health, Education, and Welfare— total (formerly Federal Security Agency)	1,314,267,671	1,966,214,946
a. Office of Education—total	38,218,252	204,336,577
(1) Agriculture and mechanical arts	5,030,000	5,051,500
(2) Vocational education	26,489,335	37,582,036
(3) School construction; survey; assistance	6,698,917	67,068,366
(4) Maintenance and operation	. . .	93,194,675
(5) Library services	. . .	1,440,000
b. Public Health Service—total	104,987,535	132,735,125
c. Social Security Administration—total	1,170,936,884	1,628,903,244
(1) Maternal and Child Health Welfare Services	22,777,724	38,251,998
(2) Public Assistance and Health	1,123,417,650	1,556,422,423
(3) Vocational Rehabilitation	24,741,510	34,228,823
d. Printing for the blind—total	125,000	240,000
4. Department of the Interior—total	21,655,190	55,102,049
a. Regular grants—wildlife, etc.	7,577,938	15,739,837
b. Shared revenues	14,077,252	39,362,212
5. Department of Labor—total	207,617,255	248,315,752
a. Unemployment Compensation and Employment Service Administration		
6. Treasury Department		
a. Unemployment Trust Fund	. . .	71,195,220
7. Federal Civil Defense Administration	. . .	8,647,943
8. Federal Power Commission—shared revenues	28,315	32,980
9. Housing and Home Finance Agency	6,366,604	117,613,537
10. Tennessee Valley Authority—shared revenues	. . .	4,744,401
11. Veterans' Administration	14,537,415	8,217,579
12. Miscellaneous grants	722,288	54,059,450
13. Grand total of payments—Part A	$2,234,699,542	$4,064,190,041

Table 17-1   (*Continued*)

	1950 (*actual*)	1957 (*actual*)
Part B. Payments to Individuals Within States		
14. Department of Agriculture—total	$289,297,937	$867,297,937
a. Conservation; sugar	289,951,995	288,302,866
b. Soil bank; aid to drought-stricken areas	. . .	578,995,071
15. Department of Commerce—total	. . .	250,613
a. In 1950 amount was spent for public roads and forest highways	26,916,655	
16. Department of Defense—total	132,166,305	504,388,072
17. Department of Health, Education, and Welfare—total	19,681,917	128,377,038
a. Research grants to national institutes	17,098,343	82,517,308
b. Training grants	491,489	30,528,569
c. Fellowship awards	2,092,085	9,868,654
d. Office of Vocational Rehabilitation	. . .	5,462,507
18. Department of Labor—total	905,964	78,426,796
a. Unemployment compensation to veterans	. . .	53,210,349
b. Unemployment compensation to federal employees	. . .	25,216,447
c. Unemployment benefits to seamen	905,964	
19. Atomic Energy Commission—fellowship and assistance to schools	. . .	3,943,551
20. National Science Foundation—total	. . .	33,623,204
a. Research grants	. . .	31,490,219
b. Fellowship awards	. . .	2,132,985
21A. Veterans' Administration—total	2,817,191,109	787,952,527
a. (Automobiles and readjustment benefits)		
21B. General Services Administration payments to individuals for disaster and emergency relief	460,932	
22. Grand total—Part B, payments to individuals within the States	$3,287,321,201	$2,404,259,738
23. Grand total (Parts A and B) Payments to states and local units of government and payments to individuals within states	$5,522,020,743	$6,468,449,760

SOURCE: *Annual Report of the Secretary of the Treasury on the State of the Finances.* Data supplied by Orlando F. Furno, Specialist in State Educational Finance, Department of Health, Education, and Welfare, U.S. Office of Education, Washington, D.C.

Students of school finance will recognize the same purposes running through the grants for other purposes that have operated in the field of education: stimulation of matters of national concern, equalization, and (largely theoretical) the use of federal taxation to reach sources difficult for the states to tap efficiently. An additional interest that education has seemed to seek to avoid is what Studenski calls "establishment of cooperative Federal-state support and administration of services vested within joint Federal-state interest." [26]

The earlier studies in the "federal-state relations series," the authors believe, suffered from concern with this fourth purpose, a purpose the authors suggest as one to avoid in aid for education. It may account for what appears to be a tendency to shy away from thoroughgoing analyses of objective measures of need and ability, since "joint Federal-state interest" may connote a degree of interest in Federal control not desired in the educational field. The later studies, however, indicate a clearer differentiation of the basic purposes of tax sharing and equalization, embracing the whole of state and local government. For example, House Report No. 2533 is a particularly good presentation of the range of issues and concerns shared by education and other state and local government functions.[27] This report is a fruit of the long series of efforts to develop a better integration of federal and state governments, beginning, as the report points out, with President Theodore Roosevelt's Conference of Governors in 1908, and culminating, after twenty intermediate steps, (a) in the staffing of the President's office "for attention to intergovernmental relations" (1956), (b) in the extension of the joint federal-state bill drafting program (1956), and (c) in the Joint Federal-State Action Committee (1957).[28]

In reading this report it is not difficult to see an approach to the tax-collection problem far more embracing than can be made through aid to education. But the recommendations do not reflect any such major concern as yet arising from these studies.[29] Rather, there is a series of useful but extremely limited recommendations (a) on how to write special aid laws, (b) on strengthening the staff in the President's office and (c) on matters of administrative housekeeping. In the hiatus a plethora of limited federal-aid proposals, in education as in other fields, continues to come forward.

Those educational-aid proposals, with the tax-collection and distribution purposes central, favor the flat-grant idea. However, in the second session of the 85th Congress three bills were introduced which were searching for a way to return the income tax to the source states.

Thought of as a complete system of aid, as is pointed out in earlier chapters, the flat grant falls short on the equalization side, unless it is sufficient to pay the whole cost of the operation of the function. The flat grant is a gesture that gains its support from the fact that it bows toward

---

[26] Paul Studenski, "Federal Grants-in-aid," *National Tax Journal,* vol. II, no. 3, September, 1949.

[27] Thirtieth Report by the Committee on Government Operations, House Report No. 2533, August 1958, pp. 23–26.

[28] *Ibid.,* pp. 61–77.   [29] *Ibid.,* pp. 51–52.

a need that is as yet not carefully defined. Since in education we do not suffer this handicap, there would appear to be no justification for stopping with the equalization incident to a system of flat grants.

Proposals for federal aid on a flat grant basis such as that made by Beardsley Ruml are of a similar character.[30] Ruml proposed $80 per pupil. This amount supplemented by present expenditures typical in some of the poorest states would not provide an acceptable level of support according to any defensible standards. Accordingly as a basis of assessing an acceptable minimum of educational support, it would be grossly inadequate. Approximately two-thirds of the total of three billion dollars involved would be shared taxes, defensible only in terms of tax reform, not in terms of educational need except indirectly. The only defense for the two-thirds that would be shared taxes, other than political, would be in the establishment of the position that the states are not able to reach their own resources. In other words, the lion's share of flat grant federal aid is aid only in the sense that the federal government rather than the states collects the taxes within the states and turns the revenue over to them. The net equalizing effect resulting from the distribution on a population basis is relatively small. Accordingly, unless our purpose is *tax reform*, not financing education, such a plan suggests the story of burning the house to roast a pig.

If indeed it can be established that we need to move not only from the local community to the state, but from the state to the nation for the collection of major non-property taxes, such a proposal takes on merit as a means of providing more wholesome conditions not only for education but also for all other state and local government. In accepting support for such moves from economists we should at least examine whether their purpose fully recognizes the particular major problems of school finance. To do otherwise may lead educators to accept a major role in tax reform ahead of the time when the public will be alert to appreciate that it is tax reform and not education.

But these studies do throw light on the problems common to all state and local government functions. For example, Mushkin's study of the incidence of benefit from federal spending and the supplying of revenue by the various states indicates that federal spending within the states is rather closely related to population. Thus the vast federal expenditure has an equalizing effect. From Mushkin's figures it can be deduced that about 60 per cent of the taxes goes back to the states they came from, while 40 per cent goes in inverse proportion to taxpaying ability.[31]

[30] Beardsley Ruml, "Federal Support for the Public Schools," *Education Digest,* October, 1957.

[31] Selma Mushkin, *Illustrative Estimates of Federal Expenditures and Revenues by States,* U.S. Department of Health, Education, and Welfare, Division of Public Health Methods, Washington, 1956.

THE DECADE OF THE 1950s

The high point of the trend toward equalization came with the Taft bill in 1949. The Taft bill called for equalization of the Mort-Lawler Type I plan, plus a small flat grant to all states. It was free from controls. It defined a foundation expenditure level and it measured need and ability objectively. This bill passed the Senate but failed of passage in the House of Representatives.

During the intervening years there has been a return to programs with the design less apparent, none of which have been passed by either house. And there has been a new proliferation of special-aid proposals: for school buildings and for scholarships particularly.

In an address before a conference on Education and Science in the United States held at Harvard University in the summer of 1958, Elliott R. Richardson, Assistant Secretary of Health, Education, and Welfare, gave as his concept of the preferred function of the national government the stimulation of action in specific areas of need.[32] Secretary Folsom, in an interview given at the time of his return to private life, spoke of the purpose of the scholarship bill (a form of which was enacted in 1958) as "much broader than the scholarship or the aid-to-science bill people think it is. It is an all-around bill to strengthen education and to prevent waste of the 200,000 talented youths who drop out of school before college." [33]

This return to the special emphasis may be a tactical maneuver of the times recognizing the failure of the nation to formulate a conception of education strong enough to overcome in the public mind the blocks posed by unresolved issues such as private versus public education and integration.

A LOOK AHEAD

While the battle for ascendancy of the principle of equalization of an adequate foundation program of education throughout the United States over the idea of the promotion of special national interests through special aids seemed, for the moment at least, to have been won, both the multiplicity of special-aid bills, on the one hand, and the failure of Congress to pass a general-aid bill of the equalization type, on the other, indicates that this battle was but a skirmish.

But there are signs too of a continued awareness of the need for a broader approach. The 1955 White House Conference report states:

[32] *Proceedings of the Conference on Education and Science in the United States,* Harvard University, 1958.
[33] *New York Times,* August 1, 1958.

This Committee is presenting no recommendation concerning Federal aid for school operation. Reports from State conferences and reports from the participants in the White House Conference on Education indicate great division of opinion on this subject. The reports also indicate that there is much greater public interest in Federal aid for school building construction than aid for school operation.[34]

Beardsley Ruml in 1957 proposed a flat grant of $80 per census child. This is the Mort-Lawler Type III applied to a low foundation level. Its parentage is in the tax sharing tradition.[35]

The Educational Policies Commission report, *The Contemporary Challenge to American Education,* says, "Substantial improvement in the financial status of education is clearly called for. This must involve greatly increased support of all levels of government and bold attacks on the problem of paying for education." [36]

A panel of the National Conference on School Finance Problems held in 1958 reports the following: "The consensus of the group in regard to this question was that federal financial support should be in the nature of a large-fund program with the allocations distributed on the basis of school-age population. The group believed that the need for financial support for education had grown so great that it could be met only by a massive infusion of federal funds to state and local school systems." [37]

In the panel's report submitted by Dr. Lindman the following statements appear: "It was pointed out that a flat grant of $25 per child of school age would be the equivalent, for the state of Delaware, to 0.85 per cent of the federal income and employment tax receipts for 1957 in that state while the same $25 grant per child of school age in Mississippi would amount to over 12.16 per cent of the federal income and employment tax receipts. Similar figures given were for New York, 1.14 per cent; and for South Carolina, 9.17 per cent." [38]

". . . It was pointed out that the return of 1 per cent of the individual income and employment taxes for the fiscal year ended 1959 in Delaware would amount to $31.72 per child of school age and in New York to $27.76 per child of school age. In contrast, Mississippi would receive only $2.22 per child, South Carolina $2.94, and Arkansas $3.06." [39]

[34] The Committee for the White House Conference, *A Report to the President,* Government Printing Office, Washington, April, 1956.

[35] Beardsley Ruml, *op. cit.*

[36] National Education Association, Educational Policies Commission, *The Contemporary Challenge to American Education,* Washington, 1958.

[37] *Proceedings of the National Conference on School Finance Problems,* May 22–23, 1958, Sponsored by The Committee on Tax Education and School Finance, National Education Association, Washington, p. 33.

[38] *Ibid.,* p. 33.

[39] *Ibid.,* p. 33.

A different and refreshing note was sounded by Seymour Harris in an address delivered in New York City in the spring of 1958. He suggested that the federal government dedicate to education about 7 per cent of the increase in the gross national product, adding to it each year as the amount increases. This "hostage to fortune" principle, exemplified in the dedication of a set percentage of state revenues by the Missouri Constitution, may well warrant a more important place in our national thinking.

Students of the problem of federal aid may well give thoughtful consideration to the possibilities of a farseeing and constructive approach designed to dramatize the national interest in such matters as a fundamental preparation for our technological age (science, mathematics, technology), a thoroughgoing mastery of our arts of communication, a more widespread sharing of the knowledge of the world we live in, as well as those special matters of consideration in the past, such as health. Recognition of purposes of such scope could be made without the spelling-out characteristic of a special-aid law. It could use the same measure of need and ability as a general-aid law. This would seem to apply whether these matters were dealt with individually or in combination. The technological, communication, and health phases of a $400 foundation program would require more than $6 billion of expenditure annually. To equalize this on the meagerest plan would require nearly $2 billion of federal aid. With mathematics, English, science, and the work arts out of the way, the social studies and humanities could have to themselves the lion's share of the resources in the poor states.

Something of this may be discerned in the discussion of federal aid in the Rockefeller Report.[40] In juxtaposition should be placed the idea of the Udall bill (H.R. 2279) introduced in 1958 and sponsored by the Council of Chief State School Officers, and the N.E.A.-sponsored bill (Murray-Metcalf). These bills are similar in pattern to the Ruml proposal, discussed elsewhere. Their significance is that they are entirely divorced from the vectorialism of the special-aid idea.

Perhaps the first hint of a more vigorous national policy may be read into the preamble of the National Defense Education Act of 1958: "The Congress reaffirms the principle and declares that the States and local communities have and must retain control over and primary responsibility for public education. The national interest requires, however, that the Federal Government give assistance to education for programs which are important to our defense."

But this conception will have to broaden a great deal before it becomes a national purpose capable of bringing education out of its pres-

[40] Rockefeller Brothers Fund, Inc.: *The Pursuit of Excellence*, Education and the Future of America, Doubleday & Company, Inc., New York, 1958.

ent category of emphasis as a minor part of that small per cent of the national budget allocated to health, welfare, and personal security of the people—a smaller proportion of a minor aspect of the budget than Harris proposes as a dedicated proportion of the increase in the gross national product.

SUMMARY

The part that the federal government has played in financing schools has been a varied one. In recent years there have been several attempts to see its place in the structural pattern. At present there is still conflict with respect to the proper role. There is a widely held belief that the federal government should play an important part in equalizing educational support, but there is still a widespread belief that its major role should be that of stimulating desirable adaptations in the school system, by means of aids granted for particular activities or areas. There are indications that it may be more feasible to combine the two roles than students of the problem have supposed.

Recent studies differ mainly in their emphasis on the degree to which federal aid should be associated with federal control.

As far as equalization is concerned, it would seem to be feasible for the federal government to assure a minimum level in the poorest states without complete equalization of the burden. However, there is considerable support for the idea of using federal tax-collecting machinery to administer the newer types of taxes, distributing the yield back to all the states by taking over a considerable portion of the total cost of a defensible foundation program in all the states.

In recent years there has been a great deal of activity on the part of national agencies and private groups looking toward a more systematic treatment of federal-state financial relations. On the whole these activities have tended to ignore the long history of development in education and may endanger the unique place for education in the governmental picture built up over the years of the history of the Republic.

QUESTIONS FOR STUDY AND DISCUSSION

1. In the light of this chapter, analyze the latest federal equalization bill before Congress.

2. State the conflict in purpose that is still found in the discussions of federal aid to education.

3. How does the hypothesis of separability of support and control bear upon the question of federal aid?

4. Appraise the Smith-Hughes Law in terms of its use of devices proposed as facilitating the separation of support and control.

5. What was the purpose of the Smith-Hughes Law? How effectively has it helped to diffuse vocational education in your state? Are there indications that it has drawn support from other activities? Has it effectively reached the poorer communities in your state?

6. What are the effects of using school census as the basic measure of educational need in place of enrollment or average daily attendance?

7. Compare the compliance features of the most recent federal-aid bills to those proposed by the Advisory Committee on Education (see pages 314–315).

8. What would be the advantages from the control point of view to limiting federal aid to the special areas suggested on page 325? What case can you make, from the standpoint of national interest, for federal aid to each of the special areas listed as possible subjects of special aid on page 325? How would you square such a proposal with what has been said in this book concerning special aids?

SELECTED REFERENCES

Allen, Hollis P.: *The Federal Government and Education,* McGraw-Hill Book Company, Inc., New York, 1950.

Ashby, Lyle W.: *The Efforts of the States to Support Education as Related to the Adequacy of Financial Support Provided and the Ability of the States to Support Education,* National Education Association, Washington, 1936.

Burke, Arvid J.: *Financing Public Schools in the United States,* Harper & Brothers, New York, 1957.

Chism, Leslie L.: *The Economic Ability of the States to Finance Public Schools,* Bureau of Publications, Teachers College, Columbia University, New York, 1936.

Committee on Government Operations: *Federal–State–Local Relations: Federal Grants-in-aid,* Government Printing Office, Washington, 1958.

Committee on Intergovernmental Relations: *The Impact of Federal Grants-in-aid on Structure and Function of State and Local Government,* Government Printing Office, Washington, June, 1955.

Council of State Governments: "Federal-State Relations," *Senate Document 81,* 81st Congress, 1st Session, Government Printing Office, Washington, 1949.

Ginzberg, Eli, and Douglas W. Bray: *The Uneducated,* Columbia University Press, New York, 1953.

Harris, Seymour E.: *How Shall We Pay for Education?* Harper & Brothers, New York, 1948.

Hearings before a Subcommittee of the Committee on Education and Labor, House of Representatives, 85th Congress, Second Session, Government Printing Office, Washington, 1958.

Hunt, Herold C., and Paul R. Pierce: *The Practice of School Administration,* Houghton Mifflin Company, Boston, 1958.

Hutchins, Clayton D.: *Federal Funds for Education,* U.S. Department of Health, Education, and Welfare, Office of Education Bulletin 1956, No. 5.

Maxwell, James A.: *The Fiscal Impact of Federalism,* Harvard University Press, Cambridge, Mass., 1946.

Miller, Van, and Willard S. Spalding: *The Public Administration of American Schools,* 2nd ed., World Book Co., Yonkers, N.Y., 1958.

Mort, Paul R.: *Federal Support for Public Education,* Bureau of Publications, Teachers College, Columbia University, New York, 1936.

————, and Eugene S. Lawler: *Principles and Methods of Distributing Federal Aid for Education,* Report of the Advisory Committee on Education, Staff Study 5, Government Printing Office, Washington, 1939.

Mushkin, Selma: *Illustrative Estimates of Federal Expenditures and Revenues by States,* U.S. Department of Health, Education, and Welfare, 1956. (Mimeographed.)

National Advisory Committee on Education: "Federal Relations to Education," *Report of the Committee,* Part I, Washington, 1931.

National Education Association, *Public Opinion Polls on American Education,* Washington, May, 1958.

Norton, John K., and M. A. Norton: *Wealth, Children and Education,* Bureau of Publications, Teachers College, Columbia University, New York, 1938.

Quattlebaum, Charles A.: *Federal Aid to Students for Higher Education,* Government Printing Office, Washington, 1956.

————: *Development of Scientific, Engineering and Other Professional Manpower,* Government Printing Office, Washington, 1957.

Reavis, William C.: "Federal Aid for Education," *Annals of the American Academy of Political and Social Science,* Philadelphia, 1949, vol. 265, pp. 56–60.

Ruml, Beardsley: "Federal Support for the Public Schools," *Education Digest,* October, 1957.

Studenski, Paul: "Federal Grants-in-aid," *National Tax Journal,* vol. II, no. 3, September, 1949.

U.S. Commission on Organization of the Executive Branch of the Government: *The Hoover Commission Report,* McGraw-Hill Book Company, Inc., New York, 1949.

U.S. Office of Education: *Federal Funds for Education, 1954–55 and 1955–56,* Washington, 1956.

PART FIVE

Operational finance

Operational finance as treated in Chapters 18 through 25 deals with the fiscal management of school systems as it is carried on in the local administrative units. These chapters cover many of the aspects of business administration but are not intended to be all-inclusive of this area and no attempt is made to draw a sharp distinction between finance and business administration. Operational finance is limited to those phases of business administration which deal with budgeting, accounting, auditing, fiscal statements and reports, expenditures for personnel services, school supply management, property management, and indebtedness. Other problems of school business administration are treated only to the extent that they are involved in fiscal administration.

18. A design for local financial administration

THE DESIGN for local financial administration described in this chapter presents an over-all view of the principles and procedures that enter into the local operation of schools. The design deals with broad concepts of administration into which the various separate tasks must be fitted. It embraces the concepts of education as a state function, local autonomy, and principles and agencies of administration that enter into the day-to-day operation of the schools.

In somewhat more detail the design shows the seeming paradox that education is a state function, but that it is administered largely in the local communities. It presents the two types of agencies that are involved in administration (namely, state and local) and considers the principles upon which financial operation is based and which are essential to its efficiency and purpose. It then goes on to the operational functions which set forth the two major purposes, planning and evaluation, and finally it embraces the many mechanized tasks that must be performed in the day-to-day operation of the schools. Figure 18-1 shows the interrelationship of the conceptual basis and operational principles, the operational functions, and the mechanized tasks in local school finance. The chapters that follow take up the various aspects of planning, evaluation, and handling the mechanized tasks.

AN ILLUSTRATION

In the present-day complex of educational administration it is often difficult to see the design as it has developed and as it is in operation. It may be helpful to consider the control of schools in an earlier day when both the school and its administration were relatively simple. Indeed a

331

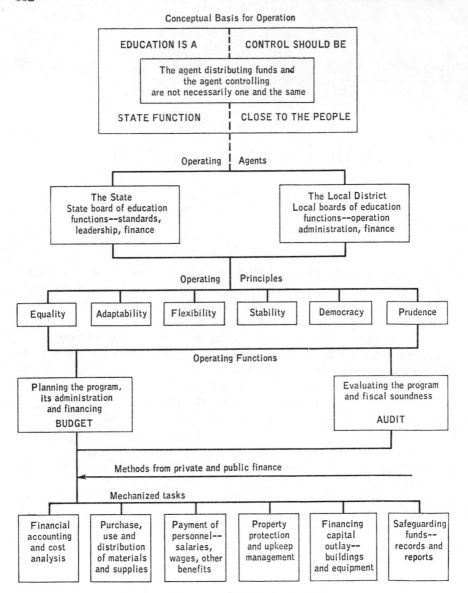

Fig. 18-1   A conceptual design for local finance.

vestige of this early simplicity is still to be found in many one-teacher school districts of today.

As the school system grew from small beginnings so did the machinery of financial administration. When the educational activities were limited as in the case of one-teacher districts, the task of determining the financial policy and of keeping a record of transactions was a far cry from the complex mechanism that we find in our large school systems of today. At that time the school directors brought their plans to the school meetings. The amount to be paid to the teacher, and likely as not the teacher to be employed, were discussed by the whole company. It was obvious to all that some provision had to be made for heating and that books and chalk and a few other supplies had to be purchased. In terms of the problem that they faced, there was a perfect example of what local financial practice ought to be. The community itself understood its educational program and in the light of it planned its financial program. New proposals were balanced against the tax rate. The cost in tax rate of a new roof or of a globe or of new maps could be computed in terms of what it would mean in personal sacrifice and a choice was made between individual expenditures and public expenditures. The picture given by David Grayson in his essay, "The Politician," while it glorifies the school meeting, nevertheless brings out beautifully what we are striving for in all our financial processes: [1]

Baxter's lamp is, somehow, inextricably associated in my mind with politics. Being busy farmers, we hold our caucuses and other meetings in the evening and usually in the schoolhouse. The schoolhouse is conveniently near to Baxter's shop, so we gather at Baxter's shop. Baxter takes his lamp down from the bracket above his bench, reflector and all, and you will see us, a row of dusky figures, Baxter in the lead, proceeding down the roadway to the schoolhouse. Having arrived, some one scratches a match, shields it with his hand (I see yet the sudden fitful illumination of the brown-bearded, watchful faces of my neighbors!) and Baxter guides us into the schoolhouse—with its shut-in dusty odors of chalk and varnished desks and—yes, leftover lunches!

Baxter's lamp stands on the table, casting a vast shadow of the chairman on the wall.

"Come to order," says the chairman, and we have here at this moment in operation the greatest institution in this round world: the institution of free self-government. Great in its simplicity, great in its unselfishness! And Baxter's old lamp with its smoky tin reflector, is not that the veritable torch of our liberties?

This, I forgot to say, though it makes no special difference—a caucus would be the same—is a school meeting.

You see, ours is a prolific community. When a young man and a young

[1] David Grayson, *Adventures in Contentment*, Doubleday & Company, Inc., New York, 1907, 1935, pp. 224–227.

woman are married they think about babies; they want babies, and what is more, they have them! and love them afterwards! And having babies, there must be a place to teach them to live.

Without more explanation you will understand that we needed an addition to our schoolhouse. A committee reported that the amount required would be $800. We talked it over. The Scotch Preacher was there with a plan which he tacked up on the blackboard and explained to us. He told us of seeing the stone-mason and the carpenter, he told us what the seats would cost, and the door knobs and the hooks in the closet. We are a careful people; we want to know where every penny goes!

"If we put it all in the budget this year what will that make the rate?" inquires a voice from the end of the room.

We don't look around; we know the voice. And when the secretary has computed the rate, if you listen closely you can almost hear the buzz of multiplications and additions which is going on in each man's head as he calculates exactly how much the addition will mean to him in taxes on his farm, his daughter's piano, his wife's top-buggy.

And many a man is saying to himself:

"If we build this addition to the schoolhouse, I shall have to give up the new overcoat I have counted upon, or Amanda won't be able to get the new cooking-range."

That's *real* politics: the voluntary surrender of some private good for the upbuilding of some community good. It is in such exercises that the fibre of democracy grows sound and strong. There is, after all, in this world no real good for which we do not have to surrender something. In the city the average voter is never conscious of any surrender. He never realizes that he is giving anything himself for good schools or good streets. Under such conditions how can you expect self-government? No service, no reward!"

It is more than likely that the treasurer kept the money in his personal account or in his strongbox and sometimes he kept the accounts in his head. The people depended upon his integrity rather than on accounts or depositories for the safety of their funds. Sometimes this confidence was misplaced. From the abuses there grew up the state-wide safeguards that we know today. In the larger communities, where the job was more complicated and where the school board had power to act for the community itself, the advisability of keeping records became apparent. From this evolved the various systems of accounting and management discussed in Chapter 21.

The student today does not see the simple well-balanced processes that existed in the early school meeting. He sees complex mechanized systems of budget making, accounting, and reporting—often without a realization of the fact that they gain their meaning from basic educational principles. In many instances, actual practice may have drawn heavily on private enterprise or public finance, but always the meaning of it is derived from educational principles.

A BASIS FOR THE DESIGN

In Chapter 2 of this volume we noted and discussed the basic concept of education as a state function, the concept of "home rule," and that of the independence of finance and control. Here we discuss the place of these concepts in the design for local financial administration. The concept of education as a state function recognizes education as a responsibility of all the people of the state and the machinery through which the people express themselves comprises constitutions, legislatures, referendums, and the state and local boards of education. While these principles have been upheld many times in court cases and are generally recognized by students of educational administration and finance, they may not always be clear to those who have been delegated to carry on local administration and control. The delegation of control has gone so far that we speak of local autonomy, that the schools should be kept close to the people. This concept of education has a historic background. The early colonial schools were essentially local enterprises, even with the growth of state supervision, state finance, and state administration. We cherish the concept of communities exercising a large share of the control over their schools.

Another concept that flows from the legal fact that education is a state function and the belief that the schools should be kept close to the people is the separability of finance and control. The oft repeated statement that he who holds the purse strings exercises the control need not necessarily be true. While a large measure of control is given to the local schools units, it is not practical to expect these same units to pay for their schools in their entirety. In recent years there has come to be more understanding of the principles involved here. We think today of the local school units as exercising a large measure of control, but we also see the necessity of state support being used to aid districts to finance their schools as the local communities, through due legal processes, see fit to promote their program.

As we have seen, the framework in which the local school organization operates is defined by the legal principle that education is a state function and by the derivative of the democratic principle that control should be kept close to the people. The doctrine that there is no inherent right to home rule (Chapter 2), applying as it does to all phases of government, amplifies the legal fact that education is a state function. How then can we operate education as a state function and still keep control close to the people? We can achieve this result through the basic theory that the state does not necessarily work through a central agency and that, therefore, the agency used to collect the taxes need not necessarily be one and the same as the agency that controls the program. This is the hypothesis of the separability of control and finance.

OPERATING AGENCIES

There has grown up in this country a system of local and state school administration. All states in the Union have state departments of education and all states have local units of administration. Despite the differences that there may be in the state structure of local unit and state organization, there is a common pattern of state and local operation.

To serve the educational program, there must be cooperation between the agencies of local jurisdiction and the agency of state-wide jurisdiction. This is true in fiscal administration as in all aspects of administration. All of our educational problems and financial problems have this two-fold aspect—the one local and the other state. They are essentially local problems that have their roots in the state structure of organization, support, and control. The state authority is concerned with the setting up of standards and minimum requirements, leadership, and the provision of financial school support, whereas the local authorities are concerned with the day-to-day processes of maintaining the schools; providing buildings and equipment; employing teachers and paying their salaries; keeping buildings warm, clean, and in good repair; and in a thousand ways maintaining the smooth operation of the educational program.

Local and state educational policies and purposes overlap at many points and are so interwoven that they cannot easily be separated in practice. Attempts to separate the two aspects of administration are generally regarded as unsatisfactory because they lead to arbitrary distinctions in which the primary function of the school may be lost sight of in the engrossing details of local operation. All of our problems have this twofold aspect, one the function of the state and the other the function of the local communities. It is important that school administrators, when dealing with financial problems, have a clear understanding of the responsibility of each of the agencies—state and local.

From the principle that state and local agencies of administration are corelative flows our conceptual design of local financial administration in which there are, of necessity, officials on different government levels engaged in certain administrative tasks. Our chief concern here is to see how local officials, boards of education, superintendents, and other administrative personnel fit into the total picture of fiscal administration.

Agencies of Local Jurisdiction

Boards of education, as agencies of control, are usually given considerable discretion in carrying out the provisions of local autonomy. In the discharge of their duties, they are controlled not only by the administrative organization, the line of authority, but also by certain unwritten standards accepted by the people of the community which require them to exercise their authority to seek the greatest good of all the people of the community. While there must be drawn lines of authority and lines of responsibility in the structure of administration, this authority in a democracy must be shared by many persons and should not be exercised to its full extent, except in emergencies, by the group in which the control is legally established. This is true in financial administration as in all administration.

Although it is true that there are many lay boards of education which assume the duties of fiscal administration of schools, it is now generally recognized that this is not their function and that they can best serve the schools by acting in a legislative capacity as representatives of the people of their districts. With respect to school districts which are too small to employ competent educational leadership, the solution does not lie in the assumption of any of the administrative duties by the board, but rather in the reorganization of those districts into larger ones that will be able to provide competent leadership. In the city school districts there is usually a clear distinction between the functions of the board of education and those of the executive officer employed by the board.

The best practice indicates that boards of education generally recognize their functions as those of general oversight and control, such as those of a board of directors of a business concern, but not management of the schools themselves. In the discharge of their duties they should employ an executive officer, a superintendent of schools, give him full power and responsibility, and hold him accountable for the successful operation of all departments of the school system. The board must also see that buildings are provided, teachers employed, materials and supplies purchased, and funds made available for the operation of the schools.

The superintendent of schools as the executive officer of the board of education should be responsible for all phases of school administration. When business administration or any other aspect of administration is carried on by specialized personnel, such personnel should be directly responsible to the superintendent. Business and financial phases of conducting a school system are truly educational in nature and cannot be separated from the purposes they are intended to serve. Collecting, safeguarding, and expending school funds are important, but only to the end that they serve the educational program. The preparation and administration of a school budget is meaningless unless it is very closely related to the educational program it is intended to promote. Accounting of school funds and computing school costs are significant because they make information available for management.

As in the case of boards of education, the superintendent of schools is in the line of authority extending from the people of the district and the board of education down to the teachers and pupils.[2] In a unitary system of education, all personnel of the school are responsible to him, and in the exercise of his authority, the principle of sharing responsibility with others is important in the democratic administration of the school. Thus, many persons in the school and community will have a share in the preparation of the budget, building planning, and selection of supplies and equipment. Throughout the wide range of planning and executing the business functions, these cooperative relations will operate.

Agency of State-wide Jurisdiction

In the organization of state boards of education and state departments of education, there is a growing tendency to divorce this organization from state politics. In a large number of states the chief state school officer is still elected by popular vote. State boards of education are constituted in a number of different ways. In some cases members are elected and in others they are appointed, or they may be both elected and appointed. There seems to be emerging a rather clear-cut pattern of how the state educational branch should be organized. Perhaps state organization could learn much from the evolution of local school organization and preserve the principles described above as they relate to the local board of education and the superintendent of schools.

Whatever may be the organization of the state department of education, its functions are rather clear-cut in terms of the school system of the state. As already stated, these functions may be summed up briefly as the setting of standards, the exercise of educational leadership, and the provision of school support. Long lists could be made of specific functions of state departments of education and functions of local school units, but it is perhaps sufficient to point out that each of these agencies has a part to play in practically every phase of administration and finance. The important point is the definition of what is the state's part and what is the local unit's part. Such definition determines to a large extent the degree of local autonomy left to the districts.

OPERATING PRINCIPLES

The principles of educational administration referred to in Chapter 2 of this volume apply throughout the whole matrix of financial operation. They are the principles of equality, adaptability, flexibility, stability, democracy, and prudence. When applied here as elsewhere, there must be a balance among them. In order that the purposes of education may be

[2] By virtue of his office the superintendent has also certain direct responsibilities to state agencies.

realized, operational finance should strive to maintain equality of opportunity for all pupils within the local district, just as this principle applies to the equality of opportunity among districts on the state level. The principle of adaptability would dictate that school systems be modified from time to time to make them conform with changing social demands. The procedures and practices of financial operation should be flexible rather than rigid. Over a period of time there should be a degree of stability which will carry the program forward from year to year. In the administration of the entire program the principles of democracy loom large. It deals with persons and how they should be treated, the conditions under which they can make their best contributions. The principle of prudence refers to local administration in that it is always desirable to secure the best results for the money expended. It signifies wise management and careful attention to the details.

In the application of the principles stated above, four of them have a large impact on educational purposes: equality, adaptability, flexibility, and stability. Two have to do with methods of procedure: democracy and prudence. In the operation of the local school system then, we have always before us the need to consider equality, adaptability, flexibility, and stability in the educational program itself and to consider how to achieve these in line with the democratic and prudential principles.

OPERATIONAL FUNCTIONS

All of the financial activities have two functions to serve: (1) the development, adoption, and administration of the budget; and (2) making the necessary provisions for proper evaluation and appraisal through the audit and other means.

The budget is the work program. In its operation we have essentially nothing more than what occurred at the school district meeting. The evaluation of the budget and of the financial program is an outside check of honesty and fiscal soundness. It flows from the prudential principle and from the concept of the school district as a state agency. To make possible the budget and the audit we need to know about tax sources, we need adequate accounting and cost analysis, we need statements and reports which today serve partially the purposes of the district meetings, and we need systematic ways of managing salaries, supplies, properties, and school indebtedness. These are the mechanized tasks, the reason for which is that the budget and evaluation functions may be exercised.

Need for Planning

The school budgetary procedure is essentially one of financial planning for education. Need for planning arises from a number of sources that have been widely recognized and have their roots in the social, economic,

and political structure of our times. Among these may be mentioned:
(1) changes in population, such as the migration from rural areas to
urban centers, the movement of population from highly congested cities
to suburban areas, population movement from one section of the country
to another, the increase or decrease in the birth rate, and subsequent
changes in the age distribution of school population; (2) new demands
made upon education by the changing conditions of employment and
the demands for the extension of the educational program for young
people and adults; (3) general inefficiency of financial management resulting from the great decentralization of control of public schools, lack
of leadership in many districts, and the inadequacy of financial support
to maintain programs.

In any adequate program of fiscal planning, one must consider needs
and resources—local, state and national needs and local resources supplemented by state and national sharing of the burden. Such a program
of planning will include a much longer time than one year; it will project
the program into the future. It is a comprehensive long-term plan for
education.

Planning as Policy Making

The financial administration of the local school system involves the
formation of policies in the various areas of management. These policies
must be so formulated as to insure continuity in the procedures followed
year after year. It is a shortsighted policy, indeed, that does not provide
for the continued operation of the educational program from one budget
period to another in an unbroken sequence. Lack of planning in the
day-to-day policy of financing the schools has been responsible for waste
and inefficiency in the management of school money. Long-term local
planning will give consideration to such problems as the following: (1)
How can income and expenditures be managed so that excessive borrowing for current purposes or the carrying of large balances may be avoided?
(2) Have school funds been safeguarded so that losses or misappropria-
tions are avoided? (3) Are certain items in the annual budget parts of
long-range programs? (4) What improvements in accounting, cost
analysis, auditing, and reporting are needed to make these procedures
more efficient? (5) Have salary schedules for school employees been
constructed and administered so as to attract and retain the best personnel? (6) Have the school plant needs been adequately cared for? (7)
Is indebtedness systematically handled so that it does not threaten the
ongoing program? (8) Has the policy for education been such as to utilize
all elements in the community, and has it been democratic rather than
promotional?

In all matters of fiscal planning, significance and purpose may be gained by orienting the plan with respect to the principles of school administration discussed in another chapter of this volume. It is only when educators have in mind certain guiding principles or criteria that successive changes which they are called upon to make in the structure of administration of schools will add up to form a more adequate system for meeting community needs. Without such orientation, changes may be but a patchwork of unrelated practices over an inadequate foundation.

Evaluation of the Program

Parallel with planning, or rather a part of planning, is a constant evaluation of practices and procedures as the plans are carried forward. While there are a number of methods in public school systems for determining the goodness of the plan and the fiscal soundness of the school system, we usually think of the external audit as an important means by which this evaluation is made. In addition to the external audit, certain internal audits and some continuing audits and preaudits of budget are also needed. The annual report is in a sense the statement of how well the budget has been carried out. While it is not expected that there should be complete agreement between the amounts in the various budget categories and the amounts set forth in the annual report, the two should be checked against each other.

The operational functions, then, are planning and evaluation. Planning the entire school program is not merely a matter of preparing the annual budget document. It is a continuous process that goes on from one school year to another. It is the reason why we set up budget calendars to show when the various processes in budgetary procedure should be carried on. Evaluation is likewise a continuous process. While the annual audit may be a periodic check, there is need for sound day-to-day accounting and continuous internal audit to see that the funds are properly received and expended and that proper accounting of them is made.

While budgeting and auditing in public schools differ in many respects from budgeting and auditing in private enterprises and in other public finance, there are many close parallels. School budgeting, school planning, and evaluation have derived much from the methods of private business and public finance in general.

MECHANIZED TASKS

In order to carry on the operational functions adequately, we need certain mechanized tasks. To make possible the budget and the audit, we need to know about tax sources; we need adequate accounts and cost analysis; we need statements and reports; we need systematic ways of managing salaries, supplies, properties, and school indebtedness. These are the mechanized tasks associated with the budget and audit functions.

As pointed out and discussed in later chapters, budgetary procedures must be carried on in many details and involve the work of many officials. They are details of receipts and expenditures, general condition of the district, and the forecasting of what the schools will cost in the fiscal period ahead.

An actual accounting is essentially the keeping of records of income and expenditures classified in many ways so as to become readily available for analysis and management. In addition to the records of income and expenditures, a number of subsidiary accounts must be kept such as those to facilitate purchasing of materials and supplies, and records of the payments made. The detail of financial analysis that should be possible through the financial accounting system is almost unlimited if the accounts are properly coded and recorded in such a way that those in charge can readily make the analysis desired.

It is also necessary that policies be adopted for the payment of school personnel, for their retirement, and for other benefits that surround their employment. A system of records known as payroll procedures is necessary to keep proper account of payment to various groups of the school personnel.

The purchase of the many items of materials and supplies needed in a school system requires a comprehensive program of classification, of procedures for initiating purchases, for securing bids, for making payments, for storage of supplies, and for their distribution.

Every school system has much money invested in property, buildings, grounds, equipment, and the like. While property accounting in the public school system is not parallel to property accounting in a private business enterprise, there nevertheless should be records of the various pieces of property, their condition, period of life over which the assets may be used, and other facts to determine the need for their replacement.

Every school must make expenditures for capital outlay, new buildings, alterations of present buildings, new sites or extension of sites, new equipment or replacement of equipment, all of which require proper management and often must be paid for through special funds.

Another group of mechanized tasks is that of safeguarding school funds, seeing that all receipts have been collected, that those in charge of receiving money are properly protected under bond, that the depositories in which the money is placed have been properly safeguarded, that other means have been taken to prevent loss or misuse of funds. This also involves a proper system of records and reports. These in brief are the mechanized tasks that must be carried on in order that the entire local financial operation may go on smoothly, with efficiency and without loss.

SUMMARY

The conceptual design of local school financial administration is intended to show the over-all framework in which the board of education and the superintendent of schools carry on their tasks. It extends from the legal fact that education is a state function; the principle that the schools should be kept close to the people; the fact of separability of finance and control. It embraces the operating agents, state and local; the operational principles of equality, adaptability, flexibility, stability, democracy, and prudence; the operational functions of planning and evaluation as carried on largely through the budget and the audit; and finally, the numerous mechanized tasks that must be performed to make information available to those who would plan and evaluate the goodness of their school systems.

All of this involves continuous planning. No part of the system can operate separately. It should be a well-integrated matrix for the functioning of the schools.

QUESTIONS FOR STUDY AND DISCUSSION

1. Outline the organization and the powers and duties of the state board of education and chief state school officer in your state.

2. Outline the organization of a city school system with which you are familiar. How do lay advisory groups fit into this picture?

3. Outline in some area the separation of functions as between the state and the local unit in the administration of schools. Give examples for such areas as the employment of personnel, the construction of buildings, etc.

4. What is the agency responsible for auditing school accounts in your state? What other agencies for checking on honesty and fiscal soundness are there?

5. What organizations or agencies in your state are concerned with state-wide planning for the improvement of education?

SELECTED REFERENCES

American Association of School Administrators: *School Boards in Action,* Twenty-fourth Year Book, Washington, 1946.

American Association of School Administrators: *Staff Relations in School Administration,* Thirty-third Year Book, Washington, 1955.

American Association of School Administrators: *School Board Superintendent Relations,* Thirty-fourth Year Book, Washington, 1956.

American Association of School Administrators: *The Superintendent as Instructional Leader,* Thirty-fifth Year Book, Washington, 1957.

Fowlkes, J. G., and G. E. Watson: "School Finance and Local Planning,"

Studies in Educational Administration, Proceedings, Midwest Administration Center, 1957, p. 486.

Hagman, Harlan L.: The Administration of American Public Schools, McGraw-Hill Book Company, Inc., New York, 1951.

Koopman, G. Robert, Alice Miel, and Paul J. Misner: *Democracy in School Administration,* Appleton-Century-Crofts, Inc., New York, 1943, p. 330.

Mort, Paul R., and Donald H. Ross: *Principles of School Administration,* McGraw-Hill Book Company, New York, 1957.

National Education Association, Educational Policies Commission: *The Unique Function of Education in American Democracy,* Washington, 1937.

————: *The Structure and Administration of Education in American Democracy,* Washington, 1938.

Sears, Jesse B.: *The Nature of the Administrative Process,* McGraw-Hill Book Company, Inc., New York, 1950.

Studenski, Paul, and Paul R. Mort: *Centralized vs. Decentralized Government in Relation to Democracy,* Bureau of Publications, Teachers College, Columbia University, New York, 1941.

19. Budgeting school funds

THE DESIRABILITY of some form of budgetary procedure for public schools has long been recognized. There has never been dissent from the premise that school expenditures can be made more effectively when available funds are apportioned among the various items necessary for the efficient conduct of the school system and that serious effort should be made to restrict expenditures to the various estimated amounts set forth in the adopted budget.

In view of the rising expenditures for public schools, it seems strange that more serious attention has not been given to budgetary procedure as a phase of financial administration. It is only comparatively recently that research studies attacking the different phases of school budgeting have appeared, but already sufficient progress has been made to point out clearly the broad outline of desirable budgetary procedures. Moreover, such research has been valuable in locating weaknesses in the school finance structure and in the inprovement of cost analysis and budgetary administration.

DEFINITION OF THE BUDGET

In the broad sense of the term, the word "budget" means a plan, a plan for financing a school system for a period of time in the future, usually one year. This plan is usually evidenced by a "budget document" which is the exhibit that shows the plan in all of its details. The term "budgetary procedures" is used to indicate the steps that the administrator and the board of education take in planning the budget from beginning to end. While we sometimes use the terms interchangeably, it should be clearly understood that the three terms refer to various aspects of budgeting. We very frequently think of the budget as the budget document which gives the outline of the plan for financing the school system.

345

Ultimately the budget is a balancing of the positive factors flowing from educational objectives and a willingness and capacity to support schools. Neither the educational program nor the independent estimates of financial resources can be considered alone. Budgetary procedure should be such that the resulting budget plan expresses the amount of money that the community is willing to spend in the light of the kind of educational program it wishes to support.

DEVELOPMENT OF SCHOOL BUDGETING

A study of the development of budgeting shows that it had its origin in business and industry from which it spread to state and national governments and then to local subdivisions of the states—cities, counties, and school districts. Budgeting in public schools was first developed in urban schools where the procedure is now well established. From these it spread to the various other types of local school units until gradually it has become recognized as a necessary and desirable financial procedure in all local school units. Practically all of the fifty states now require some form of budget or estimate of receipts and expenditures from certain or all of their local school units, but in many cases the requirements fall far short of desirable budgetary procedures.

A beginning in state budgetary procedure for schools may be found in the laws of some of the states that prescribe the extent of itemization of the amounts of money to be raised for the ensuing fiscal period. Such laws are usually not very specific and prescribe only that certain amounts be raised or certain tax rates be imposed for specific items, such as teachers' salaries, maintenance of the school, building and repair of school houses. In some states this practice has led to the creation of several different funds from which the various items of current expenditure are paid. The most common practice perhaps is that of setting up two funds, one for current expenditures and the other for capital expenditures. While some fund accounting may be justified, it is doubtful whether many different funds under current expenditures are justified. It is now generally recognized that a well-planned and a well-administered school budget accomplishes the purposes for which separate funds were originally provided.

One of the first comprehensive studies of school budgetary practices was made by Twente [1] in 1922. In this study a summary of budgetary practices in 363 cities revealed a variety of procedures, both in the budgetary requirements imposed on the local school units by city charters and state authorities and in the budgetary practices that were fol-

[1] John W. Twente, *Budgetary Procedure for a Local School System*, Capitol City Press, Montpelier, Vt., 1922.

lowed by local school boards. The study further showed that budgetary practices in public schools were relatively undeveloped and nonstandardized. Twente's study was a pioneer effort that pointed out the need for research in this phase of educational administration.

DeYoung's [2] study in 1932 repeated some phases of Twente's study by sampling 813 cities in different parts of the United States. The result of this study shows more uniformity in state requirements and the practices followed by the cities, although considerable variation was noted. Much information assembled in this study and in the follow-up one conducted three years later is included in *Budgeting in Public Schools*.[3]

Chase and Morphet [4] showed that in 1947–1948 school officials were fully responsible for the preparation and approval of school budgets in thirty-one states. In eleven states other approving bodies such as the county commissioners, the city council, or the budget commission had the responsibility for approval of separate items or budget totals; and in five states, budget reviewing bodies had responsibility for total amounts only.

Although budgeting is one of the newer developments in public school administration, the procedure has been sufficiently well recognized to insure its thorough establishment in the more progressive school systems. In fact, there is a growing tendency to require a budget in all school districts within states, although there may be some variation among the districts within a state. The relatively large demand now placed upon the schools—the rising school costs and the increased number of children in the schools—makes it imperative that school boards and school administrators study their programs to select the elements that in their judgment yield the greatest returns to the children of the community, and that their budgets reflect the educational objectives of the schools and of the community.

FUNCTIONS OF THE BUDGET

The budget has several definite purposes to serve in defining the school program in terms of the amount of money to be spent and the amount to be derived from the different sources. More specifically, one might think of the functions of the budget as the following: (1) It projects the school program accepted by the board and the community

[2] Chris A. DeYoung, *Budgetary Practices in Public School Administration*, Northwestern University Studies, Evanston, Ill., 1932.

[3] Chris A. DeYoung, *Budgeting in Public Schools,* The Odyssey Press, Inc., New York, 1936.

[4] Francis S. Chase, Research Director, and Edgar L. Morphet, Associate Director, *The Forty-eight State School Systems,* Council of State Governments, Chicago, 1949.

into the future for the specified period of time, usually one year. (2) It shows what revenue is anticipated and from what sources it is derived. (3) It shows in some detail the estimates of expenditure for the various items of the school program and for the school system as a whole. (4) It shows the amount of money that must be raised locally as well as the tax rate for raising it. (5) It aids the administration in conducting the school program in accordance with the accepted plan.

Budgetary planning is a continuous process that goes on throughout the school year. It is not merely an activity to be engaged in shortly before the new fiscal year. There is hardly a time when the collection of budget information is not in order. In fact, many school systems set up definite budgetary calendars which specify months and dates on which certain activities are to be carried on. This procedure is useful for securing the information upon which the budget document is built before it is presented to the board of education and the public prior to the opening of the fiscal year.

Budgetary procedure may be thought of as a cycle of operations that passes through certain definite steps: preparation, presentation and adoption, administration, and appraisal. One or another of these phases is usually in process at any time throughout the year.

AGENCIES OF BUDGETARY PROCEDURE

While school budgeting is usually thought of as a local function, that is, a function of local boards of education and superintendent of schools, it should be remembered that every step in its planning has its roots in the state structure of education. This state and local aspect of budgeting is set forth in Figure 19-1 which shows how the procedure has a basis in state organization and control structure, as well as in the local school unit.

In most states some form of budget is required of all school districts, but this requirement varies greatly and often involves only a statement of receipts and expenditures. In other cases, the budgetary procedure is quite definitely specified. In any case the state requirement is but the skeleton of procedure which must be clothed with the flesh and blood of desirable financial practices to make budgeting really significant.

The variation in the legal provisions of rules and regulations established by state departments of education and state boards of education concerning budgetary procedure in the several states may be grouped roughly under the following types: (1) Comprehensive school budget laws and regulations outlining in detail the various steps in the procedure, such provisions applying to all or certain classes of school districts. (2) General provisions of law regarding budgets that apply to all local governments as well as to school districts. (3) State laws and regulations that relate mainly to the method of raising revenue and in which mention of the budget or estimate is but incidental. (4) Legal provisions that do not mention budget or estimates at all but specify the method of raising revenue for schools and set tax limitations and other items that relate to budgeting. Under these general types of provisions, school budgeting is carried on in the local units of the states. The provisions of the first type mentioned are the only ones that are really satisfactory, because they relate directly to the purpose for which the budget is made, to support the educational program.

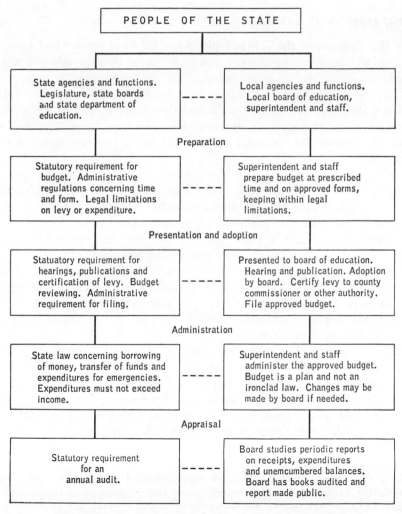

Fig. 19-1 Budgetary procedure in the state organization.

These provisions of law are in line with the concept that the educational system regards the people of the school district as representative of all the people of the state. In accord with this concept it is a matter of prudence for the state to require a considerable period to be consumed in making the budget. During this period there should be opportunity for an interplay of public opinion, fostered by hearings and publicity, so that the forming of the budget becomes the focal point of interaction among community, professional staff, and board of education, and so that the end result may be a common understanding of a program approved by those who undertake to support it.

BUDGETING AS PLANNING

In the diagram of the conceptual design for local operational finance outlined in the preceding chapter, it may be noted that the school budget stands out as having a unique place. This unique position is to convey the impression that into budgeting must go the planning of the entire school system—from what is taught and how it is taught to what it will cost and where the money is to come from. Perhaps no other phase of local school financial operation requires so much planning as does the school budget.

Budget planning is not alone the responsibility of the administrative staff and the board of education, but should to a large extent involve the citizens of the community. To facilitate extensive community participation, the board of education should set up special techniques and see that laymen are encouraged to participate. Numerous examples are found in school systems where lay advisory groups and special committees study certain school problems and make recommendations to the board. When such groups function well they are of considerable assistance in bringing new ideas to the board and in serving as a sounding board for the community. The board of education, however, must always remain the final authority for decision making.[5]

The well-prepared budget document reveals the planning that has gone into it and shows not only what is to be supported and how, but to a considerable extent the individuals and groups who have participated in the planning. The procedure of preparing a budget well in advance of the time of its adoption involves many persons both professional and lay. Figure 19-2 shows the sequence of budget development in one of the

[5] Central School Boards Committee for Educational Research, *Budgeting Practices in Central Schools: A Report of Current Practices in Budget Making as Educational Planning in Central Schools of New York State*, 525 West 120 St., New York, 1952.

O. E. Hill, *Citizens at Work: A Description of Lay Participation in the Cleveland Heights Public School System*, Associated Public School Systems, 525 West 120 St., New York, 1956.

larger New Jersey communities, giving the legal requirements, the operational policy, the voluntary community organizations involved, and the time prior to voting on the budget.[6]

Required by law	Operational policy	Voluntary community organization	Time prior to voting on the budget
	Superintendent sends out instructions and forms (initial action)		9 months
	Total staff participation (staff conferences)		9-8 months
	Principals' and department heads' participation (judgmental action on staff requests)		8 months
	Preparation of working copy (superintendent and his staff screen and scale requests)		7-6 months
	Superintendent's staff confers with principals and department heads (explanation of decisions taken)		6-5 months
	Board of education participation (examines decisions of the superintendent)		5-4 months
	Distribution of the tentative plan (administration and public coverage)	Budget committee, parent-teacher associations (initial action)	4 months
		Budget committee, parent-teacher associations (reports to the board of education)	
		Education committee, chamber of commerce (limited-interest group)	
		Taxpayers' protective association (limited-interest group)	2 months
		The council of neighborhood associations (greater-interest group)	
		The staff (limited-interest groups)	
	Board of education deliberations (desire further to involve the people)		8-5 weeks
		Parent-teacher associations meetings (approval of budget committee reports)	6 weeks
Preparation and submission of proposed budget to the board of school estimate (by the board of education			3 weeks
The budget hearing by the board of school estimate (before the people)			1 week
Adoption of the budget (the people's representatives)			0

Fig. 19-2 Sequence of budget development and adoption in a New Jersey school district. (From Alfred Miller, *Patterns in School District Budget Making*, Institute of Administrative Research, Teachers College, Columbia University, New York, 1959.)

The various steps in operational policy and participation of voluntary community groups are in a sense a calendar to be followed by the budget maker. The nature of this procedure may vary somewhat from one state

[6] Alfred Miller, "Patterns in School District Budget Making," Institute of Administrative Research, Teachers College, Columbia University, New York, 1959.

to another, depending upon the legal requirements, but in general such a procedural pattern is highly desirable. This pattern is shown in Figure 19-2.

PREPARATION OF THE BUDGET DOCUMENT

The procedure for making and administering a school budget document involves both legislative and executive functions. Certain parts of the work can be carried on only by those competent in school administration, whereas other parts are properly the work of lay boards of education. The preparation of the budget plan and detailed estimates is generally regarded as an executive function which should be carried on by the superintendent of schools and his staff. The broad policies of the school districts and the decision regarding the amounts of money to be raised in the locality are thought of as legislative functions. In making the budget based upon the policies adopted, the technical details become a matter for the school executive to handle.

The preparation of a school budget consists of the formulation of three plans: (1) the educational plan, which defines the policies of the school and the school program that is to be carried on; (2) the expenditure plan, which translates the educational program into costs; and (3) the financing plan which sets forth the means of meeting the cost of the educational plan.

The Educational Plan

The educational or work plan of the budget shows the scope of the school program proposed for the ensuing year. It is a most important part of the budget and serves as a basis for the spending and financing plans. It corresponds to the specifications for the construction of a building. These educational specifications reflect the policies of education in the community, as they are based on past experience and project the plan into the future. This part of the budget will show the educational organization that is to be carried on during the proposed budget year; the number of pupils to be served; the number and kinds of personnel to be employed and the services to be performed by each.

This work program may be set up by types of school organization, such as elementary schools, junior high schools, senior high schools, junior colleges, and adult education. It is a condensed statement of the educational program that will be carried forward and at every point relates the program to cost. The well-built educational plan inspires confidence in the budget maker and does much to interpret the budget to the board of education and to the public. Mention of this phase of the budget is almost entirely absent in state requirements. Its development has grown out of the best practices of city school budgeting.

It Reflects the Educational Philosophy. The educational plan of the budget should set forth in some detail the educational objectives to be achieved by the schools. It is in a sense a statement of educational philosophy that has been adopted by the board of education, the administrative and teaching staffs, and the community. The educational philosophy is usually developed over a period of time, and takes on a rather definite character. The budget should reflect this philosophy and show how it influences the work of the schools in the fiscal period ahead. This is the part of the budget that is usually lacking or developed in the least detail. A few budgets show clearly what the educational objectives are and how they are to be achieved. They set forth purposes of education, the special needs of the community, the type of school organization, the extent of the school program (both for lower grades and upper grades), the school personnel that is to carry on the program, their salaries and other special benefits they are to receive, the qualifications of teachers, the nature of school supplies and services, the number of pupils to be served, and, to some extent, the size of classes or the number of pupils per teacher, teaching materials, books, supplies, etc., and the kind of a school plant that is planned for the educational program.

It Shows Planning. It becomes evident that, if the educational program is to set forth the kind of school program that the community wants and for which it is willing to pay, continuous planning throughout the year is essential. Such planning is carried on by many people in the school system in the community and with the aid and assistance of a number of others from entirely outside the school system. It involves state regulations, state laws, and often an intimate knowledge of the financial support of the schools on a state-wide basis.

It Interprets the Budget. In recent years a number of city school systems have developed justification budgets in which the figures are reduced to a minimum and much of the actual work of the school is shown by means of pictures taken from classrooms and activities in which pupils participate. Through this type of presentation, the educational plan of the school is brought into the foreground, whereas the statistical data are given as supporting information. While this is essentially a phase of presentation of the budget to the public, it does show the extent to which the educational program may be developed as a part of the regular budget document.

It Encourages Citizen Participation. It seems probable that the justification budget is the first step in an important new phase of budgetary preparation extending the opportunities for participation of staff and public. As school systems become more concerned with public participation in the development of the educational policy, the budget presentation process emerges as one of the most significant ones in administration. This is in great contrast to the attitude held in most communities in the past where the board of education and the administrative staff have tended to consider concern with educational matters by voluntary groups as something to be minimized. It indicates a growing realization that the voluntary group plays a very important part in our governmental system and has throughout history.

Considerable experimentation has been carried on in certain school systems to indicate the place and purpose of groups of citizens in budget making. It is perhaps in the setting up of the educational plan that citizens can be most helpful, since it is this phase of the school program with which they are most directly concerned. When we consider this phase of budgetary planning, it becomes obvious that the later step of presentation and adoption of the budget comes much too late. Participation of citizen groups should be an early step in budgeting and a continuous one, especially in the development of the educational plan.

Grierson's [7] study gives useful guide lines developed from the study of lay participation in budget making. It shows the purposes of lay participation to be to provide understanding, ideas, mutual appreciation, help for school board members, evaluation aid, moral and financial support, relief from unjustified attacks, and a training ground for school board members. Rather detailed information is given on the structure and formation of lay groups, how they should function, results that may be expected, and lay-board relationships.

There is every indication that this emphasis on operational democracy in the budget-development process will pay off prudentially and in improved adaptability as well as in the important fruits of the democratic process itself, harvested by the persons participating in it. Such work makes tremendous demands upon administration, such great demands, in fact, that it probably requires more expenditure for administration than has customarily been made for budget development or for promoting lay participation.

The development of such budget-developing procedures need not be left entirely to the discretion of boards of education and administrators. Typically, laws specifying that the superintendent of schools shall develop the budget stop with this statement. In many cases, this is interpreted by the superintendent of schools to make it a very special, individual, and private matter, probably in many cases owing to shortage of clerical help rather than to any particular opposition to the principle of democratic operation. The situation can be ameliorated, it would seem, by making

[7] Harry W. Grierson, "School Budget Making: Its Potential for Improving the Quality of Education," unpublished doctoral project, Teachers College, Columbia University, New York, 1956.

the provision in the state school code and state school board regulations more specific as to the scope of participation in the budget-making process.

The Expenditure Plan

The translation of the educational program into an expenditure program is the technical part of budget making. It must be based upon accurate past experiences and estimates of cost that prevail at the time. For example, the cost of personal services in the expenditure program must be based on the salary schedules adopted and the placement of various personnel on these salary schedules. It requires information that has been collected over a period of time and reflects any changes that may be needed from one year to another. The work of making the estimates of materials and supplies to be purchased may be facilitated by use of a system of blanks on which the needs of each department are entered by teachers and principals to be compiled and entered in the larger items by the superintendent and his staff. Estimates of materials and supplies should be based on accepted standards of quality and standards of consumption previously accepted by the board of education.

Budget Workbook. It becomes quite obvious in making a budget that the data that have been assembled over a period of time in the form of a budget workbook provide an invaluable source of material from which to make the detailed estimates. Such a budget workbook has been advocated for some time and is actually kept by a number of school systems, although the idea has not received very wide acceptance.

It is entirely possible for the administrator to make what might be termed a lump-sum budget in which only the largest items of expenditure are estimated and set forth in a brief analysis of total expenditures needed. Such lump-sum budgets are usually based upon the preceding year or years, without much analysis of the educational program. In contrast to this method, the specific translation of the educational program into expenditures requires much more work and must necessarily extend over a period of time. By the use of a workbook the expenditure program can be very detailed and very carefully analyzed. It must be broken down into the large character categories of expenditure such as administration or general control, instruction, auxiliary services, operation of plant, maintenance of plant, fixed charges, capital outlay, and debt service. But this is only the beginning of the classification. Each of the major categories of expenditure will need to be broken down into the details set forth in the accounting system and placed in their proper positions in the budget document.

Comparison with Past Year. The expenditure program is often set forth in tabular form. It shows the expenditures by detailed items for the current budget, the year preceding the year in which the budget is made, and for one or two years preceding. While every budget is a unique document and should attempt to set forth the cost of the program proposed, it is often helpful to compare the items of expenditure in the proposed budget with those in the past years. Any large deviations will at once show a change in the educational program, changes in costs, and other conditions which the budget should set forth.

Too much emphasis cannot be placed upon the coordination of the expenditure program in detail with the figures set forth in the financial accounting system for the preceding years. In fact, the budget is based on the detailed analysis of the accounts and no satisfactory budget can be prepared without a thoroughgoing method of financial accounting and cost analysis.

Flexibility in Budgeting. Some flexibility in the expenditure program must always be maintained. One method of carrying this out is to set forth certain additional expenditures that are desirable and still others that may be carried forward if funds permit. Some budgets carry an extra column showing desirable expenditures with reference to notes detailing special studies by citizens' groups which recommend more expenditure than the budget proposes. Certain contingency allowances are often found in budgets, although the amount set aside for this purpose should not be large. Too large an emergency fund may encourage superficial estimates.

A rather common practice in school budgeting is for school officials to pad their budgets. This is usually done by overemphasizing the items of expenditure and underemphasizing the sources of receipts. Neither of these practices is considered desirable in setting up an honest budget. Every effort should be made to set forth the costs just as accurately as possible. If unforeseen conditions occur during the budget year, special means must be provided for taking care of them.

Translating Program into Cost. The expenditure plan consists of the analysis of the cost of the educational program proposed. It is in reality a translation of the educational program into cost. In formulating this plan, it is best to begin with the educational program as outlined and then to determine as nearly as possible what it will cost to carry out such a program. This is the ideal situation. In actual practice, however, the educational program, the expenditure program, and the financing program must all be worked out together. While some administrators prefer to begin with the financing program to determine the receipts and then build the expenditure program and the educational program to fit it, this is not considered to be the best practice. Usually there is and always should be some flexibility in the financing program which makes it possible more or less accurately to carry out the educational program as originally planned.

In preparing the estimates of expenditure it is desirable to have them listed by main character categories for a number of years past. Such expenditures are guides for building the expenditure plan for the proposed budget. Care should be exercised, however, in carrying forward the figures or percentages of past years into the budget year without an adequate consideration of changes in the educational plan that may be needed or demanded by the community.

Subdivision of Expenditures. The first subdivision as suggested above is to estimate the expenditures by a classification of purpose for which money is spent—administration or general control, instruction, auxiliary services, (other subdivisions may be used here), operation of plant, maintenance of plant, fixed charges, capital outlay, and debt service. In building the expenditure program, the different funds must be taken into consideration since often income and expenditures for certain funds may not be transferred readily to other funds. In the main, it is wise to keep current expenditures separate from capital outlay and debt service. Further subdivisions of the main categories may be made, e.g., grade levels of the school system: kindergarten, primary, elementary, junior high school, senior high school, junior college; functions, such as supervision, attendance service, health service, etc.; or objects, such as mimeograph paper, printing, advertising, etc.

In comparing the expenditure program for the budget year with that of preceding years, both amounts and percentages should be shown, since this aids the administrator in pointing out or determining trends.

The principle here is essentially a prudential one. It is one of good sound management and maintaining a balance between what is desirable in the educational program and what is wise in terms of tax burden on the community. The expenditure program should be made as accurately as possible, and the expenditures should not be estimated in general only.

After the general estimates of expenditures are made, there might be several tabulations of much more detailed estimates breaking down each item of expenditure into various categories and into quite detailed lists. Sufficient explanation should accompany the expenditures lists to justify any large increases or decreases in particular items. Such explanation must be made at some time or another, and it is wise to include it in the budget document.

The Financing Plan

The financing plan is necessary to complete the picture of budgeting for education in a community. It shows the income of the schools from all sources. The local school unit usually has some tax leeway between the amounts levied and the tax limitation imposed by law or approved by public opinion. If the amounts to be levied are shown to be fairly consistent over a period of years, the program is more likely to be accepted than if the needs fluctuate greatly.

Some items in the financing plan must necessarily be taken into consideration at an early stage in the budget making. This may be true for certain fixed amounts of income such as state aid or amounts due from taxation when specific limitations are imposed. Better practice, however, is to estimate first the educational plan and its cost and then to fit the financing plan to the educational plan in the best manner possible.

The financing plan should show the extent to which the funds due the schools have been collected and paid into the school treasury in past years. If those who are responsible for budget preparation can show the board of education that they fully understand all aspects of the financing plan, they are more likely to win acceptance for their program.

Revenue Must Be Adequate. Not only must revenue be estimated accurately, but the expected revenue must fully satisfy the demands of the expenditure plan. When the budget becomes unbalanced, it ceases to fulfill its functions. This responsibility for estimating the needed receipts is usually placed by law on the board of education. This phase, as some other phases of budgetary procedure, is an executive one, which should be placed largely in the hands of the superintendent of schools under the direction of the board of education. It is of interest to note that in many states the executive function of preparing the budget and the legislative function of approving the budget are both stated as a responsibility of the board of education.

Fiscal and School Years. Another problem that arises in connection with the estimation of school revenue is the discrepancy that sometimes exists between the tax year and the fiscal year of the school system. It is now becoming more and more recognized that the tax year and the school year, as well as the fiscal year for state and other local governments, should coincide as nearly as possible. More and more the school year is coming to extend from July 1 to June 30, but this is not always the case in the fiscal year of the state and counties. Wherever there is a discrepancy between the tax year and the school year, sufficient leeway must be allowed to permit the accumulation of funds from tax sources to take care of school expenditures until another tax period arrives. This means that the receipts must often show a balance or a carry-over fund, sometimes called an interim fund, from one year to another. It must be a regular part of the budget because of the discrepancy in dates of income and expenditure. This illustration of the differences between the state fiscal year and the school fiscal year is but one example of the dependence of budget making upon state regulations.

State Services. In addition to establishing the framework of budget development, the state can be of service in assisting communities in other important processes. One of the most common of these is to provide forms to be used by local communities in developing the budget instrument. Other types of helpful state services may be rendered by the state departments of education by providing consultative service to local school boards and superintendents, and prebudget conferences held under the leadership of the state departments of education. The latter plan has been utilized in a number of states. Such services, of course, must be safeguarded in the same way as state audits as discussed in Chapter 25. It is easy for central officers to come to the conclusion that their judgments on a great many matters which by law are left to the boards of education are superior to those of the boards of education simply because as state officers they are listened to. This danger is not so likely to occur in the development of forms and procedures. Accordingly, such supplementary service to most school districts may well be limited to forms and procedures and to the provision of comparative data.

FORMAT OF THE BUDGET

The format of the budget document is prescribed by law or state regulations in more or less detail in most of the states. The form of the budget usually prescribed makes provision for the funds to be kept with some subdivisions and the main items of proposed expenditures and anticipated receipts. Printed forms for reporting to state agencies are in use in approximately three-fourths of the states. These forms are largely lists of expenditures and receipts. Occasionally other items are included.

While it is necessary to have some form for reporting the budget to state agencies, such reports are necessarily brief and should not be taken to comprise the local budget. The school district budget must be much more detailed and must contain much more explanatory and supplementary material than is necessary in any state form.

Although the form of the budget varies from one local unit to another and from one state to another, there are nevertheless certain large groups of informational items that are common to most forms and should be included. The four groups of items may be summarized as (1) the budget message, (2) the general budget summary, (3) the estimates of receipts and expenditures and (4) the supporting schedules. These groups of items may not always appear in the order given and often one or more may be given special emphasis, depending upon the needs and conditions in the school system.

Budget Message

The budget message consists of the written explanatory and interpretative material given by the budget maker to the group that approves the budget and to the public. The budget message is a means of vitalizing the financial plan, and enables the budget maker to present his proposals in understandable, meaningful language to laymen, whether they are members of the legislative body or taxpayers. It is in reality a means of breaking away from the technical vocabulary of the accountant and the statistician.

Among the subsections that should be included in the budget message are the following: (1) a statement showing the financial condition of the district at the close of the fiscal year, whether it is one of solvency or indebtedness, and showing also the amount of balance or of indebtedness and the chief reasons for the condition; (2) a statement of the educational policy of the board of education for the next fiscal year or for a longer period (if any change in policy is contemplated, its probable effect on the financial situation should be given); (3) a statement of the educational task to be undertaken by the school district (essentially a verbal description of the educational plan); (4) a statement showing the capital expenditures program to be undertaken and the reason for such expenditures; and (5) a statement setting forth any other conditions that may be foreseen and that are likely to influence school costs.

Budget Summary

The budget summary should show proposed expenditures and anticipated revenue in convenient form for comparison. It is often helpful to list this information on facing pages of the budget document. The summary might show the following: (1) the anticipated revenue from all sources during the fiscal period and the amount of the balance or deficit at the beginning of the fiscal year; (2) the proposed expenditures for all purposes during the fiscal year, usually listed by broad categories; (3) increase or decrease in major items of expenditure for two or three years past; (4) sufficient explanatory material to accompany the estimates either in footnotes or before or after the tables to make each item clear.

List of Expenditures and Receipts

The list of expenditures and receipts should be sufficiently detailed to enable the board of education or a reviewing body to follow up any item of cost. The classifications of expenditures prescribed by the state should be used, but supplementary classifications are frequently desirable. All accounts should be coded for ready reference. Other breakdowns may be necessary depending upon the detail to which the budget maker may wish to analyze receipts and expenditures.

Supporting Schedules

In addition to the material already indicated as a part of the budget document, it is often very helpful, especially in long-term planning, to include certain supporting schedules which show expenditures for a period of time that help the budget maker in determining the amount to be expended in a particular year. Among such supporting schedules may be found the following: (1) an analysis of teachers' salary schedules showing the number and variety of teaching positions and the placement of teachers on the schedule; (2) an analysis of the cost of other personal services, such as those of janitors, engineers, bus drivers, repairmen, watchmen, matrons, cafeteria managers, etc., and the salary schedules for other persons employed in the system; (3) detailed analysis of the quantity of materials and supplies used during the fiscal year together with certain standards of computation; (4) the long-term program of maintenance of the school plant; (5) the bonding plan of the schools for a period of years in the future, showing the schedule of bond retirement and interest payments; (6) certain tabulations of unit costs; (7) comparative data on wealth and school costs with other comparable school systems (See Chapter 7).

The budget document should be bound with a protective cover, include a table of contents, a letter of transmittal and an index.

PRESENTATION AND APPROVAL OF THE BUDGET

Budget presentation like budget preparation is an executive function to be carried on by the chief executive officer of the board of education, the superintendent of schools. This phase of the procedure is more dependent on state laws and state regulations than is that of preparation, nevertheless it is largely a local function. The completed budget should be accompanied by a program of interpretation to the board of education, the schools, and the public. The document itself carries some interpretative material in the budget message, but this must be supplemented with oral interpretation and other forms of publicity. A considerable number of states now require publication of the proposed budget or a public hearing.

The time of presentation of the budget is one that varies among the states and often no specific time is given for this step. As a general rule, it may be stated that the budget should be presented to the board of education, the reviewing body, if such there is, and the public long enough before the date for adoption to give ample time for study and interpretation that these groups may wish to make. (See Figure 19-2.)

Publication and Hearings

Publication in one form or another is required in a number of the states. Such publication usually precedes and always should precede the adoption of the budget. Newspaper publication, posting the estimates in prominent places in the district, and placing the budget on file for public inspection are among the more important methods of satisfying this requirement. Public hearings are required in a number of states. Both publication of the budget and public hearings on the budget may be thought of as minimum provisions for public participation in budgetary procedure.

Approval of the Budget

Although the final adoption of the budget is usually in the hands of the local boards of education, there are many exceptions to this procedure. In states where local boards of education are partially fiscally dependent on other groups or boards, there may often be considerable delay. For some time there has been a tendency toward legislation tending to restrict local boards with respect to budgetary estimates by limiting them in the amount of local taxes that may be levied. Most of this legislation seems to be prompted by the need, as the legislators see it, for restriction or control of educational expenditures.

If local control over education is to be maintained, it is essential that the final adoption or approval of the budget remain essentially a local function. This function must be recognized in the laws of the state, even in those states in which there is a reviewing body outside the board of education. The integrity of the school system, the responsibility of those in charge, and the potentialities of home rule are realized when local decisions are made by school authorities who are responsible to the people. This fact is recognized in the laws of many states, although there are numerous responsibilities for budgets given to agencies entirely apart from the board of education.

A number of tabulations have been made of the various agencies that are responsible for budget approval. A study by Chase and Morphet for the years 1947 and 1948,[8] showed that in thirty-one states the school board was legally responsible for the approval of the school budget; in seventeen states, the county commissioners, city council, or budget commission had some responsibility for approval, although the degree of responsibility of these officials varied greatly.[8a]

[8] Francis S. Chase and Edgar L. Morphet, *The Forty-eight State School Systems,* Council of State Governments, Chicago, 1949, pp. 157–158.

[8a] Facts on certain aspects of budgeting were pointed out by Walter C. Reusser in "Better Budgets," *Nation's Schools,* November, 1935; December, 1935; January, 1936.

State Review of School Budgets

A study shows that in thirty-six states a copy of the budget must be filed with a state agency.[9] Most of these are either state departments of education, departments of public instruction, or tax commissions. The extent of authority these agencies generally have over school district budgets is limited. In less than a half-dozen does any state agency hold the power of approval of the amount of money to be spent. Where state controls are present it is possible that not enough attention has been given to possibilities of placing budget approval on the people themselves. When this responsibility is taken away from the people and put in a representative board, such as the board of education, then the old principle of checks and balances comes into play; where the budget, on the other hand, still remains in the hands of the people, as in the New England town meetings, in New York district meetings, and in small districts and small cities in many parts of the country, state budget approval boards have not developed and these districts have been generally free from review by county or city officials.

ADMINISTRATION OF THE BUDGET

The steps of budget preparation, presentation, and adoption complete the formal construction and acceptance of the budget plan. The real test of any budget comes in its administration. The best budget will fail if it is not well administered, and even a poor budget may succeed in the hands of a competent administrator. As a rule, fewer state regulations and legal provisions surround the administration of the school budget than its preparation and approval; however, certain well-defined provisions of budget administration are evident.

The administration of the school budget is essentially the carrying out of the plan of receiving and accounting for the receipts that are due the schools and of making expenditures for personnel, materials, supplies, etc., from day to day as the school year progresses.

Administration, an Executive Function

The administration of the school budget, like its preparation, is generally regarded as an executive function to be performed by the superintendent of schools or a member of his staff. Good practice would hold that budget approval and certain phases of appraisal are policy-making functions to be performed by the board of education.

In the legal provisions of the various states this distinction is practically

[9] Clayton D. Hutchins and Albert R. Munse, *Public School Finance Programs in the United States,* U.S. Office of Education, 1954, p. 52.

nonexistent. In most cases, the boards of education are charged with responsibility of administering the budget, as they have also been charged with the preparation and approval of this document. In only a few states is the superintendent of schools named as a responsible party along with the board of education for the administration of the budget. In practice, however, it is general for the board of education to delegate the responsibility of administration to the superintendent and his staff.

It is interesting that so few states mention the superintendent. This may be a vestige of an earlier form of organizational structure of education which permitted large numbers of school districts to operate without the leadership of a superintendent of schools, and in which boards of education were charged with the administration of the schools. In a relatively large number of states no mention was made in the statutory provisions in regard to the administration of the budget, but it was assumed that boards had this authority by implication, since they were the responsible representatives of the people.

In the states that have adopted comprehensive budget laws for school units, some limit boards of education rigidly to the budgetary statement as adopted whereas in others, boards give relatively little attention to budgets after they are made and adopted, as there are no provisions that compel the board to live within the budgetary amounts. In the latter cases, budgets are merely for the purpose of determining the amount of tax money to be raised locally.

New Mexico is an example of a state that compels boards to keep within their budgets, whereas in Arizona the budgets are not regulatory of expenditures. It is doubtful whether the best results can be achieved and whether budgets can ever be made really functional by the application of laws and regulations that require boards to make and keep within their adopted statements if at the same time there is no provision for adequate educational leadership and if there is no professional responsibility for prudential management in the local schools units. A budget is an instrument for management and is not effective in those units where provision is not made for the exercise of local initiative through efficient educational leadership.

Meeting Emergency Needs

One aspect of budgetary administration that is somewhat more definitely prescribed by the states is the manner in which school boards may meet emergency needs. The three most frequently found provisions are (1) placing an emergency fund in the school budget, (2) providing for additional taxation or appropriation, and (3) borrowing money on the credit of the district to meet current needs. In at least eleven states the state budgetary forms provide for an emergency fund in the school budget. In Kansas and California the emergency fund is equal to 10 per cent of the entire budget, while in New Jersey this fund is limited to 1 per cent of the total. The laws of some states prohibit the inclusion of an emergency fund in school budgets.

In some states an emergency fund can be raised by a special tax not to exceed a certain rate, but again the approval of the electors is required for this fund. In New Mexico, the state tax commission can approve a transfer from the county emergency fund to the school district. In some of those states in which money is appropriated to the schools by the city or town officials, emergencies are met by additional appropriations.

Borrowing for Current Needs

Perhaps the most frequently used method of meeting emergency expenditures is by borrowing money on the credit of the district. Such indebtedness can be liquidated by making a higher regular tax levy during the next fiscal period or by means of a special tax. This is more frequently done when the emergency expenditure is for the erection of new buildings or the rebuilding of structures, than when it is for current operation. In the former case, the provisions for raising money for capital expenditures are usually sufficient to cover the needs.

In the administration of a budget there may be times when bills must be paid although there are insufficient funds on hand with which to meet the obligations. This is particularly likely to occur at times between periods of annual or semiannual payments of taxes or of the distribution of state aid. So acute may this problem become that most states have made some provision for current borrowing, but the provisions are usually surrounded with definite requirements. The three most commonly found methods of enabling school districts to meet their current obligations throughout the year are (1) issuing anticipation warrants, (2) borrowing money on the credit of the district, and (3) carrying relatively large balances.

During the depression, issuing warrants in anticipation of tax collections was frequently practiced as a means for paying current obligations. In some of the states a limit was placed on the amount of such warrants that might be issued. This method of financing was permitted by one or all types of districts in two-thirds of the states. Less frequently this method is still employed by many school districts throughout the country.

A number of states provide in their laws for the borrowing of money by school districts for meeting current expenditures. Some permit such borrowing to pay teachers' salaries and other current expenses, but the amount so borrowed may often not exceed a stated per cent of the comparable expenditures of the preceding year. Another method is for districts to borrow money from banks, from individuals, or from the next year's revenue to the amount of the maximum nonbonded indebtedness of the district during the preceding year.

Relative to the disposition of unexpended balances at the close of the fiscal year, three methods are in use: (1) the appropriation of such balances to the next fiscal year, (2) lapse of appropriations or the reversion of any balances to the general fund from which paid, and (3) the transfer of such to another fund that may be carried into the next fiscal period.

The transfer of money from one budget item to another is generally permitted at the discretion of boards of education; specific restrictions are, however, placed upon the transfer of money from one fund to another. In many states budgetary provisions allow for free transfer among budget items.

Transfer of money from the incidental fund to the building fund may be made in Missouri for the purpose of necessary repairs to school buildings, and any balance in the building fund may be transferred back to the incidental fund. The Iowa provision is somewhat similar—surpluses in the general fund may be transferred to the schoolhouse fund by the board of education, but transfers from the schoolhouse fund to the general fund may be made only by majority vote of the electors of the district.

Boards in Control

Budgetary procedure as it is now developing seems to assume that neither school boards nor executives will be able to exercise competent judgment again until a new year rolls around. But a lively, adaptable school system will have need of funds to buy unforeseen, unthought-of materials and services. Adaptability would dictate that every budget should have a considerable contingent fund that can be used without too much red tape to assist a teacher or a principal or an administrative officer to carry forward experimental work. Of course, much of this can be budgeted, but if the system is not static or is not on the way to becoming static, needs of this sort will arise to which the school board or the administration should be in a position to respond.

There may be real danger in the fact that the application of budgeting was expanded during a period of retrenchment. Budgetary procedure must therefore continuously be scanned lest its larger purpose be forgotten—to serve as a device implementing the school district as an agent of the state (all the people). If the budget should become a strait jacket, it would destroy much of the good of local initiative. In such case it would seem to be better to save the time of school boards and the expense of hundreds or thousands of budget accounts, tax levies, etc., and handle the whole educational system with one budget and one set of accounts, that is, as a state-operated system.

Good budget administration means efficiency and planning. To carry out these functions to any great extent would seem to go contrary to the criterion of adaptability in the local school system, since too much adherence to efficiency and preplanning might handicap the fruition of new ideas. Often teachers plan new projects or approaches to their teaching which require the expenditure of funds not previously budgeted. To deny such experimentation goes contrary to the principle of adaptability. Some flexibility is needed for teachers to carry on their best work, and provision should be made for some unforeseen contingencies.

The following taken from one of the early studies of adaptability highlights the human side of budget administration:

Where these attitudes are found in a professional staff there is lack of tension that can be readily sensed—an environment itself a contributor to the mental health of teachers, pupils and community—a sanctuary from strains and stresses—a good place to be. Such teachers do not fear to go to authority for they do not go for authority, they go for wise counsel, sure that it will be forthcoming. If small additional materials or funds are required—and it is often the lack of small sums that impedes the enthusiast—the administrator will find them. If it isn't in his contingent fund he will have someone to turn to. For he knows that the confidence that the act expresses is infinitely more important than the material or the fund itself. Many an enthusiastic teacher has had his spirits irreparably dampened by having an administrator prove to him that what he requests is not needed.[10]

APPRAISAL OF THE BUDGET

The appraisal of the budget is an evaluation of the budget plan to determine how accurately receipts and expenditures have been projected for the fiscal period. It is essentially the determination of the goodness of the budget, how well it has been made, and how it agrees with actual administration.

There are a number of methods by which budgets may be appraised, both the budget document and the procedure involved in making and administering the budget. The use of these methods may differ somewhat dependent upon the point of view of those making the appraisal, whether it be made by a professional school administrator or by laymen. For example, a school business manager may judge the success of his budget by the extent to which his estimates of receipts and expenditures agree with the actual amounts received and expended. A well-made budget under favorable circumstances will agree very closely with the actual figures shown in the annual report. Although this method of judg-

[10] Paul R. Mort and Francis G. Cornell, *American Schools in Transition,* Bureau of Publications, Teachers College, Columbia University, New York, 1941.

ing a budget has value and encourages accuracy in making the estimates, one must remember that it is not possible to foresee all the conditions which may arise during the fiscal year and that frequently considerable discrepancy between estimates and expenditures and receipts may be justified. Over a period of years, however, there will be sufficient agreement between estimates and expenditures to provide a reliable working basis for the preparation of subsequent budgets.

In states where the laws require that expenditures be limited to income, there is no choice in the matter of exceeding the budgetary allowances, faulty as these may sometimes be. When the funds are expended, the school program must be curtailed or stopped altogether. Under such circumstances there is usually a tendency for those making the budget to allow for plenty of leeway between estimated expenditures and estimated income, so that there is likely to be a balance at the end of the year. This tends to defeat accurate budget making and may consequently lead to expenditures at the close of the year, when funds remain in the treasury, that would not be made at all under more accurate budgeting. In this case, prudence defeats itself.

A number of appraisal forms have been devised for judging the merits of the budget document as an instrument in financial management. The great variation in the form and content of school budgets makes this type of appraisal somewhat difficult to apply to budgets prepared for different communities. Used in the same community over a period of years, such means of appraisal have considerable validity in pointing out weaknesses and omissions in the budget document. Grierson made an analysis of budget format and content and an outline for a citizens' budget review that gives useful information for the evaluation of the budget document by lay groups.[11]

SUMMARY

The school budget is essentially a plan for financing the schools for a period of time in the future. The plan is evidenced by a budget document. Budgetary procedure involves the cycle of operations that embrace preparation, approval, administration, and appraisal of the budget plan.

Budget preparation is essentially an executive function. It embraces planning three types of program—the educational program which sets forth the kind of schools to be carried on and the general policies of the board of education, the expenditures plan which is essentially an estimate of the cost of the educational program, and the financial plan which shows

[11] Harry W. Grierson, "School Budget Making: Its Potential for Improving the Quality of Education," unpublished doctoral project, Teachers College, Columbia University, New York, 1956.

how funds will be obtained during the ensuing fiscal period. In practice, the three programs are coordinated to form an integrated whole.

The second step in the cyclic operations, budget presentation and approval, consists essentially of making known to the board of education or other agency and to the public what is proposed for the ensuing fiscal period. As far as possible, the community should participate through budget recommendations, publication of the budget, and budget hearings.

The budgeting plan, however carefully prepared and however effectively presented, does not become operative until it is administered. In this step of the procedure, the executive officer of the board will have great responsibilities for effective and economical management. He must carry on the functions of making the expenditures in accordance with the budgetary appropriations, periodic reporting to the board of education, borrowing for current needs, transfer of funds, and the like. If unforeseen expenditures become necessary, he must call upon the board of education for consideration of such needs.

The final step of budgetary procedure is that of appraisal. This is an attempt to determine the effectiveness of the budget plan, both in preparation and administration. The annual audit of school accounts and the periodic reports made through the year are means of appraising the budget plan and the manner of its execution.

QUESTIONS FOR STUDY AND DISCUSSION

1. Show how budgetary procedure is carried on in a particular state with which you are familiar. Indicate the provisions of the law and the various steps that the budget maker must follow in the complete preparation and administration of the budget.

2. From a set of school accounts, prepare a budget document for that school. Indicate how the budgetary procedure is to be carried on.

3. Analyze a number of school budgets made for different school systems. Point out clearly the educational plan, the expenditure plan, and the financing plan in each budget. What material comprises the budget message?

4. How are budgets approved in your state? To what extent are there state or local agencies outside the board of education that must approve the budget? If there are any such agencies, to what extent have they control over the budget?

5. Selecting a particular school district with which you are familiar, show what information should be given in the educational plan of the budget.

6. Plan a presentation of a budget at a budget hearing. Select materials that are likely to be of greatest interest to the public. Assume a fair audience at the budget hearing.

7. Analyze several school budgets and prepare a brief justification budget based on one of them. Select descriptive material and brief financial presentation that is most likely to be of interest to the public.

8. Show what agencies beside the administration of the school and board of education are likely to be involved in preparing a budget. Assume a certain situation with which you are familiar.

9. Why are budgeting and auditing thought of as more important than the mechanized tasks shown in the conceptual design of local financial administration in the preceding chapter? What is the relation of budgeting to the democratic process? What is the value of drawing public support into the budgetary procedure at several points?

10. What are the relative merits in budget administration of carrying large balances or borrowing money for current expenditures in periods of low income?

SELECTED REFERENCES

Ackerly, Harold E.: "The Budget Procedure: Step by Step," *School Executive,* 67:46–47, November, 1947.

American Association of School Administrators: *School Boards in Action,* Twenty-fourth Yearbook, Washington, 1946, pp. 153–155.

———: *Public Relations for American Schools,* Twenty-eighth Yearbook, Washington, 1950.

Anderson, Walter A., "Functions in School Budget Making," *School Executive,* 67:52–53, November, 1947.

Associated Public School Systems, *Everybody Invests in Our Public Schools,* 525 West 120th Street, New York, 1955.

Barry, Royal P.: "Budget Accounting," Proceedings of the Seventy-fifth Annual Convention of School Business Officials, Kalamazoo, Mich., 1951, pp. 151–156. Also in *Nation's Schools,* vol. 47, pp. 37–39, February, 1951.

Burke, Arvid J.: *Financing Public Schools in the United States,* Harper & Brothers, New York, 1957.

Central School Boards Committee for Educational Research, *Budgeting Practices in Central Schools: A Report of Current Practices in Budget Making as Educational Planning in Central Schools of New York State,* 525 West 120th Street, New York, 1952.

Clark, Zenas R.: "Necessary Information for Making the Budget," *School Executive,* vol. 67, p. 48, November, 1947.

Cremin, Lawrence A., and Merle L. Barrowman: *Public Schools in Our Democracy,* New York, The Macmillan Company, 1956.

DeYoung, Chris A.: *Budgeting in Public Schools,* The Odyssey Press, Inc., New York, 1936.

Engelhardt, N. L.: "The School Budget as an Administrative Control," *School Executive,* vol. 67, p. 44, November, 1947.

Grierson, Harry W: "School Budget Making: Its Potential for Improving the Quality of Education," unpublished doctoral project, Teachers College, Columbia University, New York, 1956.

Hill, O. E: *Citizens at Work: A Description of Lay Participation in the Cleveland Heights Public School System,* Associated Public School Systems, 525 West 120th St., New York, 1956.

Johns, R. L., and E. L. Morphet (eds.): *Problems and Issues in Public School Finance,* chap. X, "The Budgetary Process," Bureau of Publications, Teachers College, Columbia University, New York, 1952.

Lewis, John W.: "The Operation of the Budget," *School Executive,* vol. 67, p. 51, November, 1947.

Linn, Henry H.: *School Business Administration,* The Ronald Press Company, New York, 1956, chap. V, "The School Budget."

Lutz, Charles D.: "Long Range and Annual Budgeting in Gary," *American School Board Journal,* vol. 120, pp. 22–23, June, 1950.

McCunn, Gromand J.: "Presenting the Budget to the Board and the Community," *School Executive,* vol. 67, p. 54, November, 1947.

Metropolitan School Study Council, *What Do They Learn About Education?* 525 West 120th Street, New York, 1955.

Mort, Paul R., and Donald H. Ross: *Principles of School Administration,* McGraw-Hill Book Co., Inc., New York, 1957 (see index).

Reusser, Walter C.: "Better Budgets," *Nation's Schools,* vol. 16, no. 5, pp. 35–36, November, 1935; vol. 16, no. 6, pp. 33–34, December, 1935; vol. 17, no. 1, pp. 33–34, January, 1936.

Rosenstengel, William E., and Jefferson N. Eastmond: *School Finance: Its Theory and Practice,* chap. X, "Budgetary Procedures," The Ronald Press Company, New York, 1957.

20. Financial accounting

FINANCIAL accounting is a prudential function that has for its purpose the recording and analysis of receipts and expenditures of the school system for use in operation, reporting and budgeting. It also serves as a means of rendering an account of stewardship and of a general financial management and as a basis for appraisal studies. As one of the mechanized tasks of a school system, it should embrace a degree of uniformity among school systems and states in order that the data obtained may be comparable. This degree of uniformity, however, need not go beyond the purpose of reporting to state and national agencies. The amount of detail in the accounting system must always vary with the purposes of the administration, the size of the school system, and the educational structure within which the accounting is carried on. It is important that uniformity should not be stressed at the expense of service to the educational program, because this service must remain flexible in order that it may facilitate the changing conceptions of education.

During periods of rapid increase in school enrollment and costs, it becomes necessary to provide administrative devices for the management and protection of the large sums of money collected and expended by school officials. In many districts better methods of accounting and procedures for reporting are needed. Methods yielding cost figures that are not comparable among cities and states are of little or no value. Uniformity of classification of receipts and expenditures, definitions of terms, and standardization of accounts are needed.

TRENDS IN FINANCIAL ACCOUNTING

Financial accounting for schools in cities, states, and the nation had its beginnings in a number of more or less distinct movements that started many years ago. Among the more important of these were the efforts of

372

such organizations as the National Education Association and the National Association of Public School Business Officials to establish a uniform basis for the reporting of school financial statistics and for the standardization of terminology, forms, and methods. Other factors were the influence of municipal accounting methods and the examples of business and private enterprise. Some of these factors have tended to retard progress in the achievement of uniformity.

Among the various steps in the development of financial accounting might be mentioned the reports of the National Education Association from 1860 to 1885 which revealed many efforts to bring a degree of uniformity into this phase of educational administration.[1] The determination of what classification of accounts to use, how the accounts may be made most serviceable to the schools, and what derived statistics to compute, occupied the thought of educators and laymen at this time. Out of these efforts grew certain concepts of standard terminology such as current expenditures, capital outlay, operation of plant, supplies, and equipment, etc.

In 1912, the United States Bureau of Education in cooperation with the Bureau of Census, the Association of School Accounting Officers, and the Department of Superintendence of the National Education Association[2] published a set of report forms which brought about substantial agreement in practices, especially in the definition of terms, the classification of receipts and expenditures, and the general procedures for handling accounts.

Hutchinson's work in 1914 reviewed school costs and accounting in cities of 10,000 to 100,000 population.[3] This author found wide variation in almost all kinds of account forms used, and summed up the four chief deficiencies as follows: (1) No attempt was made to account for revenue accruing and expenses incurred; (2) There was no attempt to distinguish expenditures for maintenance from expenditures for capital outlay; (3) No city showed the total expenditures for each type of school; and (4) No school showed the total amount spent for each character of expenditure. In view of the fact that there was no uniformity in the ac-

[1] National Education Association, "School Statistics," *Proceedings*, 1860, pp. 253–258; National Education Association, Department of School Superintendence, "Statistics of School Attendance," *Proceedings*, 1871, pp. 225–226; National Education Association, "Reforms Needed in Educational Statistics," *Proceedings*, 1885, pp. 482–489; Washington.

[2] U.S. Bureau of Education, "Report of the Committee on Uniform Records and Reports," *Bulletin*, 1912, No. 3, Government Printing Office, Washington, 1912, pp. 13–17, 36–46.

[3] J. Howard Hutchinson, *School Costs and School Accounting*, Contributions to Education 62, Bureau of Publications, Teachers College, Columbia University, New York, 1914, p. 98.

counting forms used or in the items carried on them, he proposed a system of financial accounting that would serve the following purposes: (1) To provide a complete history of all transactions from their beginning to their completion; (2) To make it possible to account for funds in terms of specific purposes of expenditure; (3) To assist the administrative officers in judging whether the school services rendered were made at the lowest cost compatible with efficiency.

Further refinements in the method of school accounting and reporting were made by the Committee on Uniform Records and Reports of 1921 [4] and the National Education Association report of 1927.[5] Both of these reports emphasize the importance of reporting school fiscal information to the United States Bureau of Education, but neither was in any sense a complete system of financial accounting. Case [6] made important contributions to financial accounting in the clarification of the classes of expenditure by character, function, object, and location. A number of other authors made contributions to the field of financial accounting. Among these were Peel,[7] Engelhardt and Engelhardt,[8] and Engelhardt and Von Borgersrode.[9]

In the early 1930s Fowlkes described accounting procedures and developed a set of forms for school use.[10] His work was based on the classification of accounts recommended by the United States Bureau of Education and drew from the work already done in this field. As stated by the author, it was different from the work of others in that it contained a glossary of accounting terminology, provided for the accounting of both expenditures and disbursements, provided for advancements, treated budgetary procedure, and contained several mechanical devices in the ledger sheets that facilitate the use of the forms.

In 1940 the report of the Advisory Committee on School Records and Reports of the United States Office of Education made recommendations

[4] Arthur B. Moehlman, "Revision of School Accounting Report," *American School Board Journal*, vol. 64, pp. 24–25, 121–122, 125, May, 1922.

[5] National Education Association, Research Division, "School Records and Reports," *Research Bulletin*, Washington, vol. 5, pp. 226–346, November, 1927.

[6] Hiram C. Case, *Handbook of Instructions for Recording Disbursements for School Purposes*, C. F. Williams and Sons, Inc., Albany, N.Y., 1916.

[7] Arthur J. Peel, *Simplified School Accounting*, The Bruce Publishing Company, Milwaukee, Wis., 1925.

[8] N. L. Engelhardt and Fred Engelhardt, *Public School Business Administration*, Bureau of Publications, Teachers College, Columbia University, New York, 1927.

[9] Fred Engelhardt and Fred Von Borgersrode, *Accounting Procedure for School Systems*, Bureau of Publications, Teachers College, Columbia University, New York, 1927.

[10] John Guy Fowlkes, *Principles and Practices of Financial Accounting for Schools*, also, *Practical School Financial Accounting System*, E. M. Hale and Company, Publishers, Eau Claire, Wis., 1934

for changes in the accounting classification of certain items of expenditure.[11] Among these was the division of the heading "auxiliary services" into three subheads (1) school services, (2) transportation, and (3) community services, to replace the two former classifications of auxiliary agencies and coordinate activities. Work on the improvement of school financial accounting systems continued under the leadership of the United States Office of Education, and in 1953 a handbook on *The Common Core of State Educational Information* was issued.[12] Again in 1957 a second handbook on *Financial Accounting for Local and State School Systems* was published.[13] The latter handbook made many improvements in accounting procedures and introduced a number of new accounts. The discussion of receipts and expenditures in this chapter is based on this handbook.

During the decades when school accounting was developed, many states placed uniform accounting systems in operation. In these systems were incorporated some of the best features developed by individuals and committees, and in addition, adaptations were made to a variety of conditions. In all these efforts the United States Office of Education played an important part in achieving uniformity and simplicity.

In the evolution of practices and procedures of financial accounting for schools, a number of different points of view were developed with respect to the bases on which an accounting system should be founded. Among them may be mentioned the accrual basis and the cash basis. The accrual basis takes into consideration everything that has worth or value—all assets, liabilities, deferred payments, and accounts payable. It is the basis of business accounting. On the cash basis, only actual income and payments are considered and no account is taken of deferred payments, receipts due but not collected, and short-term loans.

Some authors support the imputed economic-cost theory by drawing an analogy between public schools and commercial accounting and include depreciation in the computed per pupil costs. Others take the position that the economic cost of the schools consists of services and goods used up in operation, the use of land occupied by schools, and the use of capital invested in schools. This economic cost is to be liquidated through the utilization of productive capacity, the improvement of demand for

[11] U.S. Office of Education, *Financial Accounting for Public Schools*, Preliminary Report of National Advisory Committee on School Records and Reports, Circular 204, Federal Security Agency, Washington, 1940.

[12] Paul L. Reason, Emory M. Foster, and Robert F. Will, *The Common Core of State Educational Information*, Handbook I, Bulletin 1953, No. 8, U.S. Office of Education, Washington, 1953.

[13] Paul L. Reason and Alvius L. White, *Financial Accounting for Local and State School Systems*, Handbook II, Bulletin 1957, No. 4, U.S. Office of Education, Washington, 1957.

necessities and luxuries, development of thrift, the control of population, the professionalization of vocations, and the growth of economic intelligence.

School accounts differ from business accounts in that the concept of proprietary interest does not apply. Thus, it is desirable not to use the balance sheet, but rather to replace it by a statement of assets and liabilities. The operating statement presents a picture of the financial status of the school at any one time. It is misleading to place in one statement the assets and liabilities drawn from different funds. For example, sinking-fund assets usually cannot be used for the payment of current indebtedness, and the value of buildings and grounds does not constitute an asset to offset bonded indebtedness.

CRITERIA OF GOOD FINANCIAL ACCOUNTING

A number of principles or criteria of a good accounting system point up the purposes of accounting and assist the administrator in judging the adequacy of his own system. Among these characteristics may be mentioned completeness, ease of securing information from records, uniformity of keeping the accounts, simplicity of accounts and records, and the degree of permanency desired.

Completeness

It is important that a complete record be maintained of every financial transaction. This usually begins with the voucher or order authorizing payment and follows through to the final payment by check. It should be possible to trace all receipts and expenditures that have been made in the school system. This is not only important for purposes of local management, but necessary for auditing the accounts by an outside agency. Under this criterion fall the method of classifying and recording receipts, the method of classifying and recording expenditures, and all the subsidiary records and accounts that go with the system of financial accounting.

Ease of Securing Information

It is essential in any financial accounting system that the desired information on receipts, expenditures, or any transaction be readily available. The information should be secured quickly and easily by the secretary or clerk in charge of the accounting office. This is also true of statements and reports, recapitulations, summaries, annual reports, and reports on budgets. Readily available information is likely to be used more than information which requires some computation and some time to secure. If the information that can be secured from the financial accounting system is to be of its maximum value, it should be obtainable promptly when needed.

Simplicity of Records and Reports

It is desirable that any financial accounting system should be as simple and direct as possible. This does not mean that completeness should be sacrificed to simplicity, but it does mean that other things being equal the simplest methods of keeping the records and accounts are the best. All forms in the accounting system should be such that the bookkeeper and others in charge can understand how they are to be used and fill in the information, or make the analyses required, in the minimum amount of time and with the highest degree of accuracy. It should not be necessary for the business manager or an accountant to give close supervision to the accounting system. This principle applies to the method of keeping the books, whether by long hand methods or by machine accounting.

Uniformity of Forms and Procedures

The financial accounting system used in the schools of any state should be as nearly uniform as possible. If the financial data for a state are to be meaningful, they should be collected in a similar manner; the classification of accounts, accounting terminology, and the procedure of recording the data should be carried on uniformly in all school systems. This principle also applies to uniformity among states for information that is submitted to the United States Office of Education. Uniformity in the basic accounts is highly desirable; thereafter any school may make further classifications or analyses of its own receipts or expenditures. But in broad outline, there should be identity in the facts and data reported. This principle should apply to schools in all types of districts within a state, to large schools and small ones, in those in which there is a complete accounting office and in those in which accounting is carried on in less extensive form. In most states school statistics are not entirely uniform in all districts, and among states there is frequently a lack of uniformity in the basic information that is compiled. Differences in methods of recording or errors in recording original data cannot later be corrected.

Degree of Permanency Required

The school accounting system should provide for the degree of permanency required in the various types of accounts. Certain basic records of transactions should be kept in such a way that they can be filed for future reference. The filing system should be compact and should not occupy more space than is necessary, so that data may be kept on hand for as many years as the school system desires to keep them. Certainly, information must be kept for a period of at least five years. Some data should be kept longer. Certain statistics might be kept indefinitely. The accounting office should distinguish between information that is to be kept for a short time and that which should be retained permanently.

ACCOUNTING AND BUDGETING

Accounting and budgeting are closely related and interdependent. Without an adequate accounting system, good budgeting is impossible. Many of the more recently developed state and local accounting systems provide for budgetary forms containing the same classification of receipts and expenditures as are found in the accounting system—an arrangement that facilitates comparison throughout.

The classification of receipts in the budget should be the same as that in the cash receipts ledger, and the classification of expenditures should follow the basic accounts. In the budget, expenditures are further classed as (1) current expenditures, including general control, instruction, auxiliary agencies, coordinate activities, operation, maintenance, and fixed charges; (2) capital outlay; and (3) debt service. Different funds are shown by receipts and expenditures for each.

The close relationship of the budget to the accounting system is one that is not always appreciated—sometimes not considered. The budget items provide the initial entries in the distribution ledger and serve as the basis for checking actual expenditures against estimated ones, thus showing the balance unexpended. The accounting system and cost analysis based upon it make possible the construction of an accurate budget for the next fiscal period.

ACCOUNTING RECORDS

Accurate accounting records should be kept of all receipts and expenditures as money is received and paid out. There should also be the basic documents for the authorization of expenditures and for payment of liabilities. In this group of records are those which order payment to persons for services and those for the purchase of materials and supplies. Liabilities for personal services are incurred when contracts are made. Those with teachers constitute by far the largest item of expenditure. Nonteaching personnel such as janitors, custodians, matrons, and other full-time workers usually have less formal contracts but the records nevertheless should show accurately the liabilities incurred. Part-time and temporary workers frequently do not have contracts, but are employed by letter or on the basis of work orders. The latter form is used mostly for the employment of skilled and unskilled labor on particular jobs.

Along with the record of money received and expended there should be a detailed classification of receipts and expenditures according to the classification set up in the accounting system. Usually receipts are listed by type and by sources in a distribution of receipts ledger. Expenditures are recorded in a distribution of expenditures ledger which shows the main expenditure accounts.

Another division that must be made accurately is that which records the different funds that the school system may utilize. Fund accounting requires that receipts and expenditures of each fund must be kept separately. This may vary with the requirements in different states, but usually there is a separation of at least the funds for current expenditure or general operation and the funds for expenditures for buildings and equipment. The reason for fund accounting is that the sources of income and the items of expenditure that may be made from the funds are often prescribed by law.

CODING ACCOUNTS

The main purpose of coding accounts is to facilitate the classification of the expenditures and receipts. Usually the books are set up in such a way that the main items of receipts and expenditures appear on the ledger sheet in various columns. This is shown in some detail on the ledger sheets for the classification of receipts and expenditures. No set of ledger sheets can take care of all the possible classifications that the school system may desire to make. For this reason, a system of coding accounts has been introduced. When properly followed, the code system provides for classification in much greater detail than can be made on the accounting ledgers. Systems for coding accounts differ greatly among states, but it is generally agreed that some system is desirable.

One system of code symbols employs four digit numbers as suggested by Engelhardt and Engelhardt.[14] Receipts are coded as follows: 1,000 to 1,499, revenue receipts; 1,500 to 1,899, nonrevenue receipts; 1,900 to 1,999, revolving fund or transfer fund receipts. The code for expenditures suggested by these authors is by character as follows: 100, general control; 200, instruction; 300, auxiliary agencies; 400, coordinate activities; 500, operation of plant; 600, maintenance of plant; 700, fixed charges; 800 debt service; 900, capital outlay; 1, stores; 50, revolving fund. Other symbols may be used for still other classifications, such as organization units or types of activities, instructional departments, and functions.

The United States Office of Education suggests a simple code to accompany the receipts and expenditures accounts.[15] By this plan revenue receipts are in the 10 to 40 series, nonrevenue receipts in the 50 to 70 series,

[14] Engelhardt and Engelhardt, *op. cit.*
[15] Reason and White, *op. cit.*

and income transfer accounts in the 80 to 90 series. Expenditures are coded as follows: 100 series, administration; 200, instruction; 300 to 400, attendance and health service; 500, pupil transportation service; 600, operation of plant; 700, maintenance of plant; 800, fixed charges; 900 to 1,000, food service and student body activities; 1,100, community service; 1,200, capital outlay; 1,300, debt service from current funds; 1,400, outgoing transfer accounts. This code also uses a series of letters to subdivide accounts.

CLASSIFICATION OF RECEIPTS

School receipts are usually derived from a number of sources, such as property taxation, state appropriations, permanent funds, county sources, and a variety of others. The relative amounts derived from each source depend upon the revenue system of the particular state in which the school system is located. Local property taxation is the major source in some states, whereas in others a substantial portion comes from state non-property taxes, appropriations from the general fund of the state, and receipts from permanent funds. For purposes of record and analysis, school receipts should be grouped according to three generally accepted classifications: (1) revenue, nonrevenue, and revolving fund or transfer accounts, (2) political subdivision from which derived, and (3) specific sources of the money.

Revenue, Nonrevenue, and Incoming Transfer Receipts

The basic classification of receipts places each of them in one of three major groups: revenue, nonrevenue, and incoming transfer accounts. This classification does not refer to the source of the funds or the purposes for which the money may be used but to the nature of the receipts, the regularity or irregularity with which they may be expected, and their relationship to the assets and liabilities of the local unit. Revenue receipts are those which represent additions to cash and do not increase the indebtedness or decrease the assets of the districts. They consist of such items of receipt as tax collections, state aid, and income from permanent funds, all of which may be expected to flow into the treasury rather regularly. Nonrevenue receipts consist of money received which either incurs an obligation that must be met at some future date, or changes the form of an asset from property to cash and thereby decreases the value of school property. Examples of nonrevenue receipts are loans, sale of bonds, and sale of property. They are irregular and are not additions to school money in the sense of revenue receipts, because additional receipts are needed to offset them or assets must be decreased to produce them.

It is important to note that the classification of receipts as to revenue or nonrevenue is determined from the standpoint of the school district receiving the money. An example of a nonrevenue receipt is money borrowed by a school district from the state that must in turn be repaid. An example of a revenue receipt is money received by a school district as a grant that need not be repaid at any future time.

Transfer accounts or revolving funds are net profits from such accounts as the sale of books, supplies, cafeteria, and lunch rooms. They might also include amounts received by a school district in the state for education provided in schools of the receiving district to pupils from the paying district. This is in reality a payment for services rendered. From the standpoint of the state such accounts are actually transfers of funds between school districts and it is necessary in a local district to identify them by having a separate classification known as incoming transfer accounts.

Receipts from Political Subdivisions

Various governmental units from which school money is received constitute a classification that is useful in charting receipts for a period of years. The major units are federal, state, county, and local. The local unit may be the district township, municipality, or town. When classifying receipts under these headings care should be taken to ascertain the sources of the money and to distinguish between the unit as the source of the funds and the unit as an agency for collection only. For example, when poll taxes are collected by the county and returned to the district where collected they should be classed as funds derived from the local district. Again the state may serve in a similar capacity, but when the state collects taxes on one basis and distributes the money to school districts on another basis the amounts received by the districts should be placed under state receipts.

Classification by Source

Classification by source shows the amount of money a district receives from each of the specific sources such as the various taxes—local, county, and state—the different funds from which state aid is paid, and all local sources both revenue and nonrevenue. This classification usually groups receipts as revenue and nonrevenue, listing under each the amount from each source. Such a classification may be suggested in the most general outline only since there is wide variation among states. State accounting systems must be relied upon to furnish the items in the classification but the extent to which state practices have been brought into harmony with an accepted standard is helpful.

The outline of basic receipts accounts is that suggested by the United States Office of Education in its Handbook II, *Financial Accounting for*

Local and State School Systems.[16] This classification shows the three major series for classifying receipts as revenue, nonrevenue, and incoming transfers. The classification of receipts accounts follows:

Revenue receipts, 10 to 40 series
    10   Revenue from local sources
          11   Taxation and appropriations received
          12   Tuition from patrons
          13   Transportation fees from patrons
          14   Other revenue from other sources
    20   Revenue from intermediate sources
    30   Revenue from state sources
    40   Revenue from federal sources
Nonrevenue receipts, 50 to 70 series
    50   Sale of bonds
    60   Loans
    70   Sale of school property insurance adjustments
Incoming transfer accounts, 80 to 90 series
    80   Amounts received from other school districts in the state
    90   Amounts received from school districts in another state

This system of the classification of receipts may be used with almost any form of local school accounting. The suggestion made in the manual cited gives only basic classification and does not suggest the particular type of account forms to be used. The form of the ledger sheets for accounting for receipts is not suggested here since there is great variation in state accounting forms. The books based upon the accounts described in Handbook II must be adapted to the state accounting system.

The basic classification of receipts may be subdivided as much as necessary. All receipts are recorded on the receipts ledger on the date the money is received. Space is provided for distribution among the principal subdivisions of revenue, nonrevenue, and incoming transfer accounts. Further subdivisions are made by means of numbers or code entries and should be totaled and checked at the close of each month. When receipts must be kept separate by different funds, the same forms may be used for each fund. The keeping of many separate funds should be avoided except where state law requires fund accounting as when building funds are set up separately from current funds.

CLASSIFICATION OF EXPENDITURES

Several methods might be used for classifying school expenditures but the most widely accepted one is that based on the character classification or some modification of it. The useful subclassification of expenditures is that of current expenditures, capital expenditures, and debt service.

[16] *Ibid.,* pp. 6–7.

These are usually recognized in any accounting system and totals may readily be derived from the classification. For example, in the basic expenditure accounts listed below, all series 100 through 1,100 are essentially current expenditures while series 1,200 is capital outlay; 1,300, debt service; and 1,400, outgoing transfer accounts. The series of accounts for expenditures suggested by the United States Office of Education suggests a somewhat different classification than that used formally in many state accounting systems. Under the expenditure accounts suggested in the 1957 handbook, the major character classes are somewhat different from those suggested in the earlier reports. For example, there are separate accounts for attendance and health services, food services and student body activities, and community services, making a total of nine major classifications under current expenditures. This classification of major current expenditure accounts is listed below.

Administration, 100 series; instruction, 200; attendance and health service, 300 to 400; pupil transportation service, 500; operation of plant, 600; maintenance of plant, 700; fixed charges, 800; food service and student body activities, 900 to 1,000; community service, 1,100; capital outlay, 1,200; debt service from current funds, 1,300; and outgoing transfer accounts, 1,400.

This classification by function and object is of value in management and cost analysis. Provision is usually made in larger school systems for classifying expenditures in at least three ways by means of a code. The numbers suggested by the United States Office of Education plan would also serve this purpose. The functional classification consists of such items as administration, attendance, maintenance, janitorial service, and supervisory service. The object classification groups expenditures by items such as advertising, accounting, clerical work, express, freight, lighting, printing, supplies, and textbooks. Usually separate ledger sheets are provided in the distribution ledger for each of the major character classifications, or it may be possible to combine two accounts on one ledger sheet as is sometimes done. Further subdivision of the items of expenditure is made by means of a code. Subdivision of the basic character classes varies somewhat among the states that have adopted uniform accounting systems, not only in the amount of detail but also in the terminology used. Such systems are becoming more uniform and complete than they once were.

Administration

Administration consists of those activities which have for their purpose the general regulation, direction, and control of the affairs of the school district that are district-wide and not confined to one school, subject, or phase of school activity.

Under this heading may be placed expenditures for general regulation and direction of the school such as (1) execution of policies that provide the educational and financial conditions under which the teachers and pupils may carry on the work of the schools to the best advantage, (2) creation of channels through which the educational program may be initiated promptly and effectively, (3) provision for channels through which information may be transmitted to the central office and from the central office to the staff, (4) attainment of operational standards of achievement, (5) preparation of statements and reports, (6) research, and (7) publicity.

Several methods of subdividing administration are possible. The United States Office of Education suggests three divisions: salaries, contracted services, and other expenses. These may be further subdivided to show the expenditures for the board of education, the office of the superintendent, and the office of business administration. The basic classification under administration is shown in the following outline:

Administration, 100 Series
   110   Salaries
          110a   Board of education
          110b   Board secretary's office
          110c   Treasurer's office
          110d   School elections
          110e   Tax collection
          110f   Legal services
          110g   Superintendent's office
          110h   Personnel office
          110i   Public relations
          110j   Centralized research
          110k   Census enumeration
          110l   Office of business administration
          110m   Fiscal control
          110n   Administration of buildings and grounds
          110o   Purchasing office
          110p   Printing and publishing
          110q   Other salaries for administration
   120   Contracted services
   130   Other expenses
          130a   Board of education
          130b   Board secretary's office
          130c   Treasurer's office
          130d   School elections
          130e   Tax collection
          130f   Legal services
          130g   Superintendent's office
          130h   Personnel office
          130i   Public relations
          130j   Centralized research
          130k   Census enumeration
          130l   Office of business administration

130m   Fiscal control
130n   Administration of buildings and grounds
130o   Purchasing office
130p   Printing and publishing
130q   Miscellaneous expenses for administration

Instruction

Instruction consists of those activities dealing directly with or aiding teaching of pupils or improving the quality of teaching. These are the activities of teachers, principals, consultants, supervisors, and guidance personnel. It includes all regular and special teachers on the instructional staff, such as study-hall teachers, counselors, librarians, guidance workers, psychologists, auditorium teachers, and the like.

When any of the teachers or supervisors divide their time between teaching and administration their salaries should be prorated on the basis of time spent in each kind of service. General heading of instruction also includes the teaching materials, such as textbooks, expense for school libraries, and services for the improvement of teaching. The classification of expenditure accounts for instruction is shown below:

Instruction, 200 Series
  210   Salaries
      211   Principals
      212   Consultants or supervisors
      213   Teachers
      214   Other instructional staff
          214a   School librarians
          214b   Audiovisual personnel
          214c   Guidance personnel
          214d   Psychological personnel
          214e   Television instructional personnel
      215   Secretarial and clerical assistants
          215a   Principal's office
          215b   Consultants or supervisors
          215c   Teachers
          215d   Other instructional staff
      216   Other salaries for instruction
  220   Textbooks
  230   School libraries and audiovisual materials
      230a   School library books
      230b   Periodicals and newspapers
      230c   Audiovisual materials
      230d   Other school library expenses
  240   Teaching supplies
  250   Other expenses
      250a   Supplies
      250b   Travel
      250c   Miscellaneous expenses

Attendance and Health Services

This subdivision in the character classification of expenditures replaces a portion of the classification formerly known as auxiliary services, or as auxiliary agencies and coordinated activities. There are two major divisions under this category: attendance, and health services—the 300 series and the 400 series. The main subdivisions are salaries and other expenses of attendance services, and salaries and other expenses of health services. The subgrouping of salaries and expenses may be further subdivided. This character classification embraces all expenditures for the two major items, attendance and health services. The outline is shown below:

Attendance and Health Services, 300 to 400 Series
```
300   Attendance services
      310   Salaries
            310a   Attendance personnel
            310b   Secretarial and clerical personnel
            310c   Other salaries
      320   Other expenses
            320a   Supplies
            320b   Travel
            320c   Miscellaneous expenses
400   Health services
      410   Salaries
            410a   Professional and technical health personnel
                   410a–1   School physicians, including psychiatrists
                   410a–2   School dentists
                   410a–3   School nurses
                   410a–4   School dental hygienists
                   410a–5   Other professional and technical health personnel
            410b   Nonprofessional and nontechnical health personnel
      420   Other expenses
            420a   Supplies
            420b   Travel
            420c   Miscellaneous expenses
```

Pupil Transportation Services

This category formerly was one of the subdivisions under auxiliary services. The importance of accurate records of pupil transportation makes it necessary to have more detailed classification of expenditures in this area and this separate account is desirable. Under this category are listed all salaries of persons having to do with pupil transportation whether they are supervisors, drivers, mechanics, clerks, or others. There is also an account for contracted service, for replacement of vehicles, for insurance, for expenditures in lieu of transportation, and other expenses of operation and maintenance. The subdivisions of pupil transportation services are listed below:

Pupil Transportation Services, 500 Series
510 Salaries
    510a Supervisors
    510b Drivers
    510c Mechanics and other garage employees
    510d Clerks and other employees
520 Contracted services and public carriers
530 Replacements of vehicles
    530a Cash purchase
    530b Lease-purchase and installment-purchase
540 Pupil transportation insurance
550 Expenditures in lieu of transportation
560 Other expenses for operation and maintenance
    560a Gasoline
    560b Lubricants
    560c Tires and tubes
    560d Repair parts
    560e Supplies and expenses for garage operation
    560f Garage and garage equipment repairs
    560g Maintenance of vehicles by private garages
    560h Rent
    560i Miscellaneous expenses

Operation of Plant

Under operation of plant should be entered expenditures for keeping the physical plant open and in use. It includes the salaries of janitors, custodians, and other workers; the cost of fuel, power, light, janitor supplies of all types; care of grounds; telephone; freight, express, and drayage when not allocated to items for which they are incurred.

In this group of accounts are included all current expenses for operation of the plant for the school system except direct expense for pupil transportation, food service, student body activities, and community service. It includes the school plant, central administration offices, warehouse, garage, maintenance shop, teacherages, student dormitories, and other such buildings.

The housing of teachers and students, if rent or fees are collected, is accounted for through clearing accounts and only net expenditures for operation are recorded here. Investment properties are also handled through clearing accounts. The outline of the accounts for operation of plant is listed below:

Operation of Plant, 600 Series
610 Salaries
    610a Plant engineers

610b   Custodial services
610c   Care of grounds
610d   Other salaries for operation of plant
620   Contracted services
630   Heat for buildings
640   Utilities, except heat for buildings
640a   Water and sewerage
640b   Electricity
640c   Gas
640d   Telephone and telegraph
640e   Other utilities
650   Supplies, except utilities
650a   Custodial supplies
650b   Supplies for operation of vehicles
650c   Supplies for care of grounds
650d   Other supplies for operation of plant
660   Other expenses

Maintenance of Plant

Maintenance of plant and equipment means the upkeep of the physical facilities through repair and replacement to keep property in good condition and at equal value. The term maintenance should not be confused with current expenditures as this term is sometimes used nor with operation of plant and capital outlay. For example, grading and seeding lawns for the first time should be charged to capital outlay but keeping lawns in good condition through mowing and raking should be charged to operation of plant. If a portion of the lawn is winterkilled and must be reseeded, that cost is charged to maintenance of sites. Repairs that restore property to its original value are maintenance but if the repair or replacement adds to the value of the property, that portion of the cost which represents an additional value should be charged to capital outlay. When old equipment is turned in and credited on purchases of new equipment the entire amount is charged to capital outlay. The major subdivisions under maintenance of plant are for work, materials, and supplies. The subdivisions under this category are shown below:

Maintenance of Plant, 700 Series
710   Salaries
710a   Grounds
710b   Buildings
710c   Repair of equipment
710d   Manufacture of replacements of equipment
720   Contracted services
720a   Grounds
720b   Buildings
720c   Repair of equipment
730   Replacements of equipment

        730a   Instructional equipment
        730b   Noninstructional equipment
740   Other expenses
        740a   Grounds
        740b   Buildings
        740c   Repair of equipment
        740d   Manufacture of replacements of equipment

Fixed Charges

Fixed charges accounts include stable, recurring expenditures such as insurance, rents, taxes, and pensions. When insurance premiums are fairly uniform from year to year the entire amount should be charged to the year in which the payment is made, but if premiums are paid for the current year and for one or more years in advance, only the amount for the current year should be charged here. The advance payment should be placed under "clearing account, prepaid insurance premiums." This applies to accounting on the accrual basis. If the accounting is on the cash basis the entire amount is charged to the year in which the payment is made. Payments made by the district to teacher retirement funds and direct pensions to teachers should be entered here but not the portion of the teacher's salary deducted for retirement as these amounts are entered under regular salaries.

All forms of insurance expenditures are included here whether they are for property insurance, employees' insurance, liability insurance, or fidelity bond premiums; also expenditures from current funds for judgments against the school district that are not covered by liability insurance are entered here. Rental of land and buildings, interest on current loans, and other types of fixed charges are in this classification. The outline of expenditures for fixed charges is shown below:

Fixed Charges, 800 Series
   810   School district contributions to employee retirement
        810a   State, county, or local retirement funds
        810b   Social security
        810c   Pension payments
   820   Insurance and judgments
        820a   Property insurance
        820b   Employee insurance
        820c   Liability insurance
        820d   Fidelity bond premiums
        820e   Judgments
   830   Rental of land and buildings
        830a   Land and buildings for instructional purposes
        830b   Land and buildings for noninstructional purposes
   840   Interest on current loans
   850   Other fixed charges

Current Expenditures per Pupil

It should be observed that if the calculation of current expenditures per pupil is desired such expenditures should include only administration, instruction, attendance and health services, pupil transportation services, operation of plant, maintenance of plant, and fixed charges. These are the 100 through 800 series of accounts and are included here in determining such expenditures because of their direct relationship and essentiality to the educational program. Excluded in determining current expenditures per pupil are food services and student body activities, community services, capital outlay, debt services, and outgoing transfer accounts. These are the 900 through 1,400 series.

Food Services and Student Body Activities

It should be observed that expenditures for food services and student body activities may be handled in three different ways: (1) entirely supported by the revenue produced through the activity; (2) partly supported by direct expenditure from appropriation and tax money and partly by revenue produced through the activity itself, and (3) entirely supported by expenditure from appropriation and tax money. The manner in which this group of accounts is utilized is dependent upon the method of financing used and whether separate funds are established for these activities. For example, if food services are financed wholly or partly by revenue produced through the operation of the program, the expenditures for food services, for which reimbursement is received from sale of lunches or from state and federal grants, and the revenue from the operation of the program are handled through clearing accounts. Direct expenses for food services for community activities are not recorded under this account but rather under community services.

Student body activities are services for public school pupils, such as interscholastic athletics, entertainments, publications, clubs, bands, orchestra, and other activities that are managed by the student body under guidance and direction of adults and are not part of the regular instructional program. Here again such activities may be handled in different ways but if a student body activity is financed wholly or partially by revenue produced through the operation of the activity, the gross expenditures for the activity, for which total or partial reimbursement is to be received from fees or similar sources, and the revenue from the operation of the activity are handled through "clearing accounts, student body activities."

Provision is made in the regular accounts of the board of education for food service and student body activities because, although they usually take in a certain amount of money and have certain contributions made to them, the board of education accounts must usually be utilized for payment of a portion of these expenditures. The outline of expenditures for food services and student body activities is shown below:

Food Services and Student Body Activities, 900–1000 Series
  900 Food Services
      910 Salaries
      920 Other expenses
      930 Expenditures to cover deficit of a separate food services fund or accounts
  1000 Student Body activities
      1010 Salaries
      1020 Other expenses
      1030 Expenditures to cover deficits of student body activities funds or accounts

Community Services

Community services are those activities provided by the school district for the community as a whole or some segment of the community, excluding public school and adult education programs operated by the school district. In this category are included all salaries and all extensions except contributions to retirement insurance. Retirement funds are recorded under fixed charges. The various subdivisions of community services are shown below:

Community Services, 1100 Series
  1110 Recreation
      1110a Salaries
      1110b Other expenses
  1120 Civic activities
      1120a Salaries
      1120b Other expenses
  1130 Public libraries
      1130a Salaries
      1130b Books, periodicals, and newspapers
      1130c Other expenses
  1140 Custodial and detention care of children
      1140a Salaries
      1140b Other expenses
  1150 Welfare activities
      1150a Salaries
      1150b Other expenses
  1160 Non-public school pupils
      1161 Instructional services
          1161a Textbooks
          1161b Other expenses
      1162 Attendance and health services
          1162a Attendance
          1162b Health
      1163 Transportation services

Capital Outlay

Capital outlay expenditures are those which are made for the acquisition of fixed assets or additions to fixed assets. They include the acquisition of new land and sites, new buildings and equipment, additions and alterations to old buildings, and other relatively large items that increase the value of school property. This category does not include the expenditures for school supplies and for maintenance. The distinction between equipment and supplies is often difficult to make and for that reason many state accounting systems provide lengthy lists of items in each category.

Under capital outlay are also included items such as the salary of architects and engineers and other personnel employed for building planning, and expenditures for the initial installation or the extension of service systems. The upkeep of service systems, however, is charged under maintenance of plant.

Expenditures for the replacement of a building which has been totally destroyed are placed under capital outlay but the repair of damaged buildings is maintenance except when additions are made to the plant. Insurance adjustment received for loss or damage of property is placed under "clearing accounts, insurance adjustment."

Capital outlay expenditures may be made from current revenue or from the sale of bonds. The classification of expenditures has no reference to the source of the funds. Although payments to public school housing authorities or similar agencies may appear to be capital outlay it is suggested that they be recorded under debt service. The subdivisions in capital outlay are shown below:

Capital Outlay, 1200 Series
    1210   Sites
             1210a   Professional services
             1210b   Sites and site additions
             1210c   Improvements to sites
    1220   Buildings
             1220a   Professional services
             1220b   New buildings and building additions
             1220c   Remodeling
    1230   Equipment
             1230a   Professional services
             1230b   Administration
             1230c   Instruction
             1230d   Attendance and health
             1230e   Pupil transportation
             1230f   Operation of plant
             1230g   Maintenance of plant
             1230h   Food services and student body activities

      1230i   Community services
      1230j   Investment property

Debt Service from Current Funds

Debt service includes expenditures for the retirement of debt and expenditures for interest on debt except principal and interest on current loans and money borrowed and paid back during the same fiscal year. Money borrowed and paid back during the same fiscal year is handled under "clearing accounts, current and short-term loans." Interest on such loans is recorded under "fixed charges, interest on current loans."

It should be observed that this heading includes expenditures for debt service from current funds. Current funds consist of money received during the current fiscal year from the revenue receipts which can be used to pay obligations currently due and surpluses reappropriated for the current fiscal year. Payments from sinking funds and refunding of bonds are handled through clearing accounts. The main subdivisions under debt service from current funds are shown below:

Debt Service from Current Funds, 1300 Series
  1310   Principal of debt
        1310a   Bonds
        1310b   Short-term loans
        1310c   Long-term loans
        1310d   Warrant or bills of preceding years
  1320   Interest on debt
        1320a   Bonds
        1320b   Short-term loans
        1320c   Long-term loans
  1330   Amounts paid into sinking funds
  1340   Expenditures to school housing authority or similar agency
        1340a   Principal
        1340b   Interest
  1350   Other debt service

Outgoing Transfer Accounts

The United States Office of Education suggests a category for outgoing transfer accounts to include expenditures made to other school districts or administrative units. Some of the reasons for this special category of expenditures are: (1) Such expenditures are usually made in lieu of many different expense items, they may cut across other expenditure classifications and are not readily chargeable to any one classification; (2) There are actually no membership or attendance data to which the paying district can relate these expenditures; and (3) From the standpoint of the state or the nation such expenditures represent transfer of funds between school districts and in order to avoid duplication in consolidated data it is necessary to identify such expenditures. The major classification of outgoing accounts is listed below:

Outgoing Transfer Accounts, 1400 Series
    1410   Expenditures to other school districts or administrative units in the state
            1410a   Tuition
            1410b   Transportation
            1410c   Miscellaneous
    1420   Expenditures to school districts or administrative units in another state
            1420a   Tuition
            1420b   Transportation
            1420c   Miscellaneous
    1430   Tuition to other than public schools
            1430a   Private nonsectarian schools
            1430b   Individuals

Prorating Expenditures

As the public schools offer to more and more groups in the community such services as adult education and the extension of public education to encompass grades 13 and 14, there are likely to be many expenditures which cut across the outlined accounts as given in this chapter. For this reason it is desirable, if accurate costs are to be derived, that certain expenditures be prorated among the categories. For example, a teacher spends one-half of his time in the high school grades 9 to 12 and one-half of his time in a junior college, grades 13 and 14; his salary would be prorated, one-half to high school costs and one-half to junior college costs.

The method of proration depends upon the nature of the expenditure. Some of the more common bases used for prorating are time consumed, floor area, average daily membership or average daily attendance, hour consumption, number of pupils, mileage, and quantity consumed. Such proration should be made at the time the original expenditure is made, dividing the expenditure among the categories and indicating by code the accounts to which charged. Over a period of time standards for proration may be established in a school system. It is usually desirable to use rather simple divisions such as one-half, one-fourth, or one-fifth if time is involved. If other methods of prorating are used the division may be stated more accurately. The alternative to proration would be to charge the item to the category to which the largest proportion is chargeable. As an approximate method this may serve in some school systems, although exact figures cannot be obtained by this method.

CLEARING ACCOUNTS

There are a number of accounts in a school district which have been known as revolving fund accounts, advancement accounts, or clearing accounts. These accounts involve receipt and expenditure of money outside the regular board of education receipts and expenditures classifications. Sometimes such accounts have been termed internal accounts. The classification "clearing accounts" is a somewhat broader term and includes all types of accounts that are kept in connection with the regular receipts and expenditures accounts. They embrace the recording of gross amounts received and paid out for such purposes as food services, student body activities, the purchase and sale of textbooks, refunding of bonds, the purchase and sale of securities, trust funds, and property rentals.

It may readily be observed that these accounts have a definite place in the school district books because sometimes considerable amounts of money are received and expended in the cycle of operations of the activities embraced in the accounts. When all receipts and expenditures for these accounts are carried in the regular books of the school district, they are likely to distort the financial picture with respect to amount available for expenditure by the board of education. The transactions in question generally concern the following: (1) activities financed wholly or in part by a revenue produced by the activity, (2) repayments or advancements, (3) abatements, (4) exchange of one asset or liability for another asset or liability, (5) interfund transfers, (6) current loans, and (7) insurance adjustments.

If any of these activities are subsidized by the board of education, the accounts are cleared at the end of the year and any net balance is recorded under the regular receipts and any net deficits under the regular classification of expenditures. If such accounts are not subsidized by the board of education, any balance or deficit at the end of the year is carried over in the accounts of the next fiscal year. The classification of clearing accounts is shown below:

Clearing Accounts, 1500–1900 Series
    1500   Asset accounts
            1510   Petty-cash fund
            1520   Stores
            1530   Prepaid insurance premiums
            1540   Prepaid rent
            1550   Securities
                   1550a   Money received
                   1550b   Money paid out
            1560   Sinking-fund account
                   1560a   Money received
                   1560b   Money paid out
                          1560b–1   Bonds
                          1560b–2   Interest
    1600   Liability accounts
            1610   Current and short-term loans
                   1610a   Money received
                   1610b   Money paid out
            1620   Deductions from payroll
                   1620a   Money received
                   1620b   Money paid out

1700   Food services operation accounts
     1710   Money received
          1711   Money received from the state
               1711a   State
               1711b   Federal
          1712   Money received from other sources
               1712a   Money received from the sale of food
               1712b   Miscellaneous sources
     1720   Money paid out
          1720a   Salaries
          1720b   Food
          1720c   Additional equipment
          1720d   Replacement of equipment
          1720e   Other expenses
1800   Other operation accounts
     1810   Student body activities
          1811   Athletics
               1811a   Money received
               1811b   Money paid out
          1812   School entertainments
               1812a   Money received
               1812b   Money paid out
          1813   School publications
               1813a   Money received
               1813b   Money paid out
          1814   School clubs and other cocurricular activities
               1814a   Money received
               1814b   Money paid out
     1820   Materials for resale
          1820a   Money received
          1820b   Money paid out
     1830   Textbooks
          1830a   Money received
          1830b   Money paid out
     1840   Operation of investment properties
          1840a   Money received
          1840b   Money paid out
1900   Miscellaneous accounts
     1910   Refunding bonds
          1910a   Money received
          1910b   Money paid out
     1920   Abatements
          1920a   Money received
          1920b   Money paid out
     1930   Insurance adjustments
          1930a   Money received
          1930b   Money paid out
     1940   Interfund transfers
          1940a   Money received
          1940b   Money paid out

INCURRING AND MEETING LIABILITIES

In addition to the classification of receipts and expenditures and a proper entry of figures in the various categories, it is necessary for the accounting system to have subsidiary accounts which provide for the incurring and meeting of liabilities. Under this heading should be placed the entire procedure for making purchases of one kind or another and the procedure for paying personnel. These are generally known as purchasing procedures and payroll procedures.

Liabilities for personal services are incurred when contracts are drawn. Those with teachers constitute by far the largest item of expenditure. Nonteaching personnel such as janitors, custodians, matrons, and other full-time workers usually have contracts and may be paid on the basis of a salary schedule adopted for the particular group of workers. Part-time and temporary workers frequently do not have contracts but are employed by letter or voucher on the basis of work orders. The latter form is used mostly for the employment of skilled and unskilled labor on particular jobs.

Work orders usually state the type of work to be done, the specific jobs, the hours or days to be devoted to the job, the rate of pay, and the time when work should be completed. As stated before, much work can be accomplished merely by an informal agreement; however, a simple form of contract or work order is desirable.

Purchase Accounting

The first step in the purchasing of materials and supplies is usually the requisition, arising in the school department for which the purchase is made. The second step is the preparation of the bid form if bids are to be secured. Usually, bids are required if the order for materials exceeds a certain amount, say $500 or $1,000. The next step is the preparation of the purchase order, or the voucher authorizing the purchase and payment, and the record incident to the purchase. The requisition initiates the purchase, gives a description of the items to be purchased, and the necessary specifications. This form is usually sent by the department to the central office. The requisition is not an order but a request to the central office. It is usually made out in duplicate or triplicate, depending upon the number of copies needed for filing. In the central office the requisitions are checked against the available funds and, if the materials or supplies requisitioned are to be purchased on bids, the bid form is prepared and sent to the vendors. This form gives the specifications for the purchase to be made. When bids are received, the successful bidder is sent a purchase order for the goods. This is the instrument which incurs the liability, although it is subject to certain correction in the amount of the expenditure. The purchase order is made out in as many copies as are necessary for proper filing. Requisition, bid, and purchase order forms are shown in Chapter 23.

When the accounting for the purchasing of materials and supplies is well organized, each step clearly defined, and adequate records kept, any purchase can be traced from its initiation to the final payment of the goods. This is essential in maintaining good relations with personnel within the school as well as with vendors and their representatives.

Although the requisition and purchase orders are essential steps in the procedure for procuring goods and services, the instrument authorizing payment is usually referred to as the voucher. There are several types of vouchers in common use, among which are the check, order, or warrant; the voucher check; and the voucher jacket. The check or school order is more commonly used in small school systems where the accounting procedure is relatively simple. It consists of a check or order, usually with some space on it to show the account classification to which the expenditure should be charged. The voucher check is a combination of the check and an attached portion on which are recorded the details concerning the payment, such as discounts, amount actually paid, purchase order number, and invoice number. The voucher portion is detached before presentation for payment. The voucher jacket, as the name implies, is a jacket or folded paper on the obverse side of which is recorded the necessary information concerning the purchase. On the reverse side may be the name of the school unit for which the purchase is made and on the inside is a list of items as shown on the distribution ledger with convenient space for entering the amount of the payment that should be charged to each account. A voucher jacket is convenient for school systems that use the check or school order for payment of bills. The jacket may be folded in such a way as to form a pocket into which may be placed the requisition, purchase order, invoice, cancelled check, and any other matter relating to the purchase. Vouchers are numbered serially and filed in that order with a cross index to the vendor's file or other classification.

Payroll Accounting

The proper management of payroll procedure is an essential part in the maintenance of the morale of the teaching staff and other school employees. The annual salary, the monthly salary, the time of payment, deductions for absences or illnesses, deductions for retirement provisions, withholding tax, and similar items should be clearly stated in the contract entered into by the school employees and the board of education. In addition to the contractual agreement there should be given to each employee clear instructions concerning the operation of the salary schedule, additions and deductions made, school board policies and the like. In order to carry out the contractual obligations without delay, the school must set up a thoroughgoing procedure of accounting and provision for payment of salaries at such times as they are called for in the agreement. The preparation of a payroll and the accurate accounting for the absences of teachers or other employees due to illness or other causes must be made. The compensation of substitute teachers and additional workers must be computed and checks should be drawn and delivered with dispatch.

The work of preparing the payroll is a function of the central office but the necessary information must be supplied by principals of the various schools and by the superintendent of schools. The principals must provide the information concerning teacher absences, substitute teaching, and the proportion of time spent by teachers in the various divisions of the school system. Such information should be reported to the payroll office accurately and regularly, as it is the basis for making deductions and for the allocation of cost to the different units of the system. Any change of status of a teacher, either in salary or in position, as well as the established policies of salary payments as set forth in contracts, should be reported by the superintendent of schools. The chief custodian or superintendent of buildings and grounds should make reports on his employees and workers, both full-time and part-time. Payroll accounting forms should be cumulative in order to reduce duplication in entering names and other essential data. A payroll calculator should be available showing the amount of the deductions for different purposes and the amount actually paid teachers.

MACHINE ACCOUNTING

In many of the smaller school systems, the manner of keeping the various accounts and records by hand posting seems to be quite adequate. In the larger systems, however, when the operations are multiplied many times, it may be desirable to use machine accounting. It is difficult to say when a school system is large enough to justify machine accounting, but several factors must be taken into consideration in making this decision. Among these factors are the size of the school system and the number of different accounts that must be kept, the cost of clerical help for hand posting as compared with the cost for machine posting, the specific jobs or tasks that are to be carried on by machines, and the number of different records that must be kept.

There are on the market many different kinds of accounting machines which may be adapted for school use. The boards of education and school administrators who are interested in machine accounting should decide on what they want done by machine accounting and should then confer with some of the leading firms that manufacture machine accounting equipment to see that they receive the kind of equipment that will best carry on the particular jobs that they wish done. Careful analysis of the entire accounting procedure is necessary before a school system enters upon the machine accounting operations.

COST ANALYSIS

The information provided in the financial accounting system is basic for studies of cost of the educational program. Such studies have their greatest value for school administrators who are responsible for financial management and for the determination of school policies. For these purposes, the analysis of annual statements and periodic reports is needed to show trends of past periods as well as to reveal current financial conditions. Accurate analysis of cost is essential to effective control of the educational enterprise and is an aid in explaining the work of the schools to those who are interested. The accounting system should provide the necessary information to answer such questions as the following: (1) What has been the annual cost of education in the community during preceding years, and what is it likely to be during the next fiscal period? (2) How does the cost of education in one community compare with that in other similar communities? (3) What is the cost of education as compared with the cost of the various other types of public services that are maintained? (4) What is the cost of the various types of educational services that the schools provide? (5) What is the cost of the various educational departments maintained and the cost of teaching the various subjects? (6) What is the cost of maintaining such services as transportation of pupils, maintenance of isolated pupils' payments in lieu of transportation, and maintenance of summer playgrounds? (7) What is the cost of education in relation to the resources of the community and the state?

Value of Cost Studies

The knowledge of the cost of an element in the school program is a factor in the determination of the policy that is adopted for its management. The knowledge that dental service in a school costs a given amount is a factor in determining how such service is to be administered. The information that the cost of teaching English is only one-half as much as that of teaching chemistry may be helpful in the administration of the school that offers these subjects. In both situations the cost is not the only factor to be considered, but it is one of the important factors on which information is needed for the management of a school.

The detailed study of costs in a school system may frequently reveal ways and means whereby economies can be effected, either by securing the same materials or services at a lower cost or by securing better materials or services for the same cost. When, for example, it is possible to purchase supplies of standard quality at a lower cost through consolidation of one-room rural schools, the economy should be considered. Good economy is always in order. Only when savings of money are made at the expense of vital elements in the education program is economy decried as the "bogus" kind. Knowledge of the facts relative to cost is necessary in order to economize wisely.

The cost of the various elements in the school program is a necessary item in case changes in the program are contemplated. Before new courses are offered or additional activities are initiated, the superintendent and the board of education may be called upon to answer questions concerning the cost of the offering or activity. Moreover, cost figures for past years are needed for predicting the expenditures that will be necessary in the budget for the ensuing year, for estimating the additional revenue that will be required because of increases in school enrollment, or for calculating future building needs.

Comparative Costs

Facts on comparative cost throw light on what is current practice, but these should not be interpreted as setting a standard to which all schools should conform. Variation from school to school is to be expected. When a particular community is greatly out of line with others that are similar, it may mean only that reasons should be sought for the variation. Differences in the school program and in the conditions under which programs are carried on will account for some of the variations.

Much of the complaint that is made concerning higher educational costs reflects the point of view of local taxpayers who see only the proportion of their tax bills that is devoted to school purposes. Frequently one-third to one-half of local taxes levied and collected is for education. This is in part due to the fact that a relatively large share of school revenue has been left to the local school units which are almost entirely dependent upon the property tax for their funds. What is lost sight of is the fact that there are many other sources of public revenue utilized mainly by federal and state governments which are productive of large sums of money but many of which are more indirect than the property tax or which reach a relatively small proportion of taxpayers. It is manifestly unfair to education in districts where 50 per cent of the local tax goes for schools to say that education costs as much as all other governmental functions put together. Such objections come from local taxpayers who see from their tax bills what the schools are costing but who seldom complain of the cost of highways or governmental services since only a

small part of the cost of these objects may appear on the property tax
bill.

A better method of comparison of school costs with costs for other
local and state governments would be to show the proportion that schools
are costing of total public money spent. Frequently this may be within
a state for all local and state expenditures. The cost for schools would
be a much smaller proportion than when it is compared with the amount
of property tax collected.

Another very common method of comparing costs is from one school
system to another. A caution should be mentioned in this respect. School
costs are usually not comparable unless the school systems themselves are
comparable. Differences in size of schools and scope of programs frequently make it impossible to make a fair comparison. Methods of
processing data to make fair comparisons possible are given in Chapter 7.

Unit Costs

Perhaps the most important consideration in the computation of unit
costs is the selection of appropriate units to express costs. In stating the
cost of teaching, the per pupil unit has been one of the most widely
used. Pupil costs may be expressed in terms of kinds of pupil measures
such as the average daily attendance, the average daily membership, or,
better, some weighted pupil measure as described in Chapter 7. When
computing the cost of operation and maintenance of school plant, for
example, it is obvious that the pupil measure is not the satisfactory one
to use, but rather the number of square feet or cubic feet of building
space. In the case of heating the amount of space to be heated, the number
of cubic feet is a satisfactory measure. In the case of janitorial service,
cleaning and the like, the amount of floor space is obviously more appropriate than any other.

SUMMARY

Financial accounting for public school systems has developed greatly
in recent decades. The basic principles of accounting—the classification
of receipts and expenditures according to the purposes, character or object for which the expenditures are made—have become more clearly
recognized. Much progress has been made by the United States Office of
Education in the preparation and distribution of handbooks that provide
the basis upon which accounting should be made and Handbook II, referred to in this chapter, gives a comprehensive classification of receipts,
expenditures, and clearing accounts.

Financial accounting provides the information upon which efficient
management depends, makes possible cost accounting, and shows in

detail the receipts by general classification and the sources from which funds are derived. The expenditure classification provides the basis for budgeting and auditing and shows the cost of the various character categories of school expenditure as well as the cost for different departments and grade levels.

Although school financial accounting draws upon the principles and practices of accounting in private industry and of municipal and governmental accounting, it has developed a distinctive set of accounts peculiar to the nature of the enterprise. In this development certain agencies such as the National Education Association, the National Association of Public School Business Officials and the United States Office of Education have given outstanding leadership. The efforts of these organizations have been supplemented by a large number of individual studies made in different states. A rather comprehensive and complete set of financial accounts is now available for school use.

School accounting in its better form as practiced today in most city school systems embraces: (1) the original records of all financial transactions, including such documents as the voucher, the purchase order, the bid form, requisitions, and invoices; (2) complete records of all receipts classified by principal sources and of all expenditures classified and coded by purpose, instructional function, and object; (3) the necessary books and records for various individuals, such as the clerk or secretary of a school district and a treasurer, as required by law in many states; (4) the complete system of monthly and annual reports to the board of education and the annual reports to state and national agencies.

School financial accounting may be on the cash basis, that is, recording all cash payments received and all cash expenditures made at the time of receipt or purchase; or it may be on an accrual basis under which revenues are recorded when earned or when levies are made and expenditures are recorded as soon as they result in liabilities, regardless of when the revenue is actually received or the payment is actually made.

The increased importance placed upon receipts from other school districts, such as tuition, transportation, and other miscellaneous receipts, has led to a classification of such receipts under incoming transfer accounts. Under expenditures such categories as food service and student body activities are receiving more emphasis than formerly. This is because such activities are usually supported in part by self-sustaining accounts and in part by expenditures made by the school district. Because such services are to the community as a whole, with the possible exception of public school and adult education programs operated by the school district, the category *outgoing transfer accounts* provides for payments to other school districts for tuition, transportation, and other miscellaneous purposes. It also includes payments to individuals and nonsectarian schools. A system of clearing accounts has been set up to take care of such items as petty cash funds, stores, prepaid insurance premiums, prepaid rent, securities, and sinking fund. Other accounts in this general category are set up for other operating accounts and miscellaneous accounts.

QUESTIONS FOR STUDY AND DISCUSSION

1. What are the purposes of financial accounting? Show how these purposes are realized in the financial accounting used in schools in your state.

2. Show the trends of school costs in your state from 1900 to the present time. Use total costs, current expenditures, or teachers' salary costs. Plot the trend on coordinate sheets.

3. From handbooks of financial accounting systems or from local school systems show the following: (*a*) proration of superintendent's salary and office expense when he engages in both educational and business administration, (*b*) distinction between replacement and new equipment, (*c*) distinction between items of equipment and supply.

4. Show several types of vouchers. What type is used in your state? What is the form of the voucher register?

5. Secure copies of all financial accounting records in your state. Examine them carefully and compare them with the accounting classification as shown in this chapter.

6. Show how the purposes of financial accounting are realized in your state. What reports are made? What analyses of cost are made on a state-wide basis.

7. What clearing accounts are kept in the accounting system of your state? Are these separated out or are they placed in the regular categories of current and capital expenditures?

8. In the distribution of expenditures, to which character category and subdivision would you charge the following:

   a. Five gallons of ink for general use throughout the school system.
   b. Five gallons of paint for interior work on an elementary school building.
   c. Refreshments for a board of education party.
   d. Uniforms for the football team.
   e. A load of lumber for woodworking shops.
   f. Twelve new brooms and twelve floor mops.
   g. Part-time salary for a city librarian.
   h. Ballots for a board election.
   i. Fifty auditorium chairs, one-half as replacement and one-half as additional equipment.

9. Study the development of financial accounting for public schools by comparing United States Office of Education reports—Circular No. 204, 1940; Handbook I, *The Common Core of State Educational Information*, 1953; and Handbook II, *Financial Accounting for Local and State School Systems*, 1957— and handbook used in your state.

10. Show by example a number of items of expenditure from a school system, either actual or hypothetical, and indicate how they should be prorated. Show also how unit costs should be computed for various items of expenditure.

SELECTED REFERENCES

Engelhardt, Fred, and Fred Von Borgersrode: *Accounting Procedure for School Systems*, Bureau of Publications, Teachers College, Columbia University, New York, 1927.

Engelhardt, N. L., and Fred Engelhardt: *Public School Business Administration*, Bureau of Publications, Teachers College, Columbia University, New York, 1927.

Fowlkes, John Guy: *Principles and Practices of Financial Accounting for Schools*, Eau Claire, Wis., E. M. Hale and Co., Publishers, 1934.

Linn, Henry H.: *School Business Administration*, chap. 6, The Ronald Press Company, New York, 1956.

Reason, Paul L., Emory M. Foster, and Robert F. Will: *The Common Core of State Educational Information*, Handbook I, U.S. Office of Education, Washington, 1953.

―――, and Alvius L. White: *Financial Accounting for Local and State School Systems*, Handbook II, U.S. Office of Education, Washington, 1953.

Rosenstengel, William E., and Jefferson N. Eastman: *School Finance*, chaps. 11 and 12, The Ronald Press Company, New York, 1957.

Tidwell, Sam B.: "Fundamental School Fund Accounting," *American School Board Journal*, May, 1957, pp. 37–38.

U.S. Office of Education: *Financial Accounting for Public Schools*, Preliminary Report of the National Advisory Committee on School Records and Reports, Circular 204, Federal Security Agency, Washington, 1940.

21. Finance and personnel service

CURRENT expenditures may be divided for budgeting, accounting, and reporting purposes into two groups—those for personal services and those for materials and supplies. The first group of these expenditures is by far the larger, constituting probably three-fourths of the total. Of the expenditures for personal services the salaries of teachers frequently constitute a large part. Salaries of other employees such as janitors, engineers, bus drivers, etc., are as a rule relatively small except in those districts having extensive transportation programs. Consideration of the school personnel in relation to finance is important not only because of the relatively large payments that are made for personal services, but also because the quality of education depends to a large extent upon the qualifications of the personnel employed.

Nowhere in the system is financial expenditure more directly related to the quality of education than in the financing of personnel, especially the teaching personnel. Some of the areas of personnel administration that are directly concerned with financial management are teachers' salary schedules, leaves of absence, retirement, and certain other teacher benefits.

Perhaps one of the most common criticisms one hears of school salaries is that they are too low. Studies show that teachers' salaries have been low as compared with other professional workers for a long period of time. While there is some fluctuation, the general trend has put them somewhere between wages of skilled and unskilled workers.

TREND OF TEACHERS' SALARIES

Although the trend of teachers' salaries from 1919 to 1957 was generally upward, it was marked by certain short-time fluctuations and by certain constant differentials throughout the period. Short-time fluctua-
406

tions may appear in a school system during times of local economic change or changes in the revenue system or under changing conditions of supply. For the nation as a whole, the most noticeable fluctuations were during the period of the depression in the early 1930s when salaries decreased rapidly to about 1935 and rose steadily to about 1942, after which increases accelerated during the postwar period. This general trend held for all types of schools throughout the various regions of the United States.

Salary Variations in City School Systems

The constant differentials in teachers' salaries are those present in the different levels of the educational program such as among elementary schools, junior high schools, and senior high schools, and the differences in schools of different size. The general tendency has been that teachers in the upper grades, especially the senior high schools, have been paid higher salaries than those in junior high or elementary schools. Again, teachers in the larger city school systems have been paid higher salaries than those in the smaller cities or in rural areas. Perhaps there is a relationship here between salary and the qualifications of teachers, although in individual cities or school systems this may not be the case. The present tendency toward the single salary schedule should do much to offset differences in salaries among teachers of different grade levels but with the same qualifications. Also, teachers of the same qualifications in different size school systems should be paid more nearly equal salaries.

The trend of teacher's salaries from 1929–1930 to 1953–1954 as shown in a recent United States Office of Education publication [1] shows that in the former year the expenditure for salaries of the instructional staff was $1,250,427,194 whereas in the latter it was $4,200,542,046. To put it another way, the earlier expenditures were but 29.8 per cent of the later expenditures. Another comparison can be made between the average salary per instructional staff member in 1929–1930 and that in 1953–1954. This includes all members of the instructional staff in the various states and levels of education. In 1929–1930 this average salary was $1,420 whereas in the 1953–1954 it was $3,825 or the earlier figures were 37.1 per cent of the later salaries, an increase of nearly three times during the period.

Salaries as Percentage of Current Expenditures

Still another indication of the trend of salaries is shown in the percentage of total current expenditures devoted to salaries of the instruc-

[1] Clayton D. Hutchins and Albert R. Munse, *Trends in Significant Facts on School Finance, 1929–30 to 1953–54,* U.S. Office of Education, Circular No. 498, Washington, 1957.

tional staff for the same period of time. This shows that in 1929–1930, 67.8 per cent of current expenditures was used for the salaries of teachers, whereas in 1953–1954, 61 per cent of current expenditures was used for salaries, a decrease of 6.8 per cent.

Another comparison of salary trends is revealed in the bulletins of the Research Division of the National Education Association which show that the average salary for teachers in elementary schools in cities of 30,000 to 100,000 population in 1940–1941 was $1,608 whereas in 1956–1957 it was $4,454, an increase of 177 per cent. In junior high schools in cities of the same size, the average salary of teachers in the former year was $1,847 while in the latter it was $4,783, a 159 per cent increase. In senior high schools the average salary in 1940–1941 was $2,039 whereas in 1956–1957 it was $5,135, an increase of 151.8 per cent.[2]

Variations in Teachers' Salaries among States

When comparing the various states with respect to salaries paid teachers, an estimated average salary is used. This estimated average salary varies greatly among the states. For example, in 1957–1958 the five states that paid the highest average salaries to classroom teachers in public schools were: California, $5,750; New York, $5,687; Delaware, $5,450; New Jersey, $5,210; and Washington, $5,175. The five states that paid the lowest average salaries were: South Carolina, $3,250; South Dakota, $3,250; Arkansas, $3,180; Kentucky, $3,125; and Mississippi, $2,525. During the same year the average for the United States was $4,520. Utah had an estimated average salary for classroom teachers of $4,650; Ohio, $4,525; Indiana, $4,500; Louisiana, $4,450.

When one considers the estimated average salaries of the entire instructional staff in public schools for the same year he finds that these averages are somewhat higher since they include administrative officers. California ranks first with $5,925 and Mississippi is the lowest with $2,650. The average for the United States was $4,650.[3]

FACTORS AFFECTING TEACHERS' SALARIES

A consideration of the factors that underlie teachers' salaries shows that the employment and retention of efficient teachers must be accompanied by salaries that are commensurate with the services they render, adequate to maintain a satisfactory standard of living, and comparable to salaries paid employees in other occupations and professions that require

[2] National Education Association, Research Division: "Salaries and Salary Schedules of Urban School Employees, 1956–57," *Research Bulletin,* vol. 35, no. 2, p. 74, Washington, April, 1957.

[3] National Education Association, *Ranking of the States,* Washington, 1957.

similar training. The relation of teachers' salaries to general economic conditions reveals that salaries tend to fluctuate with such conditions, somewhat as do wages of skilled and unskilled workers. In periods of economic stress, teachers' salaries tend to become lower and in periods of inflation they rise, although the range may not be as great as in the case of wages and there may be more lag in the salary levels.

Economic Changes

During the economic depression of the 1930s, the average salaries of teachers dropped considerably below the figures reached in 1930–1931. For example, the average teachers' salaries in that year for elementary school teachers in cities of 30,000 to 100,000 population was $1,609, whereas four years later they had dropped to $1,412 and did not again reach the predepression level until 1940–1941. Similarly, the average of junior high school teachers' salaries in cities of the same size dropped from $1,860 to $1,612 and were back up to $1,847 in 1940–1941. The average salary for senior high school teachers in the same group of cities dropped from $2,111 in 1930–1931 to $1,834 in 1934–1935 and were up to $2,039 in 1940–1941.[4]

In times of rising income and costs, salaries rise rapidly and are likely to remain at a high level. This is shown in the trend from 1946–1947 to 1956–1957. During this period, the average salary of elementary school teachers in cities of 30,000 to 100,000 increased from $2,288 to $4,454. Junior high school teachers' salaries in the same group of cities increased from $2,546 to $4,787. Senior high school teachers' salaries in this group of cities rose from $2,774 in 1946–1947 to $5,135 in 1956–1957.[5]

Not only do periods of depression and prosperity affect teachers' salaries, but the general level of prices has a direct effect upon them. While salaries have increased in dollars, it is not at all certain that in gross dollars they rise or fall with the purchasing power of the dollar.

Supply and Demand

The supply and demand of teachers is also related to salaries paid. When the supply exceeds the demand as it did during the 1930 depression, there is a tendency to reduce salaries, whereas in times when the demand exceeds the supply as during World War II, there is a tendency for salaries to rise. Periodic studies are needed to show the relation of the supply of teachers to the demand, and measures should be taken to maintain a fair balance between the number of persons entering the

[4] National Education Association, *Research Bulletin*, Washington, vol. 50, no. 2, and vol. 23, no. 1, March, 1937, and February, 1945.

[5] National Education Association, *Research Bulletin*, Washington, vol. 27, no. 2, and vol. 35, no. 2, April, 1949, and April, 1957.

profession and the need for teachers in the different grades in the elementary schools and the various teaching fields in the high schools. Such a balance can be maintained only by cooperative efforts among all the agencies concerned with the problem—state departments of education, teacher education institutions, and officials in school systems. Programs of guidance, recruitment, and selection of prospective teachers will do much to regulate the supply to meet the demand.

Supply and demand is not concerned only with the number of teachers needed and the number entering the profession. In many fields, well-qualified teachers have always been difficult to secure. While there has been a gradual increase in the qualifications of teachers in past decades, there are still many states in which a relatively large proportion of elementary school teachers do not have the Bachelor's degree. This may be a partial explanation for the lower salaries paid in elementary schools than in high schools, since more elementary teachers lack degrees than do high school teachers. As we approach more uniform qualifications of teachers throughout a school system for different grade levels and different types of positions, there should be a tendency to maintain salaries more uniformly throughout the system.

Salaries in Other Occupations

The importance of considering the adequacy of salaries of teachers with that of earnings in other professions and occupations is evident when one realizes that teaching requires a considerably larger number of new entrants than most other working groups. In order to attract a sufficient number of recruits with adequate training, teaching must pay salaries at least comparable to those paid other workers of equal training and ability. This has not been the case in the past and probably does not obtain today. Clark's work on the income of workers in selected occupations for the years 1920 to 1936 shows the following average annual earnings in different occupations: [5a] medicine, $4,850; law, $4,730; dentistry, $4,170; engineering, $4,410; architecture, $3,820; college teaching, $3,050; social work, $1,650; journalism, $2,120; ministry, $1,980; library work, $2,020; public school teaching, $1,350; skilled trades, $1,430; nursing, $1,310; unskilled labor, $795; farming, $580; farm labor, $485. Although some of the figures are based on estimates, they show a general situation that has obtained over a period of years. Public school teaching salaries were considerably below those for the professions listed except nursing, which was only slightly below teaching. Skilled trades were somewhat higher than public school teaching, and only unskilled labor, farming, and farm labor were definitely below.

[5a] Harold F. Clark, *Life Earnings in Selected Occupations in the United States*, Harper & Brothers, New York, 1937.

In recent years when all salaries and earnings have been greatly increased in amount, many of the same differences have been present. A *Special Memo* of the National Education Association shows comparisons of estimated average salaries of teachers and other groups of workers. Data are shown for years from 1929 to 1955. In 1955, the average estimated salary for teachers for the calendar year was $4,012. The average for all persons working for wages or salaries was $3,830. Employees in manufacturing averaged $4,597. Figures are also shown for three non-salaried professional practitioners: dentists, lawyers, and physicians, but these figures are not complete after 1951. The average earning of dentists is shown as $7,820; of lawyers, $8,855; and of physicians, $13,432. Further comparisons of teachers' salaries with the other occupations show the following: (1) In 1939 teachers' salaries compared more favorably than in 1929 with salaries in all other occupational groups; (2) In 1945 teachers' salaries compared less favorably than in 1929 with salaries of all other occupations except lawyers; (3) In 1950 teachers' salaries compared more favorably than in 1929 with other occupational groups except physicians; (4) By 1955 teachers' salaries compared more favorably than in 1929 with all other occupational groups; however, the 1955 salaries of teachers compared less favorably than in 1939 with all groups except civilian employees of the federal government.[5b]

Cost of Living

Another factor that enters into the determination of teacher's salaries is the cost of living that this class of workers must maintain. At any given time there may be a considerable difference in living costs in various communities within a state. Usually cost of living is higher in the larger cities and their suburbs than in the smaller ones or in the rural areas.

It should be noted that in the determination of a cost-of-living index to be used for the adjustment of teachers' salaries, a like standard of living is normally assumed. It is only partially true that a like standard of living can be maintained by teachers in different communities. Both the cost of living and the standard of living must be taken into consideration. While it is generally assumed that teachers should live on an adequately professional standard, it is often difficult to determine what this standard is in a particular community. In any community such factors as the cost of housing and the cost of transportation may vary greatly from similar costs in other communities. Similarly, such costs may be higher in more densely populated areas than in more sparsely populated ones. The choice of living in a particular locality in close proximity to one's place of work or to shopping centers, schools, and

[5b] National Education Association, "Economic Status of Teachers in 1956–57," *Special Memo*, Washington, February, 1957, pp. 17–18.

churches may make a marked difference in the cost of living that a teacher must maintain.

Other cost-of-living adjustments are frequently made in teachers' salaries as when an extra amount is added in a particular school system because of changes in economic conditions. Often there are additional salary payments made in response to the general increase in price levels from one year to the next. These various uses of the term "cost of living" may lead to confusion unless one is careful to distinguish between them.[6]

Public Opinion

Often a marked difference in salaries paid teachers in a community seems to be due to the commonly accepted practice in that community. Some pay higher salaries than others because it has been customary, and people of the community apparently recognize that better teachers can be secured if their salary levels are higher than elsewhere. This is not alone the policy of the board of education but seems to reflect general community attitude.

This attitude as well as the policies of boards of education may at times be influenced by the demands made by individual teachers or by certain groups. This is especially true in times of extreme teacher shortage when teachers are in a position to demand higher salaries than they would be in times of greater supply.

Perhaps the matter of public opinion can be influenced to some extent by enlisting more citizen participation in the making of school policies, and certainly by a program designed to increase public understanding of the work of the schools. It is only as public opinion permits the payment of higher salaries that boards of education can establish such a policy.

Proportion of Women in Teaching

In the past, men have been paid more than women for public school teaching. The relatively larger proportion of women than men in the teaching profession has been one reason for keeping salaries at a relatively lower average than they might otherwise have been. The trend, however, is strongly in favor of paying women salaries equal to those of men. Many salary schedules are eliminating the sex differential entirely, but as long as salaries are based upon qualifications and the qualifications of women are somewhat lower than those of men, there is likely to be some difference between the salaries of the sexes.

[6] A useful method of comparing the purchasing power of what the community is spending with expenditures in earlier years has been developed by Woollatt and is reproduced in chap. 7.

The policy of paying women lower salaries than those of men probably stems from an earlier time when salaries were closer to the subsistence level than they are now. Many women voluntarily worked for lower salaries than were needed for men, although this is not entirely a sex differential. As salaries are advanced to a more professional level, it may be expected that the differential in salaries as between men and women will disappear.

Education, A Public Service

The nature of education as a public service and the fact that salaries of teachers are paid from the proceeds of taxes are factors that probably do not permit as high salary levels as are paid many workers in business or industry. Other professions, such as law and medicine, that are on a private-fee basis are in a better position to adjust their income than is teaching, although the large differentials shown by earlier investigators among salaries in different occupations are becoming less apparent. If the profession of teaching is to maintain capable young people with relatively high training, the salaries of this group of workers must be brought up to a level that will attract and hold them in the profession.

TEACHERS' SALARY SCHEDULES

A consideration of teachers' salary schedules includes both the local salary schedules used in city or rural school districts and state-wide salary schedules. Salary schedules have been developed largely in local school systems where they are now rather generally accepted in most communities. In all except some of the small districts and rural areas, salary schedules are found. In a few cases, state minimum-salary schedules have been adopted as the local salary schedule. For most school districts, the question is not one of whether to schedule salaries, but rather one of determining what salary schedule is best for the particular district. Many kinds of schedules have been built on the basis of such factors as the preparation of teachers, experience, subjects and grade levels taught, and others.

State-adopted salary schedules vary from provisions for a relatively low salary for all teachers to more or less complete schedules based on preparation and experience. In all cases, state salary schedules must be regarded as minimums and for that reason salaries stated are usually lower than those in effect in city salary schedules.

Salary schedules are most often developed for teachers. Schedules for other personnel, such as custodians, secretaries, and other administrative personnel, are used in some of the larger cities but not in all cases even in city school systems. Salary schedules have been regarded as the policy of the community and the board of education. They reflect the citizens' attitude toward the schools and what they are willing to pay to maintain good schools.

Values of Salary Schedules

The scheduling of teachers' salaries has beneficial results to the school employees, the administrators, and the community. For the individual teacher, a salary schedule replaces the individual bargaining basis for determining salary. The schedule states the amount that teachers who have certain training and experience will be paid. This enables teachers to know in advance what their salaries will be and how they may expect to progress in the school system. It gives them the assurance that they will be treated fairly and offers a measure of economic security in their work as a career and enables them to plan accordingly. When teachers are on a salary schedule there is a reduction in the feeling of competition that may exist among them within a school system. The steps in advancement are clearly set forth for teachers to follow. It is generally admitted that a teachers' salary schedule improves the teacher morale and the general working conditions of the staff in a school system.

Teachers' salary schedules are of value to administrators because they show clearly the accepted policy of the school with regard to payment of salary. It enables the administrator as budget maker to plan for the expense of personnel and when correlated with other educational policies, it enables him to predict personnel expenditures in future years. The administrator can thus plan for education in the community in a way that he could not do as well without the salary schedule. It relieves both administrators and boards of education from the necessity of making decisions each time new teachers are employed or presently employed teachers are reengaged for successive years.

A local salary schedule is essential for the community because it shows in advance what the people are willing to pay and what kind of teachers are likely to be attracted to the school system. It also shows the educational qualifications which the community desires. When members of the community participate in the formulation of salary schedules, there is better understanding and wider acceptance of salary policy than there would be otherwise. This is a very important way for communities to participate in the making of school policy.

Types of Salary Schedules

Several types of salary schedule are in use in school systems throughout the country. Perhaps the most widely accepted is the single salary schedule or the one based upon preparation and experience. Other types less frequently found are those based on preparation and position or on position alone.

Single Salary Schedule. The single salary schedule, or "preparation and experience" type, is one in which the several groups of teachers are differentiated by the amount of professional preparation they have completed. The grade level of subjects taught is not taken into consideration. Such schedules usually have several levels of preparation, such as less than four years of training, the Bachelor's degree or four years, the Master's degree or five years, and six years or more. Sometimes there is more than one level below the Bachelor's degree and likewise there may be more than one level above the Master's degree. The Bachelor's and Master's degree levels, however, are the most commonly accepted ones. In each case the beginning salary is determined for teachers without experience, usually with a differential among the salary classes. From this beginning salary, teachers progress year after year by annual increments until the maximum salary for their class is reached.

It is of interest to note that the single salary schedule has been very widely adopted in recent decades. For example, in 1940–1941, 31.3 per cent of the salary schedules reviewed by the Research Division of the National Education Association were of this type, whereas in 1950–1951, 97.1 per cent were single salary schedules.[7]

This single salary schedule recognizes the necessity for equal preparation of teachers in the lower and upper grades of the elementary school and the secondary school and emphasizes preparation and experience as the principal factors that determine the salaries of teachers at any time, although it may contain other provisions. Such a schedule enables teachers to make professional advancement while teaching on a particular grade level or in any high school subject and does not encourage the practice that is sometimes followed of moving teachers to higher grade levels in order to increase their salaries. It also eliminates the practice of paying elementary teachers lower salaries than junior high school and senior high school teachers because of their positions.

Although the past fifty years have shown remarkable improvement in teacher preparation, one may ask why the profession of teaching permits its workers to practice with such widely varying preparation. The preparation type schedules encourage higher levels of preparation by offering greater financial rewards, but this differs from the practice in many other professions in which the standard professional preparation is required before the person may begin his work. There is much to be said for the completion of a standard four-year or five-year professional-training program for all prospective teachers before they enter upon teaching. Even with such preparation, beginning teachers must learn

[7] National Education Association, *Research Bulletin*, vol. 35, no. 2, *op. cit.*, p. 90.

much through experience. To compromise with the initial preparation means greater uncertainty in the possible success of the new entrants to the profession. If single salary schedules are tending in the direction of a minimum standard preparation level, their popularity will do much to make teaching more professional than it has been in the past.

Position Schedule. Salary schedules known as the "position type" establish salaries in terms of the positions which teachers hold, such as those in the elementary school, the junior high school, the senior high school, or certain groups of special teachers. The initial salaries, the number and amount of increments for experience, and the maximum salaries in these schedules determine the extent to which teachers may progress in their positions. This is one of the older forms of scheduling, and although it is not in general use among city school systems, certain features of it still prevail. Perhaps one reason for this form of schedule is based upon the fact that formerly less preparation was required in the elementary schools than in the junior high schools or the senior high schools, and this differential in preparation was considered as the basis for a differential in salary. As teachers in all grades come to have better preparation, this form of salary schedule may be expected to become less prevalent.

Position-Preparation Schedule. The position-preparation type of schedule recognizes both professional preparation and the position of the teacher. This schedule is in reality a variation of the position type schedule since the basic teaching groups are established for elementary schools, for junior high schools, and senior high schools, but within each group variations are made to recognize different levels of preparation. Such schedules may include many of the preparation levels found in single salary schedules, but in addition to the differential among preparation levels, there are also the differentials among position groups. It embodies features of both the single salary schedule and the position schedule, but does not go all the way on either basis. Its use as a transition type of schedule between the position type and the preparation type may be one reason for its introduction, but like the position type schedule, the number of school systems using it are rapidly decreasing in number.

Factors in Salary Schedules

There are many variations in the structure of local teachers' salary schedules, but they have many things in common—minimum salaries for different salary classes, a number of increments between the minimum and maximum salaries, and certain maximum salaries. Other variations may include the differential for the length of the school year, either nine months or twelve months, certain merit provisions, and such features as extra pay for extra work or allowance for dependents.

Minimum Salaries. Determining the minimum salary to be paid teachers in any type of schedule for a particular school system depends upon many factors, such as the economic condition in the district and the state, salaries paid teachers in other school systems, and the salaries paid workers in other professions. The weights given to these factors are not always equal, as at any time some may be more important than others or their relative importance may change from year to year. Regardless of the figures used, the minimum salary should be sufficient to enable the teachers to maintain a standard of living commensurate with their position.

It may be argued that present minimum salaries paid teachers without experience, except such experience as they may have had in practice teaching courses or in short periods of intern teaching, should not be high, since no school can expect high quality of service from such teachers. Relatively low beginning salary with ample opportunities to advance, and to advance further than most schedules now permit, would be an inducement for those who look at teaching as a life profession. It may also be argued that a relatively high minimum salary will bring into the profession more persons who might look to other work, and although many teachers do not remain long in the profession, the high minimum salary tends to attract capable persons who will serve the schools well if only for a short time.

A recent publication of the Research Division of the National Education Association [8] shows that in 303 urban school districts of 30,000 to 100,000 in population salary schedules usually establish five classes—the lowest preparation, usually less than four years of college; the Bachelor's degree or four years; the Master's degree or five years; six years; and the highest preparation level, usually above six years. Minimum salaries for each of these classes for the year 1957–1958 are shown as follows: lowest level, $3,400; Bachelor's degree or four years, $3,800; Master's degree or five years, $4,050; six years, $4,400; and the highest level, if above six years, $4,525.

In contrast to the average figures shown above it is of interest to show here minimum salaries paid in schools of the Metropolitan School Study Council, all of which are on a relatively high expenditure level. These minimum salaries for the year 1957–1958 were as follows: for teachers with four years of training the median was $4,200; for teachers with five years of training, $4,500; for six years of training, $4,900; and for Doctor's degree or equivalent, $5,300. [9]

[8] National Education Association, Research Division, "Salary Schedules for Classroom Teachers, 1957–58, Urban School District 30,000 to 100,000 in Population," Washington, October, 1957, p. 25.

[9] Metropolitan School Study Council, *Financing Council Schools, 1957–58*, New York, 1957.

Salary Increments. The number, size, and spacing of salary increments vary among schedules in city school systems, the number ranging from eight or nine to fourteen or fifteen. The median number of increments in the tabulation of salaries reported by the Research Division of the National Education Association is twelve. These increments may vary in amount from $50 to $400. An average increment is somewhere between $200 and $300. Variations in this respect do not point to very clear purposes in providing a salary schedule from low to high salaries, whether the purpose is to attract capable persons of good preparation, to increase the tenure of teachers, to reward teachers for long and faithful service, or to achieve a combination of these purposes.

Another consideration in determining the number and size of the salary increments is the value of experience in teaching. It is generally believed that teaching experience is most valuable in perhaps the first five years; thereafter, it might still be of value but to a lesser degree. This might indicate larger increments in the early years and relatively smaller increments in later years. Another point of view is to distinguish between the increments of increase for experience and those for professional advancement. If a teacher secures more preparation, he is automatically moved to another salary class, but within the same salary class it may be shown that some teachers make more professional advancement than do others. If this is to be recognized, a professional-advancement increment, either in the earlier or later years of teaching, would be larger for teachers making more professional advancement than for those making less.

If education is to become truly professional, it must attract more capable, well-trained persons who make a life career of teaching than we have had in the past. For such persons the beginning salary is not so important perhaps as the possibility of advancement and the ultimate compensation that may be anticipated. To achieve these ends, salary schedules should provide for a wide range between minimum and maximum salaries with increments adequate for advancement from a reasonable minimum to a satisfactory maximum that is two or three times as high as the minimum. Most salary schedules do not meet this standard.

Maximum Salaries. Maximum salaries for teachers generally set upper limits that represent the ability of the community to support education. Such maximums should be sufficiently high to hold capable teachers who wish to remain in the profession and make a life work of teaching. Maximum salaries are more likely to affect those of high qualification and long experience and persons who are well established in the community. Some school systems set "supermaximums" for teachers of outstanding ability, whereas in others no maximum is set. The National Education Association study cited shows maximum salaries for the different classes to be as follows: for the lowest preparation level, below the Bachelor's degree, the maximum is $4,800; Bachelor's degree or four years, $5,738; Master's degree or five years, $6,200; six years, $6,820; and the highest level of preparation of above six years, $6,900.[10]

Maximum salaries in schools of the Metropolitan School Study Council show considerably higher medians. They are as follows: for four years of training, $7,100; five years of training, $7,650; six years of training, $8,100; Doctor's degree or equivalent, $8,650.[11]

Having teachers divided into certain grades has been advocated and practiced to some extent, e.g., new entrants into the profession are classed as beginning teachers who will advance regularly on the salary schedule for a period of years. Their maximum salary may be relatively low. The next grade may be experienced teachers who will advance on the schedule for longer periods of time, but for whom there will be a maximum sufficiently high to retain them in the profession. The third grade may be that of master teacher for whom there should be no maximum. The determination of maximum salaries is one which is closely related to the whole pattern of salary payments, minimum salaries, number and amount of increments, spacing of increments, and perhaps other features that are included in a salary schedule.

Length of Working Year. A number of salary schedules make a difference in salary on the basis of length of the contract period of the teacher. While regular teachers may be working during a nine- or ten-month school year, others may be employed for the full year of twelve months. This usually applies to administrative officers and sometimes to those in the business management or certain supervisory positions. While there has been some discussion concerning the operation of schools for a longer period of time—on eleven-month or twelve-month contracts—there is relatively little of this found in present teachers' salaries. In a number of cases, teachers are paid additional salaries for special work done during the summer months, such as the conduct of summer sessions.

Salary and Merit. In recent years there has been much discussion concerning the relationship between the quality of service or merit of a teacher and his salary. Many types of teacher evaluation and rating have been devised in an effort to determine quality of service for purposes of salary payment. The principle is one that has considerable validity, but the chief difficulty encountered is the means of evaluating quality of service. Some of the devices in salary schedules for rewarding merit are the recommendations of administrative officers for normal progress on the salary schedule, double increments for meritorious serv-

[10] National Education Association, *Salary Schedules for Classroom Teachers, 1957–58, op. cit.*

[11] *Financing Council Schools, op. cit.*

ice, and higher maximums for teachers of outstanding service. The methods of determining the quality of service of teachers are rating scales, recommendations of administrative officers, and judgments of teacher committees. In some salary schedules, there are provisions for regular advancement of all teachers for a number of years beyond which there are certain merit levels into which only teachers of recognized ability and quality of service may enter. In effect this fixes different maximum salaries for teachers of different quality of service.

There is really a very splendid merit system in operation in the United States because of the fact that teachers can move rather readily from place to place and from state to state. A teacher beginning with a very low minimum salary in one school system, for example, could, if sufficiently meritorious, find himself eventually on a salary schedule in another state that is very much higher. A really meritorious teacher can advance professionally during his working lifetime much more rapidly than is provided for by the salary schedule of most school districts.

Special groups of public school employees—principals, supervisors, special teachers, and administrative officers—are frequently paid on the basis of separate salary schedules. When this is done, the minimum and maximum salaries are usually higher than for classroom teachers. Another method is to use the regular teachers' salary schedules, but to pay such officers additional increments because of the nature of their special assignments. In some cases, the salaries of such school employees are fixed by the administrative office and the board of education independently of the salary schedule.

Extra Pay for Extra Work. In theory it would be desirable to equalize the working load of teachers as nearly as possible and to pay all teachers on the basis of the salary schedule. This is often impossible because of the varying duties that different groups of teachers must perform. In some salary schedules, provision is made for extra pay for extra duties assigned to teachers. This is particularly true in the case of athletic coaches, and perhaps to a lesser degree to certain other types of special subject or activity teachers. It is usually defended on the basis that such special teachers spend an unusual amount of time directing their activities and that their working day is not comparable to that of the regular classroom teacher. Theoretically, such extra pay is withheld when the teacher is again assigned to a regular position. Overemphasis upon this provision may lead to a general payment of higher salaries to men than to women even though the schedule purports to pay them on the same basis. This problem is a very difficult one to handle, and it is almost impossible at times to draw the line between those who should receive extra pay and those who should not.

Allowance for Dependents. In past years there has been some tendency among school districts to allow extra compensation for teachers with dependents. This provision has applied alike to men and women according to the number of dependents supported by them. It doubtless arose at a time when salaries were relatively low, perhaps on a subsistence basis, and when it was necessary to pay men teachers higher salaries than women teachers in order to retain them in the system. But as salaries have increased, the necessity for this provision is less than it once was. Perhaps when salaries can be placed on a truly professional basis, it will not be necessary to pay extra amounts for teachers with dependents. This provision is almost entirely absent in the payment of instructors in institutions of higher learning.

Adjustment of Salary Schedules. Salary schedules are in reality a device for payment of teachers according to a definite policy as it has developed in the individual communities. As economic conditions change or as communities grow in population or for many other reasons it is necessary periodically to reevaluate salary schedules and to make adjustments in them to express accurately the ability and willingness of the communities to support their schools. Similarly, adjustments in salary schedules may be needed when the policy of the administration changes to reflect differences in the qualification of teachers employed, or in the recognition of differentials that should be made between minimum and maximum salaries, or for other reasons. The salary schedule in itself does not constitute a complete personnel program. It reflects only that aspect of the program which deals with the compensation of personnel. Occasionally, it may be necessary to adjust the salary schedule to bring salaries more nearly in agreement with those paid in other school districts within the area. A desirable feature would be to have comparable salaries offered not only throughout the school district, but throughout a county or state. The changing attitude of a community toward its schools is another factor that may require adjustment in salary schedules. A community usually pays for the services that it values most highly.

STATE MINIMUM-SALARY SCHEDULES

Minimum salaries are guaranteed to teachers by law in a number of states. Sometimes these state salary schedules are used in determining the amount of state appropriation due to a particular district. The theory underlying such provision is that all teachers in the state should be guaranteed at least a minimum salary. The effectiveness of the provision depends much upon the type of minimum-salary provisions in the state school systems.

The various types of state minimum-salary standards may be classified as: (1) minimum salaries with recognition of preparation and experience, (2) minimum salaries fixed on the basis of two or more flat rates with no credit for experience, (3) minimum salaries fixed as a single flat-rate amount, and (4) salary allotments specified as a part of state aid, but not as minimum salaries.

The Research Division of the National Education Association [12] shows a tabulation of the minimum annual salaries for teachers as required by state laws in 1957–1958. Thirty-three states had minimum salaries for teachers prescribed by law. Only two states showed flat-rate minimum salaries; the others had two or more salary classes for beginning teachers.

Thirty-one states gave minimum salaries for beginning teachers with the Bachelor's degree, or four years of training. These salaries ranged from $810 to $4,200. Twenty-three states showed beginning salaries for teachers with Master's degree, or five years of training, ranging from $2,200 to $4,000. Twenty states showed maximum salaries for teachers with Bachelor's degree or four years of training, from $2,400 to $5,800. Seventeen states showed maximum salaries for teachers with Master's degree or five years of training, from $2,600 to $6,400.

The Committee on Tenure of the National Education Association [13] made an extensive study of minimum-salary laws in the course of which opinions concerning the advantages and disadvantages were gathered from many of the states. A summary of these opinions shows that the two outstanding disadvantages which have been mentioned are as follows: (1) there is a danger that the minimum salary may become the maximum salary paid by communities, and (2) minimum salary laws do not provide for the differences in the worth of teachers with the same amount of training and experience and do not consider cost of living and other variable factors. The second objection, however, refers more to uniform state-wide schedules than to minimum salary laws.

The advantages of minimum salary laws are summarized under the following five points: (1) minimum-salary laws help prevent extreme cuts during the worst of depression years, (2) minimum-salary laws have been particularly effective in certain Southern states in raising the salary of Negro teachers, (3) minimum-salary laws help to attract competent people to the teaching profession, (4) minimum-salary laws prevent bargaining with teachers at salaries below a reasonable rate, (5) minimum-salary laws have been a help in improving the teaching service in very small schools.

[12] National Education Association, *Minimum Annual Salaries for Teachers as Required by State Law, 1956–57 and 1957–58*, Washington, December, 1957.

[13] National Education Association, Committee on Tenure, *Minimum Salary Laws for Teachers*, Washington, January, 1937, p. 23.

Another point that should be considered in relation to state salary schedules is their use in determining a foundation program of education. One point of view is that the state salary schedule determines the total amount of money that should be allotted for teachers' salaries when the number of employees in each salary classification has been determined. As Chapter 16 shows, this policy may be quite upsetting to the equalization objective. The opposite point of view is expressed when a foundation program of education is established on the basis of well-defined measures of educational need and this foundation program is supported jointly by local contributions and state aid. The latter point of view is based upon the theory that communities can and will pay adequate salaries if the money is available. The growing tendency for states to establish foundation programs would indicate that this point of view is preferable.

SALARIES OF NONTEACHING PERSONNEL

There is considerable variation among school districts in the salaries and salary policies adopted for the payment of nonteaching school employees. It is difficult to show schedules for such employees because of the lack of uniformity in the classification of employees and in the salary rates determined for each classification.

Salaries of maintenance personnel, such as those engaged chiefly in cleaning and caring for school buildings and grounds, in heating and ventilation of school buildings, in repair and improvement of school buildings, and others not engaged in the above classes, have been tabulated by the Department of Research and Service, American Federation of State, County, and Municipal Employees.[14]

This publication shows hours of work, overtime, sick leave, vacation, holidays, shift differentials, group hospitalization and surgical insurance, retirement, civil service, and basis for promotion of noncertified school employees in forty-five cities. It also shows the salaries paid for various types of positions such as secretaries, accountants, business office employees, attendance officers, janitors, engineers, maintenance employees, mechanics, carpenters, and others. The classification of positions varies so widely that any listing would be incomplete. Salaries are usually stated in either monthly or annual amounts.

The National Education Association shows tabulations of salaries paid clerical and secretarial employees and operation and maintenance em-

[14] American Federation of State, County, and Municipal Employees, Department of Research and Service, *Comparative Salaries and Working Conditions for Non-Certified School Employees,* Part III, Cities with Population of 50,000 to 100,000, M901, OEIU-39, AFL-CIO, May 16, 1956.

ployees in urban school systems of over 30,000 population.[15] Such workers are usually divided into several classes with minimum salaries for each class depending upon work and experience. More or less complete salary schedules are shown for 220 urban school districts, but the classification of such employees varies so greatly that no one type of salary schedule would be applicable to all.

The following recommendations have been proposed by Phay as desirable standards for salary schedules for custodial workers.[16]

1. Definite salary schedules should be provided for custodians.

2. Salary schedules for custodians should be made cooperatively and participants should properly represent all divisions of the custodial staff.

3. Rules of promotion should be established and made known.

4. Salary schedules should be made that will attract "career" custodians.

5. The maximum salaries for custodians should be determined by the amount necessary for a "health and decency" standard of living as determined by the Heller Committee or by other equally reliable groups.

6. Salary schedules for custodians should have from three to five yearly increments.

7. Increments should be large enough to be "felt."

8. Salary increments should be granted annually. In some cases increments should be denied for just cause but only upon the written recommendation of the supervisor.

9. All custodial positions should be classified and a distinct salary scale made for each classification.

10. At least once in five years appraisal should be made of the appropriateness of the basic salary rates and of the job classifications.

11. Salary schedules should provide for cost-of-living adjustments.

TEACHER RETIREMENT

Teacher retirement provisions of one form or another have been recognized in most of the states for a relatively long period of time. Some states have excellent teacher-retirement plans in operation, whereas in others they are less well developed. The recent provision for including teachers under federal social security has been adopted by many states and provides an addition to existing teacher-retirement plans.

---

[15] National Education Association, *Rates of Pay for School Clerical and Secretarial Employees in Urban School Districts of 30,000 in Population,* 1952–53, Circular No. 8, and *Rates of Pay for Operation and Maintenance Employees in Urban School Districts, 1952–1953,* Circular No. 9, Washington, 1953.

[16] John E. Phay, "Custodial Personnel Administration," *American School Board Journal,* vol. 116, pp. 33–35, April, 1948.

Under teacher-retirement provisions, it is generally recognized that teachers pay a certain proportion of the cost and that the school districts pay the remainder. Sometimes teachers pay 50 per cent and school districts 50 per cent, although this may differ according to the type of retirement provisions in effect. Teacher-retirement provisions should be regarded as a part of the general administration of personnel. Inadequate provisions for retirement may keep teachers in the classroom beyond the period of competency and may engender in them a feeling of insecurity which is not conducive to the employment of new personnel or the retention of persons in the system.

Many of the early retirement plans did not provide sufficient security for teachers. Many of them required relatively low contributions on the part of teachers, but as a result provided rather restricted benefits. An adequate plan of teacher retirement would require a contribution of perhaps 5 per cent of a teacher's salary to be matched by a similar amount by the school district. An individual account should be maintained for each teacher and the amount of his contributions and earnings should be credited to him for retirement purposes. Teacher-retirement plans usually carry disability benefits and death benefits, both of which are desirable, to provide the maximum security for the teacher and his dependents.

It is sufficient to consider at this point that teacher retirement is an item in the total program of the welfare of teachers and that the amount of money contributed by the district toward such plans is an investment in the security and well-being of teachers employed. Total amount of money involved in retirement plans is usually not large as compared with total educational expenditures, but for the money expended, retirement provisions yield large dividends in teacher security.

LEAVES OF ABSENCE

The practice of granting leaves of absence either with pay or without pay so commonly found in institutions of higher education, is becoming more and more general practice in the larger city school systems. Some school districts grant sabbatical leaves of absence with pay ranging from 40 to 60 per cent of salary for a school year. Such leaves are usually granted for purposes of increasing teacher preparation or as a reward for service when the time is spent in further study, travel, or other activities that may accrue to the benefit of the schools.

Most school systems provide some sick leave, that is, absences on full pay for a period of time. The most common provision for sick leave is an allowance of five to ten days with full pay for illness, although there is a growing tendency to increase this time to three or four weeks. In many cases, sick leave is cumulative up to a certain length of time, say one month or six weeks. While such provisions are desirable for short illnesses, they do not provide for any protracted illnesses. These must be taken care of through disability benefits in teacher-retirement provisions.

SUMMARY

Financing school personnel services is important because salaries constitute the largest single item of school expenditure and upon this item of expenditure more than any other the quality of service depends.

Teachers' salaries have improved markedly in the past decade and compare more favorably with salaries paid in other comparable work than they did formerly.

Teachers' salary schedules are now generally in use. It is no longer a question of whether or not to schedule salaries but rather one of the kind of salary schedule to be placed in operation. There are three general types of such schedules that may be characterized as: (1) the single salary schedule or the preparation schedule, (2) the position schedule, and (3) the position-preparation schedule. The number of school systems that have adopted the single salary schedule has increased greatly during the postwar period until it is fair to say that in a typical school system in cities of over 30,000 the single salary schedule is by far the predominating one. Factors within salary schedules such as minimum salaries, number and size of increments, and maximum salaries have become more uniform although many variations still persist. Other features of salary schedules are extra pay given teachers for dependents, sex differentials which are still quite common, and cost-of-living adjustments which have been made in many schedules during the postwar period. Provision for extra pay for extra duties has been made in a number of them.

The relating of salaries to quality of service of teachers, theoretically a desirable provision, appears to be gaining in favor in spite of the fact that it has met with considerable opposition. The opposition seems to be centered in the difficulty of evaluating the quality of teaching. This has not been done with any degree of satisfaction to the profession. Special groups of teachers, such as principals, supervisors, and special teachers, are usually paid on separate salary schedules and are given special increments above the regular schedule. In thirty-six states minimum-salary schedules have been adopted by law. These usually state the beginning salary for one or more classifications of teachers, the number of increments, and the maximum salaries that may be attained. A few states still have a single flat-rate minimum salary.

Salary schedules for custodial and other nonteaching groups have not been as generally used as for teachers although their popularity is increasing. Salary schedules for such employees tend to place such positions more in line with recognized occupations than they were in former times when salaries were low and fixed for each individual worker.

Another very important feature in the financing of school personnel is the provision for teacher retirement. Most of the states have some form of teacher retirement under which both the teacher and the school district or the state contribute in the provision for the retirement.

Other desirable features in financing personnel are adequate provision for leaves of absence, provision for sick leave, and for substitute teaching.

QUESTIONS FOR STUDY AND DISCUSSION

1. From city or state reports, study the trend of teachers' salaries in your state. Plot the average salaries of different groups of teachers for a period of years.

2. Compare the salaries of teachers with those of certain other occupations in your community. What type of work commands higher pay? What types command lower pay?

3. Study a number of salary schedules and the tabulations of salary schedules in city school systems of the National Education Association to show minimum salaries, number of increments, and maximum salaries.

4. Summarize the arguments for and against equal pay for men and women with the same preparation and the same type of position.

5. Cite illustrations of the different kinds of salary schedules described in this chapter. In many cases, a salary schedule may contain provisions of more than one type.

6. From recent literature summarize the practices of evaluating teachers for purposes of salary increases. Tell the advantages and disadvantages of different methods of evaluation.

7. Summarize the advantages and disadvantages of minimum state-wide salary laws. Show the application of such standards to salaries paid in a particular state.

8. Cite illustrations of salaries paid to nonteaching school employees. To what extent are salary schedules used? What are the provisions and advantages and disadvantages?

9. Study salary schedules of educational administrators, supervisors, and special personnel not directly engaged in classroom activities, as tabulated in the salary tabulations of the National Education Association. Compare salaries of such personnel with those of classroom teachers.

10. What are the provisions for retirement and other benefits for teachers in your state?

SELECTED REFERENCES

Beecher, Dwight E.: "The New York Plan of Rewarding Good Teaching," *American School Board Journal,* vol. 119, pp. 35–37, October, 1949.

Burke, Arvid J.: "New State Minimum Salary Schedules and their Financing," *American School Board Journal,* vol. 16, pp. 29–30, February, 1948.

Burke, Arvid J.: *Financing Public Schools in the United States,* Harper and Brothers, New York, 1957.

Elsbree, Willard S., and E. Edmund Reutter, *Staff Personnel in the Public Schools,* Prentice-Hall, Inc., Englewood Cliffs, N.J., 1954.

Furno, Orlando F.: *Twenty Years of Teachers Salaries in Schools of the Metropolitan School Study Council,* Institute of Administrator Research, Teachers College, Columbia University, New York, 1958.

Johns, R. L., and Edgar L. Morphet: *Problems and Issues in Public School Finance,* Bureau of Publications, Teachers College, New York, Columbia University, 1952, chap. XI, pp. 359–396.

Metropolitan School Study Council: *Financing Council Schools 1957–1958,* New York, 1957.

Morphet, Edgar L.: "State Responsibility for Salaries," *School Executive,* vol. 67, pp. 31–33, February, 1948.

National Education Association, Research Division: "Salaries and Salary Schedules of Urban School Employees, 1956–57," *Research Bulletin,* vol. 35, no. 2, Washington, April, 1957.

————: "Salary Schedules for Classroom Teachers, 1957–58, Urban School Districts 30,000 to 100,000 in Population," *Research Bulletin,* Washington, October, 1957.

————: "Salary Schedules for Classroom Teachers, 1957–58, Urban School Districts 100,000 and Over," Washington, September, 1957.

————: "Economic Status of Teachers in 1956–57," *Special Memo,* Washington, February, 1957.

Rosenstengel, William E., and Jefferson N. Eastmond: *School Finance,* The Ronald Press Company, New York, 1957, chap. 17, pp. 327–348.

22. Financing capital outlay

Present-day school programs require much more extensive investments in building facilities and equipment than did programs in a former generation. The newer types of program that place more emphasis on pupil activity require larger classrooms and more specialized facilities than ever before. Major items of capital outlay such as school sites, school buildings, and school equipment require a relatively large expenditure which boards of education must supply if the program is to operate smoothly and efficiently and the maximum educational opportunity is to be afforded the children.

Problems of providing school plant facilities have been greatly accentuated in recent years because of the growth in school population, inflated building costs, and the lag that has been present in an effort to keep school facilities apace with growing needs of the school system. During the postwar period when the birth rate increased rapidly in most parts of the country the schools soon noted the increased enrollments. Many districts were ill prepared to cope with the oncoming numbers of children in the lower elementary grades. Since that time this increase has been noted in the high school and is reaching into higher education. So greatly have building costs increased that it became virtually impossible for many districts to provide the funds needed to remodel old structures or to build new ones. This has created a lag in school construction that has been present since the war and is not yet fully met in many districts.

For example, in 1925–1926 capital outlay amounted to $411 million or about one-fifth of total expenditures.[1] These expenditures declined during the time of the depression so that in 1933–1934 they were only $59 million. Thereafter, they rose steadily but again declined during the

[1] U.S. Office of Education, *Biennial Survey of Education in the United States, 1952–54*, "Statistics of State School Systems," Government Printing Office, Washington, 1956, chap. 2, pp. 94–95.

period of World War II, so that in 1943–1944 only $54 million were spent for this purpose. Since that time capital outlay expenditures have risen sharply. Recently they have amounted to approximately 23 per cent of total expenditures.

Most of this capital outlay was achieved through borrowing with the result that school indebtedness increased in two decades from approximately $3.1 billion to about $6.9 billion. Indebtedness declined in the depression and again during World War II but this was more than offset by the earlier and later increases.

If school boards are to discharge their responsibilities by providing buildings and equipment for children and youth of the community, they should be guided by the principle of stability which would dictate that rather constant increase be made in capital expenditures from year to year. This, however, may vary greatly from one community to another since conditions are not the same in different parts of the county and the means of financing capital outlay may differ greatly from one state to another. Where expenditures for capital outlay are financed through bond issues, a degree of stability may be achieved by spreading the payments over a period of time and by adjusting the schedules in such a way that a fairly constant rate of taxation is needed to liquidate the indebtedness. Boards of education as the representatives of the people of the community should discharge this function in accordance with legislative requirements and the principles of democracy and prudence. The retirement of bonded indebtedness should be adjusted to the needs and abilities of the particular school district, usually over periods of time considerably shorter than the calculated life of the buildings or equipment provided.

Borrowing money for public school buildings and equipment has become a serious problem as the need for school facilities has increased, prices of both labor and materials have greatly increased, and in many cases the assessed valuations of the school districts have not kept pace with these increases. All this has led to more state financing of capital outlay than formerly, sometimes through state loan funds and again through state grants for school building construction.

FINANCING SCHOOL BUILDING CONSTRUCTION

Unlike the financing of current expenditures which may be met by fairly uniform tax rates from one year to another, capital expenditures may require greater amounts during periods of construction than can be met from annual tax resources. This is especially true in the smaller districts where buildings are constructed at relatively long intervals of time.

Even in some of the larger districts the building needs may become more pressing at certain times than at others.

Because the construction of buildings makes relatively large expenditure demands on the local units, a number of different plans have been adopted for financing capital outlay. In the local districts two of the methods most generally used are: (1) the pay-as-you-go plan and (2) the bonding plan. Each of these plans has certain advantages and disadvantages that must be taken into account in deciding which should be used in a particular situation; moreover, a number of other factors must be considered such as the size of the school system, the tax resources of the local unit, the tax levies that have been made for capital outlay and debt service, the type of building to be constructed, increase or decrease in school population, changes in taxable wealth of the community, and other social and economic changes. Careful survey of the community to ascertain these various factors is necessary to make a wise choice of financing plans in the district. The small school district that erects a building every ten, fifteen, or twenty years must adopt a plan to meet its own peculiar need.

The limitation placed upon the amount of money that may be raised by taxation in any one year may further influence whether to "pay as you go" or to bond.

The policy of erecting buildings by units may make possible their financing during a shorter period than would be necessary were the complete building to be erected at once. Large school systems in which the construction of one or more buildings is an annual occurrence may well adopt a plan that would be quite impossible in smaller districts.

Financing Plans in Local Districts

The two plans mentioned earlier in this chapter, pay-as-you-go and bonding, for the financing of building construction from current income or spreading the cost over a period of time, are designed specifically for use when capital outlay must be made from local district funds. As a variation of the bonding plan the building reserve plan permits spreading the burden over a period of time before the buildings are erected, whereas under the bonding plan the burden is spread over a period of time after the buildings have been constructed and while they are in use. The combination of the two plans may often be desirable. Three important considerations in the selection of a plan or combination of plans are: (1) the total cost of financing including construction costs and carrying costs, (2) distribution of the burden on the taxpayer, whether it be for one or more years before or after construction, and (3) the assurance offered by the various plans that school buildings will be provided when needed. The relative merits of these plans must be considered under good management for obviously the poorest plan may be best when it is most efficiently administered and even the best plan may result in waste and burden on the taxpayers when it is poorly administered.

Pay-as-you-go Plan

Under the pay-as-you-go plan are usually included all the financial arrangements by which the school buildings are paid for during the period of their construction. It is obvious that in small school systems this plan would require a relatively large tax levy in one or two years, a condition that makes it wholly impracticable for a large number of districts. In the larger districts, where building construction is more or less continuous and in which the building program involves the erection of one or more units each year, this plan may be quite acceptable, and because of the elimination of the carrying charges, it may result in a smaller total capital outlay and debt-service cost than would the bonding plan.

Difficulty may be encountered in inaugurating a plan of financing buildings currently because of the policy of the district in past years. If a district has issued bonds and is paying for the buildings and equipment it is using on a long-term plan, it would be assuming a double burden to initiate a policy of pay-as-you-go or of setting up a building reserve fund. Any such change in policy must be made with due regard for past obligations that have been assumed. If a district can begin with a "clean slate" and need not consider existing outstanding indebtedness, a pay-as-you-go policy is much easier to initiate. Moreover, changes in enrollment, wealth of the community, or general economic conditions may cause variations in the need for construction and may place a greater burden on certain periods than on others and thus prevent a complete pay-as-you-go program. As a supplement to other plans, however, it has many advantages.

There are two types of saving claimed for the pay-as-you-go plan: (1) avoiding the interest on debt and, (2) saving from better prudential oversight (avoidance of extravagances). Before one can determine the saving in money to the community he should know the value of the money to the taxpayer, who could retain it in his own business when payments are deferred.

Often boards of education are less willing to approve extensive plans when payment must be made immediately and there is no opportunity to defer the burden to some future time. Although there is no doubt much merit in the pay-as-you-go plan of financing as a check on extravagance, it may at times result in inadequate provision for housing the schools, which in the long run may cost more than the original expenditure it was intended to prevent. There the principle of prudence must dictate the extent to which economy is desirable and necessary.

The alleged disadvantage of the pay-as-you-go plan is that it does not give the greatest assurance that funds will be available and, hence, that the building needs of a community will be met. The variability in tax rates that will result and the failure of the plan even in some of the largest cities, where it may be expected to operate best, are other arguments against it. In assessing the relative merits of the pay-as-you-go and the bonding plans, it may be shown that the large tax burden which falls on one or two years may in reality not produce the revenue needed and thus may interfere seriously with the building needs of a community.

If, for example, a community has for years levied a tax of 10 cents per $100 for a long-term bond issue, it does not follow that a tax of 50 cents per $100 would raise five times the amount in one year even if that rate were theoretically possible. Each new increase in the tax rate imposes a proportionally greater burden upon the taxpayer and decreases the possibility that the tax will be collected. The stability of a tax is violated when there are large fluctuations in the rates imposed.

Although it is in the smaller communities that greatest difficulty is experienced in financing buildings on the annual basis, there are instances of the failure of this plan in large districts. When a district experiences increased need for school construction or when it changes from bonding to pay-as-you-go it is sometimes impossible to raise the necessary revenue and in consequence building must be postponed for a time. When further postponement of the improvements becomes impossible, it is necessary to resort to issuing bonds in order to raise the needed funds. Changing economic and social conditions frequently result in greater building needs than can be anticipated. The reduction in school building construction during the depression and during World War II caused a greater need in later years than would have occurred otherwise. Such variations make it necessary to supplement the pay-as-you-go plan with others.

Bonding Plan

The practice of borrowing money for the erection of school buildings has been approved so generally that it is now used in most communities and has received more widespread acceptance than has any other plan. It is generally more feasible than pay-as-you-go, and although it results in a greater total cost, it has the advantage of spreading the cost over a period of years. The use of the bonding plan in preference to any other must be determined in part by the type of bonds to be issued, but one may state the merits of the plan on the basis of the practice that may be expected to ensue. In many districts, school administrators are faced with a situation in which outstanding indebtedness has been created and must be liquidated before any current financing can be substituted. Here the bonding plan should be used as a supplement. Moreover, there may be the situation in which a large amount of permanent improvement has become obsolete and must be replaced in a relatively short period.

The chief advantages of the bonding plan are the stability that is maintained in the revenue system, the assurance it gives that the building needs of a community will be met, and the equitable distribution of the cost of a building on the generation of taxpayers who use it and whose children benefit by the new structure.

When bond issues are liquidated on a serial plan, or when a sinking fund is created for their redemption, a relatively small tax rate for paying the interest and the matured bonds or making the sinking-fund payments may be maintained throughout the period of the bonds. The burden during any one year is relatively small and does not seriously disrupt the revenue-raising system. It is a principle of good financial management to keep rates of taxation from marked and arbitrary fluctuation.

The fact that new buildings will be needed in the future as existing ones become obsolete or worn out requires a plan that will ensure construction when it is needed. Long-term financing at relatively low annual cost seems to be the best way of assuring that future buildings will be constructed. The spread of the cost of an improvement over a period of twenty to thirty years results in more equitable distribution of the tax burden, although there may be a greater total cost to the community.

The disadvantages of the bonding plan most frequently advanced are the greater total cost to the community and the alleged tendency toward extravagance under the deferred-payment plan. That bonding has often proved to be expensive in practice cannot be denied, but most of this added cost has been due to poor management, resulting in the necessity for issuing refunding bonds. There are instances on record in which refunding bonds were issued two and three times and in which the interest costs amounted to several times the cost of the original bond. Such mismanagement of indebtedness is fortunately becoming less frequent as serial bonds are used to a greater extent.

The argument that deferred-payment plans tend to cause extravagance in building construction has led many to advocate current financing for schools and other governmental enterprises. It is held that taxpayers and boards of education will scrutinize budgets and building projects more closely when they know that they must be paid for from current funds.

A special case under the bonding plan is that of setting up a building reserve fund in anticipation of meeting school building needs. Usually such a plan provides only a part of the funds and bonding is still necessary. The plan is essentially that of setting aside a certain amount of money each year from current tax sources and investing the money in interest-bearing securities until the time when it is needed for construction. By this plan the cost is spread over a period of time before construction.

The building reserve fund is closely related to the depreciation reserve fund. The former is usually applied to the financing of additional buildings required because of increases in enrollment or changes in program, whereas the latter is applied to the replacement of worn-out or obsolete structures. Theoretically, financing school building construction might well be carried on by a combination of the building reserve and bonding plans, but in practice there are some rather serious objections to building reserve funds of any considerable size.

If a depreciation or reserve fund is accumulated during the period of usefulness of the asset, a considerable amount will be available when replacement is necessary. Such a plan calls for relatively small reserve payments which would be further augmented by interest earnings. However, such earnings in times of low interest rates and the need for safe investment of public funds would be relatively small. Advocates of the plan have claimed that it is cheaper in the long run, avoids the misuse of credit, and encourages economy. The first claim, namely, that it is cheaper for the community to accumulate a building reserve fund than to borrow, must be studied in the light of the cost to the taxpayer for the prior collection of taxes. Money may be worth more in the hands of taxpayers than the board would be required to pay for borrowing.

The difference in time of tax collections between the reserve fund plan and the borrowing plan may result in a greater total cost under the former than under the latter. If, for example, one compares the cost of a reserve fund built up over a ten-year period preceding the construction of a building with the cost of a ten-year serial bonding plan following construction, imputed interest on tax collection would be based on a ten-year period on all payments, less interest earned from investment. This might amount to more than the total interest costs on the debt, payment on which would begin the first year and be completed in ten years.

Limitation on Bonded Indebtedness

All states in the union have placed limitations on indebtedness that may be created for the construction of school buildings. These limitations vary widely among the states, ranging from 2 per cent in Indiana and Kentucky to 50 per cent of the assessed valuation in Minnesota.[2] Such limitations expressed in percentage of the taxable assessed valuation are less than 6 per cent in twelve states, from 6 to 9 per cent in fourteen states, from 9 to 12 per cent in thirteen states and more than 12 per cent in nine states.

[2] Clayton D. Hutchins and Albert R. Munse, *Public School Finance Programs in the United States*, U.S. Office of Education, 1954.

Some variations may be noted such as in the case of Illinois where there is a 5 per cent limitation on either elementary or high school districts but the total indebtedness on any piece of property for school construction may be 10 per cent. There is also a limitation in this state on the maximum levy that may be made for debt service. Maryland has no limitation on bonded indebtedness but bond issues must be approved by the state legislature. A county referendum may also be required. In Texas there is no absolute limitation; however, the state cannot purchase school bonds that exceed 7 per cent of the valuation. Debt-service levies are limited to 5 mills. The state of Virginia has a limitation of 18 mills for cities but there is no prescribed limit on indebtedness of county school districts. By constitutional amendment, the debt limitation in South Dakota was recently raised from 5 to 10 per cent. Also in Wyoming, a constitutional amendment increased the limitation from 6 to 10 per cent.

Legal debt limits are fixed by the constitution in twenty states and by state statute in twenty-nine states. New York and Montana have both a constitutional and a statutory limitation.

The practice of limiting bonded indebtedness of school districts for construction purposes grew rapidly in the latter half of the nineteenth century. It was a result of increased expansion in school construction and perhaps of inept administration of bonded indebtedness.

In the years following World War II when building costs increased greatly and assessed valuation did not keep pace with rising prices, many school districts found themselves in a position in which they could not provide the necessary school buildings within their bonding capacity. Under such conditions, limitations on bonded indebtedness, even in states where the limitations were fairly high, tended to handicap many districts in providing the new construction needed. It is true that in many cases the indebtedness has been reduced but even with such reduction, increased building costs have made such a demand upon districts that their bonding capacities have been insufficient to meet the needs. To overcome such limitations, it has been suggested that unit construction be resorted to and that bonds be issued for a relatively short term with maximum annual retirement schedules.

Another factor that operates to the disadvantage of customary bond limitations is the fact that assessed valuations in the various states are not directly comparable and when bond limitations are stated in terms of a percentage of the assessed valuation, there may arise a situation in which a low maximum per cent limitation is combined with the low assessed valuation. This makes adequate building virtually impossible, especially in communities of rapidly growing population. Tax rates are of little significance unless they are considered in terms of the amount of money which they produce. There are four solutions to this problem, all of which have been used in recent years: (1) to raise the limits; (2) to make the limits apply to full valuation, regardless of ratios of assessed to true value; (3) to use a building authority to which the district pays rent, thus circumventing the limits; (4) to provide state aid for building construction.

In addition to the limitations stated in the constitution or statutes of the state, there are a number of cases in which state agencies have power to limit school indebtedness. Among these states are Colorado, Florida, Kansas, Massachusetts, New Hampshire, New Jersey, New York, and Texas. In these states the state agencies also have power to approve higher limits under certain emergency conditions.[3]

Types of Bonds

Different kinds of bonds may be classed according to the type of corporation issuing them, the security of principal, the conditions attending payment of interest, and the conditions attending the payment of the principal. In a consideration of bonds issued by school districts, the most important type of classification is that which deals with the conditions for payment of principal and interest.

According to the classification of method of payment of principal there are two chief types: the term bond or sinking-fund bond and the serial bond. A term bond is one which is issued for a period of years, the entire principal being payable at the end of the term and no part of the principal being payable before the end of the term unless the bonds also contain the callable feature. Interest payments may be made annually or semiannually. Frequently term bonds are accompanied by a provision that a sinking fund must be created which will yield a sufficient amount to retire the bonds when they become due. Interest payments on sinking-fund bonds may be made annually or semiannually, but the whole principal is payable at one time, that is, at the end of the term.

The serial bond is one that is retired by payments at certain regular intervals, usually one or more bonds coming due each year throughout the entire term. Interest payments are made annually or semiannually as the bonds may require.

The classification of bonds according to conditions of payment of interest includes two chief types: coupon bonds and registered bonds. Coupon bonds are negotiable instruments and do not show the name of the owner. Interest payments are made on surrender of the coupons that are attached to the bonds. Such bonds are usually not registered with respect to payment of either principal or interest. Registered bonds are issued in the name of the purchaser and interest payments are made to him when they come due. Transfer of registered bonds is made in the

[3] *Ibid.*

home office of the bonding company. In addition to the above two types, bonds may be registered as to principal but not as to interest or they may be interchangeable, either registered or coupon, at the option of the purchaser.

Most school districts now issue serial bonds for relatively short terms. This provides for more rapid payment of principal and more recovery of bonding capacity and is a distinct advantage in a growing community. Serial bonds may be adjusted for any type of schedule for the payment of principal that may be needed in the particular type of school district.

Advantages and Disadvantages of Various Types

A generation ago, the term bond was widely used in financing school buildings. It is difficult to understand why this type of bond should have received such general acceptance unless it is that from the lender's point of view it represents a more stable investment than do the other types and frequently has been purchased at a somewhat lower interest rate. Its most serious disadvantage lies in the fact that the entire principal must be paid at one time or in a relatively short period of time. Its cost is also considerably greater than that of the other types.

When the term bond is accompanied by a sinking fund there appear to be many advantages in that it combines the features of a long-term bond with a systematic annual provision for building up the fund for its retirement. In actual practice, however, many of these advantages have not been realized. The most serious objections attending the creation and maintenance of a sinking fund may be summarized as follows: (1) with changing economic conditions payments to the sinking fund may not always be made in sufficient amounts; (2) changes in the personnel of the board of education may result in changes in policy during the period in which the sinking fund is built up; (3) tendency to reduce current taxation rather than to provide for the payment of an indebtedness that is ten or fifteen years distant is frequently very strong and may result in insufficient funds accumulated; (4) the creation of a sinking fund requires that the board of education invest the funds in safe and profitable investments; (5) there is always the danger of loss attendant on the building up and maintenance of any public trust or endowment fund.

On the whole, it would appear that the disadvantages of a sinking-fund plan of bonding would greatly outweigh the advantages that such bonds may have. In fact, in some states opposition to this method is so strong that the creation of sinking funds is illegal.

The serial type of bond appears to correct most of the weaknesses of the sinking-fund type. Provision is made for the systematic payment of one or more bonds each year in such a manner that at the end of the period the entire amount has been retired. Some of the more obvious advantages of serial bonds are: (1) the annual payments may be arranged in such a manner as to provide for a wide variety of conditions found in local districts; (2) larger payments may be made early in the period, the payments may be equal throughout the period, or larger payments may be made toward the end of the period; (3) the tax rate for bond retirement and bond interest may be kept fairly uniform throughout the period thus avoiding any excessive rate in one or more years; (4) the systematic plan of payment is contained in the bond issue itself and obviates the necessity of creating a sinking fund; (5) the entire issue is set up at the time it is sold and there is no opportunity for changes in school board policy to affect the retirement of any of the bonds; (6) the gradual reduction of interest rates throughout the period presents a saving in money from this type of bond as compared with a straight term bond.

Serial bonds are required by law in thirty-four states whereas in fourteen states serial bonds are not definitely required.

The term of years for which serial bonds are issued varies greatly among the states. The usual term is from fifteen to fifty years. The average term for school bonds is approximately twenty-six years.[4] In six states there is no limitation on the maximum number of years that school bonds may run. Maryland and New Jersey limit bond issues for certain districts to fifteen years. Twenty to twenty-five years is a frequently mentioned term. Few states permit forty years, and Maine is the only one that permits fifty-year bond issues.

Another type of borrowing for capital outlay is the maintenance by states of school building funds for the purpose of lending money to the districts for building construction. This is really a variation of state programs of financing school construction described earlier in this chapter. In effect, this plan is in operation in states that have a considerably large permanent school fund which permits investment in school district bonds. There is, however, little difference in rates so that it becomes a matter of lending money to small school districts that cannot establish a credit rating comparable with the larger ones. The real advantage in this plan becomes evident only when states can lend money to school districts at a lower rate of interest but this sometimes is in conflict with the credit rating of districts.

Interest rates on school bonds usually depend upon several factors. Small districts generally are required to pay higher rates of interest than are large districts with better credit ratings. The type of bond, whether it be serial or sinking fund or the combination of the two, may also affect interest ratings. Such variations in the interest rates can often be avoided by the careful study of all factors.

[4] *Ibid.*

Another very important consideration in the determining of interest rates is the current market value of school bonds. With some study of the bond market it is usually possible for school districts to take advantage of the market in such a way that their bond issues are sold at a reasonable rate of interest.

Schedule of Payment for Serial Bonds

Although serial bonds present many advantages over other types, efficient debt management depends quite as much upon the schedules for payment that are adopted as upon the types of bond issued. Poorly planned schedules of bond retirement may work as much hardship upon a district as would term bonds with the optional clause after ten years, or again, a well managed sinking-fund bond issue may place less burden upon a district than a poorly planned serial bond issue.

A number of factors enter into consideration of the way in which serial bonds are to be retired throughout the period. Among these are population changes of the school districts, changes in school enrollment, changes in property valuation in the district, tax rates for schools and for other governmental purposes, existing indebtedness of the district and of the city or other governmental units, and the policies of the community with respect to indebtedness. Careful study of all these conditions will indicate the best schedule for a particular community at a particular time. Serial bond issues may be scheduled for retirement in a variety of different ways and the schedules may be adjusted to meet varying local conditions. These three general plans are commonly followed: (1) equal annual payments on principal; (2) equal annual payments of principal and interest; and (3) irregular payments on principal.

Where the school population is fairly stable or increasing at a relatively slow rate and where school buildings need not be constructed to take care of large additional numbers of pupils, the method of arranging serial bonds on the basis of equal annual payments on principal appears to be satisfactory. Because of the varying amounts of interest, somewhat larger payments for interest and principal would be made in the beginning of the period than toward the end. This differential may be an advantage in offsetting any additional upkeep for maintenance of the buildings as they grow older. It also provides for possibility of erection of additional buildings before the end of the term. It has the advantage of keeping the tax rates for bond redemption and bond interest fairly uniform.

Under the plan of providing approximately equal total annual payments of principal and interest, the payments on the principal would be relatively smaller in the early years and larger in the later ones. The extent to which the total annual payments may be equal will depend upon the denomination of the bonds. An index of payment may be established for the retirement of serial bonds based on different rates of interest and different lengths of term. Such a bond retirement schedule would require an approximately uniform tax rate for bond redemption and interest over the period.

Various other provisions may be included in the bond retirement schedules for accelerating or decelerating the payments on the principal. In the case of rapidly increasing assessed valuation it may be possible to place the larger payments toward the end of the period without materially increasing the tax rate whereas in a community where there is a decreasing assessed valuation it may be desirable to place the larger payments in the earlier years, thus decreasing the total annual payments toward the end of the period. Such a plan would make it easier to fit new issues into outstanding ones without placing too great a burden upon the taxpayers. Various combinations of these methods are possible depending upon the particular community conditions that prevail.

The method of using unequal annual payments on the principal is suggested largely for the purpose of fitting new bond issues into existing indebtedness in a school district. If there is an indebtedness to run for a number of years that consumes considerable portions of the tax rate for bonded indebtedness it may be necessary to fit new issues into existing ones by permitting no payment on principal until the old issues have been paid. Interest on the new issue must be paid from the beginning. Later larger payments on the new issue can be made or payments on principal and interest can be equalized for the remainder of the period. If, for example, a bond issue of some $100,000 remains in a school district for a period of four years, the new issue would not begin payment on principal until the fifth year and if it is a ten-year issue, the new principal would be paid in six annual payments.

It may be observed that serial bond plans provide for great flexibility in adjusting the payments of new issues to already existing indebtedness in the district and to varying conditions and needs for future bond issues.

Prudent management is of the utmost importance in the handling of bonded indebtedness and bond retirement. Table 22-1 shows an amortization schedule derived from the formula showing annuities whose value at compound interest is one. The table shows the index, the average payment per year and total for all years, the rates of interest from 2 to 5 per cent and for terms of ten to thirty years. The payments are based upon the amounts for each $1,000 of indebtedness. Such an amortization schedule must, of course, be adjusted to fit the denominations of the bonds.

Table 22-1 Amortizing Schedule, Indices of Amortization Factors,
Average Annual and Total Costs Per $1,000 *

	10 years	15 years	20 years	30 years
2 per cent index	0.1113265	0.0778254	0.0611567	0.0446499
Average per year	$ 111.33	$ 77.83	$ 61.16	$ 44.65
Total—all years	1,113.30	1,167.45	1,223.20	1,339.50
3 per cent index	0.1172305	0.0837665	0.0672157	0.0510192
Average per year	$ 117.23	$ 83.77	$ 67.22	$ 51.02
Total—all years	1,172.30	1,256.55	1,344.40	1,530.60
4 per cent index	0.1232909	0.0899411	0.0735817	0.0578300
Average per year	$ 123.29	$ 89.94	$ 73.58	$ 57.83
Total—all years	1,232.90	1,349.10	1,471.60	1,734.90
5 per cent index	0.1295045	0.0963422	0.0802425	0.0650514
Average per year	$ 129.50	$ 96.34	$ 80.24	$ 65.05
Total—all years	1,295.00	1,445.10	1,604.80	1,951.50

* N. E. Viles, *Local School Construction Programs,* Bulletin, 1957, No. 20, U.S. Office of Education, Washington, 1957, p. 54.

Approval by the Electorate

One of the general requirements for the issuing of bonds by school corporations is that the issue be approved by the people of the district at an election called for the purpose or at any regular election. The theory back of this requirement is that popular approval acts as a check upon amounts that may be issued and that it is a pledge of good faith on the part of the people where property is taxed to redeem the bonds and pay the interest. In some states, the fact that property owners are taxed for the redemption of bonds has been interpreted to mean that only property owners may vote on bond issues. This position is hardly warranted in view of the fact that some taxes are shifted to non-property owners and that no property qualification is required for general elections. In some cases, such statutes have been declared unconstitutional by the supreme courts of the states.

In a number of states there are other specifications for issuing bonds such as state approval and the securing of state assistance before the people of the district vote upon the bond issue. In twenty-one states, state approval of local bond issues is required. In twelve the approval must be secured before the election is held and in six states school district bond issues must first be offered to the state agency. In four states there is state assistance in the sale of school bonds.[5]

[5] Hutchins and Munse, *op. cit.,* p. 49.

Preparation of Bond Issues

In the preparation of bond issues there are numerous details to which the school officials must give their attention. They should have knowledge of the information that should be made available to the public as well as that required for the preparation of the prospectus to be made available to the bond purchasers. They should also be familiar with the legal requirements and restrictions concerning bonding in the state.

With respect to the type of information that should be made available to the public, the superintendent and board of education should make a thorough survey of the school needs in the community. The survey should take into consideration the population trends, both total and school, which have taken place during the past years and it should estimate the changes that will be likely to occur in the future. The survey should also determine the most desirable location and size of each new building to be erected, together with the number of pupils and grades to be housed in each. Complete data should be available with respect to the changes in the valuation of property and in tax rates that have taken place in past years and that will be needed in future years. There should also be noted any change in economic conditions that is likely to influence the future building needs of the community or the ability to pay.

When this information has been assembled it should be presented to the public. The manner of presenting the information to the public will vary according to local conditions. In general, it is better to place such items before the board of education and the public in a continuous program of the interpretation of the schools than to concentrate upon it too intensively at the time immediately preceding the vote on the bond issue. The entire program of public relations is one of very great importance in securing confidence and the willingness of the community to vote the necessary bonds for adequate housing of the school program.

Information need to prepare the prospectus of the bonds to be sold should be placed in the hands of such technical assistants as may be necessary to prepare an attractive and accurately descriptive brochure of the bond issue. In the preparation of such a prospectus, state departments of education are often in a position to give information which may be needed to secure the best rates for bond issues.

Voting School Bonds

Legal restrictions may differ in the different states and sometimes even among different districts in the same state. Much will depend upon the custom of voting bonds that is in effect at the time the issue is to be sold. School bonds are normally issued to be sold but sales are not limited to the state of origin. Bond buyers must often depend upon the financial integrity of the local district and upon compliance with state regulations. Bond prices and interest rates may be affected by state authorization and the manner in which they are to be paid.

The percentage of the voters required for the approval of a bond issue may vary from state to state. In some cases it may be a simple majority, whereas in other states a two-thirds majority is required. Local officers must be sure to satisfy themselves that all legal requirements are complied with before the vote on bonds is called. Before calling for a bond election district officials should make certain that all the necessary information—such as assessed valuation, bonding capacity of the district, proper authorization of the issue by the board, the attorney's report, and the types of bonds to be sold—is made known to the voters before they are asked to vote at the polls.

In most states school bonds cannot be sold for less than par value. Where it is permissible to sell them below par value, there are usually certain other restrictions. These regulations are intended to protect school districts in the disposition of their bonds. When a district has approved a bond issue, selling below par would result in securing less money than was originally intended or in the necessity of selling more bonds than were approved in order to realize the amount of money needed.

Maximum legal interest rates on school bonds differ in the various states, although the larger school districts can usually take advantage of the bond market and sell at considerably lower rates of interest than the legal rate.

State Service to Local Districts

As mentioned in the preceding section, state departments of education may render valuable service to school districts in the preparation and sale of bond issues. Sometimes this service may be rendered directly by the state department of education and again it may be rendered by other state agencies through the cooperation of the state departments. In either case, state agencies may give supervision to school districts in this matter which is usually rather closely circumscribed by legal restrictions. One of the areas in which state agencies may give service to local districts is in the interpretation of the legal requirements and in setting forth the steps by which the district may proceed in the voting and sale of bond issues. There are usually legal requirements with respect to notice of time, places of voting, manner of voting, and persons who may vote. Some of the state departments have issued detailed instructions covering all these matters and offering examples of the various notices.

In some of the state departments, legal and technical services are provided for the administration of school bond issues. These are services which individual schools might find difficult to secure otherwise at reasonable cost. State regulations and supervision of school bond issues may further serve as a means of maintaining the credit of local districts and may, in some cases, prevent the unwise management of bonding and consequent pyramiding of indebtedness. Such service is beneficial not only to local districts but to the state.

SUMMARY

The greatly increased capital expenditures of school districts make it essential that adequate programs of financing capital outlay be established and maintained.

Financing plans in local districts are largely pay-as-you-go or bonding or some combination or modification of the two. Pay-as-you-go seems to be applicable only to the large school districts where considerable construction is carried on each year. In most of the smaller schools and even in some large city districts, bonding plans are necessary. While there are advantages and disadvantages in each type, by far the most school building construction is financed through the issuing of bonds.

School district bonds now generally issued are of the serial type although there may be some term bonds secured by sinking funds. It is obvious that the serial bond has distinct advantages over the term bond. Moreover, the manner of payment of principal and interest may be so arranged as to become adapted to local community needs. It is necessary that state regulations respecting the type of bonds that may be issued, the length of the term for which they may run, approval by the electorate or some state agency, preparation of the bond prospectus, the manner of voting the bonds, the sale of bonds, and other details of local administration be carefully adhered to. Where state service in the issuing of bonds is available, school districts should take advantage of such service.

The principle of prudence is the most important one operating in the management of local school indebtedness. Although the procedure is governed rather rigidly by state requirements, there is nevertheless a large opportunity for school officials to exercise efficient management of their indebtedness.

QUESTIONS FOR STUDY AND DISCUSSION

1. To what extent is capital outlay financed through current school funds? What type of expenditures may be made and what restrictions are there in your state?

2. Summarize the advantages and disadvantages of state programs of financing capital outlay and local district plans.

3. Summarize the conditions of financing capital outlay through state plans in one or more states with which you are familiar.

4. What are the relative merits and limitations of the bonding plan for the financing of school buildings? Consider the plan from the standpoint of the total cost, the burden on the taxpayer, and the assurance that your building needs will be met.

5. What types of bonds may be issued by school districts in your state? Are serial bonds compulsory? What is the legal limitation on the amount of indebtedness that may be incurred by the various school districts? Compare it with limitations in other states.

6. Select a community with which you are familiar and outline for it a plan for the retirement of a bond issue, the amount of which would be adequate for the construction of new school buildings. Determine the type of bonds to be used and the schedule for retirement.

7. Outline the various legal requirements that must be met in voting a bond issue in your state. Consider the requirements for the election, who may vote, vote required to carry the election, notices that must be given, and the like.

8. Outline the information that should be given to the public concerning bond issues in a community with which you are familiar. Consider, also, the information needed for the bond prospectus.

9. Outline a prospectus of bonds to be sold by a school district, giving all of the essential information.

SELECTED REFERENCES

American Association of School Administrators: *American School Buildings,* Twenty-seventh Yearbook, Washington, 1949.

Barr, William M.: "The Capital Need and Taxpaying Ability of Indiana Public Schools," doctor's thesis, Indiana University, Bloomington, Ind., 1953.

Burke, Arvid J.: *Financing Public Schools in the United States,* Harper & Brothers, New York, 1957, chap. 17.

———: "Some Proposals for Better Financing of School House Construction," *Nation's Schools,* vol. 53, pp. 48–51, February, 1954.

Close, Wendell C.: "Effective Marketing of School Bonds," *California Journal of Education Research,* vol. 5, pp. 51–56, March, 1954.

Johns, R. L., and Edgar L. Morphet (eds.): *Problems and Issues of Public School Finance,* Bureau of Publications, Teachers College, Columbia University, New York, 1952, chap. 12.

Linn, Henry H.: *School Business Administration,* The Ronald Press Company, New York, 1956, chap. 12.

Rosenstengel, William Everett, and Jefferson N. Eastmond: *School Finance,* The Ronald Press Company, New York, 1957, chap. 15.

U.S. Office of Education: *State Provisions for Financing Public School Capital Outlay Programs,* Bulletin, 1951, No. 6, Washington, 1951.

Viles, N. E.: *Local School Construction Programs,* U.S. Office of Education, Bulletin, 1957, No. 20, Washington, 1957.

23. Supply and equipment management

MANAGEMENT of school supplies and equipment is one of the mechanized tasks that should be performed with efficiency and dispatch in order that the teaching personnel may have the necessary materials with which to carry on the day-to-day work of education. This phase of administration is usually handled by personnel in the business office where the various steps in the procedure are carried on. School material supply and equipment management is but one phase of material management in public schools. The entire scope of such administration includes the procurement of the necessary materials for maintenance and operation equipment and supplies, and in a general sense the procurement of all the physical facilities, with the exception of new buildings and sites, needed for the conduct of the schools.

School supply and equipment management embraces a number of steps in which are included the procedures of purchasing, receiving, storing, and distribution of materials and supplies. Each of these steps should be carried on with efficiency and dispatch in order that the necessary materials may be available when needed.

TRENDS IN SCHOOL SUPPLY MANAGEMENT

In the schools of an earlier day, the materials, equipment, supplies, and textbooks needed were relatively few in number and their management relatively simple. A few items of school furniture, books, and fuel were about the only materials and supplies required in many of the schools. Costs of such items constituted a relatively small part of the total school budget.

As the work of education expanded, as the number of persons served

447

increased, and as programs became more extensive, more and more specialized items of supply and equipment became necessary. Today one finds hundreds of different items in the storeroom of a modern school system. Although the supply budget has greatly increased, it still constitutes a relatively small proportion of the total operating budget.

Efficient management is an important phase of supply administration since proper selection, purchase, and use of materials may greatly enhance the effectiveness of the work of the capable teacher and greatly facilitate pupil learning.

The organization and administration of the supply department should be in harmony with the educational purposes of the school system. The department should be closely integrated with the administration of personnel, and curriculum, and should be under the direction of a business official who is directly responsible to the superintendent of schools. The whole cycle of operations should stress economy, utility, and purpose. The steps in the cycle of operation must vary somewhat from one school system to another, but the essential features of cooperative centralized management and procedure in purchasing and distribution should be preserved.

The chief problems that arise in the purchasing of materials and supplies in the public school system are the determination of the kinds of materials and supplies that will best serve the needs, the adoption of adequate specifications, and efficient methods of purchasing, storing, and distribution. The wide range of items used—including those for instruction, general control, operation, maintenance, and auxiliary services—presents a long and varied list.

The whole procedure of selection, purchasing, storing, and distribution of materials and supplies, including textbooks, should be carried on in accordance with certain recognized standards that have been developed in practice.

SUPPLIES AND EQUIPMENT

The great variety of items required in a school system necessitates making a distinction between what might be termed items of equipment and items of supply. One reason for this distinction is that in any accounting system, school equipment, whether it is new or replacement, is classified differently from items of supply. The classification is not difficult to make as between the large pieces of school equipment and the smaller items of instructional supply, but there will always be some items that will cause confusion unless a clearly defined classification has been adopted. For the sake of uniformity in accounting, it is often desirable to have definitions of items of supply and items of equipment. Usually supplies are defined as nonpermanent materials, exclusive of textbooks, that are used for instruction or maintenance or operation of the schools. The definition embraces those items that are consumed or used up in a relatively short period of time. It may also embrace small items that are easily lost or broken. Examples of materials consumed in use are such things as paper, pens, crayons, ink, fuel, lumber, cleaning materials, and materials for maintenance. Examples of items that have a relatively short life are such things as brooms, blackboard erasers, rulers, and other similar articles. Materials that are fragile or easily broken might be such items as laboratory glassware and home economics supplies.

There have developed many variations of this general definition. Some have proposed that items costing more than ten dollars and having a life of more than ten years should be classified as equipment, whereas others have proposed that the limit be set at five dollars and a life of five years or more. These are arbitrary distinctions and are made only for the purpose of convenience. In a 1957 report, the United States Office of Education defined supplies as material items of an expendable nature that are consumed, worn out, or deteriorated in use or items that lose their identity through fabrication or incorporation into different or more complex systems. Equipment is defined as material items of a nonexpendable nature such as a built-in facility, a movable or fixed unit of furniture or furnishings, an instrument or apparatus, a machine, an instructional skilled-training device or a set of small articles whose parts are replaceable or repairable, the whole retaining its identity and utility over a period of time.[1] Whatever standard is adopted, it should be uniform throughout the school and preferably throughout the state. Lists of items of supply and equipment are usually a part of state-wide uniform accounting systems and provide a guide for distinguishing between the two categories.

Textbooks are usually placed in a class by themselves since they must be distinguished from library books and other reference books. Textbooks furnished by the school to the pupil usually serve for a limited period depending upon their binding and extent of use. A period of three years is generally considered as the life of a textbook used by the pupils. Reference books and library books have a longer life, and for that reason would qualify as equipment rather than supplies. Expenditures for books for public libraries are usually classed as expenditures for auxiliary services.

Studies by Brickell,[2] Teresa,[2] Campbell,[2] and Bothwell[3] indicate that

[1] Paul Reason and Alvius L. White, *Financial Accounting for Local and State School Systems*, State Educational Records and Reports Series, Handbook II, U.S. Office of Education, Washington, 1957, pp. 222–223.

[2] See Donald H. Ross (ed.), *Administration for Adaptability*, Metropolitan School Study Council, New York, 1958, pp. 370–372.

[3] Bruce K. Bothwell, *Creative Expenditures for Quality Education*, Associated Public School Systems, New York, 1958.

there is considerable significance in those small items of expenditure associated with efforts to enhance the quality of the educational program. Their findings counsel a special coding that will facilitate assembling these items from the various categories where they are normally classified—often in the subitem "miscellaneous." As is pointed out in Chapter 7, expenditure for such items is one of the facts of great yield for predicting the quality of the schooling. Bothwell gives the following as examples of items in this category. Note that they are not by any means limited to supplies and equipment.

Quality Improvement	*Quality Related*
Art and Music Supplies	Medical and Dental
Audio-Visual Supplies	Assembly Program
Field Trips	Board Travel
Health and Physical Education	Staff Travel
Supplementary Readers	Staff Memberships
Library Books	Public Relations
Science Supplies	Research and In-service Training
Guidance Supplies	
Manual and Practical Arts	

SELECTION OF SUPPLIES AND EQUIPMENT

The great variation in the amount and kind of instructional supplies and equipment used in public schools suggests that sufficient attention be given this phase of school administration so that all necessary items may be available. The first step in selection procedure for the supply department is for teachers, janitors, maintenance personnel, clerks, and others who use the items to be involved so that the best selection may be made without excessive duplication in the number and kinds of items. Standardized supply lists have the advantage of avoiding unnecessary duplication of items that vary slightly in their specifications, and provide a ready reference for those who are to select the various items.

Standardization of both quality and quantity according to definite criteria means economy in purchase. Among such criteria may be mentioned adaptability, quality, and use. One of the first requirements for selection of supplies and materials is that the items should be adapted for use in the school program for which they are intended. This requires a careful analysis of the work to be done on different grade levels and for different subjects.

Every item of supply may be purchased in many different grades of quality and the selection for a particular purpose should be in harmony with the quality that is best adapted for the particular use. For example, one may find teachers desiring paper for pupil use that varies greatly in quality, size, packaging, and other features. As far as possible, the quality of materials and supplies best adapted for a particular purpose should be used widely throughout the system under similar conditions. This makes it unnecessary to purchase many different items where one standardized item might well serve a much wider use.

A periodic inspection should be made of storerooms and warehouses as well as classrooms to ascertain what items of supply are in most demand, to check the items of supply that may be on hand but not used, and to see that supplies are not hoarded. By careful attention to such details, the items necessary can be provided without waste and within the budgetary requirements of the school system.

It should be emphasized that although standardized lists of supplies are desirable for the purpose of reducing to a minimum the number of different items that should be purchased, care should be taken to avoid any curtailment of supplies that may be needed in programs and may not be on the standardized list. Frequently, teachers develop projects in connection with their classroom activities which demand special materials and supplies, somewhat different from those on the standardized list. When this occurs, special requisitions should be made out by the building principal for the materials that are needed. This provides for flexibility in a supply list and leads to revised supply lists developed through experience.

Criteria for the Selection of Equipment

As in the selection of supplies, it is important that criteria be developed for the selection of equipment. All equipment used in the school system should be adequate for the purpose for which it is to be used and economical in operation and in cost. A number of criteria for the selection of equipment have been suggested. These are as follows:

1. Equipment should be secured at the lowest cost consistent with quality and utilization.

2. Equipment should be of such quality in its materials, construction, and workmanship as to give evidence of strength and durability.

3. The utility or value of equipment with reference to its particular use should be consistent with the cost and results to be secured.

4. The educational value of equipment should, in the greatest degree possible, contribute to the educational program.

5. There should be a degree of standardization of certain essential specifications in equipment materials and design which will make for some uniformity as to construction, without necessarily determining the specific brand or make.

6. The reliability and integrity of the vendor should be considered with regard to financial stability, dependability, and the proper attitude toward the product.

7. Ability of the vendor to service his product is an important consideration when purchasing equipment.

8. Economy and long life factors of equipment through the servicing which may be done by the maintenance department of the school should be considered.

9. The effect of any piece of equipment on the use or wear of other equipment should be considered.

10. There should be safeguards and protection of funds through specific and clearly worded contracts and agreements.

STANDARDS AND SPECIFICATIONS

In order to meet the criteria described above, it is essential that an accurate description of each item be made. Such descriptions are called specifications. They describe in detail the kinds of materials and supplies that are needed in the school system.

Standards of Quality

While it may be desirable to revise the specifications from time to time as experience is gained in the use of the materials, it is needless to mention that specifications for each item should be complete, that they should include enough details so that there can be no substitution of items of different quality from that intended. The following is an example of incomplete specifications:

Number needed	Article and specifications	Unit price
1	Foot rules, hardwood, graduated to fourths and inches on one side	About $0.10

Here is the same article specified in full:

Number needed	Article	Specifications	Unit price
1	Foot rules	Select rock maple, 1⅛ in. wide, with double scale divided into eighths and running opposite directions. Opposite side graduated into ½, ¼ ft. Varnished, weight per dozen, 1½ lb.	$0.25

Such specifications or definitions of the standard of quality desired for any item on the list as it has been developed by teachers, principals, and supervisors is necessary to insure that the right quality of merchandise be supplied. Complete specifications are needed when more than one firm is asked to bid on the supplies or when the same articles are purchased year after year. One cannot always depend upon trade names or brands alone without knowing more specifically the details of construction, composition, and nature of goods. As materials are tested through use in the school system, or through special laboratory tests whenever this is feasible, a standard of quality may be determined which is best adapted to the needs of the school and of those using the materials.

Standards of Quantity

It is quite as important that school systems develop standards of quantity for each item used as it is that standards of quality be determined. Without such standards, there is likely to be great variation in the amount of supplies used by various teachers within the school system without any apparent reason for the difference. When materials are of a desired quality, it should be relatively easy to determine the amount of any item that will be used in each grade under a given school program. The purpose of setting up these standards is not to place a limitation upon the supplies that may be used by a class, but rather to determine units of consumption that will simplify the estimation of needs.

Many items of supply may be eliminated through careful standardization. The result is a reduction in the number of different items on the supply list. In one school system it was found that many items of school supply were eliminated through standardization, the number being reduced from 124 to 68, or by 45 per cent. The process should eliminate only unnecessary supplies, not any that are needed by the pupils. The elimination of items is often brought about because they have been requisitioned by a relatively small number of teachers. When agreement is reached concerning any item, it is usually found that a much smaller number of different items meets all needs.

Although there are certain administrative advantages in the computation of the average quantities of supplies used by each pupil, some may see in this practice an overstandardization of supply lists and, consequently, limitations in the flexibility of the service of the supply department to the instructional program. This, of course, is not what is intended when standards of quantity are developed; their chief purpose is to facilitate the computation of the amounts of each item needed for the succeeding fiscal period. Nevertheless, there may be some school systems in which administrators and teachers feel that a more flexible plan is essential for the conduct of the best instructional program. One such variation is to give each principal a supply allowance to be spent in the purchase of materials and supplies particularly adapted to the various activities and projects that he wishes to carry on in his building. This plan has much to recommend it, because of the many possibilities it affords and the consequent adaptation it permits to the work of a particular teacher, grade, or subject matter field. The greater supply amounts required by one teacher may be offset by lesser amounts others may desire. By this method all selection is made cooperatively between teachers and administrative officials and all purchases are made through the central office.

For a number of years Ardsley, New York, has followed the rewarding practice of earmarking for each teacher annually an amount of money in addition to the regular supply allotment. Each teacher is permitted to purchase, either directly or through the office, anything he needs. If he makes the purchases personally, he submits a bill for reimbursement. Unused balances are added to the following year's allotment. With special permission the allotments for two or three years in the future may be drawn on to make possible a purchase requiring more than one year's special allotment.

It should be emphasized here that school systems should not fix arbitrarily certain quantities of supplies to be used in any particular grade, subject, or period of time. This practice may unnecessarily limit or handicap the program of education. If the principle of adaptability is to be served, there should be sufficient leeway in the quantity and quality of supplies to permit carrying out the program as planned in a particular grade or subject.

A balance must be maintained between the proper degree of centralization and decentralization in school supply management. In large school systems where supply management is highly centralized, there may be a degree of rigidity in the entire procedure that often fails to meet the needs of individual teachers. Obviously, a high degree of decentralization is wasteful, since it does not permit quantity purchasing. The advantages of each plan should be taken into consideration and adaptations made to the school system in question. Any system of supply management will require some modification in different school systems. In general it may be said that the system is best which best serves the schools and effects economies.

PURCHASING SCHOOL SUPPLIES AND EQUIPMENT

Purchasing school supplies, materials, and equipment should be in the hands of a centralized purchasing department through which all orders are handled. In large school systems, this may require the service of a purchasing agent and several assistants, such as bookkeepers and accountants, whereas in small school systems, purchasing must be handled by an assistant or secretary working under the direction of the super-

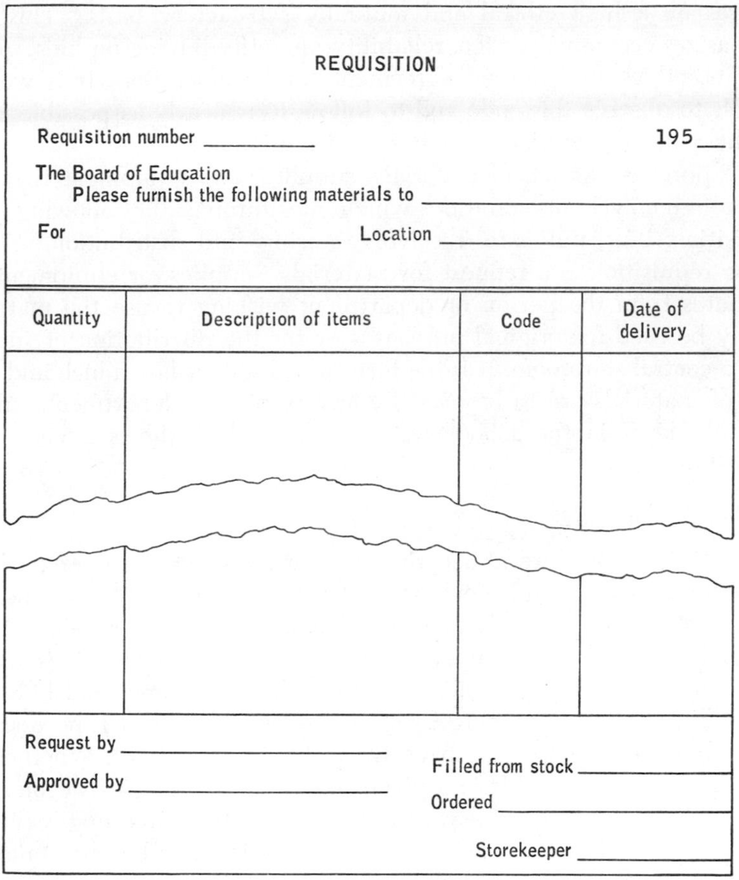

REQUISITION

Requisition number ________ 195__

The Board of Education
Please furnish the following materials to ________

For ________ Location ________

Quantity	Description of items	Code	Date of delivery

Request by ________

Approved by ________

Filled from stock ________

Ordered ________

Storekeeper ________

Fig. 23-1 Requisition form.

intendent of schools. Centralization is important for the reason that all orders, specifications, contracts, and other records can be filed in one place in order that ready access may be had to them at any time.

In most school systems, it will be found to be advantageous to purchase materials and supplies in quantities and at times well in advance of the opening of the school year in order that they may be available when needed.

The buying-selling code for schools prepared in 1954 by the American

Association of School Administrators, the Association of School Business Officials, and the National School Board Association and the National School Service Institute sets forth certain principles which are designed to promote economy, to increase service, to insure reliability, to facilitate purchase and delivery practices, and establish buying and selling procedures on a high ethical and mutually satisfactory basis.[4] This code emphasizes economy, service, reliability, quantity buying on bids, quality benefits, ethics, and mutual agreements and cooperation. It is well for schools to observe this code and to follow it as nearly as possible in the purchase of all materials, supplies, and equipment.

The purchase of school materials, supplies, and equipment is carried on through a cycle of operations which goes through the following steps: requisition, bids, purchase, receiving, storing, and distribution.

The requisition is a request for materials, supplies, or equipment and originates from the person or department wishing to use the materials. It may be used for original purchases or for the distribution of supplies from a central storeroom. It is the form which shows how much and what kind of materials are to be used by any particular department, subject, or grade level in the school system. Figure 23-1 shows a convenient requisition form.

Purchasing on Bids

The entire procedure of securing bids and awarding contracts should be outlined in rules and regulations of the board of education and may often contain many details over and beyond state requirements. When materials, supplies, and equipment are purchased on bids it is usually done only after careful specifications have been prepared and bids have been secured from a number of vendors. In some states, it is necessary to secure bids on all purchases over a certain stated amount. Whether this legal requirement prevails in a given community or not, it is economical and good practice to purchase through competitive bidding since this usually results in lower prices and standards may be maintained if specifications are properly made.

When vendors are asked to bid on a supply list, they must be furnished with copies of the exact specification for each item. Such specifications should be up to date and on file in the purchasing office. This office should also have lists of reliable vendors in order that the bids may be secured promptly and from vendors of established reputation. In a regular designated meeting of the board of education, bids should be opened, the selection of vendors made, and contracts awarded to the successful bidders. Usually contracts are let to the vendor submitting the lowest bids;

[4] Henry H. Linn, *School Business Administration*, The Ronald Press Company, New York, 1956, p. 277.

however, other considerations may enter into the selection. Figure 23-2 shows a convenient form for bidding on items.

BID FORM

Bid number _____

Board of Education _____ 195__

To_____ Address _____

Please quote lowest prices on the materials and supplies described below. The Board of Education reserves the right to reject any or all bids. The conditions under which the bids are made are given on the reverse side of this sheet. Bids will be received at the office of the Board of Education until _____ 195__.

_____   _____
Secretary Board of Education   President Board of Education

Unit	Quantity	Description of items	Unit price	Amount

_____
Firm making the bid

Fig. 23-2   Bid form.

Purchasing Procedure

When bids have been opened and the selection of a vendor has been made, the contract with a successful bidder may vary from a formal contract to a more or less informal agreement. In the case of large purchases, it is often desirable to have the vendor give bond in such amount as to insure delivery in the required quantity and quality. Less formal contracts or agreements may be made when a single delivery is involved or when the total amount of the purchase is small.

The board of education should always reserve the right to reject any or all bids. This enables them to make a somewhat better selection of firms with which they may wish to place contracts. In the case of substitute materials offered by certain firms, the board of education should retain the right of acceptance or rejection.

Fig. 23-3 Purchase order.

When the successful bidder has been selected, the purchasing office fills out the purchase order which again should contain the essential information regarding the purchase. The purchase order is usually prepared in three or four copies on paper of different colors. The original copy is sent to the vendor, one copy is filed as an unpaid bill, one is sent to the warehouse, and one is filed in the purchasing department according to the number of the purchase order to be used for future reference. As in the case of the bid form, the purchase order may vary, but it should contain the essential information. Figure 23-3 shows an illustration of a simple type of purchase order.

In some areas it has been customary to resort to cooperative buying by a number of school districts joining in the purchase of materials and supplies. This is usually a good plan for the smaller school systems or for rural school districts since it permits them to take advantage of quantity purchasing. Reports of such cooperative purchasing indicate a saving in money and the purchase of material of a better quality than would be possible if each school district purchased separately.

STORAGE OF MATERIALS AND SUPPLIES

On receipt of each shipment all materials and supplies should be consigned to a central receiving storehouse where items are unpacked and contents carefully noted in order that claims may be filed promptly. In large school systems where it may be desirable to store the supplies in various buildings, this step should be taken only after goods have been checked in at the central storeroom or the receiving department.

The matter of proper storage of materials and supplies is as important in small as in large school systems, because approximately the same percentage of the budget is spent for these items.

Centralized Storage

Larger school systems usually have a central storeroom or warehouse from which all supplies are delivered to the several schools at a later date. This is a convenient place for receiving and checking goods. In school systems where facilities are available, tests may be made of the quality of the various supply items. In school systems where facilities are not available, such testing might be done by state agencies or agencies of the state university. Some school systems use the facilities of high school laboratories for making the more simple tests.

When materials are stored in a central storeroom or storehouse, it becomes necessary to devise some means for the distribution of materials and supplies to the different parts of the school system where they may be needed. This is usually done by periodic deliveries to the various school buildings, the time of delivery depending upon the items requisitioned by the schools and the organization of the delivery system. While there are obvious advantages to centralized storage, there is the added cost of delivering the goods to the various divisions of the school system.

Decentralized Storage

The plan of storing materials, supplies, and equipment in the various school buildings rather than in one centrally located warehouse is usually carried on by schools where the central storeroom is not available or where space is available in the various buildings. This method locates materials and supplies in more accessible storerooms and does not require as much delivery as the central storage plan. It is obviously impossible to place a sufficient quantity of materials in each building so that a central storeroom will not be required. The decentralized plan may eliminate some costs of overhead and may save time in securing the materials when needed.

Classroom Storage

Regardless of whether the school system uses centralized or decentralized storage, it is necessary to have some materials and supplies in the classroom or in rooms readily accessible to classrooms. Usually this type of storage space is limited and relatively small amounts of supplies may be kept readily accessible to the classrooms. The advantage of this plan is that the more commonly used items will be readily available when needed without the necessity of requisitions, deliveries, and elaborate records.

Storeroom Requirements

Storerooms should be ample in size, conveniently located, clean, and dry. The storeroom should be furnished with shelves and bins or other convenient compartments in which the various items are kept. Ample protection of materials and supplies in storerooms would require that they be fireproof and free from deteriorating influences.

The location and size of storerooms depends largely upon the plan in use in a particular school system. It is likely that a combination of centralized and decentralized plans for storing materials and supplies will be found most satisfactory in many school districts.

Storeroom Records

Accurate records of materials, supplies, and equipment on hand in the central storeroom is an important phase of supply management. The person in charge of supplies should be responsible for all material, supplies, and equipment purchased by the school system, regardless of where such materials and supplies are stored. In each storeroom there should be an accurate perpetual inventory of all materials on hand. This inventory should have space for entering the amount of each supply on hand, addition to supply, distribution of materials and supplies made, and the balance on hand at any time.

When materials are received they should be carefully checked against the invoice and each item should be entered on its proper perpetual inventory card. Likewise when requisitions are received and deliveries made, each item distributed should again be checked off on this sheet so that a balance can be struck at any time showing the number of pieces of any item on hand. Figure 23-4 illustrates a perpetual inventory card.

Date	Amount on hand	Amount received	Order number	Amount distributed	Requisition number	School unit	Amount on hand

Storeroom _____

Storekeeper _____

Fig. 23-4   Perpetual inventory sheet.

Inventory for supplies may not be needed. There should, nevertheless, be a plan of accounting for stores. In its simplest form, such a plan would consist of a stores ledger and periodic inventories of materials and supplies on hand. Those materials and supplies received should be entered on the stores ledger and those delivered to teachers and other school personnel should be credited to the building or organization for which they are intended. The same method should be followed in handling janitor supplies. Any unused materials should be returned to the storeroom and the account added to the quantity on hand. Only through such systematic methods of accounting can waste be avoided.[5]

[5] William E. Arnold, William B. Castetter, Walter C. Reusser, and Roman J. Verhaalen, "Business Management: Safeguarding School Funds and Property," chap. XIII in R. L. Johns and E. L. Morphet (eds.), *Problems and Issues in Public School Finance*, Bureau of Publications, Teachers College, Columbia University, New York, 1952.

TEXTBOOKS

A rather specialized category of school materials and supplies is that of textbooks. Procedures should be developed for the selection, purchase, and distribution of textbooks which will function smoothly and efficiently. There is considerable difference among states in the requirements for the selection and purchase of textbooks. Regardless of whether textbooks are selected on a state basis or whether they are entirely a matter of local concern, it is desirable that the selection be made locally by a committee of teachers who follow definite criteria for choosing books in different fields. Frequently score cards are used whereby different school readers, for example, are evaluated. When textbooks are provided by the school district, as they are now in most cases, it is desirable to initiate a definite budget that provides either for annual purchase charged to current expenditures or for purchases charged in part to current funds and in part prepaid account. For example, if a large order of textbooks is purchased in one year and is intended to serve for a three-year period, one-third of the cost is charged to current expenditure and two-thirds to the prepaid account. Books that are repaired or become obsolete and must be replaced, as well as any losses that may occur, are charged to current expenses for free textbooks.

When the district provides free textbooks, it is essential that an accurate, comprehensive record of books assigned to pupils be kept. This not only prevents loss but permits a charge to be made to pupils who may mistreat or lose books. In case books are purchased by the school district and resold to pupils, as may be the case with workbooks or similar materials, a system of internal accounting should provide the necessary records. Net receipts or deficits only should be charged against current receipts or costs.

Procedures for purchasing textbooks may follow very closely the regular purchasing procedures of the school system, but there may be certain differences that should be emphasized. Practices in the schools, such as local adoptions, may dictate that certain books be purchased from a given publisher for the length of the period of adoption. As in all purchasing, advantage should be taken of school discounts.

SUMMARY

The provision of materials, supplies, and equipment for school systems affords many opportunities for service to the educational program; it makes possible economy and prudent management. Frequently savings can be made through wise selection, standardization, and quantity purchasing. The entire procedure should be developed and set forth in rules and regulations which will serve as a guide for the formulation of better procedures. The distinction between equipment and supplies and the compilation of suggestive lists of such materials aid in the classification of many items. The entire procedure is a cyclic one beginning with selection and proceeding through the development of standards of quality and quantity, purchasing, storage, and finally distribution and records of the many items that fall under these categories.

Selection is essentially a cooperative enterprise among those who carry on the instructional, operational, and maintenance programs. All materials, equipment, and supplies should be chosen with a view to service for the purpose for which they are selected. Standards of quality are defined by written specifications for each item. Standards of quantity developed over a period of time aid in budgeting and distribution of supplies. Both are devices in prudential management. Purchasing by means of bids and buying in large quantities are both economies. Storage and distribution are essential steps in the system of supply management.

The selection, purchase, and distribution of textbooks present problems that may differ somewhat from the regular procedures of purchasing materials and supplies. An important reason for this is that textbooks are usually the concern of the state more than other materials and supplies. The same general principle, however, with respect to selection, purchase, storage, and distribution should be followed as in the cases of other materials.

QUESTIONS FOR STUDY AND DISCUSSION

1. Show by examples how the standardization of supply lists has brought about better materials and supplies and has proved a real economy.

2. Trace the various steps in the procedure of purchasing, receiving, storing, and distributing school materials and supplies.

3. Cite examples of cooperative buying of school materials and supplies. Show how such cooperation results in increased quality and economy.

4. Give illustrations of complete and incomplete specifications. Show the possible results of incomplete specifications when bids are let to a number of different firms.

5. Are there any laws or state regulations in your state concerning the purchase of school equipment and supplies? Are bids required for purchases made in excess of certain amounts?

6. Show how the principles of buying school supplies outlined in this chapter can be applied efficiently to small school systems. What adaptation should be made?

7. Make a survey of equipment and supplies used in one grade or department in a local school system. What items are supplied by the school and what items are provided by the pupils?

8. Outline the state requirements for the selection and purchase of textbooks in one or more states. What are the provisions and what special funds, if any, are available for this purpose?

9. Prepare a plan for textbook selection which may be used by a group of teachers or administrators for the selection of textbooks in a local school system.

10. Prepare a plan of textbook accounting in a school system that provides free textbooks to pupils. What records are needed? How does the plan operate?

SELECTED REFERENCES

Balluff, Louis N.: "Using a Comparative Check List of Construction Costs," *American School and University*, American School Publishing Corp., New York, 1957–1958, pp. 267–272.

Barbour, Julius E.: "Stretching the School Dollar," *Nation's Schools*, vol. 44, p. 584, August, 1949.

Burke, Arvid J.: *Financing Public Schools in the United States*, Harper & Brothers, New York, 1951, chap. 19, pp. 506, 532.

Clark, Harold F.: "Bond Rates, Building Costs and School Plant Financing," *American School and University*, American School Publishing Corp., New York, 1957–1958, pp. 262–266.

Hunt, Harold C., and Alfred H. Clark: "Efficient Use of Supplies and Equipment," *School Executive*, vol. 67, pp. 43–44, July, 1948.

Johns, R. L., and E. L. Morphet (eds.): *Problems and Issues of Public School Finance*, Bureau of Publications, Teachers College, Columbia University, New York, 1952, chap. 13, pp. 429–463.

Linn, Henry H.: *School Business Administration*, The Ronald Press Company, New York, 1956, chaps. 9 and 10, pp. 250–311.

Little, Thomas C.: "Measuring Efficiency in School Supply Purchasing," *American School Board Journal*, vol. 117, pp. 25–27, December, 1948.

"Maintenance Practices, A Symposium," *American School and University*, American School Publishing Corp., New York, 1957–1958, pp. 273–284.

Murray, John J., and Winfield F. Holzapfel: "Management of Supplies and Repairs," *School Executive*, vol. 67, pp. 40–41, July, 1948.

"Purchasing Habits of Schools Surveyed," *School Executive*, vol. 66, p. 59, January, 1949.

Rickets, Roy S.: "Proposed Set of Guides Distinguishes Between Supplies and Equipment," *Nation's Schools*, vol. 58, no. 1, pp. 70–72, July, 1956.

Rosenstengel, William E., and Jefferson N. Eastmond: *School Finance*, The Ronald Press Company, New York, 1957, chap. 20, pp. 382–409.

"School Purchasing Agent," *American School Board Journal*, vol. 114, pp. 50–51, June, 1947.

Yerge, Clyde S.: "Purchasing Supplies and Equipment," *School Executive*, vol. 67, pp. 38–39, July, 1948.

24. School property management

THE MANAGEMENT of school property—land, buildings, and equip-ment—is a phase of business administration that is very important for carrying on the educational program. While large expenditures must necessarily be made for the employment of personnel for instruction, the best returns for such expenditures cannot be realized unless the physical plant contributes maximally to the objectives of education. The deter-mination of the amount and kind of school properties that are needed, their adaptation to the program of education, and the adequate protection and maintenance of the plant constitute the subject of this chapter.

The care and maintenance of school property as a phase of business administration has not always been sufficiently emphasized by school officials. When cash is converted into goods, sites, buildings, and equip-ment, the essential values remain and must be protected and accounted for as truly as before such conversion. Frequently when buildings are erected or equipment purchased and payment made, insufficient atten-tion is given to the material values. Perhaps one reason for this apparent lack of appreciation of the importance of plant values lies in the fact that school property does not bear the same fiscal relationship to the school enterprise as does property in private business. In the latter case, the adequacy of the plant contributes directly to production and in turn produces greater income from which the property is maintained or re-placed. Obsolete or poorly maintained equipment will soon be revealed in the production and sales departments, whereas an adequate plant, well maintained, will increase the efficiency of the enterprise. Property, thus, pays its own way in business. In the case of school property, it should be realized that adequate plant facilities contribute to the effi-ciency of the program but there may not be a direct increase in money income. School property must be maintained by funds derived from taxation or from other revenue sources. Such expenditures of public money

465

must be justified, plant values maintained and well managed, adequate records kept, repairs and replacements made in order that the physical facilities may contribute their share in the education of children. Expenditure for the school plant is one of the ways in which the school enterprise contributes directly to the quality of education.

VALUE OF SCHOOL PROPERTY

For purposes of management, maintenance, insurance, reporting, and planning for future buildings, it is essential that the value of school property be known and accurate accounts kept. When school buildings are purchased or new ones constructed, an estimate of their probable costs must be made in planning for the financing of the capital expenditure. The relationship of the cost of upkeep of buildings and equipment to their original cost, the age of the buildings, and the type of construc-

Table 24-1   Value of School Property *

Year	Total reported value of school property, thousands	Value per pupil enrolled
1920	$2,409,719	$112
1925	4,252,329	172
1930	6,211,328	241
1936	6,731,324	255
1940	7,635,112	346
1946	8,190,858	351
1948	9,212,746	385
1950	11,396,804	454
1952	13,954,650	525

* U.S. Office of Education, Biennial Survey of Education in the United States, *Statistics of State School Systems,* 1952–54, chap. 2, pp. 26–27. *Statistics of State School Systems,* 1947–48, chap. 2, p. 90. *Statistics of State School Systems,* 1945–46, chap. 2, p. 13. *Statistics of State School Systems,* 1939–40 and 1941–42, vol. II, chap. 3, p. 32. *Statistics of State School Systems,* 1935–36. *Bulletin,* 1937, vol. II, no. 2, chap. 2, p. 55. *Bulletin,* 1931, vol. II, no. 20, chap. 2, pp. 40–41. Washington, D.C.

tion should also be known to administrative officials. In the event of destruction by fire, windstorm, flood, or other causes, insurance adjustments are facilitated when school administrators have available all the data relating to original cost, depreciation, and subsequent changes to the plant. Also, state and national authorities require periodic statements of the value of school property and equipment. The lack of accurate records in many school units has called into question the reliability of the figures submitted in such reports. Knowledge of the value of school lands, buildings, and equipment serve the most useful purpose when school administrators use the information for estimating future needs and in maintaining and operating the plant.

The rapid increase in the value of school property since 1920 is shown in Table 24-1. The figures reflect changes in price levels as well as in the improvement of plant facilities. Taking the gross figures without correction for purchasing power of the dollar, the value of school property in 1952, the latest year for which nationwide figures were available, was more than 5 times as much as the value reported in 1920. The number of pupils enrolled during the same time increased even more, resulting in a per pupil value of about 4.7 times as much. This means that not only were provisions made for more pupils but those that were housed were cared for better.

The greater adequacy of school properties per pupil, as reflected in Table 24-1, has been brought about to a large extent by the reduction in the number of school districts. In 1931–1932 there were 127,422 districts, whereas in 1953–1954, there were only 62,969. This means the elimination of a large number of rural school buildings. For example, in 1931–1932 there were 143,391 one-teacher schools, whereas in 1953–1954 there were only 42,825 such schools.[1]

PLANT PROGRAMS

It is a basic principle of school plant planning that structures be so designed as to house best the particular types of school programs that are to be carried on within their walls. Planning a school building program is placing the materials—brick, stone, steel, wood, glass—about the school program. While this has reference particularly to the construction of new buildings or to major remodeling of old structures, there are many school buildings in use that may not be ideal because of a number of factors beyond the immediate control of the board of trustees or the community. At any time present school buildings must be used by administrators and teachers in such a way as to make the best use of them and to bring out their maximum values in service.

Plant Planning

When a new structure is to be erected there should be a thorough survey of the school and of the community in order to note any changes in the school program or characteristics in the community which might call for a particular type of structure. When this is done by the school administration, and in many cases by consultants from outside the district,

[1] Association of School Business Officials, Committee on Insurance Research, *Research Committee Report on School Fire Insurance, 1938–1945*, Kalamazoo, Mich., 1948.

a better over-all assessment of school and community needs may be obtained than when planning the building is left to the administrator and the architect.

Because in most communities school buildings are rather permanent and are not readily changed it is highly important that the maximum planning be done before structures are erected. Such planning will take into consideration the increase or decrease in the school population of the district, and the prediction of school population in the years ahead. It will also take into consideration the financial capacity of the district in order that the best school structures may be obtained for the money spent.

Many of the newer buildings are constructed in such a manner that they are flexible and adjustments may be made for a changing program. Room changes are easily possible and the addition of more classrooms can be made if, and when, the need for them arises.

Utilization of Facilities

Frequently what appears to be a crowded condition in a school building is in reality a relatively low degree of room utilization. This is due to a number of factors among which may be the type of building, the extent to which it is adapted for the program it is to house, the equipment in the room, and the school schedule in use. There are two methods of measuring the utilization of school buildings: first, measurement in terms of percentage of classroom utilization, and second, the percentage of pupil-station utilization.

Room utilization is greatly affected by the kind of equipment in the room. In rooms that may be readily adapted for different classes, utilization is usually higher than in rooms furnished with special equipment such as laboratories. It is highly desirable that special rooms be so constructed as to provide for multiple use. Science laboratories, for example, may be equipped with combination-type desks to make them serviceable for courses in physics, chemistry, biology, and general science, in lecture recitation and laboratory work. In small schools it is impossible to attain the same degree of room utilization that would be possible in the large schools. Usually room utilization is lower in high schools than in elementary schools, because in the former classes may not be scheduled for every hour of the day, whereas in the latter a group of pupils usually occupies the room throughout the school day. The percentage of room utilization is the measure most commonly employed in both elementary and high schools. This is obtained by dividing the number of hours per week that classes occupy the various rooms by the total number of hours throughout a period of one week. The percentage of room utilization is usually less than 100, especially in high schools. A utilization of 70 to 90 per cent would be desirable.

The second method of measuring utilization of school buildings is in terms of the number of pupil stations used for a period of one week. The percentage of all pupil stations (seats or desks) that are in use is the percentage of pupil-station utilization of the building. The most important factor in determining pupil-station utilization is the size of classes in relation to the size of rooms. The better that the class size is adjusted to room size, the higher the percentage of pupil-station utilization. In small high schools there may be considerable unused space in any classroom period, because of small classes. Pupil-station utilization is usually lower than room utilization, although there may be cases in elementary schools that are overcrowded where the actual pupil-station utilization may exceed 100 per cent.

MAINTENANCE OF SCHOOL PLANT

Because of the capital outlay involved and relative infrequency of construction of school buildings in many districts, the problem of preservation of the investment through effective maintenance is a serious responsibility. In addition to the need for conservation of the plant, school plant care is important to the welfare of pupils. Inadequate sanitation, glaring lights, and uncontrolled noises often are definite health hazards. From this point of view adequate plant maintenance is a safeguard to the pupils and is important in their educational progress. In spite of the many reasons for adequate maintenance that may be given, it is not uncommon to find school buildings in poor repair, deteriorated through neglect, and often involving definite health hazards.

The policy adopted by the board of education for the maintenance and upkeep of the school buildings becomes one of major importance in providing for the maximum utility of the school plant. A comprehensive program of maintaining school buildings should be planned for a period of time so that the cost may be spread over a number of years and not be too great a drain upon the current budget for any one year. Painting, roofing, upkeep for classrooms and laboratories, furniture, and other more or less regularly recurring maintenance items may be taken care of at periodic times, and may thus provide regular employment of the maintenance staff. In small school systems where maintenance must be done at least in part by the regular custodial staff, there should be a planned program of summer work for the upkeep of buildings. When such a policy is initiated, the maintenance budget may be kept fairly constant from year to year.

In the larger school systems it may be desirable to have a centralized shop in which much of the work of day-to-day maintenance is carried on by a special staff. One such plan is to have a building supervisor with assistants who are skilled in different types of repair work—carpentry, plumbing, electrical work, painting, and heating and ventilating. Such a maintenance department can do all but the most extensive jobs.

An adequate budget should be set up so that it is definitely known what funds are available for the maintenance of the different school buildings in the system. The maintenance budget is an example of long-range planning, and when such maintenance is placed on a schedule, most of it can be carried on as needed, with only minor deviations to meet emergencies. There should also be periodic inspection of the buildings to reveal any unscheduled maintenance needs. Under an adequate program of maintenance, depreciation of school buildings and equipment may be largely offset by keeping property in such a state of repair as to preserve its serviceability.

OPERATION OF SCHOOL PLANT

No attempt is made in this section to summarize the details of good plant operation since there is considerable literature on the subject. It is perhaps sufficient to state that methods of treating floors and other types of cleaning, methods of operating heating and ventilating systems, and the care of school grounds present many details which should be studied carefully by custodians and others in charge of the program of school plant operation. The emphasis here is on general management and organization of personnel and equipment. In larger systems where there is a superintendent of buildings and grounds, he may have under his supervision various groups of personnel for carrying on the several jobs of operation. In smaller school systems, the custodial staff or janitors must carry on the work of operation of the school plant.

Regardless of the titles given to personnel—whether they are called custodians, engineers, janitors, or by some other title—they should be well trained for their work and should have their jobs well outlined for them. Their number should be determined by the amount of space to be cared for by the custodial staff. A well-trained custodial staff not only keeps buildings warm, clean, and serviceable, but does much to preserve the structures and their equipment. A training program is often an investment rather than an expenditure when considering the total cost of operation of the school plants.

The cost of effective operation, whether it be in terms of personnel or of buying fuel and other such items of operation, is an important factor in the preservation of plant values and in the day-to-day housekeeping within the school building. It is a means of extending the life of a building and often pays dividends by making even old buildings more serviceable than they would be without adequate operation and maintenance care.

INSURANCE OF SCHOOL PLANT

For the proper preservation of school plant values property should be protected against losses through fire, tornado, earthquake, explosion, or other unforeseen circumstances. In any such disaster the loss may be partial or total depending upon the nature of the cause and the construction of school buildings. Prudent management would dictate that some method of protection be instituted.

Two possible methods are by insurance and by the creation of a reserve fund. In many school districts where building construction is carried on relatively infrequently, the loss may be so great the replacement cannot be made from current funds. In such cases programs of insurance are necessary. In large districts where building programs are carried on almost continually, protection may be afforded through current funds or reserve funds. This kind of protection is sometimes termed self-insurance. For most school districts, however, a sound policy of insurance would seem to afford the best type of protection against losses.

Purposes of Insurance

The main purposes of insurance are (1) protection of the community against losses through fire or other means of destruction, (2) protection of personnel in the school, and (3) assurance that losses will be met through the systematic provision of insurance funds.

In most school districts a school building that is lost through fire, tornado, earthquake, or other catastrophe must be replaced from district funds raised by direct taxes or by issuing bonds. In some states aid of an emergency nature is provided for rebuilding school structures thus destroyed. But even in such cases a portion of the loss is sustained by the district.

In an adequate program of insurance there is usually some inspection of buildings that may reduce fire hazards of many kinds. This is protection to children, teachers, and other workers in and about the school building. A systematic study of conditions that affect school insurance may not only reduce costs but makes possible more and better protection.

Methods of Insurance

There are several methods by which school buildings are insured against losses. Among these are insurance with commercial companies and state insurance.

Commercial Companies. Most school buildings are insured through commercial companies of two types, (1) stock companies and (2) mutuals, reciprocals, and cooperatives. A stock company is an organization based on capital stock of the company which is available to pay losses when premiums collected are insufficient. When the company earns a profit, a dividend is paid to the stockholders. In mutual companies policy holders take the place of the stockholders and there is no capital stock. The losses sustained are paid from premiums and when these are not sufficient to meet the losses, policy holders may be assessed. Some mutual companies are nonassessable, which means that no additional assessments can be made to pay losses. Reciprocal companies have many of the characteristics of mutual companies, except that business is usually conducted by an attorney. Cooperatives are similar to mutuals. Losses are paid through accumulated premiums and when they are not sufficient policy holders are liable to assessment.

In addition to the types of company mentioned above that are primarily concerned with the insurance of property, there are a number of other national or regional organizations in the insurance industry. Among these are organizations that are supported by a number of insurance companies and have for their purpose the formulation of building codes and fire protection standards. Others test materials and equipment with reference to fire protection. Some companies are engaged entirely in the work of making rates on a national or regional scale. Still others deal entirely with adjustment of losses.

State Insurance. State-wide plans for the insurance of school buildings have been organized in a number of the states. Some of these plans have been generally successful and have resulted in a saving of insurance costs to school districts. Among the states are North Carolina, South Carolina, Wisconsin, North Dakota, Alabama, Florida, and Vermont. South Carolina was the first state to establish a state insurance fund— in 1900. From very small beginnings, this fund has gradually increased to over $100,000,000 with considerable profit accumulated over the years. In a study by Garnett, the history of some twenty state public property insurance plans is given, showing that they have operated with varying degrees of success.[2]

That more states have not taken advantage of state-wide plans for public school insurance may be owing to some of the disadvantages that have been mentioned in the literature. Among these may be the difficulty of legislative management, the time it takes to initiate a complete plan, and the maintenance of a high degree of solvency that is necessary for such insurance funds.

The legislation providing for the organization and operation of state insurance funds differs among the states. It is difficult to suggest any characterization that will embrace all of the provisions. Sometimes such

[2] Garnett, Percy F.: *The History of Various State Insurance Experiments,* Los Angeles Board of Fire Underwriters of the Pacific, 1939.

plans exclude certain types of risk to make them safer, but on the whole there seems to be considerable justification for the establishment of state insurance plans.

Self-insurance. The method of state insurance described above is in reality a variation of what is often termed self-insurance. Under this plan, the state may assume the risk for all or a certain proportion of school losses or again the local districts may assume the losses. In case of state buildings, such as college buildings, the state assumes the loss. The theory back of self-insurance is that the state or the administrative unit is both the owner and the protecting agency, and that more economical protection may be secured by assuming the risk than by paying insurance premiums. The feasibility of self-insurance depends upon many conditions, such as the number and distribution of buildings, financial resources of the school district, and the experience that a district has had in the past concerning fire and other types of property losses.

In certain school districts where there are many buildings and where school construction is going on almost continuously, it may be feasible for the district to assume the risk. The district must assess the possibility of replacing lost buildings either from current or reserved funds or from other sources of funds, the amount of saving that would be involved by assuming the risk, and the reserve bonding capacity available at any time. Usually small school districts find it difficult to assume the risk and are more or less dependent upon insurance programs, either through commercial companies or through a state agency.[3]

TYPES OF INSURANCE

Of the many different kinds of insurance that may be carried on school buildings, perhaps the most common types are flat-rate insurance, co-insurance, and extended coverage. Insurance on property only is considered here. Liability insurance is a topic dealt with under personnel administration.

Flat-rate Insurance

Flat-rate insurance may be thought of as a certain amount of insurance taken on a particular building. If, for example, a school building is appraised for $750,000 as its present worth, the board of education may decide to insure it for $500,000 and pay the premiums on that amount. In the event of loss, the company pays losses in full up to $500,000. This would also be true in case of a complete loss. The face value of the policy only would be recoverable. Depending upon the laws

[3] American Association of School Administrators, *Managing the School District Insurance Program*, Washington, 1953, pp. 22–23.

of the state, it is frequent that a company would not pay more than the actual worth of the building. Such a regulation would need to be observed at the time the insurance policy on the building is written.

Such insurance might be desirable in the case of some buildings, but much would depend upon the type of construction and whether it is fireproof. Flat-rate insurance is usually purchased at a somewhat higher premium than other types, especially coinsurance.

Coinsurance

The plan of coinsurance has been rather extensively adopted by school districts in many states. It is essentially a plan to prevent the under-insurance of school property. It makes the school district coinsurer with the company. Coinsurance may be carried for a given percentage of the present worth or sound value of a building. The coinsurance clause establishes this percentage at 70 per cent, 80 per cent, or 90 per cent. Such insurance is usually accompanied by what is known as a reduced-rate clause. The district agrees to insure buildings at 80 per cent of their value in the case of 80 per cent coinsurance. The district is covered to that extent of the value of the building, and in the case of partial loss, complete coverage is secured. The chief benefit of coinsurance is the reduction in rate as compared with flat-rate insurance.

For example, if a school building has an insurable value of $500,000 and is insured for $400,000 under an 80 per cent coinsurance contract, the owner becomes coinsurer in name only. If he purchases less than 80 per cent of the value of the building, say for example, $300,000 of protection, he is coinsurer for that part of the 80 per cent as per contract that he failed to purchase. In other words, the company carries three-fourths and the owner one-fourth of the risk. In the case of a loss of $60,000, the company pays three-fourths, or $45,000, and owner would bear the one-fourth, or $15,000, of the loss. In case of a complete loss, the company pays up to the face value of the policy, or $300,000, and the owner assumes the balance of the loss. If the owner purchases the full 80 per cent coinsurance, or $400,000, the company pays all of any loss up to the face of the policy of $400,000.[4]

Extended Coverage

The ordinary insurance policy for fire and lightning does not neces-sarily cover damage from other causes such as explosion, windstorm, hail, smoke, vehicle, or aircraft. Damage from such causes is usually secured through what is known as extended coverage that may be ob-tained in connection with a fire insurance policy at an additional pre-

[4] American Association of School Administrators, *Managing the School District Insurance Program*, Washington, 1953.

mium. Boards of education should study their insurance policies on property rather closely to see what type of insurance they actually have.

Boards of education may vary in the amount of extended coverage they desire to carry. Usually such coverage is for the same amount of protection as the fire and lightning policies on which the extended coverage is endorsed.

ADMINISTRATION OF THE INSURANCE PROGRAM

Although school buildings as a class of public property have not suffered as much loss as other types of public buildings, such losses do occur and often when the district is least financially able to replace the structure. A considerable number of school buildings are destroyed by fire each year, and often the insurance is not adequate to replace the buildings.

For insurance purposes, school buildings are usually classified by insurance underwriters as fireproof, brick, and frame construction. A fireproof building is one that has walls of brick, stone, or solid concrete with floors, roofs, and principal partitions made of brick, tile, or reinforced concrete. Very little wood trim is found on such buildings. Brick buildings are those that have walls of brick, stone, or reinforced concrete but with wood interior. They frequently have frame additions. A frame building is one that is built of wood. Outside walls and inside walls may be entirely of wood or they may be hollow tile or concrete block with brick veneer. Exterior may be of wood covered with stucco.

For fire insurance purposes, buildings are also classified as being in protected or unprotected areas. A protected risk is one that is located within a certain distance, usually about a city block, from a fire hydrant with town or city water supply and within a certain distance of a regularly equipped fire department. Risks that do not have this type of protection are classified as unprotected.

The problem of determining the insurable value of a school building is one that requires considerable thought and study. Usually one thinks of a building's value in terms of its present worth or sound value. Present worth or sound value has been taken as the replacement cost minus depreciation and deduction of the value of certain noninsurable portions of the building. The insurable value is the value that is commonly accepted as the basis for writing insurance policies. The replacement value of a building is usually determined by an appraisal, made either through appraisal companies, architects, or construction companies. Where the actual cost is known, it may be possible to determine replacement value by the use of an index of original cost, the index to correct for changes in construction costs over the years.

Usually the replacement value of a building for insurance purposes is reduced by a depreciation figure based on the original cost. The annual depreciation of a building is computed by dividing the cost by the life of the building. If a $300,000 building were estimated as having a life of fifty years and a salvage value of $50,000, depreciation would be $5,000 per year. The estimate of the replacement value of building minus the depreciation would result in the present worth or sound value of the building. Insurable value of a building would be the present worth minus such items that are considered noninsurable as excavations, foundation walls, and underground plumbing.

Kinds of Policies

There are a number of different kinds of fire insurance policies commonly written for school districts. Among these may be listed the specific policy, the specific schedule policy, and the blanket policy. The choice as to which of these types a school should purchase depends upon local conditions. In the case of a small school where there are only one or two buildings, the specific policy may be desirable. This is a policy written on a specific building in a specific location. It may cover the building alone or the building and its contents. The rate is determined for that particular building and the conditions surrounding it.

Under the specific schedule policy more than one school building and its contents may be insured, each building insured for a specified amount at a specified rate. The premiums for all buildings are added and the sum divided by the total coverage to arrive at an average rate. This plan provides one policy for all buildings but each building is insured for a specified amount. The chief advantage in this type of insurance is in the administration of the program. In cities where there are many buildings, it is much easier to handle the insurance program in this manner.

Blanket insurance operates somewhat the same as the specific schedule policies, but covers different buildings at different locations in a single policy. The average rate is determined as in the specific schedule policy. Losses on specific buildings are determined in terms of the loss and the value of the building. Usually coinsurance is carried on buildings covered by blanket policies.

Boiler insurance is usually written as separate policies since this type of coverage is ordinarily not included in extended coverage. Boiler insurance usually includes the damage done to boilers through explosion or other accident and also covers damage to buildings done by boiler explosion. There is less danger of boiler explosion in the present-day low-pressure types of boiler as compared with the high-pressure boilers more frequently used in former years. Perhaps one of the most important advantages of boiler insurance is the periodic inspection that accompanies this type of policy.

PROPERTY RECORDS

Perhaps no other aspect of financial accounting in public schools has received less attention than that of the accounting for school property. When state grants are made or bond issues sold for the construction of school buildings, it is the concern of boards of education and administrators to preserve the property values in the buildings and equipment realized from the funds received.

Some writers have made a distinction between wasting assets and permanent assets to distinguish between school sites which may be thought of as permanent assets and school buildings and equipment that depreciate in value which are thought of as wasting assets. One difference is that wasting assets must be replaced through the expenditure of capital at some future time. Moreover, throughout the life of such an asset, it is necessary to keep it in a proper condition of maintenance. Thus it becomes an important consideration in the management of property values, termination of depreciation, maintenance, and replacement.

Classification of Property

As suggested above, it may be desirable for a school district to classify the various items of property in order to keep a better accounting of the various kinds. Such classifications are necessary to determine rates of depreciation, maintenance, and the like. One commonly accepted classification of school property is that given below:

1. School sites and school lands including playgrounds, athletic fields, and other grounds used for school purposes.

2. School structures including elementary and high school buildings and other accessory buildings such as shops, teacherages, dormitories, or others needed in the school program.

3. Permanent school equipment including such items as built-in furniture, electrical wiring and fixtures, fences, walks, heating and ventilating systems and equipment, and sanitary equipment.

4. All types of movable equipment in school use such as office equipment and furniture, laboratory and special room equipment, school buses and automobiles, and movable equipment used in operation and maintenance of plant.

5. Various types of equipment in storage including items similar to those in 4 above but not in use at the time.

6. School textbooks and library books including all those furnished by the district and used by pupils as well as those in libraries, in circulation, and in storage.

Types of Records

The various kinds of records of school property needed to provide a complete and readily available list of all items include the property ledger, the property inventory, and insurance record. Others may seem desirable in larger school systems, but these three seem to supply most of the needed information. The keeping of these records does not entail much clerical work, since most of the entries are made infrequently.

The property ledger is a record of items by the classification given above or by other satisfactory classification or description and includes the year when purchased and installed, the cost, the annual depreciation, additions or subtractions, and depreciated values. It is often difficult to state the present value of a piece of property because of the difficulty of arriving at a satisfactory figure, but original cost, salvage value, life of the asset, and depreciation are some of the basic data needed. Figure 24-1 shows one form of the property ledger.

The property inventory is a record of the amount of each item of land, buildings, or equipment, together with other information concerning its description, location, and value. An accurate inventory of all property owned by the school district is the only means of keeping track of the various items of school furniture, apparatus, library books, typewriters and other office equipment; maintenance and janitorial equipment; school buses; equipment for upkeep; and numerous other items that are needed in the operation of the school system. Daily use of equipment, especially the smaller movable articles, often results in moving pieces from one part of the school system to another and unless an accurate record is kept, property is likely to be misplaced or lost. Considerable time and work may be involved in setting up an inventory for the first time, but when once established it is relatively simple to keep. Addition of new items is made at the time of purchase. Items broken or worn out or traded in for new ones are removed from the inventory at regular intervals. Periodic inspection reveals the location of items and enables those in charge of the inventory to make the necessary corrections. Items should not be moved from one room to another without an entry on the inventory. Figure 24-2 shows one form of property inventory.

In order that all information concerning the insurance program can be readily available, two kinds of records should be kept, one of buildings and equipment and the other of insurance policies. In the first record space is provided for the name and location of the building, the type of construction, the insurable value of the building and its contents, and

	Building or equipment items	Code	Date of acquisition	Original cost	Estimated value at beginning of year	Additions	Replacement and repairs	Deductions of losses	Depreciation	Estimated value at end of year

Fig. 24-1 Property ledger.

	Description of article	Date of purchase	Unit cost	Number on hand and location											
				1950-1951 Number	Room	1951-1952 Number	Room	1952-1953 Number	Room	1953-1954 Number	Room	1954-1955 Number	Room	1955-1956 Number	Room

Fig. 24-2 Property inventory.

the amount of insurance carried on each for both building and contents, insurance rates, and the type of insurance carried. The second type of record gives information for each insurance policy and contains such information as the date of the policy, the term of insurance, the expiration date of the policy, the policy number, the property insured, amount of insurance premium, and name and address of the agent from whom the policy was taken. Figure 24-3 shows a record of insurance by policies.

SUMMARY

Property management has for its purpose the maintenance of building and equipment in good condition for maximum service. Because of great increase in plant and equipment values in recent decades, this phase of business administration assumes increased importance. Plant values must be analyzed, maintained, and protected if they are to contribute to educational objectives.

The total value of school property from 1920 to 1952 increased about 5.8 times in current dollars and the value of school property per pupil during the same period increased about 4.7 times.

When planning a school plant program a number of factors should be taken into consideration, among them the community characteristics, the school population, present school facilities, utilization of present facilities, flexibility of construction, financial capacity of the district, and the long-range projection of what is likely to be the situation in the community in future years.

School plant maintenance and operation are important considerations in preserving school plant values. Adequate and regular maintenance does much to preserve such values, and adequate operation of the plant is essential to keep buildings warm, clean, and in healthful condition to achieve maximum educational results.

The proper protection of school plant values requires that a program of insurance be available to the school district. Insurance may be carried through commercial companies, state plans, or self-insurance. Many different kinds and types of insurance should be studied carefully in order that maximum protection at reasonable cost may be achieved for the various structures in the school system.

The principal types of property records include the property register, the property inventory, and insurance records. The amount and time of clerical help involved in keeping such records is relatively small in comparison to the value of having such information readily at hand for purposes of management.

Name and location	Date of appraisal	Type of construction	Building			Contents			
			Insurable value	Amount of insurance	Insurance rate	Insurable value	Amount of insurance	Insurance rate	Class of insurance

Date of policy	Name and address of company	Policy number	Property insured	Amount of insurance	Premium	Term of insurance	Expiration of policy	Rate of insurance	Name and address of agent

Fig. 24-3 Records of insurance.

QUESTIONS FOR STUDY AND DISCUSSION

1. Study one or more school districts with which you are familiar and give some description and evaluation of the property in each. Resort to records of property values if they are available.

2. Study one or more school districts with which you are familiar and for a period of time note the program of school plant construction. Has this plant program followed the characteristics developed in this chapter?

3. Study the utilization of a school building or a portion of it, both in terms of room utilization and pupil-station utilization. What is an optimum percentage of utilization in elementary school buildings and in high school buildings?

4. Outline a maintenance program for school buildings in a community of some 50,000 population. What are the different maintenance jobs? Which ones might be done in summer and which should be carried on throughout the school year?

5. Study the operation costs in one or more school districts. Note the various items of expenditure under operation and compare the cost of these items with the total cost of the current budget.

6. Study one or more school buildings to determine the depreciation for a period of years by using the straight line method. Note also the salvage value after the estimated life of the buildings.

7. Study the insurance practices in your community and state. What types of insurance are commonly carried? What legal restrictions are placed on the insurance of school property?

8. What is the cost of insurance in several kinds of school districts with which you are familiar? Would it be feasible for any district to assume its own risk?

9. What are some of the factors in a school district that contribute to the reduction of insurance rates?

10. Study one or more school systems to determine the kinds of property records that are kept. Study the property ledger and the property inventory in a number of districts in your state.

SELECTED REFERENCES

American Association of School Administrators: *Managing the School District Insurance Program,* Washington, 1953.

Burke, Arvid J.: *Financing Public Schools in the United States,* Harper & Brothers, New York, 1951, pp. 525–528.

Johns, R. L., and Edgar L. Morphet (eds.): *Problems and Issues of Public School Finance,* Bureau of Publications, Teachers College, Columbia University, New York, 1952, pp. 443–449.

Kent, John R.: "The Administration of Public School Insurance Affairs," doctor's thesis, Stanford University, Stanford, Cal., 1954.

Linn, Henry H. (ed.): *School Business Administration,* The Ronald Press Company, New York, 1956, chap. 11, pp. 312–341.

MacConnell, James D.: *Planning for School Buildings,* Prentice-Hall, Inc., Englewood Cliffs, N.J., 1957.

Perkins, Laurence B.: *Work Place for Learning,* Reinhold Publishing Corporation, New York, 1957.

Rosenstengel, William E., and Jefferson N. Eastmond: *School Finance,* The Ronald Press Company, New York, 1957, chap. 18, pp. 349–372.

Sumption, Merle R., and Jack L. Landes: *Planning Functional School Buildings,* Harper & Brothers, New York, 1957.

25. Auditing, reporting, and safeguarding school funds

Throughout Part Five of this volume, chapters are devoted to various aspects of business administration carried on in the conceptual design of local operational finance. This final chapter is devoted to auditing, reporting, and safeguarding school funds. Auditing is the verification of the records kept in the accounting system of the school; reporting follows accounting in the preparation and transmission of periodic summaries; and safeguarding school funds involves receiving, depositing, and protecting school funds.

AUDITING SCHOOL FUNDS

The school audit is essentially an appraisal of the financial records and financial management of a school district. Audits are usually required by state authorities and are of importance in establishing confidence in the school authorities on the part of the public. Audits made by competent, disinterested persons serve to satisfy all state and local requirements. Although the value of the audit has long been recognized and has been clearly defined in business, there does not seem to be any uniformity of practice among school districts within most states or among states.

Auditing is a branch of accounting as developed in business and has become clearly recognized and differentiated from accounting. School auditing differs from auditing in private enterprise only as the functions of school accounting differ from the functions of business accounting. In both cases, the audit may be thought of as a verification of the books, records, and accounts made by competent persons outside the enterprise. Quite as important as audits made by competent public accountants outside the school system is the practice of internal auditing performed by a competent person on the administrative staff of the local school system. Auditing may thus be viewed as an examination of the books both from within the system and from without.

From the point of view of auditors from outside the school system, the purpose is verification of accounts as they have been kept by others, such verification being made by disinterested parties for the determination of validity and accuracy of the records. Such statements prove helpful both to the administrative officials and to the public and lead to an understanding of the financial status of the schools. For the purpose of maintaining internal audits, the school business accounting department usually engages a person to be in charge of performing the work of auditing and accounting. Such audits are continuous and comprise the setting up and carrying out of various internal checks and make for frequent more or less complete audits.

Purpose of Audits

In recent decades there has been a significant change in the purposes for which audits are made. The early conception of an auditing was largely that of the detection of fraud and error. This has been extended to encompass ascertainment of the factual conditions of the school's finances. In business the audit would also seek to determine the earnings of the enterprise. The knowledge of financial conditions is of importance both to those interested in the enterprise and to those concerned directly with its management. In a school district the information made available by the audit serves as a basis for prudential management and for giving the general public a statement of the financial conditions of the district.

To these purposes should be added the moral effect that an audit has upon those who handle the funds. There is likely to be less fraud and error when those in charge know that a periodic statement will be made public. Also the auditor is in a position to recommend practices and procedures that will result in more efficient administration and protection of funds.

In keeping with the demands of local initiative, it is essential to develop within the school unit the responsibility for keeping accounts and handling funds and for the economical administration of such funds. The work of inspection and verification, either by independent local auditors or by state authorities, should become a minor function in school administration rather than a major one. It should become merely a confirmation of correct business methods and local responsibility assumed by the administrative officials.

Types of Audits

As already stated, school audits are made by auditors both from within the school system and from without. To these two types may be added a number of other kinds of audits such as the preaudit, the current audit, the operational audit, and the postaudit. The preaudit is essentially an audit of accounts as set up in the budget and seeks to determine as accurately as possible all expenditures and funds available to meet the necessary costs. Preaudits are usually made by agencies within the school system and may be thought of as a type of internal audit. The current audit is essentially an internal, continuous audit that is carried on as the accounts are kept. It is also thought of as the operational audit. The postaudit is a verification of accounts, usually at the end of the fiscal period. It may be carried on by state agencies or by independent auditing agencies. The postaudit is made annually, biennially, or at other periodic times as may be required by law, or in the absence of legal requirement, by policy of the board of education.

Practice in School Auditing

Present practice of auditing school accounts varies considerably among the states. Thirty-two states and the District of Columbia require that school districts have periodic financial audits. Seven states require audits in some districts only, and nine states do not require periodic financial audits.[1]

With reference to the frequency of audit in those states which require them the annual audit is the most prevalent. Some states require that audits be made every two years, Michigan every three years, and Idaho every four years. Missouri requires that audits be made upon petition, and in the District of Columbia, the audit is a continuous one.

The auditors designated by state law for making school district audits vary as greatly as other features in legal auditing provisions. Frequently, a state agency carries on this function. This may be either the office of the state auditor, department of finance, the auditor of public accounts, state examiner, state tax commissioner, state department of education, or some other state agency. In a few states, county officers are designated as the auditing agents, but an increasing number of state independent auditing agencies are designated.

Auditing Agencies

The auditors designated by local school administrative units and by states reveal a variety of different agencies responsible for this task.

[1] Clayton D. Hutchins and Albert R. Munse, *Public School Finance Programs in the United States,* U.S. Office of Education, 1954, p. 53.

They range from competent certified public accountants to laymen.

Where state departments of education have the facilities for making annual audits of the accounts of school districts, this service is a valuable one and can be rendered at a lower cost than would be possible for districts to secure from independent auditors. Moreover, it has the advantage that persons in the departments are familiar with educational practices in the states and can frequently make suggestions relative to accounting methods and procedures and check various requirements for the administration of funds. Such service is particularly valuable to small school units where improvements in accounting are most needed and where school officials are most likely to change more frequently than in large ones. State department authorities sometimes act as instructors for new officials and may render valuable service in their supervision of the accounts. There is a possible danger that auditing officials may not stay within the bounds of financial advice and proper auditing but may overstep their prudential functions.

In a few states, county authorities are designated as auditors of school accounts. It would seem that in many cases such officers may not be qualified to carry on the functions of an auditor. In other cases the county superintendent assumes this function, but this seems undesirable since he is both an executive officer and the auditor of his own accounts. Moreover, he may not be competent to make the audit since it is a duty for which he has not been especially trained.

Irrespective of state requirements local school boards in many cases select auditing agencies to make annual examination of their accounts. Many of the small school districts still follow the practice of selecting electors at the annual meeting to audit the accounts. Such examinations do not meet any of the requirements of a technical audit.

In practice, the certified public accountant has generally been considered the most efficient, capable auditor of school accounts. He is thoroughly trained in accounting and has usually had wide experience in the auditing of various types of public and private accounts.

Auditing and Policy Making

In the emphasis placed upon state-wide auditing by central agencies there has grown the danger that auditing practices may develop into certain undesirable controls of school policy which are quite foreign to good educational administration. Such a condition is perhaps most likely to arise when the auditing agency is outside the department of education and when there is a lack of coordination between the department of education and the department that is responsible for auditing.

But there is a danger in giving auditing authority to any state agency unless it is strictly limited to the generally accepted criteria of auditing.

There is always the temptation for the overzealous to make an issue over new items of expenditure made in good faith by the board of education. When this occurs there may be a threat to the authority of the board of education that will effectively eliminate experimentation in new areas. Auditing that gets into this realm strikes at the growing edge of the school system and slows down adaptations in their most critical stage.

The present authors have been concerned over this tendency of auditors to get out of bounds. As they have observed this development, they have become stronger for the position that the state auditing of educational accounts should be eliminated and that school districts, instead, should be required to provide commercial audits. If there are to be state audits, there is little that individual school districts can do to keep auditing within bounds. In general two lines of procedure would seem possible. First, the law providing the audits should be specific as to the scope, and second, the law governing powers of school boards should be clarified to give school boards power over the educational program except where the law states specific prohibitions. Locally, school boards and school officials should be alert to challenge auditors' recommendations with respect to *ultra vires* acts. Presumably, the auditor's judgment on such matters is no better than that of other citizens. If the judgment goes contrary to that of responsible authorities, the auditor should be expected to take the board to court to get the decision by the only agency that is (or should be) competent to give an ultimate decision.

COMPLETENESS OF AUDIT

The character of the audit report is usually not specified by state law but is left to the auditing agencies, whether independent auditors or state agencies. Norman suggests a number of criteria that should govern the enactment of auditing laws and which would make the audit more complete. Among these are the following: [2] (1) an examination and analysis of all sources of income; (2) the verification of disbursements; (3) the reconciliation of budget items with actual receipts and disbursements; (4) a report of the budget procedures employed in the school district; (5) an examination of the legal authorization of all local school expenditures; (6) an examination of the board of education minutes, insurance policies, contracts, and deeds (titles) to real estate; (7) the verification of assets and liabilities, bank balances, etc.; (8) an analysis of the school bond indebtedness; (9) an examination of capital assets, inventory, surpluses, accounts, vouchers payable; (10) verification of all

[2] Loyal V. Norman, "Scope, Conduct, and Report of the School Audit," *American School Board Journal*, vol. 127, pp. 44–45, October, 1953.

accounts paid with the examination of invoices; (11) a report of whether the fiscal affairs of the district have been administered according to law; (12) an examination of the accounting system; (13) a report of the soundness of the school board business practices and procedures; (14) a report of search for matters not on the books, for errors of method and fact.

Norman reports that in one state school auditors are required to examine attendance records of the district. It is doubtful whether such matters fall under the scope of the auditor or whether it would be better to leave them entirely to the school authorities. Norman states further:

While thirty-six states provide by law for the auditing of school district financial accounting, nineteen of them require that a report be made of such audit. For the sake of consistency, if for no other cause, it would appear that the statutes should require auditors to include in their written report all items defined within the scope of such office. Notwithstanding, considerable variance exists among the state laws in this respect. Not one state law specifically requires that an audit report for all factors embraced in the preview of the audit.[3]

FINANCIAL REPORTS AND REPORTING

Financial statements and reports of the condition of an enterprise constitute an essential element in the continuing public support of that enterprise. In this respect, schools are not different from any other public agency or institution.

Reporting has its roots in the financial accounting system, which, when properly set up and carried out, makes possible the analysis of cost for the system and its various parts and shows at any time the relation between income and expenditures. The data thus revealed by the accounting system should then be presented clearly and forcibly to the various groups who need the information and to those who support the education program.

The Functions of Reporting

The functions of school financial reporting may be stated as follows: (1) to present clearly the financial condition of the school district at any time, especially at the close of the fiscal year, and to show the assets and liabilities of each fund maintained by the district, including the internal accounts; (2) to show in detail and in summary form the facts concerning income and expenditures and the cost of the various activities and services of the school; (3) to present fiscal information required for making reports to state and national agencies; and (4) to give fiscal

[3] The present authors take issue on this item. This is where the auditor becomes a walking court.

information to the general public for the purpose of cultivating better understanding of the schools on the part of parents, taxpayers, and other lay groups.

While these purposes are generally recognized, there is much to be desired in the way of school reporting. Careful study is needed of the kinds of material that should be used and the most effective methods of presentation to the different groups interested in the schools. Different kinds of reports are needed for administrative officers and boards of education who usually require detailed tabular information of receipts and expenditures. The public requires only a broad overview of the purposes and methods of public education and of school finance. Often this information can be presented in pictorial or graphic form, making it easier to follow than long detailed tables. The data required by state and national agencies should be readily available from the accounting system and should be given in such a way that it corresponds with similar information recorded from other school districts and states. It is only through uniform reporting that national statistics have any validity.

Trends in School Reporting

Reports of city school superintendents to boards of education are of long standing and constitute a form of reporting prevalent throughout the second half of the nineteenth century. They usually contained descriptions of the schools and devoted considerable space to new theories of education. Financial data did not occupy a prominent place although total receipts and expenditures, classified by a number of major items such as teachers' salaries, cost per school and cost per pupil, were frequently included.

Since this early period, much has been done to improve school reporting, although there is yet a lack of uniformity in the data presented by various districts in state reports and by state reports submitted to the United States Office of Education.

Two publications of the United States Office of Education [4] outline the various items of educational information that should be reported by states to the federal government and thus constitute a goal toward which school district reporting should be directed. The manual for financial accounting shows in greater detail the kind of accounts that should be kept in every school system. These reports show clearly the recent trend in school reporting, not only for financial but other types

[4] Paul L. Reason, Emory M. Foster, and Robert F. Will, *Common Core of State Educational Information,* Handbook I, Bulletin, 1953, No. 8, U.S. Office of Education, 1953. Paul L. Reason and Alvius L. White, *Financial Accounting for Local and State School Systems,* Handbook II, Bulletin 1957, No. 4, U.S. Office of Education, Washington, 1957.

of information, and should go far toward securing greater uniformity in the reporting of school information.

The broad concept of public relations and a better understanding of the necessity of interpreting the schools to the various groups within and without the school system have resulted in a clearer recognition that the older forms of reporting as exemplified in the annual school report did not serve adequately the needs of the administration, the board of education, or the public. No one report addressed to all three groups can serve any group well since the different reports require different information. The information must vary from broad general statements of the cost of the school, designed for the public, to detailed unit cost of various materials and services given separately.

It is probable that commercial advertising has had an effect upon financial statements and reports issued by schools for the enlightenment of the public, although such methods are not widely adopted. Indeed, there has been some disagreement concerning the use of commercial advertising methods by the schools. While the purpose of school reporting is somewhat different from the purposes of commercial advertising, many of the methods of the latter might serve to sharpen school reporting. That, for some reason or other, the schools have been slow to take advantage of the methods of commercial advertising and sales promotion is very apparent today, although this may not be entirely the fault of school administrators and boards of education. Fundamental differences between commercial enterprises operating for profit and schools operating as a public service may be such that they do not permit the same promotional activities. School executives could, however, study with profit the results of research in advertising, such as those in the measurement of attention, interest, and memory, the value of color and white space, and the appeal made by different types of materials.

Types of Fiscal Statements and Reports

Various types of fiscal statements and reports that should be made for the school administration have already been pointed out and the purposes of them given. Within these types there may be several different kinds adapted specifically to the purposes they are to serve.

Reports to the Administration. At regular intervals, usually once a month, the administrative officers and board of education should have statements showing the relation of expected income to actual receipts and total current expenditures to appropriations. Such statements may show in detail the receipts from different sources and expenditures by functions or character categories. Since the data for these statements are drawn from the accounting records, it is important that the accounts be kept in such a manner as to enable the person in charge to make them

quickly and accurately. In addition to the reports mentioned there should
be periodic reports of assets, liabilities, receipts, expenditures, school
property, stores, bonds, sinking funds, special funds, budget, ability to
pay, cost audit, and specialized activities.

Although the time of making these reports varies in different school
systems and with the requirements of the respective states, several of
them are made annually, whereas others have greater meaning when
made monthly or for shorter periods than one year. Among the annual

Assets	Amount	Liabilities	Amount

General fund:
  Cash
  Taxes due but not
    collected
  State appropriation
    due but not paid
  Accounts receivable
  Stores
  Prepaid fixed charges
    Total
 	
Building fund:
  Cash
  Transfers due from
    other funds
  Stores
  Bonds authorized
    but not sold
    Total
 	
Bonded indebtedness:
  Cash in sinking funds
  Transfers due from
    other funds
  Investments
  Interest accrued
    not due
  Excess of liabilities
    Total
		General fund:
		  Accounts payable
		  Short-term loans
		  Amounts due other
		    funds
		  Excess of general
		    fund assets
		    Total
		
		Building fund:
		  Accounts payable
		  Contracts outstanding
		  Excess of building
		    fund assets
		    Total
		
		Bonded indebtedness:
		  Bonds outstanding
		  Serial issues
		  Sinking fund issues
		    Total	

Fig. 25-1   Statement of assets and liabilities.

statements are those of assets and liabilities, total receipts and expenditures, budgets, and the like. Periodic reports include monthly statements
of tax collections plus receipts from all other sources and statements of
expenditures compared with budgetary appropriations.

The balance sheet as sometimes used in school accounting does not
appear to be applicable in the sense that it is used in business, but
rather the concept is more that of a statement of assets and liabilities
for each separate fund and for the district as a whole. Figure 25-1 shows

the form of an annual statement of assets and liabilities for the general, building, and bonded indebtedness funds.

Statements of property and plant values are useful in an over-all picture of school assets but they should be kept separate from current funds, building funds, and bond funds. Statements of the value of property showing original cost, additions, depreciation, and present value should be available for appraisal and insurance purposes.

Statements of receipts and expenditures reveal the current financial situation in summary form in annual statements made for the various agencies to which the schools must report. Such statements may be in more or less detail varying from a simple summary for several years past to detailed annual costs. The summaries for a number of years are needed

Source of income	July	Aug	Sept	Oct	Nov	June	Total for year
Federal sources							
Vocational educ.							
Other							
State sources							
Permanent funds							
Appropriations							
Other							

Fig. 25-2   Monthly statement of receipts.

as supporting material to justify school budgets, for determining trends, and for general management. Statements of outstanding indebtedness for a number of years show the complete history of a bond issue or the projection of unpaid obligations into future years and thus become a part of the long-term planning program.

Among the periodic statements made to the board of education are: (1) the monthly statements of receipts, (2) the monthly statements of expenditures in comparison with budgetary appropriations, and (3) the monthly statements of taxes collected. Statements of receipts keep the board informed on conditions of current financing, such as tax collections, need for borrowing money, the balance on hand, and the current condition of other income. Often it is desirable to give a summary of conditions as revealed in previous reports and of the more significant changes that have taken place since the last report was made. Receipts for the various funds give additional information on the current status of financing schools. Figure 25-2 shows a form for reporting monthly the receipts from various sources.

The monthly statements of expenditures, budgetary appropriations, and unexpended balance, under the various subdivisions of the accounts, serve as a control of expenditures and reveal the extent to which funds are administered in accordance with budgetary allowance. Figure 25-3 shows a comparative statement of budgetary allotments, expenditures made, and unexpended balances for any month.

Periodic records of utmost importance, and ones that have perhaps not been sufficiently emphasized, are the minutes of the board of education. Since boards speak only through their minutes, these basic records embody the policies of the board and are the expression of the governing body of the schools. In them is the authorization to employ teachers and to pay their salaries in accordance with the adopted schedule, to

Summary for month				Date				
Budget classification	Amount budgeted	Additions in month	Total available	Accounts paid	Accounts payable	Total expenditures	Balance on hand	

Fig. 25-3   Monthly budget statement.

purchase school sites, to build and equip school buildings, to borrow money and to determine the amount that shall be raised by local taxation, to prepare and administer the school budget, and to carry on all functions within the jurisdiction of the school.

Since the school board minutes are public records, and in some states must be published in their entirety or in summary form, they should be open to the public for inspection and study, although few citizens may take the time to visit the administrative office for this purpose. The practice of publishing a booklet of the policies and regulations of the board of education in which are set forth the policies of this body in a form that is readily available to teachers and citizens is to be recommended. Since the policies of the board should be known by members of the community, the rules and regulations are the best means of conveying this information. Figure 25-4 shows in part the two forms of recording minutes of meetings of the board of education.

Reports to State and National Agencies. Reports made by school systems to state departments of education serve the functions of (1) keeping the state fiscal and other data up to date for purposes of providing complete information regarding the schools and for reporting to federal agencies, (2) providing comparative statistics of the local units, and (3)

RECORD OF MEMBERS PRESENT

| No. | Kind of meeting | Place | Time A.M. P.M. | Date |

Members

| Present | Absent |

Marginal index

(a)

NOTES OF MINUTES OF BOARD OF EDUCATION MEETING

Hour _____

Date _____

Action no. _____

| Names of members | Motion vote | Record of motion |

(b)

Fig. 25-4 Minutes of board of education (two forms).

computing state aid to local units. State administration and leadership are dependent upon such information in order to perform properly the functions of state departments of education.

Here again the two bulletins cited from the United States Office of

Education [5] contain recommendations as to the kinds of educational information that should be included in the reports and the underlying accounts that should be kept to provide the information. There is need for further development among the states of such accounting systems that incorporate enough common features to make reporting to the United States Office of Education complete and uniform. State report forms should be geared to the system of financial accounting required from all local units. If any modification must be made for small school systems, it should be by decreasing the amount of detail in the subdivisions of the accounting classification, without changing the classification. At least the basic items of receipts and expenditures should be the same.

Reports to the Public. This information should constitute a part of the interpretive material that flows regularly from schools to the general public. Too frequently, school financial data are presented only when support for special education projects is sought or when general increases in local taxation are needed. Such special presentations of needs may be valuable in campaigns for better schools but they would undoubtedly be more effective when supplemented by a regular program of interpretation. In order to be more significant, school fiscal statistics must be related to the regular work of the school. Parents and taxpayers must be shown what activities and educational projects are carried on and what each costs, how the school dollar is raised and how it is expended, and what results are achieved through the expenditure.

The agencies through which fiscal data are reported to the public are the same as those used for the dissemination of all other information concerning the schools. Most frequently used are the newspapers, school publications, special bulletins, annual budget reports, and annual reports of the board of education. In addition to the avenues for dissemination of information through the printed page and through pictorial materials, there are the various persons who may appear before public gatherings at more or less frequent intervals. School board members, superintendents, and principals, as well as teachers, may report orally on the work of the school to parent-teacher meetings, civic organizations and other lay groups.

One of the most effective means of bringing school information to the public is through the pupils themselves. High school pupils should be made familiar with the work of the schools and with their cost and the means by which they are financed. No units of instruction in the social studies are more valuable than those dealing with the purposes of education, the work of the elementary and the secondary schools, the relationship of the schools to all other community enterprises, the essentials

[5] *Ibid.*

of taxation, and the fundamentals of school finance. Both teachers and pupils might profit greatly by an intensive study of such materials, not only because of their value for interpreting the schools to the public, but because such units contain information that is based directly upon the experience of the people of the community and the state in the conduct of one of the most important governmental activities, public education.

The need for popular bulletins and reports on various phases of education was emphasized in a bulletin of the United States Office of Education in the following statement: [6]

Education, one of the most fundamental aspects of our society, receives relatively little attention by the layman outside of sensational occurrences which are played up by newspapers and magazines. It is recognized that factual material is in and of itself of little direct appeal and further that information on education has to compete in the reader's interest and time with the great bulk of advertising and popular fiction prepared by those who are expert in appealing to reading attention and time. It is believed that a matter of such fundamental concern to the American people as education should receive expert professional attention and service from the standpoint of popularization and competition with commercial published materials to the end that education will occupy a larger place in the understanding of every American citizen. Those who are charged directly with the responsibility for the progress of education are not discharging their duty to the people who look to them for leadership if they do not keep the public duly informed, not only of the current status of education but of its trends, problems and needs.

SAFEGUARDING SCHOOL FUNDS

In addition to the collection of all income due the school districts and the wise management of temporary loans to pay current bills, there must be adequate provisions for safeguarding and protecting public school money that is kept on hand. Although the necessity for the protection of school funds has long been recognized, states have been relatively slow to make adequate provisions and to set up suitable safeguards. The two main types of provisions needed are those for adequate bonding of school officials charged with the custody of school funds, and adequate protection in the form of securities or guarantees required of depositories handling the funds. Many of the internal checks, such as internal auditing, provide further safeguards to the management of school funds.

[6] U.S. Office of Education, "Proposals Relating to the Statistical Function of the U.S. Office of Education," *Report of the National Conference on the Office of Education Statistical Program*, Bulletin No. 2, 1946, Washington, 1946.

Custody of School Funds

Following the receipt of school funds a number of problems arise relative to their management during the interval between receipt and disbursement. One of these is the selection of the proper school official to receive the money and to have custody of the funds. Among the states there is much variation relative to what official should be charged with this responsibility. The school district treasurer is perhaps the most commonly mentioned person. Often county officials and sometimes tax collectors have custody of the funds and sometimes it is a county official who is not at all connected with the schools.

Perhaps the school treasurer and the school clerk, as officers of the school corporation, are the persons who most frequently have custody of the school funds. The school treasurer is the person who receives the money and makes the deposits and also writes the checks for the disbursements. The school clerk, sometimes designated as secretary, keeps a record of receipts and expenditures. In short, he does the bookkeeping for the district. Sometimes he is an officer in the office of the superintendent of schools or the board of education. Even in large city school systems where all the accounting and fiscal transactions are done through the business office there still prevails the custom of designating a member of the board of education as the treasurer. In the smaller school districts where the school treasurer and the school clerk are different individuals there is provision for cross-checking between the individuals which in itself acts as a safeguard.

The school board treasurer is usually a member of the board of education and is charged with the responsibility of receiving and depositing funds and writing checks for the expenditure of school money whether he actually performs these functions or not.

Where the school clerk and the school treasurer are combined in one official, both the accounting function and the custody of funds function is vested in this one person. It has the advantage of combining various aspects of the accounting procedure with respect to receipts and disbursements. This person receives school money from the hands of the tax collector, from state aid, and from other sources that pay money to the school treasurer. He then deposits it in a bank or trust company. The treasurer keeps the accounts for the school district and writes the checks which may be countersigned by a member of the board of education. This system would seem to work well where the clerk-treasurer is a competent accountant or bookkeeper but this is often not the case.

Another rather common plan for providing for the custody of school funds is to use a regularly elected county official. In some states where school districts are county-wide or where there are county high school districts, the county treasurer frequently serves as the treasurer of the school districts. Under such circumstances he collects the tax money and deposits it to the credit of the school district. The governmental officers who serve as school treasurers, however, do not keep the accounts for the school district and it is necessary to have a clerk or secretary in the board of education or the superintendent's office to carry out this function. In many states the governmental treasury system is used for certain or all school districts.

Still another method that has been advocated, although not widely used, for the custody of school funds is to place this function in a school depository, a bank, or a trust company that serves as the treasurer of the school district. Under such circumstances the depository receives the money directly from the tax collector and deposits it to the credit of the school district. The official of the depository writes all checks or warrants on the order of the school business office or the school clerk. This plan has been advocated by some writers, but it has not become widespread in use.

Bonding School Officials

Regardless of what plan is used for the custody of school funds, in practically all states school officials are held responsible for the school money in their charge by giving bond for the faithful performance of their duties. Bonds given by school officers may be of the personal surety type or of the corporate surety type.

Of these two, the corporate surety bond has come into much more general use than the personal surety bond which is one of the older types. A number of writers have analyzed the relative advantages and disadvantages of personal surety bonds and corporate surety bonds. In brief they are as follows: The chief alleged merits of personal surety bonds are that they are cheaper for the school district and afford a type of privacy which may not be the case with corporate surety bonds. Their chief disadvantage is that there is no real guarantee that in case of loss the person who acts as surety may provide the money to make up the loss. Changes in personnel often cause conditions that require new personal sureties.

From all points of view, the advantages of corporate surety bonds are so great for a school district that it is the only type of bond which should be required of school officials. A corporate surety company usually makes a thorough investigation of the official, has a definite rate depending upon the amount of money that is handled, and carries on the security of the official in a businesslike way. The alleged disadvantages of this type of bond are that it costs too much or that in some cases the surety company may avoid payment, which is not often the case. When reputable companies are dealt with, the advantages greatly outweigh the alleged disadvantages. The corporate surety bond has the advantages of greater certainty of payment in case of loss than the personal bond and a strict examination and investigation of school officials and an examination of the accounting and safeguarding procedures in a school district.

There are several types of corporate bonds among which may be mentioned: (1) the individual bond, which is written to cover a specific individual; (2) the name schedule bond, which is usually written to cover a number of employees but in each case the employees are named and surety is obtained for these persons only; (3) the positions bond, which covers a number of school employees usually in different positions but not by name; (4) the blanket type of bond, which covers all school employees in a given organization, without specifying positions or name; (5) the statutory bond, which is required by law and may not differ greatly from those already mentioned; and (6) public official bonds, which are required by law and usually specify faithful performance of duty as well as accountability for money received.[7]

A somewhat different form of state requirement for bonding school officials is a plan that has been developed in North Dakota in which the state has undertaken the bonding of public officials in amounts ordinarily required by statutes or determined by local governmental units. These bonds are usually written regardless of the amount, and are secured through the state bonding plan. Premiums are paid from state funds, but it is unlawful to pay the premiums on corporate bonds from public funds. The rates for bonds issued by the state are usually about one-half the rate of corporate surety companies.

The amount of bond to be given by a school official who is in charge of funds differs among the different states and school districts within a state. The conditions under which bond is given may differ considerably and may include such factors as the number of losses, the amount of money handled, the kind of accounting system kept, internal checks and audits made, the direct responsibility of the employee for collecting and depositing money, the record of the employee and other types of safety devices used. It has been proposed that the penalty bond of a school district treasurer be set at about 5 per cent of the total amount of money handled or about 20 per cent of the maximum amount on hand at any one time, whichever is the larger figure. For a smaller district, some modification of this rule must be made.

[7] S. C. Joyner, "Schools Need Fidelity Bond Protection," *American School Board Journal,* vol. 108, p. 25, February, 1944. "Best Type of Fidelity Bonds for School," *American School Board Journal,* vol. 108, p. 41, March, 1944. "Court Decisions and Their Effect on School Fidelity Bonding," *American School Board Journal,* vol. 108, p. 91, April, 1944.

Experience has shown that in the bonding of school officials it seems desirable that the amount of the bond should be at least equal to the amount of money that the school official handles during a thirty-day period. This might give adequate protection for a school district at normal times but would seem to be insufficient for times when large amounts of money are received, such as during tax collection periods.

School Fund Depositories

Usually every dollar of school money is placed in a school depository for at least a short period of time. The selection of a depository or depositories is a function of the board of education and should be made with consideration for the amount of money to be kept on hand, the method of securing funds in the depository, and the reputation of the institution serving as depository. Sometimes the selection of the depository is made on the basis of bids received although this may not often be possible because in many communities the selection of depositories is limited.

A number of methods of securing money in depositories have been in use in the different states. Sometimes corporate depository bonds are given; again, collateral covering the amount of money on hand is deposited with the school district; more recently the Federal Deposit Insurance Corporation has undertaken to insure bank deposits up to $10,000 for any one account. Some writers question the advisability of requiring banks or trust companies to give security for public deposits on the basis that collateral deposited for such funds has a tendency to weaken the security of private deposits. In many cases a school would do well to select more than one depository in which to keep school money.

Some years ago, a number of states instituted state-wide guarantee plans for the protection of public funds. Such plans were organized in Oklahoma, Kansas, Nebraska, Mississippi, North Dakota, South Dakota, and Washington. The record of these state funds has not been very good, and in most cases they have either failed or have been discontinued. An exception to these state guarantee plans is that which was set up in the state of Iowa in 1925, known as the Iowa State Sinking Fund for Public Deposits.[8] This sinking fund was built up through a charge on the interest earnings of public deposits. There is also a provision that when the fund reaches the amount of $500,000 no more collections will be made until the fund is again reduced to $250,000 when a small assessment on interest charges can again be made. This sinking fund for public deposits, of course, applies to all public deposits, not only that of school districts, and seems to have worked very well over a long period of time.

[8] State of Iowa, "School Laws in 1935," Section 7421-AL7420-B12, pp. 320–328.

Administrative Safeguards

In addition to the practice of designating certain officials as custodians of the school money, requiring them to give surety bonds, and making provision for guarantees of the funds deposited in banks or trust companies, it is considered desirable to set up certain administrative safeguards within the school system. Among these may be mentioned: (1) an adequate school financial accounting system and an adequate system of checks; (2) preaudits on school budgets and on annual reports; (3) periodic reports of the condition of the school funds, the amounts expended, and the balances remaining under the different budgetary categories; (4) publicity on the financial condition of the school district to inform the public as well as the board of education; (5) the proper supervision of internal and external audits of school accounts; and (6) the proper investment of any sinking funds or reserve funds kept on hand. It is also considered good practice to have two separate and independent sets of records of receipts and disbursements and the separation of authority to expend money from the custody of the money, and the requirement that at least two persons take part in the act of disbursing the funds.

SUMMARY

The school audit is essentially an appraisal of the financial records and financial management of the school district. It has for its purpose the verification of accounts and setting forth the financial condition of the school district.

Audits may be thought of as external and internal—the external being made by independent auditors or by some state agencies, whereas internal audits are the continuous verification of accounts within the district. Auditing is required by law in thirty-three states, usually annually by various state agencies or independent auditors. Those who are engaged in making school audits should be careful to distinguish between auditing and policy making. Policy making is a function of the board of education and not of the auditor.

As in any business, regular reports of financial transactions and of the work of the schools should be made. Reporting is usually considered of three kinds—to the administration, to state and national agencies, and to the public. The first two types are rather detailed and statistical in nature, whereas the latter is descriptive and interpretive rather than statistical.

Care should be observed in gathering school statistics that definitions are complied with and that the data gathered for purposes of state and national reporting are uniform. Reporting to the administration is largely for purposes of management, and reporting to the public is for purposes of developing understanding of the schools and their programs.

Every dollar of school money must be collected, accounted for, and placed in a depository until the money is used. Questions of safeguarding school funds in terms of bonding school officials, selection of depositories, and protection of funds in them are important to prudential management and are the responsibility of boards of education and administrators.

The custody of school funds is usually the responsibility of the school treasurer or the school secretary-treasurer who may or may not be a member of the board of education. All officials who are charged with the collection of and accounting for school money should be bonded by adequate corporate surety bonds. School fund depositories should be carefully selected and protection should be secured for the funds in the depositories. Such protection may be by corporate depository bonds, collateral, and the Federal Deposit Insurance Corporation.

In addition to the safeguards mentioned above, there must be a number of administrative checks to be observed in the accounting and handling of school money, such as preaudits of budgets, periodical reports, publicity of the financial condition of the district, and proper supervision of internal accounts.

QUESTIONS FOR STUDY AND DISCUSSION

1. Study the school laws of a number of states and make a summary concerning the requirements for audits of school accounts. Note particularly the auditing agencies, the time and frequency of making audits, the type of audits required, and the form of the audit report.

2. Secure one or more copies of audit reports of school systems or other local governments as prepared in your state. Study these audit reports in the light of the school laws and the purposes and methods of auditing described in this chapter.

3. Evaluate the independent audit and the audit made by state educational agencies. Set forth the merits and limitations of each. Which do you consider preferable?

4. Secure a number of annual reports of boards of education. Note the kind of fiscal information given in them and the manner in which the data are presented.

5. Analyze current issues of newspapers to discover what information regarding the schools is published. What financial data are presented? Are they adequate to give the public an understanding of the cost of education?

6. Study the methods of writing school board minutes and show how such basic records can be improved.

7. Summarize the provisions for school fund custody in your state. Do they differ for the various local units? If you consider the provisions inadequate,

what recommendations would you make? What are the provisions in your state for bonding school officials or those who receive and disburse the school funds? What types of bond are required for the various officials and in what amounts?

8. What safeguards are required for school funds in local depositories? What amount of collateral or bond is given? Is the situation wholly satisfactory? If not, make recommendations for improvement.

9. List any other administrative safeguards that are placed about school funds in your state. Show the extent to which each is used and give the relative success of each.

SELECTED REFERENCES

Arnold, William E., William B. Castetter, Walter C. Reusser, and Roman J. Verhaalen, "Business Management: Safeguarding School Funds and Property," chap. XIII in R. L. Johns and E. L. Morphet (eds.), *Problems and Issues in Public School Finance,* Bureau of Publications, Teachers College, Columbia University, New York, 1952.

Chambers, J. L.: "Public School Auditing Practices in the United States," *American School Board Journal,* vol. LXXXV, pp. 41–43, September, 1932.

Hamilton, Robert R., and Paul R. Mort: *The Law and Public Education,* The Foundation Press, Chicago, 1959.

Harvard, J.: *Financing Public Schools in the United States,* Harper & Brothers, New York, 1951, pp. 551–561.

Johns, R. L., and E. L. Morphet (eds.): *Problems and Issues in Public School Finance,* Bureau of Publications, Teachers College, Columbia University, New York, 1952, chap. 12, pp. 432–443, and chap. 14, pp. 472–477.

Kilpatrick, Edward W.: *Advantages of an Independent Annual Audit of School Accounts,* Proceedings of the Association of School Business Officials of the United States and Canada, 1952, pp. 223–226.

Linn, Henry H.: *School Business Administration,* The Ronald Press Company, New York, 1956, chap. 7, pp. 219–223.

Norman, Loyal V.: "Model State School Audit Statute," *School Executive,* vol. 73, pp. 80–82, March, 1954.

————: "Scope, Conduct, and Report of the School Audit," *American School Board Journal,* vol. 127, pp. 44–45, October, 1953.

Index